P9-ARR-677

The Editors

JAMES F. LOUCKS is Associate Professor of English at The Ohio State University, Newark. He received his Ph.D. from The Ohio State University. He is the co-author (wth Richard D. Altick) of *Browning's Roman Murder Story: A Reading of "The Ring and the Book"* and is the author of articles on Victorian and twentieth-century literature.

ANDREW M. STAUFFER is Associate Professor of English at Boston University. He received his Ph.D. from the University of Virginia. He is the author of *Anger, Revolution, and Romanticism* and has published many articles on Romantic and Victorian poetry.

W. W. NORTON & COMPANY, INC.
Also Publishes

THE NORTON ANTHOLOGY OF AFRICAN AMERICAN LITERATURE
edited by Henry Louis Gates Jr. and Nellie Y. McKay et al.

THE NORTON ANTHOLOGY OF AMERICAN LITERATURE
edited by Nina Baym et al.

THE NORTON ANTHOLOGY OF CHILDREN'S LITERATURE
edited by Jack Zipes et al.

THE NORTON ANTHOLOGY OF CONTEMPORARY FICTION
edited by R. V. Cassill and Joyce Carol Oates

THE NORTON ANTHOLOGY OF ENGLISH LITERATURE
edited by M. H. Abrams and Stephen Greenblatt et al.

THE NORTON ANTHOLOGY OF LITERATURE BY WOMEN
edited by Sandra M. Gilbert and Susan Gubar

THE NORTON ANTHOLOGY OF MODERN AND CONTEMPORARY POETRY
edited by Jahan Ramazani, Richard Ellmann, and Robert O'Clair

THE NORTON ANTHOLOGY OF POETRY
edited by Margaret Ferguson, Mary Jo Salter, and Jon Stallworthy

THE NORTON ANTHOLOGY OF SHORT FICTION
edited by R. V. Cassill and Richard Bausch

THE NORTON ANTHOLOGY OF THEORY AND CRITICISM
edited by Vincent B. Leitch et al.

THE NORTON ANTHOLOGY OF WORLD LITERATURE
edited by Sarah Lawall et al.

THE NORTON FACSIMILE OF THE FIRST FOLIO OF SHAKESPEARE
prepared by Charlton Hinman

THE NORTON INTRODUCTION TO LITERATURE
edited by Alison Booth, J. Paul Hunter, and Kelly J. Mays

THE NORTON INTRODUCTION TO THE SHORT NOVEL
edited by Jerome Beaty

THE NORTON READER
edited by Linda H. Peterson and John C. Brereton

THE NORTON SAMPLER
edited by Thomas Cooley

THE NORTON SHAKESPEARE, BASED ON THE OXFORD EDITION
edited by Stephen Greenblatt et al.

For a complete list of Norton Critical Editions, visit
www.wwnorton.com/college/english/nce_home.htm

A NORTON CRITICAL EDITION

ROBERT BROWNING'S
POETRY

AUTHORITATIVE TEXTS

CRITICISM

SECOND EDITION

Selected and Edited by

JAMES F. LOUCKS

THE OHIO STATE UNIVERSITY OF NEWARK

and

ANDREW M. STAUFFER

BOSTON UNIVERSITY

W. W. NORTON & COMPANY

New York • London

W. W. Norton & Company has been independent since its founding in 1923, when William Warder Norton and Mary D. Herter Norton first published lectures delivered at the People's Institute, the adult education division of New York City's Cooper Union. The Nortons soon expanded their program beyond the Institute, publishing books by celebrated academics from America and abroad. By mid-century, the two major pillars of Norton's publishing program—trade books and college texts—were firmly established. In the 1950s, the Norton family transferred control of the company to its employees, and today—with a staff of four hundred and a comparable number of trade, college, and professional titles published each year—W. W. Norton & Company stands as the largest and oldest publishing house owned wholly by its employees.

Copyright © 2007, 1979 by W. W. Norton & Company, Inc.

All rights reserved.
Printed in the United States of America.

Every effort has been made to contact the copyright holders of each of the
selections. Rights holders of any selections not credited should contact
W. W. Norton & Company, Inc. for a correction to be made in the next printing
of our work.

The text of this book is composed in Fairfield Medium
with the display set in Bernhard Modern.
Composition by PennSet, Inc.
Manufacturing by the Courier Companies—Westford Division.
Book design by Antonina Krass.
Production manager: Benjamin Reynolds.

Library of Congress Cataloging-in-Publication Data
Browning, Robert, 1812–1889.
[Poems. Selections]
Robert Browning's poetry : authoritative texts, criticism / selected
and edited by James F. Loucks and Andrew M. Stauffer.—2nd ed.
p. cm.— (A Norton critical edition)

ISBN-13: 978-0-393-92600-2 (pbk.)
ISBN-10: 0-393-92600-1 (pbk.)

1. Browning, Robert, 1812–1889—Criticism and interpretation.
I. Loucks, James F. II. Stauffer, Andrew M., 1968– III. Title.

PR4202.L59 2006
821'.8—dc22

2006047308

W. W. Norton & Company, Inc., 500 Fifth Avenue, New York, N.Y. 10110-0017
www.wwnorton.com

W. W. Norton & Company Ltd., Castle House,
75/76 Wells Street, London W1T 3QT

2   3   4   5   6   7   8   9   0

Contents

Criticism

Preface

In preparing this second edition of *Robert Browning's Poetry*, we have been mindful that a quarter of a century has elapsed since the first edition was issued, during which period both readers' tastes and scholars' critical approaches have evolved. We have tried to improve the appeal and relevance of this Norton Critical Edition while preserving many of the strengths of the first edition. Accordingly, we have made a handful of significant changes in the selection of poems, while radically altering the selection of modern criticism. Notably, we have printed the early poem *Pauline* in its entirety; dropped Book VI ("Caponsacchi") in favor of Book VII ("Pompilia") in *The Ring and the Book*; and removed "Saul" and "James Lee's Wife" to make room for several other poems we wished to include. Our hope is that this volume will serve as a wide-ranging and usable testament to Browning's poetic achievement.

The texts have been completely reset and re-proofed since the first edition. We have thoroughly amended the annotations, continuing to avoid interpretive notes while providing information intended to clarify Browning's references and vocabulary. Our sense is that readers new to Browning are too often daunted by a mass of footnotes that seem to confirm rumors of the poet's obscurity and difficulty. Therefore, as a general rule, and in the interest of readability, we have chosen to err on the side of annotating too lightly. With few exceptions, we have not, in the notes themselves, cited our many predecessors in Browning scholarship upon whose work these notes frequently depend. The date of each work's composition, whether known or conjectured, is printed after the text on the left-hand side. If a version appeared in print prior to book publication, that date appears on the right. In excerpted passages, the lines are numbered in accordance with the full text, for ease of reference.

We have left unchanged the selection of Victorian opinions on Browning's work, deeming that these remain among the most valuable and telling reactions of the period. However, we have overhauled the "Modern Essays in Criticism" completely, in an attempt to bring the edition up to the present moment in Browning's critical heritage. Only classic essays by Robert Langbaum and Harold Bloom remain from the first edition. The other essays represent a range of some of the best criticism on Browning in recent years, from a number of theoretical perspectives and across a range of Browning's poetry. The work of Isobel Armstrong and Herbert Tucker has been the most influential; and we are pleased to include essays by other scholars who have changed the ways we think about Browning and his art: Susan Brown, Erik Gray, Stefan Hawlin, Daniel Karlin, Catherine Maxwell, and Jennifer Wagner-Lawlor. Other important work that could not be included can be found listed in the Selected Bibliography, which has been thoroughly revised for this edition.

The list of scholars to whom we owe debts is long: the work of Richard Altick, A. K. Cook, W. C. DeVane, William Irvine, Roma King, and Park Honan was crucial to the preparation of the first edition and remains so here. We have also profited from the first-rate scholarship in the editions of Tim Burnett, Thomas J. Collins, Stefan Hawlin, Ian Jack, Robert Inglesfield, Daniel Karlin, Michael Meredith, and John Woolford. For more direct advice and assistance, we would like to thank David Latané, Jack Kolb and Chip Tucker. Cara Norris was invaluable as a research assistant in our preparations. Brian Baker, of W. W. Norton, has been an encouraging and helpful guide throughout the process, and he has our thanks.

The Texts of
THE POEMS

A Note on the Texts

The order of the poems is that of their initial publication in book form; the text followed, however, is the "Fourth and complete edition" of 1888–94 in seventeen volumes, all but the last having been supervised by Browning in the final months of his life. Alert and meticulous even in old age, Browning supplied the publisher, Smith, Elder, and Company, with a list of corrections—mostly in punctuation—that he wished to make in the first ten volumes of the 1889 reprint. Since not every correction was made (or made accurately) by the publisher, we have taken the course of emending the 1888–89 text in accordance with Browning's extant corrigenda, rather than relying on the 1889 reprint. Though the corrigenda sent to Smith, Elder have not been recovered, two presumably parallel sets of corrections in Browning's hand remain, differing in only a few particulars; these may be found in a list in the Brown University Library, and in the Dykes Campbell copy of the 1888–89 edition in the British Museum. We are indebted to Philip Kelley and William S. Peterson for their convenient tabulation of Browning's final revisions (*Browning Institute Studies*, 1 [1973], 109–17).

Browning's own corrections have been made silently. Below are listed our own verbal emendations; the edition followed, where relevant, is given in parentheses:

Cristina, 1. 63: "the next life" for "next life" (1849).

Bishop Blougram's Apology, 1. 608: "soil" for "soul" (1885).

Bishop Blougram's Apology, 1. 759:

"other" for "others" (1855).

The Ring and the Book, X.1141: "law's" for "laws."

The rare misspellings and obvious errors of punctuation in the 1888–89 edition have been silently corrected. Two peculiarities of Smith, Elder's house styling have been normalized: the inverted commas used to begin every line of continuous quoted material are suppressed; and the irregular practice of numbering half-lines of *The Ring and the Book* is not followed. The line numbering in that poem follows that of the "Florentine Edition."

3

The Experimental Phase
(1833–45)

PAULINE; A FRAGMENT OF A CONFESSION

(1833; final version 1888)

Published anonymously when Browning was twenty-one years old, *Pauline* records various early crises of the poet's intellectual and creative development, with particular reference to his reading of the "Sun-treader," Percy Bysshe Shelley (1792–1822), an early hero of Browning's. Although ostensibly dramatic in form, the poem cleaves fairly closely to autobiography, and the personally reticent Browning later came to regard it with "extreme repugnance." *Pauline* was positively but slightly noticed by reviewers in 1833, and did not sell well at all. However, John Stuart Mill read it with great interest and annotated it closely, and sent his copy back to Browning. Mill wrote at the end of the volume, "With considerable poetic powers, this writer seems to me possessed with a more intense and morbid self-consciousness than I ever knew in a sane human being." Browning suppressed *Pauline* until 1868, when he reluctantly included a revised version of this "crude preliminary sketch" in an edition of his collected works. Our text is from the 1888 collected *Poetical Works*, for which Browning again revised the poem, "experience helping, in some degree, the helplessness of juvenile haste and heat in their untried adventure long ago."

> Plus ne suis ce que j'ai été
> Et ne le sçaurois jamais être.—MAROT[1]

NON dubito, quin titulus libri nostri raritate sua quamplurimos alliciat ad legendum: inter quos nonnulli obliquæ opinionis, mente languidi, multi etiam maligni, et in ingenium nostrum ingrati accedent, qui temeraria sua ignorantia, vix conspecto titulo clamabunt Nos vetita docere, hæresium semina jacere: piis auribus offendiculo, præclaris ingeniis scandalo esse: . . . adeo conscientiæ suæ consulentes, ut nec Apollo, nec Musæ omnes, neque Angelus de cœlo me ab illorum execratione vindicare queant: quibus et ego nunc consulo, ne scripta nostra legant, nec intelligant, nec meminerint: nam noxia sunt, venenosa sunt: Acherontis ostium est in hoc libro, lapides loquitur, caveant, ne cerebrum illis excutiat. Vos autem, qui æqua mente ad legendum venitis, si tantam prudentiæ discretionem adhibueritis, quantam in melle legendo apes, jam securi legite. Puto namque vos et utilitatis haud parum et voluptatis plurimum accep-

---

1. Epigraph by Clément Marot (1496–1544), "I am no longer what I have been, and would never know how to be again."

5

turos. Quod si qua repereritis, quæ vobis non placeant, mittite illa,
nec utimini. NAM ET EGO VOBIS ILLA NON PROBO, SED NARRO. Cætera
tamen propterea non respuite . . . . . Ideo, si quid liberius dictum sit,
ignoscite adolescentiæ nostræ, qui minor quam adolescens hoc opus
composui.—*Hen. Corn. Agrippa, De Occult. Philosoph. in Præfat.*[2]

LONDON: *January* 1833.
V. A. XX.

[This introduction would appear less absurdly pretentious did it ap-
ply, as was intended, to a completed structure of which the poem was
meant for only a beginning and remains a fragment.]

Pauline, mine own, bend o'er me—thy soft breast
Shall pant to mine—bend o'er me—thy sweet eyes,
And loosened hair and breathing lips, and arms
Drawing me to thee—these build up a screen
To shut me in with thee, and from all fear;   5
So that I might unlock the sleepless brood
Of fancies from my soul, their lurking-place,
Nor doubt that each would pass, ne'er to return
To one so watched, so loved and so secured.
But what can guard thee but thy naked love?   10
Ah dearest, whoso sucks a poisoned wound
Envenoms his own veins! Thou art so good,
So calm—if thou shouldst wear a brow less light
For some wild thought which, but for me, were kept
From out thy soul as from a sacred star!   15
Yet till I have unlocked them it were vain
To hope to sing; some woe would light on me;
Nature would point at one whose quivering lip
Was bathed in her enchantments, whose brow burned
Beneath the crown to which her secrets knelt,   20
Who learned the spell which can call up the dead,
And then departed smiling like a fiend
Who has deceived God,—if such one should seek
Again her altars and stand robed and crowned
Amid the faithful! Sad confession first,   25

2. Latin introduction adapted from the preface to Cornelius Agrippa's *De Occulta Philosophia*
(1531): 'I have no doubt that the title of our book may by its unusual character entice very
many to read it, and that among them some of biased opinions, with weak minds—many
even hostile and churlish—will attack our genius, who in the rashness of their ignorance will
cry out, almost before they have read the title, that we are teaching forbidden things, are
scattering the seeds of heresies, that we are an annoyance to righteous ears, to enlightened
minds an object of offence; so taking care for their consciences that neither Apollo, nor all
the Muses, nor an angel from heaven could save me from their execration. To these I now
give counsel not to read our book, neither to understand it nor remember it; for it is harm-
ful, poisonous; the gate of Hell is in this book; it speaks of stones—let them beware lest by
them it beat out their brains. But if you who come to its perusal with unprejudiced minds
will exercise as much discernment and prudence as bees gathering honey, then read with
safety. For I think you will receive not a little of instruction and a great deal of enjoyment.
On the other hand, if you find things which do not please you, pass over them and make no
use of them. FOR I DO NOT RECOMMEND THESE THINGS TO YOU: I MERELY TELL YOU OF THEM.
Yet do not on that account reject the rest. Therefore if anything has been said rather freely,
forgive my youth; I wrote this work when I was less than a youth' (F. A. Pottle's translation).
The note "V[ixeram] A[annos] XX." means Browning was 20 when he wrote the poem.

Remorse and pardon and old claims renewed,
Ere I can be—as I shall be no more.

I had been spared this shame if I had sat
By thee for ever from the first, in place
Of my wild dreams of beauty and of good,   30
Or with them, as an earnest of their truth:
No thought nor hope having been shut from thee,
No vague wish unexplained, no wandering aim
Sent back to bind on fancy's wings and seek
Some strange fair world where it might be a law;   35
But, doubting nothing, had been led by thee,
Thro' youth, and saved, as one at length awaked
Who has slept through a peril. Ah vain, vain!

Thou lovest me; the past is in its grave
Tho' its ghost haunts us; still this much is ours,   40
To cast away restraint, lest a worse thing
Wait for us in the dark. Thou lovest me;
And thou art to receive not love but faith,
For which thou wilt be mine, and smile and take
All shapes and shames, and veil without a fear   45
That form which music follows like a slave:
And I look to thee and I trust in thee,
As in a Northern night one looks alway
Unto the East for morn and spring and joy.
Thou seest then my aimless, hopeless state,   50
And, resting on some few old feelings won
Back by thy beauty, wouldst that I essay
The task which was to me what now thou art:
And why should I conceal one weakness more?

Thou wilt remember one warm morn when winter   55
Crept aged from the earth, and spring's first breath
Blew soft from the moist hills; the black-thorn boughs,
So dark in the bare wood, when glistening
In the sunshine were white with coming buds,
Like the bright side of a sorrow, and the banks   60
Had violets opening from sleep like eyes.
I walked with thee who knew'st not a deep shame
Lurked beneath smiles and careless words which sought
To hide it till they wandered and were mute,
As we stood listening on a sunny mound   65
To the wind murmuring in the damp copse,
Like heavy breathings of some hidden thing
Betrayed by sleep; until the feeling rushed
That I was low indeed, yet not so low
As to endure the calmness of thine eyes.   70
And so I told thee all, while the cool breast
I leaned on altered not its quiet beating:
And long ere words like a hurt bird's complaint

Bade me look up and be what I had been,
I felt despair could never live by thee: 75
Thou wilt remember. Thou art not more dear
Than song was once to me; and I ne'er sung
But as one entering bright halls where all
Will rise and shout for him: sure I must own
That I am fallen, having chosen gifts   80
Distinct from theirs—that I am sad and fain
Would give up all to be but where I was,
Not high as I had been if faithful found,
But low and weak yet full of hope, and sure
Of goodness as of life—that I would lose   85
All this gay mastery of mind, to sit
Once more with them, trusting in truth and love
And with an aim—not being what I am.

Oh Pauline, I am ruined who believed
That though my soul had floated from its sphere   90
Of wild dominion into the dim orb
Of self—that it was strong and free as ever!
It has conformed itself to that dim orb,
Reflecting all its shades and shapes, and now
Must stay where it alone can be adored.   95
I have felt this in dreams—in dreams in which
I seemed the fate from which I fled; I felt
A strange delight in causing my decay.
I was a fiend in darkness chained for ever
Within some ocean-cave; and ages rolled,   100
Till through the cleft rock, like a moonbeam, came
A white swan to remain with me; and ages
Rolled, yet I tired not of my first free joy
In gazing on the peace of its pure wings:
And then I said "It is most fair to me,   105
Yet its soft wings must sure have suffered change
From the thick darkness, sure its eyes are dim,
Its silver pinions must be cramped and numbed
With sleeping ages here; it cannot leave me,
For it would seem, in light beside its kind,   110
Withered, tho' here to me most beautiful."
And then I was a young witch whose blue eyes,
As she stood naked by the river springs,
Drew down a god: I watched his radiant form
Growing less radiant, and it gladdened me;   115
Till one morn, as he sat in the sunshine
Upon my knees, singing to me of heaven,
He turned to look at me, ere I could lose
The grin with which I viewed his perishing:
And he shrieked and departed and sat long   120
By his deserted throne, but sunk at last
Murmuring, as I kissed his lips and curled
Around him, "I am still a god—to thee."

Still I can lay my soul bare in its fall,
Since all the wandering and all the weakness   125
Will be a saddest comment on the song:
And if, that done, I can be young again,
I will give up all gained, as willingly
As one gives up a charm which shuts him out
From hope or part or care in human kind.   130
As life wanes, all its care and strife and toil
Seem strangely valueless, while the old trees
Which grew by our youth's home, the waving mass
Of climbing plants heavy with bloom and dew,
The morning swallows with their songs like words,   135
All these seem clear and only worth our thoughts:
So, aught connected with my early life,
My rude songs or my wild imaginings,
How I look on them—most distinct amid
The fever and the stir of after years!   140

I ne'er had ventured e'en to hope for this,
Had not the glow I felt at HIS award,[3]
Assured me all was not extinct within:
HIS whom all honour, whose renown springs up
Like sunlight which will visit all the world,   145
So that e'en they who sneered at him at first,
Come out to it, as some dark spider crawls
From his foul nets which some lit torch invades,
Yet spinning still new films for his retreat.
Thou didst smile, poet, but can we forgive?   150

Sun-treader, life and light be thine for ever!
Thou art gone from us; years go by and spring
Gladdens and the young earth is beautiful,
Yet thy songs come not, other bards arise,
But none like thee: they stand, thy majesties,   155
Like mighty works which tell some spirit there
Hath sat regardless of neglect and scorn,
Till, its long task completed, it hath risen
And left us, never to return, and all
Rush in to peer and praise when all in vain.   160
The air seems bright with thy past presence yet,
But thou art still for me as thou hast been
When I have stood with thee as on a throne
With all thy dim creations gathered round
Like mountains, and I felt of mould[4] like them,   165
And with them creatures of my own were mixed,
Like things half-lived, catching and giving life.
But thou art still for me who have adored
Tho' single, panting but to hear thy name
Which I believed a spell to me alone,   170

3. The awarding of posthumous fame to the poet Shelley.
4. Form or essence.

Scarce deeming thou wast as a star to men!
As one should worship long a sacred spring
Scarce worth a moth's flitting, which long grasses cross,
And one small tree embowers droopingly—
Joying to see some wandering insect won   175
To live in its few rushes, or some locust
To pasture on its boughs, or some wild bird
Stoop for its freshness from the trackless air:
And then should find it but the fountain-head,
Long lost, of some great river washing towns   180
And towers, and seeing old woods which will live
But by its banks untrod of human foot,
Which, when the great sun sinks, lie quivering
In light as some thing lieth half of life
Before God's foot, waiting a wondrous change;   185
Then girt with rocks which seek to turn or stay
Its course in vain, for it does ever spread
Like a sea's arm as it goes rolling on,
Being the pulse of some great country—so
Wast thou to me, and art thou to the world!   190
And I, perchance, half feel a strange regret
That I am not what I have been to thee:
Like a girl one has silently loved long
In her first loneliness in some retreat,
When, late emerged, all gaze and glow to view   195
Her fresh eyes and soft hair and lips which bloom
Like a mountain berry: doubtless it is sweet
To see her thus adored, but there have been
Moments when all the world was in our praise,
Sweeter than any pride of after hours.   200
Yet, sun-treader, all hail! From my heart's heart
I bid thee hail! E'en in my wildest dreams,
I proudly feel I would have thrown to dust
The wreaths of fame which seemed o'erhanging me,
To see thee for a moment as thou art.   205

And if thou livest, if thou lovest, spirit!
Remember me who set this final seal
To wandering thought—that one so pure as thou
Could never die. Remember me who flung
All honour from my soul, yet paused and said   210
"There is one spark of love remaining yet,
For I have nought in common with him, shapes
Which followed him avoid me, and foul forms
Seek me, which ne'er could fasten on his mind;
And though I feel how low I am to him,   215
Yet I aim not even to catch a tone
Of harmonies he called profusely up;
So, one gleam still remains, although the last."
Remember me who praise thee e'en with tears,
For never more shall I walk calm with thee;   220

Thy sweet imaginings are as an air,
A melody some wondrous singer sings,
Which, though it haunt men oft in the still eve,
They dream not to essay; yet it no less
But more is honoured. I was thine in shame,[5]   225
And now when all thy proud renown is out,
I am a watcher whose eyes have grown dim
With looking for some star which breaks on him
Altered and worn and weak and full of tears.

Autumn has come like spring returned to us,   230
Won from her girlishness; like one returned
A friend that was a lover, nor forgets
The first warm love, but full of sober thoughts
Of fading years; whose soft mouth quivers yet
With the old smile, but yet so changed and still!   235
And here am I the scoffer, who have probed
Life's vanity, won by a word again
Into my own life—by one little word
Of this sweet friend who lives in loving me,
Lives strangely on my thoughts and looks and words,   240
As fathoms down some nameless ocean thing
Its silent course of quietness and joy.
O dearest, if indeed I tell the past,
May'st thou forget it as a sad sick dream!
Or if it linger—my lost soul too soon   245
Sinks to itself and whispers we shall be
But closer linked, two creatures whom the earth
Bears singly, with strange feelings unrevealed
Save to each other; or two lonely things
Created by some power whose reign is done,   250
Having no part in God or his bright world.
I am to sing whilst ebbing day dies soft,
As a lean scholar dies worn o'er his book,
And in the heaven stars steal out one by one
As hunted men steal to their mountain watch.   255
I must not think, lest this new impulse die
In which I trust; I have no confidence:
So, I will sing on fast as fancies come;
Rudely, the verse being as the mood it paints.

I strip my mind bare, whose first elements   260
I shall unveil—not as they struggled forth
In infancy, nor as they now exist,
When I am grown above them and can rule—
But in that middle stage when they were full
Yet ere I had disposed them to my will;   265
And then I shall show how these elements
Produced my present state, and what it is.

5. I.e., I was your disciple when you were neglected.

I am made up of an intensest life,
Of a most clear idea of consciousness
Of self, distinct from all its qualities,   270
From all affections, passions, feelings, powers;
And thus far it exists, if tracked, in all:
But linked, in me, to self-supremacy,
Existing as a centre to all things,
Most potent to create and rule and call   275
Upon all things to minister to it;
And to a principle of restlessness
Which would be all, have, see, know, taste, feel, all—
This is myself; and I should thus have been
Though gifted lower than the meanest soul.   280

And of my powers, one springs up to save
From utter death a soul with such desire
Confined to clay—of powers the only one
Which marks me—an imagination which
Has been a very angel, coming not   285
In fitful visions but beside me ever
And never failing me; so, though my mind
Forgets not, not a shred of life forgets,
Yet I can take a secret pride in calling
The dark past up to quell it regally.   290

A mind like this must dissipate itself,
But I have always had one lode-star; now,
As I look back, I see that I have halted
Or hastened as I looked towards that star—
A need, a trust, a yearning after God: 295
A feeling I have analysed but late,
But it existed, and was reconciled
With a neglect of all I deemed his laws,
Which yet, when seen in others, I abhorred.
I felt as one beloved, and so shut in   300
From fear: and thence I date my trust in signs
And omens, for I saw God everywhere;
And I can only lay it to the fruit
Of a sad after-time that I could doubt
Even his being—e'en the while I felt   305
His presence, never acted from myself,
Still trusted in a hand to lead me through
All danger; and this feeling ever fought
Against my weakest reason and resolve.

And I can love nothing—and this dull truth   310
Has come the last: but sense supplies a love
Encircling me and mingling with my life.

These make myself: I have long sought in vain
To trace how they were formed by circumstance,

Yet ever found them mould my wildest youth   315
Where they alone displayed themselves, converted
All objects to their use: now see their course!

They came to me in my first dawn of life
Which passed alone with wisest ancient books
All halo-girt with fancies of my own;   320
And I myself went with the tale—a god
Wandering after beauty, or a giant
Standing vast in the sunset—an old hunter
Talking with gods, or a high-crested chief
Sailing with troops of friends to Tenedos.[6]   325
I tell you, nought has ever been so clear
As the place, the time, the fashion of those lives:
I had not seen a work of lofty art,
Nor woman's beauty nor sweet nature's face,
Yet, I say, never morn broke clear as those   330
On the dim clustered isles in the blue sea,
The deep groves and white temples and wet caves,
And nothing ever will surprise me now—
Who stood beside the naked Swift-footed,[7]
Who bound my forehead with Proserpine's[8] hair.   335

And strange it is that I who could so dream
Should e'er have stooped to aim at aught beneath—
Aught low or painful; but I never doubted:
So, as I grew, I rudely shaped my life
To my immediate wants; yet strong beneath   340
Was a vague sense of power though folded up—
A sense that, though those shades and times were past,
Their spirit dwelt in me, with them should rule.

Then came a pause, and long restraint chained down
My soul till it was changed. I lost myself,   345
And were it not that I so loathe that loss,
I could recall how first I learned to turn
My mind against itself; and the effects
In deeds for which remorse were vain as for
The wanderings of delirious dream; yet thence   350
Came cunning, envy, falsehood, all world's wrong
That spotted me: at length I cleansed my soul.
Yet long world's influence remained; and nought
But the still life I led, apart once more,
Which left me free to seek soul's old delights,   355
Could e'er have brought me thus far back to peace.

6. A small island to which the Greek chiefs sailed in order to fool the Trojans into thinking they had abandoned the siege of Troy.
7. Hermes, the messenger of the Greek gods.
8. Queen of the underworld and wife of Pluto, lord of the dead.

As peace returned, I sought out some pursuit;
And song rose, no new impulse but the one
With which all others best could be combined.
My life has not been that of those whose heaven   360
Was lampless save where poesy shone out;
But as a clime where glittering mountain-tops
And glancing sea and forests steeped in light
Give back reflected the far-flashing sun;
For music (which is earnest[9] of a heaven,   365
Seeing we know emotions strange by it,
Not else to be revealed,) is like a voice,
A low voice calling fancy, as a friend,
To the green woods in the gay summer time:
And she fills all the way with dancing shapes   370
Which have made painters pale, and they go on
Till stars look at them and winds call to them
As they leave life's path for the twilight world
Where the dead gather. This was not at first,
For I scarce knew what I would do. I had   375
An impulse but no yearning—only sang.

And first I sang as I in dream have seen
Music wait on a lyrist for some thought,
Yet singing to herself until it came.
I turned to those old times and scenes where all   380
That's beautiful had birth for me, and made
Rude verses on them all; and then I paused—
I had done nothing, so I sought to know
What other minds achieved. No fear outbroke
As on the works of mighty bards I gazed,   385
In the first joy at finding my own thoughts
Recorded, my own fancies justified,
And their aspirings but my very own.
With them I first explored passion and mind,—
All to begin afresh! I rather sought   390
To rival what I wondered at than form
Creations of my own; if much was light
Lent by the others, much was yet my own.

I paused again: a change was coming—came:
I was no more a boy, the past was breaking   395
Before the future and like fever worked.
I thought on my new self, and all my powers
Burst out. I dreamed not of restraint, but gazed
On all things: schemes and systems went and came,
And I was proud (being vainest of the weak)   400
In wandering o'er thought's world to seek some one
To be my prize, as if you wandered o'er
The White Way[1] for a star.

9. Promise.
1. Milky Way.

                                    And my choice fell
Not so much on a system as a man²—
On one, whom praise of mine shall not offend,   405
Who was as calm as beauty, being such
Unto mankind as thou to me, Pauline,—
Believing in them and devoting all
His soul's strength to their winning back to peace;
Who sent forth hopes and longings for their sake,   410
Clothed in all passion's melodies: such first
Caught me and set me, slave of a sweet task,
To disentangle, gather sense from song:
Since, song-inwoven, lurked there words which seemed
A key to a new world, the muttering   415
Of angels, something yet unguessed by man.
How my heart leapt as still I sought and found
Much there, I felt my own soul had conceived,
But there living and burning! Soon the orb
Of his conceptions dawned on me; its praise   420
Lives in the tongues of men, men's brows are high
When his name means a triumph and a pride,
So, my weak voice may well forbear to shame
What seemed decreed my fate: I threw myself
To meet it, I was vowed to liberty,   425
Men were to be as gods and earth as heaven,
And I—ah, what a life was mine to prove!
My whole soul rose to meet it. Now, Pauline,
I shall go mad, if I recall that time!

    Oh let me look back ere I leave for ever   430
The time which was an hour one fondly waits
For a fair girl that comes a withered hag!
And I was lonely, far from woods and fields,
And amid dullest sights, who should be loose
As a stag; yet I was full of bliss, who lived   435
With Plato and who had the key to life;
And I had dimly shaped my first attempt,
And many a thought did I build up on thought,
As the wild bee hangs cell to cell; in vain,
For I must still advance, no rest for mind.   440

'Twas in my plan to look on real life,
The life all new to me; my theories
Were firm, so them I left, to look and learn
Mankind, its cares, hopes, fears, its woes and joys;
And, as I pondered on their ways, I sought   445
How best life's end might be attained—an end
Comprising every joy. I deeply mused.

2. Shelley.

And suddenly without heart-wreck I awoke
As from a dream: I said "'Twas beautiful,
Yet but a dream, and so adieu to it!"   450
As some world-wanderer sees in a far meadow
Strange towers and high-walled gardens thick with trees,
Where song takes shelter and delicious mirth
From laughing fairy creatures peeping over,
And on the morrow when he comes to lie   455
For ever 'neath those garden-trees fruit-flushed
Sung round by fairies, all his search is vain.
First went my hopes of perfecting mankind,
Next—faith in them, and then in freedom's self
And virtue's self, then my own motives, ends   460
And aims and loves, and human love went last.
I felt this no decay, because new powers
Rose as old feelings left—wit, mockery,
Light-heartedness; for I had oft been sad,
Mistrusting my resolves, but now I cast   465
Hope joyously away: I laughed and said
"No more of this!" I must not think: at length
I looked again to see if all went well.

My powers were greater: as some temple seemed
My soul, where nought is changed and incense rolls   470
Around the altar, only God is gone
And some dark spirit sitteth in his seat.
So, I passed through the temple and to me
Knelt troops of shadows, and they cried "Hail, king!
We serve thee now and thou shalt serve no more!   475
Call on us, prove us, let us worship thee!"
And I said "Are ye strong? Let fancy bear me
Far from the past!" And I was borne away,
As Arab birds[3] float sleeping in the wind,
O'er deserts, towers and forests, I being calm.   480
And I said "I have nursed up energies,
They will prey on me." And a band knelt low
And cried "Lord, we are here and we will make
Safe way for thee in thine appointed life!
But look on us!" And I said "Ye will worship   485
Me; should my heart not worship too?" They shouted
"Thyself, thou art our king!" So, I stood there
Smiling—oh, vanity of vanities[4]!
For buoyant and rejoicing was the spirit
With which I looked out how to end my course;   490
I felt once more myself, my powers—all mine;
I knew while youth and health so lifted me
That, spite of all life's nothingness, no grief
Came nigh me, I must ever be light-hearted;
And that this knowledge was the only veil   495

3. Birds of paradise, which according to legend were footless and thus lived always in flight.
4. Ecclesiastes 1:2: "Vanity of vanities; all is vanity."

Betwixt joy and despair: so, if age came,
I should be left—a wreck linked to a soul
Yet fluttering, or mind-broken and aware
Of my decay. So a long summer morn
Found me; and ere noon came, I had resolved   500
No age should come on me ere youth was spent,
For I would wear myself out, like that morn
Which wasted not a sunbeam; every hour
I would make mine, and die.

                              And thus I sought
To chain my spirit down which erst[5] I freed   505
For flights to fame: I said "The troubled life
Of genius, seen so gay when working forth
Some trusted end, grows sad when all proves vain—
How sad when men have parted with truth's peace
For falsest fancy's sake, which waited first   510
As an obedient spirit when delight
Came without fancy's call: but alters soon,
Comes darkened, seldom, hastens to depart,
Leaving a heavy darkness and warm tears.
But I shall never lose her; she will live   515
Dearer for such seclusion. I but catch
A hue, a glance of what I sing: so, pain
Is linked with pleasure, for I ne'er may tell
Half the bright sights which dazzle me; but now
Mine shall be all the radiance: let them fade   520
Untold—others shall rise as fair, as fast!
And when all's done, the few dim gleams transferred,"—
(For a new thought sprang up how well it were,
Discarding shadowy hope, to weave such lays
As straight encircle men with praise and love,   525
So, I should not die utterly,—should bring
One branch from the gold forest, like the knight
Of old tales, witnessing I had been there)—
"And when all's done, how vain seems e'en success—
The vaunted influence poets have o'er men!   530
'T is a fine thing that one weak as myself
Should sit in his lone room, knowing the words
He utters in his solitude shall move
Men like a swift wind—that tho' dead and gone,
New eyes shall glisten when his beauteous dreams   535
Of love come true in happier frames than his.
Ay, the still night brings thoughts like these, but morn
Comes and the mockery again laughs out
At hollow praises, smiles allied to sneers;
And my soul's idol ever whispers me   540
To dwell with him and his unhonoured song:
And I foreknow my spirit, that would press

5. Formerly.

First in the struggle, fail again to make
All bow enslaved, and I again should sink.

"And then know that this curse will come on us,   545
To see our idols perish; we may wither,
No marvel, we are clay, but our low fate
Should not extend to those whom trustingly
We sent before into time's yawning gulf
To face what dread may lurk in darkness there.   550
To find the painter's glory pass, and feel
Music can move us not as once, or, worst,
To weep decaying wits ere the frail body
Decays! Nought makes me trust some love is true,
But the delight of the contented lowness   555
With which I gaze on him I keep for ever
Above me; I to rise and rival him?
Feed his fame rather from my heart's best blood,
Wither unseen that he may flourish still."
Pauline, my soul's friend, thou dost pity yet   560
How this mood swayed me when that soul found thine,
When I had set myself to live this life,
Defying all past glory. Ere thou camest
I seemed defiant, sweet, for old delights
Had flocked like birds again; music, my life,   565
Nourished me more than ever; then the lore
Loved for itself and all it shows—that king[6]
Treading the purple calmly to his death,
While round him, like the clouds of eve, all dusk,
The giant shades of fate, silently flitting,   570
Pile the dim outline of the coming doom;
And him[7] sitting alone in blood while friends
Are hunting far in the sunshine; and the boy[8]
With his white breast and brow and clustering curls
Streaked with his mother's blood, but striving hard   575
To tell his story ere his reason goes.
And when I loved thee as love seemed so oft,
Thou lovedst me indeed: I wondering searched
My heart to find some feeling like such love,
Believing I was still much I had been.   580
Too soon I found all faith had gone from me,
And the late glow of life, like change on clouds,
Proved not the morn-blush widening into day,
But eve faint-coloured by the dying sun
While darkness hastens quickly. I will tell   585
My state as though 'twere none of mine—despair
Cannot come near us—this it is, my state.

---

6. Agamemnon, Greek king who was murdered after returning home from the Trojan War by
   his wife Clytemnestra and her lover Aegisthus. Cf. Aeschylus's *Agamemnon*.
7. Ajax, Greek hero who slaughtered livestock in a fit of madness, thinking he was attacking his
   former comrades who betrayed him. Cf. Sophocles's *Ajax*.
8. Orestes, son of Agamemnon and Clytemnestra, who avenges his father's murder by killing
   his mother. Cf. Aeschylus's *The Libation-Bearers*.

Souls alter not, and mine must still advance;
Strange that I knew not, when I flung away
My youth's chief aims, their loss might lead to loss   590
Of what few I retained, and no resource
Be left me: for behold how changed is all!
I cannot chain my soul: it will not rest
In its clay prison, this most narrow sphere:
It has strange impulse, tendency, desire,   595
Which nowise I account for nor explain,
But cannot stifle, being bound to trust
All feelings equally, to hear all sides:
How can my life indulge them? yet they live,
Referring to some state of life unknown.   600

My selfishness is satiated not,
It wears me like a flame; my hunger for
All pleasure, howsoe'er minute, grows pain;
I envy—how I envy him whose soul
Turns its whole energies to some one end,   605
To elevate an aim, pursue success
However mean! So, my still baffled hope
Seeks out abstractions; I would have one joy,
But one in life, so it were wholly mine,
One rapture all my soul could fill: and this   610
Wild feeling places me in dream afar
In some vast country where the eye can see
No end to the far hills and dales bestrewn
With shining towers and towns, till I grow mad
Well-nigh, to know not one abode but holds   615
Some pleasure, while my soul could grasp the world,
But must remain this vile form's slave. I look
With hope to age at last, which quenching much,
May let me concentrate what sparks it spares.

This restlessness of passion meets in me   620
A craving after knowledge: the sole proof
Of yet commanding will is in that power
Repressed; for I beheld it in its dawn,
The sleepless harpy[9] with just-budding wings,
And I considered whether to forego   625
All happy ignorant hopes and fears, to live,
Finding a recompense in its wild eyes.
And when I found that I should perish so,
I bade its wild eyes close from me for ever,
And I am left alone with old delights;   630
See! it lies in me a chained thing, still prompt
To serve me if I loose its slightest bond:
I cannot but be proud of my bright slave.
How should this earth's life prove my only sphere?

9. Legendary winged monster with a woman's head, known for tormenting its victims.

Can I so narrow sense but that in life   635
Soul still exceeds it? In their elements
My love outsoars my reason; but since love
Perforce receives its object from this earth
While reason wanders chainless, the few truths
Caught from its wanderings have sufficed to quell   640
Love chained below; then what were love, set free,
Which, with the object it demands, would pass
Reason companioning the seraphim?
No, what I feel may pass all human love
Yet fall far short of what my love should be.   645
And yet I seem more warped in this than aught,
Myself stands out more hideously: of old
I could forget myself in friendship, fame,
Liberty, nay, in love of mightier souls;
But I begin to know what thing hate is—   650
To sicken and to quiver and grow white—
And I myself have furnished its first prey.
Hate of the weak and ever-wavering will,
The selfishness, the still-decaying frame . . .
But I must never grieve whom wing can waft   655
Far from such thoughts—as now. Andromeda![1]
And she is with me: years roll, I shall change,
But change can touch her not—so beautiful
With her fixed eyes, earnest and still, and hair
Lifted and spread by the salt-sweeping breeze,   660
And one red beam, all the storm leaves in heaven,
Resting upon her eyes and hair, such hair,
As she awaits the snake on the wet beach
By the dark rock and the white wave just breaking
At her feet; quite naked and alone; a thing   665
I doubt not, nor fear for, secure some god
To save will come in thunder from the stars.
Let it pass! Soul requires another change.
I will be gifted with a wondrous mind,
Yet sunk by error to men's sympathy,   670
And in the wane of life, yet only so
As to call up their fears; and there shall come
A time requiring youth's best energies;
And lo, I fling age, sorrow, sickness off,
And rise triumphant, triumph through decay.   675

And thus it is that I supply the chasm
'Twixt what I am and all I fain would be:
But then to know nothing, to hope for nothing,
To seize on life's dull joys from a strange fear
Lest, losing them, all's lost and nought remains!   680

---

1. In classical myth, Andromeda was chained to a rock near the ocean and threatened by a sea-monster or dragon; the hero Perseus saved her. The narrator here refers to a painting of the scene by Caravaggio.

There's some vile juggle with my reason here;
I feel I but explain to my own loss
These impulses: they live no less the same.
Liberty! what though I despair? my blood
Rose never at a slave's name proud as now.   685
Oh sympathies, obscured by sophistries!—
Why else have I sought refuge in myself,
But from the woes I saw and could not stay?
Love! is not this to love thee, my Pauline?
I cherish prejudice,[2] lest I be left   690
Utterly loveless? witness my belief
In poets, though sad change has come there too;
No more I leave myself to follow them—
Unconsciously I measure me by them—
Let me forget it: and I cherish most   695
My love of England—how her name, a word
Of hers in a strange tongue makes my heart beat!

Pauline, could I but break the spell! Not now—
All's fever—but when calm shall come again,
I am prepared: I have made life my own.   700
I would not be content with all the change
One frame should feel, but I have gone in thought
Thro' all conjuncture, I have lived all life
When it is most alive, where strangest fate
New-shapes it past surmise—the throes of men   705
Bit by some curse or in the grasps of doom
Half-visible and still-increasing round,
Or crowning their wide being's general aim.
These are wild fancies, but I feel, sweet friend,
As one breathing his weakness to the ear   710
Of pitying angel—dear as a winter flower,
A slight flower growing alone, and offering
Its frail cup of three leaves to the cold sun,
Yet joyous and confiding like the triumph
Of a child: and why am I not worthy thee?   715
I can live all the life of plants, and gaze
Drowsily on the bees that flit and play,
Or bare my breast for sunbeams which will kill,
Or open in the night of sounds, to look
For the dim stars; I can mount with the bird   720
Leaping airily his pyramid of leaves
And twisted boughs of some tall mountain tree,
Or rise cheerfully springing to the heavens;
Or like a fish breathe deep the morning air
In the misty sun-warm water; or with flower   725
And tree can smile in light at the sinking sun
Just as the storm comes, as a girl would look
On a departing lover—most serene.

2. Familiar ideas, not bigotry.

Pauline, come with me, see how I could build
A home for us, out of the world, in thought!   730
I am uplifted: fly with me, Pauline!

Night, and one single ridge of narrow path
Between the sullen river and the woods
Waving and muttering, for the moonless night
Has shaped them into images of life,   735
Like the uprising of the giant-ghosts,
Looking on earth to know how their sons fare:
Thou art so close by me, the roughest swell
Of wind in the tree-tops hides not the panting
Of thy soft breasts. No, we will pass to morning—   740
Morning, the rocks and valleys and old woods.
How the sun brightens in the mist, and here,
Half in the air, like creatures of the place,
Trusting the element, living on high boughs
That swing in the wind—look at the silver spray   745
Flung from the foam-sheet of the cataract
Amid the broken rocks! Shall we stay here
With the wild hawks? No, ere the hot noon come,
Dive we down—safe! See this our new retreat
Walled in with a sloped mound of matted shrubs,   750
Dark, tangled, old and green, still sloping down
To a small pool whose waters lie asleep
Amid the trailing boughs turned water-plants:
And tall trees overarch to keep us in,
Breaking the sunbeams into emerald shafts,   755
And in the dreamy water one small group
Of two or three strange trees are got together
Wondering at all around, as strange beasts herd
Together far from their own land: all wildness,
No turf nor moss, for boughs and plants pave all,   760
And tongues of bank go shelving in the lymph,[3]
Where the pale-throated snake reclines his head,
And old grey stones lie making eddies there,
The wild-mice cross them dry-shod. Deeper in!
Shut thy soft eyes—now look—still deeper in!   765
This is the very heart of the woods all round
Mountain-like heaped above us; yet even here
One pond of water gleams; far off the river
Sweeps like a sea, barred out from land; but one—
One thin clear sheet has overleaped and wound   770
Into this silent depth, which gained, it lies
Still, as but let by sufferance; the trees bend
O'er it as wild men watch a sleeping girl,
And through their roots long creeping plants out-stretch
Their twined hair, steeped and sparkling; farther on,   775
Tall rushes and thick flag-knots have combined

3. Water.

To narrow it; so, at length, a silver thread,
It winds, all noiselessly through the deep wood
Till thro' a cleft-way, thro' the moss and stone,
It joins its parent-river with a shout.   780

Up for the glowing day, leave the old woods!
See, they part, like a ruined arch: the sky!
Nothing but sky appears, so close the roots
And grass of the hill-top level with the air—
Blue sunny air, where a great cloud floats laden   785
With light, like a dead whale that white birds pick,
Floating away in the sun in some north sea.
Air, air, fresh life-blood, thin and searching air,
The clear, dear breath of God that loveth us,
Where small birds reel and winds take their delight!   790
Water is beautiful, but not like air:
See, where the solid azure waters lie
Made as of thickened air, and down below,
The fern-ranks like a forest spread themselves
As though each pore could feel the element;   795
Where the quick glancing serpent winds his way,
Float with me there, Pauline!—but not like air.

Down the hill! Stop—a clump of trees, see, set
On a heap of rock, which look o'er the far plain:
So, envious climbing shrubs would mount to rest   800
And peer from their spread boughs; wide they wave, looking
At the muleteers who whistle on their way,
To the merry chime of morning bells, past all
The little smoking cots, mid fields and banks
And copses bright in the sun. My spirit wanders: 805
Hedgerows for me—those living hedgerows where
The bushes close and clasp above and keep
Thought in—I am concentrated—I feel;
But my soul saddens when it looks beyond:
I cannot be immortal, taste all joy.   810

O God, where do they tend—these struggling aims?*
What would I have? What is this "sleep" which seems

---

* Je crains bien que mon pauvre ami ne soit pas toujours parfaitement compris dans ce qui
reste à lire de cet étrange fragment, mais il est moins propre que tout autre à éclaircir ce qui
de sa nature ne peut jamais être que songe et confusion. D'ailleurs je ne sais trop si en cher-
chant à mieux co-ordonner certaines parties l'on ne courrait pas le risque de nuire au seul
mérite auquel une production si singulière peut prétendre, celui de donner une idée assez
précise du genre qu'elle n'a fait qu'ébaucher. Ce début sans prétention, ce remuement des
passions qui va d'abord en accroissant et puis s'apaise par degrés, ces élans de l'âme, ce re-
tour soudain sur soi-même, et par-dessus tout, la tournure d'esprit tout particulière de mon
ami, rendent les changemens presque impossibles. Les raisons qu'il fait valoir ailleurs,
et d'autres encore plus puissantes, ont fait trouver grâce à mes yeux pour cet écrit
qu'autrement je lui eusse conseillé de jeter au feu. Je n'en crois pas moins au grand principe
de toute composition—à ce principe de Shakespeare, de Rafaelle, de Beethoven, d'où il suit
que la concentration des idées est due bien plus à leur conception qu'à leur mise en exécu-
tion: j'ai tout lieu de craindre que la première de ces qualités ne soit encore étrangère à mon
ami, et je doute fort qu'un redoublement de travail lui fasse acquérir la seconde. Le mieux
serait de brûler ceci; mais que faire?

To bound all? can there be a "waking" point
Of crowning life? The soul would never rule;
It would be first in all things, it would have   815
Its utmost pleasure filled, but, that complete,
Commanding, for commanding, sickens it.
The last point I can trace is—rest beneath
Some better essence than itself, in weakness;
This is "myself," not what I think should be: 820
And what is that I hunger for but God?

My God, my God, let me for once look on thee
As though nought else existed, we alone!
And as creation crumbles, my soul's spark
Expands till I can say,—Even from myself   825
I need thee and I feel thee and I love thee.
I do not plead my rapture in thy works
For love of thee, nor that I feel as one
Who cannot die: but there is that in me
Which turns to thee, which loves or which should love.   830

Why have I girt myself with this hell-dress?
Why have I laboured to put out my life?
Is it not in my nature to adore,
And e'en for all my reason do I not
Feel him, and thank him, and pray to him—now?   835
Can I forego the trust that he loves me?
Do I not feel a love which only ONE . . .
O thou pale form, so dimly seen, deep-eyed!

Je crois que dans ce qui suit il fait allusion à un certain examen qu'il fit autrefois de l'âme, ou plutôt de son âme, pour découvrir la suite des objets auxquels il lui serait possible d'atteindre, et dont chacun une fois obtenu devait former une espèce de plateau d'où l'on pouvait apercevoir d'autres buts, d'autres projets, d'autres jouissances qui, à leur tour, devaient être surmontés. Il en résultait que l'oubli et le sommeil devaient tout terminer. Cette idée, que je ne saisis pas parfaitement, lui est peut-être aussi inintelligible qu'à moi.

PAULINE.[4]

4. This note, written by Browning, can be translated as follows: "I am very much afraid that my poor friend is not always to be perfectly understood in what remains to be read of this strange fragment, but he is less fitted than anyone else to clarify what from its nature can ever be only dream and confusion. Besides I am not sure whether in seeking better to integrate certain parts, one would not risk damaging the only merit to which so singular a production can pretend, that of giving a precise enough idea of the kind that has only been sketched. This unpretentious beginning, this stirring of the passions which first increases and then gradually subsides, these impulses of the soul, this sudden return on himself, and, above all, the exceptional nature of my friend's spirit, make changes almost impossible. The reasons he advances elsewhere, and others still more powerful, have made me appreciate this composition that I should otherwise have advised him to burn. I do not believe any the less in the grand principle of all composition—that principle of Shakespeare, of Raphael, of Beethoven, from which it follows that the concentration of ideas owes much more to their conception than to their execution: I have every reason to fear that the first of these qualities is still strange to my friend, and I very much doubt that a doubling of effort would make him acquire the second. The best thing would be to burn this; but what can one do?
   I believe that in what follows he refers to a certain examination that he once made of the soul, or rather of his own soul, to discover the succession of goals which it would be possible for him to attain, and of which each, once obtained, would be a sort of plateau from which one could discern other ends, other projects, other pleasures, that should in their turn be surmounted. The conclusion was that oblivion and sleep ought to end everything. This idea, which I do not perfectly grasp, is perhaps as unintelligible to him as to me" (Pettigrew's translation).

I have denied thee calmly—do I not
Pant when I read of thy consummate power,   840
And burn to see thy calm pure truths out-flash
The brightest gleams of earth's philosophy?
Do I not shake to hear aught question thee?
If I am erring save me, madden me,
Take from me powers and pleasures, let me die   845
Ages, so I see thee! I am knit round
As with a charm by sin and lust and pride,
Yet though my wandering dreams have seen all shapes
Of strange delight, oft have I stood by thee—
Have I been keeping lonely watch with thee   850
In the damp night by weeping Olivet,[5]
Or leaning on thy bosom, proudly less,
Or dying with thee on the lonely cross,
Or witnessing thine outburst from the tomb.

A mortal, sin's familiar friend, doth here   855
Avow that he will give all earth's reward,
But to believe and humbly teach the faith,
In suffering and poverty and shame,
Only believing he is not unloved.

And now, my Pauline, I am thine for ever!   860
I feel the spirit which has buoyed me up
Desert me, and old shades are gathering fast;
Yet while the last light waits, I would say much,
This chiefly, it is gain that I have said
Somewhat of love I ever felt for thee   865
But seldom told; our hearts so beat together
That speech seemed mockery; but when dark hours come,
And joy departs, and thou, sweet, deem'st it strange
A sorrow moves me, thou canst not remove,
Look on this lay I dedicate to thee,   870
Which through thee I began, which thus I end,
Collecting the last gleams to strive to tell
How I am thine, and more than ever now
That I sink fast: yet though I deeplier sink,
No less song proves one word has brought me bliss,   875
Another still may win bliss surely back.
Thou knowest, dear, I could not think all calm,
For fancies followed thought and bore me off,
And left all indistinct; ere one was caught
Another glanced; so, dazzled by my wealth,   880
I knew not which to leave nor which to choose,
For all so floated, nought was fixed and firm.
And then thou said'st a perfect bard was one
Who chronicled the stages of all life,
And so thou bad'st me shadow[6] this first stage.   885

5. Mountain ridge near Jerusalem, overlooking Gesthemene, where Christ suffered. See Mark
   14:26–42.
6. Depict.

'T is done, and even now I recognize
The shift, the change from last to past—discern
Faintly how life is truth and truth is good.
And why thou must be mine is, that e'en now
In the dim hush of night, that I have done,   890
Despite the sad forebodings, love looks through—
Whispers,—E'en at the last I have her still,
With her delicious eyes as clear as heaven
When rain in a quick shower has beat down mist,
And clouds float white above like broods of swans.   895
How the blood lies upon her cheek, outspread
As thinned by kisses! only in her lips
It wells and pulses like a living thing,
And her neck looks like marble misted o'er
With love-breath,—a Pauline from heights above,   900
Stooping beneath me, looking up—one look
As I might kill her and be loved the more.

So, love me—me, Pauline, and nought but me,
Never leave loving! Words are wild and weak,
Believe them not, Pauline! I stained myself   905
But to behold thee purer by my side,
To show thou art my breath, my life, a last
Resource, an extreme want: never believe
Aught better could so look on thee; nor seek
Again the world of good thoughts left for mine!   910
There were bright troops of undiscovered suns,
Each equal in their radiant course; there were
Clusters of far fair isles which ocean kept
For his own joy, and his waves broke on them
Without a choice; and there was a dim crowd   915
Of visions, each a part of some grand whole:
And one star left his peers and came with peace
Upon a storm, and all eyes pined for him;
And one isle harboured a sea-beaten ship,
And the crew wandered in its bowers and plucked   920
Its fruits and gave up all their hopes of home;[7]
And one dream came to a pale poet's sleep,
And he said, "I am singled out by God,
No sin must touch me." Words are wild and weak,
But what they would express is,—Leave me not,   925
Still sit by me with beating breast and hair
Loosened, be watching earnest by my side,
Turning my books or kissing me when I
Look up—like summer wind! Be still to me
A help to music's mystery which mind fails   930
To fathom, its solution, no mere clue!
O reason's pedantry, life's rule prescribed!
I hopeless, I the loveless, hope and love.

---

7. Alluding to the sojourn of Odysseus and his crew on the island of the lotus-eaters in
Homer's *Odyssey* IX.

Wiser and better, know me now, not when
You loved me as I was. Smile not! I have   935
Much yet to dawn on you, to gladden you.
No more of the past! I'll look within no more.
I have too trusted my own lawless wants,
Too trusted my vain self, vague intuition—
Draining soul's wine alone in the still night,   940
And seeing how, as gathering films arose,
As by an inspiration life seemed bare
And grinning in its vanity, while ends
Foul to be dreamed of, smiled at me as fixed
And fair, while others changed from fair to foul   945
As a young witch turns an old hag at night.
No more of this! We will go hand in hand,
I with thee, even as a child—love's slave,
Looking no farther than his liege commands.

And thou hast chosen where this life shall be: 950
The land[8] which gave me thee shall be our home,
Where nature lies all wild amid her lakes
And snow-swathed mountains and vast pines begirt
With ropes of snow—where nature lies all bare,
Suffering none to view her but a race   955
Or stinted or deformed, like the mute dwarfs
Which wait upon a naked Indian queen.
And there (the time being when the heavens are thick
With storm) I'll sit with thee while thou dost sing
Thy native songs, gay as a desert bird   960
Which crieth as it flies for perfect joy,
Or telling me old stories of dead knights;
Or I will read great lays to thee—how she,[9]
The fair pale sister, went to her chill grave
With power to love and to be loved and live: 965
Or we will go together, like twin gods
Of the infernal world, with scented lamp
Over the dead, to call and to awake,
Over the unshaped images which lie
Within my mind's cave: only leaving all,   970
That tells of the past doubt. So, when spring comes
With sunshine back again like an old smile,
And the fresh waters and awakened birds
And budding woods await us, I shall be
Prepared, and we will question life once more,   975
Till its old sense shall come renewed by change,
Like some clear thought which harsh words veiled before;
Feeling God loves us, and that all which errs
Is but a dream which death will dissipate.
And then what need of longer exile? Seek   980
My England, and, again there, calm approach

8. Switzerland.
9. Antigone, in Sophocles's play, sacrifices herself to defend the honor of her dead brother.

All I once fled from, calmly look on those
The works of my past weakness, as one views
Some scene where danger met him long before.
Ah that such pleasant life should be but dreamed!   985

But whate'er come of it, and though it fade,
And though ere the cold morning all be gone,
As it may be;—tho' music wait to wile,
And strange eyes and bright wine lure, laugh like sin
Which steals back softly on a soul half saved,   990
And I the first deny, decry, despise,
With this avowal, these intents so fair,—
Still be it all my own, this moment's pride!
No less I make an end in perfect joy.
E'en in my brightest time, a lurking fear   995
Possessed me: I well knew my weak resolves,
I felt the witchery that makes mind sleep
Over its treasure, as one half afraid
To make his riches definite: but now
These feelings shall not utterly be lost,   1000
I shall not know again that nameless care
Lest, leaving all undone in youth, some new
And undreamed end reveal itself too late:
For this song shall remain to tell for ever
That when I lost all hope of such a change,   1005
Suddenly beauty rose on me again.
No less I make an end in perfect joy,
For I, who thus again was visited,
Shall doubt not many another bliss awaits,
And, though this weak soul sink and darkness whelm,   1010
Some little word shall light it, raise aloft,
To where I clearlier see and better love,
As I again go o'er the tracts of thought
Like one who has a right, and I shall live
With poets, calmer, purer still each time,   1015
And beauteous shapes will come for me to seize,
And unknown secrets will be trusted me
Which were denied the waverer once; but now
I shall be priest and prophet as of old.

Sun-treader, I believe in God and truth   1020
And love; and as one just escaped from death
Would bind himself in bands of friends to feel
He lives indeed, so, I would lean on thee!
Thou must be ever with me, most in gloom
If such must come, but chiefly when I die,   1025
For I seem, dying, as one going in the dark
To fight a giant: but live thou for ever,
And be to all what thou hast been to me!
All in whom this wakes pleasant thoughts of me

Know my last state is happy, free from doubt   1030
Or touch of fear. Love me and wish me well.

RICHMOND:
October 22, 1832.

FROM *PARACELSUS* (1835)[1]

Part II

* * *

I hear a voice, perchance I heard[2]
Long ago, but all too low,
So that scarce a care it stirred
If the voice were real or no:
I heard it in my youth when first   285
The waters of my life outburst:
But, now their stream ebbs faint, I hear
That voice, still low, but fatal-clear—
As if all poets, God ever meant
Should save the world, and therefore lent   290
Great gifts to, but who, proud, refused
To do his work, or lightly used
Those gifts, or failed through weak endeavour,
So, mourn cast off by him for ever,—
As if these leaned in airy ring   295
To take me; this the song they sing.

"Lost, lost! yet come,
With our wan troop make thy home.
Come, come! for we
Will not breathe, so much as breathe   300
Reproach to thee,
Knowing what thou sink'st beneath.
So sank we in those old years,
We who bid thee, come! thou last
Who, living yet, hast life o'erpast.   305
And altogether we, thy peers,
Will pardon crave for thee, the last
Whose trial is done, whose lot is cast
With those who watch but work no more,
Who gaze on life but live no more.   310
Yet we trusted thou shouldst speak

1. Browning's first acknowledged work, the ambitious dialogue-poem *Paracelsus* (1835) was a
critical if not popular success, setting the young poet before the London literary world. His
essentially romantic vision led him to portray Paracelsus (1493–1541), Renaissance al-
chemist and reformer of medicine and pharmacology, as a Promethean hero on an obsessive,
failed quest for universal knowledge.
2. This lyric is sung by an Italian poet, Aprile, whom Paracelsus encounters in Constantinople.
The two characters are complementary: just as Paracelsus aspires to know all, Aprile "would
love infinitely, and be loved" (II.420).

The message which our lips, too weak,
Refused to utter,—shouldst redeem
Our fault: such trust, and all a dream!
Yet we chose thee a birthplace   315
Where the richness ran to flowers:
Couldst not sing one song for grace?
Not make one blossom man's and ours?
Must one more recreant[3] to his race
Die with unexerted powers,   320
And join us, leaving as he found
The world, he was to loosen, bound?
Anguish! ever and for ever;[4]
Still beginning, ending never.
Yet, lost and last one, come!   325
How couldst understand, alas,
What our pale ghosts strove to say,[5]
As their shades did glance and pass
Before thee night and day?
Thou wast blind as we were dumb: 330
Once more, therefore, come, O come!
How should we clothe, how arm the spirit
Shall next thy post of life inherit—
How guard him from thy speedy ruin?
Tell us of thy sad undoing   335
Here, where we sit, ever pursuing
Our weary task, ever renewing
Sharp sorrow, far from God who gave
Our powers, and man they could not save!"

* * *

Part IV

* * *

                                        [He sings.
Heap cassia, sandal-buds and stripes[6]   190
    Of labdanum, and aloe-balls,
Smeared with dull nard an Indian wipes
    From out her hair: such balsam falls
    Down sea-side mountain pedestals,
From tree-tops where tired winds are fain,   195
Spent with the vast and howling main,
To treasure half their island-gain.

And strew faint sweetness from some old
    Egyptian's fine worm-eaten shroud

---

3. Unfaithful.
4. Cf. Shelley, *Prometheus Unbound*, I.23: "alas, pain, pain ever, for ever!"
5. The "pale ghosts" recall the horde of the Indifferent in the Vestibule of Dante's hell (*Inferno*, III).
6. In the presence of his friend Festus, Paracelsus bids farewell to his youthful fancies, represented in the first stanza by exotic spices. Cf. *Paradise Lost*, V.292–93: "groves of myrrh, / And flowering odours, cassia, nard, and balm."

Which breaks to dust when once unrolled;[7]   200
   Or shredded perfume, like a cloud
From closet long to quiet vowed,
With mothed[8] and dropping arras[9] hung,
Mouldering her lute and books among,
As when a queen, long dead, was young.   205

* * *

[He sings.

Over the sea our galleys went,[1]   450
With cleaving prows in order brave
To a speeding wind and a bounding wave,
   A gallant armament:
Each bark built out of a forest-tree
   Left leafy and rough as first it grew,   455
And nailed all over the gaping sides,
Within and without, with black bull-hides,
Seethed in fat and suppled in flame,
To bear the playful billows' game:
So, each good ship was rude to see,   460
Rude and bare to the outward view,
   But each upbore a stately tent
Where cedar pales[2] in scented row
Kept out the flakes of the dancing brine,
And an awning drooped the mast below,   465
In fold on fold of the purple fine,
That neither noontide nor starshine
Nor moonlight cold which maketh mad,
   Might pierce the regal tenement.[3]
When the sun dawned, oh, gay and glad   470
We set the sail and plied the oar;
But when the night-wind blew like breath,
For joy of one day's voyage more,
We sang together on the wide sea,
Like men at peace on a peaceful shore;   475
Each sail was loosed to the wind so free,
Each helm made sure by the twilight star,
And in a sleep as calm as death,
We, the voyagers from afar,
   Lay stretched along, each weary crew   480
In a circle round its wondrous tent
Whence gleamed soft light and curled rich scent,
   And with light and perfume, music too:
So the stars wheeled round, and the darkness past,
And at morn we started beside the mast,   485
And still each ship was sailing fast.

---

7. Renaissance physicians used pulverized Egyptian mummies for medicinal purposes.
8. Moth-eaten.
9. Tapestry.
1. After singing this allegorical song to Festus, Paracelsus comments: "The sad rhyme of the men who proudly clung / To their first fault and withered in their pride" (526–27).
2. Poles.
3. I.e., the "stately tent" of line 13.

Now, one morn, land appeared—a speck
Dim trembling betwixt sea and sky:
"Avoid it," cried our pilot, "check
   The shout, restrain the eager eye!"   490
But the heaving sea was black behind
For many a night and many a day,
And land, though but a rock, drew nigh;
So, we broke the cedar pales away,
Let the purple awning flap in the wind,   495
   And a statue bright was on every deck!
We shouted, every man of us,
And steered right into the harbour thus,
With pomp and pæan[4] glorious.

A hundred shapes of lucid stone!   500
   All day we built its shrine for each,
A shrine of rock for every one,
Nor paused till in the westering sun
   We sat together on the beach
To sing because our task was done.   505
When lo! what shouts and merry songs!
What laughter all the distance stirs!
A loaded raft with happy throngs
Of gentle islanders!
"Our isles are just at hand," they cried,   510
   "Like cloudlets faint in even sleeping
Our temple-gates are opened wide,
   Our olive-groves thick shade are keeping
For these majestic forms"—they cried.
Oh, then we awoke with sudden start   515
From our deep dream, and knew, too late,
How bare the rock, how desolate,
Which had received our precious freight:
   Yet we called out—"Depart!
Our gifts, once given, must here abide.   520
   Our work is done; we have no heart
To mar our work,"—we cried.[5]

     * * *

Part V

     * * *

Thus the Mayne glideth[6]
Where my Love abideth.
Sleep's no softer: it proceeds   420
On through lawns, on through meads,

4. Song of praise or triumph.
5. The voyagers have left their "precious freight" on the wrong (deserted) island, but are too
weary to move their gifts to where the "gentle islanders" await them.
6. Festus sings to comfort the dying Paracelsus. Before joining the Rhine, the Mayne (Main)
river flows through Würzburg, where Paracelsus had studied some thirty years before, and
had known happiness with Festus and his wife Michal.

On and on, whate'er befall,
Meandering and musical,
Though the niggard pasturage
Bears not on its shaven ledge   425
Aught but weeds and waving grasses
To view the river as it passes,
Save here and there a scanty patch
Of primroses too faint to catch
A weary bee.   430
Paracelsus.   More, more; say on!
Festus.   And scarce it pushes
Its gentle way through strangling rushes
Where the glossy kingfisher
Flutters when noon-heats are near,
Glad the shelving banks to shun,   435
Red and steaming in the sun;
Where the shrew-mouse with pale throat
Burrows, and the speckled stoat;
Where the quick sandpipers flit
In and out the marl[7] and grit   440
That seems to breed them, brown as they:
Nought disturbs its quiet way,
Save some lazy stork that springs,
Trailing it with legs and wings,
Whom the shy fox from the hill   445
Rouses, creep he ne'er so still.
                    * * *
I knew, I felt, (perception unexpressed,[8]
Uncomprehended by our narrow thought,
But somehow felt and known in every shift   640
And change in the spirit,—nay, in every pore
Of the body, even,)—what God is, what we are,
What life is—how God tastes an infinite joy
In infinite ways—one everlasting bliss,
From whom all being emanates, all power   645
Proceeds; in whom is life for evermore,
Yet whom existence in its lowest form
Includes; where dwells enjoyment there is he:
With still a flying point of bliss remote,
A happiness in store afar, a sphere   650
Of distant glory in full view; thus climbs
Pleasure its heights for ever and for ever.
The centre-fire heaves underneath the earth,
And the earth changes like a human face;
The molten ore bursts up among the rocks,   655
Winds into the stone's heart, outbranches bright
In hidden mines, spots barren river-beds,
Crumbles into fine sand where sunbeams bask—
God joys therein. The wroth sea's waves are edged

7. Silt.
8. In this, his dying speech, Paracelsus reviews his life and celebrates God's "scheme of being."

With foam, white as the bitten lip of hate,   660
When, in the solitary waste, strange groups
Of young volcanos come up, cyclops-like,
Staring together with their eyes on flame—
God tastes a pleasure in their uncouth pride.
Then all is still; earth is a wintry clod: 665
But spring-wind, like a dancing psaltress,[9] passes
Over its breast to waken it, rare verdure
Buds tenderly upon rough banks, between
The withered tree-roots and the cracks of frost,
Like a smile striving with a wrinkled face;   670
The grass grows bright, the boughs are swoln with blooms
Like chrysalids impatient for the air,
The shining dorrs[1] are busy, beetles run
Along the furrows, ants make their ado;
Above, birds fly in merry flocks, the lark   675
Soars up and up, shivering for very joy;
Afar the ocean sleeps; white fishing-gulls
Flit where the strand is purple with its tribe
Of nested limpets; savage creatures seek
Their loves in wood and plain—and God renews   680
His ancient rapture. Thus he dwells in all,
From life's minute beginnings, up at last
To man—the consummation of this scheme
Of being, the completion of this sphere
Of life: whose attributes had here and there   685
Been scattered o'er the visible world before,
Asking to be combined, dim fragments meant
To be united in some wondrous whole,
Imperfect qualities throughout creation,
Suggesting some one creature yet to make,   690
Some point where all those scattered rays should meet
Convergent in the faculties of man.
Power—neither put forth blindly, nor controlled
Calmly by perfect knowledge; to be used
At risk, inspired or checked by hope and fear: 695
Knowledge—not intuition, but the slow
Uncertain fruit of an enhancing toil,
Strengthened by love: love—not serenely pure,
But strong from weakness, like a chance-sown plant
Which, cast on stubborn soil, puts forth changed buds   700
And softer stains, unknown in happier climes;
Love which endures and doubts and is oppressed
And cherished, suffering much and much sustained,
And blind, oft-failing, yet believing love,
A half-enlightened, often-chequered trust:—   705
Hints and previsions of which faculties,
Are strewn confusedly everywhere about

9. Woman playing a psaltery, a string instrument.
1. Dorbeetle, European dung beetle.

The inferior natures, and all lead up higher,
All shape out dimly the superior race,
The heir of hopes too fair to turn out false,   710
And man appears at last. So far the seal
Is put on life; one stage of being complete,
One scheme wound up: and from the grand result
A supplementary reflux of light,
Illustrates[2] all the inferior grades, explains   715
Each back step in the circle. Not alone
For their possessor dawn those qualities,
But the new glory mixes with the heaven
And earth; man, once descried, imprints for ever
His presence on all lifeless things: the winds   720
Are henceforth voices, wailing or a shout,
A querulous mutter or a quick gay laugh,
Never a senseless gust now man is born.
The herded pines commune and have deep thoughts,
A secret they assemble to discuss   725
When the sun drops behind their trunks which glare
Like grates of hell: the peerless cup afloat
Of the lake-lily is an urn, some nymph
Swims bearing high above her head: no bird
Whistles unseen, but through the gaps above   730
That let light in upon the gloomy woods,
A shape peeps from the breezy forest-top,
Arch with small puckered mouth and mocking eye.
The morn has enterprise, deep quiet droops
With evening, triumph takes the sunset hour,   735
Voluptuous transport ripens with the corn
Beneath a warm moon like a happy face:
—And this to fill us with regard for man.
With apprehension of his passing worth,
Desire to work his proper nature out,   740
And ascertain his rank and final place,
For these things tend still upward, progress is
The law of life, man is not Man as yet.
Nor shall I deem his object served, his end
Attained, his genuine strength put fairly forth,   745
While only here and there a star dispels
The darkness, here and there a towering mind
O'erlooks its prostrate fellows: when the host
Is out at once to the despair of night,
When all mankind alike is perfected,   750
Equal in full-blown powers—then, not till then,
I say, begins man's general infancy.
For wherefore make account of feverish starts
Of restless members of a dormant whole,
Impatient nerves which quiver while the body   755
Slumbers as in a grave? Oh long ago

2. Casts light upon.

The brow was twitched, the tremulous lids astir,
The peaceful mouth disturbed; half-uttered speech
Ruffled the lip, and then the teeth were set,
The breath drawn sharp, the strong right-hand
    clenched stronger,   760
As it would pluck a lion by the jaw;
The glorious creature laughed out even in sleep!
But when full roused, each giant-limb awake,
Each sinew strung, the great heart pulsing fast,
He shall start up and stand on his own earth,   765
Then shall his long triumphant march begin,
Thence shall his being date,—thus wholly roused,
What he achieves shall be set down to him.
When all the race is perfected alike
As man, that is; all tended to mankind,   770
And, man produced, all has its end thus far:
But in completed man begins anew
A tendency to God. Prognostics told
Man's near approach; so in man's self arise
August anticipations, symbols, types   775
Of a dim splendour ever on before
In that eternal circle life pursues.
For men begin to pass their nature's bound,
And find new hopes and cares which fast supplant
Their proper joys and griefs; they grow too great   780
For narrow creeds of right and wrong, which fade
Before the unmeasured thirst for good: while peace
Rises within them ever more and more.
Such men are even now upon the earth,
Serene amid the half-formed creatures round   785
Who should be saved by them and joined with them.
Such was my task, and I was born to it—
Free, as I said but now, from much that chains
Spirits, high-dowered but limited and vexed
By a divided and delusive aim,   790
A shadow mocking a reality
Whose truth avails not wholly to disperse
The flitting mimic called up by itself,
And so remains perplexed and nigh put out
By its fantastic fellow's wavering gleam.   795
I, from the first, was never cheated thus;
I never fashioned out a fancied good
Distinct from man's; a service to be done,
A glory to be ministered unto
With powers put forth at man's expense, withdrawn   800
From labouring in his behalf; a strength
Denied that might avail him. I cared not
Lest his success ran counter to success
Elsewhere: for God is glorified in man,
And to man's glory vowed I soul and limb.   805
Yet, constituted thus, and thus endowed,

I failed: I gazed on power till I grew blind.
Power; I could not take my eyes from that:
That only, I thought, should be preserved, increased
At any risk, displayed, struck out at once—   810
The sign and note and character of man.
I saw no use in the past: only a scene
Of degradation, ugliness and tears,
The record of disgraces best forgotten,
A sullen page in human chronicles   815
Fit to erase. I saw no cause why man
Should not stand all-sufficient even now,
Or why his annals should be forced to tell
That once the tide of light, about to break
Upon the world, was sealed within its spring: 820
I would have had one day, one moment's space,
Change man's condition, push each slumbering claim
Of mastery o'er the elemental world
At once to full maturity, then roll
Oblivion o'er the work, and hide from man   825
What night had ushered morn. Not so, dear child
Of after-days, wilt thou reject the past
Big with deep warnings of the proper tenure
By which thou hast the earth: for thee the present
Shall have distinct and trembling beauty, seen   830
Beside that past's own shade when, in relief,
Its brightness shall stand out: nor yet on thee
Shall burst the future, as successive zones
Of several wonder open on some spirit
Flying secure and glad from heaven to heaven: 835
But thou shalt painfully attain to joy,
While hope and fear and love shall keep thee man!
All this was hid from me: as one by one
My dreams grew dim, my wide aims circumscribed,
As actual good within my reach decreased,   840
While obstacles sprung up this way and that
To keep me from effecting half the sum,
Small as it proved; as objects, mean within
The primal aggregate, seemed, even the least,
Itself a match for my concentred strength—   845
What wonder if I saw no way to shun
Despair? The power I sought for man, seemed God's.
In this conjuncture, as I prayed to die,
A strange adventure made me know, one sin
Had spotted my career from its uprise;   850
I saw Aprile—my Aprile there!
And as the poor melodious wretch disburthened
His heart, and moaned his weakness in my ear,
I learned my own deep error; love's undoing
Taught me the worth of love in man's estate,   855
And what proportion love should hold with power
In his right constitution; love preceding

Power, and with much power, always much more love;
Love still too straitened in his present means,
And earnest for new power to set love free.   860
I learned this, and supposed the whole was learned:
And thus, when men received with stupid wonder
My first revealings, would have worshipped me,
And I despised and loathed their proffered praise—
When, with awakened eyes, they took revenge   865
For past credulity in casting shame
On my real knowledge, and I hated them—
It was not strange I saw no good in man,
To overbalance all the wear and waste
Of faculties, displayed in vain, but born   870
To prosper in some better sphere: and why?
In my own heart love had not been made wise
To trace love's faint beginnings in mankind,
To know even hate is but a mask of love's,
To see a good in evil, and a hope   875
In ill-success; to sympathize, be proud
Of their half-reasons, faint aspirings, dim
Struggles for truth, their poorest fallacies,
Their prejudice and fears and cares and doubts;
All with a touch of nobleness, despite   880
Their error, upward tending all though weak,
Like plants in mines which never saw the sun,
But dream of him, and guess where he may be,
And do their best to climb and get to him.
All this I knew not, and I failed. Let men   885
Regard me, and the poet dead long ago
Who loved too rashly; and shape forth a third
And better-tempered spirit, warned by both:
As from the over-radiant star too mad
To drink the life-springs, beamless thence itself—   890
And the dark orb which borders the abyss,
Ingulfed in icy night,—might have its course
A temperate and equidistant world.
Meanwhile, I have done well, though not all well.
As yet men cannot do without contempt;   895
'T is for their good, and therefore fit awhile
That they reject the weak, and scorn the false,
Rather than praise the strong and true, in me:
But after, they will know me. If I stoop
Into a dark tremendous sea of cloud,   900
It is but for a time; I press God's lamp
Close to my breast; its splendour, soon or late,
Will pierce the gloom: I shall emerge one day.
You understand me? I have said enough?
    Festus. Now die, dear Aureole!
    Paracelsus.   Festus, let my hand—   905
This hand, lie in your own, my own true friend!
Aprile! Hand in hand with you, Aprile!
Festus. And this was Paracelsus!

FROM *SORDELLO* (1840)

When after six years of composition—and painstaking revision—the ambitious narrative poem *Sordello* was published in 1840, it was greeted with howls of protest or derision because of its obscurity of style and allusion. Browning wrote to Macready that it was "praised by the units, cursed by the tens, and unmeddled with by the hundreds!" Despite generous praise from the great modern American poet Ezra Pound, *Sordello* remains among the most neglected of Browning's works, an irony since the poem provides a comprehensive view of the author's mind and art in his early phase. The historical context of *Sordello* is the strife between two rival factions, the Guelphs and the Ghibellines, in northern Italy in the early thirteenth century. The protagonist is Sordello, a troubadour praised by Dante but otherwise obscure; Browning makes this figure his type of "Poet-as-Hero." Arthur Symons' characterization of the poem as a "psychological epic" is apt, for the focus is the developing conflict within Sordello between egoism and sympathy, art and society, contemplation and action—an internecine struggle that finally kills the hero. This passage, excerpted from Book II, concerns Sordello's attitudes toward his art after he wins a song-contest in the Mantuan court by defeating his rival, Eglamor. Browning's own marginal glosses are helpful: "He has loved song's results, not song; so, must effect this [song] to obtain those [results]. He succeeds a little, but fails more; tries again, is no better satisfied, and declines from the ideal of song. What is the world's recognition worth? How poet no longer in unity with man, the whole visible Sordello goes wrong."

* * *

> The evening star was high
> When he reached Mantua, but his fame arrived
> Before him: friends applauded, foes connived,
> And Naddo[1] looked an angel, and the rest
> Angels, and all these angels would be blest   480
> Supremely by a song—the thrice-renowned
> Goito-manufacture.[2] Then he found
> (Casting about to satisfy the crowd)
> That happy vehicle, so late allowed,
> A sore annoyance; 't was the song's effect   485
> He cared for, scarce the song itself: reflect!
> In the past life, what might be singing's use?
> Just to delight his Delians,[3] whose profuse
> Praise, not the toilsome process which procured
> That praise, enticed Apollo: dreams abjured,   490
> No overleaping means for ends—take both
> For granted or take neither! I am loth
> To say the rhymes at last were Eglamor's;[4]
> But Naddo, chuckling, bade competitors

1. Naddo is "busiest of the tribe/Of genius-haunters" (*Sordello*, II.821–22).
2. Goito was Sordello's birthplace.
3. Natives of Delos, birthplace of Apollo, god of song.
4. Sordello used his competitor's rhymes in composing his song, presumably indicating a lack of inspiration.

Go pine; "the master certes meant to waste   495
No effort, cautiously had probed the taste
He'd please anon: true bard, in short,—disturb
His title if they could; nor spur nor curb,
Fancy nor reason, wanting in him; whence
The staple of his verses, common sense: 500
He built on man's broad nature—gift of gifts,
That power to build! The world contented shifts
With counterfeits enough, a dreary sort
Of warriors, statesmen, ere it can extort
Its poet-soul—that's, after all, a freak   505
(The having eyes to see and tongue to speak)
With our herd's stupid sterling happiness
So plainly incompatible that—yes—
Yes—should a son of his improve the breed
And turn out poet, he were cursed indeed!"   510
"Well, there's Goito and its woods anon,
If the worst happen; best go stoutly on
Now!" thought Sordello.
                            Ay, and goes on yet!
You pother with your glossaries to get
A notion of the Troubadour's intent   515
In rondel, tenzon, virlai or sirvent[5]—
Much as you study arras[6] how to twirl
His angelot,[7] plaything of page and girl
Once; but you surely reach, at last,—or, no!
Never quite reach what struck the people so,   520
As from the welter of their time he drew
Its elements successively to view,
Followed all actions backward on their course,
And catching up, unmingled at the source,
Such a strength, such a weakness, added then   525
A touch or two, and turned them into men.
Virtue took form, nor vice refused a shape;
Here heaven opened, there was hell agape,
As Saint this simpered past in sanctity,
Sinner the other flared portentous by   530
A greedy people. Then why stop, surprised
At his success? The scheme was realized
Too suddenly in one respect: a crowd
Praising, eyes quick to see, and lips as loud
To speak, delicious homage to receive,   535
The woman's breath to feel upon his sleeve,
Who said, "But Anafest—why asks he less
Than Lucio, in your verses?[8] how confess,

5. Conventional French forms. *Rondel*: a lyric of ten or thirteen lines on two rhymes, the first
two lines becoming the refrain. *Tenzon*: a "contention" or imaginary verbal exchange upon
some question of love or conduct. *Virlai*: or virelai, a complicated fixed form with refrains.
Sirvent: Old Provençal poem in strophes, satiric or vituperative in tone, often about current
events.
6. Tapestries.
7. Stringed, lute-like instrument.
8. I.e., "why does my lover (Anafest) speak less passionately than the Lucio of your poem?"

It seemed too much but yestereve!"—the youth,
Who bade him earnestly, "Avow the truth!   540
You love Bianca, surely, from your song;
I knew I was unworthy!"—soft or strong,
In poured such tributes ere he had arranged
Ethereal ways to take them, sorted, changed,
Digested. Courted thus at unawares,   545
In spite of his pretensions and his cares,
He caught himself shamefully hankering
After the obvious petty joys that spring
From true life, fain relinquish pedestal
And condescend with pleasures—one and all   550
To be renounced, no doubt; for, thus to chain
Himself to single joys and so refrain
From tasting their quintessence, frustrates, sure,
His prime design; each joy must he abjure
Even for love of it.
     He laughed: what sage   555
But perishes if from his magic page
He look because, at the first line, a proof
'T was heard salutes him from the cavern roof?
"On! Give yourself, excluding aught beside,
To the day's task; compel your slave provide   560
Its utmost at the soonest; turn the leaf
Thoroughly conned. These lays of yours, in brief—
Cannot men bear, now, something better?—fly
A pitch beyond this unreal pageantry
Of essences? the period sure has ceased   565
For such: present us with ourselves, at least,
Not portions of ourselves, mere loves and hates
Made flesh: wait not!"
      Awhile the poet waits
However. The first trial was enough:
He left imagining, to try the stuff   570
That held the imaged thing, and, let it writhe
Never so fiercely, scarce allowed a tithe
To reach the light—his Language. How he sought
The cause, conceived a cure, and slow re-wrought
That Language,—welding words into the crude   575
Mass from the new speech round him, till a rude
Armour was hammered out, in time to be
Approved beyond the Roman panoply[9]
Melted to make it,—boots not. This obtained
With some ado, no obstacle remained   580
To using it; accordingly he took
An action with its actors, quite forsook
Himself to live in each, returned anon
With the result—a creature, and, by one
And one, proceeded leisurely to equip   585

9. Latin, or perhaps Provençal, forerunners of the vernacular Italian.

Its limbs in harness of his workmanship.
"Accomplished! Listen, Mantuans!" Fond essay![1]
Piece after piece that armour broke away,
Because perceptions whole, like that he sought
To clothe, reject so pure a work of thought   590
As language: thought may take perception's place
But hardly co-exist in any case,
Being its mere presentment—of the whole
By parts, the simultaneous and the sole
By the successive and the many. Lacks   595
The crowd perception? painfully it tacks
Thought to thought, which Sordello, needing such,
Has rent perception into: it's to clutch
And reconstruct—his office to diffuse,
Destroy: as hard, then, to obtain a Muse   600
As to become Apollo. "For the rest,
E'en if some wondrous vehicle[2] expressed
The whole dream, what impertinence in me
So to express it, who myself can be
The dream! nor, on the other hand, are those   605
I sing to, over-likely to suppose
A higher than the highest I present
Now, which they praise already: be content
Both parties, rather—they with the old verse,
And I with the old praise—far go, fare worse!"   610
A few adhering rivets loosed, upsprings
The angel, sparkles off his mail,[3] which rings
Whirled from each delicatest limb it warps;
So might Apollo from the sudden corpse
Of Hyacinth[4] have cast his luckless quoits.   615
He set to celebrating the exploits
Of Montfort[5] o'er the Mountaineers.

                             Then came
The world's revenge: their pleasure, now his aim
Merely,—what was it? "Not to play the fool
So much as learn our lesson in your school!"   620
Replied the world. He found that, every time
He gained applause by any ballad-rhyme,
His auditory recognized no jot
As he intended, and, mistaking not
Him for his meanest hero, ne'er was dunce   625
Sufficient to believe him—all, at once.
His will . . . conceive it caring for his will!
—Mantuans, the main of them, admiring still

1. Foolish attempt.
2. Poetic form.
3. Sheds his armor.
4. Youth loved by both Apollo and Zephyrus. The latter out of jealousy blew a quoit thrown by
   Apollo so that it struck Hyacinthus, his partner in the game, instantly killing him.
5. Simon de Montfort, in the early thirteenth century, led a crusade to suppress the heretical
   Albigenses, whose strongholds were the mountainous regions of southern France and north-
   ern Italy. This crusade, noted for its cruelty, was associated with the end of the Provençal
   troubadours.

How a mere singer, ugly, stunted, weak,
Had Montfort at completely (so to speak)   630
His fingers' ends; while past the praise-tide swept
To Montfort, either's share distinctly kept:
The true meed for true merit!—his abates
Into a sort he most repudiates,
And on them angrily he turns. Who were   635
The Mantuans, after all, that he should care
About their recognition, ay or no?
In spite of the convention months ago,
(Why blink the truth?) was not he forced to help
This same ungrateful audience, every whelp   640
Of Naddo's litter, make them pass for peers
With the bright band of old Goito years,
As erst he toiled for flower or tree? Why, there
Sat Palma![6] Adelaide's funereal hair
Ennobled the next corner. Ay, he strewed   645
A fairy dust upon that multitude,
Although he feigned to take them by themselves;
His giants dignified those puny elves,
Sublimed their faint applause. In short, he found
Himself still footing a delusive round,   650
Remote as ever from the self-display
He meant to compass, hampered every way
By what he hoped assistance. Wherefore then
Continue, make believe to find in men
A use he found not?
                         Weeks, months, years went by   655
And lo, Sordello vanished utterly,
Sundered in twain; each spectral part at strife
With each; one jarred against another life;
The Poet thwarting hopelessly the Man—
Who, fooled no longer, free in fancy ran   660
Here, there: let slip no opportunities
As pitiful, forsooth, beside the prize
To drop on him some no-time and acquit
His constant faith (the Poet-half's to wit—
That waiving any compromise between   665
No joy and all joy kept the hunger keen
Beyond most methods)—of incurring scoff
From the Man-portion—not to be put off
With self-reflectings by the Poet's scheme,
Though ne'er so bright. Who sauntered forth in dream,   670
Dressed any how, nor waited mystic frames,
    Immeasurable gifts, astounding claims,
    But just his sorry self?—who yet might be
    Sorrier for aught he in reality
    Achieved, so pinioned Man's the Poet-part,   675

6. Daughter of Eccelino by Agnes Este, and resident at Adelaide's court. Palma is loved by Sor-
   dello, who finds her beauty an inspiration. Neither woman is actually present, but Sordello's
   poetry makes it seem as if they are.

Fondling, in turn of fancy, verse; the Art
Developing his soul a thousand ways—
Potent, by its assistance, to amaze
The multitude with majesties, convince
Each sort of nature that the nature's prince   680
Accosted it. Language, the makeshift, grew
Into a bravest of expedients, too;
Apollo, seemed it now, perverse had thrown
Quiver and bow away, the lyre alone
Sufficed. While, out of dream, his day's work went   685
To tune a crazy tenzon or sirvent—
So hampered him the Man-part, thrust to judge .
Between the bard and the bard's audience, grudge
A minute's toil that missed its due reward!
But the complete Sordello, Man and Bard,   690
John's cloud-girt angel,[7] this foot on the land,
That on the sea, with, open in his hand,
A bitter-sweeting of a book—was gone.

* * *

PIPPA PASSES (1841)[1]

Persons

PIPPA	JULES
OTTIMA	PHENE
SEBALD	*Austrian Police*
Foreign Students	BLUPHOCKS
GOTTLIEB	LUIGI *and his* Mother
SCHRAMM	*Poor Girls*

MONSIGNOR *and his Attendants*

Introduction

NEW YEAR'S DAY AT ASOLO IN THE TREVISAN[2]

SCENE.—*A large mean airy chamber. A girl,* PIPPA, *from the Silk-mills,
springing out of bed.*

Day!
Faster and more fast,
O'er night's brim, day boils at last:
Boils, pure gold, o'er the cloud-cup's brim
Where spurting and suppressed it lay,   5

---

7. Revelation 10:1–3. A mighty angel came down from heaven. "And he had in his hand a little
book open: and he set his right foot upon the sea, and his left foot on the earth. . . ."
1. *Pippa Passes* was published in 1841 as the first of a series of eight pamphlets with the general title *Bells and Pomegranates*. A product of Browning's first Italian visit in 1838, the play is set in Asolo, near Venice, where the poet was collecting materials for *Sordello* (1840).
2. Province of Treviso, north of Venice.

For not a froth-flake touched the rim
Of yonder gap in the solid gray
Of the eastern cloud, an hour away;
But forth one wavelet, then another, curled,
Till the whole sunrise, not to be suppressed,   10
Rose, reddened, and its seething breast
Flickered in bounds, grew gold, then overflowed the world.

Oh, Day, if I squander a wavelet of thee,
A mite of my twelve hours' treasure,
The least of thy gazes or glances,   15
(Be they grants thou art bound to or gifts above measure)
One of thy choices or one of thy chances,
(Be they tasks God imposed thee or freaks[3] at thy pleasure)
—My Day, if I squander such labour or leisure,
Then shame fall on Asolo, mischief on me!   20

Thy long blue solemn hours serenely flowing,
Whence earth, we feel, gets steady help and good—
Thy fitful sunshine-minutes, coming, going,
As if earth turned from work in gamesome mood—
All shall be mine! But thou must treat me not   25
As prosperous ones are treated, those who live
At hand here, and enjoy the higher lot,
In readiness to take what thou wilt give,
And free to let alone what thou refusest;
For, Day, my holiday, if thou ill-usest   30
Me, who am only Pippa,—old-year's sorrow,
Cast off last night, will come again to-morrow:
Whereas, if thou prove gentle, I shall borrow
Sufficient strength of thee for new-year's sorrow.
All other men and women that this earth   35
Belongs to, who all days alike possess,
Make general plenty cure particular dearth,
Get more joy one way, if another, less:
Thou art my single day, God lends to leaven
What were all earth else, with a feel of heaven,—   40
Sole light that helps me through the year, thy sun's!
Try now! Take Asolo's Four Happiest Ones—
And let thy morning rain on that superb
Great haughty Ottima; can rain disturb
Her Sebald's homage? All the while thy rain   45
Beats fiercest on her shrub-house window-pane,
He will but press the closer, breathe more warm
Against her cheek; how should she mind the storm?
And, morning past, if mid-day shed a gloom
    O'er Jules and Phene,—what care bride and groom   50
    Save for their dear selves? 'T is their marriage-day;
    And while they leave church and go home their way,

3. Capricious actions.

Hand clasping hand, within each breast would be
Sunbeams and pleasant weather spite of thee.
Then, for another trial, obscure thy eve   55
With mist,—will Luigi and his mother grieve—
The lady and her child, unmatched, forsooth,
She in her age, as Luigi in his youth,
For true content? The cheerful town, warm, close
And safe, the sooner that thou art morose,   60
Receives them. And yet once again, outbreak
In storm at night on Monsignor, they make
Such stir about,—whom they expect from Rome
To visit Asolo, his brothers' home,
And say here masses proper to release   65
A soul from pain,—what storm dares hurt his peace?
Calm would he pray, with his own thoughts to ward
Thy thunder off, nor want the angels' guard.
But Pippa—just one such mischance would spoil
Her day that lightens the next twelvemonth's toil   70
At wearisome silk-winding, coil on coil!
    And here I let time slip for nought!
Aha, you foolhardy sunbeam, caught
With a single splash from my ewer!
You that would mock the best pursuer,   75
Was my basin over-deep?
One splash of water ruins you asleep,
And up, up, fleet your brilliant bits
Wheeling and counterwheeling,
Reeling, broken beyond healing: 80
Now grow together on the ceiling!
That will task your wits.
Whoever it was quenched fire first, hoped to see
Morsel after morsel flee
As merrily, as giddily . . .   85
Meantime, what lights my sunbeam on,
Where settles by degrees the radiant cripple?
Oh, is it surely blown, my martagon?[4]
New-blown and ruddy as St. Agnes'[5] nipple,
Plump as the flesh-bunch on some Turk bird's poll![6]   90
Be sure if corals, branching 'neath the ripple
Of ocean, bud there,—fairies watch unroll
Such turban-flowers; I say, such lamps disperse
Thick red flame through that dusk green universe!
I am queen of thee, floweret!   95
And each fleshy blossom
Preserve I not—(safer
Than leaves that embower it,
Or shells that embosom)

---

4. Kind of lily, also called Turk's cap.
5. Virgin martyr, killed at the age of twelve or thirteen for refusing to marry.
6. Turkey's head.

—From weevil and chafer?[7]   100
Laugh through my pane then; solicit the bee;
Gibe him, be sure; and, in midst of thy glee,
Love thy queen, worship me!

—Worship whom else? For am I not, this day,
Whate'er I please? What shall I please to-day?   105
My morn, noon, eve and night—how spend my day?
To-morrow I must be Pippa who winds silk,
The whole year round, to earn just bread and milk:
But, this one day, I have leave to go,
And play out my fancy's fullest games;   110
I may fancy all day—and it shall be so—
That I taste of the pleasures, am called by the names
Of the Happiest Four in our Asolo!
See! Up the hill-side yonder, through the morning,
Some one shall love me, as the world calls love: 115
I am no less than Ottima, take warning!
The gardens, and the great stone house above,
And other house for shrubs, all glass in front,
Are mine; where Sebald steals, as he is wont,
To court me, while old Luca yet reposes: 120
And therefore, till the shrub-house door uncloses,
I . . . what now?—give abundant cause for prate
About me—Ottima, I mean—of late,
Too bold, too confident she'll still face down
The spitefullest of talkers in our town.   125
How we talk in the little town below!
   But love, love, love—there's better love, I know!
This foolish love was only day's first offer;
I choose my next love to defy the scoffer:
For do not our Bride and Bridegroom sally   130
Out of Possagno church[8] at noon?
Their house looks over Orcana valley:
Why should not I be the bride as soon
As Ottima? For I saw, beside,
Arrive last night that little bride—   135
Saw, if you call it seeing her, one flash
Of the pale snow-pure cheek and black bright tresses,
Blacker than all except the black eyelash;
I wonder she contrives those lids no dresses!
—So strict was she, the veil   140
Should cover close her pale
Pure cheeks—a bride to look at and scarce touch,
Scarce touch, remember, Jules! For are not such
Used to be tended, flower-like, every feature,
As if one's breath would fray the lily of a creature?   145

7. Two species of beetle.
8. A church designed by the sculptor Antonio Canova (1757–1822), born at Possagno, near
   Treviso.

A soft and easy life these ladies lead:
Whiteness in us were wonderful indeed.
Oh, save that brow its virgin dimness,
Keep that foot its lady primness,
Let those ankles never swerve   150
From their exquisite reserve,
Yet have to trip along the streets like me,
All but naked to the knee!
How will she ever grant her Jules a bliss
So startling as her real first infant kiss?   155
Oh, no—not envy, this!

—Not envy, sure!—for if you gave me
Leave to take or to refuse,
In earnest, do you think I'd choose
That sort of new love to enslave me?   160
Mine should have lapped me round from the beginning;
As little fear of losing it as winning:
Lovers grow cold, men learn to hate their wives,
And only parents' love can last our lives.
At eve the Son and Mother, gentle pair,   165
Commune inside our turret: what prevents
My being Luigi? While that mossy lair
Of lizards through the winter-time is stirred
With each to each imparting sweet intents
For this new-year, as brooding bird to bird—   170
(For I observe of late, the evening walk
Of Luigi and his mother, always ends
Inside our ruined turret, where they talk,
Calmer than lovers, yet more kind than friends)
—Let me be cared about, kept out of harm,   175
And schemed for, safe in love as with a charm;
Let me be Luigi! If I only knew
What was my mother's face—my father, too!
  Nay, if you come to that, best love of all
Is God's; then why not have God's love befall   180
Myself as, in the palace by the Dome,[9]
Monsignor?—who to-night will bless the home
Of his dead brother; and God bless in turn
That heart which beats, those eyes which mildly burn
With love for all men! I, to-night at least,   185
Would be that holy and beloved priest.

Now wait!—even I already seem to share
In God's love: what does New-year's hymn declare?
What other meaning do these verses bear?

> *All service ranks the same with God:*   190
> *If now, as formerly he trod*

---

9. Cathedral.

Paradise, his presence fills
Our earth, each only as God wills
Can work—God's puppets, best and worst,
Are we; there is no last nor first.   195

Say not "a small event!" Why "small"?
Costs it more pain that this, ye call
A "great event," should come to pass,
Than that? Untwine me from the mass
Of deeds which make up life, one deed   200
Power shall fall short in or exceed!

And more of it, and more of it!—oh yes—
I will pass each, and see their happiness,
And envy none—being just as great, no doubt,
Useful to men, and dear to God, as they!   205
A pretty thing to care about
So mightily, this single holiday!
But let the sun shine! Wherefore repine?
—With thee to lead me, O Day of mine,
Down the grass path grey with dew,   210
Under the pine-wood, blind with boughs,
Where the swallow never flew
Nor yet cicala[1] dared carouse—
No, dared carouse!

                          [*She enters the street.*]

Part I

MORNING

SCENE.—*Up the Hill-side, inside the Shrub-house.* LUCA's *wife,* OTTIMA, *and her paramour, the German* SEBALD.

SEBALD. [*sings*].

          Let the watching lids wink!
          Day's a-blaze with eyes, think!
          Deep into the night, drink!

OTTIMA. Night? Such may be your Rhine-land nights perhaps;
     But this blood-red beam through the shutter's chink   5
     —We call such light, the morning: let us see!
     Mind how you grope your way, though! How these tall
     Naked geraniums straggle! Push the lattice
     Behind that frame!—Nay, do I bid you!—Sebald,
     It shakes the dust down on me! Why, of course   10
     The slide-bolt catches. Well, are you content,
     Or must I find you something else to spoil?

1. Cicada, locust.

'riends, my Sebald! Is 't full morning?
ık then!
                      Ay, thus it used to be.
       ɔuse was, I remember, shut   15
   ɪnɪd-day; I observed that, as I strolled
On mornings through the vale here; country girls
Were noisy, washing garments in the brook,
Hinds drove the slow white oxen up the hills:
But no, your house was mute, would ope no eye.   20
And wisely: you were plotting one thing there,
Nature, another outside. I looked up—
Rough white wood shutters, rusty iron bars,
Silent as death, blind in a flood of light.
Oh, I remember!—and the peasants laughed   25
And said, "The old man sleeps with the young wife."
This house was his, this chair, this window—his.
OTTIMA. Ah, the clear morning! I can see St. Mark's;[2]
That black streak is the belfry. Stop: Vicenza
Should lie . . . there's Padua, plain enough, that blue!   30
Look o'er my shoulder, follow my finger!
SEBALD.   Morning?
It seems to me a night with a sun added.
Where's dew, where's freshness? That bruised plant, I bruised
In getting through the lattice yestereve,
Droops as it did. See, here's my elbow's mark   35
I' the dust o' the sill.
OTTIMA.   Oh, shut the lattice, pray!
SEBALD. Let me lean out. I cannot scent blood here,
Foul as the morn may be.
                    There, shut the world out!
How do you feel now, Ottima? There, curse
The world and all outside! Let us throw off   40
This mask: how do you bear yourself? Let's out
With all of it.
OTTIMA.   Best never speak of it.
SEBALD. Best speak again and yet again of it,
Till words cease to be more than words. "His blood,"
For instance—let those two words mean "His blood"   45
And nothing more. Notice, I'll say them now,
"His blood."
OTTIMA.   Assuredly if I repented
The deed—
SEBALD.   Repent? Who should repent, or why?
What puts that in your head? Did I once say
That I repented?   50
OTTIMA.   No, I said the deed . . .
SEBALD. "The deed" and "the event"—just now it was
"Our passion's fruit"—the devil take such cant!

---

2. Cathedral in Venice. Vicenza and Padua are to the south.

Say, once and always, Luca was a wittol,[3]
I am his cut-throat, you are . . .
OTTIMA.   Here's the wine;
I brought it when we left the house above,   55
And glasses too—wine of both sorts. Black?[4] White then?
SEBALD. But am not I his cut-throat? What are you?
OTTIMA. There trudges on his business from the Duomo[5]
Benet the Capuchin,[6] with his brown hood
And bare feet; always in one place at church,   60
Close under the stone wall by the south entry.
I used to take him for a brown cold piece
Of the wall's self, as out of it he rose
To let me pass—at first, I say, I used:
Now, so has that dumb figure fastened on me,   65
I rather should account the plastered wall
A piece of him, so chilly does it strike.
This, Sebald?
SEBALD.   No, the white wine—the white wine!
Well, Ottima, I promised no new year
Should rise on us the ancient shameful way;   70
Nor does it rise. Pour on! To your black eyes!
Do you remember last damned New Year's day?
OTTIMA. You brought those foreign prints. We looked at them
Over the wine and fruit. I had to scheme
To get him from the fire. Nothing but saying   75
His own set wants the proof-mark,[7] roused him up
To hunt them out.
SEBALD.   'Faith, he is not alive
To fondle you before my face.
OTTIMA.   Do you
Fondle me then! Who means to take your life
For that, my Sebald?
SEBALD.   Hark you, Ottima!   80
One thing to guard against. We'll not make much
One of the other—that is, not make more
Parade of warmth, childish officious coil,[8]
Than yesterday: as if, sweet, I supposed
Proof upon proof were needed now, now first,   85
To show I love you—yes, still love you—love you
In spite of Luca and what's come to him
—Sure sign we had him ever in our thoughts,
White sneering old reproachful face and all!
We'll even quarrel, love, at times, as if   90
We still could lose each other, were not tied
By this: conceive you?

3. Man who knows his wife is unfaithful.
4. Red wine (Italian *vino nero*).
5. Cathedral.
6. Branch of the Franciscan order of friars.
7. Sign on a print showing it to be one of the first from the plate, and consequently valuable.
8. Fuss.

OTTIMA.   Love!

SEBALD.   Not tied so sure.
  Because though I was wrought upon, have struck
  His insolence back into him—am I
  So surely yours?—therefore forever yours?   95

OTTIMA. Love, to be wise, (one counsel pays another)
  Should we have—months ago, when first we loved,
  For instance that May morning we two stole
  Under the green ascent of sycamores—
  If we had come upon a thing like that   100
  Suddenly . . .

SEBALD.   "A thing"—there again—"a thing!"

OTTIMA. Then, Venus' body, had we come upon
  My husband Luca Gaddi's murdered corpse
  Within there, at his couch-foot, covered close—
  Would you have pored upon it? Why persist   105
  In poring now upon it? For 't is here
  As much as there in the deserted house:
  You cannot rid your eyes of it. For me,
  Now he is dead I hate him worse: I hate . . .
  Dare you stay here? I would go back and hold   110
  His two dead hands, and say, "I hate you worse,
  Luca, than . . ."

SEBALD.   Off, off—take your hands off mine,
  'T is the hot evening—off! oh, morning is it?

OTTIMA. There's one thing must be done; you know what thing.
  Come in and help to carry. We may sleep   115
  Anywhere in the whole wide house to-night.

SEBALD. What would come, think you, if we let him lie
  Just as he is? Let him lie there until
  The angels take him! He is turned by this
  Off from his face beside,[9] as you will see.   120

OTTIMA. This dusty pane might serve for looking glass.
  Three, four—four grey hairs! Is it so you said
  A plait of hair should wave across my neck?
  No—this way.

SEBALD.   Ottima, I would give your neck,
  Each splendid shoulder, both those breasts of yours,   125
  That this were undone! Killing! Kill the world,
  So Luca lives again!—ay, lives to sputter
  His fulsome dotage on you—yes, and feign
  Surprise that I return at eve to sup,
  When all the morning I was loitering here—   130
  Bid me despatch my business and begone.
  I would . . .

OTTIMA.   See!

SEBALD.   No, I'll finish. Do you think
  I fear to speak the bare truth once for all?
  All we have talked of, is, at bottom, fine

9. There is an old superstition that a murdered man looks to the sky for vengeance.

To suffer; there's a recompense in guilt;   135
One must be venturous and fortunate:
What is one young for, else? In age we'll sigh
O'er the wild reckless wicked days flown over;
Still, we have lived: the vice was in its place.
But to have eaten Luca's bread, have worn   140
His clothes, have felt his money swell my purse—
Do lovers in romances sin that way?
Why, I was starving when I used to call
And teach you music, starving while you plucked me
These flowers to smell!
OTTIMA.   My poor lost friend!
SEBALD.   He gave me   145
  Life, nothing less: what if he did reproach
  My perfidy, and threaten, and do more—
  Had he no right? What was to wonder at?
  He sat by us at table quietly:
  Why must you lean across till our cheeks touched?   150
  Could he do less than make pretence to strike?
  'T is not the crime's sake—I'd commit ten crimes
  Greater, to have this crime wiped out, undone!
  And you—O how feel you? Feel you for me?
OTTIMA. Well then, I love you better now than ever,   155
  And best (look at me while I speak to you)—
  Best for the crime; nor do I grieve, in truth,
  This mask, this simulated ignorance,
  This affectation of simplicity,
  Falls off our crime; this naked crime of ours   160
  May not now be looked over: look it down!
  Great? let it be great; but the joys it brought,
  Pay they or no its price? Come: they or it!
  Speak not! The past, would you give up the past
  Such as it is, pleasure and crime together?   165
  Give up that noon I owned my love for you?
  The garden's silence: even the single bee
  Persisting in his toil, suddenly stopped,
  And where he hid you only could surmise
  By some campanula[1] chalice set a-swing.   170
  Who stammered—"Yes, I love you?"
SEBALD.   And I drew
  Back; put far back your face with both my hands
  Lest you should grow too full of me—your face
  So seemed athirst for my whole soul and body!
OTTIMA. And when I ventured to receive you here,   175
  Made you steal hither in the mornings—
SEBALD.   When
  I used to look up 'neath the shrub-house here,
  Till the red fire on its glazed windows spread
  To a yellow haze?

1. Bell-flower.

OTTIMA.   Ah—my sign was, the sun
　Inflamed the sere side of yon chestnut-tree   180
　Nipped by the first frost.
SEBALD.   You would always laugh
　At my wet boots: I had to stride thro' grass
　Over my ankles.
OTTIMA.   Then our crowning night!
SEBALD. The July night?
OTTIMA.   The day of it too, Sebald!
　When heaven's pillars seemed o'erbowed with heat,   185
　Its black-blue canopy suffered descend
　Close on us both, to weigh down each to each,
　And smother up all life except our life.
　So lay we till the storm came.
SEBALD.   How it came!
OTTIMA. Buried in woods we lay, you recollect;   190
　Swift ran the searching tempest overhead;
　And ever and anon some bright white shaft
　Burned thro' the pine-tree roof, here burned and there,
　As if God's messenger thro' the close wood screen
　Plunged and replunged his weapon at a venture,   195
　Feeling for guilty thee and me: then broke
　The thunder like a whole sea overhead—
SEBALD. Yes!
OTTIMA. —While I stretched myself upon you, hands
　To hands, my mouth to your hot mouth, and shook
　All my locks loose, and covered you with them—   200
　You, Sebald, the same you!
SEBALD.   Slower, Ottima!
OTTIMA. And as we lay—
SEBALD.   Less vehemently! Love me!
　Forgive me! Take not words, mere words, to heart!
　Your breath is worse than wine! Breathe slow, speak slow!
　Do not lean on me!
OTTIMA.   Sebald, as we lay,   205
　Rising and falling only with our pants,
　Who said, "Let death come now! 'T is right to die!
　Right to be punished! Nought completes such bliss
　But woe!" Who said that? Who said that?
SEBALD.   How did we ever rise?
　Was't that we slept? Why did it end?
OTTIMA.   I felt you   210
　Taper into a point the ruffled ends
　Of my loose locks 'twixt both your humid lips.
　My hair is fallen now: knot it again!
SEBALD. I kiss you now, dear Ottima, now and now!
　This way? Will you forgive me—be once more   215
　My great queen?
OTTIMA.   Bind it thrice about my brow;
　Crown me your queen, your spirit's arbitress,
　Magnificent in sin. Say that!

SEBALD.   I crown you
  My great white queen, my spirit's arbitress,
  Magnificent . . .   220
     [From without is heard the voice of PIPPA, *singing—]*

       The year's at the spring
       And day's at the morn;
       Morning's at seven;
       The hill-side's dew-pearled;
       The lark's on the wing;   225
       The snail's on the thorn:
       God's in his heaven—
       All's right with the world!

                     *[*PIPPA *passes.]*
SEBALD. God's in his heaven! Do you hear that? Who spoke?
  You, you spoke!
OTTIMA.   Oh—that little ragged girl!   230
  She must have rested on the step: we give them
  But this one holiday the whole year round.
  Did you ever see our silk-mills—their inside?
  There are ten silk-mills now belong to you.
  She stoops to pick my double heartsease[2] . . . Sh!   235
  She does not hear: call you out louder!
SEBALD.   Leave me!
  Go, get your clothes on—dress those shoulders!
OTTIMA.   Sebald?
SEBALD. Wipe off that paint! I hate you.
OTTIMA.   Miserable!
SEBALD. My God, and she is emptied of it now!
  Outright now!—how miraculously gone   240
  All of the grace—had she not strange grace once?
  Why, the blank cheek hangs listless as it likes,
  No purpose holds the features up together,
  Only the cloven brow and puckered chin
  Stay in their places: and the very hair,   245
  That seemed to have a sort of life in it,
  Drops, a dead web!
OTTIMA.   Speak to me—not of me!
SEBALD. —That round great full-orbed face, where not an angle
  Broke the delicious indolence—all broken!
OTTIMA. To me—not of me! Ungrateful, perjured cheat!   250
  A coward too: but ingrate's worse than all.
  Beggar—my slave—a fawning, cringing lie!
  Leave me! Betray me! I can see your drift!
  A lie that walks and eats and drinks!
SEBALD.   My God!
  Those morbid olive faultless shoulder-blades—   255
  I should have known there was no blood beneath!
OTTIMA. You hate me then? You hate me then?

2. Kind of violet or pansy.

SEBALD.   To think
   She would succeed in her absurd attempt,
   And fascinate by sinning, show herself
   Superior—guilt from its excess superior   260
   To innocence! That little peasant's voice
   Has righted all again. Though I be lost,
   I know which is the better, never fear,
   Of vice or virtue, purity or lust,
   Nature or trick! I see what I have done,   265
   Entirely now! Oh I am proud to feel
   Such torments—let the world take credit thence—
   I, having done my deed, pay too its price!
   I hate, hate—curse you! God's in his heaven!
OTTIMA.   —Me!
   Me! no, no, Sebald, not yourself—kill me!   270
   Mine is the whole crime. Do but kill me—then
   Yourself—then—presently—first hear me speak!
   I always meant to kill myself—wait, you!
   Lean on my breast—not as a breast; don't love me
   The more because you lean on me, my own   275
   Heart's Sebald! There, there, both deaths presently!
SEBALD. My brain is drowned now—quite drowned: all I feel
   Is . . . is, at swift-recurring intervals,
   A hurry-down within me, as of waters
   Loosened to smother up some ghastly pit: 280
   There they go—whirls from a black fiery sea!
OTTIMA. Not me—to him, O God, be merciful!

    Talk by the way, while PIPPA *is passing from the hill-side to Or-
    cana. Foreign* STUDENTS *of painting and sculpture, from Venice,
    assembled opposite the house of* JULES, *a young French statuary,
    at Possagno.*

1st STUDENT. Attention! My own post is beneath this window, but the
pomegranate clump yonder will hide three or four of you with a lit-
tle squeezing, and Schramm and his pipe must lie flat in the bal-
cony. Four, five—who's a defaulter? We want everybody, for Jules
must not be suffered to hurt his bride when the jest's found out.

2nd STUDENT. All here! Only our poet's away—never having much
meant to be present, moonstrike him! The airs of that fellow, that
Giovacchino! He was in violent love with himself, and had a fair
prospect of thriving in his suit, so unmolested was it,—when sud-
denly a woman falls in love with him, too; and out of pure jealousy
he takes himself off to Trieste,[3] immortal poem and all: whereto is
this prophetical epitaph appended already, as Bluphocks assures
me,—"Here a mammoth-poem lies, Fouled to death by butterflies."
His own fault, the simpleton! Instead of cramp couplets, each like a
knife in your entrails, he should write, says Bluphocks, both classi-
cally and intelligibly.—Æsculapius,[4] *an Epic. Catalogue of the drugs:*

---

3. City on the Adriatic across from Venice.
4. God of medicine. "Catalogue" refers to the epic convention of the catalogue or list of heroes.

Hebe's[5] *plaister—One strip Cools your lip. Phœbus'*[6] *emulsion—One bottle Clears your throttle. Mercury's*[7] *bolus—One box Cures* . . .

3rd STUDENT. Subside, my fine fellow! If the marriage was over by ten o'clock, Jules will certainly be here in a minute with his bride.

2nd STUDENT. Good!—only, so should the poet's muse have been universally acceptable, says Bluphocks, *et canibus nostris*[8] . . . and Delia not better known to our literary dogs than the boy Giovacchino!

1st STUDENT. To the point, now. Where's Gottlieb, the newcomer? Oh,—listen, Gottlieb, to what has called down this piece of friendly vengeance on Jules, of which we now assemble to witness the winding-up. We are all agreed, all in a tale, observe, when Jules shall burst out on us in a fury by and by: I am spokesman—the verses that are to undeceive Jules bear my name of Lutwyche—but each professes himself alike insulted by this strutting stone-squarer, who came alone from Paris to Munich, and thence with a crowd of us to Venice and Possagno here, but proceeds in a day or two alone again—oh, alone indubitably!—to Rome and Florence. He, forsooth, take up his portion with these dissolute, brutalized, heartless bunglers!—so he was heard to call us all: now, is Schramm brutalized, I should like to know? Am I heartless?

GOTTLIEB. Why, somewhat heartless; for, suppose Jules a coxcomb as much as you choose, still, for this mere coxcombry, you will have brushed off—what do folks style it?—the bloom of his life. Is it too late to alter? These love-letters now, you call his—I can't laugh at them.

4th STUDENT. Because you never read the sham letters of our inditing which drew forth these.

GOTTLIEB. His discovery of the truth will be frightful.

4th STUDENT. That's the joke. But you should have joined us at the beginning: there's no doubt he loves the girl—loves a model he might hire by the hour!

GOTTLIEB. See here! "He has been accustomed," he writes, "to have Canova's women about him, in stone, and the world's women beside him, in flesh; these being as much below, as those above, his soul's aspiration: but now he is to have the reality." There you laugh again! I say, you wipe off the very dew of his youth.

1st STUDENT. Schramm! (Take the pipe out of his mouth, somebody!) Will Jules lose the bloom of his youth?

SCHRAMM. Nothing worth keeping is ever lost in this world: look at a blossom—it drops presently, having done its service and lasted its time; but fruits succeed, and where would be the blossom's place could it continue? As well affirm that your eye is no longer in your body, because its earliest favourite, whatever it may have first loved to look on, is dead and done with—as that any affection is lost to the soul when its first object, whatever happened first to satisfy it, is

---

5. Goddess of youth, cupbearer to the gods.
6. Apollo, god of song and of healing, father of Aesculapius.
7. Messenger of the gods. His emblem is the caduceus, symbol of medicine. Bolus: large pill. The rhyming word is "pox," i.e., syphilis.
8. "And to our dogs." Cf. Virgil, *Eclogues*, III.66–67: "But my flame Amyntas comes to me unbidden: insomuch that now our dogs know not Delia better" (Mackail translation).

superseded in due course. Keep but ever looking, whether with the body's eye or the mind's, and you will soon find something to look on! Has the man done wondering at women?—there follow men, dead and alive, to wonder at. Has he done wondering at men?—there's God to wonder at: and the faculty of wonder may be, at the same time, old and tired enough with respect to its first object, and yet young and fresh sufficiently, so far as concerns its novel one. Thus . . .

1st STUDENT. Put Schramm's pipe into his mouth again! There, you see! Well, this Jules . . . a wretched fribble[9]—oh, I watched his disportings at Possagno, the other day! Canova's gallery—you know: there he marches first resolvedly past great works by the dozen without vouchsafing an eye: all at once he stops full at the *Psiche-fanciulla*[1]—cannot pass that old acquaintance without a nod of encouragement—"In your new place, beauty? Then behave yourself as well here as at Munich—I see you!" Next he posts himself deliberately before the unfinished *Pietà*[2] for half an hour without moving, till up he starts of a sudden, and thrusts his very nose into—I say, into—the group; by which gesture you are informed that precisely the sole point he had not fully mastered in Canova's practice was a certain method of using the drill in the articulation of the knee-joint—and that, likewise, has he mastered at length! Goodbye, therefore, to poor Canova—whose gallery no longer needs detain his successor Jules, the predestinated novel thinker in marble!

5th STUDENT. Tell him about the women: go on to the women!

1st STUDENT. Why, on that matter he could never be supercilious enough. How should we be other (he said) than the poor devils you see, with those debasing habits we cherish? He was not to wallow in that mire, at least: he would wait, and love only at the proper time, and meanwhile put up with the *Psiche-fanciulla*. Now, I happened to hear of a young Greek—real Greek girl at Malamocco;[3] a true Islander, do you see, with Alciphron's[4] "hair like sea-moss"—Schramm knows!—white and quiet as an apparition, and fourteen years old at farthest,—a daughter of Natalia, so she swears—that hag Natalia, who helps us to models at three *lire* an hour. We selected this girl for the heroine of our jest. So first, Jules received a scented letter—somebody had seen his Tydeus[5] at the Academy,[6] and my picture was nothing to it: a profound admirer bade him persevere—would make herself known to him ere long. (Paolina, my little friend of the *Fenice*,[7] transcribes divinely.) And in due time, the mysterious correspondent gave certain hints of her peculiar charms—the pale cheeks, the black hair—whatever, in short, had struck us in our Malamocco model: we retained her name, too—

---

9. A flirt or trifler.
1. Canova's statue of Psyche with a butterfly.
2. Statue of Mary mourning over the body of Jesus.
3. Island near Venice.
4. Greek writer of the second century C.E. who authored fictitious letters admired for their style.
5. A hero of the Theban War.
6. Venetian Accademia, the gallery of fine arts.
7. The Phoenix, theatre in Venice.

Phene, which is, by interpretation, sea-eagle. Now, think of Jules finding himself distinguished from the herd of us by such a creature! In his very first answer he proposed marrying his monitress: and fancy us over these letters, two, three times a day, to receive and despatch! I concocted the main of it: relations were in the way—secrecy must be observed—in fine, would he wed her on trust, and only speak to her when they were indissolubly united? St—st— Here they come!

6th STUDENT. Both of them! Heaven's love, speak softly, speak within yourselves!

5th STUDENT. Look at the bridegroom! Half his hair in storm and half in calm,—patted down over the left temple,—like a frothy cup one blows on to cool it: and the same old blouse that he murders the marble in.

2nd STUDENT. Not a rich vest like yours, Hannibal Scratchy![8]—rich, that your face may the better set it off.

6th STUDENT. And the bride! Yes, sure enough, our Phene! Should you have known her in her clothes? How magnificently pale!

GOTTLIEB. She does not also take it for earnest, I hope?

1st STUDENT. Oh, Natalia's concern, that is! We settle with Natalia.

6th STUDENT. She does not speak—has evidently let out no word. The only thing is, will she equally remember the rest of her lesson, and repeat correctly all those verses which are to break the secret to Jules?

GOTTLIEB. How he gazes on her! Pity—pity!

1st STUDENT. They go in: now, silence! You three,—not nearer the window, mind, than that pomegranate: just where the little girl, who a few minutes ago passed us singing, is seated!

Part II

NOON

SCENE.—*Over Orcana. The house of* JULES, *who crosses its threshold with* PHENE: *she is silent, on which* JULES *begins—*

Do not die, Phene! I am yours now, you
Are mine now; let fate reach me how she likes,
If you'll not die: so, never die! Sit here—
My work-room's single seat. I over-lean
This length of hair and lustrous front; they turn 5
Like an entire flower upward: eyes, lips, last
Your chin—no, last your throat turns: 't is their scent
Pulls down my face upon you. Nay, look ever
This one way till I change, grow you—I could
Change into you, beloved!
                                    You by me, 10
And I by you; this is your hand in mine,
And side by side we sit: all's true. Thank God!

8. Play on the name of the Italian painter Annibale Caracci (1560–1609), who began as a tailor.

I have spoken: speak you!
                                   O my life to come!
My Tydeus must be carved that's there in clay;
Yet how be carved, with you about the room?   15
Where must I place you? When I think that once
This room-full of rough block-work seemed my heaven
Without you! Shall I ever work again,
Get fairly into my old ways again,
Bid each conception stand while, trait by trait,   20
My hand transfers its lineaments to stone?
Will my mere fancies live near you, their truth—
The live truth, passing and repassing me,
Sitting beside me?
                          Now speak!
                                   Only first,
See, all your letters! Was 't not well contrived?   25
Their hiding-place is Psyche's robe; she keeps
Your letters next her skin: which drops out foremost?
Ah,—this that swam down like a first moonbeam
Into my world!
                    Again those eyes complete
Their melancholy survey, sweet and slow,   30
Of all my room holds; to return and rest
On me, with pity, yet some wonder too:
As if God bade some spirit plague a world,
And this were the one moment of surprise
And sorrow while she took her station, pausing   35
O'er what she sees, finds good, and must destroy!
What gaze you at? Those? Books, I told you of;
Let your first word to me rejoice them, too:
This minion, a Coluthus,[9] writ in red
Bistre[1] and azure by Bessarion's scribe—   40
Read this line . . . no, shame—Homer's be the Greek
First breathed me from the lips of my Greek girl!
This Odyssey in coarse black vivid type
With faded yellow blossoms 'twixt page and page,
To mark great places with due gratitude;   45
"He said, and on Antinous[2] directed
A bitter shaft" . . . a flower blots out the rest!
Again upon your search? My statues, then!
—Ah, do not mind that—better that will look
When cast in bronze—an Almaign Kaiser,[3] that,   50
Swart-green and gold, with truncheon based on hip.
This, rather, turn to! What, unrecognized?
I thought you would have seen that here you sit
As I imagined you,—Hippolyta,[4]

9. Greek poet of the sixth century C.E., whose poem, "The Rape of Helen," was discovered by
   Cardinal Bessarion in the fifteenth century (line 40). Minion: darling.
1. Dark brown.
2. One of Penelope's suitors, slain by Odysseus (Odyssey, XXII).
3. German ruler.
4. Queen of the Amazons.

Naked upon her bright Numidian[5] horse.   55
Recall you this then? "Carve in bold relief"—
So you commanded—"carve, against I come,
A Greek, in Athens, as our fashion was,
Feasting, bay-filleted[6] and thunder-free,
Who rises 'neath the lifted myrtle-branch.   60
'Praise those who slew Hipparchus!'[7] cry the guests,
While o'er thy head the singer's myrtle waves
As erst above our champion: stand up, all!' "
See, I have laboured to express your thought.
Quite round, a cluster of mere hands and arms,   65
(Thrust in all senses, all ways, from all sides,
Only consenting at the branch's end
They strain toward) serves for frame to a sole face,
The Praiser's, in the centre: who with eyes
Sightless, so bend they back to light inside   70
His brain where visionary forms throng up,
Sings, minding not that palpitating arch
Of hands and arms, nor the quick drip of wine
From the drenched leaves o'erhead, nor crowns cast off,
Violet and parsley crowns to trample on—   75
Sings, pausing as the patron-ghosts approve,
Devoutly their unconquerable hymn.
But you must say a "well" to that—say "well!"
Because you gaze—am I fantastic, sweet?
Gaze like my very life's-stuff, marble—marbly   80
Even to the silence! Why, before I found
The real flesh Phene, I inured myself
To see, throughout all nature, varied stuff
For better nature's birth by means of art:
With me, each substance tended to one form   85
Of beauty—to the human archetype.
On every side occurred suggestive germs
Of that—the tree, the flower—or take the fruit,—
Some rosy shape, continuing the peach,
Curved beewise o'er its bough; as rosy limbs,   90
Depending, nestled in the leaves; and just
From a cleft rose-peach the whole Dryad[8] sprang.
But of the stuffs one can be master of,
How I divined their capabilities!
From the soft-rinded smoothening facile chalk   95
That yields your outline to the air's embrace,
Half-softened by a halo's pearly gloom;
Down to the crisp imperious steel, so sure
To cut its one confided thought clean out
Of all the world. But marble!—'neath my tools   100
More pliable than jelly—as it were

5. North African, from present-day Algeria.
6. Crowned with bay leaves, supposed to protect the wearer against lightning.
7. Athenian tyrant whose murderers concealed their daggers in branches of myrtle at a festival.
8. Wood nymph.

Some clear primordial creature dug from depths
In the earth's heart, where itself breeds itself,
And whence all baser substance may be worked;
Refine it off to air, you may,—condense it   105
Down to the diamond;—is not metal there,
When o'er the sudden speck my chisel trips?
—Not flesh, as flake off flake I scale, approach,
Lay bare those bluish veins of blood asleep?
Lurks flame in no strange windings where, surprised   110
By the swift implement sent home at once,
Flushes and glowings radiate and hover
About its track?
                    Phene? what—why is this?
That whitening cheek, those still dilating eyes!
Ah, you will die—I knew that you would die!   115
     PHENE *begins, on his having long remained silent.*
Now the end's coming; to be sure, it must
Have ended sometime! Tush, why need I speak
Their foolish speech? I cannot bring to mind
One half of it, beside; and do not care
For old Natalia now, nor any of them.   120
Oh, you—what are you?—if I do not try
To say the words Natalia made me learn,
To please your friends,—it is to keep myself
Where your voice lifted me, by letting that
Proceed: but can it? Even you, perhaps,   125
Cannot take up, now you have once let fall,
The music's life, and me along with that—
No, or you would! We'll stay then, as we are:
Above the world.
                    You creature with the eyes!
If I could look for ever up to them,   130
As now you let me,—I believe, all sin,
All memory of wrong done, suffering borne,
Would drop down, low and lower, to the earth
Whence all that's low comes, and there touch and stay
—Never to overtake the rest of me,   135
All that, unspotted, reaches up to you,
Drawn by those eyes! What rises is myself,
Not me the shame and suffering; but they sink,
Are left, I rise above them. Keep me so,
Above the world!
                    But you sink, for your eyes   140
Are altering—altered! Stay—"I love you, love" . . .
I could prevent it if I understood:
More of your words to me: was't in the tone
Or the words, your power?
                    Or stay—I will repeat
Their speech, if that contents you! Only change   145
No more, and I shall find it presently
Far back here, in the brain yourself filled up.

Natalia threatened me that harm should follow
Unless I spoke their lesson to the end,
But harm to me, I thought she meant, not you.   150
Your friends,—Natalia said they were your friends
And meant you well,—because, I doubted it,
Observing (what was very strange to see)
On every face, so different in all else,
The same smile girls like me are used to bear,   155
But never men, men cannot stoop so low;
Yet your friends, speaking of you, used that smile,
That hateful smirk of boundless self-conceit
Which seems to take possession of the world
And make of God a tame confederate,   160
Purveyor to their appetites . . . you know!
But still Natalia said they were your friends,
And they assented though they smiled the more,
And all came round me,—that thin Englishman
With light lank hair seemed leader of the rest;   165
He held a paper—"What we want," said he,
Ending some explanation to his friends—
"Is something slow, involved and mystical,
To hold Jules long in doubt, yet take his taste
And lure him on until, at innermost   170
Where he seeks sweetness' soul, he may find—this!
—As in the apple's core, the noisome fly:
For insects on the rind are seen at once,
And brushed aside as soon, but this is found
Only when on the lips or loathing tongue."   175
And so he read what I have got by heart:
I'll speak it,—"Do not die, love! I am yours."
No—is not that, or like that, part of words
Yourself began by speaking? Strange to lose
What cost such pains to learn! Is this more right?   180

   I am a painter who cannot paint;
   In my life, a devil rather than saint;
   In my brain, as poor a creature too:
   No end to all I cannot do!
   Yet do one thing at least I can—   185
   Love a man or hate a man
   Supremely: thus my lore began.
   Through the Valley of Love I went,
   In the lovingest spot to abide,
   And just on the verge where I pitched my tent,   190
   I found Hate dwelling beside.
   (Let the Bridegroom ask what the painter meant,
   Of his Bride, of the peerless Bride!)
   And further, I traversed Hate's grove,
   In the hatefullest nook to dwell;   195
   But lo, where I flung myself prone, couched Love
   Where the shadow threefold fell.

(*The meaning—those black bride's-eyes above,*
Not a painter's lips should tell!)

"And here," said he, "Jules probably will ask,   200
"You have black eyes, Love,—you are, sure enough,
My peerless bride,—then do you tell indeed
What needs some explanation! What means this?' "
—And I am to go on, without a word—

    So, I grew wise in Love and Hate,   205
    From simple that I was of late.
    Once, when I loved, I would enlace
    Breast, eyelids, hands, feet, form and face
    Of her I loved, in one embrace—
    As if by mere love I could love immensely!   210
    Once, when I hated, I would plunge
    My sword, and wipe with the first lunge
    My foe's whole life out like a sponge—
    As if by mere hate I could hate intensely!
    But now I am wiser, know better the fashion   215
    How passion seeks aid from its opposite passion:
    And if I see cause to love more, hate more
    Than ever man loved, ever hated before—
    And seek in the Valley of Love,
    The nest, or the nook in Hate's Grove,   220
    Where my soul may surely reach
    The essence, nought less, of each,
    The Hate of all Hates, the Love
    Of all Loves, in the Valley or Grove,—
    I find them the very warders   225
    Each of the other's borders.
    When I love most, Love is disguised
    In Hate; and when Hate is surprised
    In Love, then I hate most: ask
    How Love smiles through Hate's iron casque,[9]   230
    Hate grins through Love's rose-braided mask,—
    And how, having hated thee,
    I sought long and painfully
    To reach thy heart, nor prick
    The skin but pierce to the quick—   235
    Ask this, my Jules, and be answered straight
    By thy bride—how the painter Lutwyche can hate!
  JULES *interposes.*
Lutwyche! Who else? But all of them, no doubt,
Hated me: they at Venice—presently
Their turn, however! You I shall not meet: 240
If I dreamed, saying this would wake me.
                            Keep
What's here, the gold—we cannot meet again,

---

9. Helmet that partially covers the face.

Consider! and the money was but meant
For two years' travel, which is over now,
All chance or hope or care or need of it.   245
This—and what comes from selling these, my casts
And books and medals, except . . . let them go
Together, so the produce keeps you safe
Out of Natalia's clutches! If by chance
(For all's chance here) I should survive the gang   250
At Venice, root out all fifteen of them,
We might meet somewhere, since the world is wide.
      [From without is heard the voice of PIPPA, *singing—]*

     Give her but a least excuse to love me!
     When—where—
     How—can this arm establish her above me,   255
     If fortune fixed her as my lady there,
     There already, to eternally reprove me?
       ("Hist!"—said Kate the Queen;[1]
       But "Oh!"—cried the maiden, binding her tresses,
       " 'T is only a page that carols unseen,   260
       Crumbling your hounds their messes!")

     Is she wronged?—To the rescue of her honour,
     My heart!
     Is she poor?—What costs it to be styled a donor?
     Merely an earth to cleave, a sea to part.   265
     But that fortune should have thrust all this upon her!
       ("Nay, list!"—bade Kate the Queen;
       And still cried the maiden, binding her tresses,
       " 'T is only a page that carols unseen,
       Fitting your hawks their jesses!"[2])   270
                 *[*PIPPA *passes.]*

JULES *resumes.*
What name was that the little girl sang forth?
Kate? The Cornaro, doubtless, who renounced
The crown of Cyprus to be lady here
At Asolo, where still her memory stays,
And peasants sing how once a certain page   275
Pined for the grace of her so far above
His power of doing good to, "Kate the Queen—
She never could be wronged, be poor," he sighed,
"Need him to help her!"
              Yes, a bitter thing
To see our lady above all need of us;   280
Yet so we look ere we will love; not I,
But the world looks so. If whoever loves
Must be, in some sort, god or worshipper,
The blessing or the blest one, queen or page,

---

1. Caterina Cornaro (ca. 1454–1510), Venetian queen of Cyprus. In 1488 her abdication was forced by Venice, which gave her a castle at Asolo as residence.
2. In falconry, the straps on a hawk's legs for attaching a leash.

Why should we always choose the page's part?   285
Here is a woman with utter need of me,—
I find myself queen here, it seems!
                                        How strange!
Look at the woman here with the new soul,
Like my own Psyche,—fresh upon her lips
Alit, the visionary butterfly,   290
Waiting my word to enter and make bright,
Or flutter off and leave all blank as first.
This body had no soul before, but slept
Or stirred, was beauteous or ungainly, free
From taint or foul with stain, as outward things   295
Fastened their image on its passiveness:
Now, it will wake, feel, live—or die again!
Shall to produce form out of unshaped stuff
Be Art—and further, to evoke a soul
From form be nothing? This new soul is mine!   300

Now, to kill Lutwyche, what would that do?—save
A wretched dauber, men will hoot to death
Without me, from their hooting. Oh, to hear
God's voice plain as I heard it first, before
They broke in with their laughter! I heard them   305
Henceforth, not God.
                        To Ancona[3]—Greece—some isle!
I wanted silence only; there is clay
Everywhere. One may do whate'er one likes
In Art: the only thing is, to make sure
That one does like it—which takes pains to know.   310
    Scatter all this, my Phene—this mad dream!
Who, what is Lutwyche, what Natalia's friends,
What the whole world except our love—my own,
Own Phene? But I told you, did I not,
Ere night we travel for your land—some isle   315
With the sea's silence on it? Stand aside—
I do but break these paltry models up
To begin Art afresh. Meet Lutwyche, I—
And save him from my statue meeting him?
Some unsuspected isle in the far seas!   320
Like a god going through his world, there stands
One mountain for a moment in the dusk,
Whole brotherhoods of cedars on its brow:
And you are ever by me while I gaze
—Are in my arms as now—as now—as now!   325
Some unsuspected isle in the far seas!
Some unsuspected isle in far-off seas!

Talk by the way, while PIPPA *is passing from Orcana to the Turret.*
Two or three of the Austrian Police loitering with BLUPHOCKS, *an*
English vagabond, just in view of the Turret.

3. A town on the Adriatic, south of Venice.

BLUPHOCKS.[4] So, that is your Pippa, the little girl who passed us singing? Well, your Bishop's Intendant's[5] money shall be honestly earned:—now, don't make me that sour face because I bring the Bishop's name into the business; we know he can have nothing to do with such horrors: we know that he is a saint and all that a bishop should be, who is a great man beside. *Oh were but every worm a maggot, Every fly a grig,*[6] *Every bough a Christmas faggot, Every tune a jig!* In fact, I have abjured all religions; but the last I inclined to, was the Armenian: for I have travelled, do you see, and at Koenigsberg,[7] Prussia Improper (so styled because there's a sort of bleak hungry sun there), you might remark over a venerable house-porch, a certain Chaldee[8] inscription; and brief as it is, a mere glance at it used absolutely to change the mood of every bearded passenger. In they turned, one and all; the young and lightsome, with no irreverent pause, the aged and decrepit, with a sensible alacrity: 't was the Grand Rabbi's abode, in short. Struck with curiosity, I lost no time in learning Syriac—(these are vowels, you dogs,—follow my stick's end in the mud—*Celarent, Darii, Ferio!*[9]) and one morning presented myself, spelling-book in hand, a, b, c,— I picked it out letter by letter, and what was the purport of this miraculous posy? Some cherished legend of the past, you'll say— "*How Moses hocus-pocussed Egypt's land with fly and locust,*"—or, "*How to Jonah sounded harshish, Get thee up and go to Tarshish,*"[1]— or, "*How the angel meeting Balaam, Straight his ass returned a salaam.*"[2] In no wise! "*Shackabrack—Boach—somebody or other— Isaach, Re-cei-ver, Pur-cha-ser and Ex-chan-ger of—Stolen Goods!*"[3] So, talk to me of the religion of a bishop! I have renounced all bishops save Bishop Beveridge[4]— mean to live so—and die—*As some Greek dog-sage, dead and merry, Hellward bound in Charon's wherry,*[5] *With food for both worlds, under and upper, Lupine-seed and Hecate's*[6] *supper, And never an obolus* . . . (Though thanks to you, or this Intendant through you, or this Bishop through his Intendant— I possess a burning pocketful of *zwanzigers*[7]) . . . *To pay the Stygian Ferry!*

1st POLICEMAN. There is the girl, then; go and deserve them the moment you have pointed out to us Signor Luigi and his mother. [*To*

4. "He maketh his sun to rise on the evil and on the good, and sendeth rain on the just and on the unjust" (Matthew 5:45). [*Browning's note.*] The name alludes to the *Edinburgh Review*, a journal known for its harsh criticism of poetry, whose cover was "blue-fox" (reddish-brown).
5. Superintendent of the estate.
6. Grasshopper or cricket.
7. Capital of East Prussia.
8. Aramaic vernacular, the original language of some parts of the Bible. "Syriac" in the next sentence is also an Aramaic dialect.
9. The vowels in these coined words were used as memory aids in the study of logic.
1. Actually Jonah flees to Tarshish in disobedience of the Lord's command to go to Nineveh (Jonah 1).
2. The angel of the Lord stops Balaam on the road to Moab. Balaam's ass, seeing the angel, balks and finally falls down (Numbers 22).
3. Bluphocks is presumably translating the "Chaldee inscription."
4. Eighteenth-century churchman, whose name provides Bluphocks with a pun.
5. Boat of Charon, who ferried the souls of the dead across the rivers Styx and Acheron for a fee (obolus, or coin of small value).
6. Greek goddess of the underworld. Lupine-seed: edible seed of a leguminous herb.
7. Coinage of Austria, which at the time ruled northern Italy.

the rest.] I have been noticing a house yonder, this long while: not a
shutter unclosed since morning!

2nd POLICEMAN. Old Luca Gaddi's, that owns the silk-mills here: he
dozes by the hour, wakes up, sighs deeply, says he should like to be
Prince Metternich,[8] and then dozes again, after having bidden
young Sebald, the foreigner, set his wife to playing draughts. Never
molest such a household, they mean well.

BLUPHOCKS. Only, cannot you tell me something of this little Pippa, I
must have to do with? One could make something of that name.
Pippa—that is, short for Felippa—rhyming to *Panurge consults Her-
trippa—Believest thou, King Agrippa?*[9] Something might be done
with that name.

2nd POLICEMAN. Put into rhyme that your head and a ripe muskmelon
would not be dear at half a *zwanziger!* Leave this fooling, and look
out; the afternoon's over or nearly so.

3rd POLICEMAN. Where in this passport of Signor Luigi does our
Principal instruct you to watch him so narrowly? There? What's
there beside a simple signature? (That English fool's busy watch-
ing.)

2nd POLICEMAN. Flourish all round—"Put all possible obstacles in his
way;" oblong dot at the end—"Detain him till further advices reach
you;" scratch at bottom—"Send him back on pretence of some in-
formality in the above;" ink-spirt on right-hand side (which is the
case here)—"Arrest him at once." Why and wherefore, I don't con-
cern myself, but my instructions amount to this: if Signor Luigi
leaves home to-night for Vienna—well and good, the passport de-
posed with us for our *visa* is really for his own use, they have misin-
formed the Office, and he means well; but let him stay over
to-night—there has been the pretence we suspect, the accounts of
his corresponding and holding intelligence with the Carbonari[1] are
correct, we arrest him at once, to-morrow comes Venice, and
presently Spielberg.[2] Bluphocks makes the signal, sure enough!
That is he, entering the turret with his mother, no doubt.

Part III

EVENING

SCENE.—*Inside the Turret on the Hill above Asolo.* LUIGI *and his*
MOTHER *entering.*

MOTHER. If there blew wind, you'd hear a long sigh, easing
  The utmost heaviness of music's heart.

LUIGI. Here in the archway?

MOTHER.   Oh no, no—in farther.
  Where the echo is made, on the ridge.

LUIGI.   Here surely, then.

8. Austrian statesman (1773–1859), architect of his country's reactionary foreign policy.
9. "Panurge consults Hertrippa" about his marriage in Rabelais' *Gargantua and Pantagruel*. The
  question "King Agrippa, believest thou the prophets?" is put by St. Paul (Acts 26:27).
1. Secret society of patriots aiming to liberate Italy.
2. Austrian prison.

How plain the tap of my heel as I leaped up!   5
Hark—"Lucius Junius!"[3] The very ghost of a voice
Whose body is caught and kept by . . . what are those?
Mere withered wallflowers, waving overhead?
They seem an elvish group with thin bleached hair
That lean out of their topmost fortress—look   10
And listen, mountain men, to what we say,
Hand under chin of each grave earthy face.
Up and show faces all of you!—"All of you!"
That's the king dwarf with the scarlet comb; old Franz,[4]
Come down and meet your fate? Hark—"Meet your fate!"   15
MOTHER. Let him not meet it, my Luigi—do not
    Go to his City! Putting crime aside,
    Half of these ills of Italy are feigned:
    Your Pellicos[5] and writers for effect,
    Write for effect.
LUIGI.   Hush! Say A. writes, and B.   20
MOTHER. These A.s and B.s write for effect, I say.
    Then, evil is in its nature loud, while good
    Is silent; you hear each petty injury,
    None of his virtues; he is old beside,
    Quiet and kind, and densely stupid. Why   25
    Do A. and B. not kill him themselves?
LUIGI.   They teach
    Others to kill him—me—and, if I fail,
    Others to succeed; now, if A. tried and failed,
    I could not teach that: mine's the lesser task.
    Mother, they visit night by night . . .
MOTHER.   —You, Luigi?   30
    Ah, will you let me tell you what you are?
LUIGI. Why not? Oh, the one thing you fear to hint,
    You may assure yourself I say and say
    Ever to myself! At times—nay, even as now
    We sit—I think my mind is touched, suspect   35
    All is not sound: but is not knowing that,
    What constitutes one sane or otherwise?
    I know I am thus—so, all is right again.
    I laugh at myself as through the town I walk,
    And see men merry as if no Italy   40
    Were suffering; then I ponder—"I am rich,
    Young, healthy; why should this fact trouble me,
    More than it troubles these?" But it does trouble.
    No, trouble's a bad word: for as I walk
    There's springing and melody and giddiness,   45
    And old quaint turns and passages of my youth,
    Dreams long forgotten, little in themselves,

3. Lucius Junius Brutus, who drove the Tarquins from Rome and became one of the first two
   consuls of the republic (509 B.C.E.)
4. The Austrian emperor Francis I (ruled 1804–35).
5. Silvio Pellico, Italian dramatist, patriot, and Carbonarist, had been imprisoned in the Spiel-
   berg for ten years.

Return to me—whatever may amuse me:
And earth seems in a truce with me, and heaven
Accords with me, all things suspend their strife,   50
The very cicala laughs "There goes he, and there!
Feast him, the time is short; he is on his way
For the world's sake: feast him this once, our friend!"
And in return for all this, I can trip
Cheerfully up the scaffold-steps. I go   55
This evening, mother!
MOTHER.   But mistrust yourself—
Mistrust the judgment you pronounce on him!
LUIGI. Oh, there I feel—am sure that I am right!
MOTHER. Mistrust your judgment then, of the mere means
To this wild enterprise. Say, you are right,—   60
How should one in your state e'er bring to pass
What would require a cool head, a cold heart,
And a calm hand? You never will escape.
LUIGI. Escape? To even wish that, would spoil all.
The dying is best part of it. Too much   65
Have I enjoyed these fifteen years of mine,
To leave myself excuse for longer life:
Was not life pressed down, running o'er with joy,
That I might finish with it ere my fellows
Who, sparelier feasted, make a longer stay?   70
I was put at the board-head, helped to all
At first; I rise up happy and content.
God must be glad one loves his world so much.
I can give news of earth to all the dead
Who ask me:—last year's sunsets, and great stars   75
Which had a right to come first and see ebb
The crimson wave that drifts the sun away—
Those crescent moons with notched and burning rims
That strengthened into sharp fire, and there stood,
Impatient of the azure—and that day   80
In March, a double rainbow stopped the storm—
May's warm slow yellow moonlit summer nights—
Gone are they, but I have them in my soul!
MOTHER. (He will not go!)
LUIGI.   You smile at me? 'T is true,—
Voluptuousness, grotesqueness, ghastliness,   85
Environ my devotedness as quaintly
As round about some antique altar wreathe
The rose festoons, goats' horns, and oxen's skulls.
MOTHER. See now: you reach the city, you must cross
His threshold—how?
LUIGI.   Oh, that's if we conspired!   90
Then would come pains in plenty, as you guess—
But guess not how the qualities most fit
For such an office, qualities I have,
Would little stead me, otherwise employed,
Yet prove of rarest merit only here.   95

Every one knows for what his excellence
Will serve, but no one ever will consider
For what his worst defect might serve: and yet
Have you not seen me range our coppice yonder
In search of a distorted ash?—I find   100
The wry spoilt branch a natural perfect bow.
Fancy the thrice-sage, thrice-precautioned man
Arriving at the palace on my errand!
No, no! I have a handsome dress packed up—
White satin here, to set off my black hair;   105
In I shall march—for you may watch your life out
Behind thick walls, make friends there to betray you;
More than one man spoils everything. March straight—
Only, no clumsy knife to fumble for.
Take the great gate, and walk (not saunter) on   110
Thro' guards and guards——I have rehearsed it all
Inside the turret here a hundred times.
Don't ask the way of whom you meet, observe!
But where they cluster thickliest is the door
Of doors; they'll let you pass—they'll never blab   115
Each to the other, he knows not the favourite,
Whence he is bound and what's his business now.
Walk in—straight up to him; you have no knife:
Be prompt, how should he scream? Then, out with you!
Italy, Italy, my Italy!   120
You're free, you're free! Oh mother, I could dream
They got about me—Andrea from his exile,
Pier from his dungeon, Gualtier[6] from his grave!
MOTHER. Well, you shall go. Yet seems this patriotism
   The easiest virtue for a selfish man   125
To acquire: he loves himself—and next, the world—
If he must love beyond,—but nought between:
As a short-sighted man sees nought midway
His body and the sun above. But you
Are my adored Luigi, ever obedient   130
To my least wish, and running o'er with love:
I could not call you cruel or unkind.
Once more, your ground for killing him!—then go!
LUIGI. Now do you try me, or make sport of me?
   How first the Austrians got these provinces[7] . . .   135
(If that is all, I'll satisfy you soon)
—Never by conquest but by cunning, for
That treaty whereby . . .
MOTHER.   Well?
LUIGI.   (Sure, he's arrived,
The tell-tale cuckoo: spring's his confidant,
And he lets out her April purposes!)   140
Or . . . better go at once to modern time,
He has . . . they have . . . in fact, I understand

6. Other conspirators.
7. Northern Italian lands given to Austria by the Congress of Vienna (1815).

But can't restate the matter; that's my boast:
Others could reason it out to you, and prove
Things they have made me feel.
MOTHER.   Why go to-night?   145
  Morn's for adventure. Jupiter is now
  A morning-star. I cannot hear you, Luigi!
LUIGI. "I am the bright and morning-star," saith God[8]—
  And, "to such an one I give the morning-star."
  The gift of the morning-star! Have I God's gift   150
  Of the morning-star?
MOTHER.   Chiara will love to see
  That Jupiter an evening-star next June.
LUIGI. True, mother. Well for those who live through June!
  Great noontides, thunder-storms, all glaring pomps
  That triumph at the heels of June the god   155
  Leading his revel through our leafy world.
  Yes, Chiara will be here.
MOTHER.   In June: remember,
  Yourself appointed that month for her coming.
LUIGI. Was that low noise the echo?
MOTHER.   The night-wind.
  She must be grown—with her blue eyes upturned   160
  As if life were one long and sweet surprise:
  In June she comes.
LUIGI.   We were to see together
  The Titian at Treviso.[9] There, again!
      [*From without is heard the voice of* PIPPA, *singing*—]

            A king lived long ago,
            In the morning of the world,   165
            When earth was nigher heaven than now:
            And the king's locks curled,
            Disparting o'er a forehead full
            As the milk-white space 'twixt horn and horn
            Of some sacrificial bull—   170
            Only calm as a babe new-born:
            For he was got to a sleepy mood,
            So safe from all decrepitude,
            Age with its bane, so sure gone by,
            (The gods so loved him while he dreamed)   175
            That, having lived thus long, there seemed
            No need the king should ever die.

LUIGI. No need that sort of king should ever die!

      Among the rocks his city was:

8. Revelation 22:16: "I [Jesus] . . . am . . . the bright and morning star." Also Revelation
   2:26–28: "And he that overcometh, and keepeth my works unto the end, to him will I give
   power over the nations: and he shall rule them with a rod of iron. . . . And I will give him the
   morning star."
9. Altarpiece, an *Annunciation* by the Venetian painter Titian (d. 1576) in the cathedral at Tre-
   viso.

Before his palace, in the sun,   180
He sat to see his people pass,
And judge them every one
From its threshold of smooth stone.
They haled him many a valley-thief
Caught in the sheep-pens, robber-chief   185
Swarthy and shameless, beggar-cheat,
Spy-prowler, or rough pirate found
On the sea-sand left aground;
And sometimes clung about his feet,
With bleeding lip and burning cheek,   190
A woman, bitterest wrong to speak
Of one with sullen thickset brows:
And sometimes from the prison-house
The angry priests a pale wretch brought,
Who through some chink had pushed and pressed   195
On knees and elbows, belly and breast,
Worm-like into the temple,—caught
He was by the very god,
Who ever in the darkness strode
Backward and forward, keeping watch   200
O'er his brazen bowls, such rogues to catch!
These, all and every one,
The king judged, sitting in the sun.

LUIGI. That king should still judge sitting in the sun!

His councillors, on left and right,   205
Looked anxious up,—but no surprise
Disturbed the king's old smiling eyes
Where the very blue had turned to white.
'T is said, a Python[1] scared one day
The breathless city, till he came,   210
With forky tongue and eyes on flame
Where the old king sat to judge alway,
But when he saw the sweepy hair
Girt with a crown of berries rare
Which the god will hardly give to wear   215
To the maiden who singeth, dancing bare
In the altar-smoke by the pine-torch lights,
At his wondrous forest rites,—
Seeing this, he did not dare
Approach that threshold in the sun,   220
Assault the old king smiling there.
Such grace had kings when the world begun!
                                                [PIPPA *passes.*]
LUIGI. And such grace have they, now that the world ends!
  The Python at the city, on the throne,
  And brave men, God would crown for slaying him,   225

---

1. Enormous serpent that terrorized the folk until slain by Apollo.

Lurk in bye-corners lest they fall his prey.
Are crowns yet to be won in this late time,
Which weakness makes me hesitate to reach?
'T is God's voice calls: how could I stay? Farewell!

> *Talk by the way, while* PIPPA *is passing from the Turret to the
> Bishop's Brother's House, close to the Duomo S. Maria.* POOR
> GIRLS *sitting on the steps.*

1st GIRL. There goes a swallow to Venice—the stout seafarer!   230
Seeing those birds fly, makes one wish for wings.
Let us all wish; you wish first!
2nd GIRL.   I? This sunset
To finish.
3rd GIRL. That old—somebody I know,
Greyer and older than my grandfather,
To give me the same treat he gave last week—   235
Feeding me on his knee with fig-peckers,[2]
Lampreys and red Breganze-wine, and mumbling
The while some folly about how well I fare,
Let sit and eat my supper quietly:
Since had he not himself been late this morning   240
Detained at—never mind where,—had he not . . .
"Eh, baggage, had I not!"—
2nd GIRL.   How she can lie!
3rd GIRL. Look there—by the nails!
2nd GIRL.   What makes your fingers red?
3rd GIRL. Dipping them into wine to write bad words with
On the bright table: how he laughed!
1st GIRL.   My turn.   245
Spring's come and summer's coming. I would wear
A long loose gown, down to the feet and hands,
With plaits here, close about the throat, all day;
And all night lie, the cool long nights, in bed;
And have new milk to drink, apples to eat,   250
Deuzans and junetings, leather-coats[3] . . . ah, I should say,
This is away in the fields—miles!
3rd GIRL.   Say at once
You'd be at home: she'd always be at home!
Now comes the story of the farm among
The cherry orchards, and how April snowed   255
White blossoms on her as she ran. Why, fool,
They've rubbed the chalk-mark out, how tall you were
Twisted your starling's neck, broken his cage,
Made a dung-hill of your garden!
1st GIRL.   They, destroy
My garden since I left them? well—perhaps!   260
I would have done so: so I hope they have!
A fig-tree curled out of our cottage wall;

---

2. Small birds, a delicacy, as are lamprey eels.
3. Varieties of apples.

They called it mine, I have forgotten why,
It must have been there long ere I was born:
Cric—cric—I think I hear the wasps o'erhead   265
Pricking the papers strung to flutter there
And keep off birds in fruit-time—coarse long papers,
And the wasps eat them, prick them through and through.
3rd GIRL. How her mouth twitches! Where was I?—before
She broke in with her wishes and long gowns   270
And wasps—would I be such a fool!—Oh, here!
This is my way: I answer every one
Who asks me why I make so much of him—
(If you say, "you love him"—straight "he'll not be gulled!")
"He that seduced me when I was a girl   275
Thus high—had eyes like yours, or hair like yours,
Brown, red, white,"—as the case may be: that pleases!
See how that beetle burnishes in the path!
There sparkles he along the dust: and, there—
Your journey to that maize-tuft spoiled at least!   280
1st GIRL. When I was young, they said if you killed one
Of those sunshiny beetles, that his friend
Up there, would shine no more that day nor next.
2nd GIRL. When you were young? Nor are you young, that's
      true.
How your plump arms, that were, have dropped away!   285
Why, I can span them. Cecco beats you still?
No matter, so you keep your curious[4] hair.
I wish they'd find a way to dye our hair
Your colour—any lighter tint, indeed,
Than black: the men say they are sick of black,   290
Black eyes, black hair!
4th GIRL.   Sick of yours, like enough.
Do you pretend you ever tasted lampreys
And ortolans?[5] Giovita, of the palace,
Engaged (but there's no trusting him) to slice me
Polenta[6] with a knife that had cut up   295
An ortolan.
2nd GIRL. Why, there! Is not that Pippa
We are to talk to, under the window,—quick,—
Where the lights are?
1st GIRL.   That she? No, or she would sing.
For the Intendant said . . .
3rd GIRL.   Oh, you sing first!
Then, if she listens and comes close . . . I'll tell you,—   300
Sing that song the young English noble made,
Who took you for the purest of the pure,
And meant to leave the world for you—what fun!
2nd GIRL. [sings].

4. Elegant, neat.
5. Another species of bird regarded as a delicacy.
6. Pudding made of cornmeal.

You'll love me yet!—and I can tarry
   Your love's protracted growing: 305
June reared that bunch of flowers you carry,
   From seeds of April's sowing.

I plant a heartful now: some seed
   At least is sure to strike,
And yield—what you'll not pluck indeed,   310
   Not love, but, may be, like.

You'll look at least on love's remains,
   A grave's one violet:
Your look?—that pays a thousand pains.
What's death? You'll love me yet!   315

3rd GIRL [*to* PIPPA *who approaches*]. Oh, you may come closer—we shall not eat you! Why, you seem the very person that the great rich handsome Englishman has fallen so violently in love with. I'll tell you all about it.

Part IV

NIGHT

SCENE.—*Inside the Palace by the Duomo.* MONSIGNOR, *dismissing his* ATTENDANTS.

MONSIGNOR. Thanks, friends, many thanks! I chiefly desire life now, that I may recompense every one of you. Most I know something of already. What, a repast prepared? *Benedicto benedicatur*[7] . . . ugh, ugh! Where was I? Oh, as you were remarking, Ugo, the weather is mild, very unlike winter-weather: but I am a Sicilian, you know, and shiver in your Julys here. To be sure, when 't was full summer at Messina,[8] as we priests used to cross in procession the great square on Assumption Day,[9] you might see our thickest yellow tapers twist suddenly in two, each like a falling star, or sink down on themselves in a gore[1] of wax. But go, my friends, but go! [*To the* INTENDANT.] Not you, Ugo! [*The others leave the apartment.*] I have long wanted to converse with you, Ugo.
INTENDANT. Uguccio—
MONSIGNOR. . . . 'guccio Stefani, man! of Ascoli, Fermo and Fossombruno;[2]—what I do need instructing about, are these accounts of your administration of my poor brother's affairs. Ugh! I shall never get through a third part of your accounts: take some of these dainties before we attempt it, however. Are you bashful to that degree? For me, a crust and water suffice.

7. A blessing.
8. Town in Sicily.
9. August 15. Feast celebrating the ascension of the Virgin Mary into heaven.
1. Clot.
2. Cities far to the south of Asolo, as are Forli and Cesena, mentioned later.

INTENDANT. Do you choose this especial night to question me?

MONSIGNOR. This night, Ugo. You have managed my late brother's affairs since the death of our elder brother: fourteen years and a month, all but three days. On the Third of December, I find him . . .

INTENDANT. If you have so intimate an acquaintance with your brother's affairs, you will be tender of turning so far back: they will hardly bear looking into, so far back.

MONSIGNOR. Ay, ay, ugh, ugh,—nothing but disappointments here below! I remark a considerable payment made to yourself on this Third of December. Talk of disappointments! There was a young fellow here, Jules, a foreign sculptor I did my utmost to advance, that the Church might be a gainer by us both: he was going on hopefully enough, and of a sudden he notifies to me some marvellous change that has happened in his notions of Art. Here's his letter,—"He never had a clearly conceived Ideal within his brain till to-day. Yet since his hand could manage a chisel, he has practised expressing other men's Ideals; and, in the very perfection he has attained to, he foresees an ultimate failure: his unconscious hand will pursue its prescribed course of old years, and will reproduce with a fatal expertness the ancient types, let the novel one appear never so palpably to his spirit. There is but one method of escape: confiding the virgin type to as chaste a hand, he will turn painter instead of sculptor, and paint, not carve, its characteristics,"—strike out, I dare say, a school like Correggio:[3] how think you, Ugo?

INTENDANT. Is Correggio a painter?

MONSIGNOR. Foolish Jules! and yet, after all, why foolish? He may— probably will—fail egregiously; but if there should arise a new painter, will it not be in some such way, by a poet now, or a musician (spirits who have conceived and perfected an Ideal through some other channel), transferring it to this, and escaping our conventional roads by pure ignorance of them; eh, Ugo? If you have no appetite, talk at least, Ugo!

INTENDANT. Sir, I can submit no longer to this course of yours. First, you select the group of which I formed one,—next you thin it gradually,—always retaining me with your smile,—and so do you proceed till you have fairly got me alone with you between four stone walls. And now then? Let this farce, this chatter end now: what is it you want with me?

MONSIGNOR. Ugo!

INTENDANT. From the instant you arrived, I felt your smile on me as you questioned me about this and the other article in those papers—why your brother should have given me this villa, that *podere*,[4]—and your nod at the end meant,—what?

MONSIGNOR. Possibly that I wished for no loud talk here. If once you set me coughing, Ugo!—

INTENDANT. I have your brother's hand and seal to all I possess: now ask me what for! what service I did him—ask me!

MONSIGNOR. I would better not: I should rip up old disgraces, let out my poor brother's weaknesses. By the way, Maffeo of Forli (which, I

3. Antonio Allegri (ca. 1489–1534), Italian painter who took the name of his native town.
4. Farm.

forgot to observe, is your true name), was the interdict ever taken off you, for robbing that church at Cesena?

INTENDANT. No, nor needs be: for when I murdered your brother's friend, Pasquale, for him . . .

MONSIGNOR. Ah, he employed you in that business, did he? Well, I must let you keep, as you say, this villa and that *podere*, for fear the world should find out my relations were of so indifferent a stamp? Maffeo, my family is the oldest in Messina, and century after century have my progenitors gone on polluting themselves with every wickedness under heaven: my own father . . . rest his soul!—I have, I know, a chapel to support that it may rest: my dear two dead brothers were,—what you know tolerably well; I, the youngest, might have rivalled them in vice, if not in wealth: but from my boyhood I came out from among them, and so am not partaker of their plagues.[5] My glory springs from another source; or if from this, by contrast only,—for I, the bishop, am the brother of your employers, Ugo. I hope to repair some of their wrong, however; so far as my brother's ill-gotten treasure reverts to me, I can stop the consequences of his crime: and not one *soldo*[6] shall escape me. Maffeo, the sword we quiet men spurn away, you shrewd knaves pick up and commit murders with; what opportunities the virtuous forego, the villainous seize. Because, to pleasure myself apart from other considerations, my food would be millet-cake, my dress sackcloth, and my couch straw,—am I therefore to let you, the offscouring of the earth, seduce the poor and ignorant by appropriating a pomp these will be sure to think lessens the abominations so unaccountably and exclusively associated with it? Must I let villas and *poderi* go to you, a murderer and thief, that you may beget by means of them other murderers and thieves? No—if my cough would but allow me to speak!

INTENDANT. What am I to expect? You are going to punish me?

MONSIGNOR. —Must punish you, Maffeo. I cannot afford to cast away a chance. I have whole centuries of sin to redeem, and only a month or two of life to do it in. How should I dare to say . . .

INTENDANT. "Forgive us our trespasses"?[7]

MONSIGNOR. My friend, it is because I avow myself a very worm, sinful beyond measure, that I reject a line of conduct you would applaud perhaps. Shall I proceed, as it were, a-pardoning?—I?—who have no symptom of reason to assume that aught less than my strenuousest efforts will keep myself out of mortal sin, much less keep others out. No: I do trepass, but will not double that by allowing you to trespass.

INTENDANT. And suppose the villas are not your brother's to give, nor yours to take? Oh, you are hasty enough just now!

MONSIGNOR. 1, 2—No. 3!—ay, can you read the substance of a letter, No. 3, I have received from Rome? It is precisely on the ground there mentioned, of the suspicion I have that a certain child of my late elder brother, who would have succeeded to his estates, was

5. Alluding to 2 Corinthians 6:17 and Revelation 18:4.
6. Small coin.
7. From the Lord's Prayer (Matthew 6:12).

murdered in infancy by you, Maffeo, at the instigation of my late younger brother—that the Pontiff enjoins on me not merely the bringing that Maffeo to condign punishment, but the taking all pains, as guardian of the infant's heritage for the Church, to recover it parcel by parcel, howsoever, whensoever, and wheresoever. While you are now gnawing those fingers, the police are engaged in sealing up your papers, Maffeo, and the mere raising my voice brings my people from the next room to dispose of yourself. But I want you to confess quietly, and save me raising my voice. Why, man, do I not know the old story? The heir between the succeeding heir, and this heir's ruffianly instrument, and their complot's effect, and the life of fear and bribes and ominous smiling silence? Did you throttle or stab my brother's infant? Come now!

INTENDANT. So old a story, and tell it no better? When did such an instrument ever produce such an effect? Either the child smiles in his face; or, most likely, he is not fool enough to put himself in the employer's power so thoroughly: the child is always ready to produce— as you say—howsoever, wheresoever, and whensoever.

MONSIGNOR. Liar!

INTENDANT. Strike me? Ah, so might a father chastise! I shall sleep soundly to-night at least, though the gallows await me to-morrow; for what a life did I lead! Carlo of Cesena reminds me of his connivance, every time I pay his annuity; which happens commonly thrice a year. If I remonstrate, he will confess all to the good bishop—you!

MONSIGNOR. I see through the trick, caitiff! I would you spoke truth for once. All shall be sifted, however—seven times sifted.

INTENDANT. And how my absurd riches encumbered me! I dared not lay claim to above half my possessions. Let me but once unbosom myself, glorify Heaven, and die!

Sir, you are no brutal dastardly idiot like your brother I frightened to death: let us understand one another. Sir, I will make away with her for you—the girl—here close at hand; not the stupid obvious kind of killing; do not speak—know nothing of her nor of me! I see her every day—saw her this morning: of course there is to be no killing; but at Rome the courtesans perish off every three years, and I can entice her thither—have indeed begun operations already. There's a certain lusty blue-eyed florid-complexioned English knave, I and the Police employ occasionally. You assent, I perceive—no, that's not it—assent I do not say—but you will let me convert my present havings and holdings into cash, and give me time to cross the Alps? 'T is but a little black-eyed pretty singing Felippa, gay silk-winding girl. I have kept her out of harm's way up to this present; for I always intended to make your life a plague to you with her. 'T is as well settled once and for ever. Some women I have procured will pass Bluphocks, my handsome scoundrel, off for somebody; and once Pippa entangled!—you conceive? Through her singing? Is it a bargain?

[*From without is heard the voice of* PIPPA, *singing*—]

Overhead the tree-tops meet,
Flowers and grass spring 'neath one's feet;
There was nought above me, nought below,
My childhood had not learned to know:
For, what are the voices of birds
—Ay, and of beasts,—but words, our words,
Only so much more sweet?
The knowledge of that with my life begun.
But I had so near made out the sun,
And counted your stars, the seven and one,[8]
Like the fingers of my hand:
Nay, I could all but understand
Wherefore through heaven the white moon ranges;
And just when out of her soft fifty changes
No unfamiliar face might overlook me—
Suddenly God took me.

[PIPPA *passes.*]

MONSIGNOR [*springing up*]. My people—one and all—all—within
there! Gag this villain—tie him hand and foot! He dares . . . I know
not half he dares—but remove him—quick! *Miserere mei, Domine!*[9]
Quick, I say!

SCENE.—PIPPA'S *chamber again. She enters it.*

The bee with his comb,
The mouse at her dray,[1]
The grub in his tomb,
Wile winter away;
But the fire-fly and hedge-shrew and lob-worm,[2] I pray,   5
How fare they?
Ha, ha, thanks for your counsel, my Zanze!
"Feast upon lampreys, quaff Breganze"—
The summer of life so easy to spend,
And care for to-morrow so soon put away!   10
But winter hastens at summer's end,
And fire-fly, hedge-shrew, lob-worm, pray,
How fare they?
No bidding me then to . . . what did Zanze say?
"Pare your nails pearlwise, get your small feet shoes   15
More like" . . . (what said she?)—"and less like canoes!"
How pert that girl was!—would I be those pert
Impudent staring women! It had done me,
However, surely no such mighty hurt
To learn his name who passed that jest upon me: 20
No foreigner, that I can recollect,
Came, as she says, a month since, to inspect

8. The Pleiades constellation and Aldebaran, a nearby star.
9. "Lord, have mercy on me!"
1. Nest.
2. Earth worm. Hedge-shrew: Field mouse.

Our silk-mills—none with blue eyes and thick rings
Of raw-silk-coloured hair, at all events.
Well, if old Luca keep his good intents,   25
We shall do better, see what next year brings.
I may buy shoes, my Zanze, not appear
More destitute than you perhaps next year!
Bluph . . . something! I had caught the uncouth name
But for Monsignor's people's sudden clatter   30
Above us—bound to spoil such idle chatter
As ours: it were indeed a serious matter
If silly talk like ours should put to shame
The pious man, the man devoid of blame,
The . . . ah but—ah but, all the same,   35
No mere mortal has a right
To carry that exalted air;
Best people are not angels quite:
While—not the worst of people's doings scare
The devil; so there's that proud look to spare!   40
    Which is mere counsel to myself, mind! for
I have just been the holy Monsignor:
And I was you too, Luigi's gentle mother,
And you too, Luigi!—how that Luigi started
Out of the turret—doubtlessly departed   45
On some good errand or another,
For he passed just now in a traveller's trim,
And the sullen company that prowled
About his path, I noticed, scowled
As if they had lost a prey in him.   50
And I was Jules the sculptor's bride,
And I was Ottima beside,
And now what am I?—tired of fooling.
Day for folly, night for schooling!
New year's day is over and spent,   55
Ill or well, I must be content.
    Even my lily's asleep, I vow:
Wake up—here's a friend I've plucked you!
Call this flower a heart's-ease now!
Something rare, let me instruct you,   60
Is this, with petals triply swollen,
Three times spotted, thrice the pollen;
While the leaves and parts that witness
Old proportions and their fitness,
Here remain unchanged, unmoved now;   65
Call this pampered thing improved now!
Suppose there's a king of the flowers
And a girl-show held in his bowers—
"Look ye, buds, this growth of ours,"
Says he, "Zanze from the Brenta,[3]   70
I have made her gorge polenta

3. River flowing to Venice.

Till both cheeks are near as bouncing
As her . . . name there's no pronouncing!
See this heightened colour too,
For she swilled Breganze wine   75
Till her nose turned deep carmine;
'T was but white when wild she grew.
And only by this Zanze's eyes
Of which we could not change the size,
The magnitude of all achieved   80
Otherwise, may be perceived."

Oh what a drear dark close to my poor day!
How could that red sun drop in that black cloud?
Ah Pippa, morning's rule is moved away,
Dispensed with, never more to be allowed!   85
Day's turn is over, now arrives the night's.
Oh lark, be day's apostle
To mavis, merle and throstle,[4]
Bid them their betters jostle
From day and its delights!   90
But at night, brother howlet,[5] over the woods,
Toll the world to thy chantry;
Sing to the bat's sleek sisterhoods
Full complines[6] with gallantry:
Then, owls and bats,   95
Cowls and twats,[7]
Monks and nuns, in a cloister's moods,
Adjourn to the oak-stump pantry!
     [*After she has begun to undress herself.*]
Now, one thing I should like to really know:
How near I ever might approach all these   100
I only fancied being, this long day:
—Approach, I mean, so as to touch them, so
As to . . . in some way . . . move them—if you please,
Do good or evil to them some slight way.
For instance, if I wind   105
Silk to-morrow, my silk may bind
                              [*Sitting on the bedside.*]
And border Ottima's cloak's hem.
Ah me, and my important part with them,
This morning's hymn half promised when I rose!
True in some sense or other, I suppose.   110
                              [*As she lies down.*]
God bless me! I can pray no more to-night.
No doubt, some way or other, hymns say right.

---

4. Three species of birds.
5. Owl.
6. Seventh and last of the canonical hours.
7. Browning later said he thought the word referred to part of a nun's attire.

All service ranks the same with God—
With God, whose puppets, best and worst
Are we: there is no last nor first.

FROM *DRAMATIC LYRICS* (1

My Last Duchess[1]

FERRARA

That's my last Duchess painted on the wall,
Looking as if she were alive. I call
That piece a wonder, now: Frà Pandolf's[2] hands
Worked busily a day, and there she stands.
Will 't please you sit and look at her? I said   5
"Frà Pandolf" by design, for never read
Strangers like you that pictured countenance,
The depth and passion of its earnest glance,
But to myself they turned (since none puts by
The curtain I have drawn for you, but I)   10
And seemed as they would ask me, if they durst,
How such a glance came there; so, not the first
Are you to turn and ask thus. Sir, 't was not
Her husband's presence only, called that spot
Of joy into the Duchess' cheek: perhaps   15
Frà Pandolf chanced to say "Her mantle laps
Over my lady's wrist too much," or "Paint
Must never hope to reproduce the faint
Half-flush that dies along her throat:" such stuff
Was courtesy, she thought, and cause enough   20
For calling up that spot of joy. She had
A heart—how shall I say?—too soon made glad,
Too easily impressed; she liked whate'er
She looked on, and her looks went everywhere.
Sir, 't was all one! My favour at her breast,   25
The dropping of the daylight in the West,
The bough of cherries some officious fool
Broke in the orchard for her, the white mule
She rode with round the terrace—all and each
Would draw from her alike the approving speech,   30
Or blush, at least. She thanked men,—good! but thanked
Somehow—I know not how—as if she ranked

---

1. First published with the contrasting poem, "Count Gismond" (below), under the caption "Italy and France." The duke closely resembles Alfonso II, fifth and last duke of Ferrara (1533–97), and last of the main branch of the powerful Este family, whose history Browning had studied while compiling material for his long Italian poem *Sordello* (1840). In 1558, Alfonso married Lucrezia, fourteen-year-old daughter of Cosimo I de' Medici, duke of Florence; in 1561 she died under mysterious circumstances. Several years later, the duke married the daughter of Ferdinand I, the count of Tyrol.
2. Brother Pandolf, fictitious painter from a monastic order.

My gift of a nine-hundred-years-old name
With anybody's gift. Who'd stoop to blame
This sort of trifling? Even had you skill   35
In speech—(which I have not)—to make your will
Quite clear to such an one, and say, "Just this
Or that in you disgusts me; here you miss,
Or there exceed the mark"—and if she let
Herself be lessoned so, nor plainly set   40
Her wits to yours, forsooth, and made excuse,
—E'en then would be some stooping; and I choose
Never to stoop. Oh sir, she smiled, no doubt,
Whene'er I passed her; but who passed without
Much the same smile? This grew; I gave commands;[3]   45
Then all smiles stopped together. There she stands
As if alive. Will 't please you rise? We'll meet
The company below, then. I repeat,
The Count your master's known munificence
Is ample warrant that no just pretence[4]   50
Of mine for dowry will be disallowed;
Though his fair daughter's self, as I avowed
At starting, is my object. Nay, we'll go
Together down, sir. Notice Neptune,[5] though,
Taming a sea-horse, thought a rarity,   55
Which Claus of Innsbruck[6] cast in bronze for me!

Count Gismond[1]

AIX IN PROVENCE

I

Christ God who savest man, save most
    Of men Count Gismond who saved me!
Count Gauthier, when he chose his post,
    Chose time and place and company
To suit it; when he struck at length   5
My honour, 't was with all his strength.

II

And doubtlessly ere he could draw
    All points to one, he must have schemed!
That miserable morning saw

3. The sense is ambiguous. Much later Browning said, "The commands were that she be put to death," then added, "or he might have had her shut up in a convent."
4. Claim.
5. Roman deity identified with the Greek sea god Poseidon.
6. Imaginary sculptor. The mention of Innsbruck, seat of the Tyrolean Count, is calculated to flatter.
1. Originally the companion of "My Last Duchess" under the heading "Italy and France," this poem representing medieval France. Aix, capital of Provence in the Middle Ages, reached its zenith after the twelfth century under the patronage of the houses of Aragon and Anjou.

Few half so happy as I seemed,   10
While being dressed in queen's array
To give our tourney prize away.

III

I thought they loved me, did me grace
    To please themselves; 't was all their deed;
God makes, or fair or foul, our face;   15
    If showing mine so caused to bleed
My cousins' hearts, they should have dropped
A word, and straight the play had stopped.

IV

They, too, so beauteous! Each a queen
    By virtue of her brow and breast;   20
Not needing to be crowned, I mean,
    As I do. E'en when I was dressed,
Had either of them spoke, instead
Of glancing sideways with still head!

V

But no: they let me laugh, and sing   25
    My birthday song quite through, adjust
The last rose in my garland, fling
    A last look on the mirror, trust
My arms to each an arm of theirs,
And so descend the castle-stairs—   30

VI

And come out on the morning-troop
    Of merry friends who kissed my cheek,
And called me queen, and made me stoop
    Under the canopy—(a streak
That pierced it, of the outside sun,   35
Powdered with gold its gloom's soft dun)—

VII

And they could let me take my state
    And foolish throne amid applause
Of all come there to celebrate
    My queen's-day—Oh I think the cause   40
Of much was, they forgot no crowd
Makes up for parents in their shroud!

VIII

However that be, all eyes were bent
   Upon me, when my cousins cast
Theirs down; 't was time I should present   45
   The victor's crown, but . . . there, 't will last
No long time . . . the old mist again
Blinds me as then it did. How vain!

IX

See! Gismond's at the gate, in talk
   With his two boys: I can proceed.   50
Well, at that moment, who should stalk
   Forth boldly—to my face, indeed—
But Gauthier, and he thundered "Stay!"
And all stayed. "Bring no crowns, I say!

X

"Bring torches! Wind the penance-sheet   55
   About her! Let her shun the chaste,
Or lay herself before their feet!
   Shall she whose body I embraced
A night long, queen it in the day?
For honour's sake no crowns, I say!"   60

XI

I? What I answered? As I live,
   I never fancied such a thing
As answer possible to give.
   What says the body when they spring
Some monstrous torture-engine's whole   65
Strength on it? No more says the soul.

XII

Till out strode Gismond; then I knew
   That I was saved. I never met
His face before, but, at first view,
   I felt quite sure that God had set   70
Himself to Satan; who would spend
A minute's mistrust on the end?

XIII

He strode to Gauthier, in his throat
   Gave him the lie, then struck his mouth
With one back-handed blow that wrote   75
   In blood men's verdict there. North, South,
East, West, I looked. The lie was dead.
And damned, and truth stood up instead.

XIV

This glads me most, that I enjoyed
   The heart of the joy, with my content   80
In watching Gismond unalloyed
   By any doubt of the event:
God took that on him—I was bid
Watch Gismond for my part: I did.

XV

Did I not watch him while he let   85
   His armourer just brace his greaves,[2]
Rivet his hauberk, on the fret[3]
   The while! His foot . . . my memory leaves
No least stamp out, nor how anon
He pulled his ringing gauntlets on.   90

XVI

And e'en before the trumpet's sound
   Was finished, prone lay the false knight,
Prone as his lie, upon the ground:
   Gismond flew at him, used no sleight
O' the sword, but open-breasted drove,   95
Cleaving till out the truth he clove.

XVII

Which done, he dragged him to my feet
   And said "Here die, but end thy breath
In full confession, lest thou fleet
   From my first, to God's second death!   100
Say, hast thou lied?" And, "I have lied
To God and her," he said, and died.

XVIII

Then Gismond, kneeling to me, asked
   —What safe my heart holds, though no word
Could I repeat now, if I tasked   105
   My powers for ever, to a third
Dear even as you are. Pass the rest
Until I sank upon his breast.

XIX

Over my head his arm he flung
   Against the world; and scarce I felt   110
His sword (that dripped by me and swung)

2. Leg armor worn below the knee.
3. Impatient. Hauberk: armored breastplate.

A little shifted in its belt:
For he began to say the while
How South our home lay many a mile.

XX

So 'mid the shouting multitude   115
  We two walked forth to never more
Return. My cousins have pursued
  Their life, untroubled as before
I vexed them. Gauthier's dwelling-place
God lighten! May his soul find grace!   120

XXI

Our elder boy has got the clear
  Great brow; tho' when his brother's black
Full eye shows scorn, it . . . Gismond here?
  And have you brought my tercel[4] back?
I just was telling Adela   125
How many birds it struck since May.

Incident of the French Camp[1]

I

You know, we French stormed Ratisbon:
  A mile or so away,
On a little mound, Napoleon
  Stood on our storming-day;
With neck out-thrust, you fancy how,   5
  Legs wide, arms locked behind,
As if to balance the prone brow
  Oppressive with its mind.

II

Just as perhaps he mused "My plans
  That soar, to earth may fall,   10
Let once my army-leader Lannes
  Waver at yonder wall,"—
Out 'twixt the battery-smokes there flew
  A rider, bound on bound
Full-galloping; nor bridle drew   15
  Until he reached the mound.

---

4. Male hawk. As William E. Harrold has observed, imagery from the sport of falconry attaches
  to the poem's characters throughout. In stanza I, for example, Gauthier "struck" the
  speaker's honor (*The Variance and the Unity*, [1973], p. 43).
1. Originally called "Camp (French)" and paired with the following poem entitled "Cloister
  (Spanish)"; the poems were separated in 1849 and thereafter. Napoleon's army attacked
  Ratisbon (or Regensburg in Bavaria) in April of 1809.

III

Then off there flung in smiling joy,
   And held himself erect
By just his horse's mane, a boy:
   You hardly could suspect—   20
(So tight he kept his lips compressed,
   Scarce any blood came through)
You looked twice ere you saw his breast
   Was all but shot in two.

IV

"Well," cried he, "Emperor, by God's grace   25
   We've got you Ratisbon!
The Marshal's in the market-place,
   And you'll be there anon
To see your flag-bird flap his vans[2]
   Where I, to heart's desire,   30
Perched him!" The chief's eye flashed; his plans
   Soared up again like fire.

V

The chief's eye flashed; but presently
   Softened itself, as sheathes
A film the mother-eagle's eye   35
   When her bruised eaglet breathes;
"You're wounded!" "Nay," the soldier's pride
   Touched to the quick, he said:
"I'm killed, Sire!" And his chief beside
   Smiling the boy fell dead.   40

Soliloquy of the Spanish Cloister[1]

I

Gr-r-r—there go, my heart's abhorrence!
   Water your damned flower-pots, do!
If hate killed men, Brother Lawrence,
   God's blood, would not mine kill you!
What? your myrtle-bush wants trimming?   5
   Oh, that rose has prior claims—
Needs its leaden vase filled brimming?
   Hell dry you up with its flames!

---

2. Wings. Napoleon's emblem was an eagle.
1. See note 1 to previous poem, "Incident of the French Camp."

II

At the meal we sit together:
    Salve tibi![2] I must hear   10
Wise talk of the kind of weather,
    Sort of season, time of year:
Not a plenteous cork-crop: scarcely
    Dare we hope oak-galls,[3] *I doubt:*
What's the Latin name for "parsley"?   15
What's the Greek name for Swine's Snout?[4]

III

Whew! We'll have our platter burnished,
    Laid with care on our own shelf!
With a fire-new spoon we're furnished,
    And a goblet for ourself,   20
Rinsed like something sacrificial
    Ere 't is fit to touch our chaps[5]—
Marked with L. for our initial!
    (He-he! There his lily[6] snaps!)

IV

Saint, forsooth! While brown Dolores   25
    Squats outside the Convent bank
With Sanchicha, telling stories,
    Steeping tresses in the tank,
Blue-black, lustrous, thick like horsehairs,
    —Can't I see his dead eye glow,   30
Bright as 't were a Barbary corsair's?[7]
    (That is, if he'd let it show!)

V

When he finishes refection,
    Knife and fork he never lays
Cross-wise, to my recollection,   35
    As do I, in Jesu's praise.
I the Trinity illustrate,
    Drinking watered orange-pulp—
In three sips the Arian[8] frustrate;
    While he drains his at one gulp.   40

---

2. "Hail to you" (Latin).
3. Swelling on oak leaf caused by fungi or parasites, yielding tannin used in tanning, dyeing, and the making of ink.
4. Dandelion, with an insult intended.
5. Jaws.
6. In Christian art, symbol of purity.
7. Pirate of the Barbary Coast of northeast Africa.
8. The Arians heretically rejected the orthodox doctrine of the Trinity, holding that the Son was created by and was subordinate to the Father.

VI

Oh, those melons? If he's able
　　We're to have a feast! so nice!
One goes to the Abbot's table,
　　All of us get each a slice.
How go on your flowers? None double?　　　　　　45
　　Not one fruit-sort can you spy?
Strange!—And I, too, at such trouble,
　　Keep them close-nipped on the sly!

VII

There's great text in Galatians,[9]
　　Once you trip on it, entails　　　　　　　　　50
Twenty-nine distinct damnations,
　　One sure, if another fails:
If I trip him just a-dying,
　　Sure of heaven as sure can be,
Spin him round and send him flying　　　　　　55
　　Off to hell, a Manichee?[1]

VIII

Or, my scrofulous[2] French novel
　　On grey paper with blunt type!
Simply glance at it, you grovel
　　Hand and foot in Belial's[3] gripe:　　　　　60
If I double down its pages
　　At the woeful sixteenth print[4]
When he gathers his greengages,[5]
　　Ope a sieve[6] and slip it in 't?

IX

Or, there's Satan!—one might venture　　　　　65
　　Pledge one's soul to him, yet leave
Such a flaw in the indenture
　　As he'd miss till, past retrieve,
Blasted lay that rose-acacia

9. Browning may have in mind Galatians 3:10: "For as many as are of the works of the law are under the curse: for it is written [Deuteronomy 28:15–44], Cursed is every one that continueth not in all things which are written in the book of the law to do them." The passage in Deuteronomy proceeds to list twenty-nine torments. Presumably the speaker hopes to prove Lawrence a heretic by requiring of him a deathbed interpretation of difficult Pauline doctrine such as that quoted.
1. Manichaeism was a popular dualistic heresy originating in third-century Persia, holding that Evil (Darkness) stands in eternal opposition to Good (Light). "Manichee" came to denote any dualistic philosophy considered heretical by the Roman Catholic church.
2. Morally corrupt, contaminated.
3. A prince of darkness. Cf. Milton's *Paradise Lost*, I.490–92: "*Belial* came last, than whom a Spirit more lewd/Fell not from Heaven, or more gross to love/Vice for itself."
4. The sixteenth (presumably pornographic) illustration. Woeful: bringing woe.
5. Small greenish plums.
6. Basket.

We're so proud of! *Hy, Zy, Hine* . . .[7]   70
'St, there's Vespers![8] *Plena gratiâ*
Ave, Virgo![9] Gr-r-r—you swine!

In a Gondola[1]

He sings.

I send my heart up to thee, all my heart
   In this my singing.
For the stars help me, and the sea bears part;
   The very night is clinging
Closer to Venice' streets to leave one space   5
   Above me, whence thy face
May light my joyous heart to thee its dwelling-place.

She speaks.

Say after me, and try to say
My very words, as if each word
Came from you of your own accord,   10
In your own voice, in your own way:
"This woman's heart and soul and brain
Are mine as much as this gold chain
She bids me wear; which" (say again)
"I choose to make by cherishing   15
A precious thing, or choose to fling
Over the boat-side, ring by ring."
And yet once more say . . . no word more!
Since words are only words. Give o'er![2]

Unless you call me, all the same,   20
Familiarly by my pet name,
Which if the Three[3] should hear you call,
And me reply to, would proclaim
At once our secret to them all.
Ask of me, too, command me, blame—   25
Do, break down the partition-wall
'Twixt us, the daylight world beholds
Curtained in dusk and splendid folds!
What's left but—all of me to take?
I am the Three's: prevent them, slake   30
Your thirst! 'T is said, the Arab sage,
In practising with gems, can loose

---

7. Probably a fragment of an incantation, presumably uttered to seal the pact with Satan.
8. Evening prayer, sixth canonical hour of the Breviary.
9. "Full of Grace, hail, Virgin!" Garbled Angelus prayer, which should begin *Ave Maria, gratiâ plena.*
1. The opening stanza of this lyrical drama was hastily written, at the urging of a friend, John Forster, to illustrate Daniel Maclise's painting *The Serenade*, exhibited in 1842.
2. Stop!
3. Later (lines 104–107) called Paul, Gian, and Himself (i.e., the woman's husband).

Their subtle spirit in his cruce[4]
And leave but ashes: so, sweet mage,
Leave them my ashes when thy use   35
Sucks out my soul, thy heritage!

He sings.

I

Past we glide, and past, and past!
   What's that poor Agnese doing
Where they make the shutters fast?
   Grey Zanobi's just a-wooing   40
To his couch the purchased bride:
   Past we glide!

II

Past we glide, and past, and past!
   Why's the Pucci Palace flaring
Like a beacon to the blast?   45
   Guests by hundreds, not one caring
If the dear host's neck were wried:[5]
   Past we glide!

She sings.

I

The moth's kiss, first!
Kiss me as if you made believe   50
You were not sure, this eve,
How my face, your flower, had pursed
Its petals up; so, here and there
You brush it, till I grow aware
Who wants me, and wide ope I burst.   55

II

The bee's kiss, now!
Kiss me as if you entered gay
My heart at some noonday,
A bud that dares not disallow
The claim, so all is rendered up,   60
And passively its shattered cup
Over your head to sleep I bow.

4. Crucible.
5. Wrung.

He sings.

I

What are we two?
I am a Jew,
And carry thee, farther than friends can pursue,   65
To a feast of our tribe;
Where they need thee to bribe
The devil that blasts them unless he imbibe
Thy . . . Scatter the vision for ever! And now,
As of old, I am I, thou art thou!   70

II

Say again, what we are?
The sprite of a star,
I lure thee above where the destinies bar
My plumes their full play
Till a ruddier ray
Than my pale one announce there is withering away   75
Some . . . Scatter the vision for ever! And now,
As of old, I am I, thou art thou!

He muses.

Oh, which were best, to roam or rest?
The land's lap or the water's breast?   80
To sleep on yellow millet-sheaves,
Or swim in lucid shallows just
Eluding water-lily leaves,
An inch from Death's black fingers, thrust
To lock you, whom release he must;   85
Which life were best on Summer eves?

He speaks, musing.

Lie back; could thought of mine improve you?
From this shoulder let there spring
A wing; from this, another wing;
Wings, not legs and feet, shall move you!   90
Snow-white must they spring, to blend
With your flesh, but I intend
They shall deepen to the end,
Broader, into burning gold,
Till both wings crescent-wise enfold   95
Your perfect self, from 'neath your feet
To o'er your head, where, lo, they meet
As if a million sword-blades hurled
Defiance from you to the world!

Rescue me thou, the only real!   100
And scare away this mad ideal

That came, nor motions to depart!
Thanks! Now, stay ever as thou art!

Still he muses.

I

What if the Three should catch at last
Thy serenader? While there's cast   105
Paul's cloak about my head, and fast
Gian pinions[6] me, Himself has past
His stylet[7] thro' my back; I reel;
And . . . is it thou I feel?

II

They trail me, these three godless knaves,   110
Past every church that saints and saves,
Nor stop till, where the cold sea raves
By Lido's[8] wet accursed graves,
They scoop mine, roll me to its brink,
And . . . on thy breast I sink!   115

She replies, musing.

Dip your arm o'er the boat-side, elbow-deep,
As I do: thus: were death so unlike sleep,
Caught this way? Death's to fear from flame or steel,
Or poison doubtless; but from water—feel!

Go find the bottom! Would you stay me? There!   120
Now pluck a great blade of that ribbon-grass
To plait in where the foolish jewel was,
I flung away: since you have praised my hair,
'T is proper to be choice in what I wear.

He speaks.

Row home? must we row home? Too surely   125
Know I where its front's demurely
Over the Giudecca[9] piled;
Window just with window mating,
Door on door exactly waiting,
All's the set face of a child: 130
But behind it, where's a trace
Of the staidness and reserve,
And formal lines without a curve,
In the same child's playing-face?

6. Binds.
7. Stiletto, dagger.
8. Long narrow island containing the Jewish cemetery, flooded at high tide.
9. Canal.

No two windows look one way   135
O'er the small sea-water thread
Below them. Ah, the autumn day
I, passing, saw you overhead!
First, out a cloud of curtain blew,
Then a sweet cry, and last came you—   140
To catch your lory[1] that must needs
Escape just then, of all times then,
To peck a tall plant's fleecy seeds,
And make me happiest of men.
I scarce could breathe to see you reach   145
So far back o'er the balcony
To catch him ere he climbed too high
Above you in the Smyrna peach
That quick the round smooth cord of gold,
This coiled hair on your head, unrolled,   150
Fell down you like a gorgeous snake
The Roman girls were wont, of old,
When Rome there was, for coolness' sake
To let lie curling o'er their bosoms.
Dear lory, may his beak retain   155
Ever its delicate rose stain
As if the wounded lotus-blossoms
Had marked their thief to know again!

Stay longer yet, for others' sake
Than mine! What should your chamber do?   160
—With all its rarities that ache
In silence while day lasts, but wake
At night-time and their life renew,
Suspended just to pleasure you
Who brought against their will together   165
These objects, and, while day lasts, weave
Around them such a magic tether
That dumb they look: your harp, believe,
With all the sensitive tight strings
Which dare not speak, now to itself   170
Breathes slumberously, as if some elf
Went in and out the chords, his wings
Make murmur wheresoe'er they graze,
As an angel may, between the maze
Of midnight palace-pillars, on   175
And on, to sow God's plagues, have gone
Through guilty glorious Babylon.
And while such murmurs flow, the nymph
Bends o'er the harp-top from her shell
As the dry limpet for the lymph[2]   180
Come with a tune he knows so well.
And how your statues' hearts must swell!

1. Parrot.
2. Water. Limpet: mollusk with tent-shaped shell, adhering to rocks of tidal areas.

And how your pictures must descend
To see each other, friend with friend!
Oh, could you take them by surprise,   185
You'd find Schidone's[3] eager Duke
Doing the quaintest courtesies
To that prim saint by Haste-thee-Luke![4]
And, deeper into her rock den,
Bold Castelfranco's[5] Magdalen   190
You'd find retreated from the ken[6]
Of that robed counsel-keeping Ser[7]—
As if the Tizian[8] thinks of her,
And is not, rather, gravely bent
On seeing for himself what toys   195
Are these, his progeny invent,
What litter now the board employs
Whereon he signed a document
That got him murdered! Each enjoys
Its night so well, you cannot break   200
The sport up, so, indeed must make
More stay with me, for others' sake.

She speaks.

I

To-morrow, if a harp-string, say,
Is used to tie the jasmine back
That overfloods my room with sweets,   205
Contrive your Zorzi somehow meets
My Zanze! If the ribbon's black,
The Three are watching: keep away!

II

Your gondola—let Zorzi wreathe
A mesh of water-weeds about   210
Its prow, as if he unaware
Had struck some quay or bridge-foot stair!
That I may throw a paper out
As you and he go underneath.

There's Zanze's vigilant taper; safe are we.   215
Only one minute more to-night with me?
Resume your past self of a month ago!
Be you the bashful gallant, I will be

---

3. Bartolomeo Schedoni, or Schidone (ca. 1570–1615), Italian painter. The *Duke* and other art works described here are imaginary.
4. Or "Luca-fa-presto," nickname of Luca Giordano (1632–1705), prolific Neapolitan painter whose father, it is said, constantly admonished him to hurry.
5. Birthplace of the Italian painter Giorgione (ca. 1477–1510).
6. View.
7. Sir, gentleman.
8. A painting by Titian (d. 1576), most famous painter of the Venetian school.

The lady with the colder breast than snow.
Now bow you, as becomes, nor touch my hand   220
More than I touch yours when I step to land,
And say, "All thanks, Siora!"[9]—
                              Heart to heart
And lips to lips! Yet once more, ere we part,
Clasp me and make me thine, as mine thou art!
          [*He is surprised, and stabbed.*[1]]
It was ordained to be so, sweet!—and best   225
Comes now, beneath thine eyes, upon thy breast.
Still kiss me! Care not for the cowards! Care
Only to put aside thy beauteous hair
My blood will hurt! The Three, I do not scorn
To death, because they never lived: but I   230
Have lived indeed, and so—(yet one more kiss)—can die!

Cristina[1]

I

She should never have looked at me
    If she meant I should not love her!
There are plenty . . . men, you call such,
    I suppose . . . she may discover
All her soul to, if she pleases,   5
    And yet leave much as she found them:
But I'm not so, and she knew it
    When she fixed me, glancing round them.

II

What? To fix me thus meant nothing?
    But I can't tell (there's my weakness)   10
What her look said!—no vile cant, sure,
    About "need to strew the bleakness
Of some lone shore with its pearl-seed,
    That the sea feels"—no "strange yearning
That such souls have, most to lavish   15
    Where there's chance of least returning."

III

Oh, we're sunk enough here, God knows!
    But not quite so sunk that moments,

---

9. Signora, lady.
1. Browning later said the woman was not an accomplice.
1. Originally paired with "Rudel to the Lady of Tripoli" as Part II of "Queen-Worship." A notorious coquette, Maria Cristina I (1806–78), daughter of Francis I, king of the Two Sicilies, married Ferdinand VII, king of Spain, in 1829. Upon Ferdinand's death in 1833 she became regent with absolute power; but her secret marriage to an ex-sergeant (1833) antagonized many of her supporters, and the opposition of Spain's leading general prompted her resignation in 1840.

Sure tho' seldom, are denied us,
    When the spirit's true endowments   20
Stand out plainly from its false ones,
    And apprise it if pursuing
Or the right way or the wrong way,
    To its triumph or undoing.

IV

There are flashes struck from midnights,   25
    There are fire-flames noondays kindle,
Whereby piled-up honours perish,
    Whereby swollen ambitions dwindle,
While just this or that poor impulse,
    Which for once had play unstifled,   30
Seems the sole work of a life-time
    That away the rest have trifled.

V

Doubt you if, in some such moment,
    As she fixed me, she felt clearly,
Ages past the soul existed,   35
    Here an age 't is resting merely,
And hence fleets again for ages,
    While the true end, sole and single,
It stops here for is, this love-way,
    With some other soul to mingle?   40

VI

Else it loses what it lived for,
    And eternally must lose it;
Better ends may be in prospect,
    Deeper blisses (if you choose it),
But this life's end and this love-bliss   45
    Have been lost here. Doubt you whether
This she felt as, looking at me,
    Mine and her souls rushed together?

VII

Oh, observe! Of course, next moment,
    The world's honours, in derision,   50
Trampled out the light for ever:
    Never fear but there's provision
Of the devil's to quench knowledge
    Lest we walk the earth in rapture!
—Making those who catch God's secret   55
    Just so much more prize their capture!

VIII

Such am I: the secret's mine now!
    She has lost me, I have gained her;
Her soul's mine: and thus, grown perfect,
    I shall pass my life's remainder.   60
Life will just hold out the proving
    Both our powers, alone and blended:
And then, come the next life quickly!
    This world's use will have been ended.

Johannes Agricola in Meditation[1]

There's heaven above, and night by night
    I look right through its gorgeous roof;
No suns and moons though e'er so bright
    Avail to stop me; splendour-proof[2]
I keep the broods of stars aloof: 5
For I intend to get to God,
    For 't is to God I speed so fast,
For in God's breast, my own abode,
    Those shoals of dazzling glory, passed,
    I lay my spirit down at last.   10
I lie where I have always lain,
    God smiles as he has always smiled;
Ere suns and moons could wax and wane,
    Ere stars were thundergirt, or piled
    The heavens, God thought on me his child;   15
Ordained a life for me, arrayed
    Its circumstances every one
To the minutest; ay, God said
    This head this hand should rest upon
    Thus, ere he fashioned star or sun.   20
And having thus created me,
    Thus rooted me, he bade me grow,
Guiltless for ever, like a tree
    That buds and blooms, nor seeks to know
    The law by which it prospers so: 25
But sure that thought and word and deed
    All go to swell his love for me,
Me, made because that love had need

---

1. First published with "Porphyria" ("Porphyria's Lover," below) in *The Monthly Repository* for January 1836 and signed "Z"; in *Dramatic Lyrics* (1842) the two poems are linked under the title "Madhouse Cells," but in the collections of 1863 and after, the poems are dissociated. The title figure, German Protestant reformer Johannes Agricola (born Schneider or Schnitter, 1494–1566), was the founder of Antinomianism, a heresy which held that while the unregenerate are still under the Mosaic Law, Christians are freed from it by grace, being under the Gospel alone. Moreover, good works are not efficacious; man is saved by faith alone, without regard to moral character. As C. R. Tracy has pointed out, part of Browning's intention may be to satirize the Calvinistic doctrines of election and reprobation (DeVane, pp. 124–25).
2. Echoing Shelley's "The Cloud" (1820), line 65: "Sunbeam-proof, I hang like a roof" and Shelley's *Epipsychidion* (1821), line 81: "The splendour-winged stars."

Of something irreversibly
  Pledged solely its content to be.   30
Yes, yes, a tree which must ascend,
  No poison-gourd[3] foredoomed to stoop!
I have God's warrant, could I blend
  All hideous sins, as in a cup,
  To drink the mingled venoms up;   35
Secure my nature will convert
  The draught to blossoming gladness fast:
While sweet dews turn to the gourd's hurt,
  And bloat, and while they bloat it, blast,
  As from the first its lot was cast.   40
For as I lie, smiled on, full-fed
  By unexhausted power to bless,
I gaze below on hell's fierce bed,
  And those its waves of flame oppress,
  Swarming in ghastly wretchedness;   45
Whose life on earth aspired to be
  One altar-smoke, so pure!—to win
If not love like God's love for me,
  At least to keep his anger in;
  And all their striving turned to sin.   50
Priest, doctor, hermit, monk grown white
  With prayer, the broken-hearted nun,
The martyr, the wan acolyte,[4]
  The incense-swinging child,—undone
  Before God fashioned star or sun!   55
God, whom I praise; how could I praise,
  If such as I might understand,
Make out and reckon on his ways,
  And bargain for his love, and stand,
  Paying a price, at his right hand?[5]   60

ca. 1834   1836

Porphyria's Lover[1]

The rain set early in to-night,
  The sullen wind was soon awake,
It tore the elm-tops down for spite,
  And did its worst to vex the lake:[2]

---

3. Here a symbol for the damned; mentioned in 2 Kings 4:38–41.
4. Minor church official who assists the clergy with services.
5. Symbol of election, exaltation, and power. Cf. Matthew 25:34: "Then shall the King say unto them on his right hand, Come, ye blessed of my Father, inherit the kingdom prepared for you from the foundation of the world. . . ."
1. Thought to have been written in 1834 during a brief journey to St. Petersburg, Russia (*BRP*, p. 44). First published as "Porphyria" in *The Monthly Repository* for January 1836 with "Johannes Agricola" and later with that poem under the heading "Madhouse Cells."
2. The projection of the speaker's mood onto nature anticipates Tennyson's *Maud* (1855), wherein the device—for which John Ruskin coined the pejorative term "pathetic fallacy"—is employed extensively.

I listened with heart fit to break.   5
When glided in Porphyria; straight
    She shut the cold out and the storm,
And kneeled and made the cheerless grate
    Blaze up, and all the cottage warm;
    Which done, she rose, and from her form   10
Withdrew the dripping cloak and shawl,
    And laid her soiled gloves by, untied
Her hat and let the damp hair fall,
    And, last, she sat down by my side
    And called me. When no voice replied,   15
She put my arm about her waist,
    And made her smooth white shoulder bare,
And all her yellow hair displaced,
    And, stooping, made my cheek lie there,
    And spread, o'er all, her yellow hair,   20
Murmuring how she loved me—she
    Too weak, for all her heart's endeavour,
To set its struggling passion free
    From pride, and vainer ties dissever,
    And give herself to me for ever.   25
But passion sometimes would prevail,
    Nor could to-night's gay feast restrain
A sudden thought of one so pale
    For love of her, and all in vain:
    So, she was come through wind and rain.   30
Be sure I looked up at her eyes
    Happy and proud; at last I knew
Porphyria worshipped me; surprise
    Made my heart swell, and still it grew
    While I debated what to do.   35
That moment she was mine, mine, fair,
    Perfectly pure and good: I found
A thing to do, and all her hair
    In one long yellow string I wound
    Three times her little throat around,   40
And strangled her. No pain felt she;
    I am quite sure she felt no pain.
As a shut bud that holds a bee,
    I warily oped her lids: again
    Laughed the blue eyes without a stain.   45
And I untightened next the tress
    About her neck; her cheek once more
Blushed bright beneath my burning kiss:
    I propped her head up as before,
    Only, this time my shoulder bore   50
Her head, which droops upon it still:
    The smiling rosy little head,
So glad it has its utmost will,
    That all it scorned at once is fled,
    And I, its love, am gained instead!   55

Porphyria's love: she guessed not how
   Her darling one wish would be heard.
And thus we sit together now,
   And all night long we have not stirred,
   And yet God has not said a word!   60

ca. 1834   1836

The Pied Piper of Hamelin[1]

A Child's Story

(WRITTEN FOR, AND INSCRIBED TO, W. M. THE YOUNGER)

I

Hamelin Town's in Brunswick,
   By famous Hanover city;
The river Weser, deep and wide,
Washes its wall on the southern side;
A pleasanter spot you never spied;   5
   But, when begins my ditty,
Almost five hundred years ago,
To see the townsfolk suffer so
   From vermin, was a pity.

II

   Rats!   10
They fought the dogs and killed the cats,
   And bit the babies in the cradles,
And ate the cheeses out of the vats,
   And licked the soup from the cooks' own ladles,
Split open the kegs of salted sprats,   15
Made nests inside men's Sunday hats,
And even spoiled the women's chats
     By drowning their speaking
     With shrieking and squeaking
In fifty different sharps and flats.   20

III

At last the people in a body
   To the Town Hall came flocking:
" 'T is clear," cried they, "our Mayor's a noddy;

---

1. Composed in May 1842 for Willie Macready, son of the famed actor William Charles
Macready. The boy, sick at the time, was sent the poem to illustrate. In Hamelin (Hameln),
a German town in the province of Hanover (not Brunswick), occurred a storied plague of
rats in 1284. Browning's sources for the legend are Nathaniel Wanley's *Wonders of the Little
World* (1678) and Richard Verstegen's *Restitution of Decayed Intelligence in Antiquities*
(1605).

And as for our Corporation—shocking
To think we buy gowns lined with ermine   25
For dolts that can't or won't determine
What's best to rid us of our vermin!
You hope, because you're old and obese,
To find in the furry civic robe ease?
Rouse up, sirs! Give your brains a racking   30
To find the remedy we're lacking,
Or, sure as fate, we'll send you packing!"
At this the Mayor and Corporation
Quaked with a mighty consternation.

IV

An hour they sat in council,   35
    At length the Mayor broke silence:
"For a guilder² I'd my ermine gown sell,
    I wish I were a mile hence!
It's easy to bid one rack one's brain—
I'm sure my poor head aches again,   40
I've scratched it so, and all in vain.
Oh for a trap, a trap, a trap!"
Just as he said this, what should hap
At the chamber door but a gentle tap?
"Bless us," cried the Mayor, "what's that?"   45
(With the Corporation as he sat,
Looking little though wondrous fat;
Nor brighter was his eye, nor moister
Than a too-long-opened oyster,
Save when at noon his paunch grew mutinous   50
For a plate of turtle green and glutinous)
"Only a scraping of shoes on the mat?
Anything like the sound of a rat
Makes my heart go pit-a-pat!"

V

"Come in!"—the Mayor cried, looking bigger: 55
And in did come the strangest figure!
His queer long coat from heel to head
Was half of yellow and half of red,
And he himself was tall and thin,
With sharp blue eyes, each like a pin,   60
And light loose hair, yet swarthy skin,
No tuft on cheek nor beard on chin,
But lips where smiles went out and in;
There was no guessing his kith and kin:
And nobody could enough admire   65
The tall man and his quaint attire.
Quoth one: "It's as my great-grandsire,

---

2. Gold coin, the currency of parts of medieval Europe.

Starting up at the Trump of Doom's tone,
Had walked this way from his painted tombstone!"

VI

He advanced to the council-table: 70
And, "Please your honours," said he, "I'm able,
By means of a secret charm, to draw
   All creatures living beneath the sun,
   That creep or swim or fly or run,
After me so as you never saw!   75
And I chiefly use my charm
On creatures that do people harm,
The mole and toad and newt and viper;
And people call me the Pied Piper."
(And here they noticed round his neck   80
   A scarf of red and yellow stripe,
To match with his coat of the self-same cheque;
   And at the scarf's end hung a pipe;
And his fingers, they noticed, were ever straying
As if impatient to be playing   85
Upon this pipe, as low it dangled
Over his vesture so old-fangled.)
"Yet," said he, "poor piper as I am,
In Tartary I freed the Cham,[3]
   Last June, from his huge swarms of gnats;   90
I eased in Asia the Nizam[4]
   Of a monstrous brood of vampyre-bats:
And as for what your brain bewilders,
   If I can rid your town of rats
Will you give me a thousand guilders?"   95
"One? fifty thousand!"—was the exclamation
Of the astonished Mayor and Corporation.

VII

Into the street the Piper stept,
   Smiling first a little smile,
As if he knew what magic slept   100
   In his quiet pipe the while;
Then, like a musical adept,
To blow the pipe his lips he wrinkled,
And green and blue his sharp eyes twinkled,
Like a candle-flame where salt is sprinkled;   105
And ere three shrill notes the pipe uttered,
You heard as if an army muttered;
And the muttering grew to a grumbling;
And the grumbling grew to a mighty rumbling;
And out of the houses the rats came tumbling.   110

3. Or khan, ruler of the Tartar empire in central Asia.
4. Ruler of Hyderabad, state in India.

Great rats, small rats, lean rats, brawny rats,
Brown rats, black rats, grey rats, tawny rats,
Grave old plodders, gay young friskers,
    Fathers, mothers, uncles, cousins,
Cocking tails and pricking whiskers,   115
    Families by tens and dozens,
Brothers, sisters, husbands, wives—
Followed the Piper for their lives.
From street to street he piped advancing,
And step for step they followed dancing,   120
Until they came to the river Weser,
    Wherein all plunged and perished!
—Save one who, stout as Julius Cæsar,[5]
Swam across and lived to carry
    (As he, the manuscript he cherished)   125
To Rat-land home his commentary:
Which was, "At the first shrill notes of the pipe,
I heard a sound as of scraping tripe,[6]
And putting apples, wondrous ripe,
Into a cider-press's gripe: 130
And a moving away of pickle-tub-boards,
And a leaving ajar of conserve-cupboards,
And a drawing the corks of train-oil-flasks,[7]
And a breaking the hoops of butter-casks:
And it seemed as if a voice   135
    (Sweeter far than bý harp or bý psaltery[8]
Is breathed) called out, 'Oh rats, rejoice!
    The world is grown to one vast drysaltery![9]
So munch on, crunch on, take your nuncheon,[1]
Breakfast, supper, dinner, luncheon!'   140
And just as a bulky sugar-puncheon,[2]
All ready staved, like a great sun shone
Glorious scarce an inch before me,
Just as methought it said, 'Come, bore me!'
—I found the Weser rolling o'er me."   145

VIII

You should have heard the Hamelin people
Ringing the bells till they rocked the steeple.
"Go," cried the Mayor, "and get long poles,
Poke out the nests and block up the holes!
Consult with carpenters and builders,   150
And leave in our town not even a trace
Of the rats!"—when suddenly, up the face

5. Cæsar's ship was captured in 48 B.C.E. during the siege of Alexandria, and according to leg-
   end he swam to safety carrying aloft his *Commentaries on the Gallic War.*
6. Stomach tissue of cattle, used as food.
7. Train-oil: whale oil.
8. Stringed instrument resembling the zither.
9. I.e., a place full of casks; warehouse.
1. Snack.
2. Cask of sugar.

Of the Piper perked in the market-place,
With a, "First, if you please, my thousand guilders!"

IX

A thousand guilders! The Mayor looked blue;   155
So did the Corporation too.
For council dinners made rare havoc
With Claret, Moselle, Vin-de-Grave, Hock;[3]
And half the money would replenish
Their cellar's biggest butt with Rhenish.   160
To pay this sum to a wandering fellow
With a gipsy coat of red and yellow!
"Beside," quoth the Mayor with a knowing wink,
"Our business was done at the river's brink;
We saw with our eyes the vermin sink,   165
And what's dead can't come to life, I think.
So, friend, we're not the folks to shrink
From the duty of giving you something for drink,
And a matter of money to put in your poke;[4]
But as for the guilders, what we spoke   170
Of them, as you very well know, was in joke.
Beside, our losses have made us thrifty.
A thousand guilders! Come, take fifty!"

X

The Piper's face fell, and he cried
"No trifling! I can't wait, beside!   175
I've promised to visit by dinnertime
Bagdat,[5] and accept the prime
Of the Head-Cook's pottage, all he's rich in,
For having left, in the Caliph's[6] kitchen,
Of a nest of scorpions no survivor: 180
With him I proved no bargain-driver,
With you, don't think I'll bate a stiver![7]
And folks who put me in a passion
May find me pipe after another fashion."

XI

"How?" cried the Mayor, "d'ye think I brook   185
Being worse treated than a Cook?
Insulted by a lazy ribald
With idle pipe and vesture piebald?
You threaten us, fellow? Do your worst,
Blow your pipe there till you burst!"   190

3. These and Rhenish are wines.
4. Small bag or purse.
5. Baghdad, capital of Iraq.
6. The chief Mohammedan civil and religious leader.
7. Lower my price by even a twentieth of a guilder.

XII

Once more he stept into the street
    And to his lips again
    Laid his long pipe of smooth straight cane;
And ere he blew three notes (such sweet
Soft notes as yet musician's cunning   195
    Never gave the enraptured air)
There was a rustling that seemed like a bustling
Of merry crowds justling at pitching and hustling,
Small feet were pattering, wooden shoes clattering,
Little hands clapping and little tongues chattering,   200
And, like fowls in a farm-yard when barley is scattering,
Out came the children running.
All the little boys and girls,
With rosy cheeks and flaxen curls,
And sparkling eyes and teeth like pearls,   205
Tripping and skipping, ran merrily after
The wonderful music with shouting and laughter.

XIII

The Mayor was dumb, and the Council stood
As if they were changed into blocks of wood,
Unable to move a step, or cry   210
To the children merrily skipping by,
—Could only follow with the eye
That joyous crowd at the Piper's back.
But how the Mayor was on the rack,
And the wretched Council's bosoms beat,   215
As the Piper turned from the High Street
To where the Weser rolled its waters
Right in the way of their sons and daughters!
However he turned from South to West,
And to Koppelberg Hill his steps addressed,   220
And after him the children pressed;
Great was the joy in every breast.
"He never can cross that mighty top!
He's forced to let the piping drop,
And we shall see our children stop!"   225
When, lo, as they reached the mountain-side,
A wondrous portal opened wide,
As if a cavern was suddenly hollowed;
And the Piper advanced and the children followed,
And when all were in to the very last,   230
The door in the mountain-side shut fast.
Did I say, all? No! One was lame,
    And could not dance the whole of the way;
And in after years, if you would blame
    His sadness, he was used to say,—   235
"It's dull in our town since my playmates left!

I can't forget that I'm bereft
Of all the pleasant sights they see,
Which the Piper also promised me.
For he led us, he said, to a joyous land,   240
Joining the town and just at hand,
Where waters gushed and fruit-trees grew
And flowers put forth a fairer hue,
And everything was strange and new;
The sparrows were brighter than peacocks here,   245
And their dogs outran our fallow deer,
And honey-bees had lost their stings,
And horses were born with eagles' wings:
And just as I became assured
My lame foot would be speedily cured,   250
The music stopped and I stood still,
And found myself outside the hill,
Left alone against my will,
To go now limping as before,
And never hear of that country more!"   255

XIV

Alas, alas for Hamelin!
    There came into many a burgher's pate
    A text which says that heaven's gate
    Opes to the rich at as easy rate
As the needle's eye takes a camel in![8]   260
The mayor sent East, West, North and South,
To offer the Piper, by word of mouth,
    Wherever it was men's lot to find him,
Silver and gold to his heart's content,
If he'd only return the way he went,   265
    And bring the children behind him.
But when they saw 't was a lost endeavour,
And Piper and dancers were gone for ever,
They made a decree that lawyers never
    Should think their records dated duly   270
If, after the day of the month and year,
These words did not as well appear,
"And so long after what happened here
    On the Twenty-second of July,
Thirteen hundred and seventy-six:"   275
And the better in memory to fix
The place of the children's last retreat,
They called it, the Pied Piper's Street—
Where any one playing on pipe or tabor
Was sure for the future to lose his labour.   280
Nor suffered they hostelry or tavern
    To shock with mirth a street so solemn;

8. Matthew 19:24.

But opposite the place of the cavern
　They wrote the story on a column,
And on the great church-window painted   285
The same, to make the world acquainted
How their children were stolen away,
And there it stands to this very day.
And I must not omit to say
That in Transylvania there's a tribe   290
Of alien people who ascribe
The outlandish ways and dress
On which their neighbours lay such stress,
To their fathers and mothers having risen
Out of some subterraneous prison   295
Into which they were trepanned[9]
Long time ago in a mighty band
Out of Hamelin town in Brunswick land,
But how or why, they don't understand.

XV

So, Willy, let me and you be wipers   300
Of scores out with all men—especially pipers!
And, whether they pipe us free frόm rats or frόm mice,
If we've promised them aught, let us keep our promise!

1842

FROM *DRAMATIC ROMANCES AND LYRICS*
(1845)

"How They Brought the Good
News from Ghent to Aix"[1]

[16———.]

I

I sprang to the stirrup, and Joris, and he;
I galloped, Dirck galloped, we galloped all three;
"Good speed!" cried the watch, as the gate-bolts undrew;
"Speed!" echoed the wall to us galloping through;
Behind shut the postern,[2] the lights sank to rest,   5
And into the midnight we galloped abreast.

9. Lured.
1. Working without a map, Browning had described a somewhat devious route (about 120
　miles) from Ghent, capital of East Flanders in Belgium, to Aix-la-Chapelle (Aachen) in West
　Germany.
2. Back door or gate in city wall.

II

Not a word to each other; we kept the great pace
Neck by neck, stride by stride, never changing our place;
I turned in my saddle and made its girths tight,
Then shortened each stirrup, and set the pique[3] right,   10
Rebuckled the cheek-strap, chained slacker the bit,
Nor galloped less steadily Roland a whit.

III

'T was moonset at starting; but while we drew near
Lokeren, the cocks crew and twilight dawned clear;
At Boom, a great yellow star came out to see;   15
At Düffeld, 't was morning as plain as could be;
And from Mecheln church-steeple we heard the half-chime,
So, Joris broke silence with, "Yet there is time!"

IV

At Aershot, up leaped of a sudden the sun,
And against him the cattle stood black every one,   20
To stare thro' the mist at us galloping past,
And I saw my stout galloper Roland at last,
With resolute shoulders, each butting away
The haze, as some bluff river headland its spray:

V

And his low head and crest, just one sharp ear bent back   25
For my voice, and the other pricked out on his track;
And one eye's black intelligence,—ever that glance
O'er its white edge at me, his own master, askance!
And the thick heavy spume-flakes which aye and anon
His fierce lips shook upwards in galloping on.   30

VI

By Hasselt, Dirck groaned; and cried Joris, "Stay spur!
Your Roos galloped bravely, the fault's not in her,
We'll remember at Aix"—for one heard the quick wheeze
Of her chest, saw the stretched neck and staggering knees,
And sunk tail, and horrible heave of the flank,   35
As down on her haunches she shuddered and sank.

VII

So, we were left galloping, Joris and I,
Past Looz and past Tongres, no cloud in the sky;
The broad sun above laughed a pitiless laugh,
'Neath our feet broke the brittle bright stubble like chaff;   40

---

3. Referring to the pommel of the saddle.

Till over by Dalhem a dome-spire[4] sprang white,
And "Gallop," gasped Joris, "for Aix is in sight!"

VIII

"How they'll greet us!"—and all in a moment his roan
Rolled neck and croup[5] over, lay dead as a stone;
And there was my Roland to bear the whole weight   45
Of the news which alone could save Aix from her fate,
With his nostrils like pits full of blood to the brim,
And with circles of red for his eye-sockets' rim.

IX

Then I cast loose my buffcoat,[6] each holster let fall,
Shook off both my jack-boots,[7] let go belt and all,   50
Stood up in the stirrup, leaned, patted his ear,
Called my Roland his pet-name, my horse without peer;
Clapped my hands, laughed and sang, any noise, bad or good,
Till at length into Aix Roland galloped and stood.

X

And all I remember is—friends flocking round   55
As I sat with his head twixt my knees on the ground;
And no voice but was praising this Roland of mine,
As I poured down his throat our last measure of wine,
Which (the burgesses voted by common consent)
Was no more than his due who brought good news from Ghent.   60

ca. 1844

Pictor Ignotus[1]

FLORENCE, 15——

I could have painted pictures like that youth's
    Ye praise so. How my soul springs up! No bar
Stayed me—ah, thought which saddens while it soothes!
    —Never did fate forbid me, star by star,

---

4. Dome of the Romanesque "Octagon," the Chapel in Aachen, begun by Charlemagne in 796
   and (according to tradition) housing his remains.
5. Rump.
6. Close short-sleeved leather military coat worn for defense in the seventeenth century.
7. Heavy military boots extending above the knee.
1. First of Browning's monologues on painting, "Pictor Ignotus" foreshadows the theme of "Fra
   Lippo Lippi" and "Andrea del Sarto": the indissoluble relationship of art to the moral char-
   acter of the artist. The Latin title means "painter unknown" (ignotus also means "ignoble");
   the phrase is used for anonymous works. The subtitle sets the poem in the High Renais-
   sance, a period of unparalleled achievement in painting and sculpture, when Leonardo,
   Michelangelo, and Raphael made Florence the leading art center. (If we presume the living
   "youth" envied by the speaker at the opening of his monologue to be Raphael [1483–1520],
   the poem may be set about 1508, the end of Raphael's important Florentine Period.)

To outburst on your night with all my gift   5
    Of fires from God: nor would my flesh have shrunk
From seconding my soul, with eyes uplift
    And wide to heaven, or, straight like thunder, sunk
To the centre, of an instant; or around
    Turned calmly and inquisitive, to scan   10
The license and the limit, space and bound,
    Allowed to truth made visible in man.
And, like that youth ye praise so, all I saw,
    Over the canvas could my hand have flung,
Each face obedient to its passion's law,   15
    Each passion clear proclaimed without a tongue;
Whether Hope rose at once in all the blood,
    A-tiptoe for the blessing of embrace,
Or Rapture drooped the eyes, as when her brood
    Pull down the nesting dove's heart to its place;   20
Or Confidence lit swift the forehead up,
    And locked the mouth fast, like a castle braved,[2]—
O human faces, hath it spilt, my cup?
    What did ye give me that I have not saved?
Nor will I say I have not dreamed (how well!)   25
    Of going—I, in each new picture,—forth,
As, making new hearts beat and bosoms swell,
    To Pope or Kaiser,[3] East, West, South, or North,
Bound for the calmly-satisfied great State,
    Or glad aspiring little burgh, it went,   30
Flowers cast upon the car which bore the freight,
    Through old streets named afresh from the event,[4]
Till it reached home, where learned age should greet
    My face, and youth, the star not yet distinct
Above his hair, lie learning at my feet!—   35
    Oh, thus to live, I and my picture, linked
With love about, and praise, till life should end,
    And then not go to heaven, but linger here,
Here on my earth, earth's every man my friend,—
    The thought grew frightful, 't was so wildly dear!   40
But a voice changed it. Glimpses of such sights
    Have scared me, like the revels through a door
Of some strange house of idols at its rites!
    This world seemed not the world it was before:
Mixed with my loving trusting ones, there trooped   45
    . . . Who summoned those cold faces that begun
To press on me and judge me? Though I stooped
    Shrinking, as from the soldiery a nun,

---

2. Attacked.
3. Emperor of the Holy Roman Empire. In the sixteenth century the best artists had immense prestige, attracting the patronage of rich princes and potentates ambitious for fame. Since the artist often dictated his own terms, he enjoyed unprecedented freedom.
4. Browning may have in mind Cimabue (ca. 1240–ca. 1302), whose colossal painting of the Madonna, according to Vasari, won such acclaim that the place where the painter worked was renamed Borgo Allegri, or "Joyful District." The completed painting was solemnly carried through the streets of Florence.

They drew me forth, and spite of me . . . enough!
    These buy and sell our pictures, take and give,   50
Count them for garniture and household-stuff,
    And where they live needs must our pictures live
And see their faces, listen to their prate,
    Partakers of their daily pettiness,
Discussed of,—"This I love, or this I hate,   55
    This likes[5] me more, and this affects me less!"
Wherefore I chose my portion. If at whiles
    My heart sinks, as monotonous I paint
These endless cloisters and eternal aisles
    With the same series, Virgin, Babe and Saint,   60
With the same cold calm beautiful regard,—
    At least no merchant traffics in my heart;
The sanctuary's gloom at least shall ward
    Vain tongues from where my pictures stand apart:
Only prayer breaks the silence of the shrine   65
    While, blackening in the daily candle-smoke,
They moulder on the damp wall's travertine,[6]
    'Mid echoes the light footstep never woke.
So, die my pictures! surely, gently die!
    O youth, men praise so,—holds their praise its worth?   70
Blown harshly, keeps the trump its golden cry?
    Tastes sweet the water with such specks of earth?

1844?

The Italian in England

That second time they hunted me
From hill to plain, from shore to sea,
And Austria, hounding far and wide
Her blood-hounds thro' the country-side,
Breathed hot and instant on my trace,—   5
I made six days a hiding-place
Of that dry green old aqueduct
Where I and Charles, when boys, have plucked
The fire-flies from the roof above,
Bright creeping thro' the moss they love: 10
—How long it seems since Charles was lost!
Six days the soldiers crossed and crossed
The country in my very sight;
And when that peril ceased at night,
The sky broke out in red dismay   15
With signal fires; well, there I lay
Close covered o'er in my recess,
Up to the neck in ferns and cress,

5. Pleases.
6. White limestone.

Thinking on Metternich[1] our friend,
And Charles's miserable end,   20
And much beside; two days; the third,
Hunger o'ercame me when I heard
The peasants from the village go
To work among the maize; you know,
With us in Lombardy, they bring   25
Provisions packed on mules, a string
With little bells that cheer their task,
And casks, and boughs on every cask
To keep the sun's heat from the wine;
These I let pass in jingling line,   30
And, close on them, dear noisy crew,
The peasants from the village, too;
For at the very rear would troop
Their wives and sisters in a group
To help, I knew. When these had passed,   35
I threw my glove to strike the last,
Taking the chance: she did not start,
Much less cry out, but stooped apart,
One instant rapidly glanced round,
And saw me beckon from the ground.   40
A wild bush grows and hides my crypt;
She picked my glove up while she stripped
A branch off, then rejoined the rest
With that; my glove lay in her breast.
Then I drew breath; they disappeared: 45
It was for Italy I feared.

  An hour, and she returned alone
Exactly where my glove was thrown.
Meanwhile came many thoughts: on me
Rested the hopes of Italy.   50
I had devised a certain tale
Which, when 't was told her, could not fail
Persuade a peasant of its truth;
I meant to call a freak of youth
This hiding, and give hopes of pay,   55
And no temptation to betray.
But when I saw that woman's face,
Its calm simplicity of grace,
Our Italy's own attitude
In which she walked thus far, and stood,   60
Planting each naked foot so firm,
To crush the snake and spare the worm—
At first sight of her eyes, I said,
"I am that man upon whose head
They fix the price, because I hate   65

1. Chancellor of Austria 1809–1848. The speaker is being ironic, since Italy was in revolt
against Austrian rule.

The Austrians over us: the State
Will give you gold—oh, gold so much!—
If you betray me to their clutch,
And be your death, for aught I know,
If once they find you saved their foe.   70
Now, you must bring me food and drink,
And also paper, pen and ink,
And carry safe what I shall write
To Padua, which you'll reach at night
Before the duomo² shuts; go in,   75
And wait till Tenebræ³ begin;
Walk to the third confessional,
Between the pillar and the wall,
And kneeling whisper, *Whence comes peace?*
Say it a second time, then cease;   80
And if the voice inside returns,
From Christ and Freedom; what concerns
The cause of Peace?—for answer, slip
My letter where you placed your lip;
Then come back happy we have done   85
Our mother service—I, the son,
As you the daughter of our land!"

    Three mornings more, she took her stand
In the same place, with the same eyes:
I was no surer of sun-rise   90
Than of her coming. We conferred
Of her own prospects, and I heard
She had a lover—stout and tall,
She said—then let her eyelids fall,
"He could do much"—as if some doubt   95
Entered her heart,—then, passing out,
"She could not speak for others, who
Had other thoughts; herself she knew:"
And so she brought me drink and food.
After four days, the scouts pursued   100
Another path; at last arrived
The help my Paduan friends contrived
To furnish me: she brought the news.
For the first time I could not choose
But kiss her hand, and lay my own   105
Upon her head—"This faith was shown
To Italy, our mother; she
Uses my hand and blesses thee."
She followed down to the sea-shore;
I left and never saw her more.   110

    How very long since I have thought
Concerning—much less wished for—aught

2. Italian cathedral.
3. Religious service held during Holy Week.

Beside the good of Italy,
For which I live and mean to die!
I never was in love; and since   115
Charles proved false, what shall now convince
My inmost heart I have a friend?
However, if I pleased to spend
Real wishes on myself—say, three—
I know at least what one should be.   120
I would grasp Metternich until
I felt his red wet throat distil
In blood thro' these two hands. And next,
—Nor much for that am I perplexed—
Charles, perjured traitor, for his part,   125
Should die slow of a broken heart
Under his new employers. Last
—Ah, there, what should I wish? For fast
Do I grow old and out of strength.
If I resolved to seek at length   130
My father's house again, how scared
They all would look, and unprepared!
My brothers live in Austria's pay
—Disowned me long ago, men say;
And all my early mates who used   135
To praise me so—perhaps induced
More than one early step of mine—
Are turning wise: while some opine
"Freedom grows license," some suspect
"Haste breeds delay," and recollect   140
They always said, such premature
Beginnings never could endure!
So, with a sullen "All's for best,"
The land seems settling to its rest.
I think then, I should wish to stand   145
This evening in that dear, lost land,
Over the sea the thousand miles,
And know if yet that woman smiles
With the calm smile; some little farm
She lives in there, no doubt: what harm   150
If I sat on the door-side bench,
And, while her spindle made a trench
Fantastically in the dust,
Inquired of all her fortunes—just
Her children's ages and their names,   155
And what may be the husband's aims
For each of them. I'd talk this out,
And sit there, for an hour about,
Then kiss her hand once more, and lay
Mine on her head, and go my way.   160

   So much for idle wishing—how
It steals the time! To business now.

The Englishman in Italy

PIANO DI SORRENTO

Fortù,[1] Fortù, my beloved one,
　　Sit here by my side,
On my knees put up both little feet!
　　I was sure, if I tried,
I could make you laugh spite of Scirocco.[2]　　　　5
　　Now, open your eyes,
Let me keep you amused till he vanish
　　In black from the skies,
With telling my memories over
　　As you tell your beads;[3]　　　　10
All the Plain saw me gather, I garland
　　—The flowers or the weeds.

Time for rain! for your long hot dry Autumn
　　Had net-worked with brown
The white skin of each grape on the bunches,　　　　15
　　Marked like a quail's crown,
Those creatures you make such account of,
　　Whose heads,—speckled white
Over brown like a great spider's back,
　　As I told you last night,—　　　　20
Your mother bites off for her supper.
　　Red-ripe as could be,
Pomegranates were chapping and splitting
　　In halves on the tree:
And betwixt the loose walls of great flintstone,　　　　25
　　Or in the thick dust
On the path, or straight out of the rock-side,
　　Wherever could thrust
Some burnt sprig of bold hardy rock-flower
　　Its yellow face up,　　　　30
For the prize were great butterflies fighting,
　　Some five for one cup.
So, I guessed, ere I got up this morning,
　　What change was in store,
By the quick rustle-down of the quail-nets　　　　35
　　Which woke me before
I could open my shutter, made fast
　　With a bough and a stone,
And look thro' the twisted dead vine-twigs,
　　Sole lattice that's known.　　　　40
Quick and sharp rang the rings down the net-poles,
　　While, busy beneath,
Your priest and his brother tugged at them,

1. Young girl.
2. A hot, dry, autumnal wind.
3. Rosary beads.

The rain in their teeth.
And out upon all the flat house-roofs   45
   Where split figs lay drying,
The girls took the frails[4] under cover:
   Nor use seemed in trying
To get out the boats and go fishing,
   For, under the cliff,   50
Fierce the black water frothed o'er the blind-rock.
   No seeing our skiff
Arrive about noon from Amalfi,
   —Our fisher arrive,
And pitch down his basket before us,   55
   All trembling alive
With pink and grey jellies, your sea-fruit;
   You touch the strange lumps,
And mouths gape there, eyes open, all manner
   Of horns and of humps,   60
Which only the fisher looks grave at,
   While round him like imps
Cling screaming the children as naked
   And brown as his shrimps;
Himself too as bare to the middle   65
   —You see round his neck
The string and its brass coin suspended,
   That saves him from wreck.
But to-day not a boat reached Salerno,
   So back, to a man,   70
Came our friends, with whose help in the vineyards
   Grape-harvest began.
In the vat, halfway up in our house-side,
   Like blood the juice spins,
While your brother all bare-legged is dancing   75
   Till breathless he grins
Dead-beaten in effort on effort
   To keep the grapes under,
Since still when he seems all but master,
   In pours the fresh plunder   80
From girls who keep coming and going
   With basket on shoulder,
And eyes shut against the rain's driving;
   Your girls that are older,—
For under the hedges of aloe,   85
   And where, on its bed
Of the orchard's black mould, the love-apple[5]
   Lies pulpy and red,
All the young ones are kneeling and filling
   Their laps with the snails   90
Tempted out by this first rainy weather,—
   Your best of regales,

4. Baskets.
5. Tomato.

As to-night will be proved to my sorrow,
　　When, supping in state,
We shall feast our grape-gleaners (two dozen,　　　　95
　　Three over one plate)
With lasagne so tempting to swallow
　　In slippery ropes,
And gourds fried in great purple slices,
　　That colour of popes.　　　　　　　　　　　　100
Meantime, see the grape bunch they've brought you:
　　The rain-water slips
O'er the heavy blue bloom on each globe
　　Which the wasp to your lips
Still follows with fretful persistence:　　　　　　　105
　　Nay, taste, while awake,
This half of a curd-white smooth cheese-ball
　　That peels, flake by flake,
Like an onion, each smoother and whiter;
　　Next, sip this weak wine　　　　　　　　　　110
From the thin green glass flask, with its stopper,
　　A leaf of the vine;
And end with the prickly-pear's red flesh
　　That leaves thro' its juice
The stony black seeds on your pearl-teeth.　　　　115
　　Scirocco is loose!
Hark, the quick, whistling pelt of the olives
　　Which, thick in one's track,
Tempt the stranger to pick up and bite them,
　　Tho' not yet half black!　　　　　　　　　　120
How the old twisted olive trunks shudder,
　　The medlars[6] let fall
Their hard fruit, and the brittle great fig-trees
　　Snap off, figs and all,
For here comes the whole of the tempest!　　　　125
　　No refuge, but creep
Back again to my side and my shoulder,
　　And listen or sleep.

O how will your country show next week,
　　When all the vine-boughs　　　　　　　　　130
Have been stripped of their foliage to pasture
　　The mules and the cows?
Last eve, I rode over the mountains;
　　Your brother, my guide,
Soon left me, to feast on the myrtles　　　　　　135
　　That offered, each side,
Their fruit-balls, black, glossy and luscious,—
　　Or strip from the sorbs[7]
A treasure, or, rosy and wondrous,

6. A type of apple tree.
7. Fruit trees.

Those hairy gold orbs!   140
But my mule picked his sure sober path out,
    Just stopping to neigh
When he recognized down in the valley
    His mates on their way
With the faggots and barrels of water;   145
    And soon we emerged
From the plain, where the woods could scarce follow;
    And still as we urged
Our way, the woods wondered, and left us,
    As up still we trudged   150
Though the wild path grew wilder each instant,
    And place was e'en grudged
'Mid the rock-chasms and piles of loose stones
    Like the loose broken teeth
Of some monster which climbed there to die   155
    From the ocean beneath—
Place was grudged to the silver-grey fume-weed
    That clung to the path,
And dark rosemary ever a-dying
    That, 'spite the wind's wrath,   160
So loves the salt rock's face to seaward,
    And lentisks[8] as staunch
To the stone where they root and bear berries,
    And . . . what shows a branch
Coral-coloured, transparent, with circlets   165
    Of pale seagreen leaves;
Over all trod my mule with the caution
    Of gleaners o'er sheaves,
Still, foot after foot like a lady,
    Till, round after round,   170
He climbed to the top of Calvano,
    And God's own profound
Was above me, and round me the mountains,
    And under, the sea,
And within me my heart to bear witness   175
    What was and shall be.
Oh, heaven and the terrible crystal![9]
    No rampart excludes
Your eye from the life to be lived
    In the blue solitudes.   180
Oh, those mountains, their infinite movement!
    Still moving with you;
For, ever some new head and breast of them
    Thrusts into view
To observe the intruder; you see it   185
    If quickly you turn
And, before they escape you surprise them.

8. Small evergreen trees.
9. Probably alluding to the Ptolemaic conception of the solar system, in which heavenly bodies
   are attached to crystals rotating around the earth. See also Ezekiel 1:22.

They grudge you should learn
How the soft plains they look on, lean over
   And love (they pretend)   190
—Cower beneath them, the flat sea-pine crouches,
   The wild fruit-trees bend,
E'en the myrtle-leaves curl, shrink and shut:
   All is silent and grave:
'T is a sensual and timorous beauty,   195
   How fair! but a slave.
So, I turned to the sea; and there slumbered
   As greenly as ever
Those isles of the siren, your Galli;[1]
   No ages can sever   200
The Three, nor enable their sister[2]
   To join them,—halfway
On the voyage, she looked at Ulysses—
   No farther to-day,
Tho' the small one,[3] just launched in the wave,   205
   Watches breast-high and steady
From under the rock, her bold sister
   Swum halfway already.
Fortù, shall we sail there together
   And see from the sides   210
Quite new rocks show their faces, new haunts
   Where the siren abides?
Shall we sail round and round them, close over
   The rocks, tho' unseen,
That ruffle the grey glassy water   215
   To glorious green?
Then scramble from splinter to splinter,
   Reach land and explore,
On the largest, the strange square black turret
   With never a door,   220
Just a loop to admit the quick lizards;
   Then, stand there and hear
The birds' quiet singing, that tells us
   What life is, so clear?
—The secret they sang to Ulysses   225
   When, ages ago,
He heard and he knew this life's secret
   I hear and I know.

Ah, see! The sun breaks o'er Calvano;
   He strikes the great gloom   230
And flutters it o'er the mount's summit
   In airy gold fume.
All is over. Look out, see the gipsy,

---

1. Group of three small islands in the Gulf of Salerno associated with the mythic Sirens, whose
   song lured sailors to their deaths. Cf. *Odyssey* XII–XIII.
2. Vivaro rock, which lies between the Galli and the shore.
3. Isca rock, closer to shore.

Our tinker[4] and smith,
Has arrived, set up bellows and forge,   235
    And down-squatted forthwith
To his hammering, under the wall there;
    One eye keeps aloof
The urchins that itch to be putting
    His jews'-harps[5] to proof,   240
While the other, thro' locks of curled wire,
    Is watching how sleek
Shines the hog, come to share in the windfall
    —Chew, abbot's own cheek!
All is over. Wake up and come out now,   245
    And down let us go,
And see the fine things got in order
    At church for the show
Of the Sacrament, set forth this evening.
    To-morrow's the Feast   250
Of the Rosary's Virgin[6] by no means
    Of Virgins the least,
As you'll hear in the off-hand discourse
    Which (all nature, no art)
The Dominican brother,[7] these three weeks,   255
    Was getting by heart.
Not a pillar nor post but is dizened
    With red and blue papers;
All the roof waves with ribbons, each altar
    A-blaze with long tapers;   260
But the great masterpiece is the scaffold
    Rigged glorious to hold
All the fiddlers and fifers and drummers
    And trumpeters bold,
Not afraid of Bellini nor Auber,[8]   265
    Who, when the priest's hoarse,
Will strike us up something that's brisk
    For the feast's second course.
And then will the flaxen-wigged Image[9]
    Be carried in pomp   270
Thro' the plain, while in gallant procession
    The priests mean to stomp.
All round the glad church lie old bottles
    With gunpowder stopped,
Which will be, when the Image re-enters,   275
    Religiously popped;
And at night from the crest of Calvano
    Great bonfires will hang,
On the plain will the trumpets join chorus,

4. Blacksmith.
5. Small musical instruments played with the mouth.
6. Catholic festival held on the first Sunday in October.
7. Member of the order of St. Dominic, who is said to have instituted the rosary.
8. Auber (French) and Bellini (Italian) are nineteenth-century composers.
9. Icon of the Virgin Mary.

And more poppers bang.   280
At all events, come—to the garden
    As far as the wall;
See me tap with a hoe on the plaster
    Till out there shall fall
A scorpion with wide angry nippers!   285

    —"Such trifles!" you say?
Fortù, in my England at home,
    Men meet gravely to-day
And debate, if abolishing Corn-laws[1]
    Be righteous and wise   290
—If 't were proper, Scirocco should vanish
    In black from the skies!

The Lost Leader[1]

I

Just for a handful of silver he left us,
    Just for a riband to stick in his coat—
Found the one gift of which fortune bereft us,
    Lost all the others she lets us devote;
They, with the gold to give, doled him out silver,   5
    So much was theirs who so little allowed:
How all our copper had gone for his service!
    Rags—were they purple, his heart had been proud!
We that had loved him so, followed him, honoured him,
    Lived in his mild and magnificent eye,   10
Learned his great language, caught his clear accents,
    Made him our pattern to live and to die!
Shakespeare was of us, Milton was for us,
    Burns, Shelley, were with us,—they watch from their graves!
He alone breaks from the van and the freemen,   15
    —He alone sinks to the rear and the slaves!

II

We shall march prospering,—not thro' his presence;
    Songs may inspirit us,—not from his lyre;
Deeds will be done,—while he boasts his quiescence,
    Still bidding crouch whom the rest bade aspire: 20
Blot out his name, then, record one lost soul more,
    One task more declined, one more footpath untrod,
One more devils'-triumph and sorrow for angels,
    One wrong more to man, one more insult to God!

1. English laws hindering the importation of grain. They protected domestic farmers but made
   bread more expensive. After much debate, they were repealed in 1846.
1. Browning said that he used the poet William Wordsworth "as a sort of painter's model" in
   writing this poem. Wordsworth had grown increasingly conservative over the years, and had
   recently accepted the Laureateship.

Life's night begins: let him never come back to us!   25
    There would be doubt, hesitation and pain,
Forced praise on our part—the glimmer of twilight,
    Never glad confident morning again!
Best fight on well, for we taught him—strike gallantly,
    Menace our heart ere we master his own;   30
Then let him receive the new knowledge and wait us,
    Pardoned in heaven, the first by the throne!

Home-Thoughts, from Abroad[1]

I

Oh, to be in England
Now that April's there,
And whoever wakes in England
Sees, some morning, unaware,
That the lowest boughs and the brushwood sheaf   5
Round the elm-tree bole are in tiny leaf,
While the chaffinch sings on the orchard bough
In England—now!

II

And after April, when May follows,
And the whitethroat builds, and all the swallows!   10
Hark, where my blossomed pear-tree in the hedge
Leans to the field and scatters on the clover
Blossoms and dewdrops—at the bent spray's edge—
That's the wise thrush; he sings each song twice over,
Lest you should think he never could recapture   15
The first fine careless rapture!
And though the fields look rough with hoary dew
All will be gay when noontide wakes anew
The buttercups, the little children's dower
—Far brighter than this gaudy melon-flower!   20

ca. 1845

["Here's to Nelson's Memory!"][1]

Here's to Nelson's memory!
'T is the second time that I, at sea,
Right off Cape Trafalgar here,

---

1. This title originally headed the three lyrics "Oh, to be in England," "Here's to Nelson's Memory!" and "Nobly Cape Saint Vincent."
1. This tribute to England's great naval hero was probably written while the poet was on board a ship bound for Italy in August 1845. The source of the Nelson anecdote, according to Browning, was the ship's captain (DeVane, p. 164). The poem was later placed in a group entitled "Nationality in Drinks" and called "Beer (Nelson)."

Have drunk it deep in British Beer.
Nelson for ever—any time   5
And I his to command in prose or rhyme!
Give me of Nelson only a touch,
And I save it, be it little or much:
Here's one our Captain gives, and so
Down at the word, by George, shall it go!   10
He says that at Greenwich[2] they point the beholder
To Nelson's coat, "still with tar on the shoulder:
For he used to lean with one shoulder digging,
Jigging, as it were, and zig-zag-zigging
Up against the mizen-rigging![3]   15

1844

Home-Thoughts, from the Sea

Nobly, nobly Cape Saint Vincent[1] to the North-west died away;
Sunset ran, one glorious blood-red, reeking into Cadiz Bay;
Bluish 'mid the burning water, full in face Trafalgar lay;
In the dimmest North-east distance dawned Gibraltar grand and
    gray;
"Here and here did England help me: how can I help England?"
    —say,   5
Whoso turns as I, this evening, turn to God to praise and pray,
While Jove's planet[2] rises yonder, silent over Africa.

ca. 1844

The Bishop Orders His Tomb at
Saint Praxed's Church[1]

ROME, 15——

Vanity, saith the preacher, vanity![2]
Draw round my bed: is Anselm keeping back?

2. Greenwich Hospital, then in possession of the coat worn by Nelson at the Battle of the Nile,
   August 1, 1798. He had lost his right arm as a result of his assault on Santa Cruz de Tene-
   rife, July 24, 1797.
3. Stays supporting the mizzenmast, aft or next aft of the mainmast.
1. On the southwest tip of Portugal, where Nelson won a major naval battle on February 14,
   1797. The other points named are on the Spanish coast. Nelson assisted in the bombardment
   of Cadiz (1800), and won the Battle of Trafalgar (October 21, 1805). Gibraltar was heroically
   defended in the siege of 1779 by its British governor, George Augustus Eliott (1717–90).
2. Jupiter.
1. First published in Hood's Magazine for March 1845 as "The Tomb at St. Praxed's." Like his
   archrival Gandolf, the Bishop is fictitious, a synthesis of a number of worldly cardinals of
   Renaissance Italy. The interior of the ornate little church of Santa Prassede, built in 822,
   had been restored just prior to the poet's first visit to Rome in 1844. It is named for a virgin
   saint, daughter of Pudens, a Roman senator of the second century. The splendid chapel,
   called "Garden of Paradise," is full of glittering mosaics.
2. Ecclesiastes 1:2.

Nephews—sons mine[3] . . . ah God, I know not! Well—
She, men would have to be your mother once,
Old Gandolf envied me, so fair she was!   5
What's done is done, and she is dead beside,
Dead long ago, and I am Bishop since,
And as she died so must we die ourselves,
And thence ye may perceive the world's a dream.
Life, how and what is it? As here I lie   10
In this state-chamber, dying by degrees,
Hours and long hours in the dead night, I ask
"Do I live, am I dead?" Peace, peace seems all.
Saint Praxed's ever was the church for peace;
And so, about this tomb of mine. I fought   15
With tooth and nail to save my niche, ye know:
—Old Gandolf cozened[4] me, despite my care;
Shrewd was that snatch from out the corner South
He graced his carrion with, God curse the same!
Yet still my niche is not so cramped but thence   20
One sees the pulpit o' the epistle-side,[5]
And somewhat of the choir, those silent seats,
And up into the aery dome where live
The angels, and a sunbeam's sure to lurk:
And I shall fill my slab of basalt[6] there,   25
And 'neath my tabernacle[7] take my rest,
With those nine columns round me, two and two,
The odd one at my feet where Anselm stands:
Peach-blossom marble all, the rare, the ripe
As fresh-poured red wine of a mighty pulse.[8]   30
—Old Gandolf with his paltry onion-stone,[9]
Put me where I may look at him! True peach,
Rosy and flawless: how I earned the prize![1]
Draw close: that conflagration of my church
—What then? So much was saved if aught were missed!   35
My sons, ye would not be my death? Go dig
The white-grape vineyard where the oil-press stood,
Drop water gently till the surface sink,
And if ye find . . . Ah God, I know not, I! . . .
Bedded in store of rotten fig-leaves soft,   40
And corded up in a tight olive-frail,[2]
Some lump, ah God, of *lapis lazuli*,[3]
Big as a Jew's head cut off at the nape,
Blue as a vein o'er the Madonna's breast . . .

3. Illegitimate sons.
4. Defrauded.
5. Right side as one faces the altar, where the Epistle is read at Mass; liturgically inferior to the Gospel side.
6. Dark gray to black igneous rock.
7. Canopy.
8. Pulp of the grape.
9. Inferior marble that would flake off in layers.
1. Cf. Philippians 3:14: "I press toward the mark for the prize of the high calling of God in Christ Jesus."
2. Basket.
3. Semiprecious blue stone.

Sons, all have I bequeathed you, villas, all,   45
That brave Frascati[4] villa with its bath,
So, let the blue lump poise between my knees,
Like God the Father's globe on both his hands
Ye worship in the Jesu Church[5] so gay,
For Gandolf shall not choose but see and burst!   50
Swift as a weaver's shuttle fleet our years:[6]
Man goeth to the grave, and where is he?[7]
Did I say basalt for my slab, sons? Black—
'T was ever antique-black[8] I meant! How else
Shall ye contrast my frieze[9] to come beneath?   55
The bas-relief in bronze ye promised me,
Those Pans and Nymphs[1] ye wot of, and perchance
Some tripod, thyrsus,[2] with a vase or so,
The Saviour at his sermon on the mount,
Saint Praxed in a glory,[3] and one Pan   60
Ready to twitch the Nymph's last garment off,
And Moses with the tables[4] . . . but I know
Ye mark me not! What do they whisper thee,
Child of my bowels,[5] Anselm? Ah, ye hope
To revel down my villas while I gasp   65
Bricked o'er with beggar's mouldy travertine[6]
Which Gandolf from his tomb-top chuckles at!
Nay, boys, ye love me—all of jasper,[7] then!
'T is jasper ye stand pledged to, lest I grieve.
My bath needs be left behind, alas!   70
One block, pure green as a pistachio-nut,
There's plenty jasper somewhere in the world—
And have I not Saint Praxed's ear to pray
Horses for ye, and brown Greek manuscripts,
And mistresses with great smooth marbly limbs?   75
—That's if ye carve my epitaph aright,
Choice Latin, picked phrase, Tully's[8] every word,
No gaudy ware like Gandolf's second line—

4. Fashionable resort town in the Alban Hills about fifteen miles southeast of Rome, where
stand a number of elegant villas.
5. Chiesa del Gesù, famous Jesuit church in Rome, wherein a sculpted angel (not God) holds
a large globe of *lapis lazuli.*
6. Cf. Job 7:6: "My days are swifter than a weaver's shuttle, and are spent without hope."
7. Cf. Job 21:13: "They spend their days in wealth, and in a moment go down to the grave."
See also Job 14:10.
8. Antico-nero, marble handsomer and more costly than basalt.
9. Sculptured band of stone.
1. Nymphs: Minor deities, beautiful woodland maidens. Pan: Greek god of pastures and
forests.
2. Thyrsus: Ornamented staff carried in processions by votaries of Dionysius (Bacchus), god of
wine and fertility. Tripod: stool on which sat the oracles of Apollo at Delphi.
3. Halo.
4. Stone tablets engraved with the Ten Commandments.
5. Cf. David to Absalom, his favorite son, in 2 Samuel 16:11: "Behold, my son, which came
forth of my bowels, seeketh my life."
6. Variety of limestone.
7. Semiprecious opaque quartz of several colors. The Bishop desires the translucent variety
called green chalcedony, which has a waxlike luster.
8. Marcus Tullius Cicero (106–43 B.C.E.), orator and statesman, whose prose style was much
admired in the Renaissance.

Tully, my masters? Ulpian[9] serves his need!
And then how I shall lie through centuries,   80
And hear the blessed mutter of the mass,
And see God made and eaten all day long,[1]
And feel the steady candle-flame, and taste
Good strong thick stupefying incense-smoke!
For as I lie here, hours of the dead night,   85
Dying in state and by such slow degrees,
I fold my arms as if they clasped a crook,[2]
And stretch my feet forth straight as stone can point,
And let the bedclothes, for a mortcloth,[3] drop
Into great laps and folds of sculptor's-work: 90
And as yon tapers dwindle, and strange thoughts
Grow, with a certain humming in my ears,
About the life before I lived this life,
And this life too, popes, cardinals and priests,
Saint Praxed at his sermon on the mount,[4]   95
Your tall pale mother with her talking eyes,
And new-found agate urns as fresh as day,
And marble's language, Latin pure, discreet,
—Aha, ELUCESCEBAT[5] quoth our friend?
No Tully, said I, Ulpian at the best!   100
Evil and brief hath been my pilgrimage.[6]
All *lapis*, all, sons! Else I give the Pope
My villas! Will ye ever eat my heart?
Ever your eyes were as a lizard's quick,
They glitter like your mother's for my soul,   105
Or ye would heighten my impoverished frieze,
Piece out its starved design, and fill my vase
With grapes, and add a vizor and a Term,[7]
And to the tripod ye would tie a lynx[8]
That in his struggle throws the thyrsus down,   110
To comfort me on my entablature[9]
Whereon I am to lie till I must ask
"Do I live, am I dead?" There, leave me, there!
For ye have stabbed me with ingratitude
To death—ye wish it—God, ye wish it! Stone—   115

9. Domitius Ulpianus (d. 228), Roman jurist whose style reflects the loss of the Ciceronian classical purity.
1. Reference to the doctrine of transubstantiation, the mystical conversion of bread and wine into the body and blood of Christ during Mass.
2. Shepherd's crook or crozier, symbolic of the Bishop's office.
3. Funeral pall.
4. In the Bishop's "strange thoughts," Saint Praxed's gender is reversed, and she is conflated with Jesus.
5. "He was illustrious," in the decadent Latin of Ulpian's time; Cicero would have written *elucebat*. The Bishop had spitefully ordered bad Latin for Gandolf's tomb (lines 79 and 100).
6. Genesis 47:9: "And Jacob said unto Pharaoh, The days of the years of my pilgrimage are an hundred and thirty years: few and evil have the days of the years of my life been. . . ."
7. Bust on a pedestal, of the sort erected to honor Terminus, Roman god of boundaries. Vizor: visor or mask of a helmet, a common decoration.
8. Dionysius was often represented with lynxes.
9. Here, a slab supported by columns.

Gritstone,[1] a-crumble! Clammy squares which sweat
As if the corpse they keep were oozing through—
And no more *lapis* to delight the world!
Well go! I bless ye. Fewer tapers there,
But in a row: and, going, turn your backs   120
—Ay, like departing altar-ministrants,
And leave me in my church, the church for peace,
That I may watch at leisure if he leers—
Old Gandolf, at me, from his onion-stone,
As still he envied me, so fair she was!   125

1844–45   1845

Garden Fancies

I. THE FLOWER'S NAME

I

Here's the garden she walked across,
    Arm in my arm, such a short while since:
Hark, now I push its wicket, the moss
    Hinders the hinges and makes them wince!
She must have reached this shrub ere she turned,   5
    As back with that murmur the wicket swung;
For she laid the poor snail, my chance foot spurned,
    To feed and forget it the leaves among.

II

Down this side of the gravel-walk
    She went while her robe's edge brushed the box:[1]   10
And here she paused in her gracious talk
    To point me a moth on the milk-white phlox.
Roses, ranged in variant row,
    I will never think that she passed you by!
She loves you noble roses, I know;   15
    But yonder, see, where the rock-plants lie!

III

This flower she stopped at, finger on lip,
    Stooped over, in doubt, as settling its claim;
Till she gave me, with pride to make no slip,
    Its soft meandering Spanish name: 20
What a name! Was it love or praise?
    Speech half-asleep or song half-awake?

1. Coarse sandstone.
1. Boxwood hedge.

I must learn Spanish, one of these days,
    Only for that slow sweet name's sake.

IV

Roses, if I live and do well,   25
    I may bring her, one of these days,
To fix you fast with as fine a spell,
    Fit you each with his Spanish phrase;
But do not detain me now; for she lingers
    There, like sunshine over the ground,   30
And ever I see her soft white fingers
    Searching after the bud she found.

V

Flower, you Spaniard, look that you grow not,
    Stay as you are and be loved for ever!
Bud, if I kiss you 't is that you blow not: 35
    Mind, the shut pink mouth opens never!
For while it pouts, her fingers wrestle,
    Twinkling the audacious leaves between,
Till round they turn and down they nestle—
    Is not the dear mark still to be seen?   40

VI

Where I find her not, beauties vanish;
    Whither I follow her, beauties flee;
Is there no method to tell her in Spanish
    June's twice June since she breathed it with me?
Come, bud, show me the least of her traces,   45
    Treasure my lady's lightest footfall!
—Ah, you may flout and turn up your faces—
    Roses, you are not so fair after all!

II. SIBRANDUS SCHAFNABURGENSIS[1]

I

Plague take all your pedants, say I!
    He who wrote what I hold in my hand,
Centuries back was so good as to die,
    Leaving this rubbish to cumber the land;
This, that was a book in its time,   5
    Printed on paper and bound in leather,
Last month in the white of a matin-prime[2]
    Just when the birds sang all together.

---

1. Browning apparently found a reference to Sibrandus of Aschaffenburg in Nathaniel Wanley's *Wonders of the Little World* (1667). Here he uses Sibrandus as a representative of the pedantic, dull writer.
2. Early morning.

II

Into the garden I brought it to read,
    And under the arbute and laurustine[3]   10
Read it, so help me grace in my need,
    From title-page to closing line.
Chapter on chapter did I count,
    As a curious traveller counts Stonehenge;
Added up the mortal amount;   15
    And then proceeded to my revenge.

III

Yonder's a plum-tree with a crevice
    An owl would build in, were he but sage;
For a lap of moss, like a fine pont-levis[4]
    In a castle of the Middle Age,   20
Joins to a lip of gum, pure amber;
    When he'd be private, there might he spend
Hours alone in his lady's chamber:
    Into this crevice I dropped our friend.

IV

Splash, went he, as under he ducked,   25
    —At the bottom, I knew, rain-drippings stagnate:
Next, a handful of blossoms I plucked
    To bury him with, my bookshelf's magnate;
Then I went in-doors, brought out a loaf,
    Half a cheese, and a bottle of Chablis;   30
Lay on the grass and forgot the oaf
    Over a jolly chapter of Rabelais.[5]

V

Now, this morning, betwixt the moss
    And gum that locked our friend in limbo,
A spider had spun his web across,   35
    And sat in the midst with arms akimbo:
So, I took pity, for learning's sake,
    And, *de profundis, accentibus lætis,*
Cantate![6] quoth I, as I got a rake;
    And up I fished his delectable treatise.   40

---

3. Evergreen shrub, like the arbute.
4. Drawbridge.
5. François Rabelais (c. 1490–1553), French comic writer best known for his multi-volume
   humorous and philosophical romance, *Gargantua and Pantagruel.*
6. From the depths, with joyful accents, sing! (Latin). Cf. Psalm 130.

VI

Here you have it, dry in the sun,
  With all the binding all of a blister,
And great blue spots where the ink has run,
  And reddish streaks that wink and glister
O'er the page so beautifully yellow: 45
  Oh, well have the droppings played their tricks!
Did he guess how toadstools grow, this fellow?
  Here's one stuck in his chapter six!

VII

How did he like it when the live creatures
  Tickled and toused[7] and browsed him all over,   50
And worm, slug, eft, with serious features,
  Came in, each one, for his right of trover?[8]
—When the water-beetle with great blind deaf face
  Made of her eggs the stately deposit,
And the newt borrowed just so much of the preface   55
  As tiled in the top of his black wife's closet?

VIII

All that life and fun and romping,
  All that frisking and twisting and coupling,
While slowly our poor friend's leaves were swamping
  And clasps were cracking and covers suppling!   60
As if you had carried sour John Knox[9]
  To the play-house at Paris, Vienna or Munich,
Fastened him into a front-row box,
  And danced off the ballet with trousers and tunic.

IX

Come, old martyr! What, torment enough is it?   65
  Back to my room shall you take your sweet self.
Good-bye, mother-beetle; husband-eft, *sufficit!*[1]
  See the snug niche I have made on my shelf!
A.'s book shall prop you up, B.'s shall cover you,
  Here's C. to be grave with, or D. to be gay,   70
And with E. on each side, and F. right over you,
  Dry-rot at ease till the Judgment-day!

7. Fretted, tore roughly.
8. The right to keep the treasure one finds.
9. Rigid Scottish Calvinist preacher (c. 1515–72), known for his vehement, denunciatory manner.
1. Enough (Latin).

The Laboratory[1]

ANCIEN RÉGIME

I

Now that I, tying thy glass mask[2] tightly,
May gaze thro' these faint smokes curling whitely,
As thou pliest thy trade in this devil's-smithy—
Which is the poison to poison her, prithee?

II

He is with her, and they know that I know   5
Where they are, what they do: they believe my tears flow
While they laugh, laugh at me, at me fled to the drear
Empty church, to pray God in, for them!—I am here.

III

Grind away, moisten and mash up thy paste,
Pound at thy powder,—I am not in haste!   10
Better sit thus, and observe thy strange things,
Than go where men wait me and dance at the King's.

IV

That in the mortar—you call it a gum?[3]
Ah, the brave tree whence such gold oozings come!
And yonder soft phial, the exquisite blue,[4]   15
Sure to taste sweetly,—is that poison too?

V

Had I but all of them, thee and thy treasures,
What a wild crowd of invisible pleasures!
To carry pure death in an earring, a casket,
A signet, a fan-mount, a filigree basket!   20

VI

Soon, at the King's, a mere lozenge to give,
And Pauline should have just thirty minutes to live!
But to light a pastile,[5] and Elise, with her head
And her breast and her arms and her hands, should drop dead!

1. First published in *Hood's Magazine* for June 1844. The subtitle sets the poem in France be-
fore the Revolution of 1789. Browning probably had in mind the court of Louis XIV
(1643–1715) shaken in the 1670s by a rash of poisonings traceable to Marie-Madeleine de
Brinvilliers (1630–76) and her lover Sainte-Croix, who died when his protective mask
slipped as he was preparing a poisonous mixture.
2. Chemist's protective mask.
3. Probably gum arabic, exuded by the acacia tree, used in preparing emulsions and pills.
4. Perhaps blue vitriol (copper sulfate), a poisonous compound.
5. Tablet containing aromatic substances, burned to fumigate or deodorize the air.

VII

Quick—is it finished? The colour's too grim!   25
Why not soft like the phial's, enticing and dim?
Let it brighten her drink, let her turn it and stir,
And try it and taste, ere she fix[6] and prefer!

VIII

What a drop! She's not little, no minion[7] like me!
That's why she ensnared him: this never will free   30
The soul from those masculine eyes,—say, "no!"
To that pulse's magnificent come-and-go.

IX

For only last night, as they whispered, I brought
My own eyes to bear on her so, that I thought
Could I keep them one half minute fixed, she would fall 35
Shrivelled; she fell not; yet this does it all!

X

Not that I bid you spare her the pain;
Let death be felt and the proof remain:
Brand, burn up, bite into its grace—
He is sure to remember her dying face!   40

XI

Is it done? Take my mask off! Nay, be not morose;
It kills her, and this prevents seeing it close:
The delicate droplet, my whole fortune's fee!
If it hurts her, beside, can it ever hurt me?

XII

Now, take all my jewels, gorge gold to your fill,   45
You may kiss me, old man, on my mouth if you will!
But brush this dust off me, lest horror it brings
Ere I know it—next moment I dance at the King's!

1844

---

6. Make up her mind.
7. Here in the rare sense of small and delicate (cf. French *mignon*, "darling").

Meeting at Night

I

The grey sea and the long black land;
And the yellow half-moon large and low;
And the startled little waves that leap
In fiery ringlets from their sleep,
As I gain the cove with pushing prow,   5
And quench its speed i' the slushy sand.

II

Then a mile of warm sea-scented beach;
Three fields to cross till a farm appears;
A tap at the pane, the quick sharp scratch
And blue spurt of a lighted match,   10
And a voice less loud, thro' its joys and fears,
Than the two hearts beating each to each!

Parting at Morning[1]

Round the cape of a sudden came the sea,
And the sun looked over the mountain's rim:
And straight was a path of gold for him,[2]
And the need of a world of men for me.

---

1. Answering a query in 1889, Browning said a man was the speaker in this and "Meeting at Night." This lyric "is *his* confession of how fleeting is the belief (implied in the first part) that such raptures are self-sufficient and enduring—as for the time they appear" (De Vane, p. 178).
2. The sun.

The Major Phase (1855–69)

FROM *MEN AND WOMEN* (1855)

Love Among the Ruins[1]

I

Where the quiet-coloured end of evening smiles,
    Miles and miles
On the solitary pastures where our sheep
    Half-asleep
Tinkle homeward thro' the twilight, stray or stop   5
    As they crop—
Was the site once of a city great and gay,
    (So they say)
Of our country's very capital, its prince
    Ages since   10
Held his court in, gathered councils, wielding far
    Peace or war.

II

Now,—the country does not even boast a tree
    As you see,
To distinguish slopes of verdure, certain rills   15
    From the hills
Intersect and give a name to, (else they run
    Into one)
Where the domed and daring palace shot its spires
    Up like fires   20
O'er the hundred-gated circuit of a wall

---

1. Vexed at his laziness during 1851, Browning made a New Year's resolution to write a poem each day in 1852. The vow was kept for the first three days in January, when the poet composed "Love Among the Ruins," "Women and Roses," and "Childe Roland." The setting of "Love Among the Ruins" is unspecified, but since Browning's manuscript draft of the poem (now at Harvard) is entitled "Sicilian Pastoral," ancient Syracuse may have been the site originally in mind. Reports of recent excavations at Thebes, Babylon, and Nineveh—and the poet's reading of Shelley's "Ozymandias"—doubtless contributed to this vision of bygone opulence and power. The unusual versification may owe to the poet's "pet book" as a boy, Francis Quarles's *Emblems* (1635), one lyric of which has these echoic lines:

   > Boast not thy skill; the righteous man falls oft,
   >   Yet falls but soft:
   > There may be dirt to mire him, but no stones
   >   To crush his bones. . . .
   >   (II.xiv.13–16)

Bounding all,
Made of marble, men might march on nor be pressed,
Twelve abreast.

III

And such plenty and perfection, see, of grass   25
Never was!
Such a carpet as, this summer-time, o'erspreads
And embeds
Every vestige of the city, guessed alone,
Stock[2] or stone—   30
Where a multitude of men breathed joy and woe
Long ago;
Lust of glory pricked their hearts up, dread of shame
Struck them tame;
And that glory and that shame alike, the gold   35
Bought and sold.

IV

Now,—the single little turret that remains
On the plains,
By the caper[3] overrooted, by the gourd
Overscored,   40
While the patching houseleek's[4] head of blossom winks
Through the chinks—
Marks the basement whence a tower in ancient time
Sprang sublime,
And a burning ring, all round, the chariots traced   45
As they raced,
And the monarch and his minions and his dames
Viewed the games.

V

And I know, while thus the quiet-coloured eve
Smiles to leave   50
To their folding, all our many-tinkling fleece
In such peace,
And the slopes and rills in undistinguished grey
Melt away—
That a girl with eager eyes and yellow hair   55
Waits me there
In the turret whence the charioteers caught soul
For the goal,
When the king looked, where she looks now, breathless, dumb
Till I come.   60

2. Stumps, lifeless things.
3. Low prickly Mediterranean shrub.
4. Pink-flowered European plant found on old walls and roofs.

VI

But he looked upon the city, every side,
 Far and wide,
All the mountains topped with temples, all the glades'
 Colonnades,
All the causeys,[5] bridges, aqueducts,—and then,   65
 All the men!
When I do come, she will speak not, she will stand,
 Either hand
On my shoulder, give her eyes the first embrace
 Of my face,   70
Ere we rush, ere we extinguish sight and speech
 Each on each.

VII

In one year they sent a million fighters forth
 South and North,
And they built their gods a brazen pillar high   75
 As the sky,
Yet reserved a thousand chariots in full force—
 Gold, of course.
Oh heart! oh blood that freezes, blood that burns!
 Earth's returns   80
For whole centuries of folly, noise and sin!
 Shut them in,
With their triumphs and their glories and the rest!
 Love is best.

1852

A Lovers' Quarrel[1]

I

Oh, what a dawn of day!
How the March sun feels like May!
 All is blue again
 After last night's rain,
And the South dries the hawthorn-spray.   5
 Only, my Love's away!
I'd as lief that the blue were grey.

---

5. Causeways, raised roads.
1. The autobiographical element here is unmistakable. Browning and his wife differed strongly on the topics mentioned: Napoleon III and spiritualism. See Daniel Karlin's essay in this volume, pp. 610–21, for more on this poem.

II

Runnels,[2] which rillets swell,
Must be dancing down the dell,
    With a foaming head   10
    On the beryl[3] bed
Paven smooth as a hermit's cell;
    Each with a tale to tell
Could my Love but attend[4] as well.

III

Dearest, three months ago!   15
    When we lived blocked-up with snow,—
    When the wind would edge
    In and in his wedge,
In, as far as the point could go—
    Not to our ingle,[5] though,   20
Where we loved each the other so!

IV

Laughs with so little cause!
We devised games out of straws.
    We would try and trace
    One another's face   25
In the ash, as an artist draws;
    Free on each other's flaws,
How we chattered like two church daws![6]

V

What's in the "Times"?—a scold
At the Emperor deep and cold;   30
    He has taken a bride
    To his gruesome side,
That's as fair as himself is bold:
    There they sit ermine-stoled,
And she powders her hair with gold.[7]   35

VI

Fancy the Pampas' sheen!
Miles and miles of gold and green
    Where the sunflowers blow
    In a solid glow,

2. Rivulets; rillets are small rivulets.
3. Hard mineral often used as a gem.
4. Heed.
5. Hearth.
6. Jackdaws, resembling crows.
7. The opulent wedding of Napoleon III to Eugénie de Montijo, a Spanish countess, was reported in the [London] *Times* for January 31 and February 1, 1853.

And—to break now and then the screen—   40
　　Black neck and eyeballs keen,
Up a wild horse leaps between![8]

VII

Try, will our table turn?
Lay your hands there light, and yearn
　　　　Till the yearning slips   45
　　　　Thro' the finger-tips
In a fire which a few discern,
　　And a very few feel burn,
And the rest, they may live and learn![9]

VIII

Then we would up and pace,   50
For a change, about the place,
　　　　Each with arm o'er neck:
　　　　'T is our quarter-deck,[1]
We are seamen in woeful case.
　　　　Help in the ocean-space!   55
Or, if no help, we'll embrace.

IX

See, how she looks now, dressed
In a sledging-cap and vest!
　　　　'T is a huge fur cloak—
　　　　Like a reindeer's yoke   60
Falls the lappet[2] along the breast:
　　　　Sleeves for her arms to rest,
Or to hang, as my Love likes best.

X

Teach me to flirt[3] a fan
As the Spanish ladies can,   65
　　　　Or I tint your lip
　　　　With a burnt stick's tip
And you turn into such a man!
　　　　Just the two spots that span
Half the bill of the young male swan.   70

8. In the *Times* for February 18, 1853, was a report of an attack on Buenos Aires by *gauchos*, cowboys of the *pampas*.
9. Spiritualism in its various forms—including rapping and table-turning—was at this time a craze in Florence. To Browning's dismay Elizabeth came to believe in it.
1. After part of ship's upper deck, reserved for officers. The lovers' snowbound cottage is compared to a storm-tossed ship.
2. Decorative flap or fold in a garment.
3. Flick or wave.

XI

Dearest, three months ago
When the mesmerizer[4] Snow
    With his hand's first sweep
    Put the earth to sleep:
'T was a time when the heart could show   75
    All—how was earth to know,
'Neath the mute hand's to-and-fro?

XII

Dearest, three months ago
When we loved each other so,
    Lived and loved the same   80
    'Till an evening came
When a shaft from the devil's bow
    Pierced to our ingle-glow,
And the friends were friend and foe!

XIII

Not from the heart beneath—   85
'T was a bubble born of breath,
    Neither sneer nor vaunt,
    Nor reproach nor taunt.
See a word, how it severeth!
    Oh, power of life and death   90
In the tongue, as the Preacher saith![5]

XIV

Woman, and will you cast
For a word, quite off at last
    Me, your own, your You,—
    Since, as truth is true,   95
I was You all the happy past—
    Me do you leave aghast
With the memories We amassed?

XV

Love, if you knew the light
That your soul casts in my sight,   100
    How I look to you
    For the pure and true
And the beauteous and the right,—
    Bear with a moment's spite
When a mere mote threats the white!   105

4. Mesmerism: precursor of hypnotism.
5. Proverbs 18:21: "Death and life are in the power of the tongue."

XVI

What of a hasty word?
Is the fleshy heart not stirred
   By a worm's pin-prick
   Where its roots are quick?
See the eye, by a fly's foot blurred—   110
   Ear, when a straw is heard
Scratch the brain's coat of curd![6]

XVII

Foul be the world or fair
More or less, how can I care?
   'T is the world the same   115
   For my praise or blame,
And endurance is easy there.
   Wrong in the one thing rare—
Oh, it is hard to bear!

XVIII

Here's the spring back or close,   120
When the almond-blossom blows:
   We shall have the word
   In a minor third[7]
There is none but the cuckoo knows:
   Heaps of the guelder-rose![8]   125
I must bear with it, I suppose.

XIX

Could but November come,
Were the noisy birds struck dumb
   At the warning slash
   Of his driver's-lash—   130
I would laugh like the valiant Thumb[9]
   Facing the castle glum
And the giant's fee-faw-fum!

XX

Then, were the world well stripped
Of the gear wherein equipped   135
   We can stand apart,
   Heart dispense with heart
In the sun, with the flowers unnipped,—
   Oh, the world's hangings ripped,
We were both in a bare-walled crypt!   140

6. Whitish substance of the brain.
7. Interval between cuckoo's notes (here three semitones).
8. Shrub having clusters of white flowers and small red fruit.
9. Tom Thumb, from Henry Fielding's *Tom Thumb, a Tragedy* (1730).

XXI

Each in the crypt would cry
"But one freezes here! and why?
    When a heart, as chill,
    At my own would thrill
Back to life, and its fires out-fly?   145
    Heart, shall we live or die?
The rest, . . . settle by-and-by!"

XXII

So, she'd efface the score,
And forgive me as before.
    It is twelve o'clock: 150
    I shall hear her knock
In the worst of a storm's uproar,
    I shall pull her through the door,
I shall have her for evermore!

ca. 1853

Up at a Villa—Down in the City[1]

(AS DISTINGUISHED BY AN ITALIAN PERSON OF QUALITY)

I

Had I but plenty of money, money enough and to spare,
The house for me, no doubt, were a house in the city-square;
Ah, such a life, such a life, as one leads at the window there!

II

Something to see, by Bacchus,[2] something to hear, at least!
There, the whole day long, one's life is a perfect feast;   5
While up at a villa one lives, I maintain it, no more than a
    beast.

III

Well now, look at our villa! stuck like the horn of a bull
Just on a mountain-edge as bare as the creature's skull,
Save a mere shag of a bush with hardly a leaf to pull!
—I scratch my own, sometimes, to see if the hair's turned   10
    wool.

1. The setting is probably the Tuscan hills near Siena, where the Brownings had taken a villa in
   the fall of 1850.
2. Common Italian oath: *per Bacco!*

IV

But the city, oh the city—the square with the houses! Why?
They are stone-faced, white as a curd, there's something to take
    the eye!
Houses in four straight lines, not a single front awry;
You watch who crosses and gossips, who saunters, who hurries by;
Green blinds, as a matter of course, to draw when the sun gets
    high;   15
And the shops with fanciful signs which are painted properly.

V

What of a villa? Though winter be over in March by rights,
'T is May perhaps ere the snow shall have withered well off the
    heights:
You've the brown ploughed land before, where the oxen steam
    and wheeze,
And the hills over-smoked behind by the faint grey olive-trees.   20

VI

Is it better in May, I ask you? You've summer all at once;
In a day he leaps complete with a few strong April suns.
'Mid the sharp short emerald wheat, scarce risen three fingers
    well,
The wild tulip, at end of its tube, blows out its great red bell
Like a thin clear bubble of blood, for the children to pick and
    sell.   25

VII

Is it ever hot in the square? There's a fountain to spout and
    splash!
In the shade it sings and springs; in the shine such foam-bows
    flash
On the horses with curling fish-tails, that prance and paddle and
    pash[3]
Round the lady atop in her conch—fifty gazers do not abash.
Though all that she wears is some weeds round her waist in a
    sort of sash.   30

VIII

All the year long at the villa, nothing to see though you linger,
Except yon cypress that points like death's lean lifted forefinger.
Some think fireflies pretty, when they mix i' the corn and mingle,
Or thrid[4] the stinking hemp till the stalks of it seem a-tingle.
Late August or early September, the stunning cicala[5] is shrill,   35

3. Here, beat with hooves.
4. Thread through.
5. Locust.

And the bees keep their tiresome whine round the resinous firs
  on the hill.
Enough of the seasons,—I spare you the months of the fever and
  chill.

IX

Ere you open your eyes in the city, the blessed church-bells begin:
No sooner the bells leave off than the diligence[6] rattles in:
You get the pick of the news, and it costs you never a pin.   40
By-and-by there's the travelling doctor gives pills, lets blood, draws
  teeth;
Or the Pulcinello-trumpet[7] breaks up the market beneath.
At the post-office such a scene-picture—the new play, piping hot!
And a notice how, only this morning, three liberal thieves[8] were
  shot.
Above it, behold the Archbishop's most fatherly of rebukes,   45
And beneath, with his crown and his lion, some little new law
  of the Duke's![9]
Or a sonnet with flowery marge, to the Reverend Don So-and-so
Who is Dante, Boccaccio, Petrarca, Saint Jerome and Cicero,
"And moreover," (the sonnet goes rhyming,) "the skirts of Saint
  Paul has reached,
Having preached us those six Lent-lectures more unctuous than
  ever he preached."   50
Noon strikes,—here sweeps the procession! our Lady borne
  smiling and smart
With a pink gauze gown all spangles, and seven swords stuck in
  her heart![1]
Bang-whang-whang goes the drum, *tootle-te-tootle* the fife;[2]
No keeping one's haunches still: it's the greatest pleasure in life.

X

But bless you, it's dear—it's dear! fowls, wine, at double the rate.   55
They have clapped a new tax upon salt, and what oil pays
  passing the gate
It's a horror to think of. And so, the villa for me, not the city!
Beggars can scarcely be choosers: but still—ah, the pity, the pity!
Look, two and two go the priests, then the monks with cowls and
  sandals,
And the penitents dressed in white shirts, a-holding the yellow
  candles;   60
One, he carries a flag up straight, and another a cross with handles,

6. Public stagecoach.
7. Trumpet announcing a puppet show; the buffoon Pulcinello is the forerunner of Punch.
8. I.e., opponents of Austrian rule in Italy.
9. Upon his restoration in 1849 (with Austrian support), Leopold II, Grand Duke of Tuscany,
   dashed liberal hopes by enacting such repressive "little new law[s]" as the repeal in 1852 of
   the Tuscan constitution.
1. Symbol of St. Mary's seven sorrows.
2. Browning in 1864: "Do you see the 'Edinburg [*sic*] [*Review*]' that says all my poetry is
   summed up in 'Bang whang, whang, goes the Drum?' " (*Dearest Isa*, p. 196).

And the Duke's guard brings up the rear, for the better prevention
    of scandals:
Bang-whang-whang goes the drum, *tootle-te-tootle* the fife.
Oh, a day in the city-square, there is no such pleasure in life!

ca. 1850

A Woman's Last Word

I

    Let's contend no more, Love,
        Strive nor weep:
    All be as before, Love,
        —Only sleep!

II

    What so wild as words are?   5
        I and thou
    In debate, as birds are,
        Hawk on bough![1]

III

    See the creature stalking
        While we speak!   10
    Hush and hide the talking,
        Cheek on cheek!

IV

    What so false as truth is,
        False to thee?
    Where the serpent's tooth is   15
        Shun the tree—

V

    Where the apple reddens
        Never pry—
    Lest we lose our Edens,
        Eve and I.   20

VI

    Be a god and hold me
        With a charm!
    Be a man and fold me
        With thine arm!

1. As the hawk perches near the oblivious birds, so may love be threatened by discord.

VII

Teach me, only teach, Love!   25
  As I ought
I will speak thy speech, Love,
  Think thy thought—

VIII

Meet, if thou require it,
  Both demands,   30
Laying flesh and spirit
  In thy hands.

IX

That shall be to-morrow
  Not to night:
I must bury sorrow   35
  Out of sight:

X

—Must a little weep, Love,
  (Foolish me!)
And so fall asleep, Love,
  Loved by thee.   40

Fra Lippo Lippi[1]

I am poor brother Lippo, by your leave!
You need not clap your torches to my face.
Zooks,[2] what's to blame? you think you see a monk!
What, 't is past midnight, and you go the rounds,
And here you catch me at an alley's end   5
Where sportive ladies leave their doors ajar?
The Carmine's my cloister: hunt it up,

1. "Fra Lippo Lippi," Browning's most forceful statement upon the relation of art to life, is set in Florence near the middle of the fifteenth century. Browning's main source for the life of the painter-monk Fra Lippo Lippi (ca. 1406–69) is the sketch in Giorgio Vasari's *Lives of the Painters*. The accuracy of this account is questioned by modern scholars, and only the facts that seem well established are given here. Born in Florence, Lippi was orphaned at the age of two and was left in the hands of a poor aunt. In 1421 he was registered in the community of the Carmelite friars of S. Maria del Carmine in Florence, where he remained until 1432. His earliest known work, the *Reform of the Carmelite Rule* (ca. 1432), bore the influence of Masaccio, whom Lippi had watched at work in the Brancacci chapel of the Carmine (1426–27). After leaving the monastery he worked for a time in Padua, then returned to Florence, where he won the patronage of Cosimo de' Medici. In 1442 he was made rector of S. Quirico at Legnaia, but was dismissed for misconduct in 1455. While acting as chaplain of the convent of S. Margherita in Florence he eloped with a nun, Lucrezia Buti, who bore Filippino (ca. 1457–1504), himself a notable painter. From 1452–64 Lippi painted a series of monumental frescoes in the choir of the cathedral at Prato, near Florence; they are considered his greatest achievement. Though he painted exclusively religious subjects, his work is rich in human content.
2. "Gadzooks": a mild oath.

Do,—harry out, if you must show your zeal,
Whatever rat, there, haps on his wrong hole,
And nip each softling of a wee white mouse,   10
Weke, weke, that's crept to keep him company!
Aha, you know your betters! Then, you'll take
Your hand away that's fiddling on my throat,
And please to know me likewise. Who am I?
Why, one, sir, who is lodging with a friend   15
Three streets off—he's a certain . . . how d'ye call?
Master—a . . . Cosimo of the Medici,[3]
I' the house that caps the corner. Boh! you were best!
Remember and tell me, the day you're hanged,
How you affected such a gullet's-gripe![4]   20
But you, sir, it concerns you that your knaves
Pick up a manner nor discredit you:
Zooks, are we pilchards,[5] that they sweep the streets
And count fair prize what comes into their net?
He's Judas to a tittle, that man is!   25
Just such a face! Why, sir, you make amends.
Lord, I'm not angry! Bid your hangdogs[6] go
Drink out this quarter-florin[7] to the health
Of the munificent House that harbours me
(And many more beside, lads! more beside!)   30
And all's come square again. I'd like his face—
His, elbowing on his comrade in the door
With the pike and lantern,—for the slave that holds
John Baptist's[8] head a-dangle by the hair
With one hand ("Look you, now," as who should say)   35
And his weapon in the other, yet unwiped!
It's not your chance to have a bit of chalk,
A wood-coal or the like? or you should see!
Yes, I'm the painter, since you style me so.
What, brother Lippo's doings, up and down,   40
You know them and they take[9] you? like enough!
I saw the proper twinkle in your eye—
'Tell you, I liked your looks at very first.
Let's sit and set things straight now, hip to haunch.
Here's spring come, and the nights one makes up bands   45
To roam the town and sing out carnival,[1]
And I've been three weeks shut within my mew,[2]
A-painting for the great man, saints and saints
And saints again. I could not paint all night—

---

3. Cosimo the Elder (1389–1464), Florentine banker, virtual ruler of the city, and its leading
   art patron.
4. I.e., how you enjoyed grabbing people by their throats.
5. Sardines, small fish.
6. Degraded, ashamed men.
7. Florentine coin.
8. See note to line 196.
9. Please.
1. Festival of merrymaking before Lent.
2. Cage. According to Vasari, Lippi tolerated his confinement for only "a few days," not three
   weeks.

Ouf! I leaned out of window for fresh air.   50
There came a hurry of feet and little feet,
A sweep of lute-strings, laughs, and whifts of song,[3]—
Flower o' the broom,
Take away love, and our earth is a tomb!
Flower o' the quince,   55
I let Lisa go, and what good in life since?
Flower o' the thyme—and so on. Round they went.
Scarce had they turned the corner when a titter
Like the skipping of rabbits by moonlight,—three slim shapes,
And a face that looked up . . . zooks, sir, flesh and blood,   60
That's all I'm made of! Into shreds it went,
Curtain and counterpane and coverlet,
All the bed-furniture—a dozen knots,
There was a ladder! Down I let myself,
Hands and feet, scrambling somehow, and so dropped,   65
And after them. I came up with the fun
Hard by Saint Laurence,[4] hail fellow, well met,—
Flower o' the rose,
If I've been merry, what matter who knows?
And so as I was stealing back again   70
To get to bed and have a bit of sleep
Ere I rise up to-morrow and go work
On Jerome[5] knocking at his poor old breast
With his great round stone to subdue the flesh,
You snap me of the sudden. Ah, I see!   75
Though your eye twinkles still, you shake your head—
Mine's shaved[6]—a monk, you say—the sting's in that!
If Master Cosimo announced himself,
Mum's the word naturally; but a monk!
Come, what am I a beast for? tell us, now!   80
I was a baby when my mother died
And father died and left me in the street.
I starved there, God knows how, a year or two
On fig-skins, melon-parings, rinds and shucks,
Refuse and rubbish. One fine frosty day,   85
My stomach being empty as your hat,
The wind doubled me up and down I went.
Old Aunt Lapaccia trussed me with one hand,
(Its fellow was a stinger as I knew)
And so along the wall, over the bridge,   90
By the straight cut to the convent. Six words there,
While I stood munching my first bread that month:
"So, boy, you're minded," quoth the good fat father
Wiping his own mouth, 't was refection-time,—

---

3. The interspersed songs are imitations of *stornelli*, three-line Italian folk songs improvised on rhymes set by flower names.
4. Church of San Lorenzo.
5. St. Jerome (ca. 347–ca. 420), zealous defender of monasticism and celibacy, and one of Lippi's more incongruous subjects. The *St. Jerome in Penitence* is highly praised by Vasari.
6. The crowns of monks' heads were shaved (tonsured) to betoken vows of chastity, poverty, and obedience.

"To quit this very miserable world?   95
Will you renounce" . . . "the mouthful of bread?" thought I;
By no means! Brief, they made a monk of me;
I did renounce the world, its pride and greed,
Palace, farm, villa, shop and banking-house,
Trash, such as these poor devils of Medici   100
Have given their hearts to—all at eight years old.
Well, sir, I found in time, you may be sure,
'T was not for nothing—the good bellyful,
The warm serge and the rope that goes all round,
And day-long blessed idleness beside!   105
"Let's see what the urchin's fit for"—that came next.
Not overmuch their way, I must confess.
Such a to-do! They tried me with their books:
Lord, they'd have taught me Latin in pure waste!
Flower o' the clove,   110
All the Latin I construe is, "amo" I love!
But, mind you, when a boy starves in the streets
Eight years together, as my fortune was,
Watching folk's faces to know who will fling
The bit of half-stripped grape-bunch he desires,   115
And who will curse or kick him for his pains,—
Which gentleman processional and fine,[7]
Holding a candle to the Sacrament,
Will wink and let him lift a plate and catch
The droppings of the wax to sell again,   120
Or holla for the Eight[8] and have him whipped,—
How say I?—nay, which dog bites, which lets drop
His bone from the heap of offal in the street,—
Why, soul and sense of him grow sharp alike,
He learns the look of things, and none the less   125
For admonition from the hunger-pinch.
I had a store of such remarks, be sure,
Which, after I found leisure, turned to use.
I drew men's faces on my copy-books,
Scrawled them within the antiphonary's marge,[9]   130
Joined legs and arms to the long music-notes,
Found eyes and nose and chin for A's and B's,
And made a string of pictures of the world
Betwixt the ins and outs of verb and noun,
On the wall, the bench, the door. The monks looked black.   135
"Nay," quoth the Prior, "turn him out, d'ye say?
In no wise. Lose a crow and catch a lark.
What if at last we get our man of parts,
We Carmelites, like those Camaldolese[1]
And Preaching Friars,[2] to do our church up fine   140

7. Dressed in ecclesiastical garb for a procession.
8. Florentine magistrates.
9. Margin of a hymn book.
1. Order of monks housed at the convent of the Camaldoli, near Florence.
2. Dominicans, officially named "Order of Friars Preachers," founded 1215.

And put the front on it that ought to be!"
And hereupon he bade me daub away.
Thank you! my head being crammed, the walls a blank,
Never was such prompt disemburdening.
First, every sort of monk, the black and white,[3]   145
I drew them, fat and lean: then, folk at church,
From good old gossips waiting to confess
Their cribs[4] of barrel-droppings, candle-ends,—
To the breathless fellow at the altar-foot,
Fresh from his murder, safe[5] and sitting there   150
With the little children round him in a row
Of admiration, half for his beard and half
For that white anger of his victim's son
Shaking a fist at him with one fierce arm,
Signing himself[6] with the other because of Christ   155
(Whose sad face on the cross sees only this
After the passion of a thousand years)
Till some poor girl, her apron o'er her head,
(Which the intense eyes looked through) came at eve
On tiptoe, said a word, dropped in a loaf,   160
Her pair of earrings and a bunch of flowers
(The brute took growling), prayed, and so was gone.
I painted all, then cried " 'T is ask and have;
Choose, for more's ready!"—laid the ladder flat,
And showed my covered bit of cloister-wall.   165
The monks closed in a circle and praised loud
Till checked, taught what to see and not to see,
Being simple bodies,—"That's the very man!
Look at the boy who stoops to pat the dog!
That woman's like the Prior's niece[7] who comes   170
To care about his asthma: it's the life!"
But there my triumph's straw-fire flared and funked;[8]
Their betters took their turn to see and say:
The Prior and the learned pulled a face
And stopped all that in no time. "How? what's here?   175
Quite from the mark of painting, bless us all!
Faces, arms, legs and bodies like the true
As much as pea and pea! it's devil's-game![9]
Your business is not to catch men with show,
With homage to the perishable clay,   180
But lift them over it, ignore it all,
Make them forget there's such a thing as flesh.
Your business is to paint the souls of men—
Man's soul, and it's a fire, smoke . . . no, it's not . . .

3. Colors worn by Dominicans and Carmelites, respectively.
4. Petty thefts.
5. The church was a sanctuary outside civil jurisdiction.
6. With sign of the Cross.
7. Probably euphemism for mistress.
8. Went out in smoke.
9. What follows is a delineation of the monastic ideal of painting—the mode of Fra Angelico
   and Lorenzo Monaco (see lines 235–36)—that was to be supplanted by the natural style of
   Lippi and his contemporaries.

It's vapour done up like a new-born babe—   185
(In that shape when you die it leaves your mouth)
It's . . . well, what matters talking, it's the soul!
Give us no more of body than shows soul!
Here's Giotto,[1] with his Saint a-praising God,
That sets us praising,—why not stop with him?   190
Why put all thoughts of praise out of our head
With wonder at lines, colours, and what not?
Paint the soul, never mind the legs and arms!
Rub all out, try at it a second time.
Oh, that white smallish female with the breasts,   195
She's just my niece . . . Herodias,[2] I would say,—
Who went and danced and got men's heads cut off!
Have it all out!" Now, is this sense, I ask?
A fine way to paint soul, by painting body
So ill, the eye can't stop there, must go further   200
And can't fare worse! Thus, yellow does for white
When what you put for yellow's simply black,
And any sort of meaning looks intense
When all beside itself means and looks nought.
Why can't a painter lift each foot in turn,   205
Left foot and right foot, go a double step,
Make his flesh liker and his soul more like,
Both in their order? Take the prettiest face,
The Prior's niece . . . patron-saint—is it so pretty
You can't discover if it means hope, fear,   210
Sorrow or joy? won't beauty go with these?
Suppose I've made her eyes all right and blue,
Can't I take breath and try to add life's flash,
And then add soul and heighten them threefold?
Or say there's beauty with no soul at all—   215
(I never saw it—put the case the same—)
If you get simple beauty and nought else,
You get about the best thing God invents:
That's somewhat: and you'll find the soul you have missed,
Within yourself, when you return him thanks.   220
"Rub all out!" Well, well, there's my life, in short,
And so the thing has gone on ever since.
I'm grown a man no doubt, I've broken bounds:
You should not take a fellow eight years old
And make him swear to never kiss the girls.   225
I'm my own master, paint now as I please—
Having a friend, you see, in the Corner-house!
Lord, it's fast holding by the rings in front—
Those great rings serve more purposes than just
To plant a flag in, or tie up a horse!   230

1. Giotto di Bondone (ca. 1267–1337), whose paintings of St. Francis are described in Vasari, was the most important medieval Italian artist.
2. Rather, Herodias' daughter Salome (the error is Vasari's as well as the Prior's). Her dancing so pleased Herod that he promised her whatever she wished; upon Herodias' instruction she demanded the head of John the Baptist (Matthew 14:3–12). Lippi soon corrects the Prior's self-betraying identification, calling the niece "patron-saint" (line 209).

And yet the old schooling sticks, the old grave eyes
Are peeping o'er my shoulder as I work,
The heads shake still—"It's art's decline, my son!
You're not of the true painters, great and old;
Brother Angelico's[3] the man, you'll find;   235
Brother Lorenzo[4] stands his single peer:
Fag on at flesh, you'll never make the third!"
Flower o' the pine,
You keep your mistr . . . manners, and I'll stick to mine!
I'm not the third, then: bless us, they must know!   240
Don't you think they're the likeliest to know,
They with their Latin? So, I swallow my rage,
Clench my teeth, suck my lips in tight, and paint
To please them—sometimes do and sometimes don't;
For, doing most, there's pretty sure to come   245
A turn, some warm eve finds me at my saints—
A laugh, a cry, the business of the world—
(*Flower o' the peach,*
Death for us all, and his own life for each!)
And my whole soul revolves, the cup runs over,   250
The world and life's too big to pass for a dream,
And I do these wild things in sheer despite,
And play the fooleries you catch me at,
In pure rage! The old mill-horse, out at grass
After hard years, throws up his stiff heels so,   255
Although the miller does not preach to him
The only good of grass is to make chaff.
What would men have? Do they like grass or no—
May they or mayn't they? all I want's the thing
Settled for ever one way. As it is,   260
You tell too many lies and hurt yourself:
You don't like what you only like too much,
You do like what, if given you at your word,
You find abundantly detestable.
For me, I think I speak as I was taught;   265
I always see the garden[5] and God there
A-making man's wife: and, my lesson learned,
The value and significance of flesh,
I can't unlearn ten minutes afterwards,

        You understand me: I'm a beast, I know.   270
But see, now—why, I see as certainly
As that the morning-star's about to shine,
What will hap some day. We've a youngster here
Comes to our convent, studies what I do,
Slouches and stares and lets no atom drop: 275

---

3. The monastic name of Giovanni de Fiesole (ca. 1400–1455), perhaps the chief painter of
   the late medieval period, whose style influenced Lippi's work of the 1440s. It is said he was
   so devout he painted while kneeling.
4. Lorenzo Monaco (ca. 1370–ca. 1425), Camaldolese monk who exerted an important influ-
   ence on Lippi's early work.
5. Of Eden.

His name is Guidi[6]—he'll not mind the monks—
They call him Hulking Tom, he lets them talk—
He picks my practice up—he'll paint apace,
I hope so—though I never live so long,
I know what's sure to follow. You be judge!   280
You speak no Latin more than I, belike;
However, you're my man, you've seen the world
—The beauty and the wonder and the power,
The shapes of things, their colours, lights and shades,
Changes, surprises,—and God made it all!   285
—For what? Do you feel thankful, ay or no,
For this fair town's face, yonder river's line,
The mountain round it and the sky above,
Much more the figures of man, woman, child,
These are the frame to? What's it all about?   290
To be passed over, despised? or dwelt upon,
Wondered at? oh, this last of course!—you say.
But why not do as well as say,—paint these
Just as they are, careless what comes of it?
God's works—paint any one, and count it crime   295
To let a truth slip. Don't object, "His works
Are here already; nature is complete:
Suppose you reproduce her—(which you can't)
There's no advantage! you must beat her, then."
For, don't you mark? we're made so that we love   300
First when we see them painted, things we have passed
Perhaps a hundred times nor cared to see;
And so they are better, painted—better to us,
Which is the same thing. Art was given for that;
God uses us to help each other so,   305
Lending our minds out. Have you noticed, now,
Your cullion's[7] hanging face? A bit of chalk,
And trust me but you should, though! How much more,
If I drew higher things with the same truth!
That were to take the Prior's pulpit-place,   310
Interpret God to all of you! Oh, oh,
It makes me mad to see what men shall do
And we in our graves! This world's no blot for us,
Nor blank; it means intensely, and means good:
To find its meaning is my meat and drink.   315
"Ay, but you don't so instigate to prayer!"
Strikes in the Prior: "when your meaning's plain
It does not say to folk—remember matins,[8]
Or, mind you fast next Friday!" Why, for this
What need of art at all? A skull and bones,   320
Two bits of stick nailed crosswise, or, what's best,

6. Tommaso Guidi (1401–ca. 1428), a pioneer of Italian Renaissance painting; known as Masaccio ("Sloppy Tom") because of his careless living habits. Following the annotation in his edition of Vasari, Browning erred in regarding Masaccio as Lippi's pupil, whereas the converse is true.
7. Base fellow.
8. Morning services.

A bell to chime the hour with, does as well.
I painted a Saint Laurence[9] six months since
At Prato, splashed the fresco[1] in fine style:
"How looks my painting, now the scaffold's down?"   325
I ask a brother: "Hugely," he returns—
"Already not one phiz[2] of your three slaves
Who turn the Deacon off his toasted side,
But's scratched and prodded to our heart's content,
The pious people have so eased their own   330
With coming to say prayers there in a rage:
We get on fast to see the bricks beneath.
Expect another job this time next year,
For pity and religion grow i' the crowd—
Your painting serves its purpose!" Hang the fools!   335

—That is—you'll not mistake an idle word
Spoke in a huff by a poor monk, God wot,
Tasting the air this spicy night which turns
The unaccustomed head like Chianti wine!
Oh, the church knows! don't misreport me, now!   340
It's natural a poor monk out of bounds
Should have his apt word to excuse himself:
And hearken how I plot to make amends.
I have bethought me: I shall paint a piece[3]
. . . There's for you![4] Give me six months, then go, see   345
Something in Sant' Ambrogio's! Bless the nuns!
They want a cast o' my office,[5] I shall paint
God in the midst, Madonna and her babe,
Ringed by a bowery flowery angel-brood,
Lilies and vestments and white faces, sweet   350
As puff on puff of grated orris-root[6]
When ladies crowd to Church at midsummer.
And then i' the front, of course a saint or two—
Saint John,[7] because he saves the Florentines,
Saint Ambrose,[8] who puts down in black and white   355
The convent's friends and gives them a long day,
And Job, I must have him there past mistake,
The man of Uz (and Us without the z,
Painters who need his patience).[9] Well, all these
Secured at their devotion, up shall come   360
Out of a corner when you least expect,

9. Martyred deacon of Pope Sixtus II, who according to legend was broiled to death on a grid-
   iron (ca. 258); he is said to have told his persecutors to turn him over since he was done on
   one side.
1. Painting on fresh plaster.
2. Physiognomy, or face (slang).
3. The promised altarpiece is the *Coronation of the Virgin*, commissioned in 1441 for the
   church of the Sant' Ambrogio nunnery in Florence.
4. There's a gift of sorts for you.
5. Sample of my work.
6. Root of the iris, used in perfumes and sachets.
7. The Baptist, patron saint of Florence.
8. Bishop of Milan, Ambrose (ca. 339–397) was one of the four great Church Fathers.
9. "Ye have heard of the patience of Job . . ." (James 5:11). Uz: Job's homeland (Job 1:1).

As one by a dark stair into a great light,
Music and talking, who but Lippo! I!—
Mazed, motionless and moonstruck—I'm the man!
Back I shrink—what is this I see and hear?   365
I, caught up with my monk's-things by mistake,
My old serge gown and rope that goes all round,
I, in this presence, this pure company!
Where's a hole, where's a corner for escape?
Then steps a sweet angelic slip of a thing   370
Forward, puts out a soft palm—"Not so fast!"
—Addresses the celestial presence, "nay—
He made you and devised you, after all,
Though he's none of you! Could Saint John there draw—
His camel-hair[1] make up a painting-brush?   375
We come to brother Lippo for all that,
Iste perfecit opus!"[2] So, all smile—
I shuffle sideways with my blushing face
Under the cover of a hundred wings
Thrown like a spread of kirtles[3] when you're gay   380
And play hot cockles,[4] all the doors being shut,
Till, wholly unexpected, in there pops
The hothead husband! Thus I scuttle off
To some safe bench behind, not letting go
The palm of her, the little lily thing   385
That spoke the good word for me in the nick,
Like the Prior's niece . . . Saint Lucy,[5] I would say.
And so all's saved for me, and for the church
A pretty picture gained. Go, six months hence!
Your hand, sir, and good-bye: no lights, no lights!   390
The street's hushed, and I know my own way back,
Don't fear me! There's the grey beginning. Zooks!

1853?

A Toccata of Galuppi's[1]

I

Oh Galuppi, Baldassaro, this is very sad to find!
I can hardly misconceive you; it would prove me deaf and blind;
But although I take your meaning, 't is with such a heavy mind!

1. "And John [the Baptist] was clothed with camel's hair . . ." (Mark 1:6).
2. Means either "this man executed the work" or "this man caused the work to be done." The words appear on a scroll in the lower right hand of the *Coronation* near the head of a kneeling figure Browning, following tradition, supposed to be Lippi. The figure is actually that of the convent's benefactor, the Canon Francesco Maringhi, who "caused the work to be done."
3. Gowns or skirts.
4. Game like blindman's buff; here, euphemism for sexual escapade.
5. Virgin martyr, killed ca. 304; she is patron of the eyes. In the *Coronation* St. Lucy appears in the right foreground.
1. As a boy Browning had the best professional instruction in music; his study of music theory (under John Relfe, musician to George III) is reflected in stanzas 7–9. Browning was competent at the piano and the organ, and in his repertoire were the toccatas of Baldassare

II

Here you come with your old music, and here's all the good it
  brings.
What, they lived once thus at Venice where the merchants were
  the kings,   5
Where Saint Mark's[2] is, where the Doges used to wed the sea
  with rings?[3]

III

Ay, because the sea's the street there; and 't is arched by . . .
  what you call
. . . Shylock's bridge[4] with houses on it, where they kept the
  carnival:
I was never out of England—it's as if I saw it all.

IV

Did young people take their pleasure when the sea was warm in
  May?   10
Balls and masks begun at midnight, burning ever to mid-day,
When they made up fresh adventures for the morrow, do you
  say?

V

Was a lady such a lady, cheeks so round and lips so red,—
On her neck the small face buoyant, like a bell-flower on its bed,
O'er the breast's superb abundance where a man might base his
  head?   15

VI

Well, and it was graceful of them—they'd break talk off and
  afford
—She, to bite her mask's black velvet—he, to finger on his
  sword,
While you sat and played Toccatas, stately at the clavichord?[5]

Galuppi (1706–85), a prolific Venetian composer best known for his comic operas. "As for
Galuppi," Browning wrote in 1887, "I had once in my possession two huge manuscript vol-
umes almost exclusively made up of his 'Toccata-pieces'—apparently a slighter form of the
Sonata to be 'touched' lightly off." No single work of Galuppi's, however, was the basis for
the poem. A toccata (literally, "touch-piece") is a keyboard composition in free style with full
chords and running passages. By Galuppi's time the Italian toccata had declined into a rapid
type for exhibiting the performer's virtuosity (*Harvard Dictionary of Music*, 2nd ed.).
    See Stefan Hawlin's essay in this volume, pp. 622–33, for more on this poem.
2. Ornate church named for the patron saint of Venice and containing his relics. Galuppi was
  named *maestro di cappella* at St. Mark's in 1762.
3. To symbolize Venetian maritime power, the doge or chief magistrate, in an opulent annual
  ceremony, "wed" the sea by casting a consecrated gold ring into the waters of the Lido chan-
  nel.
4. Bridge of the Rialto across the Grand Canal, associated with Shylock because it is men-
  tioned by that character in Shakespeare's *The Merchant of Venice* (I.iii.107).
5. Precursor of the piano, its strings hit by metal pins.

VII

What? Those lesser thirds so plaintive, sixths diminished,[6] sigh
   on sigh,
Told them something? Those suspensions,[7] those solutions—
   "Must we die?"   20
Those commiserating sevenths[8]—"Life might last! we can but try!"

VIII

"Were you happy?"—"Yes."—"And are you still as happy?"—"Yes.
   And you?"
—"Then, more kisses!"—"Did *I* stop them, when a million
   seemed so few?"
Hark, the dominant's[9] persistence till it must be answered to!

IX

So, an octave struck the answer. Oh, they praised you, I dare say!   25
"Brave[1] Galuppi! that was music! good alike at grave and gay!
I can always leave off talking when I hear a master play!"

X

Then they left you for their pleasure: till in due time, one by one,
Some with lives that came to nothing, some with deeds as well
   undone,
Death stepped tacitly and took them where they never see the
   sun.   30

XI

But when I sit down to reason, think to take my stand nor swerve,
While I triumph o'er a secret wrung from nature's close reserve,
In you come with your cold music till I creep thro' every nerve.

XII

Yes, you, like a ghostly cricket, creaking where a house was
   burned:
"Dust and ashes, dead and done with, Venice spent what Venice
   earned.   35
The soul, doubtless, is immortal—where a soul can be discerned.

---

6. Diminished sixth: interval of one semi-tone less than a minor sixth; presumably the musical equivalent of a "sigh." Lesser third: interval of three semi-tones, showing the key to be minor; called "plaintive third" because supposed to evoke moods of tenderness or grief.
7. Notes held over from one chord into another, producing a momentary discord and suspending the concord that the ear expects; the resolution ("solution") is the passage of a chord from dissonance to consonance.
8. Perhaps diminished sevenths, producing mild discord.
9. Probably the "dominant seventh," so called because the chord is built on the fifth or "dominant" degree of the scale. The natural resolution (or "answer") is into the triad on C, which Galuppi strikes an octave above the first presentation of the theme, giving the toccata's close the effect of utter finality.
1. Excellent.

XIII

"Yours for instance: you know physics, something of geology,
Mathematics are your pastime; souls shall rise in their degree;
Butterflies may dread extinction,—you'll not die, it cannot be!

XIV

"As for Venice and her people, merely born to bloom and drop,   40
Here on earth they bore their fruitage, mirth and folly were the
    crop:
What of soul was left, I wonder, when the kissing had to stop?

XV

"Dust and ashes!" So you creak it, and I want the heart to scold.
Dear dead women, with such hair, too—what's become of all the
    gold
Used to hang and brush their bosoms? I feel chilly and grown
    old.   45

ca. 1853

By the Fire-Side[1]

I

How well I know what I mean to do
    When the long dark autumn-evenings come:
And where, my soul, is thy pleasant hue?
    With the music of all thy voices, dumb
In life's November too!   5

II

I shall be found by the fire, suppose,
    O'er a great wise book as beseemeth age,
While the shutters flap as the cross-wind blows
    And I turn the page, and I turn the page,
Not verse now, only prose!   10

III

Till the young ones whisper, finger on lip,
    "There he is at it, deep in Greek:
Now then, or never, out we slip
    To cut from the hazels by the creek
A mainmast for our ship!"   15

1. Though a dramatic monologue, this poem strongly reflects Browning's personal experience and attitudes, and was probably inspired by an 1853 excursion with his wife to a ruined chapel on a mountain path near Bagni di Lucca in Italy (DeVane, pp. 221–22).

IV

I shall be at it indeed, my friends:
    Greek puts already on either side
Such a branch-work forth as soon extends
    To a vista opening far and wide,
And I pass out where it ends.   20

V

The outside-frame, like your hazel-trees:
    But the inside-archway widens fast,
And a rarer sort[2] succeeds to these,
    And we slope to Italy at last
And youth, by green degrees.   25

VI

I follow wherever I am led,
    Knowing so well the leader's hand:
Oh woman-country, wooed not wed,
    Loved all the more by earth's male-lands,
Laid to their hearts instead!   30

VII

Look at the ruined chapel again
    Half-way up in the Alpine gorge!
Is that a tower, I point you plain,
    Or is it a mill, or an iron-forge
Breaks solitude in vain?   35

VIII

A turn, and we stand in the heart of things;
    The woods are round us, heaped and dim;
From slab to slab how it slips and springs,
    The thread of water single and slim,
Through the ravage some torrent brings!   40

IX

Does it feed the little lake below?
    That speck of white just on its marge
Is Pella;[3] see, in the evening-glow,
    How sharp the silver spear-heads charge
When Alp meets heaven in snow!   45

2. Rarer than hazels; presumably the olives of Italy.
3. Village on the Lago d' Orta in Piedmont.

X

On our other side is the straight-up rock;
　　And a path is kept 'twixt the gorge and it
By boulder-stones where lichens mock
　　The marks on a moth, and small ferns fit
Their teeth to the polished block.　　　　　　　　　　50

XI

Oh the sense of the yellow mountain-flowers,
　　And thorny balls, each three in one,
The chestnuts throw on our path in showers!
　　For the drop of the woodland fruit's begun,
These early November hours,　　　　　　　　　　　55

XII

That crimson the creeper's leaf across
　　Like a splash of blood, intense, abrupt,
O'er a shield else gold from rim to boss,[4]
　　And lay it for show on the fairy-cupped
Elf-needled mat of moss,　　　　　　　　　　　　60

XIII

By the rose-flesh mushrooms, undivulged
　　Last evening—nay, in to-day's first dew
Yon sudden coral nipple bulged,
　　Where a freaked[5] fawn-coloured flaky crew
Of toadstools peep indulged.　　　　　　　　　　65

XIV

And yonder, at foot of the fronting ridge
　　That takes the turn to a range beyond,
Is the chapel reached by the one-arched bridge
　　Where the water is stopped in a stagnant pond
Danced over by the midge.[6]　　　　　　　　　　70

XV

The chapel and bridge are of stone alike,
　　Blackish-grey and mostly wet;
Cut hemp-stalks steep in the narrow dyke.[7]
　　See here again, how the lichens fret
And the roots of the ivy strike!　　　　　　　　　75

---

4. Raised ornament on shield.
5. Streaked with color.
6. Tiny fly.
7. Small pond.

XVI

Poor little place, where its one priest comes
    On a festa-day,[8] if he comes at all,
To the dozen folk from their scattered homes,
    Gathered within that precinct small
By the dozen ways one roams—   80

XVII

To drop from the charcoal-burners' huts,
    Or climbing from the hemp-dressers' low shed,
Leave the grange where the woodman stores his nuts,
    Or the wattled cote[9] where the fowlers spread
Their gear on the rock's bare juts.   85

XVIII

It has some pretension too, this front,
    With its bit of fresco[1] half-moon-wise
Set over the porch, Art's early wont:
    'T is John in the Desert,[2] I surmise,
But has borne the weather's brunt—   90

XIX

Not from the fault of the builder, though,
    For a pent-house[3] properly projects
Where three carved beams make a certain show,
    Dating—good thought of our architect's—
'Five, six, nine, he lets you know.   95

XX

And all day long a bird sings there,
    And a stray sheep drinks at the pond at times;
The place is silent and aware;
    It has had its scenes, its joys and crimes,
But that is its own affair.   100

XXI

My perfect wife, my Leonor,[4]
    Oh heart, my own, oh eyes, mine too,
Whom else could I dare look backward for,
    With whom beside should I dare pursue
The path grey heads abhor?   105

8. Feast day, or religious holiday.
9. Light thatched shelter.
1. Painting made on fresh plaster.
2. John the Baptist in the wilderness.
3. Protective roof.
4. The faithful wife in Beethoven's opera *Fidelio*.

XXII

For it leads to a crag's sheer edge with them;
    Youth, flowery all the way, there stops—
Not they; age threatens and they contemn,
    Till they reach the gulf wherein youth drops,
One inch from life's safe hem!   110

XXIII

With me, youth led . . . I will speak now,
    Now longer watch you as you sit
Reading by fire-light, that great brow
    And the spirit-small hand propping it,
Mutely, my heart knows how—   115

XXIV

When, if I think but deep enough,
    You are wont to answer, prompt as rhyme;
And you, too, find without rebuff
    Response your soul seeks many a time
Piercing its fine flesh-stuff.   120

XXV

My own, confirm me! If I tread
    This path back, is it not in pride
To think how little I dreamed it led
    To an age so blest that, by its side,
Youth seems the waste instead?   125

XXVI

My own, see where the years conduct!
    At first, 't was something our two souls
Should mix as mists do; each is sucked
    In each now: on, the new stream rolls,
Whatever rocks obstruct.   130

XXVII

Think, when our one soul understands
    The great Word which makes all things new,[5]
When earth breaks up and heaven expands,
    How will the change[6] strike me and you
In the house not made with hands?[7]   135

---

5. Revelation 21:5: "And he that sat upon the throne said, Behold, I make all things new."
6. Resurrection. See 1 Corinthians 15:51: "We shall not all sleep, but we shall all be changed."
7. 2 Corinthians 5:1: "We have a building of God, an house not made with hands, eternal in
   the heavens."

XXVIII

Oh I must feel your brain prompt mine,
  Your heart anticipate my heart,
You must be just before, in fine,
  See and make me see, for your part,
New depths of the divine!   140

XXIX

But who could have expected this
  When we two drew together first
Just for the obvious human bliss,
  To satisfy life's daily thirst
With a thing men seldom miss?   145

XXX

Come back with me to the first of all,
  Let us lean and love it over again,
Let us now forget and now recall,
  Break the rosary in a pearly rain,
And gather what we let fall!   150

XXXI

What did I say?—that a small bird sings
  All day long, save when a brown pair
Of hawks from the wood float with wide wings
  Strained to a bell: 'gainst noon-day glare
You count the streaks and rings.   155

XXXII

But at afternoon or almost eve
  'T is better; then the silence grows
To that degree, you half believe
  It must get rid of what it knows,
Its bosom does so heave.   160

XXXIII

Hither we walked then, side by side,
  Arm in arm and cheek to cheek,
And still I questioned or replied,
  While my heart, convulsed to really speak,
Lay choking in its pride.   165

XXXIV

Silent the crumbling bridge we cross,
  And pity and praise the chapel sweet,
And care about the fresco's loss,

And wish for our souls a like retreat,
And wonder at the moss.

170

XXXV

Stoop and kneel on the settle[8] under,
   Look through the window's grated square:
Nothing to see! For fear of plunder,
   The cross is down and the altar bare,
As if thieves don't fear thunder.

175

XXXVI

We stoop and look in through the grate,
   See the little porch and rustic door,
Read duly the dead builder's date;
   Then cross the bridge that we crossed before,
Take the path again—but wait!

180

XXXVII

Oh moment, one and infinite!
   The water slips o'er stock and stone;
The West is tender, hardly bright:
   How grey at once is the evening grown—
One star, its chrysolite![9]

185

XXXVIII

We two stood there with never a third,
   But each by each, as each knew well:
The sights we saw and the sounds we heard,
   The lights and the shades made up a spell
Till the trouble grew and stirred.

190

XXXIX

Oh, the little more, and how much it is!
   And the little less, and what worlds away!
How a sound shall quicken content to bliss,
   Or a breath suspend the blood's best play,
And life be a proof of this!

195

XL

Had she willed it, still had stood the screen
   So slight, so sure, 'twixt my love and her:
I could fix her face with a guard between,
   And find her soul as when friends confer,
Friends—lovers that might have been.

200

8. Bench.
9. Olive green stone, used as gem.

XLI

For my heart had a touch of the woodland-time,
    Wanting to sleep now over its best.
Shake the whole tree in the summer-prime,
    But bring to the last leaf no such test!
"Hold the last fast!" runs the rhyme.   205

XLII

For a chance to make your little much,
    To gain a lover and lose a friend,
Venture the tree and a myriad such,
    When nothing you mar but the year can mend:
But a last leaf—fear to touch!   210

XLIII

Yet should it unfasten itself and fall
    Eddying down till it find your face
At some slight wind—best chance of all!
    Be your heart henceforth its dwelling-place
You trembled to forestall!   215

XLIV

Worth how well, those dark grey eyes,
    That hair so dark and dear, how worth
That a man should strive and agonize,
    And taste a veriest hell on earth
For the hope of such a prize!   220

XLV

You might have turned and tried a man,
    Set him a space to weary and wear,
And prove which suited more your plan,
    His best of hope or his worst despair,
Yet end as he began.   225

XLVI

But you spared me this, like the heart you are,
    And filled my empty heart at a word.
If two lives join, there is oft a scar,
    They are one and one, with shadowy third[1]
One near one is too far.   230

---

1. The Browning love letters several times mention a "third person," an imaginary outsider who
objectively views their courtship.

XLVII

A moment after, and hands unseen
    Were hanging the night around us fast;
But we knew that a bar was broken between
    Life and life: we were mixed at last
In spite of the mortal screen.   235

XLVIII

The forests had done it; there they stood;
    We caught for a moment the powers at play:
They had mingled us so, for once and good,
    Their work was done—we might go or stay,
They relapsed to their ancient mood.   240

XLIX

How the world is made for each of us!
    How all we perceive and know in it
Tends to some moment's product thus,
    When a soul declares itself—to wit,
By its fruit,[2] the thing it does!   245

L

Be hate that fruit or love that fruit,
    It forwards the general deed of man,
And each of the Many helps to recruit
    The life of the race by a general plan;
Each living his own, to boot.   250

LI

I am named and known by that moment's feat;
    There took my station and degree;
So grew my own small life complete,
    As nature obtained her best of me—
One born to love you, sweet!   255

LII

And to watch you sink by the fire-side now
    Back again, as you mutely sit
Musing by fire-light, that great brow
    And the spirit-small hand propping it,
Yonder, my heart knows how!   260

2. See Matthew 7:16: "Ye shall know them by their fruits."

LIII

So, earth has gained by one man the more,
   And the gain of earth must be heaven's gain too;
And the whole is well worth thinking o'er
   When autumn comes: which I mean to do
One day, as I said before.   265

1853?

Mesmerism[1]

I

All I believed is true!
   I am able yet
   All I want, to get
By a method as strange as new:
Dare I trust the same to you?   5

II

If at night, when doors are shut,
   And the wood-worm picks,
   And the death-watch[2] ticks,
And the bar has a flag of smut,
And a cat's in the water-butt—   10

III

And the socket floats and flares,
   And the house-beams groan,
   And a foot unknown
Is surmised on the garret-stairs,
And the locks slip unawares—   15

IV

And the spider, to serve his ends,
   By a sudden thread,
   Arms and legs outspread,
On the table's midst descends,
Comes to find, God knows what friends!—   20

---

1. One of several pseudo-sciences fashionable in mid-Victorian England, mesmerism (or "animal magnetism") takes its name from Franz Anton Mesmer (1733–1815), who claimed powers of influencing others hypnotically. Elizabeth Barrett Browning defended the practice; many of her peers, including Dickens and George Eliot, shared her fascination with it, while Browning himself remained skeptical.
2. The sound of a death-watch beetle, believed to be a sign of imminent death.

V

If since eve drew in, I say,
   I have sat and brought
   (So to speak) my thought
To bear on the woman away,
Till I felt my hair turn grey—   25

VI

Till I seemed to have and hold,[3]
   In the vacancy
   'Twixt the wall and me,
From the hair-plait's chestnut gold
To the foot in its muslin fold—   30

VII

Have and hold, then and there,
   Her, from head to foot,
   Breathing and mute,
Passive and yet aware,
In the grasp of my steady stare—   35

VIII

Hold and have, there and then,
   All her body and soul
   That completes my whole,
All that women add to men,
In the clutch of my steady ken[4]—   40

IX

Having and holding, till
   I imprint her fast
   On the void at last
As the sun does whom he will
By the calotypist's[5] skill—   45

X

Then,—if my heart's strength serve,
   And through all and each
   Of the veils I reach
To her soul and never swerve,
Knitting an iron nerve—   50

3. Cf. "to have and to hold," in "The Form of the Solemnization of Matrimony" in *Book of Common Prayer.*
4. View.
5. Calotype paper was patented in 1841 by Fox Talbot, English inventor of photography (Daguerre, his French contemporary, used a different process). Produced by light acting upon paper coated with silver iodide, the calotype image was fixed by immersing the paper in a solution of sodium hyposulfite.

XI

Command her soul to advance
  And inform the shape
  Which has made escape
And before my countenance
Answers me glance for glance—   55

XII

I, still with a gesture fit
  Of my hands that best
  Do my soul's behest,
Pointing the power from it,
While myself do steadfast sit—   60

XIII

Steadfast and still the same
  On my object bent,
  While the hands give vent
To my ardour and my aim
And break into very flame[6]—   65

XIV

Then I reach, I must believe,
  Not her soul in vain,
  For to me again
It reaches, and past retrieve
Is wound in the toils I weave;   70

XV

And must follow as I require,
  As befits a thrall,
  Bringing flesh and all,
Essence and earth-attire,
To the source of the tractile[7] fire;   75

XVI

Till the house called hers, not mine,
  With a growing weight
  Seems to suffocate
If she break not its leaden line
And escape from its close confine.   80

6. Probably refers to "odyl," a mesmeric influence, announced as a discovery in 1845 by Karl
   von Reichenbach. It was believed to repose in certain crystals and magnets, as well as in per-
   sons endowed with mesmeric powers. Some claimed to see it as a flame. E. B. Browning
   mentions Reichenbach in a letter of 1846 and in her *Aurora Leigh* (1856), vii. 566.
7. Having the power of attraction.

XVII

Out of doors into the night!
    On to the maze
    Of the wild wood-ways,
Not turning to left nor right
From the pathway, blind with sight—   85

XVIII

Making thro' rain and wind
    O'er the broken shrubs,
    'Twixt the stems and stubs,
With a still, composed, strong mind,
Nor a care for the world behind—   90

XIX

Swifter and still more swift,
    As the crowding peace
    Doth to joy increase
In the wide blind eyes uplift
Thro' the darkness and the drift!   95

XX

While I—to the shape, I too
    Feel my soul dilate
    Nor a whit abate,
And relax not a gesture due,
As I see my belief come true.   100

XXI

For, there! have I drawn or no
    Life to that lip?
    Do my fingers dip
In a flame which again they throw
On the cheek that breaks a-glow?   105

XXII

Ha! was the hair so first?
    What, unfilleted,[8]
    Made alive, and spread
Through the void with a rich outburst,
Chestnut gold-interspersed?   110

8. Unbound.

XXIII

Like the doors of a casket-shrine,[9]
  See, on either side,
  Her two arms divide
Till the heart betwixt makes sign,
Take me, for I am thine!   115

XXIV

"Now—now"—the door is heard!
  Hark, the stairs! and near—
  Nearer—and here—
"Now!" and at call the third
She enters without a word.   120

XXV

On doth she march and on
  To the fancied shape;
  It is, past escape,
Herself, now: the dream is done
And the shadow and she are one.   125

XXVI

First I will pray. Do Thou
  That ownest the soul,
  Yet wilt grant control
To another, nor disallow
For a time, restrain me now!   130

XXVII

I admonish me while I may,
  Not to squander guilt,
  Since require Thou wilt
At my hand its price one day!
What the price is, who can say?   135

9. A cabinet, containing a shrine, which is closed when not in use.

An Epistle[1]

Containing the
Strange Medical Experience of Karshish, the Arab Physician

Karshish, the picker-up of learning's crumbs,[2]
The not-incurious in God's handiwork
(This man's-flesh he hath admirably made,
Blown like a bubble, kneaded like a paste,
To coop up and keep down on earth a space   5
That puff of vapour from his mouth, man's soul)
—To Abib, all-sagacious in our art,
Breeder in me of what poor skill I boast,
Like me inquisitive how pricks and cracks
Befall the flesh through too much stress and strain,   10
Whereby the wily vapour fain would slip
Back and rejoin its source before the term,—
And aptest in contrivance (under God)
To baffle it by deftly stopping such:—
The vagrant Scholar to his Sage at home   15
Sends greeting (health and knowledge, fame with peace)
Three samples of true snakestone[3]—rarer still,
One of the other sort, the melon-shaped,
(But fitter, pounded fine, for charms than drugs)
And writeth now the twenty-second time.   20

    My journeyings were brought to Jericho:
Thus I resume. Who studious in our art
Shall count a little labour unrepaid?
I have shed sweat enough, left flesh and bone
On many a flinty furlong of this land.   25
Also, the country-side is all on fire
With rumours of a marching hitherward:
Some say Vespasian[4] cometh, some, his son.
A black lynx snarled and pricked a tufted ear;
Lust of my blood inflamed his yellow balls: 30
I cried and threw my staff and he was gone.
Twice have the robbers stripped and beaten me,
And once a town declared me for a spy;
But at the end, I reach Jerusalem,
Since this poor covert where I pass the night,   35
This Bethany, lies scarce the distance thence
A man with plague-sores at the third degree
Runs till he drops down dead. Thou laughest here!

1. The title refers to an imaginary encounter between an itinerant Arab medical researcher and Lazarus in C.E. 66, long after the latter was raised from the dead by Jesus (John 11: 1–44). The conflict experienced by Karshish—that of positivism opposed by the will to believe—was shared by many of Browning's contemporaries.
2. This epithet is evidently a translation of the writer's name, for "Karshish" derives from an Arabic word meaning "one who gathers." He and his teacher Abib are fictitious.
3. Supposed to cure snake bites.
4. Roman emperor (from C.E. 69–79) who as Nero's general invaded Palestine in 67–68; his son Titus destroyed Jerusalem in 70.

'Sooth, it elates me, thus reposed and safe,
To void the stuffing of my travel-scrip[5]   40
And share with thee whatever Jewry yields.
A viscid choler[6] is observable
In tertians,[7] I was nearly bold to say;
And falling-sickness[8] hath a happier cure
Than our school wots of: there's a spider here   45
Weaves no web, watches on the ledge of tombs,
Sprinkled with mottles on an ash-grey back;
Take five and drop them . . . but who knows his mind,
The Syrian runagate[9] I trust this to?
His service payeth me a sublimate[1]   50
Blown up his nose to help the ailing eye.
Best wait: I reach Jerusalem at morn,
There set in order my experiences,
Gather what most deserves, and give thee all—
Or I might add, Judæa's gum-tragacanth[2]   55
Scales off in purer flakes, shines clearer-grained,
Cracks 'twixt the pestle and the porphyry[3]
In fine[4] exceeds our produce. Scalp-disease
Confounds me, crossing so with leprosy—
Thou hadst admired one sort I gained at Zoar[5]—   60
But zeal outruns discretion. Here I end.

    Yet stay: my Syrian blinketh gratefully,
Protesteth his devotion is my price—
Suppose I write what harms not, though he steal?
I half resolve to tell thee, yet I blush,   65
What set me off a-writing first of all.
An itch I had, a sting to write, a tang!
For, be it this town's barrenness—or else
The Man had something in the look of him—
His case has struck me far more than 't is worth.   70
So, pardon if—(lest presently I lose
In the great press of novelty at hand
The care and pains this somehow stole from me)
I bid thee take the thing while fresh in mind,
Almost in sight—for, wilt thou have the truth?   75
The very man is gone from me but now,
Whose ailment is the subject of discourse.
Thus then, and let thy better wit help all!

    'Tis but a case of mania—subinduced
By epilepsy, at the turning-point   80

5. Pouch.
6. Gummy fluid.
7. Fevers recurring every third day.
8. Epilepsy.
9. Vagabond, fugitive.
1. Refined drug.
2. Soothing medicinal gum.
3. I.e., mortar.
4. In short.
5. Ancient town near Dead Sea on Jordanian border.

Of trance prolonged unduly some three days:
When, by the exhibition[6] of some drug
Or spell, exorcization, stroke of art
Unknown to me and which 't were well to know,
The evil thing out-breaking all at once   85
Left the man whole and sound of body indeed,—
But, flinging (so to speak) life's gates too wide,
Making a clear house of it too suddenly,
The first conceit[7] that entered might inscribe
Whatever it was minded on the wall   90
So plainly at that vantage, as it were,
(First come, first served) that nothing subsequent
Attaineth to erase those fancy-scrawls
The just-returned and new-established soul
Hath gotten now so thoroughly by heart   95
That henceforth she will read or these or none.
And first—the man's own firm conviction rests
That he was dead (in fact they buried him)
—That he was dead and then restored to life
By a Nazarene physician of his tribe: 100
—'Sayeth, the same bade "Rise," and he did rise.
"Such cases are diurnal,"[8] thou wilt cry.
Not so this figment!—not, that such a fume,[9]
Instead of giving way to time and health,
Should eat itself into the life of life,   105
As saffron tingeth flesh, blood, bones and all!
For see, how he takes up the after-life.
The man—it is one Lazarus a Jew,
Sanguine, proportioned, fifty years of age,
The body's habit wholly laudable,   110
As much, indeed, beyond the common health
As he were made and put aside to show.
Think, could we penetrate by any drug
And bathe the wearied soul and worried flesh,
And bring it clear and fair, by three days' sleep!   115
Whence has the man the balm that brightens all?
This grown man eyes the world now like a child.
Some elders of his tribe, I should premise,
Led in their friend, obedient as a sheep,
To bear my inquisition. While they spoke,   120
Now sharply, now with sorrow,—told the case,—
He listened not except I spoke to him,
But folded his two hands and let them talk,
Watching the flies that buzzed: and yet no fool.
And that's a sample how his years must go.   125
Look, if a beggar, in fixed middle-life,
Should find a treasure,—can he use the same

6. Application.
7. Conception, notion.
8. Everyday, commonplace.
9. Delusion.

With straitened habits and with tastes starved small,
And take at once to his impoverished brain
The sudden element that changes things,   130
That sets the undreamed-of rapture at his hand
And puts the cheap old joy in the scorned dust?
Is he not such an one as moves to mirth—
Warily parsimonious, when no need,
Wasteful as drunkenness at undue times?   135
All prudent counsel as to what befits
The golden mean, is lost on such an one:
The man's fantastic will is the man's law.
So here—we call the treasure knowledge, say,
Increased beyond the fleshy faculty—   140
Heaven opened to a soul while yet on earth,
Earth forced on a soul's use while seeing heaven:
The man is witless of the size, the sum,
The value in proportion of all things,
Or whether it be little or be much.   145
Discourse to him of prodigious armaments
Assembled to besiege his city now,
And of the passing of a mule with gourds—
'T is one! Then take it on the other side,
Speak of some trifling fact,—he will gaze rapt   150
With stupor at its very littleness,
(Far as I see) as if in that indeed
He caught prodigious import, whole results;
And so will turn to us the bystanders
In ever the same stupor (note this point)   155
That we too see not with his opened eyes.
Wonder and doubt come wrongly into play,
Preposterously, at cross purposes.
Should his child sicken unto death,—why, look
For scarce abatement of his cheerfulness,   160
Or pretermission[1] of the daily craft!
While a word, gesture, glance from that same child
At play or in the school or laid asleep,
Will startle him to an agony of fear,
Exasperation, just as like. Demand   165
The reason why—" 't is but a word," object—
"A gesture"—he regards thee as our lord[2]
Who lived there in the pyramid alone,
Looked at us (dost thou mind?) when, being young,
We both would unadvisedly recite   170
Some charm's beginning, from that book of his,
Able to bid the sun throb wide and burst
All into stars, as suns grown old are wont.
Thou and the child have each a veil alike
Thrown o'er your heads, from under which ye both   175
Stretch your blind hands and trifle with a match

1. Omission.
2. Teacher.

Over a mine of Greek fire,[3] did ye know!
He holds on firmly to some thread of life—
(It is the life to lead perforcedly)
Which runs across some vast distracting orb   180
Of glory on either side that meagre thread,
Which, conscious of, he must not enter yet—
The spiritual life around the earthly life:
The law of that is known to him as this,
His heart and brain move there, his feet stay here.   185
So is the man perplext with impulses
Sudden to start off crosswise, not straight on,
Proclaiming what is right and wrong across,
And not along, this black thread through the blaze—
"It should be" baulked by "here it cannot be."   190
And oft the man's soul springs into his face
As if he saw again and heard again
His sage that bade him "Rise" and he did rise.
Something, a word, a tick o' the blood within
Admonishes: then back he sinks at once   195
To ashes, who was very fire before,
In sedulous recurrence to his trade
Whereby he earneth him the daily bread;
And studiously the humbler for that pride,
Professedly the faultier that he knows   200
God's secret, while he holds the thread of life.
Indeed the especial marking of the man
Is prone submission to the heavenly will—
Seeing it, what it is, and why it is.
'Sayeth, he will wait patient to the last   205
For that same death which must restore his being
To equilibrium, body loosening soul
Divorced even now by premature full growth:
He will live, nay, it pleaseth him to live
So long as God please, and just how God please.   210
He even seeketh not to please God more
(Which meaneth, otherwise) than as God please.
Hence, I perceive not he affects to preach
The doctrine of his sect whate'er it be,
Make proselytes as madmen thirst to do: 215
How can he give his neighbour the real ground,
His own conviction? Ardent as he is—
Call his great truth a lie, why, still the old
"Be it as God please" reassureth him.
I probed the sore as thy disciple should: 220
"How, beast," said I, "this stolid carelessness
Sufficeth thee, when Rome is on her march
To stamp out like a little spark thy town,
Thy tribe, thy crazy tale and thee at once?"

---

3. Incendiary mixture used by the Byzantine Greeks to burn enemy ships; invented much later
than the time of the poem.

He merely looked with his large eyes on me.   225
The man is apathetic, you deduce?
Contrariwise, he loves both old and young,
Able and weak, affects the very brutes
And birds—how say I? flowers of the field[4]—
As a wise workman recognizes tools   230
In a master's workshop, loving what they make.
Thus is the man as harmless as a lamb:
Only impatient, let him do his best,
At ignorance and carelessness and sin—
An indignation which is promptly curbed: 235
As when in certain travel I have feigned
To be an ignoramus in our art
According to some preconceived design,
And happened to hear the land's practitioners
Steeped in conceit sublimed[5] by ignorance,   240
Prattle fantastically on disease,
Its cause and cure—and I must hold my peace!

    Thou wilt object—Why have I not ere this
Sought out the sage himself, the Nazarene
Who wrought this cure, inquiring at the source,   245
Conferring with the frankness that befits?
Alas! it grieveth me, the learned leech[6]
Perished in a tumult[7] many years ago,
Accused,—our learning's fate,—of wizardry,
Rebellion, to the setting up a rule   250
And creed prodigious as described to me.
His death, which happened when the earthquake fell
(Prefiguring, as soon appeared, the loss
To occult learning in our lord the sage
Who lived there in the pyramid alone)   255
Was wrought by the mad people—that's their wont!
On vain recourse, as I conjecture it,
To his tried virtue, for miraculous help—
How could he stop the earthquake?[8] That's their way!
The other imputations must be lies: 260
But take one, though I loathe to give it thee,
In mere respect for any good man's fame.
(And after all, our patient Lazarus
Is stark mad; should we count on what he says?
Perhaps not: though in writing to a leech   265
'T is well to keep back nothing of a case.)
This man so cured regards the curer, then,
As—God forgive me! who but God himself,

---

4. Matthew 6:28: "Consider the lilies of the field, how they grow; they toil not, neither do they spin. . . ."
5. Ironic reference to the chemical process of purification by distillation.
6. Physician.
7. Pilate delivered Jesus to the people after "a tumult was made." See Matthew 27:24.
8. The earthquake occurred at Jesus' death—not before, as Karshish presumes (Matthew 27:51).

Creator and sustainer of the world,
That came and dwelt in flesh on it awhile!   270
—'Sayeth that such an one was born and lived,
Taught, healed the sick, broke bread at his own house,
Then died, with Lazarus by, for aught I know,
And yet was . . . what I said nor choose repeat,
And must have so avouched himself, in fact,   275
In hearing of this very Lazarus
Who saith—but why all this of what he saith?
Why write of trivial matters, things of price
.Calling at every moment for remark?
I noticed on the margin of a pool   280
Blue-flowering borage, the Aleppo[9] sort,
Aboundeth, very nitrous. It is strange!

   Thy pardon for this long and tedious case,
Which, now that I review it, needs must seem
Unduly dwelt on, prolixly set forth!   285
Nor I myself discern in what is writ
Good cause for the peculiar interest
And awe indeed this man has touched me with.
Perhaps the journey's end, the weariness
Had wrought upon me first. I met him thus: 290
I crossed a ridge of short sharp broken hills
Like an old lion's cheek teeth. Out there came
A moon made like a face with certain spots
Multiform, manifold and menacing:
Then a wind rose behind me. So we met   295
In this old sleepy town at unaware,
The man and I. I send thee what is writ.
Regard it as a chance, a matter risked
To this ambiguous Syrian—he may lose,
Or steal, or give it thee with equal good.   300
Jerusalem's repose shall make amends
For time this letter wastes, thy time and mine;
Till when, once more thy pardon and farewell!

   The very God! think, Abib; dost thou think?
So, the All-Great, were the All-Loving too—   305
So, through the thunder comes a human voice
Saying, "O heart I made, a heart beats here!
Face, my hands fashioned, see it in myself!
Thou hast no power nor mayst conceive of mine,
But love I gave thee, with myself to love,   310
And thou must love me who have died for thee!"
The madman saith He said so: it is strange.

ca. 1854

---

9. "Aleppo": Syrian town. "Blue-flowering borage": herb used as stimulant.

My Star[1]

All that I know
  Of a certain star
Is, it can throw
  (Like the angled spar)[2]
Now a dart of red,   5
  Now a dart of blue,[3]
Till my friends have said
  They would fain see, too,
My star that dartles[4] the red and the blue!
Then it stops like a bird; like a flower, hangs furled: 10
  They must solace themselves with the Saturn above it.
What matter to me if their star is a world?
Mine has opened its soul to me; therefore I love it.

"Childe Roland to the Dark Tower Came"[1]

(See Edgar's song in "LEAR")

I

My first thought was, he lied in every word,
  That hoary cripple, with malicious eye
Askance to watch the working of his lie
On mine, and mouth scarce able to afford
  Suppression of the glee, that pursed and scored   5
  Its edge, at one more victim gained thereby.

1. According to tradition the star is the poet's wife. When asked for his autograph, Browning customarily wrote out this lyric.
2. Shard of a crystalline mineral, like a prism.
3. The imagery of the poem probably derives from a letter of Elizabeth Barrett to Browning: "Love, I have learnt to believe in. I see the new light which Reichenbach shows pouring forth visibly from these chrystals [sic] tossed out. But when you say that the blue, I see, is red, and that the little chrystals are the fixed stars of the Heavens, how am I to think of you but that you are deluded . . . mistaken?" (April 21, 1846; Kintner, II.640). The chemist Karl von Reichenbach (1788–1869) claimed to have discovered a mesmeric influence emanating from certain crystals as light.
4. Shoots forth repeatedly.
1. In 1887, when asked whether he agreed with a certain allegorical analysis of this poem, Browning said, "Oh, no, not at all. Understand, I don't repudiate it, either. I only mean I was conscious of no allegorical intention in writing it. . . . Childe Roland came upon me as a kind of dream. I had to write it, then and there, and I finished it in the same day, I believe. But it was simply that I had to do it. I did not know then what I meant beyond that, and I'm sure I don't know now. But I am very fond of it" (1887; DeVane, p. 229). When a churchman asked if the poem's meaning could be summed up in the phrase, "He that endureth to the end shall be saved," Browning replied, "Yes, just about that" (1888; DeVane, p. 231).
    Scores of possible literary sources for "Childe Roland" have been suggested, despite Browning's repeated denial of any source other than the one cited in the subtitle, Edgar's song in *King Lear* (III.iv.182–84): "Childe Rowland to the dark tower came, / His word was still, 'Fie, foh, and fum, / I smell the blood of a British man.' " Edgar at this point in the play has taken the guise of a mad beggar, "Poor Tom," who describes his torment to King Lear: "Who gives any thing to poor Tom? whom the foul fiend hath led through fire and through flame, through [ford] and whirlpool, o'er bog and quagmire; . . . made him proud of heart, to ride on a bay trotting-horse over four-inch'd bridges, to course his own shadow for a traitor" (III.iv.51–58).
    "Childe" is the title of a young warrior awaiting knighthood. Roland is a hero of the medieval French *Chanson de Roland* and of Ariosto's *Orlando Furioso* (1532).

II

What else should he be set for, with his staff?
  What, save to waylay with his lies, ensnare
  All travelers who might find him posted there,
And ask the road? I guessed what skull-like laugh   10
Would break, what crutch 'gin write my epitaph
  For pastime in the dusty thoroughfare,

III

If at his counsel I should turn aside
  Into that ominous tract which, all agree,
  Hides the Dark Tower. Yet acquiescingly   15
I did turn as he pointed: neither pride
Nor hope rekindling at the end descried,
  So much as gladness that some end might be.

IV

For, what with my whole world-wide wandering,
  What with my search drawn out thro' years, my hope   20
  Dwindled into a ghost not fit to cope
With that obstreperous joy success would bring,—
I hardly tried now to rebuke the spring
  My heart made, finding failure in its scope.

V

As when a sick man very near to death[2]   25
  Seems dead indeed, and feels begin and end
  The tears and takes the farewell of each friend,
And hears one bid the other go, draw breath
Freelier outside, ("since all is o'er," he saith,
  "And the blow fallen no grieving can amend;")   30

VI

While some discuss if near the other graves
  Be room enough for this, and when a day
  Suits best for carrying the corpse away,
With care about the banners, scarves and staves:
And still the man hears all, and only craves   35
  He may not shame such tender love and stay.

VII

Thus, I had so long suffered in this quest,
  Heard failure prophesied so oft, been writ

2. Lines 25–30 echo John Donne's "A Valediction: Forbidding Mourning," lines 1–4: "As virtu-
ous men pass mildly away, / And whisper to their souls to go, / Whilst some of their sad
friends do say, / 'The breath goes now,' and some say, 'No,' . . . ."

So many times among "The Band"—to wit,
The knights who to the Dark Tower's search addressed   40
Their steps—that just to fail as they, seemed best,
And all the doubt was now—should I be fit?

VIII

So, quiet as despair, I turned from him,
That hateful cripple, out of his highway
Into the path he pointed. All the day   45
Had been a dreary one at best, and dim
Was settling to its close, yet shot one grim
Red leer to see the plain catch its estray.[3]

IX

For mark! no sooner was I fairly found
Pledged to the plain, after a pace or two,   50
Than, pausing to throw backward a last view
O'er the safe road, 't was gone; grey plain all round:
Nothing but plain to the horizon's bound.
I might go on; nought else remained to do.

X

So, on I went. I think I never saw   55
Such starved ignoble nature; nothing throve:
For flowers—as well expect a cedar grove!
But cockle, spurge,[4] according to their law
Might propagate their kind, with none to awe,[5]
You'd think; a burr had been a treasure-trove.   60

XI

No! penury, inertness and grimace,
In some strange sort, were the land's portion. "See
Or shut your eyes," said Nature peevishly,
"It nothing skills:[6] I cannot help my case:
'T is the Last Judgment's fire must cure this place,   65
Calcine[7] its clods and set my prisoners free."

XII

If there pushed any ragged thistle-stalk
Above its mates, the head was chopped; the bents[8]
Were jealous else. What made those holes and rents

---

3. A stray domestic animal.
4. Weeds.
5. Nothing to check their growth.
6. It makes no difference.
7. Burn to a powder.
8. Coarse grasses.

In the dock's⁹ harsh swarth leaves, bruised as to baulk   70
All hope of greenness? 't is a brute must walk
     Pashing¹ their life out, with a brute's intents.

XIII

As for the grass, it grew as scant as hair
     In leprosy; thin dry blades pricked the mud
     Which underneath looked kneaded up with blood.   75
One stiff blind horse, his every bone a-stare,
Stood stupefied, however he came there:
     Thrust out past service from the devil's stud!

XIV

Alive? he might be dead for aught I know,
     With that red gaunt and colloped² neck a-strain,   80
     And shut eyes underneath the rusty mane;
Seldom went such grotesqueness with such woe;
I never saw a brute I hated so;
     He must be wicked to deserve such pain.

XV

I shut my eyes and turned them on my heart.   85
     As a man calls for wine before he fights,
     I asked one draught of earlier, happier sights,
Ere fitly I could hope to play my part.
Think first, fight afterwards—the soldier's art:
     One taste of the old time sets all to rights.   90

XVI

Not it! I fancied Cuthbert's reddening face
     Beneath its garniture of curly gold,
     Dear fellow, till I almost felt him fold
An arm in mine to fix me to the place,
That way he used. Alas, one night's disgrace!   95
     Out went my heart's new fire and left it cold.

XVII

Giles then, the soul of honour—there he stands
     Frank as ten years ago when knighted first.
     What honest man should dare (he said) he durst.³
Good—but the scene shifts—faugh! what hangman-hands   100
Pin to his breast a parchment? His own bands
     Read it. Poor traitor, spit upon and curst!

9. Coarse weedy plant.
1. Beating down, mashing.
2. In folds or ridges. The horse was inspired by a figure in a tapestry of Browning's.
3. Cf. *Macbeth*, I.vii.46–47: "I dare do all that may become a man; / Who dares do more is none."

XVIII

Better this present than a past like that;
  Back therefore to my darkening path again!
  No sound, no sight as far as eye could strain.   105
Will the night send a howlet[4] or a bat?
I asked: when something on the dismal flat
  Came to arrest my thoughts and change their train.

XIX

A sudden little river crossed my path
  As unexpected as a serpent comes.   110
  No sluggish tide congenial to the glooms;
This, as it frothed by, might have been a bath
For the fiend's glowing hoof—to see the wrath
  Of its black eddy bespate[5] with flakes and spumes.

XX

So petty yet so spiteful! All along,   115
  Low scrubby alders kneeled down over it;
  Drenched willows flung them headlong in a fit
Of mute despair, a suicidal throng:
The river which had done them all the wrong,
  Whate'er that was, rolled by, deterred no whit.   120

XXI

Which, while I forded,—good saints, how I feared
  To set my foot upon a dead man's cheek,
  Each step, or feel the spear I thrust to seek
For hollows, tangled in his hair or beard!
—It may have been a water-rat I speared,   125
  But, ugh! it sounded like a baby's shriek.

XXII

Glad was I when I reached the other bank.
  Now for a better country. Vain presage!
  Who were the strugglers, what war did they wage,
Whose savage trample thus could pad the dank   130
Soil to a plash?[6] Toads in a poisoned tank,
  Or wild cats in a red-hot iron cage—

XXIII

The fight must so have seemed in that fell cirque.[7]
  What penned them there, with all the plain to choose?

4. Owl.
5. Spattered.
6. Mire.
7. Terrible arena.

No foot-print leading to that horrid mews,[8]   135
None out of it. Mad brewage set to work
Their brains, no doubt, like galley-slaves the Turk
Pits for his pastime, Christians against Jews.

XXIV

And more than that—a furlong on—why, there!
   What bad use was that engine for, that wheel,   140
   Or brake,[9] not wheel—that harrow fit to reel
Men's bodies out like silk? with all the air
Of Tophet's[1] tool, on earth left unaware,
   Or brought to sharpen its rusty teeth of steel.

XXV

Then came a bit of stubbed ground, once a wood,   145
   Next a marsh, it would seem, and now mere earth
   Desperate and done with; (so a fool finds mirth,
Makes a thing and then mars it, till his mood
Changes and off he goes!) within a rood[2]—
   Bog, clay and rubble, sand and stark black dearth.   150

XXVI

Now blotches rankling, coloured gay and grim,
   Now patches where some leanness of the soil's
   Broke into moss or substances like boils;
Then came some palsied oak, a cleft in him
Like a distorted mouth that splits its rim   155
   Gaping at death, and dies while it recoils.

XXVII

And just as far as ever from the end!
   Nought in the distance but the evening, nought
   To point my footstep further! At the thought,
A great black bird, Apollyon's[3] bosom-friend,   160
Sailed past, nor beat his wide wing dragon-penned
   That brushed my cap—perchance the guide I sought.

XXVIII

For, looking up, aware I somehow grew,
   'Spite of the dusk, the plain had given place
   All round to mountains—with such name to grace   165

8. Cage or enclosure.
9. Toothed machine for processing flax.
1. Hell's.
2. Quarter acre.
3. Or Abaddon, meaning "destroyer." In Revelation 9:11 he is "the angel of the bottomless pit."
In *Pilgrim's Progress*, Part I, the "foul fiend" Apollyon has "wings like a dragon."

Mere ugly heights and heaps now stolen in view.
How thus they had surprised me,—solve it, you!
    How to get from them was no clearer case.

XXIX

Yet half I seemed to recognize some trick
    Of mischief happened to me, God knows when—   170
    In a bad dream perhaps. Here ended, then,
Progress this way. When, in the very nick
Of giving up, one time more, came a click
    As when a trap shuts—you're inside the den!

XXX

Burningly it came on me all at once,   175
    This was the place! those two hills on the right,
    Crouched like two bulls locked horn in horn in fight;
While to the left, a tall scalped mountain . . . Dunce,
Dotard, a-dozing at the very nonce,[4]
    After a life spent training for the sight!   180

XXXI

What in the midst lay but the Tower[5] itself?
    The round squat turret, blind as the fool's heart,[6]
    Built of brown stone, without a counterpart
In the whole world. The tempest's mocking elf
Points to the shipman thus the unseen shelf[7]   185
    He strikes on, only when the timbers start.

XXXII

Not see? because of night perhaps?—why, day
    Came back again for that! before it left,
    The dying sunset kindled through a cleft:
The hills, like giants at a hunting, lay,   190
Chin upon hand, to see the game at bay,—
    "Now stab and end the creature—to the heft!"[8]

XXXIII

Not hear? when noise was everywhere! it tolled
    Increasing like a bell. Names in my ears
    Of all the lost adventurers my peers,—   195
How such a one was strong, and such was bold,

4. Crucial moment.
5. According to Browning this setting was based on "some recollection of a strange solitary lit-
   tle tower I have come upon more than once in Massa-Carrara, in the midst of low hills . . ."
   (New Letters, p. 173). See "The Englishman in Italy," lines 219ff.
6. Cf. Psalms 14:1: "The fool hath said in his heart, There is no God."
7. Sandbank or rock ledge.
8. Hilt.

And such was fortunate, yet each of old
  Lost, lost! one moment knelled the woe of years.

XXXIV

There they stood, ranged along the hill-sides, met
  To view the last of me, a living frame   200
For one more picture! in a sheet of flame
I saw them and I knew them all. And yet
Dauntless the slug-horn[9] to my lips I set,
  And blew. *"Childe Roland to the Dark Tower came."*

1852

Respectability[1]

I

Dear, had the world in its caprice
  Deigned to proclaim "I know you both,
  Have recognized your plighted troth,
Am sponsor for you: live in peace!"—
How many precious months and years   5
  Of youth had passed, that speed so fast,
  Before we found it out at last,
The world, and what it fears?

II

How much of priceless life were spent
  With men that every virtue decks,   10
  And women models of their sex,
Society's true ornament,—
Ere we dared wander, nights like this,
  Thro' wind and rain, and watch the Seine,
  And feel the Boulevart[2] break again   15
To warmth and light and bliss?

III

I know! the world proscribes not love;
  Allows my finger to caress
  Your lips' contour and downiness,
Provided it supply a glove.   20

---

9. *Slughorn* is an archaic form of *slogan* ("battle cry"): Chatterton uses the word in this way. A *slughorn* is also a stunted or deformed cow's horn (Roberts, 757). The legendary Roland, badly outnumbered by the Saracens at Roncesvalles, thrice sounded his horn "Olivant" to communicate his plight to Charlemagne. The blasts were so loud the birds fell dead and the Saracens drew back in terror. After the battle Roland died.
1. The poem is set in Paris, 1852; the speaker is a man.
2. Boulevard.

The world's good word!—the Institute![3]
Guizot receives Montalembert![4]
Eh? Down the court three lampions[5] flare:
Put forward your best foot!

ca. 1852

A Light[1] Woman

I

So far as our story approaches the end,
   Which do you pity the most of us three?—
My friend, or the mistress of my friend
   With her wanton eyes, or me?

II

My friend was already too good to lose,   5
   And seemed in the way of improvement yet,
When she crossed his path with her hunting-noose
   And over him drew her net.

III

When I saw him tangled in her toils,
   A shame, said I, if she adds just him   10
To her nine-and-ninety other spoils,
   The hundredth for a whim!

IV

And before my friend be wholly hers,
   How easy to prove to him, I said,
An eagle's the game her pride prefers,   15
   Though she snaps at a wren instead!

V

So, I gave her eyes my own eyes to take,
   My hand sought hers as in earnest need,
And round she turned for my noble sake,
   And gave me herself indeed.   20

3. The lovers are approaching the august Institut de France, the agency governing France's learned societies, including (since 1795) the intellectually conservative Académie Française.
4. On February 5, 1852, the statesman François Guizot (1787–1874) was required by custom to deliver a speech welcoming his bitter opponent, the historian Charles Montalembert (1810–70) into the Académie Française upon the latter's election. Browning attended the ceremony.
5. Lamps.
1. The word suggests both frivolousness and sexual promiscuity.

VI

The eagle am I, with my fame in the world,
     The wren is he, with his maiden face.
—You look away and your lip is curled?
     Patience, a moment's space!

VII

For see, my friend goes shaking and white;   25
     He eyes me as the basilisk:[2]
I have turned, it appears, his day to night,
     Eclipsing his sun's disk.

VIII

And I did it, he thinks, as a very thief:
     "Though I love her"—that, he comprehends—   30
"One should master one's passions, (love, in chief)
     And be loyal to one's friends!"

IX

And she,—she lies in my hand as tame
     As a pear late basking over a wall;
Just a touch to try and off it came;   35
     'T is mine,—can I let it fall?

X

With no mind to eat it, that's the worst!
     Were it thrown in the road, would the case assist?
'T was quenching a dozen blue-flies' thirst
     When I gave its stalk a twist.   40

XI

And I,—what I seem to my friend, you see:
     What I soon shall seem to his love, you guess:
What I seem to myself, do you ask of me?
     No hero, I confess.

XII

'T is an awkward thing to play with souls,   45
     And matter enough to save one's own:
Yet think of my friend, and the burning coals
     He played with for bits of stone!

---

2. Fabulous reptile, supposed capable of killing its victims with a stare.

XIII

One likes to show the truth for the truth;
   That the woman was light is very true: 50
But suppose she says,—Never mind that youth!
   What wrong have I done to you?

XIV

Well, any how, here the story stays,
   So far at least as I understand;
And, Robert Browning, you writer of plays,[3]   55
   Here's a subject made to your hand!

The Statue and the Bust[1]

There's a palace in Florence, the world knows well,
And a statue watches it from the square,
And this story of both do our townsmen tell.

Ages ago, a lady there,
At the farthest window facing the East   5
Asked, "Who rides by with the royal air?"

The bridesmaids' prattle around her ceased;
She leaned forth, one on either hand;
They saw how the blush of the bride increased—

They felt by its beats her heart expand—   10
As one at each ear and both in a breath
Whispered, "The Great-Duke Ferdinand."

That self-same instant, underneath,
The Duke rode past in his idle way,
Empty and fine like a swordless sheath.   15

Gay he rode, with a friend as gay,
Till he threw his head back—"Who is she?"
—"A bride the Riccardi brings home to-day."

Hair in heaps lay heavily
Over a pale brow spirit-pure—   20
Carved like the heart of the coal-black tree,

---

3. Wry reference to Browning's lack of success as a dramatist.
1. Here Browning retells an old Florentine legend, imaginatively adding a della Robbia bust of
the lady to the "empty shrine" (line 189) faced by the equestrian statue of the Grand-Duke
Ferdinand de' Medici (1549–1609), ruler of Florence 1587–1609. The statue, by Giovanni
da Bologna (John of Douai, 1529–1608) stands in the Piazza della Annunziata. The palace
of the first line, called the Riccardi-Manelli palace, was not actually acquired by the Riccardi
(the family into which the lady married) until 1800.
   The rhyme scheme of the poem, though not the meter, is that of *terza rima*.

Crisped like a war-steed's encolure[2]—
And vainly sought to dissemble[3] her eyes
Of the blackest black our eyes endure.

And lo, a blade for a knight's emprise   25
Filled the fine empty sheath of a man,—
The Duke grew straightway brave and wise.

He looked at her, as a lover can;
She looked at him, as one who awakes:
The past was a sleep, and her life began.   30

Now, love so ordered for both their sakes,
A feast was held that selfsame night
In the pile[4] which the mighty shadow makes.

(For Via Larga is three-parts light,
But the palace overshadows one,   35
Because of a crime which may God requite!

To Florence and God the wrong was done,
Through the first republic's murder there
By Cosimo and his cursed son.[5]

The Duke (with the statue's face in the square)   40
Turned in the midst of his multitude
At the bright approach of the bridal pair.

Face to face the lovers stood
A single minute and no more,
While the bridgroom bent as a man subdued—   45

Bowed till his bonnet brushed the floor—
For the Duke on the lady a kiss conferred,
As the courtly custom was of yore.

In a minute can lovers exchange a word?
If a word did pass, which I do not think,   50
Only one out of the thousand heard.

That was the bridegroom. At day's brink
He and his bride were alone at last
In a bedchamber by a taper's blink.

---

2. Curled like a war horse's mane.
3. Conceal.
4. The Medici (later Medici-Riccardi) palace in the Via Larga, now Via Cavour. Browning apparently did not know this palace was closed throughout Ferdinand's lifetime.
5. Florence was a model republic until it came under the absolute rule of the Medici, beginning with Cosimo the Elder (1389–1464).

Calmly he said that her lot was cast,   55
That the door she had passed was shut on her
Till the final catafalk[6] repassed.

The world meanwhile, its noise and stir,
Through a certain window facing the East,
She could watch like a convent's chronicler.   60

Since passing the door might lead to a feast,
And a feast might lead to so much beside,
He, of many evils, chose the least.

"Freely I choose too," said the bride—
"Your window and its world suffice,"   65
Replied the tongue, while the heart replied—

"If I spend the night with that devil twice,
May his window serve as my loop of hell
Whence a damned soul looks on paradise!

"I fly to the Duke who loves me well,   70
Sit by his side and laugh at sorrow
Ere I count another ave-bell.[7]

" 'T is only the coat of a page to borrow,
And tie my hair in a horse-boy's trim,
And I save my soul—but not to-morrow"—   75

(She checked herself and her eye grew dim)
"My father tarries to bless my state:
I must keep it one day more for him.

"Is one day more so long to wait?
Moreover the Duke rides past, I know;   80
We shall see each other, sure as fate."

She turned on her side and slept. Just so!
So we resolve on a thing and sleep:
So did the lady, ages ago.

That night the Duke said, "Dear or cheap   85
As the cost of this cup of bliss may prove
To body or soul, I will drain it deep."

And on the morrow, bold with love,
He beckoned the bridegroom (close on call,
As his duty bade, by the Duke's alcove)   90

---

6. Carriage on which a coffin rests during a state funeral.
7. Prayer bell rung morning and evening.

And smiled " 'T was a very funeral,
Your lady will think, this feast of ours,—
A shame to efface, whate'er befall!

"What if we break from the Arno[8] bowers,
And try if Petraja,[9] cool and green,   95
Cure last night's fault with this morning's flowers?"

The bridegroom, not a thought to be seen
On his steady brow and quiet mouth,
Said, "Too much favour for me so mean!

"But, alas! my lady leaves[1] the South;   100
Each wind that comes from the Apennine[2]
Is a menace to her tender youth:

"Nor a way exists, the wise opine,
If she quits her palace twice this year,
To avert the flower of life's decline."   105

Quoth the Duke, "A sage and a kindly fear.
Moreover Petraja is cold this spring:
Be our feast to-night as usual here!"

And then to himself—"Which night shall bring
Thy bride to her lover's embraces, fool—   110
Or I am the fool, and thou art the king!

"Yet my passion must wait a night, nor cool—
For to-night the Envoy arrives from France[3]
Whose heart I unlock with thyself, my tool.

"I need thee still and might miss perchance.   115
To-day is not wholly lost, beside,
With its hope of my lady's countenance:

"For I ride—what should I do but ride?
And passing her palace, if I list,[4]
May glance at its window—well betide!"   120

So said, so done: nor the lady missed
One ray that broke from the ardent brow,
Nor a curl of the lips where the spirit kissed.

8. River flowing through Florence.
9. Suburb of Florence on the southern slopes of Mount Morello.
1. Comes from.
2. Mountain range north of Florence.
3. Ferdinand wanted France as ally to offset Spanish influence in Italy.
4. Choose.

Be sure that each renewed the vow,
No morrow's sun should arise and set   125
And leave them then as it left them now.

But next day passed, and next day yet,
With still fresh cause to wait one day more
Ere each leaped over the parapet.

And still, as love's brief morning wore,   130
With a gentle start, half smile, half sigh,
They found love not as it seemed before.

They thought it would work infallibly,
But not in despite of heaven and earth:
The rose would blow[5] when the storm passed by.   135

Meantime they could profit in winter's dearth
By store of fruits that supplant the rose:
The world and its ways have a certain worth:

And to press a point while these oppose
Were simple policy; better wait: 140
We lose no friends and we gain no foes.

Meantime, worse fates than a lover's fate,
Who daily may ride and pass and look
Where his lady watches behind the grate!

And she—she watched the square like a book   145
Holding one picture and only one,
Which daily to find she undertook:

When the picture was reached the book was done,
And she turned from the picture at night to scheme
Of tearing it out for herself next sun.   150

So weeks grew months, years; gleam by gleam
The glory dropped from their youth and love,
And both perceived they had dreamed a dream;

Which hovered as dreams do, still above:
But who can take a dream for a truth?   155
Oh, hide our eyes from the next remove!

One day as the lady saw her youth
Depart, and the silver thread that streaked
Her hair, and, worn by the serpent's tooth,

5. Burst into flower.

The brow so puckered, the chin so peaked,—   160
And wondered who the woman was,
Hollow-eyed and haggard-cheeked,

Fronting her silent in the glass—
"Summon here," she suddenly said,
"Before the rest of my old self pass,   165

"Him, the Carver, a hand to aid,
Who fashions the clay no love will change,
And fixes a beauty never to fade.

"Let Robbia's[6] craft so apt and strange
Arrest the remains of young and fair,   170
And rivet them while the seasons range.

"Make me a face on the window there,
Waiting as ever, mute the while,
My love to pass below in the square!

"And let me think that it may beguile   175
Dreary days which the dead must spend
Down in their darkness under the aisle,

"To say, 'What matters it at the end?
I did no more while my heart was warm
Than does that image, my pale-faced friend.'   180

"Where is the use of the lip's red charm,
The heaven of hair, the pride of the brow,
And the blood that blues the inside arm—

"Unless we turn, as the soul knows how,
The earthly gift to an end divine?   185
A lady of clay is as good, I trow."

But long ere Robbia's cornice, fine,
With flowers and fruits which leaves enlace,
Was set where now is the empty shrine—

(And, leaning out of a bright blue space,   190
As a ghost might lean from a chink of sky,
The passionate pale lady's face—

Eyeing ever, with earnest eye
And quick-turned neck at its breathless stretch,
Some one who ever is passing by—)   195

6. Luca della Robbia (1399–1482), head of a family workshop famed for its glazed terra cotta objects.

The Duke had sighed like the simplest wretch
In Florence, "Youth—my dream escapes!
Will its record stay?" And he bade them fetch

Some subtle moulder of brazen shapes—
"Can the soul, the will, die out of a man   200
Ere his body find the grave that gapes?

"John of Douay shall effect my plan,
Set me on horseback here aloft,
Alive, as the crafty sculptor can,

"In the very square I have crossed so oft: 205
That men may admire, when future suns
Shall touch the eyes to a purpose soft,

"While the mouth and the brow stay brave in bronze—
Admire and say, 'When he was alive
How he would take his pleasure once!'   210

"And it shall go hard but I contrive
To listen the while, and laugh in my tomb
At idleness which aspires to strive."

So! While these wait the trump of doom,
How do their spirits pass, I wonder,   215
Nights and days in the narrow room?

Still, I suppose, they sit and ponder
What a gift life was, ages ago,
Six steps out of the chapel yonder.

Only they see not God, I know,   220
Nor all that chivalry of his,
The soldier-saints who, row on row,

Burn upward each to his point of bliss—
Since, the end of life being manifest,
He had burned his way thro' the world to this.   225

I hear you reproach, "But delay was best,
For their end was a crime."—Oh, a crime will do
As well, I reply, to serve for a test,

As a virtue golden through and through,
Sufficient to vindicate itself   230
And prove its worth at a moment's view!

Must a game be played for the sake of pelf?[7]
Where a button goes, 't were an epigram
To offer the stamp of the very Guelph.[8]

The true has no value beyond the sham: 235
As well the counter as coin, I submit,
When your table's a hat, and your prize a dram.[9]

Stake your counter as boldly every whit,
Venture as warily, use the same skill,
Do your best, whether winning or losing it,   240

If you choose to play!—is my principle.
Let a man contend to the uttermost
For his life's set prize, be it what it will!

The counter our lovers staked was lost
As surely as if it were lawful coin: 245
And the sin I impute to each frustrate ghost

Is—the unlit lamp and the ungirt loin,[1]
Though the end in sight was a vice,[2] I say.
You of the virtue (we issue join)[3]
How strive you? *De te, fabula.*[4]   250

How It Strikes a Contemporary[1]

I only knew one poet in my life:
And this, or something like it, was his way.

You saw go up and down Valladolid,[2]
A man of mark, to know next time you saw.

---

7. Money.
8. It would be a joke ("epigram") to play the game with silver coins ("stamp of the very Guelph") if any sort of counter would do. The Guelphs were a powerful faction in medieval Italy.
9. Drink.
1. Luke 12:35–36: "Let your loins be girded about, and your lights burning; and ye yourselves like unto men that wait for their lord, when he will return from the wedding. . . ." The duke and the lady, Browning implies, are spiritually indifferent and thus unprepared to render their account before Christ.
2. "Crime" in first edition.
3. Take issue with, dispute.
4. *Quid rides? Mutato nomine de te / fabula narratur:* "Why do you laugh? Change the name, and the tale is about you" (Horace, *Satires,* I.i. 69–70).
1. May be a product of Browning's reflections on poetry and the poet while writing the *Essay on Shelley* (published 1852), particularly in defining the "subjective" poet; see the excerpt from the *Essay* in this edition. Cf. his letter of 1855 to John Ruskin: "A poet's affair is with God, to whom he is accountable, and of whom is his reward . . ." (W. G. Collingwood, *Life and Work of John Ruskin* [London, 1893] I: 234). Browning never visited Spain; the setting at Valladolid and other details may have been drawn from Lesage's *Gil Blas,* which the poet had read in 1835 (DeVane, pp. 236–37).
2. Town in north-central Spain, once the Castilian royal seat.

His very serviceable suit of black   5
Was courtly once and conscientious still,
And many might have worn it, though none did:
The cloak, that somewhat shone and showed the threads,
Had purpose, and the ruff, significance.
He walked and tapped the pavement with his cane,   10
Scenting the world, looking it full in face,
An old dog, bald and blindish, at his heels.
They turned up, now, the alley by the church,
That leads nowhither; now, they breathed themselves
On the main promenade just at the wrong time: 15
You'd come upon his scrutinizing hat,
Making a peaked shade blacker than itself
Against the single window spared some house
Intact yet with its mouldered Moorish work,—
Or else surprise the ferrel[3] of his stick   20
Trying the mortar's temper 'tween the chinks
Of some new shop a-building, French and fine.
He stood and watched the cobbler at his trade,
The man who slices lemons into drink,
The coffee-roaster's brazier, and the boys   25
That volunteer to help him turn its winch.
He glanced o'er books on stalls with half an eye,
And fly-leaf ballads[4] on the vendor's string,
And broad-edge bold-print posters by the wall.
He took such cognizance of men and things,   30
If any beat a horse, you felt he saw;
If any cursed a woman, he took note;
Yet stared at nobody,—you stared at him,
And found, less to your pleasure than surprise,
He seemed to know you and expect as much.   35
So, next time that a neighbour's tongue was loosed,
It marked the shameful and notorious fact,
We had among us, not so much a spy,
As a recording chief-inquisitor,
The town's true master if the town but knew![5]   40
We merely kept a governor for form,
While this man walked about and took account
Of all thought, said and acted, then went home,
And wrote it fully to our Lord the King
Who has an itch to know things, he knows why,   45
And reads them in his bedroom of a night.
Oh, you might smile! there wanted not a touch,
A tang of . . . well, it was not wholly ease
As back into your mind the man's look came.
Stricken in years a little,—such a brow   50
His eyes had to live under!—clear as flint

3. Ferrule, or metal tip.
4. Broadsides, popular verse printed on large folio sheets.
5. Cf. the final sentence of Shelley's *A Defence of Poetry* (1840): "Poets are the unacknowl-
edged legislators of the world."

On either side the formidable nose
Curved, cut and coloured like an eagle's claw.
Had he to do with A.'s surprising fate?
When altogether old B. disappeared   55
And young C. got his mistress,—was't our friend,
His letter to the King, that did it all?
What paid the bloodless man for so much pains?
Our Lord the King has favourites manifold,
And shifts his ministry some once a month;   60
Our city gets new governors at whiles,—
But never word or sign, that I could hear,
Notified to this man about the streets
The King's approval of those letters conned[6]
The last thing duly at the dead of night.   65
Did the man love his office? Frowned our Lord,
Exhorting when none heard—"Beseech me not!
Too far above my people,—beneath me!
I set the watch,—how should the people know?
Forget them, keep me all the more in mind!"   70
Was some such understanding 'twixt the two?

          I found no truth in one report at least—
That if you tracked him to his home, down lanes
Beyond the Jewry,[7] and as clean to pace,
You found he ate his supper in a room   75
Blazing with lights, four Titians[8] on the wall,
And twenty naked girls to change his plate!
Poor man, he lived another kind of life
In that new stuccoed third house by the bridge,
Fresh-painted, rather smart than otherwise!   80
The whole street might o'erlook him as he sat,
Leg crossing leg, one foot on the dog's back,
Playing a decent cribbage with his maid
(Jacynth, you're sure her name was) o'er the cheese
And fruit, three red halves of starved winter-pears,   85
Or treat of radishes in April. Nine,
Ten, struck the church clock, straight to bed went he.

          My father, like the man of sense he was,
Would point him out to me a dozen times;
" 'St—'St," he'd whisper, "the Corregidor!"[9]   90
I had been used to think that personage
Was one with lacquered breeches, lustrous belt,
And feathers like a forest in his hat,
Who blew a trumpet and proclaimed the news,
Announced the bull-fights, gave each church its turn,   95
And memorized[1] the miracle in vogue!

6. Read closely.
7. Ghetto, or Jewish quarter.
8. Paintings by the Italian master Titian (d. 1576), famed for his glowing colors.
9. Chief magistrate.
1. Celebrated.

He had a great observance from us boys;[2]
We were in error; that was not the man.

I'd like now, yet had haply been afraid,
To have just looked, when this man came to die,   100
And seen who lined the clean gay garret-sides
And stood about the neat low truckle-bed,
With the heavenly manner of relieving guard.[3]
Here had been, mark, the general-in-chief,
Thro' a whole campaign of the world's life and death,   105
Doing the King's work all the dim day long,
In his old coat and up to knees in mud,
Smoked like a herring, dining on a crust,—
And, now the day was won, relieved at once!
No further show or need for that old coat,   110
You are sure, for one thing! Bless us, all the while
How sprucely we are dressed out, you and I!
A second, and the angels alter that.
Well, I could never write a verse,—could you?
Let's to the Prado[4] and make the most of time.   115

ca. 1852

The Last Ride Together

I

I said—Then, dearest, since 't is so,
Since now at length my fate I know,
Since nothing all my love avails,
Since all, my life seemed meant for, fails,
    Since this was written and needs must be—   5
My whole heart rises up to bless
Your name in pride and thankfulness!
Take back the hope you gave,—I claim
Only a memory of the same,
—And this beside, if you will not blame,   10
    Your leave for one more last ride with me.

II

My mistress bent that brow of hers;
Those deep dark eyes where pride demurs
When pity would be softening through,
Fixed me a breathing-while or two   15
    With life or death in the balance: right!
The blood replenished me again;

2. I.e., the boys paid him due reverence.
3. I.e., angels would come to relieve him of his duties.
4. The town's promenade.

My last thought was at least not vain:
I and my mistress, side by side
Shall be together, breathe and ride,   20
So, one day more am I deified.
    Who knows but the world may end to-night?

III

Hush! if you saw some western cloud
All billowy-bosomed, over-bowed
By many benedictions—sun's   25
And moon's and evening-star's at once—
    And so, you, looking and loving best,
Conscious grew, your passion drew
Cloud, sunset, moonrise, star-shine too,
Down on you, near and yet more near,   30
Till flesh must fade for heaven was here!—
Thus leant she and lingered—joy and fear!
    Thus lay she a moment on my breast.

IV

Then we began to ride. My soul
Smoothed itself out, a long-cramped scroll   35
Freshening and fluttering in the wind.
Past hopes already lay behind.
    What need to strive with a life awry?
Had I said that, had I done this,
So might I gain, so might I miss.   40
Might she have loved me? just as well
She might have hated, who can tell!
Where had I been now if the worst befell?
    And here we are riding, she and I.

V

Fail I alone, in words and deeds?   45
Why, all men strive and who succeeds?
We rode; it seemed my spirit flew,
Saw other regions, cities new,
    As the world rushed by on either side.
I thought,—All labour, yet no less   50
Bear up beneath their unsuccess.
Look at the end of work, contrast
The petty done, the undone vast,
    This present of theirs with the hopeful past!
    I hoped she would love me; here we ride.   55

VI

What hand and brain went ever paired?
What heart alike conceived and dared?

What act proved all its thought had been?
What will but felt the fleshly screen?
    We ride and I see her bosom heave.   60
There's many a crown for who can reach.
Ten lines, a statesman's life in each!
The flag stuck on a heap of bones,
A soldier's doing! what atones?
They scratch his name on the Abbey-stones.[1]   65
    My riding is better, by their leave.

VII

What does it all mean, poet? Well,
Your brains beat into rhythm, you tell
What we felt only; you expressed
You hold things beautiful the best,   70
    And pace them in rhyme so, side by side.
'T is something, nay 't is much: but then,
Have you yourself what's best for men?
Are you—poor, sick, old ere your time—
Nearer one whit your own sublime   75
Than we who never have turned a rhyme?
    Sing, riding's a joy! For me, I ride.

VIII

And you, great sculptor—so, you gave
A score of years to Art, her slave,
And that's your Venus, whence we turn   80
To yonder girl that fords the burn![2]
    You acquiesce, and shall I repine?
What, man of music, you grown grey
With notes and nothing else to say,
Is this your sole praise from a friend,   85
"Greatly his opera's strains intend,
But in music we know how fashions end!"[3]
    I gave my youth; but we ride, in fine.[4]

IX

Who knows what's fit for us? Had fate
Proposed bliss here should sublimate[5]   90
My being—had I signed the bond—
Still one must lead some life beyond,
    Have a bliss to die with, dim-descried.

1. Honor him with burial in Westminster Abbey.
2. Wades across the creek.
3. Writing to Elizabeth Barrett, Browning cites a "startling axiom" of Claude Le Jeune: " 'In Music, the Beau Idéal changes every thirty years'—well, is not that *true*? The *Idea*, mind, changes,—the general standard . . .—next hundred years, who will be the Rossini?" (March 7, 1846; Kintner, I.523).
4. In short.
5. Elevate.

This foot once planted on the goal,
This glory-garland round my soul,   95
Could I descry such? Try and test!
I sink back shuddering from the quest.
Earth being so good, would heaven seem best?
    Now, heaven and she are beyond this ride.

X

And yet—she has not spoke so long!   100
What if heaven be that, fair and strong
At life's best, with our eyes upturned
Whither life's flower is first discerned,
    We, fixed so, ever should so abide?
What if we still ride on, we two   105
With life for ever old yet new,
Changed not in kind but in degree,
The instant made eternity,—
And heaven just prove that I and she
    Ride, ride together, for ever ride?   110

The Patriot[1]

AN OLD STORY

I

It was roses, roses, all the way,
    With myrtle mixed in my path like mad:
The house-roofs seemed to heave and sway,
    The church-spires flamed, such flags they had,
A year ago on this very day.   5

II

The air broke into a mist with bells,
    The old walls rocked with the crowd and cries.
Had I said, "Good folk, mere noise repels—
    But give me your sun from yonder skies!"
They had answered, "And afterward, what else?"   10

III

Alack, it was I who leaped at the sun
    To give it my loving friends to keep!
Nought man could do, have I left undone:

1. Browning, who with his wife supported the Risorgimento, the Italian struggle to throw off Austrian power, probably had in mind the events of 1848–49, when Messina, Catania, and Brescia again fell under the Grand-Duke's yoke. The poet dropped his reference to Brescia (and inferentially the patriot Arnold of Brescia) when revising the poem for his 1863 edition, presumably to give the poem a wider relevance.

And you see my harvest, what I reap
This very day, now a year is run.   15

IV

There's nobody on the house-tops now—
    Just a palsied few at the windows set;
For the best of the sight is, all allow,
    At the Shambles' Gate[2]—or, better yet,
By the very scaffold's foot, I trow.   20

V

I go in the rain, and, more than needs,
    A rope cuts both my wrists behind;
And I think, by the feel, my forehead bleeds,
    For they fling, whoever has a mind,
Stones at me for my year's misdeeds.   25

VI

Thus I entered, and thus I go:
    In triumphs, people have dropped down dead.
"Paid by the world, what dost thou owe
    Me?"—God might question; now instead,
'T is God shall repay:[3] I am safer so.   30

Master Hugues of Saxe-Gotha

I

Hist, but a word, fair and soft!
    Forth and be judged, Master Hugues!
Answer the question I've put you so oft:
    What do you mean by your mountainous fugues?[1]
See, we're alone in the loft,—   5

II

I, the poor organist here,
    Hugues, the composer of note,
Dead though, and done with, this many a year:
    Let's have a colloquy, something to quote,
Make the world prick up its ear!   10

2. A market where butchers kill and sell meat, hence a place of carnage.
3. Luke 10:35; Romans 12:19.
1. The fugue is a complicated musical form in contrapuntal style based on a short melody, the subject or theme, which is stated at the beginning by one "voice" and then taken up by the other voices in close succession. The form was freed and perfected by J. S. Bach (1685–1750), born in the duchy of Saxe-Gotha in central Germany. Browning however said in 1887 that the imaginary Hugues was not the "glorious Bach" but "one of the dry-as-dust imitators who would elaborate some such subject as [a five-note phrase] for a dozen pages together" (H. E. Greene, *PMLA*, 62 [1947], 1098).

III

See, the church empties apace:
    Fast they extinguish the lights.
Hallo there, sacristan![2] Five minutes' grace!
    Here's a crank pedal wants setting to rights,
Baulks one of holding the base.[3]   15

IV

See, our huge house of the sounds,[4]
    Hushing its hundreds at once,
Bids the last loiterer back to his bounds!
    —O you may challenge them, not a response
Get the church-saints on their rounds!   20

V

(Saints go their rounds, who shall doubt?
    —March, with the moon to admire,
Up nave, down chancel, turn transept about,
    Supervise all betwixt pavement and spire,
Put rats and mice to the rout—   25

VI

Aloys and Jurien and Just[5]—
    Order things back to their place,
Have a sharp eye lest the candlesticks rust,
    Rub the church-plate, darn the sacrament-lace,
Clear the desk-velvet of dust.)   30

VII

Here's your book, younger folks shelve!
    Played I not off-hand and runningly,
Just now, your masterpiece, hard number twelve?
    Here's what should strike, could one handle it cunningly:
Help the axe, give it a helve![6]   35

VIII

Page after page as I played,
    Every bar's rest, where one wipes
Sweat from one's brow, I looked up and surveyed,
    O'er my three claviers,[7] yon forest of pipes
Whence you still peeped in the shade.   40

2. Church custodian.
3. Prevents my playing the bass properly.
4. The organ.
5. The "church-saints" of line 20.
6. Handle. I.e., if I could grasp your purpose, I could play your fugue better.
7. Here, keyboards or "manuals."

IX

Sure you were wishful to speak?
    You, with brow ruled like a score,
Yes, and eyes buried in pits on each cheek,
    Like two great breves,[8] as they wrote them of yore,
Each side that bar,[9] your straight beak!   45

X

Sure you said—"Good, the mere notes!
    Still, couldst thou take my intent,
Know what procured me our Company's votes[1]—
    A master were lauded and sciolists shent,[2]
Parted the sheep from the goats!"   50

XI

Well then, speak up, never flinch!
    Quick, ere my candle's a snuff
—Burnt, do you see? to its uttermost inch—
    I believe in you, but that's not enough:
Give my conviction a clinch!   55

XII

First you deliver your phrase[3]
    —Nothing propound, that I see,
Fit in itself for much blame or much praise—
    Answered no less, where no answer needs be:
Off start the Two on their ways.   60

XIII

Straight must a Third interpose,
    Volunteer needlessly help;
In strikes a Fourth, a Fifth thrusts in his nose,
    So the cry's open, the kennel's a-yelp,
Argument's hot to the close.   65

XIV

One dissertates, he is candid;
    Two must discept,[4]—has distinguished;
Three helps the couple, if ever yet man did;

---

8. Old note value originally the shortest in use (Latin *brevis*, "short"), later the longest. Before 1450 it was written as a black square.
9. Vertical line marking a division in music.
1. I.e., why I was voted a "master" by the town's corporation ("Company") in a local competition.
2. Pretenders to knowledge disgraced.
3. Subject of fugue, "answered" by a second voice.
4. Disagree.

Four protests; Five makes a dart at the thing wished:
Back to One, goes the case bandied.   70

XV

One says his say with a difference;
    More of expounding, explaining!
All now is wrangle, abuse, and vociferance;
    Now there's a truce, all's subdued, self-restraining:
Five, though, stands out all the stiffer hence.   75

XVI

One is incisive, corrosive;
    Two retorts, nettled, curt, crepitant,[5]
Three makes rejoinder, expansive, explosive;
    Four overbears them all, strident and strepitant:[6]
Five . . . O Danaides, O Sieve![7]   80

XVII

Now, they ply axes and crowbars;
    Now, they prick pins at a tissue
Fine as a skein of the casuist Escobar's[8]
    Worked on the bone of a lie. To what issue?
Where is our gain at the Two-bars?[9]   85

XVIII

Est fuga, volvitur rota.[1]
    On we drift: where looms the dim port?
One, Two, Three, Four, Five, contribute their quota;
    Something is gained, if one caught but the import—
Show it us, Hugues of Saxe-Gotha!   90

XIX

What with affirming, denying,
    Holding, risposting, subjoining,[2]
All's like . . . it's like . . . for an instance I'm trying . . .
    There! See our roof, its gilt moulding and groining[3]
Under those spider-webs[4] lying!   95

5. Crackling.
6. Boisterous.
7. The daughters of Danaüs king of Argos, forced to marry, killed their husbands. Condemned in Hades to keep filling perforated water-jars, they are emblematic of futile labor.
8. Escobar y Mendoza (1589–1669), theologian noted for subtle argumentation on moral issues.
9. Double vertical bar marking end of a section or whole piece of music.
1. "There is a flight, the wheel turns." Cf. Ovid, *Metamorphoses*, IV. 461: *Volvitur Ixion et se sequiturque fugitique*: "There whirls Ixion on his wheel, both following himself and fleeing, all in one."
2. Retorting and adding.
3. Ribs covering the meeting of two intersecting vaults of a roof.
4. The spider's web as symbol of tiresome disputation may derive from Book I of Bacon's *Ad-*

XX

So your fugue broadens and thickens,
    Greatens and deepens and lengthens,
Till we exclaim—"But where's music, the dickens?
    Blot ye the gold, while your spider-web strengthens
—Blacked to the stoutest of tickens?"[5]   100

XXI

I for man's effort am zealous:
    Prove me such censure unfounded!
Seems it surprising a lover grows jealous—
    Hopes 't was for something, his organ-pipes sounded,
Tiring three boys at the bellows?   105

XXII

Is it your moral of Life?
    Such a web, simple and subtle,
Weave we on earth here in impotent strife,
    Backward and forward each throwing his shuttle,
Death ending all with a knife?   110

XXIII

Over our heads truth and nature—
    Still our life's zigzags and dodges,
Ins and outs, weaving a new legislature—
    God's gold just shining its last where that lodges,
Palled beneath man's usurpature.   115

XXIV

So we o'ershroud stars and roses,
    Cherub and trophy and garland;
Nothings grow something which quietly closes
    Heaven's earnest eye: not a glimpse of the far land
Gets through our comments and glozes.[6]   120

XXV

Ah but traditions, inventions,
    (Say we and make up a visage[7])
So many men with such various intentions,
    Down the past ages, must know more than this age!
Leave we the web its dimensions!   125

---

vancement of Learning (1605), in which the medieval schoolmen are characterized as spi-
ders who spin out "cobwebs of learning" without "substance and profit."
5. Ticking, material for bedding.
6. Glosses, interpretations.
7. Put on a solemn expression.

XXVI

Who thinks Hugues wrote for the deaf,
    Proved a mere mountain in labour?[8]
Better submit; try again; what's the clef?
    'Faith, 't is no trifle for pipe and for tabor[9]—
Four flats, the minor in F.[1]   130

XXVII

Friend, your fugue taxes the finger:
    Learning it once, who would lose it?
Yet all the while a misgiving will linger,
    Truth's golden o'er us although we refuse it—
Nature, thro' cobwebs we string her.   135

XXVIII

Hugues! I advise *meâ poenâ*[2]
    (Counterpoint glares like a Gorgon)[3]
Bid One, Two, Three, Four, Five, clear the arena!
    Say the word, straight I unstop the full-organ,
Blare out the *mode Palestrina*.[4]   140

XXIX

While in the roof, if I'm right there,
    . . . Lo you, the wick in the socket!
Hallo, you sacristan, show us a light there!
    Down it dips, gone like a rocket.
What, you want, do you, to come unawares,   145
Sweeping the church up for first morning-prayers,
And find a poor devil has ended his cares
    At the foot of your rotten-runged rat-riddled stairs?
Do I carry the moon in my pocket?[5]

ca. 1853

Bishop Blougram's Apology

"Apology" in the title means a formal defense of one's beliefs or actions.
Blougram is a fictitious Roman Catholic bishop speaking in the presence

8. "The mountains are in labor—they will give birth to a ridiculous mouse" (Horace, *Ars Poetica*, 139).
9. Small drum.
1. A difficult key.
2. At the risk of my punishment.
3. Female monster who could turn anyone looking at her to stone.
4. In the relatively severe, simple style of the school of Giovanni Pierluigi da Palestrina (ca. 1525–94), composer of religious music.
5. As R. D. Altick has shown, the line comes from Shakespeare's *Cymbeline* (III.i.42–44): "If Caesar can hide the sun from us with a blanket, or put the moon in his pocket, we will pay him tribute for light. . . ."

of a hostile agnostic journalist intent on exposing him as a hypocrite. The setting is London in the early 1850s.

"Bishop Blougram's Apology" was designedly a poem for the times. In 1850 Pope Pius IX had created a furor in England by reestablishing there the Roman Catholic hierarchy, headed by the newly installed Archbishop of Westminster, Cardinal N. P. S. Wiseman (1802–65). The prime minister wrote a scathing open letter to the Bishop of Durham (November 4, 1850), declaring that "no foreign prince or potentate will be at liberty to fasten his fetters upon a nation which has so long and so nobly vindicated its right to freedom of opinion, civil, political, and religious." When "Blougram" appeared in 1855 it was obvious, especially to Catholics, that Browning had the worldly and sophisticated Wiseman in mind as the original of the Bishop; later the poet admitted as much. But he may also have drawn from the character of the brilliant controversialist John Henry Newman (1801–90), leader of the "Oxford Movement" until his conversion to Roman Catholicism in 1845. These Anglican conservatives voiced their opinions on a wide range of ecclesiastical issues in a pamphlet series, *Tracts for the Times* (1833–41)—hence their other name, "Tractarians." In the final number of the series, "Tract XC," Newman argued that the Thirty-Nine Articles of the Anglican church conflicted in no fundamental way with Roman Catholic doctrine. The episode of "Tract XC," according to C. F. Harrold, "gave a very unflattering impression of Newman's mind and for a long time the only conception of him in the mind of the English middle-class was that of a subtle-minded ecclesiastical hair-splitter and special pleader" (*J. H. Newman* [1945], p. 43). In the process of conversion, Newman had worked out a new, unorthodox, and rhetorically sophisticated form of apologetic. At the height of the "No-Popery" panic in England, he delivered two sets of apologetic lectures: *The Difficulties of Anglicans* (1850) and *The Present Position of Catholics in England* (1851). The intellectual side of this most conspicuous Catholic spokesman probably figured, however indirectly, in the composite portrait that is Browning's Blougram.

> No more wine? then we'll push back chairs and talk.
> A final glass for me, though: cool, i' faith!
> We ought to have our Abbey[1] back, you see.
> It's different, preaching in basilicas,[2]
> And doing duty in some masterpiece   5
> Like this of brother Pugin's, bless his heart!
> I doubt if they're half baked, those chalk rosettes,
> Ciphers and stucco-twiddlings everywhere;
> It's just like breathing in a lime-kiln: eh?
> These hot long ceremonies of our church   10
> Cost us a little—oh, they pay the price,
> You take me[3]—amply pay it! Now, we'll talk.

---

1. Westminster Abbey, taken from the Roman Catholic church at the English Reformation.
2. Ancient oblong churches with nave separated from side aisles by rows of columns. Blougram goes on to ridicule the Victorian "Gothic Revival," led by English architect (and Catholic convert) A. W. N. Pugin (1812–52). Many of Pugin's churches suffered from being executed on a diminished scale, and from the introduction of shams like those named in lines 7–8.
3. Understand.

So, you despise me, Mr. Gigadibs.[4]
No deprecation,—nay, I beg you, sir!
Beside 't is our engagement: don't you know,   15
I promised, if you'd watch a dinner out,
We'd see truth dawn together?—truth that peeps
Over the glasses' edge when dinner's done,
And body gets its sop and holds its noise
And leaves soul free a little. Now's the time: 20
Truth's break of day! You do despise me then.
And if I say, "despise me,"—never fear!
I know you do not in a certain sense—
Not in my arm-chair, for example: here,
I well imagine you respect my place   25
(*Status, entourage,* worldly circumstance)
Quite to its value—very much indeed:
—Are up to the protesting eyes of you
In pride at being seated here for once—
You'll turn it to such capital account!   30
When somebody, through years and years to come,
Hints of the bishop,—names me—that's enough:
"Blougram? I knew him"—(into it you slide)
"Dined with him once, a Corpus Christi Day,[5]
All alone, we two; he's a clever man: 35
And after dinner,—why, the wine you know,—
Oh, there was wine, and good!—what with the wine . . .
'Faith, we began upon all sorts of talk!
He's no bad fellow, Blougram; he had seen
Something of mine he relished, some review: 40
He's quite above their[6] humbug in his heart,
Half-said as much, indeed—the thing's his trade.
I warrant, Blougram's sceptical at times:
How otherwise? I liked him, I confess!"
Che che,[7] my dear sir, as we say at Rome,   45
Don't you protest now! It's fair give and take;
You have had your turn and spoken your home-truths:
The hand's mine now, and here you follow suit.

Thus much conceded, still the first fact stays—
You do despise me; your ideal of life   50
Is not the bishop's: you would not be I.
You would like better to be Goethe,[8] now,
Or Buonaparte, or, bless me, lower still,
Count D'Orsay,[9]—so you did what you preferred,
Spoke as you thought, and, as you cannot help,   55

---

4. The name may come from British slang. *Gig*: "fool" and *dibs*: "money"; hence a fool who will do anything for money. A hack. (Turner, 340n.)
5. Feast honoring the Eucharist, or Lord's Supper.
6. Roman Catholics'.
7. "What, what?" (Italian exclamation of impatience or denial.)
8. Johann Wolfgang von Goethe (1749–1832), eminent German poet and man of letters.
9. Famous dandy, wit, and artist (1801–52), prominent in London society. He was an ardent Bonapartist.

Believed or disbelieved, no matter what,
So long as on that point, whate'er it was,
You loosed your mind, were whole and sole yourself.
—That, my ideal never can include,
Upon that element of truth and worth   60
Never be based! for say they make me Pope—
(They can't[1]—suppose it for our argument!)
Why, there I'm at my tether's end, I've reached
My height, and not a height which pleases you:
An unbelieving Pope won't do, you say.   65
It's like those eerie stories nurses tell,
Of how some actor on a stage played Death,
With pasteboard crown, sham orb and tinselled dart,
And called himself the monarch of the world;
Then, going in the tire-room[2] afterward,   70
Because the play was done, to shift himself,
Got touched upon the sleeve familiarly,
The moment he had shut the closet door,
By Death himself. Thus God might touch a Pope
At unawares, ask what his baubles mean,   75
And whose part he presumed to play just now.
Best be yourself, imperial, plain and true!

So, drawing comfortable breath again,
You weigh and find, whatever more or less
I boast of my ideal realized   80
Is nothing in the balance when opposed
To your ideal, your grand simple life,
Of which you will not realize one jot.
I am much, you are nothing; you would be all,
I would be merely much: you beat me there.   85

No, friend, you do not beat me: hearken why!
The common problem, yours, mine, every one's,
Is—not to fancy what were fair in life
Provided it could be,—but, finding first
What may be, then find how to make it fair   90
Up to our means: a very different thing!
No abstract intellectual plan of life
Quite irrespective of life's plainest laws,
But one, a man, who is man and nothing more,
May lead within a world which (by your leave)   95
Is Rome or London, not Fool's-paradise.
Embellish Rome, idealize away,
Make paradise of London if you can,
You're welcome, nay, you're wise.
                                    A simile!
We mortals cross the ocean of this world   100

---

1. Since the pontificate of Adrian VI of the Netherlands (1522–23), all popes had been Italian.
2. Dressing room.

Each in his average cabin of a life;
The best's not big, the worst yields elbow-room.
Now for our six months' voyage—how prepare?
You come on shipboard with a landsman's list
Of things he calls convenient: so they are!   105
An India screen is pretty furniture,
A piano-forte is a fine resource,
All Balzac's[3] novels occupy one shelf,
The new edition fifty volumes long;
And little Greek books, with the funny type   110
They get up well at Leipsic,[4] fill the next:
Go on! slabbed marble, what a bath it makes!
And Parma's pride, the Jerome,[5] let us add!
'T were pleasant could Correggio's fleeting glow
Hang full in face of one where'er one roams,   115
Since he more than the others brings with him
Italy's self,—the marvellous Modenese!—
Yet was not on your list before, perhaps.
—Alas, friend, here's the agent . . . is 't the name?
The captain, or whoever's master here—   120
You see him screw his face up; what's his cry
Ere you set foot on shipboard? "Six feet square!"
If you won't understand what six feet mean,
Compute and purchase stores accordingly—
And if, in pique because he overhauls[6]   125
Your Jerome, piano, bath, you come on board
Bare—why, you cut a figure at the first
While sympathetic landsmen see you off;
Not afterward, when long ere half seas over,[7]
You peep up from your utterly naked boards   130
Into some snug and well-appointed berth,
Like mine for instance (try the cooler jug—
Put back the other, but don't jog the ice!)[8]
And mortified you mutter "Well and good;
He sits enjoying his sea-furniture;   135
'T is stout and proper, and there's store of it:
Though I've the better notion, all agree,
Of fitting rooms up. Hang the carpenter,
Neat ship-shape fixings and contrivances—
I would have brought my Jerome, frame and all!"   140
And meantime you bring nothing: never mind—
You've proved your artist-nature: what you don't
You might bring, so despise me, as I say.

3. Honoré de Balzac (1799–1850), prolific French novelist. The new mulit-volume edition of
   his complete works began publication in 1842.
4. Tauchnitz in Leipzig, Germany, published a series of classical texts in 1849 and after.
5. The St. Jerome at Parma (called *Il Giorno* or *Day*) is the work of Correggio, the name given
   Antonio Allegri (1494–1534).
6. Examines and rejects (cf. 1. 156).
7. Midway.
8. Ice was at that time a luxury in July, when the interview takes place.

Now come, let's backward to the starting-place.
See my way: we're two college friends, suppose.   145
Prepare together for our voyage, then;
Each note and check the other in his work,—
Here's mine, a bishop's outfit; criticize!
What's wrong? why won't you be a bishop too?

Why first, you don't believe, you don't and can't,   150
(Not statedly, that is, and fixedly
And absolutely and exclusively)
In any revelation called divine.
No dogmas nail your faith; and what remains
But say so, like the honest man you are?   155
First, therefore, overhaul theology!
Nay, I too, not a fool, you please to think,
Must find believing every whit as hard:
And if I do not frankly say as much,
The ugly consequence is clear enough.   160

Now wait, my friend: well, I do not believe—
If you'll accept no faith that is not fixed,
Absolute and exclusive, as you say.
You're wrong—I mean to prove it in due time.
Meanwhile, I know where difficulties lie   165
I could not, cannot solve, nor ever shall,
So give up hope accordingly to solve—
(To you, and over the wine). Our dogmas then
With both of us, though in unlike degree,
Missing full credence—overboard with them!   170
I mean to meet you on your own premise:
Good, there go mine in company with yours!

And now what are we? unbelievers both,
Calm and complete, determinately fixed
To-day, to-morrow and for ever, pray?   175
You'll guarantee me that? Not so, I think!
In no wise! all we've gained is, that belief,
As unbelief before, shakes us by fits,
Confounds us like its predecessor. Where's
The gain? how can we guard our unbelief,   180
Make it bear fruit to us?—the problem here.
Just when we are safest, there's a sunset-touch,
A fancy from a flower-bell, some one's death,
A chorus-ending from Euripides,[9]—
And that's enough for fifty hopes and fears   185
As old and new at once as nature's self,
To rap and knock and enter in our soul,
Take hands and dance there, a fantastic ring,
Round the ancient idol, on his base again,—

9. Fifth-century B.C.E. Greek dramatist, Browning's favorite.

The grand Perhaps![1] We look on helplessly.   190
There the old misgivings, crooked questions are—
This good God,—what he could do, if he would,
Would, if he could—then must have done long since:
If so, when, where and how? some way must be,—
Once feel about, and soon or late you hit   195
Some sense, in which it might be, after all.
Why not, "The Way, the Truth, the Life?"[2]

                           —That way
Over the mountain, which who stands upon
Is apt to doubt if it be meant for a road;
While, if he views it from the waste itself,   200
Up goes the line there, plain from base to brow,
Not vague, mistakeable! what's a break or two
Seen from the unbroken desert either side?
And then (to bring in fresh philosophy)
What if the breaks themselves should prove at last   205
The most consummate of contrivances
To train a man's eye, teach him what is faith?
And so we stumble at truth's very test!
All we have gained then by our unbelief
Is a life of doubt diversifed by faith,   210
For one of faith diversifed by doubt:
We called the chess-board white,—we call it black.

    "Well," you rejoin, "the end's no worse, at least;
We've reason for both colours on the board:
Why not confess then, where I drop the faith   215
And you the doubt, that I'm as right as you?"

    Because, friend, in the next place, this being so,
And both things even,—faith and unbelief
Left to a man's choice,—we'll proceed a step,
Returning to our image, which I like.   220

    A man's choice, yes—but a cabin-passenger's—
The man made for the special life o' the world—
Do you forget him? I remember though!
Consult our ship's conditions and you find
One and but one choice suitable to all;   225
The choice, that you unluckily prefer,
Turning things topsy-turvy—they or it
Going to the ground.[3] Belief or unbelief
Bears upon life, determines its whole course,
Begins at its beginning. See the world   230
Such as it is,—you made it not, nor I;

---

1. Deathbed saying ascribed to Rabelais: *Je vais quérir un grand Peut-Être* ("I go to seek a grand Perhaps").
2. John 14:6 (Christ's self-definition).
3. To defeat.

I mean to take it as it is,—and you,
Not so you'll take it,—though you get nought else.
I know the special kind of life I like,
What suits the most my idiosyncrasy,   235
Brings out the best of me and bears me fruit
In power, peace, pleasantness and length of days.[4]
I find that positive belief does this
For me, and unbelief, no whit of this.
—For you, it does, however?—that, we'll try!   240
'T is clear, I cannot lead my life, at least,
Induce the world to let me peaceably,
Without declaring at the outset, "Friends,
I absolutely and peremptorily
Believe!"—I say, faith is my waking life: 245
One sleeps, indeed, and dreams at intervals,
We know, but waking's the main point with us
And my provision's for life's waking part.
Accordingly, I use heart, head and hand
All day, I build, scheme, study, and make friends;   250
And when night overtakes me; down I lie,
Sleep, dream a little, and get done with it,
The sooner the better, to begin afresh.
What's midnight doubt before the dayspring's faith?
You, the philosopher, that disbelieve,   255
That recognize the night, give dreams their weight—
To be consistent you should keep your bed,
Abstain from healthy acts that prove you man,
For fear you drowse perhaps at unawares!
And certainly at night you'll sleep and dream,   260
Live through the day and bustle as you please.
And so you live to sleep as I to wake,
To unbelieve as I to still believe?
Well, and the common sense o' the world calls you
Bed-ridden,—and its good things come to me.   265
Its estimation, which is half the fight,
That's the first-cabin[5] comfort I secure:
The next . . . but you perceive with half an eye!
Come, come, it's best believing, if we may;
You can't but own that!

                                   Next, concede again,   270
If once we choose belief, on all accounts
We can't be too decisive in our faith,[6]
Conclusive and exclusive in its terms,
To suit the world which gives us the good things.
In every man's career are certain points   275

---

4. Cf. Proverbs 3:16 [on wisdom]: "Length of days is in her right hand; and in her left hand riches and honour."
5. First class.
6. I.e., we dare not appear indecisive or indifferent. Cf. line 276. (The adverb "too" applies to "conclusive" and "exclusive" in the next line as well.)

Whereon he dares not be indifferent;
The world detects him clearly, if he dare,
As baffled at the game, and losing life.
He may care little or he may care much
For riches, honour, pleasure, work, repose,   280
Since various theories of life and life's
Success are extant which might easily
Comport with either estimate of these;
And whoso chooses wealth or poverty,
Labour or quiet, is not judged a fool   285
Because his fellow would choose otherwise:
We let him choose upon his own account
So long as he's consistent with his choice.
But certain points, left wholly to himself,
When once a man has arbitrated on,   290
We say he must succeed there or go hang.
Thus, he should wed the woman he loves most
Or needs most, whatsoe'er the love or need—
For he can't wed twice.[7] Then, he must avouch,
Or follow, at the least, sufficiently,   295
The form of faith his conscience holds the best,
Whate'er the process of conviction was:
For nothing can compensate his mistake
On such a point, the man himself being judge:
He cannot wed twice, nor twice lose his soul.   300

   Well now, there's one great form of Christian faith
I happened to be born in—which to teach
Was given me as I grew up, on all hands,
As best and readiest means of living by;
The same on examination being proved   305
The most pronounced moreover, fixed, precise
And absolute form of faith in the whole world—
Accordingly, most potent of all forms
For working on the world. Observe, my friend!
Such as you know me, I am free to say,   310
In these hard latter days which hamper one,
Myself—by no immoderate exercise
Of intellect and learning, but the tact
To let external forces work for me,
—Bid the street's stones be bread and they are bread;[8]   315
Bid Peter's creed, or rather, Hildebrand's,[9]
Exalt me o'er my fellows in the world
And make my life an ease and joy and pride;
It does so,—which for me's a great point gained,
Who have a soul and body that exact   320

---

7. The Catholic church does not recognize divorce.
8. Ironic echo of Matthew 4:3–4. The devil tempts Jesus, saying, "If thou be the Son of God,
   command that these stones be made bread."
9. While the creed of Peter is the absolute authority of Christ (Acts 2:36), that of Hildebrand
   (Pope Gregory VII, 1073–85) was the ascendancy of the Pope over monarchs.

A comfortable care in many ways.
There's power in me and will to dominate
Which I must exercise, they hurt me else:
In many ways I need mankind's respect,
Obedience, and the love that's born of fear: 325
While at the same time, there's a taste I have,
A toy of soul, a titillating thing,
Refuses to digest these dainties crude.
The naked life is gross till clothed upon:
I must take what men offer, with a grace   330
As though I would not, could I help it, take!
An uniform I wear though over-rich—
Something imposed on me, no choice of mine;
No fancy-dress worn for pure fancy's sake
And despicable therefore! now folk kneel   335
And kiss my hand—of course the Church's hand.
Thus I am made, thus life is best for me,
And thus that it should be I have procured;
And thus it could not be another way,
I venture to imagine.

               You'll reply,   340
So far my choice, no doubt, is a success;
But were I made of better elements,
With nobler instincts, purer tastes, like you,
I hardly would account the thing success
Though it did all for me I say.

                  But, friend,   345
We speak of what is; not of what might be,
And how 't were better if 't were otherwise.
I am the man you see here plain enough:
Grant I'm a beast, why, beasts must lead beasts' lives!
Suppose I own at once to tail and claws;   350
The tailless man exceeds me: but being tailed
I'll lash out lion fashion, and leave apes
To dock their stump[1] and dress their haunches up.
My business is not to remake myself,
But make the absolute best of what God made.   355
Or—our first simile—though you prove me doomed
To a viler berth still, to the steerage-hole,
The sheep-pen or the pig-stye, I should strive
To make what use of each were possible;
And as this cabin gets upholstery,   360
That hutch should rustle with sufficient straw.

   But, friend, I don't acknowledge quite so fast
I fail of all your manhood's lofty tastes
Enumerated so complacently,

---

1. Cut their tails short.

On the mere ground that you forsooth can find   365
In this particular life I choose to lead
No fit provision for them. Can you not?
Say you, my fault is I address myself
To grosser estimators than should judge?
And that's no way of holding up the soul,   370
Which, nobler, needs men's praise perhaps, yet knows
One wise man's verdict outweighs all the fools'—
Would like the two, but, forced to choose, takes that.
I pine among my million imbeciles
(You think) aware some dozen men of sense   375
Eye me and know me, whether I believe
In the last winking Virgin,[2] as I vow,
And am a fool, or disbelieve in her
And am a knave,—approve in neither case,
Withhold their voices though I look their way: 380
Like Verdi[3] when, at his worst opera's end
(The thing they gave at Florence,—what's its name?)
While the mad houseful's plaudits near out-bang
His orchestra of salt-box, tongs and bones,[4]
He looks through all the roaring and the wreaths   385
Where sits Rossini[5] patient in his stall.

     Nay, friend, I meet you with an answer here—
That even your prime men who appraise their kind
Are men still, catch a wheel within a wheel,[6]
See more in a truth than the truth's simple self,   390
Confuse themselves. You see lads walk the street
Sixty the minute; what's to note in that?
You see one lad o'erstride a chimney-stack;
Him you must watch—he's sure to fall, yet stands!
Our interest's on the dangerous edge of things.   395
The honest thief, the tender murderer,
The superstitious atheist, demirep[7]
That loves and saves her soul in new French books—
We watch while these in equilibrium keep
The giddy line midway: one step aside,   400
They're classed and done with. I, then, keep the line
Before your sages,—just the men to shrink
From the gross weights, coarse scales and labels broad
You offer their refinement. Fool or knave?
Why needs a bishop be a fool or knave   405

2. In *Present Position of Catholics* Newman had affirmed his belief in two miracles: "the motion of the eyes of the pictures of the Madonna in the Roman States," and the "liquefaction of the blood of St. Januarius at Naples." (For the latter miracle see lines 726–30.)
3. Giuseppe Verdi (1813–1901), leading Italian operatic composer of the time. The "worst opera" may be the early work *Macbeth*, first performed in Florence in 1847.
4. Crude percussion instruments.
5. Gioacchino Rossini (1792–1868), Italian operatic composer, who could have seen *Macbeth* since he moved to Florence in 1847.
6. I.e., they see the complexity of existence. The symbol is from Ezekiel 1:16 and 10:10.
7. Contraction of "demi-reputation," applied to immoral women.

When there's a thousand diamond weights[8] between?
So, I enlist them. Your picked twelve,[9] you'll find,
Profess themselves indignant, scandalized
At thus being held unable to explain
How a superior man who disbelieves   410
May not believe as well: that's Schelling's[1] way!
It's through my coming in the tail of time,
Nicking the minute with a happy tact.
Had I been born three hundred years ago
They'd say, "What's strange? Blougram of course believes;"   415
And, seventy years since, "disbelieves of course."
But now, "He may believe; and yet, and yet
How can he?" All eyes turn with interest.
Whereas, step off the line on either side—
You, for example, clever to a fault,   420
The rough and ready man who write apace,
Read somewhat seldomer, think perhaps even less—
You disbelieve! Who wonders and who cares?
Lord So-and-so—his coat bedropped with wax,[2]
All Peter's chains about his waist,[3] his back   425
Brave with the needlework of Noodledom[4]—
Believes! Again, who wonders and who cares?
But I, the man of sense and learning too,
The able to think yet act, the this, the that,
I, to believe at this late time of day!   430
Enough; you see, I need not fear contempt.

      —Except it's yours! Admire me as these may,
You don't. But whom at least do you admire?
Present your own prefection, your ideal,
Your pattern man for a minute—oh, make haste,   435
Is it Napoleon you would have us grow?
Concede the means; allow his head and hand,
(A large concession, clever as you are)
Good! In our common primal element
Of unbelief (we can't believe, you know—   440
We're still at that admission, recollect!)
Where do you find—apart from, towering o'er
The secondary temporary aims
Which satisfy the gross taste you despise—
Where do you find his star?—his crazy trust   445
God knows through what or in what? it's alive
And shines and leads him, and that's all we want.
Have we aught in our sober night shall point
Such ends as his were, and direct the means

8. Units of troy weight, a system for measuring precious metal and jewels.
9. Jury.
1. F. W. J. von Schelling (1775–1854), German idealist philosopher, whose continual modification of his theological views gave rise to the charge of inconsistency.
2. From devotional candles.
3. Herod bound Peter in prison with two chains (Acts 12:6).
4. Vestment (probably a chasuble) splendidly embroidered by pious fools.

Of working out our purpose straight as his,   450
Nor bring a moment's trouble on success
With after-care to justify the same?
—Be a Napoleon, and yet disbelieve—
Why, the man's mad, friend, take his light away![5]
What's the vague good o' the world, for which you dare   455
With comfort to yourself blow millions up?
We neither of us see it! we do see
The blown-up millions—spatter of their brains
And writhing of their bowels and so forth,
In that bewildering entanglement   460
Of horrible eventualities
Past calculation to the end of time!
Can I mistake for some clear word of God
(Which were my ample warrant for it all)
His puff of hazy instinct, idle talk,   465
"The State, that's I,"[6] quack-nonsense about crowns,
And (when one beats the man to his last hold)
A vague idea of setting things to rights,
Policing people efficaciously,
More to their profit, most of all to his own;   470
The whole to end that dismallest of ends
By an Austrian marriage, cant to us the Church,[7]
And resurrection of the old régime?[8]
Would I, who hope to live a dozen years,
Fight Austerlitz[9] for reasons such and such?   475
No: for, concede me but the merest chance
Doubt may be wrong—there's judgment, life to come!
With just that chance, I dare not. Doubt proves right?
This present life is all?—you offer me
Its dozen noisy years, without a chance   480
That wedding an archduchess, wearing lace,
And getting called by divers new-coined names,
Will drive off ugly thoughts and let me dine,
Sleep, read and chat in quiet as I like!
Therefore I will not.

                    Take another case;   485
Fit up the cabin yet another way.
What say you to the poets? shall we write
Hamlet, Othello—make the world our own,
Without a risk to run of either sort?

---

5. An old treatment for madness.
6. L'état, c'est moi. Attributed to Louis XIV, not to Napoleon I.
7. Napoleon I, having divorced the Empress Joséphine because she had given him no heir, married Hapsburg Archduchess Marie Louise in 1810. By "cant" in the same line Blougram means Napoleon's hypocritical dealings with the church. The Concordat (1801) allowed free exercise of Catholic worship, but made it subject to the police power of the state. Later (1809) he annexed the papal states and imprisoned the Pope.
8. Napoleon's new relation by marriage to Europe's oldest reigning dynasty symbolized to many critics a betrayal of the Revolution.
9. Town northeast of Vienna, where in 1805 Napoleon defeated the combined Russian and Austrian armies.

I can't!—to put the strongest reason first.   490
"But try," you urge, "the trying shall suffice;
The aim, if reached or not, makes great the life:
Try to be Shakespeare, leave the rest to fate!"
Spare my self-knowledge—there's no fooling me!
If I prefer remaining my poor self,   495
I say so not in self-dispraise but praise.
If I'm a Shakespeare, let the well alone;
Why should I try to be what now I am?
It I'm no Shakespeare, as too probable,—
His power and consciousness and self-delight   500
And all we want in common, shall I find—
Trying for ever? while on points of taste
Wherewith, to speak it humbly, he and I
Are dowered alike—I'll ask you, I or he,
Which in our two lives realizes most?   505
Much, he imagined—somewhat, I possess.
He had the imagination; stick to that!
Let him say, "In the face of my soul's works
Your world is worthless and I touch it not
Lest I should wrong them"—I'll withdraw my plea.   510
But does he say so? look upon his life!
Himself, who only can, gives judgment there.
He leaves his towers and gorgeous palaces[1]
To build the trimmest house in Stratford town;[2]
Saves money, spends it, owns the worth of things,   515
Giulio Romano's pictures, Dowland's[3] lute;
Enjoys a show, respects the puppets, too,
And none more, had he seen its entry once,
Than "Pandulph, of fair Milan cardinal."[4]
Why then should I who play that personage,   520
The very Pandulph Shakespeare's fancy made,
Be told that had the poet chanced to start
From where I stand now (some degree like mine
Being just the goal he ran his race to reach)
He would have run the whole race back, forsooth,   525
And left being Pandulph, to begin write plays?
Ah, the earth's best can be but the earth's best!
Did Shakespeare live, he could but sit at home
And get himself in dreams the Vatican,
Greek busts, Venetian paintings, Roman walls,   530
And English books, none equal to his own,
Which I read, bound in gold (he never did).

1. Emblems of art and unreality in Shakespeare's last play, *The Tempest* (IV.i.152).
2. In 1597 Shakespeare acquired New Place, one of the largest houses in Stratford, where he retired about 1610.
3. Romano: Italian painter (ca. 1499–1546), mentioned in Shakespeare's *The Winter's Tale* (V.ii.97). John Dowland: English lutenist and songwriter (ca. 1563–ca. 1626), praised in a sonnet by Richard Barnfield that was reprinted in an unauthorized anthology, *The Passionate Pilgrim* (1599), attributed—on its title page–to Shakespeare.
4. As "holy legate of the Pope," Cardinal Pandulph curses and excommunicates King John (Shakespeare, *King John*, III.i.173ff.).

—Terni's fall, Naples' bay and Gothard's top.[5]—
Eh, friend? I could not fancy one of these;
But, as I pour this claret, there they are: 535
I've gained them—crossed St. Gothard last July
With ten mules to the carriage and a bed
Slung inside; is my hap the worse for that?
We want the same things, Shakespeare and myself,
And what I want, I have: he, gifted more,   540
Could fancy he too had them when he liked,
But not so thoroughly that, if fate allowed,
He would not have them also in my sense.
We play one[6] game; I send the ball aloft
No less adroitly that of fifty strokes   545
Scarce five go o'er the wall so wide and high
Which sends them back to me: I wish and get.
He struck balls higher and with better skill,
But at a poor fence level with his head,
And hit—his Stratford house, a coat of arms,[7]   550
Successful dealings in his grain and wool,[8]—
While I receive heaven's incense in my nose
And style myself the cousin of Queen Bess.[9]
Ask him, if this life's all, who wins the game?

      Believe—and our whole argument breaks up.   555
Enthusiasm's the best thing, I repeat;
Only, we can't command it; fire and life
Are all, dead matter's nothing, we agree:
And be it a mad dream or God's very breath,
The fact's the same,—belief's fire, once in us,   560
Makes of all else mere stuff to show itself:
We penetrate our life with such a glow
As fire lends wood and iron—this turns steel,
That burns to ash—all's one, fire proves its power
For good or ill, since men call flare success.   565
But paint a fire, it will not therefore burn.
Light one in me, I'll find it food enough!
Why, to be Luther[1]—that's a life to lead,
Incomparably better than my own.
He comes, reclaims God's earth for God, he says,   570
Sets up God's rule again by simple means,
Re-opens a shut book,[2] and all is done.
He flared out in the flaring of mankind;[3]

---

5. The St. Gotthard pass in the Alps, linking Switzerland and Italy. Terni's fall: the famous wa-
terfall, Cascate delle Marmore, in central Italy.
6. The same.
7. In 1596 John Shakespeare, the poet's father, obtained a grant of arms; thereafter William
signed himself as "gentleman."
8. Shakespeare had purchased farmland at Stratford.
9. Since bishops comprise the aristocracy of the Roman Catholic church, Blougram is in effect
"cousin" to the English monarch, the constitutional head of the Anglican church.
1. Martin Luther (1483–1546), leader of the Reformation in Germany.
2. Luther translated the New Testament into the vernacular (1522).
3. Showed his light in an age of enlightenment.

Such Luther's luck was: how shall such be mine?
If he succeeded, nothing's left to do: 575
And if he did not altogether—well,
Strauss[4] is the next advance. All Strauss should be
I might be also. But to what result?
He looks upon no future: Luther did.
What can I gain on the denying side?   580
Ice makes no conflagration. State the facts,
Read the text right, emancipate the world—
The emancipated world enjoys itself
With scarce a thank-you: Blougram told it first
It could not owe a farthing,—not to him   585
More than Saint Paul! 't would press its pay, you think?
Then add there's still that plaguy hundredth chance
Strauss may be wrong. And so a risk is run—
For what gain? not for Luther's, who secured
A real heaven in his heart throughout his life,   590
Supposing death a little altered things.

    "Ay, but since really you lack faith," you cry,
"You run the same risk really on all sides,
In cool indifference as bold unbelief.
As well be Strauss as swing 'twixt Paul and him.   595
It's not worth having, such imperfect faith,
No more available to do faith's work
Than unbelief like mine. Whole faith, or none!"

    Softly, my friend! I must dispute that point.
Once own the use of faith, I'll find you faith.   600
We're back on Christian ground. You call for faith:
I show you doubt, to prove that faith exists.
The more of doubt, the stronger faith, I say,
If faith o'ercomes doubt. How I know it does?
By life and man's free will, God gave for that![5]   605
To mould life as we choose it, shows our choice:
That's our one act, the previous work's his own.
You criticize the soil? it reared this tree—
This broad life and whatever fruit it bears!
What matter though I doubt at every pore,   610
Head-doubts, heart-doubts, doubts at my fingers' ends,
Doubts in the trivial work of every day,
Doubts at the very bases of my soul
In the grand moments when she probes herself—
If finally I have a life to show,   615
The thing I did, brought out in evidence
Against the thing done to me underground

---

4. German scholar D. F. Strauss (1808–74), whose *Das Leben Jesu* was translated by George
Eliot into English (1846). Most influential of the "higher" (i.e., historical and interpretive)
biblical critics, Strauss concluded that the Gospels were myths rather than true historical
accounts.
5. Cf. the Thomistic doctrine that religious assent must be sufficiently free to be meritorious.

By hell and all its brood, for aught I know?
I say, whence sprang this? shows it faith or doubt?
All's doubt in me; where's break of faith in this?   620
It is the idea, the feeling and the love,
God means mankind should strive for and show forth
Whatever be the process to that end,—
And not historic knowledge, logic sound,
And methaphysical acumen, sure!   625
"What think ye of Christ,"[6] friend? when all's done and said,
Like you this Christianity or not?
It may be false, but will you wish it true?
Has it your vote to be so if it can?
Trust you an instinct silenced long ago   630
That will break silence and enjoin you love
What mortified philosophy is hoarse,
And all in vain, with bidding you despise?
If you desire faith—then you've faith enough:
What else seeks God—nay, what else seek ourselves?   635
You form a notion of me, we'll suppose,
On hearsay; it's a favourable one:
"But still" (you add), "there was no such good man,
Because of contradiction in the facts.
One proves, for instance, he was born in Rome,   640
This Blougram; yet throughout the tales of him
I see he figures as an Englishman."
Well, the two things are reconcileable.
But would I rather you discovered that,
Subjoining—"Still what matter though they be?   645
Blougram concerns me nought, born here or there."

     Pure faith indeed—you know not what you ask!
Naked belief in God the Omnipotent,
Omniscient, Omnipresent, sears too much
The sense of conscious creatures to be borne.   650
It were the seeing him, no flesh shall dare.
Some think, Creation's meant to show him forth:[7]
I say it's meant to hide him all it can,
And that's what all the blessed evil's for.
Its use in Time is to environ us,   655
Our breath, our drop of dew, with shield enough
Against that sight till we can bear its stress.
Under a vertical sun, the exposed brain
And lidless eye and disemprisoned heart
Less certainly would wither up at once   660
Than mind, confronted with the truth of him.
But time and earth case-harden us to live;
The feeblest sense is trusted most; the child

---

6. Jesus' question of the Pharisees in Matthew 22:42.
7. Blougram may have in mind the "natural theologians" of the eighteenth and early nine-
teenth centuries, who inferred from nature the providential design of a creative intelligence.

Feels God a moment, ichors o'er the place,[8]
Plays on and grows to be a man like us.   665
With me, faith means perpetual unbelief
Kept quiet like the snake 'neath Michael's foot
Who stands calm just because he feels it writhe.[9]
Or, if that's too ambitious,—here's my box[1]—
I need the excitation of a pinch   670
Threatening the torpor of the inside nose
Nigh on the imminent sneeze that never comes.
"Leave it in peace" advise the simple folk:
Make it aware of peace by itching-fits,
Say I—let doubt occasion still more faith!   675

    You'll say, once all believed, man, woman, child,
In that dear middle-age these noodles praise.[2]
How you'd exult if I could put you back
Six hundred years, blot out cosmogony,[3]
Geology, ethnology, what not,   680
(Greek endings, each the little passing-bell
That signifies some faith's about to die),[4]
And set you square with Genesis again,—
When such a traveller told you his last news,
He saw the ark a-top of Ararat[5]   685
But did not climb there since 't was getting dusk
And robber-bands infest the mountain's foot!
How should you feel, I ask, in such an age,
How act? As other people felt and did;
With soul more blank than this decanter's knob,   690
Believe—and yet lie, kill, rob, fornicate
Full in belief's face, like the beast you'd be!

    No, when the fight begins within himself,
A man's worth something. God stoops o'er his head,
Satan looks up between his feet—both tug—   695
He's left, himself, i' the middle: the soul wakes
And grows. Prolong that battle through his life!
Never leave growing till the life to come!
Here, we've got callous to the Virgin's winks[6]
That used to puzzle people wholesomely: 700

8. Ichor: a watery discharge that dries over a wound to protect it.
9. In religious art the archangel Michael is often depicted ready to slay the dragon (Satan)
   pinned beneath his foot.
1. Snuffbox.
2. At the time there was a wave of nostalgia for the Middle Ages. Blougram may have in mind
   Thomas Carlyle's *Past and Present* (1843), which in Book II praises the disciplined life of a
   medieval English monastery.
3. Scientific study of the creation of the universe. The authority of the Genesis account of the
   Creation in six days, and the concomitant belief that the earth's crust was about 6,000 years
   old, were severely shaken by the findings of geologists, who supported the theory that the
   processes of physical change took eons, not mere thousands of years.
4. Greek endings: the suffixes *gony* ("manner of coming into being") and *logy* ("science").
5. Mountain in Turkey, traditional resting place of Noah's ark (Genesis 8:4).
6. See note to line 377.

Men have outgrown the shame of being fools.
What are the laws of nature, not to bend
If the Church bid them?—brother Newman asks.[7]
Up with the Immaculate Conception,[8] then—
On the rack with faith!—is my advice.   705
Will not that hurry us upon our knees,
Knocking our breasts, "It can't be—yet it shall!
Who am I, the worm, to argue with my Pope?
Low things confound the high things!" and so forth.
That's better than acquitting God with grace   710
As some folk do. He's tried—no case is proved,
Philosophy is lenient—he may go!

    You'll say, the old system's not so obsolete
But men believe still: ay, but who and where?
King Bomba's lazzaroni[9] foster yet   715
The sacred flame, so Antonelli[1] writes;
But even of these, what ragamuffin-saint
Believes God watches him continually,
As he believes in fire that it will burn,
Or rain that it will drench him? Break fire's law,   720
Sin against rain, although the penalty
Be just a singe or soaking? "No," he smiles;
"Those laws are laws that can enforce themselves."

    The sum of all is—yes, my doubt is great,
My faith's still greater, then my faith's enough.   725
I have read much, thought much, experienced much,
Yet would die rather than avow my fear
The Naples' liquefaction[2] may be false,
When set to happen by the palace-clock
According to the clouds or dinner-time.   730
I hear you recommend, I might at least
Eliminate, decrassify[3] my faith
Since I adopt it; keeping what I must
And leaving what I can—such points as this.
I won't—that is, I can't throw one away.   735
Supposing there's no truth in what I hold
About the need of trial to man's faith,
Still, when you bid me purify the same,

7. Newman maintained that the Divine Power occasionally circumvented the natural law to effect miracles.
8. In 1854 Pius IX promulgated the dogma that the soul of the Virgin Mary was from the moment of her conception preserved from original sin by divine grace. This doctrine is not to be confused with the Virgin Birth (Matthew 1:18–23).
9. Neapolitan beggars under the despotic rule of Ferdinand II, king of the Two Sicilies. He earned the nickname "Bomba" from his bombardment of the chief cities of Sicily to quell the 1848 revolt.
1. Powerful cardinal, secretary of state to Pius IX, 1852–70.
2. The dried blood of martyr St. Januarius, or St. Gennaro, patron saint of Naples (d. 305?) is said to liquefy twice a year while on public display in the Naples cathedral. Belief in such miracles is not required of Catholics, as the Bishop implies.
3. Purify.

To such a process I discern no end.
Clearing off one excrescence to see two,   740
There's ever a next in size, now grown as big,
That meets the knife: I cut and cut again!
First cut the Liquefaction, what comes last
But Fichte's clever cut at God himself?[4]
Experimentalize on sacred things!   745
I trust nor hand nor eye nor heart nor brain
To stop betimes: they all get drunk alike.
The first step, I am master not to take.

   You'd find the cutting-process to your taste
As much as leaving growths of lies unpruned,   750
Nor see more danger in it,—you retort.
Your taste's worth mine; but my taste proves more wise
When we consider that the steadfast hold
On the extreme end of the chain of faith
Gives all the advantage, makes the difference   755
With the rough purblind mass we seek to rule:
We are their lords, or they are free of us,
Just as we tighten or relax our hold.
So, other matters equal, we'll revert
To the first problem—which, if solved my way   760
And thrown into the balance, turns the scale—
How we may lead a comfortable life,
How suit our luggage to the cabin's size.

   Of course you are remarking all this time
How narrowly and grossly I view life,   765
Respect the creature-comforts, care to rule
The masses, and regard complacently
"The cabin," in our old phrase. Well, I do.
I act for, talk for, live for this world now,
As this world prizes action, life and talk: 770
No prejudice to what next world may prove,
Whose new laws and requirements, my best pledge
To observe then, is that I observe these now,
Shall do hereafter what I do meanwhile.
Let us concede (gratuitously though)   775
Next life relieves the soul of body, yields
Pure spiritual enjoyment: well, my friend,
Why lose this life i' the meantime, since its use
May be to make the next life more intense?

   Do you know, I have often had a dream   780
(Work it up in your next month's article)
Of man's poor spirit in its progress, still

4. German idealist philosopher J. G. Fichte (1762–1814), who as professor at Jena delivered a
paper "On the Basis of Our Belief in a Divine Providence" (1798), in which he asserted that
the "living and operative moral order is itself God. We need no other God, and we cannot
conceive any other."

Losing true life for ever and a day
Through ever trying to be and ever being—
In the evolution of successive spheres—   785
Before its actual sphere and place of life,
Halfway into the next, which having reached,
It shoots with corresponding foolery
Halfway into the next still, on and off!
As when a traveller, bound from North to South,   790
Scouts[5] fur in Russia: what's its use in France?
In France spurns flannel: where's its need in Spain?
In Spain drops cloth, too cumbrous for Algiers!
Linen goes next, and last the skin itself,
A superfluity at Timbuctoo.   795
When, through his journey, was the fool at ease?
I'm at ease now, friend; worldly in this world,
I take and like its way of life; I think
My brothers, who administer the means,
Live better for my comfort—that's good too;   800
And God, if he pronounce upon such life,
Approves my service, which is better still.
If he keep silence,—why, for you or me
Or that brute beast pulled-up[6] in to-day's "Times,"
What odds is 't, save to ourselves, what life we lead?   805

    You meet me at this issue: you declare,—
All special-pleading done with—truth is truth,
And justifies itself by undreamed ways.
You don't fear but it's better, if we doubt,
To say so, act up to our truth perceived   810
However feebly. Do then,—act away!
'T is there I'm on the watch for you. How one acts
Is, both of us agree, our chief concern:
And how you'll act is what I fain would see
If, like the candid person you appear,   815
You dare to make the most of your life's scheme
As I of mine, live up to its full law
Since there's no higher law that counterchecks.
Put natural religion[7] to the test
You've just demolished the revealed with—quick,   820
Down to the root of all that checks your will,
All prohibition to lie, kill and thieve,
Or even to be an atheistic priest!
Suppose a pricking to incontinence—
Philosophers deduce you chastity   825
Or shame, from just the fact that at the first
Whoso embraced a woman in the field,
Threw club down and forewent his brains beside,

5. Rejects scornfully.
6. Arrested.
7. Natural religion laid stress on the operation of reason as a means of apprehending universal
   truth and attaining virtue, holding supernatural revelation to be unnecessary.

So, stood a ready victim in the reach
Of any brother savage, club in hand;   830
Hence saw the use of going out of sight
In wood or cave to prosecute his loves:
I read this in a French book t' other day.
Does law so analysed coerce you much?
Oh, men spin clouds of fuzz where matters end,   835
But you who reach where the first thread begins,
You'll soon cut that!—which means you can, but won't,
Through certain instincts, blind, unreasoned-out,
You dare not set aside, you can't tell why,
But there they are, and so you let them rule.   840
Then, friend, you seem as much a slave as I,
A liar, conscious coward and hypocrite,
Without the good the slave expects to get,
In case he has a master after all!
You own your instincts? why, what else do I,   845
Who want, am made for, and must have a God
Ere I can be aught, do aught?—no mere name
Want, but the true thing with what proves its truth,
To wit, a relation from that thing to me,
Touching from head to foot—which touch I feel,   850
And with it take the rest, this life of ours!
I live my life here; yours you dare not live.

　　—Not as I state it, who (you please subjoin)
Disfigure such a life and call it names,
While, to your mind, remains another way   855
For simple men: knowledge and power have rights,
But ignorance and weakness have rights too.
There needs no crucial effort to find truth
If here or there or anywhere about:
We ought to turn each side, try hard and see,   860
And if we can't, be glad we've earned at least
The right, by one laborious proof the more,
To graze in peace earth's pleasant pasturage.
Men are not angels, neither are they brutes:
Something we may see, all we cannot see.   865
What need of lying? I say, I see all,
And swear to each detail the most minute
In what I think a Pan's[8] face—you, mere cloud:
I swear I hear him speak and see him wink,
For fear, if once I drop the emphasis,   870
Mankind may doubt there's any cloud at all.
You take the simple life—ready to see,
Willing to see (for no cloud's worth a face)—
And leaving quiet what no strength can move,
And which, who bids you move? who has the right?   875
I bid you; but you are God's sheep, not mine:

8. Licentious pastoral deity of ancient Greece.

"*Pastor est tui Dominus.*"[9] You find
In this the pleasant pasture of our life
Much you may eat without the least offence,
Much you don't eat because your maw[1] objects,   880
Much you would eat but that your fellow-flock
Open great eyes at you and even butt,
And thereupon you like your mates so well
You cannot please yourself, offending them;
Though when they seem exorbitantly sheep,   885
You weigh your pleasure with their butts and bleats
And strike the balance. Sometimes certain fears
Restrain you, real checks since you find them so;
Sometimes you please yourself and nothing checks:
And thus you graze through life with not one lie,   890
And like it best.

                    But do you, in truth's name?
If so, you beat—which means you are not I—
Who needs must make earth mine and feed my fill
Not simply unbutted at, unbickered with,
But motioned to the velvet of the sward[2]   895
By those obsequious wethers'[3] very selves.
Look at me, sir; my age is double yours:
At yours, I knew beforehand, so enjoyed,
What now I should be—as, permit the word,
I pretty well imagine your whole range   900
And stretch of tether twenty years to come.
We both have minds and bodies much alike:
In truth's name, don't you want my bishopric,
My daily bread, my influence and my state?
You're young. I'm old; you must be old one day;   905
Will you find then, as I do hour by hour,
Women their lovers kneel to, who cut curls
From your fat lap-dog's ear to grace a brooch—
Dukes, who petition just to kiss your ring—
With much beside you know or may conceive?   910
Suppose we die to-night: well, here am I,
Such were my gains, life bore this fruit to me,
While writing all the same my articles
On music, poetry, the fictile[4] vase
Found at Albano, chess, Anacreon's Greek.[5]   915
But you—the highest honour in your life,
The thing you'll crown yourself with, all your days,
Is—dining here and drinking this last glass
I pour you out in sign of amity

9. "The Lord is your shepherd" (paraphrase of Psalm 23:1).
1. Stomach.
2. Choicest part of the pasture.
3. Castrated male sheep.
4. Of molded clay.
5. Anacreon: much imitated Greek lyric poet of the sixth century B.C.E. whose subjects were
   love and wine. Albano Laziale: small town in central Italy, site of ancient Roman ruins.

Before we part for ever. Of your power   920
And social influence, worldly worth in short,
Judge what's my estimation by the fact,
I do not condescend to enjoin, beseech,
Hint secrecy on one of all these words!
You're shrewd and know that should you publish one   925
The world would brand the lie—my enemies first,
Who'd sneer—"the bishop's an arch-hypocrite
And knave perhaps, but not so frank a fool."
Whereas I should not dare for both my ears
Breathe one such syllable, smile one such smile,   930
Before the chaplain who reflects myself—
My shade's so much more potent than your flesh.
What's your reward, self-abnegating friend?
Stood you confessed of those exceptional
And privileged great natures that dwarf mine—   935
A zealot with a mad ideal in reach,
A poet just about to print his ode,
A statesman with a scheme to stop this war,[6]
An artist whose religion is his art—
I should have nothing to object: such men   940
Carry the fire, all things grow warm to them,
Their drugget's[7] worth my purple, they beat me.
But you,—you're just as little those as I—
You, Gigadibs, who, thirty years of age,
Write statedly for Blackwood's Magazine,[8]   945
Believe you see two points in Hamlet's soul
Unseized by the Germans[9] yet—which view you'll print—
Meantime the best you have to show being still
That lively lightsome article we took
Almost for the true Dickens,—what's its name?   950
"The Slum and Cellar, or Whitechapel[1] life
Limned after dark!" it made me laugh, I know,
And pleased a month, and brought you in ten pounds.
—Success I recognize and compliment,
And therefore give you, if you choose, three words   955
(The card and pencil-scratch is quite enough)
Which whether here, in Dublin or New York,
Will get you, prompt as at my eyebrow's wink,
Such terms as never you aspired to get
In all our own[2] reviews and some not ours.   960
Go write your lively sketches! be the first
"Blougram, or The Eccentric Confidence"—
Or better simply say, "The Outward-bound."

---

6. Crimean War (1854–56), in which Britain joined France to preserve the Ottoman Empire
   from Russian occupation.
7. Coarse woolen fabric, in contrast to the purple cloth symbolic of a bishop's office.
8. *Blackwood's Edinburgh Magazine*, a leading periodical founded 1817.
9. Noted for painstaking scholarship. The Bishop may have in mind Georg G. Gervinus, who
   wrote a four-volume study of Shakespeare (1849–52). (Turner, 346n.)
1. One of the most degraded London slum districts at the time.
2. Roman Catholic.

Why, men as soon would throw it in my teeth
As copy and quote the infamy chalked broad   965
About me on the church-door opposite.
You will not wait for that experience though,
I fancy, howsoever you decide,
To discontinue—not detesting, not
Defaming, but at least—despising me!   970

   Over his wine so smiled and talked his hour
Sylvester Blougram, styled *in partibus*
Episcopus, nec non[3]—(the deuce knows what
It's changed to by our novel hierarchy)
With Gigadibs the literary man,   975
Who played with spoons, explored his plate's design,
And ranged the olive-stones about its edge,
While the great bishop rolled him out a mind
Long crumpled, till creased consciousness lay smooth.

   For Blougram, he believed, say, half he spoke.   980
The other portion, as he shaped it thus
For argumentatory purposes,
He felt his foe was foolish to dispute.
Some arbitrary accidental thoughts
That crossed his mind, amusing because new,   985
He chose to represent as fixtures there,
Invariable convictions (such they seemed
Beside his interlocutor's loose cards
Flung daily down, and not the same way twice)
While certain hell-deep instincts, man's weak tongue   990
Is never bold to utter in their truth
Because styled hell-deep ('t is an old mistake
To place hell at the bottom of the earth)
He ignored these,—not having in readiness
Their nomenclature and philosophy: 995
He said true things, but called them by wrong names.
"On the whole," he thought, "I justify myself
On every point where cavillers like this
Oppugn my life: he tries one kind of fence,[4]
I close, he's worsted, that's enough for him.   1000
He's on the ground: if ground should break away
I take my stand on, there's a firmer yet
Beneath it, both of us may sink and reach.
His ground was over mine and broke the first:[5]
So, let him sit with me this many a year!"   1005

----

3. Latin phrase referring to Blougram's title as bishop in a non-Catholic country (England),
   where he could have no official territory.
4. Fencing tactic. Oppugn: assail.
5. Gigadibs' ground, being abstract and idealistic, is loftier than the Bishop's pragmatic ground.

He did not sit five minutes. Just a week
Sufficed his sudden healthy vehemence.
Something had struck him in the "Outward-bound"
Another way than Blougram's purpose was:
And having bought, not cabin-furniture   1010
But settler's-implements (enough for three)
And started for Australia—there, I hope,
By this time he has tested his first plough,
And studied his last chapter of St. John.[6]

Memorabilia[1]

I

Ah, did you once see Shelley plain,
    And did he stop and speak to you?
And did you speak to him again?
    How strange it seems and new!

II

But you were living before that,   5
    And also you are living after;
And the memory I started at—
    My starting moves your laughter.

III

I crossed a moor, with a name of its own
    And a certain use in the world no doubt,   10
Yet a hand's-breadth of it shines alone
    'Mid the blank miles round about:

IV

For there I picked up on the heather
    And there I put inside my breast
A moulted feather, an eagle-feather![2]   15
    Well, I forget the rest.

ca. 1851

6. An ambiguous line which could mean (1) that Gigadibs may have ended his own critical study of "St. John" (i.e., the Gospels); or (2) that he may have reviewed the Gospels, particularly the final chapter of St. John (21). In that chapter Jesus, unrecognized by the disciples, makes himself known by telling them where to cast for a great haul of fish. Then he thrice tests Peter's love for him, each time commanding, "Feed my sheep." Perhaps Gigadibs' study of this passage amounts to an implicit "comment" on the inadequacy of Blougram's conception of his office as bishop, or Lord's shepherd.
1. Written as early as 1851, when Browning completed his *Essay on Shelley* (DeVane, p. 244). According to Browning the encounter took place in a London bookseller's shop.
2. Perhaps alluding to the opening of Shelley's *Revolt of Islam*, where the poet observes "An Eagle and a Serpent wreathed in fight," and watches fall "the shattered plumes" (stanzas 8–11). The phrase also recalls Young's *Night Thoughts*: "Had he dropt / That Eagle Genius! O had he let fall / One feather as he flew" (2:602–604).

Andrea del Sarto

(CALLED "THE FAULTLESS PAINTER")

Contrasting markedly with the exuberant "Fra Lippo Lippi," this is Browning's classic study of moral and aesthetic failure. According to tradition, Browning wrote the poem and sent it to his friend John Kenyon when he was unable to comply with the latter's request for a copy of Andrea del Sarto's self-portrait with his wife Lucrezia, which hung in the Pitti Palace, Florence.

Browning's own portrait of the Florentine painter Andrea del Sarto (1486–1531) is indebted to the somewhat biased account by Andrea's pupil Giorgio Vasari in his *Lives of the Artists* (1550, 1568). After studying for some years with Piero di Cosimo, Andrea was employed by the brotherhood of the Servites (1509–14). So excellent were his frescoes of this period that he was called *Andrea senza errori* ("Andrew the unerring"); and in that medium—painting on fresh plaster—it was said that his only rival was Raphael. Contented with his superior technical skill, he did not aspire to be either an innovator or a leader in art. In 1516 he married a handsome widow, Lucrezia del Fede, who served as model for several fine Madonnas. Vasari describes her as overbearing, jealous, and faithless, exerting a baneful influence over Andrea that cost him the respect of his associates and compromised his career. In 1518, at the invitation of Francis I, Andrea went to the royal seat at Fontainebleau, near Paris, where for the only time in his life he was adequately paid. But Lucrezia wrote Andrea such bitter letters from Florence that he resolved to go there to settle his affairs. He left Francis promising to return in a few months with statues and pictures, for which the king had provided money. With it he purchased a house and "various pleasures," never returning to France. (Modern scholars have doubted that such a misappropriation really occurred.)

In linking Andrea's artistic failure to flaws in character, Browning follows Vasari, who found the master's work, though "entirely free of errors," wanting in "ardour and animation," owing to Andrea's "timidity of mind" and utter lack of "elevation" (Vasari, III. 180).

> But do not let us quarrel any more,
> No, my Lucrezia; bear with me for once:
> Sit down and all shall happen as you wish.
> You turn your face, but does it bring your heart?
> I'll work then for your friend's friend, never fear,   5
> Treat his own subject after his own way,
> Fix his own time, accept too his own price,
> And shut the money into this small hand
> When next it takes mine. Will it? tenderly?
> Oh, I'll content him,—but to-morrow, Love!   10
> I often am much wearier than you think,
> This evening more than usual, and it seems
> As if—forgive now—should you let me sit
> Here by the window with your hand in mine
> And look a half-hour forth on Fiesole,[1]   15
> Both of one mind, as married people use,

1. Small town on a hill three miles from Florence.

Quietly, quietly the evening through,
I might get up to-morrow to my work
Cheerful and fresh as ever. Let us try.
To-morrow, how you shall be glad for this!   20
Your soft hand is a woman of itself,
And mine the man's bared breast she curls inside.
Don't count the time lost, neither; you must serve
For each of the five pictures we require:
It saves a model. So! keep looking so—   25
My serpentining[2] beauty, rounds on rounds!
—How could you ever prick those perfect ears,
Even to put the pearl there! oh, so sweet—
My face, my moon, my everybody's moon,
Which everybody looks on and calls his,   30
And, I suppose, is looked on by in turn,
While she looks—no one's: very dear, no less.
You smile? why, there's my picture ready made,
There's what we painters call our harmony!
A common greyness silvers everything,—   35
All in a twilight, you and I alike
—You, at the point of your first pride in me
(That's gone you know),—but I, at every point;
My youth, my hope, my art, being all toned down
To yonder sober pleasant Fiesole.   40
There's the bell clinking from the chapel-top;
That length of convent-wall across the way
Holds the trees safer, huddled more inside;
The last monk leaves the garden; days decrease,
And autumn grows, autumn in everything.   45
Eh? the whole seems to fall into a shape
As if I saw alike my work and self
And all that I was born to be and do,
A twilight-piece. Love, we are in God's hand.
How strange now, looks the life he makes us lead;   50
So free we seem, so fettered fast we are!
I feel he laid the fetter: let it lie!
This chamber for example—turn your head—
All that's behind us! You don't understand
Nor care to understand about my art,   55
But you can hear at least when people speak:
And that cartoon,[3] the second from the door
—It is the thing, Love! so such things should be—
Behold Madonna!—I am bold to say.
I can do with my pencil what I know,   60
What I see, what at bottom of my heart
I wish for, if I ever wish so deep—
Do easily, too—when I say, perfectly,
I do not boast, perhaps: yourself are judge,

2. Sinuous.
3. Preparatory drawing for a picture.

Who listened to the Legate's[4] talk last week,   65
And just as much they used to say in France.
At any rate 't is easy, all of it!
No sketches first, no studies, that's long past:
I do what many dream of, all their lives,
—Dream? strive to do, and agonize to do,   70
And fail in doing. I could count twenty such
On twice your fingers, and not leave this town,
Who strive—you don't know how the others strive
To paint a little thing like that you smeared
Carelessly passing with your robes afloat,—   75
Yet do much less, so much less, Someone says,
(I know his name, no matter)—so much less!
Well, less is more, Lucrezia: I am judged.
There burns a truer light of God in them,
In their vexed beating stuffed and stopped-up brain,   80
Heart, or whate'er else, than goes on to prompt
This low-pulsed forthright craftsman's hand of mine.
Their works drop groundward, but themselves, I know,
Reach many a time a heaven that's shut to me,
Enter and take their place there sure enough,   85
Though they come back and cannot tell the world.
My works are nearer heaven, but I sit here.
The sudden blood of these men! at a word—
Praise them, it boils, or blame them, it boils too.
I, painting from myself and to myself,   90
Know what I do, am unmoved by men's blame
Or their praise either. Somebody remarks
Morello's[5] outline there is wrongly traced,
His[6] hue mistaken; what of that? or else,
Rightly traced and well ordered; what of that?   95
Speak as they please, what does the mountain care?
Ah, but a man's reach should exceed his grasp,[7]
Or what's a heaven for? All is silver-grey
Placid and perfect with my art: the worse!
I know both what I want and what might gain,   100
And yet how profitless to know, to sigh
"Had I been two, another and myself,
Our head would have o'erlooked the world!" No doubt.
Yonder's a work now, of that famous youth
The Urbinate[8] who died five years ago.   105

---

4. Pope's envoy.
5. Mountain in Apennines north of Florence.
6. Its.
7. Browning's ideas on art, notably the glorification of the Imperfect, may partly derive from the great art critic John Ruskin. Cf. this passage from *The Stones of Venice* (1851–53): ". . . no good work whatever can be perfect, and *the demand for perfection is always a sign of a misunderstanding of the ends of art.* This for two reasons, both based on everlasting laws. The first, that no great man ever stops working till he has reached his point of failure; that is to say, his mind is always far in advance of his powers of execution. . . . The second reason is, that imperfection is . . . the sign of life in a mortal body, that is to say, of a state of progress and change" (II, chapter 6).
8. Raphael (Raffaello Sanzio, 1483–1520), born at Urbino.

('T is copied, George Vasari sent it me.)
Well, I can fancy how he did it all,
Pouring his soul, with kings and popes to see,
Reaching, that heaven might so replenish him,
Above and through his art—for it gives way;   110
That arm is wrongly put—and there again—
A fault to pardon in the drawing's lines,
Its body, so to speak: its soul is right,
He means right—that, a child may understand.
Still, what an arm! and I could alter it: 115
But all the play, the insight and the stretch—
Out of me, out of me! And wherefore out?
Had you enjoined them on me, given me soul,
We might have risen to Rafael, I and you!
Nay, Love, you did give all I asked, I think—   120
More than I merit, yes, by many times.
But had you—oh, with the same perfect brow,
And perfect eyes, and more than perfect mouth,
And the low voice my soul hears, as a bird
The fowler's pipe, and follows to the snare—   125
Had you, with these the same, but brought a mind!
Some women do so. Had the mouth there urged
"God and the glory! never care for gain.
The present by the future, what is that?
Live for fame, side by side with Agnolo![9]   130
Rafael is waiting: up to God, all three!"
I might have done it for you. So it seems:
Perhaps not. All is as God over-rules.
Beside, incentives come from the soul's self;
The rest avail not. Why do I need you?   135
What wife had Rafael, or has Agnolo?[1]
In this world, who can do a thing, will not;
And who would do it, cannot, I perceive:
Yet the will's somewhat—somewhat, too, the power—
And thus we half-men struggle. At the end,   140
God, I conclude, compensates, punishes.
'T is safer for me, if the award be strict,
That I am something underrated here,
Poor this long while, despised, to speak the truth.
I dared not, do you know, leave home all day,   145
For fear of chancing on the Paris lords.[2]
The best is when they pass and look aside;
But they speak sometimes; I must bear it all.
Well may they speak! That Francis, that first time,
And that long festal year at Fontainebleau![3]   150
I surely then could sometimes leave the ground,

9. Michelangelo (Michelagniolo Buonarroti, 1475–1564).
1. Raphael finally married (with reluctance), but Michelangelo said, "I have a wife too many already, namely this art, which harries me incessantly, and my works are my children . . ." (Vasari).
2. French nobles who have heard of Andrea's embezzlement.
3. Site of King Francis' royal palace, southeast of Paris.

Put on the glory, Rafael's daily wear,
In that humane great monarch's golden look,—
One finger in his beard or twisted curl
Over his mouth's good mark that made the smile,   155
One arm about my shoulder, round my neck,
The jingle of his gold chain in my ear,
I painting proudly with his breath on me,
All his court round him, seeing with his eyes,
Such frank French eyes, and such a fire of souls   160
Profuse, my hand kept plying by those hearts,—
And, best of all, this, this, this face beyond,
This in the background, waiting on my work,
To crown the issue with a last reward!
A good time, was it not, my kingly days?   165
And had you not grown restless . . . but I know—
'T is done and past; 't was right, my instinct said;
Too live the life grew, golden and not grey,
And I'm the weak-eyed bat no sun should tempt
Out of the grange[4] whose four walls make his world.   170
How could it end in any other way?
You called me, and I came home to your heart.
The triumph was—to reach and stay there; since
I reached it ere the triumph, what is lost?
Let my hands frame your face in your hair's gold,   175
You beautiful Lucrezia that are mine!
"Rafael did this, Andrea painted that;
The Roman's[5] is the better when you pray,
But still the other's Virgin was his wife—"
Men will excuse me. I am glad to judge   180
Both pictures in your presence; clearer grows
My better fortune, I resolve to think.
For, do you know, Lucrezia, as God lives,
Said one day Agnolo, his very self,
To Rafael . . . I have known it all these years . . .   185
(When the young man was flaming out his thoughts
Upon a palace-wall for Rome to see,
Too lifted up in heart because of it)
"Friend, there's a certain sorry little scrub[6]
Goes up and down our Florence, none cares how,   190
Who, were he set to plan and execute
As you are, pricked on by your popes and kings,
Would bring the sweat into that brow of yours!"
To Rafael's!—And indeed the arm is wrong.
I hardly dare . . . yet, only you to see,   195
Give the chalk here—quick, thus the line should go!
Ay, but the soul! he's Rafael! rub it out!
Still, all I care for, if he spoke the truth,
(What he? why, who but Michel Agnolo?

4. Granary.
5. Raphael's. He went to Rome in 1508 to assist in decorating St. Peter's.
6. This anecdote is related by Vasari.

Do you forget already words like those?)   200
If really there was such a chance, so lost,—
Is, whether you're—not grateful—but more pleased.
Well, let me think so. And you smile indeed!
This hour has been an hour! Another smile?
If you would sit thus by me every night   205
I should work better, do you comprehend?
I mean that I should earn more, give you more.
See, it is settled dusk now; there's a star;
Morello's gone, the watch-lights show the wall,
The cue-owls speak the name we call them by.   210
Come from the window, love,—come in, at last,
Inside the melancholy little house
We built to be so gay with. God is just.
King Francis may forgive me: oft at nights
When I look up from painting, eyes tired out,   215
The walls become illumined, brick from brick
Distinct, instead of mortar, fierce bright gold,
That gold of his I did cement them with!
Let us but love each other. Must you go?
That Cousin[7] here again? he waits outside?   220
Must see you—you, and not with me? Those loans?
More gaming debts to pay? you smiled for that?
Well, let smiles buy me! have you more to spend?
While hand and eye and something of a heart
Are left me, work's my ware, and what's it worth?   225
I'll pay my fancy. Only let me sit
The grey remainder of the evening out,
Idle, you call it, and muse perfectly
How I could paint, were I but back in France,
One picture, just one more—the Virgin's face,   230
Not yours this time! I want you at my side
To hear them—that is, Michel Agnolo—
Judge all I do and tell you of its worth.
Will you? To-morrow, satisfy your friend.
I take the subjects for his corridor,   235
Finish the portrait out of hand—there, there,
And throw him in another thing or two
If he demurs; the whole should prove enough
To pay for this same Cousin's freak. Beside,
What's better and what's all I care about,   240
Get you the thirteen scudi[8] for the ruff!
Love, does that please you? Ah, but what does he,
The Cousin! what does he to please you more?

    I am grown peaceful as old age to-night.
I regret little, I would change still less.   245
Since there my past life lies, why alter it?

7. Renaissance euphemism for "lover."
8. Silver coin worth about one dollar.

The very wrong to Francis!—it is true
I took his coin, was tempted and complied,
And built this house and sinned, and all is said.
My father and my mother died of want.   250
Well, had I riches of my own? you see
How one gets rich! Let each one bear his lot.
They were born poor, lived poor, and poor they died:
And I have laboured somewhat in my time
And not been paid profusely. Some good son   255
Paint my two hundred pictures—let him try!
No doubt, there's something strikes a balance. Yes,
You loved me quite enough, it seems to-night.
This must suffice me here. What would one have?
In heaven, perhaps, new chances, one more chance—   260
Four great walls in the New Jerusalem,[9]
Meted on each side by the angel's reed,[1]
For Leonard,[2] Rafael, Agnolo and me
To cover—the three first without a wife,
While I have mine! So—still they overcome   265
Because there's still Lucrezia,—as I choose.

Again the Cousin's whistle! Go, my Love.

ca. 1853

In a Year

I

Never any more,
    While I live,
Need I hope to see his face
    As before.
Once his love grown chill,   5
    Mine may strive:
Bitterly we re-embrace,
    Single still.

II

Was it something said,
    Something done,   10
Vexed him? was it touch of hand,
    Turn of head?
Strange! that very way
    Love begun:
I as little understand   15
    Love's decay.

9. Heaven; see Revelation 21:10–21.
1. Measured with an angel's rod.
2. Leonardo da Vinci (1452–1519).

III

When I sewed or drew,
   I recall
How he looked as if I sung,
   —Sweetly too.   20
If I spoke a word,
   First of all
Up his check the colour sprung,
   Then he heard.

IV

Sitting by my side,   25
   At my feet,
So he breathed but air I breathed,
   Satisfied!
I, too, at love's brim
   Touched the sweet: 30
I would die if death bequeathed
   Sweet to him.

V

"Speak, I love thee best!"
   He exclaimed:
"Let thy love my own foretell!"   35
   I confessed:
"Clasp my heart on thine
   Now unblamed,
Since upon thy soul as well
   Hangeth mine!"   40

VI

Was it wrong to own,
   Being truth?
Why should all the giving prove
   His alone?
I had wealth and ease,   45
   Beauty, youth:
Since my lover gave me love,
   I gave these.

VII

That was all I meant,
   —To be just,   50
And the passion I had raised,
   To content.
Since he chose to change
   Gold for dust,

If I gave him what he praised   55
   Was it strange?

VIII

Would he loved me yet,
   On and on,
While I found some way undreamed
   —Paid my debt!   60
Gave more life and more,
   Till, all gone,
He should smile "She never seemed
   Mine before.

IX

"What, she felt the while,   65
   Must I think?
Love's so different with us men!"
   He should smile:
"Dying for my sake—
   White and pink!   70
Can't we touch these bubbles then
   But they break?"

X

Dear, the pang is brief,
   Do thy part,
Have thy pleasure! How perplexed   75
   Grows belief!
Well, this cold clay clod
   Was man's heart:
Crumble it, and what comes next?
   Is it God?   80

"De Gustibus—"[1]

I

Your ghost will walk, you lover of trees,
   (If our loves remain)
   In an English lane,
By a cornfield-side[2] a-flutter with poppies.
Hark, those two in the hazel coppice—   5
A boy and a girl, if the good fates please,
   Making love, say,—
   The happier they!

---

1. "There is no disputing about tastes" (Latin).
2. A field of grain, not Indian corn.

Draw yourself up from the light of the moon,
And let them pass, as they will too soon,   10
   With the bean-flowers' boon,
   And the blackbird's tune,
   And May, and June!

II

What I love best in all the world
Is a castle, precipice-encurled,   15
In a gash of the wind-grieved Apennine.
Or look for me, old fellow of mine,
(If I get my head from out the mouth
O' the grave, and loose my spirit's bands,
And come again to the land of lands)—   20
In a sea-side house to the farther South,
Where the baked cicala[3] dies of drouth,
And one sharp tree—'t is a cypress—stands,
By the many hundred years red-rusted,
Rough iron-spiked, ripe fruit-o'ercrusted,   25
My sentinel to guard the sands
To the water's edge. For, what expands
Before the house, but the great opaque
Blue breadth of sea without a break?
While, in the house, for ever crumbles   30
Some fragment of the frescoed walls,
From blisters where a scorpion sprawls.
A girl bare-footed brings, and tumbles
Down on the pavement, green-flesh melons,
And says there's news to-day—the king[4]   35
Was shot at, touched in the liver-wing,[5]
Goes with his Bourbon arm in a sling:
—She hopes they have not caught the felons.
Italy, my Italy!
Queen Mary's saying[6] serves for me—   40
   (When fortune's malice
   Lost her—Calais)—
Open my heart and you will see
Graved inside of it, "Italy."[7]
Such lovers old are I and she: 45
So it always was, so shall ever be.[8]

3. Cicada.
4. Ferdinand II, a Bourbon, tyrannical King of the Two Sicilies.
5. Right arm.
6. In 1558 Queen Mary lost Calais, England's last French possession. She said the name of Calais would be found written on her heart after her death.
7. These two lines were inscribed on a tablet which was mounted on a wall of the Palazzo Rezzonico in Venice, where Browning died.
8. In 1855 the final phrase read "so it still shall be!"; in the 1863 collection Browning changed the wording to reflect his having left Italy after his wife's death in 1861.

Women and Roses[1]

I

I dream of a red-rose tree.
And which of its roses three
Is the dearest rose to me?

II

Round and round, like a dance of snow
In a dazzling drift, as its guardians, go   5
Floating the women faded for ages,
Sculptured in stone, on the poet's pages.
Then follow women fresh and gay,
Living and loving and loved to-day.
Last, in the rear, flee the multitude of maidens,   10
Beauties yet unborn. And all, to one cadence,
They circle their rose on my rose tree.

III

Dear rose, thy term is reached,
Thy leaf hangs loose and bleached:
Bees pass it unimpeached.[2]   15

IV

Stay then, stoop, since I cannot climb,
You, great shapes of the antique time!
How shall I fix you, fire you, freeze you,
Break my heart at your feet to please you?
Oh, to possess and be possessed!   20
Hearts that beat 'neath each pallid breast!
Once but of love, the poesy, the passion,
Drink but once and die!—In vain, the same fashion,
They circle their rose on my rose tree.

V

Dear rose, thy joy's undimmed,   25
Thy cup is ruby-rimmed,
Thy cup's heart nectar-brimmed.

VI

Deep, as drops from a statue's plinth[3]
The bee sucked in by the hyacinth,
So will I bury me while burning,   30

---

1. Written January 2, 1852 (*BRP*, p. 293).
2. Unhindered.
3. Base.

Quench like him at a plunge my yearning,
Eyes in your eyes, lips on your lips!
Fold me fast where the cincture[4] slips,
Prison all my soul in eternities of pleasure,
Girdle me for once! But no—the old measure,   35
They circle their rose on my rose tree.

VII

Dear rose without a thorn,
Thy bud's the babe unborn:
First streak of a new morn.

VIII

Wings, lend wings for the cold, the clear!   400
What is far conquers what is near.
Roses will bloom nor want beholders,
Sprung from the dust where our flesh moulders.
What shall arrive with the cycle's change?
A novel grace and a beauty strange.   45
I will make an Eve, be the artist that began her,
Shaped her to his mind!—Alas! in like manner
They circle their rose on my rose tree.

1852

Holy-Cross Day[1]

ON WHICH THE JEWS WERE FORCED TO ATTEND AN ANNUAL
CHRISTIAN SERMON IN ROME

["Now was come about Holy-Cross Day, and now must my lord preach his
first sermon to the Jews: as it was of old cared for in the merciful bowels
of the Church, that, so to speak, a crumb at least from her conspicuous
table here in Rome should be, though but once yearly, cast to the famish-
ing dogs,[2] under-trampled and bespitten-upon beneath the feet of the
guests. And a moving sight in truth, this, of so many of the besotted blind
restif and ready-to-perish Hebrews! now maternally brought—nay (for He
saith, 'Compel them to come in'[3]) haled, as it were, by the head and hair,
and against their obstinate hearts, to partake of the heavenly grace. What

4. Girdle.
1. Holy-Cross Day (September 14), one of the principal feasts of the Roman Catholic church,
originated in Jerusalem to commemorate the dedication in 335 of the churches built by the
Emperor Constantine on the sites of the Crucifixion and Holy Sepulcher. The practice of
compelling Jews to attend conversionist sermons began in the papacy of Gregory XIII
(1572–85) and continued through 1846, a few years prior to Browning's poem; several times
a year Jews were summoned to services in the church of St. Angelo in Pescheria, near the
Roman ghetto. The diary entry preceding the poem is a fiction of Browning's.
2. Cf. Matthew 15:25–27.
3. Refers to the parable of the great supper from which the invited guests all excuse them-
selves. The angry master then sends his servants to "compel them [the poor, the handi-
capped] to come in" (Luke 14:23).

awakening, what striving with tears, what working of a yeasty conscience!
Nor was my lord wanting to himself on so apt an occasion; witness the
abundance of conversions which did incontinently reward him: though
not to my lord be altogether the glory."[4]—*Diary by the Bishops' Secretary*,
1600.]

What the Jews really said, on thus being driven to church, was rather to
this effect:—

I

Fee, faw, fum! bubble and squeak![5]
Blessedest Thursday's the fat of the week.
Rumble and tumble, sleek and rough,
Stinking and savoury, smug and gruff,
Take the church-road, for the bell's due chime   5
Gives us the summons—'t is sermon-time!

II

Boh, here's Barnabas! Job, that's you?
Up stumps Solomon—bustling too?
Shame, man! greedy beyond your years
To handsel the bishop's shaving-shears?[6]   10
Fair play's a jewel! Leave friends in the lurch?
Stand on a line ere you start for the church!

III

Higgledy piggledy, packed we lie,
Rats in a hamper, swine in a stye,
Wasps in a bottle, frogs in a sieve,   15
Worms in a carcase, fleas in a sleeve.
Hist! square shoulders, settle your thumbs
And buzz for the bishop—here he comes.

IV

Bow, wow, wow—a bone for the dog!
I liken his Grace to an acorned hog.[7]   20
What, a boy at his side, with the bloom of a lass,
To help and handle my lord's hour-glass!
Didst ever behold so lithe a chine?[8]
His cheek hath laps like a fresh-singed swine.

---

4. Paraphrase of Psalm 115:1: "Not unto us, O Lord, not unto us, but unto thy name give glory
. . ."
5. Bubble and squeak: cold boiled potatoes and greens fried together.
6. Handsel: to use for the first time. The shaving of a Jew was taken as a sign of conversion.
7. Hog fattened with acorns. The Jews reject pork as unclean.
8. Cut of meat including the backbone.

V

Aaron's asleep—shove hip to haunch,   25
Or somebody deal him a dig in the paunch!
Look at the purse with the tassel and knob,
And the gown with the angel and thingumbob!
What's he at, quotha?[9] reading his text!
Now you've his curtsey[1]—and what comes next.   30

VI

See to our converts—you doomed black dozen[2]—
No stealing away—nor cog nor cozen![3]
You five, that were thieves, deserve it fairly;
You seven, that were beggars, will live less sparely;
You took your turn and dipped in the hat,   35
Got fortune—and fortune gets you; mind that!

VII

Give your first groan—compunction's at work;
And soft! from a Jew you mount to a Turk.[4]
Lo, Micah,—the selfsame beard on chin
He was four times already converted in!   40
Here's a knife, clip quick—it's a sign of grace—
Or he ruins us all with his hanging-face.[5]

VIII

Whom now is the bishop a-leering at?
I know a point where his text falls pat.
I'll tell him to-morrow, a word just now   45
Went to my heart and made me vow
I meddle no more with the worst of trades[6]—
Let somebody else pay his serenades.

IX

Groan all together now, whee—hee—hee!
It's a-work, it's a-work, ah, woe is me!   50
It began, when a herd of us, picked and placed,
Were spurred through the Corso, stripped to the waist;[7]
Jew brutes, with sweat and blood well spent
To usher in worthily Christian Lent.

9. Forsooth.
1. Genuflection.
2. Jews appointed by lot to act as though converted.
3. Neither cheat nor deceive.
4. I.e., you will rise to the status of mere barbarian in Christian eyes.
5. Shamefaced look.
6. Usury, or money-lending, which the Jew will pretend to give up. Someone else will have to finance the hypocritical bishop's love-affairs (line 48).
7. Reference to the reported substitution of Jews for horses in the annual race (*Corsa del Berberi*) at Carnival time in Rome.

X

It grew, when the hangman entered our bounds,   55
Yelled, pricked us out to his church like hounds:
It got to a pitch, when the hand indeed
Which gutted my purse would throttle my creed:
And it overflows when, to even the odd,
Men I helped to their sins help me to their God.   60

XI

But now, while the scapegoats leave our flock,
And the rest sit silent and count the clock,
Since forced to muse the appointed time
On these precious facts and truths sublime,—
Let us fitly employ it, under our breath,   65
In saying Ben Ezra's Song of Death.[8]

XII

For Rabbi Ben Ezra, the night he died,
Called sons and sons' sons to his side,
And spoke, "This world has been harsh and strange;
Something is wrong: there needeth a change.   70
But what, or where? at the last or first?
In one point only we sinned, at worst.

XIII

"The Lord will have mercy on Jacob yet,
And again in his border see Israel set.
When Judah beholds Jerusalem,   75
The stranger-seed shall be joined to them:
To Jacob's House shall the Gentiles cleave.[9]
So the Prophet saith and his sons believe.

XIV

"Ay, the children of the chosen race
Shall carry and bring them to their place: 80
In the land of the Lord shall lead the same,
Bondsmen and handmaids. Who shall blame,
When the slaves enslave, the oppressed ones o'er
The oppressor triumph for evermore?

XV

"God spoke, and gave us the word to keep,   85
Bade never fold the hands nor sleep

8. Abraham ibn Ezra (1092–1167), Jewish Bible commentator and scholar who taught in Rome after 1140. The "Song of Death" appears to be Browning's invention.
9. Lines 72–77 paraphrase Isaiah 14:1. Browning adds a phrase from Jeremiah 3:18: "In those days the house of Judah shall walk with the house of Israel."

'Mid a faithless world,—at watch and ward,
Till Christ at the end relieve our guard.
By His servant Moses the watch was set:
Though near upon cock-crow, we keep it yet.   90

XVI

"Thou! if thou wast He, who at mid-watch came,
By the starlight, naming a dubious name![1]
And if, too heavy with sleep—too rash
With fear—O Thou, if that martyr-gash
Fell on Thee coming to take thine own,   95
And we gave the Cross, when we owed the Throne—

XVII

"Thou art the Judge. We are bruised thus.
But, the Judgment over, join sides with us!
Thine too is the cause! and not more thine
Than ours, is the work of these dogs and swine,   100
Whose life laughs through and spits at their creed!
Who maintain Thee in word, and defy Thee in deed!

XVIII

"We withstood Christ then? Be mindful how
At least we withstand Barabbas[2] now!
Was our outrage sore? But the worst we spared,   105
To have called these—Christians, had we dared!
Let defiance to them pay mistrust of Thee,
And Rome make amends for Calvary!

XIX

"By the torture, prolonged from age to age,
By the infamy, Israel's heritage,   110
By the Ghetto's[3] plague, by the garb's disgrace,
By the badge of shame, by the felon's place,
By the branding-tool, the bloody whip,
And the summons to Christian fellowship,—

XX

"We boast our proof that at least the Jew   115
Would wrest Christ's name from the Devil's crew.
Thy face took never so deep a shade
But we fought them in it, God our aid!

1. Jesus, whom the Jews do not regard as their Messiah.
2. According to the New Testament, at the demand of the Jews Pilate freed the murderer
   Barabbas and crucified Jesus.
3. Jewish quarter, formally established in 1555 in Rome by papal bull. The ghetto walls were
   not removed until 1870, at which time Roman Jews were accorded civil rights.

A trophy to bear, as we march, thy band,
South, East, and on to the Pleasant Land!"[4]

120

> [*Pope Gregory XVI. abolished this bad business*
> *of the Sermon.*—R. B.][5]

ca. 1854

The Guardian-Angel[1]

A PICTURE AT FANO

I

Dear and great Angel, wouldst thou only leave
    That child, when thou hast done with him, for me!
Let me sit all the day here, that when eve
    Shall find performed thy special ministry,
And time come for departure, thou, suspending   5
Thy flight, mayst see another child for tending,
    Another still, to quiet and retrieve.

II

Then I shall feel thee step one step, no more,
    From where thou standest now, to where I gaze,
—And suddenly my head is covered o'er   10
    With those wings, white above the child who prays
Now on that tomb—and I shall feel thee guarding
Me, out of all the world; for me, discarding
    Yon heaven thy home, that waits and opes its door.

III

I would not look up thither past thy head   15
    Because the door opes, like that child, I know,
For I should have thy gracious face instead,
    Thou bird of God! And wilt thou bend me low
Like him, and lay, like his, my hands together,
And lift them up to pray, and gently tether   20
    Me, as thy lamb there, with thy garment's spread?

---

4. As Barbara Melchiori has shown, Browning adapts a passage from Jeremiah (3:17–19) in support of his final vision of unification of Christians and Jews. ". . . and all the nations shall be gathered unto it, to the name of the Lord, to Jerusalem. . . . and they [men of Judah and Israel] shall come together out of the land of the north to the land that I have given for an inheritance unto your fathers." The phrase "a pleasant land" occurs in verse 19.
5. The "bad business" ceased after 1846.
1. One of the very few poems Browning wrote during the first three years of marriage, and one of his rare autobiographical utterances. Probably composed in Ancona, Italy, in late July 1848. At Fano, near Ancona on the Adriatic, the Brownings had been admiring *L'Angelo Custode*, by the Italian painter Giovanni Francesco Barbieri (1591–1666), called Guercino ("the squint-eyed").

IV

If this was ever granted, I would rest
  My head beneath thine, while thy healing hands
Close-covered both my eyes beside thy breast,
  Pressing the brain, which too much thought expands,   25
Back to its proper size again, and smoothing
Distortion down till every nerve had soothing,
  And all lay quiet, happy and suppressed.

V

How soon all worldly wrong would be repaired!
  I think how I should view the earth and skies   30
And sea, when once again my brow was bared
  After thy healing, with such different eyes.
O world, as God has made it! All is beauty:
And knowing this, is love, and love is duty.
  What further may be sought for or declared?   35

VI

Guercino drew this angel I saw teach
  (Alfred,[2] dear friend!)—that little child to pray,
Holding the little hands up, each to each
  Pressed gently,—with his own head turned away
Over the earth where so much lay before him   40
Of work to do, though heaven was opening o'er him,
  And he was left at Fano by the beach.

VII

We were at Fano, and three times we went
  To sit and see him in his chapel there,
And drink his beauty to our soul's content   45
  —My angel[3] with me too: and since I care
For dear Guercino's fame (to which in power
And glory comes this picture for a dower,
  Fraught with a pathos so magnificent)—

VIII

And since he did not work thus earnestly   50
  At all times, and has else endured some wrong[4]—
I took one thought his picture struck from me,
  And spread it out, translating it to song.
My love is here. Where are you, dear old friend?

2. Alfred Domett (1811–87), a confidant and fellow poet, whose emigration to New Zealand is
   the subject of Browning's "Waring" (1842).
3. Browning's wife, Elizabeth.
4. Probably alludes to adverse criticism of Guercino's angels by the Brownings' friend, art critic
   Anna Jameson (*Sacred and Legendary Art* [1848] I: 82).

How rolls the Wairoa[5] at your world's far end?   55
This is Ancona, yonder is the sea.

ca. 1848

Cleon[1]

"As certain also of your own poets have said"—

Cleon the poet (from the sprinkled isles,[2]
Lily on lily, that o'erlace the sea,
And laugh their pride when the light wave lisps "Greece")—
To Protus in his Tyranny:[3] much health!

    They give thy letter to me, even now: 5
I read and seem as if I heard thee speak.
The master of thy galley still unlades
Gift after gift; they block my court at last
And pile themselves along its portico
Royal with sunset,[4] like a thought of thee: 10
And one white she-slave from the group dispersed
Of black and white slaves (like the chequer-work
Pavement, at once my nation's work and gift,
Now covered with this settle-down of doves),
One lyric[5] woman, in her crocus vest   15
Woven of sea-wools,[6] with her two white hands
Commends to me the strainer and the cup
Thy lip hath bettered ere it blesses mine.

    Well-counselled, king, in thy munificence!
For so shall men remark, in such an act   20
Of love for him whose song gives life its joy,
Thy recognition of the use of life;
Nor call thy spirit barely adequate
To help on life in straight ways, broad enough
For vulgar souls, by ruling and the rest.—   25
Thou, in the daily building of thy tower,—
Whether in fierce and sudden spasms of toil,

---

5. River in New Zealand.
1. This epistolary monologue is a formal and thematic companion to "An Epistle . . . of Karshish." The imaginary Cleon is a Greek of the late Hellenistic Age, and a contemporary of the Apostle Paul, whose European mission–including a period in Athens–commenced about C.E. 50. "Cleon" is regarded by some as Browning's reply to Matthew Arnold's *Empedocles on Etna* (1852), in which the hero, a pagan philosopher in deep despair, takes his life after painful meditation upon the human condition. The epigraph to the present poem is from Acts 17: 28: "For in him [God] we live, and move, and have our being; as certain also of your own poets have said. For we are also his offspring."
2. The Sporades, scattered islands off the Greek coast near Crete.
3. *Tyranny* in Greek means absolute power, without necessarily implying oppression. The name "Protus" means "first."
4. Crimson and purple were royal colors.
5. One who plays the lyre and sings.
6. Wools dyed with sea-purple.

Or through dim lulls of unapparent growth,
Or when the general work 'mid good acclaim
Climbed with the eye to cheer the architect,—   30
Didst ne'er engage in work for mere work's sake—
Hadst ever in thy heart the luring hope
Of some eventual rest a-top of it,
Whence, all the tumult of the building hushed,
Thou first of men mightst look out to the East: 35
The vulgar saw thy tower, thou sawest the sun.
For this, I promise on thy festival
To pour libation, looking o'er the sea,
Making this slave narrate thy fortunes, speak
Thy great words, and describe thy royal face—   40
Wishing thee wholly where Zeus lives the most,
Within the eventual element of calm.

    Thy letter's first requirement[7] meets me here.
It is as thou hast heard: in one short life
I, Cleon, have effected all those things   45
Thou wonderingly dost enumerate.
That epos[8] on thy hundred plates of gold
Is mine,—and also mine the little chant
So sure to rise from every fishing-bark
When, lights at prow, the seamen haul their net.   50
The image of the sun-god on the phare,[9]
Men turn from the sun's self to see, is mine;
The Pœcile,[1] o'er-storied its whole length,
As thou didst hear, with painting, is mine too.
I know the true proportions of a man   55
And woman also, not observed before;
And I have written three books on the soul,
Proving absurd all written hitherto,
And putting us to ignorance again.
For music,—why, I have combined the moods,[2]   60
Inventing one. In brief, all arts are mine;
Thus much the people know and recognize,
Throughout our seventeen islands. Marvel not.
We of these latter days, with greater mind
Than our forerunners, since more composite,   65
Look not so great, beside their simple way,
To a judge who only sees one way at once,
One mind-point and no other at a time,—
Compares the small part of a man of us
With some whole man of the heroic age,   70
Great in his way—not ours, nor meant for ours.

7. Inquiry. The first three inquiries are carefully answered; the fourth is dismissed in a post-
script to the letter (337ff.).
8. Heroic poem, epic.
9. Lighthouse.
1. Portico decorated with battle scenes by great artists.
2. Or modes, ancient Greek musical scales differing in the arrangement of tones and semi-
tones.

And ours is greater, had we skill to know:
For, what we call this life of men on earth,
This sequence of the soul's achievements here
Being, as I find much reason to conceive,   75
Intended to be viewed eventually
As a great whole, not analyzed to parts,
But each part having reference to all,—
How shall a certain part, pronounced complete,
Endure effacement by another part?   80
Was the thing done?—then, what's to do again?
See, in the chequered pavement opposite,
Suppose the artist made a perfect rhomb,[3]
And next a lozenge, then a trapezoid[4]—
He did not overlay them, superimpose   85
The new upon the old and blot it out,
But laid them on a level in his work,
Making at last a picture; there it lies.
So, first the perfect separate forms were made,
The portions of mankind; and after, so,   90
Occurred the combination of the same.
For where had been a progress, otherwise?
Mankind, made up of all the single men,—
In such a synthesis the labour ends.
Now mark me! those divine men of old time   95
Have reached, thou sayest well, each at one point
The outside verge that rounds[5] our faculty;
And where they reached, who can do more than reach?
It takes but little water just to touch
At some one point the inside of a sphere,   100
And, as we turn the sphere, touch all the rest
In due succession: but the finer air
Which not so palpably nor obviously,
Though no less universally, can touch
The whole circumference of that emptied sphere,   105
Fills it more fully than the water did;
Holds thrice the weight of water in itself
Resolved into a subtler element.
And yet the vulgar call the sphere first full
Up to the visible height—and after, void;   110
Not knowing air's more hidden properties.
And thus our soul, misknown, cries out to Zeus
To vindicate his purpose in our life:
Why stay we on the earth unless to grow?
Long since, I imaged, wrote the fiction out,   115
That he or other god descended here
And, once for all, showed simultaneously
What, in its nature, never can be shown,
Piecemeal or in succession;—showed, I say,

---

3. Equilateral parallelogram.
4. Quadrilateral without parallel sides. "Lozenge": diamond-shaped figure.
5. Limits.

The worth both absolute and relative   120
Of all his children from the birth of time,
His instruments for all appointed work.[6]
I now go on to image,—might we hear
The judgment which should give the due to each,
Show where the labour lay and where the ease,   125
And prove Zeus' self, the latent everywhere!
This is a dream:—but no dream, let us hope,
That years and days, the summers and the springs,
Follow each other with unwaning powers.
The grapes which dye thy wine are richer far,   130
Through culture, than the wild wealth of the rock;
The suave plum than the savage-tasted drupe;[7]
The pastured honey-bee drops choicer sweet;
The flowers turn double, and the leaves turn flowers;
That young and tender crescent-moon, thy slave,   135
Sleeping above her robe as buoyed by clouds,
Refines upon the women of my youth.
What, and the soul alone deteriorates?
I have not chanted verse like Homer, no—
Nor swept string like Terpander,[8] no—nor carved   140
And painted men like Phidias[9] and his friend:
I am not great as they are, point by point.
But I have entered into sympathy
With these four, running these into one soul,
Who, separate, ignored each other's art.   145
Say, it is nothing that I know them all?
The wild flower was the larger; I have dashed
Rose-blood upon its petals, pricked its cup's
Honey with wine,[1] and driven its seed to fruit,
And show a better flower if not so large: 150
I stand myself. Refer this to the gods
Whose gift alone it is! which, shall I dare
(All pride apart) upon the absurd pretext
That such a gift by chance lay in my hand,
Discourse of lightly or depreciate?   155
It might have fallen to another's hand: what then?
I pass too surely: let at least truth stay!

    And next, of what thou followest on to ask.
This being with me as I declare, O king,
My works, in all these varicoloured kinds,   160
So done by me, accepted so by men—

---

6. In lines 115–27, Cleon's "fiction" of a divine revelation recalls the teaching of Auguste
Comte (1798–1857), who proposed the worship of Humanity and the veneration of such
benefactors of the human race as scientists, philosophers, painters, and poets.
7. Fruit with a pit; here, bitter wild plum.
8. Musician of Lesbos in the seventh century B.C.E. said to have devised the seven-stringed
lyre.
9. Athenian sculptor and painter of the fifth century B.C.E. His "friend" is the statesman Peri-
cles (ca. 495–429 B.C.E.), who employed Phidias to help decorate Athens.
1. Modified the sweetness with dry wine.

Thou askest, if (my soul thus in men's hearts)
I must not be accounted to attain
The very crown and proper end of life?
Inquiring thence how, now life closeth up,   165
I face death with success in my right hand:
Whether I fear death less than dost thyself
The fortunate of men? "For" (writest thou)
"Thou leavest much behind, while I leave nought.
Thy life stays in the poems men shall sing,   170
The pictures men shall study; while my life,
Complete and whole now in its power and joy,
Dies altogether with my brain and arm,
Is lost indeed; since, what survives myself?
The brazen statue to o'erlook my grave,   175
Set on the promontory which I named.
And that—some supple courtier of my heir
Shall use its robed and sceptred arm, perhaps,
To fix the rope to, which best drags it down.
I go then: triumph thou, who dost not go!"   180

    Nay, thou art worthy of hearing my whole mind.
Is this apparent, when thou turn'st to muse
Upon the scheme of earth and man in chief,
That admiration grows as knowledge grows?
That imperfection means perfection hid,   185
Reserved in part, to grace the after-time?
If, in the morning of philosophy,
Ere aught had been recorded, nay perceived,
Thou, with the light now in thee, couldst have looked
On all earth's tenantry, from worm to bird,   190
Ere man, her last, appeared upon the stage—
Thou wouldst have seen them perfect, and deduced
The perfectness of others yet unseen.
Conceding which,—had Zeus then questioned thee
"Shall I go on a step, improve on this,   195
Do more for visible creatures than is done?"
Thou wouldst have answered, "Ay, by making each
Grow conscious in himself—by that alone.
All's perfect else: the shell sucks fast the rock,
The fish strikes through the sea, the snake both swims   200
And slides, forth range the beasts, the birds take flight,
Till life's mechanics can no further go—
And all this joy in natural life is put
Like fire from off thy finger into each,
So exquisitely perfect is the same.   205
But 't is pure fire, and they mere matter are;
It has them, not they it: and so I choose
For man, thy last premeditated work
(If I might add a glory to the scheme)
That a third thing should stand apart from both,   210
A quality arise within his soul,

Which, intro-active, made to supervise
And feel the force it has, may view itself,
And so be happy." Man might live at first
The animal life: but is there nothing more?   215
In due time, let him critically learn
How he lives; and, the more he gets to know
Of his own life's adaptabilities,
The more joy-giving will his life become.
Thus man, who hath this quality, is best.   220

   But thou, king, hadst more reasonably said:
"Let progress end at once,—man make no step
Beyond the natural man, the better beast,
Using his senses, not the sense of sense."
In man there's failure, only since he left   225
The lower and inconscious forms of life.
We called it an advance, the rendering plain
Man's spirit might grow conscious of man's life,
And, by new lore so added to the old,
Take each step higher over the brute's head.   230
This grew the only life, the pleasure-house,
Watch-tower and treasure-fortress of the soul,[2]
Which whole surrounding flats of natural life
Seemed only fit to yield subsistence to;
A tower that crowns a country. But alas,   235
The soul now climbs it just to perish there!
For thence we have discovered ('t is no dream—
We know this, which we had not else perceived)
That there's a world of capability
For joy, spread round about us, meant for us,   240
Inviting us; and still the soul craves all,
And still the flesh replies, "Take no jot more
Than ere thou clombst the tower to look abroad!
Nay, so much less as that fatigue has brought
Deduction to it." We struggle, fain to enlarge   245
Our bounded physical recipiency,
Increase our power, supply fresh oil to life,
Repair the waste of age and sickness: no,
It skills not![3] life's inadequate to joy,
As the soul sees joy, tempting life to take.   250
They praise a fountain in my garden here
Wherein a Naiad[4] sends the water-bow
Thin from her tube; she smiles to see it rise.
What if I told her, it is just a thread
From that great river which the hills shut up,   255
And mock her with my leave to take the same?
The artificer has given her one small tube

---

2. Cf. Tennyson's "Palace of Art" (1832): "I built my soul a lordly pleasure-house" (line 1).
3. Is of no use.
4. Water nymph, here a statue in a fountain.

Past power to widen or exchange—what boots
To know she might spout oceans if she could?
She cannot lift beyond her first thin thread:　　260
And so a man can use but a man's joy
While he sees God's. Is it for Zeus to boast,
"See, man, how happy I live, and despair—
That I may be still happier—for thy use!"
If this were so, we could not thank our lord,　　265
As hearts beat on to doing; 't is not so—
Malice it is not. Is it carelessness?
Still, no. If care—where is the sign? I ask,
And get no answer, and agree in sum,
O king, with thy profound discouragement,　　270
Who seest the wider but to sigh the more.
Most progress is most failure: thou sayest well.

　　The last point now:—thou dost except a case—
Holding joy not impossible to one
With artist-gifts—to such a man as I　　275
Who leave behind me living works indeed;[5]
For, such a poem, such a painting lives.
What? dost thou verily trip upon a word,
Confound the accurate view of what joy is
(Caught somewhat clearer by my eyes than thine)　　280
With feeling joy? confound the knowing how
And showing how to live (my faculty)
With actually living?—Otherwise
Where is the artist's vantage o'er the king?
Because in my great epos I display　　285
How divers men young, strong, fair, wise, can act—
Is this as though I acted? if I paint,
Carve the young Phœbus,[6] am I therefore young?
Methinks I'm older that I bowed myself
The many years of pain that taught me art!　　290
Indeed, to know is something, and to prove
How all this beauty might be enjoyed, is more:
But, knowing nought, to enjoy is something too.
Yon rower, with the moulded muscles there,
Lowering the sail, is nearer it than I.　　295
I can write love-odes: thy fair slave's an ode.
I get to sing of love, when grown too grey
For being beloved: she turns to that young man,
The muscles all a-ripple on his back.
I know the joy of kingship: well, thou art king!　　300

　　"But," sayest thou—(and I marvel, I repeat,
To find thee trip on such a mere word) "what
Thou writest, paintest, stays; that does not die:

---

5. A concept of immortality current in the Victorian age, notably among "unbelievers" like George Eliot and J. S. Mill.
6. The sun god Apollo, represented in art as an ideally handsome youth.

Sappho[7] survives because we sing her songs,
And Æschylus,[8] because we read his plays!"   305
Why, if they live still, let them come and take
Thy slave in my despite, drink from thy cup,
Speak in my place. Thou diest while I survive?
Say rather that my fate is deadlier still,
In this, that every day my sense of joy   310
Grows more acute, my soul (intensified
By power and insight) more enlarged, more keen;
While every day my hairs fall more and more,
My hand shakes, and the heavy years increase—
The horror quickening still from year to year,   315
The consummation coming past escape
When I shall know most, and yet least enjoy—
When all my works wherein I prove my worth,
Being present still to mock me in men's mouths,
Alive still, in the praise of such as thou,   320
I, I the feeling, thinking, acting man,
The man who loved his life so over-much,
Sleep in my urn. It is so horrible,
I dare at times imagine to my need
Some future state revealed to us by Zeus,   325
Unlimited in capability
For joy, as this is in desire for joy,
—To seek which, the joy-hunger forces us:
That, stung by straitness of our life, made strait
On purpose to make prized the life at large—   330
Freed by the throbbing impulse we call death,
We burst there as the worm into the fly,[9]
Who, while a worm still, wants his wings. But no!
Zeus has not yet revealed it; and alas,
He must have done so, were it possible!   335

    Live long and happy, and in that thought die:
Glad for what was! Farewell. And for the rest,
I cannot tell thy messenger aright
Where to deliver what he bears of thine
To one called Paulus;[1] we have heard his fame   340
Indeed, if Christus be not one with him[2]—
I know not, nor am troubled much to know.
Thou canst not think a mere barbarian Jew
As Paulus proves to be, one circumcized,[3]
Hath access to a secret shut from us?   345
Thou wrongest our philosophy, O king,
In stooping to inquire of such an one,

---

7. Poet of Lesbos (born ca. 612 B.C.E.), much admired in antiquity. Only a few fragments of her
   work have survived.
8. Athenian tragic poet (525–456 B.C.E.).
9. Butterfly.
1. St. Paul.
2. I.e., the same person as Paul.
3. I.e., of the Jewish faith.

As if his answer could impose at all!
He writeth, doth he? well, and he may write.
Oh, the Jew findeth scholars! certain slaves   350
Who touched on this same isle, preached him and Christ;
And (as I gathered from a bystander)
Their doctrine could be held by no sane man.

ca. 1854

Popularity[1]

I

Stand still, true poet that you are!
    I know you; let me try and draw you.
Some night you'll fail us: when afar
    You rise, remember one man saw you,
Knew you, and named a star!   5

II

My star, God's glow-worm! Why extend
    That loving hand of his which leads you,
Yet locks you safe from end to end
    Of this dark world, unless he needs you,
Just saves your light to spend?   10

III

His clenched hand shall unclose at last,
    I know, and let out all the beauty:
My poet holds the future fast,
    Accepts the coming ages' duty,
Their present for this past.   15

IV

That day, the earth's feast-master's brow
    Shall clear, to God the chalice raising;
"Others give best at first, but thou
    Forever set'st our table praising,
Keep'st the good wine till now!"[2]   20

1. Browning's sympathy for the neglected literary genius of the poem may partly derive from his own frustrated quest for a wide audience. In 1855, the year this poem was published, Browning was entering middle age without having achieved true popularity in either drama or poetry after two decades of writing.
2. ". . . thou hast kept the good wine until now." Words of the "ruler of the feast" to the bridegroom after Jesus' miraculous conversion of the water into wine (John 2: 1–10).

V

Meantime, I'll draw you as you stand,
   With few or none to watch and wonder:
I'll say—a fisher, on the sand
   By Tyre the old,[3] with ocean-plunder,
A netful, brought to land.   25

VI

Who has not heard how Tyrian shells
   Enclosed the blue, that dye of dyes
Whereof one drop worked miracles,
   And coloured like Astarte's eyes[4]
Raw silk the merchant sells?   30

VII

And each bystander of them all
   Could criticize, and quote tradition
How depths of blue sublimed some pall[5]
   —To get which, pricked a king's ambition;
Worth sceptre, crown and ball.   35

VIII

Yet there's the dye, in that rough mesh,
   The sea has only just o'erwhispered!
Live whelks, each lip's beard dripping fresh,
   As if they still the water's lisp heard
Through foam the rock-weeds thresh.   40

IX

Enough to furnish Solomon
   Such hangings for his cedar-house,[6]
That, when gold-robed he took the throne
   In that abyss of blue, the Spouse
Might swear his presence shone   45

X

Most like the centre-spike of gold
   Which burns deep in the blue-bell's womb,
What time, with ardours manifold,
   The bee goes singing to her groom,
Drunken and overbold.   50

3. Great city of ancient Phoenicia (now Lebanon), trade center famed for its purple dye, emblematic of royalty.
4. Semitic goddess representing the female principle.
5. Beautified a robe.
6. 1 Kings 7: Solomon's house and "porch of judgment," built of cedar; the blue wall hangings are not mentioned. The "Spouse" is Pharaoh's daughter, whom he wed and lavishly housed.

XI

Mere conchs! not fit for warp or woof![7]
  Till cunning come to pound and squeeze
And clarify,—refine to proof[8]
  The liquor filtered by degrees,
While the world stands aloof.　　　　　　　　55

XII

And there's the extract, flasked and fine,
  And priced and saleable at last!
And Hobbs, Nobbs, Stokes and Nokes[9] combine
  To paint the future from the past,
Put blue into their line.　　　　　　　　60

XIII

Hobbs hints blue,—straight he turtle eats:
  Nobbs prints blue,—claret crowns his cup:
Nokes outdares Stokes in azure feats,—
  Both gorge. Who fished the murex[1] up?
What porridge[2] had John Keats?　　　　　　　　65

Two in the Campagna[1]

I

I wonder do you feel to-day
  As I have felt since, hand in hand,
We sat down on the grass, to stray
  In spirit better through the land,
This morn of Rome and May?　　　　　　　　5

II

For me, I touched a thought, I know,
  Has tantalized me many times,
(Like turns of thread the spiders throw
  Mocking across our path) for rhymes
To catch at and let go.　　　　　　　　10

---

7. Unrefined, not ready for use in textiles.
8. To standard quality.
9. Imitators or plagiarists who batten on the "true poet's" pioneering efforts.
1. Genus of mollusc yielding purple dye, referred to in stanza VI.
2. Poor fare, symbolic of the poverty of John Keats (1795–1821), another poet who was unpopular in his day.
1. Inspired by a May 1854 outing with Elizabeth Barrett Browning in the Campagna di Roma, the plain surrounding Rome and site of the ruins of ancient Latium.

III

Help me to hold it! First it left
    The yellowing fennel, run to seed
There, branching from the brickwork's cleft,
    Some old tomb's ruin: yonder weed
Took up the floating weft,[2]   15

IV

Where one small orange cup amassed
    Five beetles,—blind and green they grope
Among the honey-meal: and last,
    Everywhere on the grassy slope
I traced it. Hold it fast!   20

V

The champaign with its endless fleece
    Of feathery grasses everywhere!
Silence and passion, joy and peace,
    An everlasting wash of air—
Rome's ghost since her decease.   25

VI

Such life here, through such lengths of hours,
    Such miracles performed in play,
Such primal naked forms of flowers,
    Such letting nature have her way
While heaven looks from its towers!   30

VII

How say you? Let us, O my dove,
    Let us be unashamed of soul,
As earth lies bare to heaven above!
    How is it under our control
To love or not to love?   35

VIII

I would that you were all to me,
    You that are just so much, no more.
Nor yours nor mine, nor slave nor free!
    Where does the fault lie? What the core
O' the wound, since wound must be?   40

2. In weaving, threads crossing from side to side.

IX

I would I could adopt your will,
   See with your eyes, and set my heart
Beating by yours, and drink my fill
   At your soul's springs,—your part my part
In life, for good and ill.   45

X

No. I yearn upward, touch you close,
   Then stand away. I kiss your cheek,
Catch your soul's warmth,—I pluck the rose[3]
   And love it more than tongue can speak—
Then the good minute goes.   50

XI

Already how am I so far
   Out of that minute? Must I go
Still like the thistle-ball, no bar,
   Onward, whenever light winds blow,
Fixed by no friendly star?[4]   55

XII

Just when I seemed about to learn!
   Where is the thread now? Off again!
The old trick! Only I discern—
   Infinite passion, and the pain
Of finite hearts that yearn.   60

1854

A Grammarian's Funeral,

SHORTLY AFTER THE REVIVAL OF LEARNING IN EUROPE[1]

Let us begin and carry up this corpse,
   Singing together.
Leave we the common crofts, the vulgar thorpes[2]

---

3. Cf. Shakespeare's *Othello*, V.ii.13–15: "When I have pluck'd thy rose, / I cannot give it vital growth again, / It needs must wither." (This echo and the next are discussed by R. D. Altick [*PLL*, 3 (1967), 79].)
4. Cf. Shakespeare's Sonnet 116: "[Love] is an ever-fixèd mark / That looks on tempests and is never shaken; / It is the star to every wand'ring bark. . . ."
1. The poem is set in fourteenth-century Italy, where the Renaissance began, marked by a humanistic revival of Greek and Latin learning. Scholars like Browning's anonymous Grammarian, who devoted their lives to the mastery of classical languages, were instrumental in the recovery of ancient texts. Though these specialists were in a sense the pioneers of the Renaissance, they inevitably became the butt of satire, as in Erasmus' *The Praise of Folly* (1510).
   The Grammarian's eulogy is sung by a band of his former students, who are carrying the corpse to its burial place atop a mountain.
2. Fields and villages of the common folk.

Each in its tether[3]
Sleeping safe on the bosom of the plain,   5
        Cared-for till cock-crow:
Look out if yonder be not day again
        Rimming the rock-row!
That's the appropriate country; there, man's thought,
        Rarer, intenser,   10
Self-gathered for an outbreak, as it is ought,
        Chafes in the censer.[4]
Leave we the unlettered plain its herd and crop;
        Seek we sepulture[5]
On a tall mountain, cried to the top,   15
        Crowded with culture!
All the peaks soar, but one the rest excels;
        Clouds overcome it;
No! yonder sparkle is the citadel's
        Circling its summit.   20
Thither our path lies; wind we up the heights:
        Wait ye the warning?[6]
Our low life was the level's and the night's;
        He's for the morning.
Step to a tune, square chests, erect each head,   25
        'Ware[7] the beholders!
This is our master, famous calm and dead,
        Borne on our shoulders.

Sleep, crop and herd! sleep, darkling thorpe and croft,
        Safe from the weather!   30
He, whom we convoy to his grave aloft,
        Singing together,
He was a man born with thy face and throat,
        Lyric Apollo![8]
Long he lived nameless: how should spring take note   35
        Winter would follow?
'Till lo, the little touch, and youth was gone!
        Cramped and diminished,
Moaned he, "New measures, other feet anon!
        My dance is finished?"   40
No, that's the world's way: (keep the mountain-side,
        Make for the city!)
He knew the signal, and stepped on with pride
        Over men's pity;
Left play for work, and grappled with the world   45
        Bent on escaping:
"What's in the scroll," quoth he, "thou keepst furled?
        Show me their shaping,

3. Small radius.
4. Seethes in the incense burner.
5. Burial place.
6. Are you ready for the signal [to begin]?
7. Show your awareness of.
8. God of the sun, order, and song (the lyre), Apollo was represented as ideally handsome.

Theirs who most studied man, the bard and sage,—
    Give!"—So, he gowned him,[9]   50
Straight got by heart that book to its last page:
    Learned, we found him.
Yea, but we found him bald too, eyes like lead,
    Accents uncertain:
"Time to taste life," another would have said,   55
    "Up with the curtain!"
This man said rather, "Actual life comes next?
    Patience a moment!
Grant I have mastered learning's crabbed text,
    Still there's the comment.[1]   60
Let me know all! Prate not of the most or least,
    Painful or easy!
Even to the crumbs I'd fain eat up the feast,
    Ay, nor feel queasy."
Oh, such a life as he resolved to live,   65
    When he had learned it,
When he had gathered all books had to give!
    Sooner, he spurned it.
Image the whole, then execute the parts—
    Fancy the fabric[2]   70
Quite, ere you build, ere steel strike fire from quartz,
    Ere mortar dab brick!

(Here's the town-gate reached: there's the market-place
    Gaping before us.)
Yea, this in him was the peculiar grace   75
    (Hearten our chorus!)
That before living he'd learn how to live—
    No end to learning:
Earn the means first—God surely will contrive
    Use for our earning.   80
Others mistrust and say, "But time escapes:
    Live now or never!"
He said, "What's time? Leave Now for dogs and apes!
    Man has Forever."
Back to his book then: deeper drooped his head: 85
    Calculus[3] racked him:
Leaden before, his eyes grew dross[4] of lead:
    Tussis[5] attacked him.
"Now, master, take a little rest!"—not he!
    (Caution redoubled,   90
Step two abreast, the way winds narrowly!)
    Not a whit troubled
Back to his studies, fresher than at first,

9. Became a scholar.
1. Textual commentary or annotation.
2. Structure.
3. *Calculus:* "the stone." Perhaps gallstones or kidney stones.
4. Waste scum on surface of molten metal.
5. Bronchial cough.

Fierce as a dragon
He (soul-hydroptic[6] with a sacred thirst)   95
Sucked at the flagon.
Oh, if we draw a circle premature,
Heedless of far gain,
Greedy for quick returns of profit, sure
Bad is our bargain!   100
Was it not great? did not he throw on God,
(He loves the burthen)—
God's task to make the heavenly period[7]
Perfect the earthen?
Did not he magnify the mind, show clear   105
Just what it all meant?
He would not discount life, as fools do here,
Paid by instalment.
He ventured neck or nothing—heaven's success
Found, or earth's failure: 110
"Wilt thou trust death or not?" He answered "Yes:
Hence with life's pale lure!"
That low man seeks a little thing to do,
Sees it and does it:
This high man, with a great thing to pursue,   115
Dies ere he knows it.
That low man goes on adding one to one
His hundred's soon hit:
This high man, aiming at a million,
Misses an unit.   120
That, has the world here—should he need the next,
Let the world mind him!
This, throws himself on God, and unperplexed
Seeking shall find him.
So, with the throttling hands of death at strife,   125
Ground he at grammar;[8]
Still, thro' the rattle, parts of speech were rife:
While he could stammer
He settled *Hoti's* business—let it be!—
Properly based *Oun*—   130
Gave us the doctrine of the enclitic *De*,[9]
Dead from the waist down.
Well, here's the platform, here's the proper place:
Hail to your purlieus,[1]
All ye highfliers of the feathered race,   135

6. Unquenchably thirsty in his soul.
7. Circuit.
8. Cf. Carlyle's denunciation of the "hidebound Pedants" of his own school days: "How can an inanimate, mechanical Gerund-Grinder . . . foster the growth of anything; much more of Mind . . .?" (*Sartor Resartus*, II.iii).
9. *Hoti, Oun, De*: Greek particles meaning respectively "that," "then," and "towards." The "enclitic *De*" is a suffix-forming particle which changes the accentual pattern in the word to which it is joined. In a letter to Tennyson, Browning said: "I wanted the grammarian 'dead from the waist down' . . . to spend his last breath on the biggest of the littlenesses; such an one is 'the enclitic δε' . . ." (July 1863).
1. Haunts.

Swallows and curlews!
Here's the top-peak; the multitude below
            Live, for they can, there:
This man decided not to Live but Know—
            Bury this man there?   140
Here—here's his place, where meteors shoot, clouds form,
            Lightnings are loosened,
Stars come and go! Let joy break with the storm,
            Peace let the dew send!
Lofty designs must close in like effects: 145
            Loftily lying,
Leave him—still loftier than the world suspects,
            Living and dying.

ca. 1854

"Transcendentalism: A Poem in Twelve Books"[1]

Stop playing, poet! May a brother speak?
'T is you speak, that's your error. Song's our art:
Whereas you please to speak these naked thoughts
Instead of draping them in sights and sounds.[2]
—True thoughts, good thoughts, thoughts fit to treasure up!   5
But why such long prolusion[3] and display,
Such turning and adjustment of the harp,
And taking it upon your breast, at length,
Only to speak dry words across its strings?
Stark-naked thought is in request enough: 10
Speak prose and hollo it till Europe hears!
The six-foot Swiss tube,[4] braced about with bark,
Which helps the hunter's voice from Alp to Alp—
Exchange our harp for that,—who hinders you?

    But here's your fault; grown men want thought, you think;   15
Thought's what they mean by verse, and seek in verse.
Boys seek for images and melody,
Men must have reason—so, you aim at men.
Quite otherwise! Objects throng our youth, 't is true;
We see and hear and do not wonder much: 20
If you could tell us what they mean, indeed!
As German Boehme[5] never cared for plants

---

1. This purports to be advice from a poet to one of his peers, the author of a long, arid philo-
   sophical poem entitled "Transcendentalism."
2. In 1853 Browning wrote his friend Joseph Milsand: "I am writing—a first step toward popu-
   larity for me—lyrics with more music and painting than before, so as to get people to hear
   and see . . ." (G&M, p. 189).
3. Introduction.
4. The alpenhorn, a kind of pastoral megaphone.
5. Jacob Boehme or Behmen (1575–1624), shoemaker and mystic of Goerlitz, Germany, who
   spoke of "communion with the Herbs and Grass of the field," during which "in his inward
   Light he saw into their Essences, Use and Properties . . ." (Works, trans. William Law,
   1764).

Until it happed, a-walking in the fields,
He noticed all at once that plants could speak,
Nay, turned with loosened tongue to talk with him.   25
That day the daisy had an eye indeed[6]—
Colloquized with the cowslip on such themes!
We find them extant yet in Jacob's prose.
But by the time youth slips a stage or two
While reading prose in that tough book he wrote   30
(Collating and emendating the same
And settling on the sense most to our mind),
We shut the clasps and find life's summer past.
Then, who helps more, pray, to repair our loss—
Another Boehme with a tougher book   35
And subtler meanings of what roses say,—
Or some stout Mage like him of Halberstadt,[7]
John, who made things Boehme wrote thoughts about?
He with a "look you!" vents a brace of rhymes,
And in there breaks the sudden rose herself,   40
Over us, under, round us every side,
Nay, in and out the tables and the chairs
And musty volumes, Boehme's book and all,—
Buries us with a glory, young once more,
Pouring heaven into this shut house of life.   45

　　So come, the harp back to your heart again!
You are a poem, though your poem's naught.
The best of all you showed before, believe,
Was your own boy-face o'er the finer chords
Bent, following the cherub at the top   50
That points to God with his paired half-moon wings.

One Word More[1]

TO E. B. B.

I

There they are, my fifty men and women
Naming me the fifty poems finished!
Take them, Love, the book and me together:
Where the heart lies, let the brain lie also.

---

6. Daisy: "day's eye."
7. Johannes Teutonicus, canon of Halberstadt, Germany. A favorite childhood book of Browning's, Nathaniel Wanley's *Wonders of the Little World* (1678), contains an account of this medieval magician.
1. This dedicatory epistle, appended to *Men and Women*, was written September 1855, after the rest of the manuscript had gone to the printer. As R. D. Altick has shown, the title derives from an 1845 letter of Elizabeth Barrett's: "Therefore we must leave this subject [of love]—& I must trust you to leave it without one word more . . ." (Kintner, I:179).

II

Rafael made a century of sonnets,[2]   5
Made and wrote them in a certain volume
Dinted with the silver-pointed pencil
Else he only used to draw Madonnas:
These, the world might view—but one, the volume.
Who that one, you ask? Your heart instructs you.   10
Did she live and love it all her life-time?
Did she drop, his lady of the sonnets,
Die, and let it drop beside her pillow
Where it lay in place of Rafael's glory,
Rafael's cheek so duteous and so loving—   15
Cheek, the world was wont to hail a painter's,
Rafael's cheek, her love had turned a poet's?

III

You and I would rather read that volume,
(Taken to his beating bosom by it)
Lean and list the bosom-beats of Rafael,   20
Would we not? than wonder at Madonnas—
Her, San Sisto names, and Her, Foligno,
Her, that visits Florence in a vision,
Her, that's left with lilies in the Louvre[3]—
Seen by us and all the world in circle.   25

IV

You and I will never read that volume.
Guido Reni, like his own eye's apple
Guarded long the treasure-book and loved it.[4]
Guido Reni dying, all Bologna
Cried, and the world cried too, "Ours, the treasure!"   30
Suddenly, as rare things will, it vanished.

V

Dante once prepared to paint an angel:[5]
Whom to please? You whisper "Beatrice."
While he mused and traced it and retraced it,
(Peradventure with a pen corroded   35

2. Vasari states that Raphael (1483–1520) was devoted to his mistress, and tradition holds that
he addressed to the lady, Margherita (called "La Fornarina"), a hundred sonnets. Only three
of Raphael's sonnets survive, with part of a fourth.
3. The four Madonnas are respectively: the *Sistine Madonna* (Dresden Gallery); the *Madonna
di Foligno* (Vatican); the *Madonna del Granduca* (Pitti, Florence); and *La Belle Jardinière*
(Louvre).
4. The manuscript of Raphael's sonnets is supposed to have passed into the hands of the Ital-
ian painter Guido Reni (1575–1642), after whose death it was lost.
5. Dante, in *Vita Nuova* (35), says that in 1291 as he began drawing a "resemblance of an an-
gel"—his lady Beatrice Portinari—he was interrupted by the appearance of "certain people
of importance." There is no evidence in *Vita Nuova* that they intended to "seize . . . the poet"
(line 48).

Still by drops of that hot ink[6] he dipped for,
When, his left-hand i' the hair o' the wicked,
Back he held the brow and pricked its stigma,
Bit into the live man's flesh for parchment,
Loosed him, laughed to see the writing rankle,   40
Let the wretch go festering through Florence)—
Dante, who loved well because he hated,
Hated wickedness that hinders loving,
Dante standing, studying his angel,—
In there broke the folk of his Inferno.   45
Says he—"Certain people of importance"
(Such he gave his daily dreadful line to)
"Entered and would seize, forsooth, the poet."
Says the poet—"Then I stopped my painting."

VI

You and I would rather see that angel,   50
Painted by the tenderness of Dante,
Would we not?—than read a fresh Inferno.

VII

You and I will never see that picture.
While he mused on love and Beatrice,
While he softened o'er his outlined angel,   55
In they broke, those "people of importance:"
We and Bice[7] bear the loss for ever.

VIII

What of Rafael's sonnets, Dante's picture?
This: no artist lives and loves, that longs not
Once, and only once, and for one only,   60
(Ah, the prize!) to find his love a language
Fit and fair and simple and sufficient—
Using nature that's an art to others,
Not, this one time, art that's turned his nature.
Ay, of all the artists living, loving,   65
None but would forego his proper dowry,—
Does he paint? he fain would write a poem,—
Does he write? he fain would paint a picture,
Put to proof art alien to the artist's,
Once, and only once, and for one only,   70
So to be the man and leave the artist,
Gain the man's joy, miss the artist's sorrow.

6. Allusion to the *Inferno*, an anachronism since Dante began the *Divine Comedy* more than
ten years after this incident.
7. Beatrice.

IX

Wherefore? Heaven's gift[8] takes earth's abatement!
He who smites the rock and spreads the water,[9]
Bidding drink and live a crowd beneath him,   75
Even he, the minute makes immortal,
Proves, perchance, but mortal in the minute,
Desecrates, belike, the deed in doing.
While he smites, how can he but remember,
So he smote before, in such a peril,   80
When they stood and mocked—"Shall smiting help us?"
When they drank and sneered—"A stroke is easy!"
When they wiped their mouths and went their journey,
Throwing him for thanks—"But drought was pleasant."
Thus old memories mar the actual triumph;   85
Thus the doing savours of disrelish;
Thus achievement lacks a gracious somewhat;
O'er-importuned brows becloud the mandate,
Carelessness or consciousness—the gesture.[1]
For he bears an ancient wrong about him,   90
Sees and knows again those phalanxed faces,
Hears, yet one time more, the 'customed prelude—
"How shouldst thou, of all men, smite, and save us?"
Guesses what is like to prove the sequel—
"Egypt's flesh-pots—nay, the drought was better."[2]   95

X

Oh, the crowd must have emphatic warrant![3]
Theirs, the Sinai-forehead's cloven brilliance,[4]
Right-arm's rod-sweep,[5] tongue's imperial fiat.
Never dares the man put off the prophet.

XI

Did he love one face from out the thousands,   100
(Were she Jethro's daughter,[6] white and wifely,
Were she but the Æthiopian bondslave,)
He would envy yon dumb patient camel,
Keeping a reserve of scanty water
Meant to save his own life in the desert;   105

8. Divine inspiration.
9. Moses smote the rock for water (Exodus 17:1–7; Numbers 20:2–13).
1. The artist's work (or "gesture") becomes careless or self-conscious when he considers his previous, thankless reception by the public.
2. Exodus 16:2–3: Moses' ungrateful people long for the good things of the past and complain of their sufferings on the desert journey.
3. Adequate grounds for faith in their "prophets" (i.e., poets).
4. When he received the Commandments atop Mt. Sinai, Moses was allowed to witness indirectly God's glory from his place in a cloven rock; after he descended "the skin of Moses' face shone" (Exodus 33: 21–23; 34:35).
5. Aaron's rod (Exodus 7; Numbers 17).
6. Zipporah, Moses' wife (Exodus 2:21); he had also married an Ethiopian woman (Numbers 12:1).

Ready in the desert to deliver
(Kneeling down to let his breast be opened)
Hoard and life together for his mistress.

XII

I shall never, in the years remaining,
Paint you pictures, no, nor carve you statues,   110
Make you music that should all-express me;
So it seems: I stand on my attainment.
This of verse alone, one life allows me;
Verse and nothing else have I to give you.
Other heights in our lives, God willing: 115
All the gifts from all the heights, your own, Love!

XIII

Yet a semblance of resource avails us—
Shade so finely touched, love's sense must seize it.
Take these lines, look lovingly and nearly,
Lines I write the first time and the last time.[7]   120
He who works in fresco, steals a hair-brush,[8]
Curbs the liberal hand, subservient proudly,
Cramps his spirit, crowds its all in little,
Makes a strange art of an art familiar,
Fills his lady's missal-marge with flowerets.   125
He who blows thro' bronze, may breathe thro' silver,
Fitly serenade a slumbrous princess.
He who writes, may write for once as I do.

XIV

Love, you saw me gather men and women,
Live or dead or fashioned by my fancy,   130
Enter each and all, and use their service,
Speak from every mouth,—the speech, a poem.
Hardly shall I tell my joys and sorrows,
Hopes and fears, belief and disbelieving:
I am mine and yours—the rest be all men's,   135
Karshish, Cleon, Norbert and the fifty.
Let me speak this once in my true person,[9]
Not as Lippo, Roland or Andrea,
Though the fruit of speech be just this sentence:
Pray you, look on these my men and women,   140
Take and keep my fifty poems finished;
Where my heart lies, let my brain lie also!
Poor the speech, be how I speak, for all things.

7. This is Browning's only poem written in trochaic pentameter, a rare metrical form.
8. Brush for painting very fine detail.
9. Alludes to Browning's wife's having urged him to speak out directly, rather than through masks of "men and women"; cf. her letter of May 25, 1846 (Kintner, II.731–32).

XV

Not but that you know me! Lo, the moon's self!
Here in London, yonder late in Florence,   145
Still we find her face, the thrice-transfigured.[1]
Curving on a sky imbrued with colour,
Drifted over Fiesole[2] by twilight,
Came she, our new crescent of a hair's-breadth.
Full she flared it, lamping Samminiato,[3]   150
Rounder 'twixt the cypresses and rounder,
Perfect till the nightingales applauded.
Now, a piece of her old self, impoverished,
Hard to greet, she traverses the houseroofs,
Hurries with unhandsome thrift of silver,   155
Goes dispiritedly, glad to finish.

XVI

What, there's nothing in the moon noteworthy?
Nay: for if the moon could love a mortal,
Use, to charm him (so to fit a fancy)
All her magic ('t is the old sweet mythos)[4]   160
She would turn a new side to her mortal,
Side unseen of herdsman, huntsman, steersman—
Blank to Zoroaster[5] on his terrace,
Blind to Galileo[6] on his turret,
Dumb to Homer,[7] dumb to Keats—him, even!   165
Think, the wonder of the moonstruck mortal—
When she turns round, comes again in heaven,
Opens out anew for worse or better!
Proves she like some portent of an iceberg
Swimming full upon the ship it founders,   170
Hungry with huge teeth of splintered crystals?
Proves she as the paved work of a sapphire
Seen by Moses when he climbed the mountain?
Moses, Aaron, Nadab and Abihu
Climbed and saw the very God, the Highest,   175
Stand upon the paved work of a sapphire.
Like the bodied heaven in his clearness
Shone the stone, the sapphire of that paved work,
When they ate and drank and saw God also![8]

---

1. The moon has passed through three phases—new or crescent, full, and waning—during the Brownings' journey from Florence to London.
2. Town three miles northeast of Florence.
3. San Miniato al Monte, church on a hill southeast of Florence.
4. The moon goddess Artemis (Diana) loved the mortal Endymion, visiting him in dreams. John Keats's *Endymion* (1818) is based on the myth; see line 165.
5. Persian prophet of the sixth century B.C.E. who founded a religion teaching the worship of Ormazd, or Ahura Mazda, a deity representing light and life.
6. Italian astronomer (1564–1642), who perfected the telescope. Just before going blind in 1637 he discovered the moon's oscillations in orbit.
7. Among the so-called Homeric Hymns is one to Artemis, identified with the moon.
8. Lines 174–79 closely paraphrase Exodus 24: 9–11.

XVII

What were seen? None knows, none ever shall know.   180
Only this is sure—the sight were other,
Not the moon's same side, born late in Florence,
Dying now impoverished here in London.
God be thanked, the meanest of his creatures
Boasts two soul-sides, one to face the world with,   185
One to show a woman when he loves her!

XVIII

This I say of me, but think of you, Love!
This to you—yourself my moon of poets!
Ah, but that's the world's side, there's the wonder,
Thus they see you, praise you, think they know you!   190
There, in turn I stand with them and praise you—
Out of my own self, I dare to phrase it.
But the best is when I glide from out them,
Cross a step or two of dubious twilight,
Come out on the other side, the novel   195
Silent silver lights and darks undreamed of,
Where I hush and bless myself with silence.

XIX

Oh, their Rafael of the dear Madonnas,
Oh, their Dante of the dread Inferno,
Wrote one song—and in my brain I sing it,   200
Drew one angel—borne, see, on my bosom!

                                               R.B.

1855

FROM *DRAMATIS PERSONAE* (1864)

Dîs aliter Visum; or, Le Byron de Nos Jours[1]

I

Stop, let me have the truth of that!
Is that all true? I say, the day
Ten years ago when both of us

1. The title points up the poem's ironies. The first half, an allusion to *Aeneid*, II. 428, means
"the gods saw it otherwise"; that is, the lovers deserved a better fate, but it was seemingly the
gods' will that their love should be coldly dissected and destroyed by the man. The second
half means "the modern Byron," referring to the very un-Byronic middle-aged poet of this
monologue, who has finally carved out a respectable literary career.
    The setting is a resort hotel in Pornic on the coast of Brittany, where the man has just
given his version of their affair. Interrupting scornfully, the woman has the last word—the
entire monologue.

Met on a morning, friends—as thus
We meet this evening, friends or what?—   5

II

Did you—because I took your arm
  And sillily smiled, "A mass of brass
That sea looks, blazing underneath!"
  While up the cliff-road edged with heath,
We took the turns nor came to harm—   10

III

Did you consider "Now makes twice
  That I have seen her, walked and talked
With this poor pretty thoughtful thing,
  Whose worth I weigh: she tries to sing;
Draws, hopes in time the eye grows nice;   15

IV

"Reads verse and thinks she understands;
  Loves all, at any rate, that's great,
Good, beautiful; but much as we
  Down at the bath-house love the sea,
Who breathe its salt and bruise its sands: 20

V

"While . . . do but follow the fishing-gull
  That flaps and floats from wave to cave!
There's the sea-lover, fair my friend!
  What then? Be patient, mark and mend!
Had you the making of your scull?"   25

VI

And did you, when we faced the church
  With spire and sad slate roof, aloof
From human fellowship so far,
  Where a few graveyard crosses are,
And garlands for the swallows' perch,—   30

VII

Did you determine, as we stepped
  O'er the lone stone fence, "Let me get
Her for myself, and what's the earth
  With all its art, verse, music, worth—
Compared with love, found, gained, and kept?   35

VIII

"Schumann's[2] our music-maker now;
   Has his march-movement youth and mouth?
Ingres's[3] the modern man that paints;
   Which will lean on me, of his saints?
Heine[4] for songs; for kisses, how?"   40

IX

And did you, when we entered, reached
   The votive frigate[5] soft aloft
Riding on air this hundred years,
   Safe-smiling at old hopes and fears,—
Did you draw profit while she preached?   45

X

Resolving, "Fools we wise men grow!
   Yes, I could easily blurt out curt
Some question that might find reply
   As prompt in her stopped lips, dropped eye,
And rush of red to cheek and brow: 50

XI

"Thus were a match made, sure and fast,
   Mid the blue weed-flowers round the mound
Where, issuing, we shall stand and stay
   For one more look at baths and bay,
Sands, sea-gulls, and the old church last—   55

XII

"A match 'twixt me, bent, wigged and lamed,
   Famous, however, for verse and worse,
Sure of the Fortieth spare Arm-chair[6]
   When gout and glory seat me there,
So, one whose love-freaks pass unblamed,—   60

XIII

"And this young beauty, round and sound
   As a mountain-apple, youth and truth

2. Robert Schumann (1810–56), German composer. Browning alludes to the stirring marches written after the Prussians confronted republican revolutionaries in Dresden, Schumann's home, in 1849.
3. Jean-Auguste-Dominique Ingres (1780–1867), much honored French painter. Though renowned for his nudes, he painted sacred subjects such as the *Martyrdom of St. Symphorian*, in the cathedral of Autun.
4. Heinrich Heine (1797–1856), German lyrical poet.
5. Offering in the form of a model ship; hence the pronoun "she."
6. Allusion to the French Academy, to which the poet is sure of election upon the death of one of its forty members.

With loves and doves, at all events
   With money in the Three per Cents,[7]
Whose choice of me would seem profound:—   65

XIV

"She might take me as I take her.
   Perfect the hour would pass, alas!
Climb high, love high, what matter? Still,
   Feet, feelings, must descend the hill:
An hour's perfection can't recur.   70

XV

"Then follows Paris and full time
   For both to reason: 'Thus with us!'
She'll sigh, 'Thus girls give body and soul
   At first word, think they gain the goal,
When 't is the starting-place they climb!   75

XVI

" 'My friend makes verse and gets renown;
   Have they all fifty years, his peers?
He knows the world, firm, quiet and gay;
   Boys will become as much one day:
They're fools; he cheats, with beard less brown.   80

XVII

" 'For boys say, *Love me or I die!*
   He did not say, *The truth is, youth*
I want, who am old and know too much;
   I'd catch youth: Lend me sight and touch!
Drop heart's blood where life's wheels grate dry!'   85

XVIII

"While I should make rejoinder"—(then
   It was, no doubt, you ceased that least
Light pressure of my arm in yours)
   " 'I can conceive of cheaper cures
For a yawning-fit o'er books and men.   90

XIX

" 'What? All I am, was, and might be,
   All, books taught, art brought, life's whole strife,
Painful results since precious, just
   Were fitly exchanged, in wise disgust,
For two cheeks freshened by youth and sea?   95

7. Her money is safely invested in Consols, British government bonds.

XX

" 'All for a nosegay!—what came first;
    With fields on flower, untried each side;
I rally, need my books and men,
    And find a nosegay': drop it, then,
No match yet made for best or worst!"   100

XXI

That ended me. You judged the porch
    We left by, Norman;[8] took our look
At sea and sky; wondered so few
    Find out the place for air and view;
Remarked the sun began to scorch;   105

XXII

Descended, soon regained the baths,
    And then, good-bye! Years ten since then:
Ten years! We meet: you tell me, now,
    By a window-seat for that cliff-brow,
On carpet-stripes for those sand-paths.   110

XXIII

Now I may speak: you fool, for all
    Your lore! WHO made things plain in vain?
What was the sea for? What, the grey
    Sad church, that solitary day,
Crosses and graves, and swallows' call?   115

XXIV

Was there nought better than to enjoy?
    No feat which, done, would make time break,
And let us pent-up creatures through
    Into eternity, our due?
No forcing earth teach heaven's employ?   120

XXV

No wise beginning, here and now,
    What cannot grow complete (earth's feat)
And heaven must finish, there and then?
    No tasting earth's true and food for men,
Its sweet in sad, its sad in sweet?   125

8. The church porch at Pornic, of Norman architecture.

XXVI

No grasping at love, gaining a share
　　O' the sole spark for God's life at strife
With death, so, sure of range above
　　The limits here? For us and love,
Failure; but, when God fails,[9] despair.　　　　130

XXVII

This you call wisdom? Thus you add
　　Good unto good again, in vain?
You loved, with body worn and weak;
　　I loved, with faculties to seek:
Were both loves worthless since ill-clad?　　　　135

XXVIII

Let the mere star-fish in his fault
　　Crawl in a wash of weed, indeed,
Rose-jacynth to the finger-tips:
　　He, whole in body and soul, outstrips
Man, found with either in default.　　　　140

XXIX

But what's whole, can increase no more,
　　Is dwarfed and dies, since here's its sphere.
The devil laughed at you in his sleeve!
　　You knew not? That I well believe;
Or you had saved two souls: nay, four.　　　　145

XXX

For Stephanie sprained last night her wrist,
　　Ankle or something. "Pooh," cry you?
At any rate she danced, all say,
　　Vilely; her vogue has had its day.
Here comes my husband from his whist.[1]　　　　150

9. When we fail God by denying love.
1. Card game with two sides of two partners. The name "whist" derives from the admonition to keep silence, and is thus appropriate to the dramatic action here.

Abt Vogler[1]

(AFTER HE HAS BEEN EXTEMPORIZING UPON THE MUSICAL
INSTRUMENT OF HIS INVENTION)

I

Would that the structure[2] brave, the manifold music I build,
　Bidding my organ obey, calling its keys to their work,
Claiming each slave of the sound, at a touch, as when Solomon
　willed
　Armies of angels that soar, legions of demons that lurk,
Man, brute, reptile, fly,[3]—alien of end and of aim,　　　　　　5
　Adverse, each from the other heaven-high, hell-deep removed,—
Should rush into sight at once as he named the ineffable Name,[4]
　And pile him a palace straight, to pleasure the princess he loved!

II

Would it might tarry like his, the beautiful building of mine,
　This which my keys in a crowd pressed and importuned to
　　raise!　　　　　　　　　　　　　　　　　　　　　　　　　10
Ah, one and all, how they helped, would dispart[5] now and now
　combine,
　Zealous to hasten the work, heighten their master his praise!
And one would bury his brow with a blind plunge down to hell,
　Burrow awhile and build, broad on the roots of things,
Then up again swim into sight, having based me my palace well,　15
　Founded it, fearless of flame, flat on the nether springs.[6]

III

And another would mount and march, like the excellent minion[7]
　he was,
　Ay, another and yet another, one crowd but with many a crest,

1. Now all but forgotten, the German organist George Joseph Vogler (1749–1814)—called
   "Abt" or "Abbé" because he had taken holy orders—was an artist of importance in his day.
   One of his legendary feats was a competition with Beethoven at a party in 1803 to settle the
   question as to which of the two was the better extemporizer. In the opinion of at least one
   trained listener, Vogler won. According to *Grove's Dictionary of Music and Musicians*, "his ex-
   tempore playing never failed to create an impression, and in the elevated fugal style he eas-
   ily distanced all rivals." Vogler not only enjoyed a long and brilliant career as a concert
   organist, but was a noted music teacher, numbering among his pupils Meyerbeer, Gans-
   bacher, and Weber. "The musical instrument of his invention" is the orchestrion, a portable
   organ nine feet square and six feet high, with nine hundred pipes and four manuals.
2. Friedrich von Schelling had called architecture "music in space, as it were a frozen music"
   (*Philosophy of Art*, trans. 1845).
3. According to Talmudic lore, Solomon received from heaven a great seal ring bearing the
   name of God. It gave him power to command supernatural forces, which helped him build
   the palace and temple at Jerusalem.
4. Jehovah or Yahweh, a name so venerated by pious Jews that it was never pronounced; sub-
   stitutes such as "Eloi" or "Ja" were used.
5. Separate.
6. The bed of hell.
7. Servant.

Raising my rampired[8] walls of gold as transparent as glass,
   Eager to do and die, yield each his place to the rest: 20
For higher still and higher (as a runner tips with fire,
   When a great illumination surprises a festal night—
Outlining round and round Rome's dome[9] from space to spire)
   Up, the pinnacled glory reached, and the pride of my soul was
     in sight.

IV

In sight? Not half! for it seemed, it was certain, to match man's
   birth,   25
   Nature in turn conceived, obeying an impulse as I;
And the emulous heaven yearned down, made effort to reach the
   earth,
   As the earth had done her best, in my passion, to scale the sky:
Novel splendours burst forth, grew familiar and dwelt with mine,
   Not a point nor peak but found and fixed its wandering star;   30
Meteor-moons, balls of blaze: and they did not pale nor pine,
   For earth had attained to heaven, there was no more near nor
     far.

V

Nay more; for there wanted not who walked in the glare and
   glow,
   Presences plain in the place; or, fresh from the Protoplast,[1]
Furnished for ages to come, when a kindlier wind should blow,   35
   Lured now to begin and live, in a house to their liking at last;
Or else the wonderful Dead who have passed through the body
   and gone,
   But were back once more to breathe in an old world worth
    their new:
What never had been, was now; what was, as it shall be anon;
   And what is,—shall I say, matched both? for I was made
    perfect too.   40

VI

All through my keys that gave their sounds to a wish of my soul,
   All through my soul that praised as its wish flowed visibly forth,
All through music and me! For think, had I painted the whole,
   Why, there it had stood, to see, nor the process so wonder-
    worth:
Had I written the same, made verse—still, effect proceeds from
   cause,
         45
   Ye know why the forms are fair, ye hear how the tale is told;
It is all triumphant art, but art in obedience to laws,
   Painter and poet are proud in the artist-list enrolled:—

---

8. Having ramparts.
9. The poet had seen St. Peter's thus illuminated at Easter 1854.
1. First creator or archetype.

VII

But here is the finger of God, a flash of the will that can,
Existent behind all laws, that made them and, lo, they are!   50
And I know not if, save in this, such gift be allowed to man,
That out of three sounds he frame, not a fourth sound, but a
   star.
Consider it well: each tone of our scale in itself is nought;
It is everywhere in the world—loud, soft, and all is said:
Give it to me to use! I mix it with two in my thought: 55
And, there! Ye have heard and seen: consider and bow the head!

VIII

Well, it is gone at last, the palace of music I reared;
Gone! and the good tears start, the praises that come too slow;
For one is assured at first, one scarce can say that he feared,
That he even gave it a thought, the gone thing was to go.   60
Never to be again![2] But many more of the kind
As good, nay, better perchance: is this your comfort to me?
To me, who must be saved because I cling with my mind
To the same, same self, same love, same God: ay, what was,
   shall be.

IX

Therefore to whom turn I but to thee, the ineffable Name?   65
Builder and maker, thou, of houses not made with hands![3]
What, have fear of change from thee who art ever the same?
Doubt that thy power can fill the heart that thy power expands?
There shall never be one lost good! What was, shall live as before;
The evil is null, is nought, is silence implying sound;   70
What was good shall be good, with, for evil so much good more;
On the earth the broken arcs; in the heaven, a perfect round.

X

All we have willed or hoped or dreamed of good shall exist;
Not its semblance, but itself; no beauty, nor good, nor power
Whose voice has gone forth, but each survives for the melodist   75
When eternity affirms the conception of an hour.
The high that proved too high, the heroic for earth too hard,
The passion that left the ground to lose itself in the sky,
Are music sent up to God by the lover and the bard;
Enough that he heard it once: we shall hear it by-and-by.   80

2. Cf. J. H. Newman: ". . . is it possible that that inexhaustible evolution and disposition of
notes . . . should be a mere sound, which is gone and perishes? Can it be that those myste-
rious stirrings of heart, and keen emotions, . . . and awful impressions from we know not
whence, should be wrought in us by what is unsubstantial, and comes and goes, and begins
and ends in itself? It is not so; it cannot be" (*Theory of Developments in Religious Doctrine*
[1843], sect. 39).
3. 2 Corinthians 5:1: "a building of God, an house not made with hands, eternal in the heav-
ens."

XI

And what is our failure here but a triumph's evidence
   For the fulness of the days? Have we withered or agonized?
Why else was the pause prolonged but that singing might issue
   thence?
Why rushed the discords in but that harmony should be prized?
Sorrow is hard to bear, and doubt is slow to clear,   85
   Each sufferer says his say, his scheme of the weal and woe:
But God has a few of us whom he whispers in the ear;
   The rest may reason and welcome: 't is we musicians know.[4]

XII

Well, it is earth with me; silence resumes her reign:
   I will be patient and proud, and soberly acquiesce.   90
Give me the keys. I feel for the common chord again,[5]
   Sliding by semitones, till I sink to the minor,—yes,
And I blunt it into a ninth, and I stand on alien ground,
   Surveying awhile the heights I rolled from into the deep;
Which, hark, I have dared and done, for my resting-place is
   found,   95
   The C Major of this life: so, now I will try to sleep.

Rabbi Ben Ezra[1]

I

   Grow old along with me!
     The best is yet to be,
The last of life, for which the first was made:
    Our times are in His hand
    Who saith "A whole I planned,   5
Youth shows but half; trust God: see all nor be afraid!"

---

4. Cf. Browning's "Parleying With Charles Avison": "There is no truer truth obtainable / By Man than comes of music" (138–39).
5. Symbolizing his transition from heaven to earth (musical ecstasy to silence), Vogler modulates stepwise ("by semitones") from the key in which he has been improvising: first he chooses a minor key (symbolic of "sorrow" or "woe" perhaps), then goes to the "alien" (i.e., middle) ground of a ninth—that is, to a discord requiring a resolution. This is produced by the modulation to C, an apt symbol both of repose and of the plane of ordinary life, since the key has no sharps or flats.
1. Browning first read the works of Abraham Ibn Ezra, or Abenezra (ca. 1090–1164) in the Vatican Library in 1853–54. Born in Toledo, Spain, the Jewish poet and scholar left his native country about 1140, traveling widely and gaining fame as a thinker, Hebrew philologist, and biblical exegete. His careful textual studies made him an important forerunner of modern biblical criticism. Philosophically he inclined toward both Neoplatonism and skepticism. Of his several hundred extant religious poems many express a yearning for Zion. Browning purports to translate the rabbi's "Song of Death" in "Holy-Cross Day" (1855).
    Part of Browning's intention, very probably, was to challenge the hedonism advocated in Edward FitzGerald's *The Rubáiyát of Omar Khayyám* (1859), the most popular poem of the Victorian age. The overwhelming optimism of "Rabbi Ben Ezra" elicited a reply, "Growing Old," from Matthew Arnold in 1867.

II

Not that, amassing flowers,
Youth sighed "Which rose make ours,
Which lily leave and then as best recall?"
Not that, admiring stars,   10
It yearned "Nor Jove, nor Mars;
Mine be some figured flame which blends, transcends them all!"

III

Not for such hopes and fears
Annulling youth's brief years,
Do I remonstrate: folly wide the mark!   15
Rather I prize the doubt
Low kinds exist without,
Finished and finite clods, untroubled by a spark.

IV

Poor vaunt of life indeed,
Were man but formed to feed   20
On joy, to solely seek and find and feast:
Such feasting ended, then
As sure an end to men;
Irks care the crop-full bird? Frets doubt the maw-crammed beast?[2]

V

Rejoice we are allied   25
To That which doth provide
And not partake, effect and not receive!
A spark disturbs our clod;
Nearer we hold of[3] God
Who gives, than of His tribes that take, I must believe.   30

VI

Then, welcome each rebuff
That turns earth's smoothness rough,
Each sting that bids nor sit nor stand but go!
Be our joys three-parts pain!
Strive, and hold cheap the strain;   35
Learn, nor account the pang; dare, never grudge the throe!

VII

For thence,—a paradox
Which comforts while it mocks,—

2. I.e., do care and doubt bother well-fed animals? This line is often cited as an instance of
Browning's tendency toward roughness of diction and syntax.
3. Are related to.

Shall life succeed in that it seems to fail:
    What I aspired to be,   40
    And was not, comforts me:[4]
A brute I might have been, but would not sink i' the scale.[5]

VIII

    What is he but a brute
    Whose flesh has soul to suit,
Whose spirit works lest arms and legs want play?   45
    To man, propose this test—
    Thy body at its best,
How far can that project thy soul on its lone way?

IX

    Yet gifts[6] should prove their use:
    I own the Past profuse[7]   50
Of power each side, perfection every turn:
    Eyes, ears took in their dole,
    Brain treasured up the whole;
Should not the heart beat once "How good to live and learn?"

X

    Not once beat "Praise be Thine!   55
    I see the whole design,
I, who saw power, see now love perfect too:[8]
    Perfect I call Thy plan:
    Thanks that I was a man!
Maker, remake, complete,—I trust what Thou shalt do!"   60

XI

    For pleasant in this flesh;
    Our soul, in its rose-mesh[9]
Pulled ever to the earth, still yearns for rest;
    Would we some prize might hold
    To match those manifold   65
Possessions of the brute,—gain most, as we did best!

XII

    Let us not always say
    "Spite of this flesh to-day
I strove, made head, gained ground upon the whole!"

4. Cf. "Saul," line 295: ". . . 't is not what man Does which exalts him, but what man Would do!"
5. The scale or chain of being.
6. The endowments of youth; cf. line 74.
7. I.e., I admit the past is full.
8. For Browning, love completes God's tripartite nature, the other two elements being power and intelligence.
9. The net of flesh, with its veins and arteries, associated with sensual pleasure.

As the bird wings and sings,   70
Let us cry "All good things
Are ours, nor soul helps flesh more, now, than flesh helps soul!"[1]

XIII

Therefore I summon age
To grant youth's heritage,
Life's struggle having so far reached its term: 75
Thence shall I pass, approved
A man, for aye removed
From the developed brute; a god though in the germ.

XIV

And I shall thereupon
Take rest, ere I be gone   80
Once more on my adventure brave and new:
Fearless and unperplexed,
When I wage battle next,
What weapons to select, what armour to indue.[2]

XV

Youth ended, I shall try   85
My gain or loss thereby;
Leave the fire ashes, what survives is gold:
And I shall weigh the same,
Give life its praise or blame:
Young, all lay in dispute; I shall know, being old.   90

XVI

For note, when evening shuts,
A certain moment cuts
The deed off, calls the glory from the grey:
A whisper from the west
Shoots—"Add this to the rest,   95
Take it and try its worth: here dies another day."

XVII

So, still within this life,
Though lifted o'er its strife,
Let me discern, compare, pronounce at last,
"This rage was right i' the main,   100
That acquiescence vain:
The Future I may face now I have proved the Past."

---

1. Here Browning differs with Ibn Ezra, who taught that the soul and body were in conflict, and that the pursuit of wisdom was necessary to hold the passions in check.
2. Put on.

XVIII

For more is not reserved
To man, with soul just nerved
To act to-morrow what he learns to-day: 105
Here, work enough to watch
The Master work, and catch
Hints of the proper craft, tricks of the tool's true play.

XIX

As it was better, youth
Should strive, through acts uncouth,   110
Toward making, than repose on aught found made:
So, better, age, exempt
From strife, should know, than tempt[3]
Further. Thou waitedest age: wait death nor be afraid!

XX

Enough now, if the Right   115
And Good and Infinite
Be named here, as thou callest thy hand thine own,
With knowledge absolute,
Subject to no dispute
From fools that crowded youth, nor let thee feel alone.   120

XXI

Be there, for once and all,
Severed great minds from small,
Announced to each his station in the Past!
Was I,[4] the world arraigned,
Were they, my soul disdained,   125
Right? Let age speak the truth and give us peace at last!

XXII

Now, who shall arbitrate?
Ten men love what I hate,
Shun what I follow, slight what I receive;
Ten, who in ears and eyes   130
Match me: we all surmise,
They this thing, and I that: whom shall my soul believe?

XXIII

Not on the vulgar mass
Called "work," must sentence pass,
Things done, that took the eye and had the price;   135

3. Attempt.
4. The word "whom" is understood as following the pronoun in this line and the next.

O'er which, from level stand,
The low world laid its hand,
Found straightway to its mind, could value in a trice:

XXIV

But all, the world's coarse thumb
And finger failed to plumb,   140
So passed in making up the main account;
All instincts immature,
All purposes unsure,
That weighed not as his work, yet swelled the man's amount:[5]

XXV

Thoughts hardly to be packed   145
Into a narrow act,
Fancies that broke through language and escaped;
All I could never be,
All, men ignored in me,
This, I was worth to God, whose wheel the pitcher shaped.   150

XXVI

Ay, note that Potter's wheel,[6]
That metaphor! and feel
Why time spins fast, why passive lies our clay,—
Thou, to whom fools propound,
When the wine makes its round,   155
"Since life fleets, all is change; the Past gone, seize to-day!"

XXVII

Fool! All that is, at all,
Lasts ever, past recall;
Earth changes, but thy soul and God stand sure:
What entered into thee,   160
That was, is, and shall be:
Time's wheel runs back or stops: Potter and clay endure.

XXVIII

He fixed thee mid this dance
Of plastic[7] circumstance,
This Present, thou, forsooth, wouldst fain arrest: 165
Machinery just meant

5. The argument here is akin to the Evangelical belief that God judges a man's intentions, not his works. This principle underlies Browning's repeated glorification of the aspirant who fails in striving loftily.
6. Browning's metaphor of the potter's wheel appears to be a reply to the *Rubáiyát*, quatrains LIX–LXVI, first edition. Cf. Ecclesiastes 2 and The Wisdom of Solomon 2.
7. Changeable in shape or form.

To give thy soul its bent,
Try thee and turn thee forth, sufficiently impressed.

XXIX

What though the earlier grooves
Which ran the laughing loves   170
Around thy base,[8] no longer pause and press?
What though, about thy rim,
Scull-things in order grim
Grow out, in graver mood, obey the sterner stress?

XXX

Look not thou down but up!   175
To uses of a cup,
The festal board, lamp's flash and trumpet's peal,
The new wine's foaming flow,
The Master's lips a-glow!
Thou, heaven's consummate cup, what need'st thou with earth's
wheel?   180

XXXI

But I need, now as then,
Thee, God, who mouldest men;
And since, not even while the whirl was worst,
Did I,—to the wheel of life
With shapes and colours rife,   185
Bound dizzily,—mistake my end, to slake Thy thirst:

XXXII

So, take and use Thy work:
Amend what flaws may lurk,
What strain o' the stuff, what warpings past the aim!
My times be in Thy hand!   190
Perfect the cup as planned!
Let age approve of youth, and death complete the same!

Caliban upon Setebos;
or, Natural Theology in the Island

"Caliban upon Setebos" has been the most widely admired poem of
Dramatis Personæ (1864). Though evidently occasioned by the intellectual
convulsion resulting from the publication in 1859 of Darwin's *The Origin
of Species*—particularly the keen debate over the "missing link" between
ape and man—"Caliban" has little to do with Darwinian theory. Rather,
Browning's subject is man's inveterate tendency to create God in his own

---

8. Of a cup being formed on the wheel; i.e., youth.

image. That the poem's intention is partly satirical is suggested by the sub-title, which alludes to one of the important forms of rational theology in the nineteenth century. *Natural Theology; or, Evidences of the Existence and Attributes of the Deity, collected from the Appearances of Nature* (1802) is the major work of an influential thinker, the latitudinarian Archdeacon William Paley (1743–1805). An elaboration of the eighteenth-century "argument from design," Paley's book professes that God's nature and purposes can be inferred empirically from natural phenomena. After drawing his famous "watchmaker-God" analogy, Paley adduces evidence of God's intelligence from the complexities of human anatomy, and His goodness from the "superaddition" of pleasure to other animal sensations. (Note that it is the prevalence of pain in his existence that forces Caliban to infer Setebos' essential cruelty.)

Several commentators have argued that another of Browning's satiric targets is orthodox Calvinism, which regarded man as depraved, and God as infinite and transcendent sovereign whose will and justice are inscrutable. The faithful, sincerely afraid of God, are impelled to repentance, which involves the denial of the flesh and the "old man" or Adam within. In accordance with God's ultimate purpose, men's souls are predestined to salvation or to condemnation and eternal death. Though Calvin insisted that man has free will, the doctrine of unconditional predestination implies that the individual exercise of free will is circumscribed by Providence. The mature Browning had largely rejected the Calvinistic elements of the Evangelical faith in which he was reared. After 1850 his stress fell heavily on the idea of a God of love.

From Calvin's thought Browning may have derived the germ of "Caliban upon Setebos." In his *Institutes* I.iii.1 ("The sense of the deity found in all men"), Calvin says, ". . . there is no nation so barbarous, no race so savage, as not to be firmly persuaded of the being of a God. Even those who in other respects appear to differ but little from brutes always retain some sense of religion. . . ." The original of Browning's brute is, of course, the spiteful humanoid of Shakespeare's *The Tempest*. Caliban, slave of the magician Prospero, is a "thing of darkness" (V.i.275). Emblematizing the bestial in man (or in theological terms, unredeemed "natural man"), Shakespeare's Caliban, all appetite and fancy, is deficient in reason and therefore ineducable. While preserving Caliban's status—and his pungent speech—Browning significantly converts him from an object of loathing to a rational creature who elicits sympathy by his groping toward transcendence of his limited sphere. See Isabel Armstrong's essay in this volume, pp. 651–59, for more on this poem.

The epigraph comes from Psalms 50:21: what God said to the wicked.

"Thou thoughtest that I was altogether such a one as thyself."

['Will[1] sprawl, now that the heat of day is best,
Flat on his belly in the pit's much mire,
With elbows wide, fists clenched to prop his chin.
And, while he kicks both feet in the cool slush,
And feels about his spine small eft-things[2] course,   5

1. He (Caliban) will. Caliban usually refers to himself in the third person. The brackets indicate that Caliban is pondering silently or perhaps whispering.
2. Lizardlike creatures.

Run in and out each arm, and make him laugh:
And while above his head a pompion-plant,[3]
Coating the cave-top as a brow its eye,
Creeps down to touch and tickle hair and beard,
And now a flower drops with a bee inside,   10
And now a fruit to snap at, catch and crunch,—
He looks out o'er yon sea which sunbeams cross
And recross till they weave a spider-web
(Meshes of fire, some great fish breaks at times)
And talks to his own self, howe'er he please,   15
Touching that other, whom his dam[4] called God.
Because to talk about Him, vexes—ha,
Could He but know! and time to vex is now,
When talk is safer than in winter-time.
Moreover Prosper and Miranda[5] sleep   20
In confidence he drudges at their task,
And it is good to cheat the pair, and gibe,
Letting the rank tongue blossom into speech.]

Setebos, Setebos, and Setebos!
'Thinketh, He dwelleth i' the cold o' the moon.   25

'Thinketh He made it, with the sun to match,
But not the stars; the stars came otherwise;
Only made clouds, winds, meteors, such as that:
Also this isle, what lives and grows thereon,
And snaky sea which rounds and ends the same.   30

'Thinketh, it came of being ill at ease:[6]
He hated that He cannot change His cold,
Nor cure its ache. 'Hath spied an icy fish
That longed to 'scape the rock-stream where she lived,
And thaw herself within the lukewarm brine   35
O' the lazy sea her stream thrusts far amid,
A crystal spike[7] 'twixt two warm walls of wave;
Only, she ever sickened, found repulse
At the other kind of water, not her life,
(Green-dense and dim-delicious, bred o' the sun)   40
Flounced back from bliss she was not born to breathe,
And in her old bounds buried her despair,
Hating and loving warmth alike: so He.

'Thinketh, He made thereat the sun, this isle,
Trees and the fowls here, beast and creeping thing.   45
Yon otter, sleek-wet, black, lithe as a leech;

3. Pumpkin vine.
4. Sycorax, a witch, mother of Caliban and votary of Setebos, a Patagonian devil-god.
5. Prospero, protagonist of *The Tempest*, and his daughter.
6. By analogical reasoning Caliban projects his own misery onto his deity. Contrast Calvin's argument that because man is miserable and corrupt he must conclude that God alone exists in perfect felicity and goodness (*Institutes*, I.i.1).
7. Icy jet of water.

Yon auk,[8] one fire-eye in a ball of foam,
That floats and feeds; a certain badger brown
He hath watched hunt with that slant white-wedge eye
By moonlight; and the pie[9] with the long tongue   50
That pricks deep into oakwarts[1] for a worm,
And says a plain word when she finds her prize,
But will not eat the ants; the ants themselves
That build a wall of seeds and settled stalks
About their hole—He made all these and more,   55
Made all we see, and us, in spite: how else?
He could not, Himself, make a second self
To be His mate; as well have made Himself:
He would not make what he mislikes or slights,
An eyesore to Him, or not worth His pains: 60
But did, in envy, listlessness or sport,[2]
Make what Himself would fain, in a manner, be—
Weaker in most points, stronger in a few,
Worthy, and yet mere playthings all the while,
Things He admires and mocks too,—that is it.   65
Because, so brave, so better though they be,
It nothing skills[3] if He begin to plague.
Look now, I melt a gourd-fruit into mash,
Add honeycomb and pods, I have perceived,
Which bite like finches when they bill and kiss,—   70
Then, when froth rises bladdery,[4] drink up all,
Quick, quick, till maggots scamper through my brain;[5]
Last, throw me on my back i' the seeded thyme,
And wanton, wishing I were born a bird.
Put case, unable to be what I wish,   75
I yet could make a live bird out of clay:
Would not I take clay, pinch my Caliban
Able to fly?—for, there, see, he hath wings,
And great comb like the hoopoe's[6] to admire,
And there, a sting to do his foes offence,   80
There, and I will that he begin to live,
Fly to yon rock-top, nip me off the horns
Of grigs[7] high up that make the merry din,
Saucy through their veined wings, and mind me not.
In which feat, if his leg snapped, brittle clay,   85
And he lay stupid-like,—why, I should laugh;
And if he, spying me, should fall to weep,
Beseech me to be good, repair his wrong,
Bid his poor leg smart less or grow again,—

8. Diving seabird.
9. Magpie, bird related to the jay.
1. Growths on trunk of the oak.
2. Cf. Shakespeare's *King Lear*, IV.i.36–37: "As flies to wanton boys, are we to the gods; / They kill us for their sport."
3. It makes no difference.
4. Bubbling.
5. In *The Tempest* Caliban worships Stephano because he "bears celestial liquor" (II.ii.117).
6. Colorful bird with large crest.
7. Crickets or grasshoppers.

Well, as the chance were, this might take or else   90
Not take my fancy: I might hear his cry,
And give the mankin three sound legs for one,
Or pluck the other off, leave him like an egg,
And lessoned he was mine and merely clay.
Were this no pleasure, lying in the thyme,   95
Drinking the mash, with brain become alive,
Making and marring clay at will? So He.

'Thinketh, such shows nor right nor wrong in Him,
Nor kind, nor cruel: He is strong and Lord.
'Am strong myself compared to yonder crabs   100
That march now from the mountain to the sea;
'Let twenty pass, and stone the twenty-first,
Loving not, hating not, just choosing so.
'Say, the first straggler that boasts purple spots
Shall join the file, one pincer twisted off;   105
'Say, this bruised fellow shall receive a worm,
And two worms he whose nippers end in red;
As it likes me each time, I do: so He.

Well, then, 'supposeth He is good i' the main,
Placable if His mind and ways were guessed,   110
But rougher than His handiwork, be sure!
Oh, He hath made things worthier than Himself,
And envieth that, so helped, such things do more
Than He who made them! What consoles but this?
That they, unless through Him, do nought at all,   115
And must submit: what other use in things?
'Hath cut a pipe of pithless elder-joint
That, blown through, gives exact the scream o' the jay
When from her wing you twitch[8] the feathers blue:
Sound this, and little birds that hate the jay   120
Flock within stone's throw, glad their foe is hurt:
Put case such pipe could prattle and boast forsooth
"I catch the birds, I am the crafty thing,
I make the cry my maker cannot make
With his great round mouth; he must blow through mine!"   125
Would not I smash it with my foot? So He.

But wherefore rough, why cold and ill at ease?
Aha, that is a question! Ask, for that,
What knows,—the something over Setebos[9]
That made Him, or He, may be, found and fought,   130
Worsted, drove off and did to nothing, perchance.
There may be something quiet o'er His head,
Out of His reach, that feels nor joy nor grief,
Since both derive from weakness in some way.

---

8. Pluck.
9. This superior force (called "Quiet" on line 137) is analogous to Aristotle's Unmoved Mover, the eternal and immaterial first cause, identified with the divine mind.

I joy because the quails come; would not joy 135
Could I bring quails here when I have a mind:
This Quiet, all it hath a mind to, doth.
'Esteemeth stars the outposts of its couch,
But never spends much thought nor care that way.
It may look up, work up,—the worse for those 140
It works on! 'Careth but for Setebos
The many-handed as a cuttle-fish,[1]
Who, making Himself feared through what He does,[2]
Looks up, first, and perceives he cannot soar
To what is quiet and hath happy life; 145
Next looks down here, and out of very spite
Makes this a bauble-world to ape yon real,[3]
These good things to match those as hips[4] do grapes.
'T is solace making baubles, ay, and sport.
Himself peeped late, eyed Prosper at his books 150
Careless and lofty, lord now of the isle:
Vexed, 'stitched a book of broad leaves, arrow-shaped,
Wrote thereon, he knows what, prodigious words;
Has peeled a wand and called it by a name;
Weareth at whiles for an enchanter's robe 155
The eyed skin of a supple oncelot;[5]
And hath an ounce[6] sleeker than youngling mole,
A four-legged serpent he makes cower and couch,
Now snarl, now hold its breath and mind his eye,
And saith she is Miranda and my wife: 160
'Keeps for his Ariel[7] a tall pouch-bill crane
He bids go wade for fish and straight disgorge;
Also a sea-beast, lumpish, which he snared,
Blinded the eyes of, and brought somewhat tame,
And split its toe-webs, and now pens the drudge 165
In a hole o' the rock and calls him Caliban;
A bitter heart that bides its time and bites.
'Plays thus at being Prosper in a way,
Taketh his mirth with make-believes: so He.

His dam held that the Quiet made all things 170
Which Setebos vexed only: 'holds not so.
Who made them weak, meant weakness He might vex.
Had He meant other, while His hand was in,
Why not make horny eyes no thorn could prick,
Or plate my scalp with bone against the snow, 175
Or overscale my flesh 'neath joint and joint,

1. Ten-armed mollusk.
2. Because Setebos shows intelligence and power but not love, Caliban responds appropriately with fear. Cf. "Cleon," in which the despairing speaker is unable to infer, from the human condition, a loving Zeus (lines 262ff.).
3. Cf. Plato's theory of Forms, developed in the *Phaedo*: there exists a transcendent world of ideal forms "imitated" in the material world.
4. Inedible fruit of the rose.
5. Ocelot, or spotted wild cat.
6. Snow leopard.
7. A spirit in Prospero's service (*Tempest*).

Like an orc's[8] armour? Ay,—so spoil His sport!
He is the One now: only He doth all.

'Saith, He may like, perchance, what profits Him.
Ay, himself loves what does him good; but why?   180
'Gets good no otherwise. This blinded beast
Loves whoso places flesh-meat on his nose,
But, had he eyes, would want no help, but hate
Or love, just as it liked him: He hath eyes.
Also it pleaseth Setebos to work,   185
Use all His hands, and exercise much craft,
By no means for the love of what is worked.
'Tasteth, himself, no finer good i' the world
When all goes right, in this safe summer-time,
And he wants little, hungers, aches not much,   190
Than trying what to do with wit and strength.
'Falls to make something: 'piled yon pile of turfs,
And squared and stuck there squares of soft white chalk,
And, with a fish-tooth, scratched a moon on each,
And set up endwise certain spikes of tree,   195
And crowned the whole with a sloth's skull a-top,
Found dead i' the woods, too hard for one to kill.
No use at all i' the work, for work's sole sake;
'Shall some day knock it down again: so He.

'Saith He is terrible: watch His feats in proof!   200
One hurricane will spoil six good months' hope.
He hath a spite against me, that I know,
Just as He favours Prosper, who knows why?
So it is, all the same, as well I find.
'Wove wattles[9] half the winter, fenced them firm   205
With stone and stake to stop she-tortoises
Crawling to lay their eggs here: well, one wave,
Feeling the foot of Him upon its neck,
Gaped as a snake does, lolled out its large tongue,
And licked the whole labour flat: so much for spite.   210
'Saw a ball[1] flame down late (yonder it lies)
Where, half an hour before, I slept i' the shade:
Often they scatter sparkles: there is force!
'Dug up a newt He may have envied once
And turned to stone, shut up inside a stone.   215
Please Him and hinder this?—What Prosper does?
Aha, if He would tell me how! Not He!
There is the sport: discover how or die!
All need not die, for of the things o' the isle
Some flee afar, some dive, some run up trees;   220
Those at His mercy,—why, they please Him most
When . . . when . . . well, never try the same way twice!

8. Sea monster.
9. Twigs.
1. Meteorite.

Repeat what act has pleased, He may grow wroth.
You must not know His ways, and play Him off,
Sure of the issue. 'Doth the like himself: 225
'Spareth a squirrel that[2] it nothing fears
But steals the nut from underneath my thumb,
And when I threat, bites stoutly in defence:
'Spareth an urchin[3] that contrariwise,
Curls up into a ball, pretending death   230
For fright at my approach: the two ways please.
But what would move my choler[4] more than this,
That either creature counted on its life
To-morrow and next day and all days to come,
Saying, forsooth, in the inmost of its heart,   235
"Because he did so yesterday with me,
And otherwise with such another brute,
So must he do henceforth and always."—Ay?
'Would teach the reasoning couple what "must" means!
'Doth as he likes, or wherefore Lord? So He.   240

'Conceiveth all things will continue thus,
And we shall have to live in fear of Him
So long as He lives, keeps His strength: no change,
If He have done His best, make no new world
To please Him more, so leave off watching this,—   245
If He surprise[5] not even the Quiet's self
Some strange day,—or, suppose, grow into it
As grubs grow butterflies: else, here are we,
And there is He, and nowhere help at all.

'Believeth with the life, the pain shall stop.   250
His dam held different, that after death
He both plagued enemies and feasted friends:
Idly![6] He does His worst in this our life,
Giving just respite lest we die through pain,
Saving last pain for worst,—with which, an end.   255
Meanwhile, the best way to escape His ire
Is, not to seem too happy.[7] 'Sees, himself,
Yonder two flies, with purple films[8] and pink,
Bask on the pompion-bell above: kills both.
'Sees two black painful beetles roll their ball   260
On head and tail as if to save their lives:
Moves them the stick away they strive to clear.

Even so, 'would have Him misconceive, suppose
This Caliban strives hard and ails no less,

---

2. In that, because.
3. Hedgehog.
4. Anger.
5. Attack.
6. I.e., Sycorax's belief in an afterlife is vain.
7. In lines 256–69 Browning seems to mock the sobriety of certain religious sects.
8. Wings.

And always, above all else, envies Him;   265
Wherefore he mainly dances on dark nights,
Moans in the sun, gets under holes to laugh,
And never speaks his mind save housed as now:
Outside, 'groans, curses. If He caught me here,
O'erheard this speech, and asked "What chucklest at?"   270
'Would, to appease Him, cut a finger off,[9]
Or of my three kid yearlings burn the best,
Or let the toothsome apples rot on tree,
Or push my tame beast for the orc to taste:
While myself lit a fire, and made a song   275
And sung it, *"What I hate, be consecrate*
To celebrate Thee and Thy state, no mate
For Thee; what see for envy in poor me?"
Hoping the while, since evils sometimes mend,
Warts rub away and sores are cured with slime,   280
That some strange day, will either the Quiet catch
And conquer Setebos, or likelier He
Decrepit may doze, doze, as good as die.

[What, what? A curtain o'er the world at once!
Crickets stop hissing; not a bird—or, yes,   285
There scuds His raven that has told Him all!
It was fool's play, this prattling! Ha! The wind
Shoulders the pillared dust, death's house o' the move,
And fast invading fires begin! White blaze—
A tree's head snaps—and there, there, there, there, there,   290
His thunder follows! Fool to gibe at Him!
Lo! 'Lieth flat and loveth Setebos!
'Maketh his teeth meet through his upper lip,
Will let those quails fly, will not eat this month
One little mess of whelks,[1] so he may 'scape!]   295

Confessions

I

What is he[1] buzzing in my ears?
    "Now that I come to die,
Do I view the world as a vale of tears?"
    Ah, reverend sir, not I!

II

What I viewed there once, what I view again   5
    Where the physic bottles stand
On the table's edge,—is a suburb lane,
    With a wall to my bedside hand.

9. Here and at the close Browning satirizes the concept of mortification or penance.
1. Shellfish.
1. The priest at hand.

III

That lane sloped, much as the bottles do,
  From a house you could descry   10
O'er the garden-wall: is the curtain blue
  Or green to a healthy eye?

IV

To mine, it serves for the old June weather
  Blue above lane and wall;
And that farthest bottle labelled "Ether"   15
  Is the house o'ertopping all.

V

At a terrace, somewhere near the stopper,
  There watched for me, one June,
A girl: I know, sir, it's improper,
  My poor mind's out of tune.   20

VI

Only, there was a way . . . you crept
  Close by the side, to dodge
Eyes in the house, two eyes except:
  They styled their house "The Lodge."

VII

What right had a lounger up their lane?   25
  But, by creeping very close,
With the good wall's help,—their eyes might strain
  And stretch themselves to Oes,

VIII

Yet never catch her and me together,
  As she left the attic, there,   30
By the rim of the bottle labelled "Ether,"
  And stole from stair to stair,

IX

And stood by the rose-wreathed gate. Alas,
  We loved, sir—used to meet:
How sad and bad and mad it was—   35
  But then, how it was sweet!

Prospice[1]

Fear death?—to feel the fog in my throat,
    The mist in my face,
When the snows begin, and the blasts denote
    I am nearing the place,
The power of the night, the press of the storm,   5
    The post of the foe;
Where he stands, the Arch Fear in a visible form,
    Yet the strong man must go:
For the journey is done and the summit attained,
    And the barriers fall,   10
Though a battle's to fight ere the guerdon be gained,
    The reward of it all.
I was ever a fighter, so—one fight more,
    The best and the last!
I would hate that death bandaged my eyes, and forbore,   15
    And bade me creep past.
No! let me taste the whole of it, fare like my peers
    The heroes of old,
Bear the brunt, in a minute pay glad life's arrears
    Of pain, darkness and cold.   20
For sudden the worst turns the best to the brave,
    The black minute's at end,
And the elements' rage, the fiend-voices that rave,
    Shall dwindle, shall blend,
Shall change, shall become first a peace out of pain,   25
    Then a light, then thy breast,
O thou soul of my soul! I shall clasp thee again,
    And with God be the rest!

Youth and Art

I

It once might have been, once only:
    We lodged in a street together,
You, a sparrow on the housetop lonely,
    I, a lone she-bird of his feather.

---

1. The title means "took forward" or "be watchful." The poem first appeared in the *Atlantic Monthly* for June 1864 but was probably written shortly after Elizabeth Barrett Browning's death in 1861. At that time Browning wrote these words from Dante into his wife's Testament: "Thus I believe, thus I affirm, thus I am certain it is, that from this life I shall pass to another, there, where that lady lives of whom my soul was enamoured" (*Convivio*, II.9).

II

Your trade was with sticks and clay,   5
    You thumbed, thrust, patted and polished,
Then laughed "They will see some day
    Smith made, and Gibson[1] demolished."

III

My business was song, song, song;
    I chirped, cheeped, trilled and twittered,   10
"Kate Brown's on the boards ere long,
    And Grisi's[2] existence embittered!"

IV

I earned no more by a warble
    Than you by a sketch in plaster;
You wanted a piece of marble,   15
    I needed a music-master.

V

We studied hard in our styles,
    Chipped each at a crust like Hindoos,
For air looked out on the tiles,
    For fun watched each other's windows.   20

VI

You lounged, like a boy of the South,
    Cap and blouse—nay, a bit of beard too;
Or you got it, rubbing your mouth
    With fingers the clay adhered to.

VII

And I—soon managed to find   25
    Weak points in the flower-fence facing,
Was forced to put up a blind
    And be safe in my corset-lacing.

VIII

No harm! It was not my fault
    If you never turned your eye's tail up   30
As I shook upon E *in alt*,[3]
    Or ran the chromatic scale up:

---

1. The English sculptor John Gibson (1790–1866), whom Browning knew well.
2. Giulia Grisi (1811–69), Italian operatic soprano.
3. High E in the music scale.

IX

For spring bade the sparrows pair,
  And the boys and girls gave guesses,
And stalls in our street looked rare   35
  With bulrush and watercresses.

X

Why did not you pinch a flower
  In a pellet of clay and fling it?
Why did not I put a power
  Of thanks in a look, or sing it?   40

XI

I did look, sharp as a lynx,
  (And yet the memory rankles)
When models arrived, some minx
  Tripped up-stairs, she and her ankles.

XII

But I think I gave you as good!   45
  "That foreign fellow,—who can know
How she pays, in a playful mood,
  For his tuning her that piano?"

XIII

Could you say so, and never say
  "Suppose we join hands and fortunes,   50
And I fetch her from over the way,
  Her, piano, and long tunes and short tunes?"

XIV

No, no: you would not be rash,
  Nor I rasher and something over:
You've to settle yet Gibson's hash,   55
  And Grisi yet lives in clover.

XV

But you meet the Prince[4] at the Board,
  I'm queen myself at *bals-paré*.[5]
I've married a rich old lord,
  And you're dubbed knight and an R.A.[6]   60

---

4. Prince Albert, Queen Victoria's husband, was interested in art.
5. Fancy-dress balls.
6. Member of the Royal Academy.

XVI

Each life unfulfilled, you see;
   It hangs still, patchy and scrappy:
We have not sighed deep, laughed free,
   Starved, feasted, despaired,—been happy.

XVII

And nobody calls you a dunce,   65
   And people suppose me clever:
This could but have happened once,
   And we missed it, lost it for ever.

A Likeness

Some people hang portraits up
In a room where they dine or sup:
   And the wife clinks tea-things under,
And her cousin, he stirs his cup,
   Asks, "Who was the lady, I wonder?"   5
" 'T is a daub John bought at a sale,"
   Quoth the wife,—looks black as thunder:
"What a shade beneath her nose!
Snuff-taking, I suppose,—"
Adds the cousin, while John's corns ail.   10

Or else, there's no wife in the case,
But the portrait's queen of the place,
   Alone mid the other spoils
Of youth,—masks, gloves and foils,
And pipe-sticks, rose, cherry-tree, jasmine,   15
   And the long whip, the tandem-lasher,
And the cast from a fist ("not, alas! mine,
   But my master's, the Tipton Slasher[1]"),
And the cards where pistol-balls mark ace,
And a satin shoe used for cigar-case,   20
And the chamois-horns ("shot in the Chablais[2]")
   And prints—Rarey[3] drumming on Cruiser,
   And Sayers, our champion, the bruiser,
And the little edition of Rabelais:
Where a friend, with both hands in his pockets,   25
   May saunter up close to examine it,
   And remark a good deal of Jane Lamb in it,
"But the eyes are half out of their sockets;
That hair's not so bad, where the gloss is,
But they've made the girl's nose a proboscis: 30

1. A boxer from Tipton.
2. French alpine district, on south side of Lake Geneva.
3. J. S. Rarey, a famed trainer of horses, one of which was named Cruiser.

Jane Lamb, that we danced with at Vichy!
What, is not she Jane? Then, who is she?"

All that I own is a print,
An etching, a mezzotint;
'T is a study, a fancy, a fiction,   35
Yet a fact (take my conviction)
Because it has more than a hint
    Of a certain face, I never
Saw elsewhere touch or trace of
In women I've seen the face of: 40
    Just an etching, and, so far, clever.

I keep my prints, an imbroglio,
Fifty in one portfolio.
When somebody tries my claret,
We turn round chairs to the fire,   45
Chirp over days in a garret,
    Chuckle o'er increase of salary,
Taste the good fruits of our leisure,
Talk about pencil and lyre,
    And the National Portrait Gallery: 50
Then I exhibit my treasure.
After we've turned over twenty,
    And the debt of wonder my crony owes
    Is paid to my Marc Antonios,
He stops me—"Festina lentè!⁴   55
What's that sweet thing there, the etching?"
How my waistcoat-strings want stretching,
    How my cheeks grow red as tomatos,
    How my heart leaps! But hearts, after leaps, ache.

"By the by, you must take, for a keepsake,   60
    That other, you praised, of Volpato's."
The fool! would he try a flight further and say—
He never saw, never before to-day,
What was able to take his breath away,
A face to lose youth for, to occupy age   65
With the dream of, meet death with,—why, I'll not engage
But that, half in a rapture and half in a rage,
I should toss him the thing's self—" 'T is only a duplicate,
A thing of no value! Take it, I supplicate!"

---

4. Make haste slowly.

Apparent Failure[1]

"We shall soon lose a celebrated building."
Paris newspaper

I

No, for I'll save it! Seven years since,
    I passed through Paris, stopped a day
To see the baptism of your Prince;[2]
    Saw, made my bow, and went my way:
Walking the heat and headache off,   5
    I took the Seine-side, you surmise,
Thought of the Congress, Gortschakoff,[3]
    Cavour's appeal and Buol's replies,[4]
So sauntered till—what met my eyes?

II

Only the Doric[5] little Morgue!   10
    The dead-house where you show your drowned:
Petrarch's Vaucluse makes proud the Sorgue[6]
    Your Morgue has made the Seine renowned.
One pays one's debt in such a case;
    I plucked up heart and entered,—stalked,   15
Keeping a tolerable face
    Compared with some whose cheeks were chalked:
Let them! No Briton's to be baulked!

III

First came the silent gazers; next,
    A screen of glass, we're thankful for;   20
Last, the sight's self, the sermon's text,
    The three men who did most abhor
Their life in Paris yesterday,
    So killed themselves: and now, enthroned
Each on his copper couch, they lay   25
    Fronting me, waiting to be owned.
I thought, and think, their sin's atoned.

---

1. Written to help save the Paris Morgue from destruction. Since the events of stanza I occurred in 1856, the date of composition is 1863.
2. Louis Napoleon (1856–79), only son of Napoleon III and the Empress Eugénie. The Brownings witnessed the baptism in Paris in June 1856.
3. The Congress of Paris met from February 25 to April 16, 1856, to settle the Crimean War; the peace treaty was signed on March 30. Prince Aleksandr Gorchakov (1798–1883) was Russian foreign minister and a leading figure of the Congress.
4. Count Cavour (1810–61), prime minister of the Italian state of Piedmont, made an appeal on behalf of his state at the Congress. Count Buot-Schauenstein (1797–1865), as chief Austrian diplomat, responded to charges leveled by Cavour and others against Austria.
5. Simplest of classical Greek architectural styles.
6. River whose source is near Vaucluse, the home of the Italian poet Petrarch (1304–74).

IV

Poor men, God made, and all for that!
   The reverence struck me; o'er each head
Religiously was hung its hat,   30
   Each coat dripped by the owner's bed,
Sacred from touch: each had his berth,
   His bounds, his proper place of rest,
Who last night tenanted on earth
   Some arch, where twelve such slept abreast,—   35
Unless the plain asphalte seemed best.

V

How did it happen, my poor boy?
   You wanted to be Buonaparte
And have the Tuileries[7] for toy,
   And could not, so it broke your heart?   40
You, old one by his side, I judge,
   Were, red as blood, a socialist,[8]
A leveller![9] Does the Empire grudge
   You've gained what no Republic missed?
Be quiet, and unclench your fist!   45

VI

And this—why, he was red in vain,
   Or black,[1]—poor fellow that is blue!
What fancy was it turned your brain?
   Oh, women were the prize for you!
Money gets women, cards and dice   50
   Get money, and ill-luck gets just
The copper couch and one clear nice
   Cool squirt of water o'er your bust,
The right thing to extinguish lust!

VII

It's wiser being good than bad;   55
   It's safer being meek than fierce:
It's fitter being sane than mad.
   My own hope is, a sun will pierce
The thickest cloud earth ever stretched;
   That, after Last, returns the First,[2]   60
Though a wide compass round be fetched;

---

7. Royal palace adjacent to the Louvre, burned in 1871; now a public garden.
8. As today, red connoted radicalism or leftism in politics.
9. One advocating removal of social inequities.
1. Red and black allude here to gambling at the roulette wheel.
2. Conflation of three biblical passages: Matthew 12:45, 19:30; Revelation 22:13.

That what began best, can't end worst,
Nor what God blessed once, prove accurst.

1863   1864

Epilogue[1]

FIRST SPEAKER, *as David*

I

On the first of the Feast of Feasts,
    The Dedication Day.[2]
When the Levites joined the Priests[3]
    At the Altar in robed array,
Give signal to sound and say,—   5

II

When the thousands, rear and van,
    Swarming with one accord
Became as a single man
    (Look, gesture, thought and word)
In praising and thanking the Lord,—   10

III

When the singers lift up their voice,
    And the trumpets made endeavour,
Sounding, "In God rejoice!"
    Saying, "In Him rejoice
Whose mercy endureth for ever!"—   15

IV

Then the Temple filled with a cloud,
    Even the House of the Lord;
Porch bent and pillar bowed:
    For the presence of the Lord,
In the glory of His cloud,   20
    Had filled the House of the Lord.

1. The first two speakers represent contrasting strains of religious thought prevalent in England
   by the mid-19th century: ritualism and rationalism, both of which are deplored by the third
   speaker, Browning in his own person. The first speaker, "David," gives the Roman
   Catholic–High Church Anglican position: the Temple is God's dwelling, and the institution is
   supported by its sacraments and hierarchies. The second speaker, "Renan," represents the skep-
   ticism and agnosticism attendant upon rational-historical criticism of Scripture. The third
   speaker argues that God continues to reveal Himself in the feeling and thought of the ordinary
   man. The poem marks the extent, by 1864, of Browning's departure from orthodox Christianity.
2. Dedication of Solomon's Temple at Jerusalem, when the Lord entered His house (1 Kings
   8,9; and 2 Chronicles 5,6).
3. Descendants of Aaron; the superior clergy. Levites: descendants of Levi, a sacred caste who
   aided the priests in ritualistic observations.

SECOND SPEAKER, *as Renan*[4]

Gone now! All gone across the dark so far,
   Sharpening fast, shuddering ever, shutting still,
Dwindling into the distance, dies that star
   Which came, stood, opened once! We gazed our fill   25
With upturned faces on as real a Face[5]
   That, stooping from grave music and mild fire,
Took in our homage, made a visible place
   Through many a depth of glory, gyre on gyre,[6]
For the dim human tribute. Was this true?   30
   Could man indeed avail, mere praise of his,
To help by rapture God's own rapture too,
   Thrill with a heart's red tinge that pure pale bliss?
Why did it end? Who failed to beat the breast,
   And shriek, and throw the arms protesting wide,   35
When a first shadow showed the star addressed
   Itself to motion, and on either side
The rims contracted as the rays retired;
   The music, like a fountain's sickening pulse,
Subsided on itself; awhile transpired   40
   Some vestige of a Face no pangs convulse,
No prayers retard; then even this was gone,
   Lost in the night at last. We, lone and left
Silent through centuries, ever and anon
   Venture to probe again the vault bereft   45
Of all now save the lesser lights, a mist
   Of multitudinous points, yet suns, men say—
And this leaps ruby, this lurks amethyst,
   But where may hide what came and loved our clay?
How shall the sage detect in yon expanse   50
   The star which chose to stoop and stay for us?
Unroll the records! Hailed ye such advance
   Indeed, and did your hope evanish thus?
Watchers of twilight, is the worst averred?
   We shall not look up, know ourselves are seen,   55
Speak, and be sure that we again are heard
   Acting or suffering, have the disk's serene[7]
Reflect our life, absorb an earthly flame,
   Nor doubt that, were mankind inert and numb,
Its core had never crimsoned all the same,   60
   Nor, missing ours, its music fallen dumb?
Oh, dread succession to a dizzy post,

4. Ernest Renan (1823–92), French scholar whose *Life of Jesus* Browning had read in 1863. Renan's purely historical interpretation of Christ's life denies any supernatural element or special revelation; his rationalistic conclusion that God had "disappeared" as a Personality informing the universe filled Renan with immense regret.
5. Of Christ.
6. Spiral. Browning may have found the word in Elizabeth Barrett Browning's *Aurora Leigh* (1856), IV.1167–68: ". . . graduating up in a spiral line / Of still expanding and ascending gyres. . . ."
7. A noun meaning "clear expanse of air," derived from Keats' "Chapman's Homer," 7–8: "Yet did I never breathe its pure serene / Till I heard Chapman speak out loud and bold."

Sad sway of sceptre whose mere touch appals,
Ghastly dethronement, cursed by those the most
On whose repugnant brow the crown next falls!   65

THIRD SPEAKER

I

Witless alike of will and way divine,
How heaven's high with earth's low should intertwine!
Friends, I have seen through your eyes: now use mine!

II

Take the least man of all mankind, as I;
Look at his head and heart, find how and why   70
He differs from his fellows utterly:

III

Then, like me, watch when nature by degrees
Grows alive round him, as in Arctic seas
(They said of old) the instinctive water flees

IV

Toward some elected point of central rock,   75
As though, for its sake only, roamed the flock
Of waves about the waste: awhile they mock

V

With radiance caught for the occasion,—hues
Of blackest hell now, now such reds and blues
As only heaven could fitly interfuse,—   80

VI

The mimic monarch of the whirlpool, king
O' the current for a minute: then they wring
Up by the roots and oversweep the thing,

VII

And hasten off, to play again elsewhere
The same part, choose another peak as bare,   85
They find and flatter, feast and finish there.

VIII

When you see what I tell you,—nature dance
About each man of us, retire, advance,
As though the pageant's end were to enhance

IX

His worth, and—once the life, his product, gained—   90
Roll away elsewhere, keep the strife sustained,
And show thus real, a thing the North but feigned—

X

When you acknowledge that one world could do
All the diverse work, old yet ever new,
Divide us, each from other, me from you,—   95

XI

Why, where's the need of Temple, when the walls
O' the world are that? What use of swells and falls
From Levites' choir, Priests' cries, and trumpet-calls?

XII

That one Face, far from vanish, rather grows,
Or decomposes but to recompose,   100
Become my universe that feels and knows.

FROM *THE RING AND THE BOOK* (1868–69)

The Ring and the Book, an epic-length poem in twelve books and Browning's acknowledged masterpiece, was published in four installments, 1868–69. It was a notable success despite its stupendous length: nearly 22,000 lines of blank verse. Browning's hold on fame was finally secured; he now rivaled his contemporary, Tennyson, and he was to enjoy two decades of lionization. The poem, which gave full scope to Browning's mind—compound as it was of earthiness and idealism, humor and high seriousness—is the product of his instinctive affinity to an obscure book and the lurid story it told. Maybe never has so ambitious a poem been based on so unpromising a subject as that of *The Ring and the Book*: an infamous triple murder that took place in Rome, 1698—once a *cause célèbre*, but a century and a half later merely a neglected chapter in the history of Roman jurisprudence. It was, as Carlyle is alleged to have said to Browning, "an old Bailey story that might have been told in ten lines, and only wants forgetting."

Browning chanced upon his source—always referred to as the Old Yellow Book—in a Florentine flea market on a June day in 1860. It was

> Small-quarto size, part print part manuscript;
> A book in shape but, really, pure crude fact
> Secreted from man's life when hearts beat hard,
> And brains, high-blooded, ticked two centuries since.
> (I.84–87)

This "pure crude fact" reposed in a bulky collection of documents—pleadings, affidavits, and letters—pertaining to a murder trial:

"*Romana Homicidiorum*"—nay,
Better translate—"A Roman murder-case:
Position of the entire criminal cause
Of Guido Franceschini, nobleman,
With certain Four the cutthroats in his pay,
Tried, all five, and found guilty and put to death
By heading or hanging as befitted ranks,
At Rome on February Twenty Two,
Since our salvation Sixteen Ninety Eight:
Wherein it is disputed if, and when,
Husbands may kill adulterous wives, yet 'scape
The customary forfeit."

(I.118–29)

His curiosity piqued, Browning quickly purchased the book, pored over its contents delightedly—for he was a connoisseur of murder stories—and pieced together the following tale of greed, deception, passion, and cruelty:

In 1693 an impoverished, middle-aged nobleman of Arezzo named Guido Franceschini married the very young Francesca Pompilia, reared as the daughter of a bourgeois Roman couple, Pietro and Violante Comparini. Guido and wife went to Arezzo, followed soon by the Comparini, who had been led to believe they were allied to moneyed nobility. Finding only genteel poverty—and what they deemed poor treatment—they angrily returned to Rome, there bringing suit for the return of Pompilia's dowry. Their case was built on Violante's late revelation that Pompilia was not their daughter after all, but that of a Roman prostitute. The girl had been purchased in order that the Comparini could lay claim to an inheritance left them on the condition they produce an heir. Enraged at the suit, Guido entered a countersuit and (according to Pompilia's testimony) proceeded to make life torturous for his lowborn child-bride through constant harassment and petty cruelties. For his part, Guido declared that Pompilia was intractable and unfaithful. Pompilia, after several thwarted escape attempts, finally fled from Arezzo toward Rome on April 28–29, 1697, in the company of a young cleric, Giuseppe Caponsacchi. (Browning significantly altered the date to April 23, St. George's Day, to romanticize the event.) Giving chase, Guido caught them in an inn at Castelnuovo, near Rome, and had them arrested for flight and adultery. Tried and convicted at Rome, Caponsacchi was relegated to Civita Vecchia for three years; pending further inquiry, Pompilia was sent to a nunnery for penitent women. Because of pregnancy, however, she was soon bound over to the Comparini, in whose custody she gave birth to a son, Gaetano, on December 18, 1697. Apprised of the event, Guido went to Rome with four henchmen, and on January 2, 1698, after gaining entry into the Comparini house by pretending to be the bearer of a message from Caponsacchi, he murdered and mutilated the Comparini, leaving Pompilia for dead with twenty-two stab wounds. She lingered on four days, telling her story before dying. Quickly apprehended, Guido and the four were tried for murder before the tribunal of the Governor in Rome. At issue in the trial was whether a husband could kill his adulterous wife *honoris causâ*—for the sake of injured honor—with impunity. Behind this lay the still unresolved question of Pompilia's guilt or innocence. After the lawyers "wrangled, brangled, jangled" for a month, the court on February 18 found Guido guilty and sentenced him to be beheaded, his accomplices to be hanged. Pleading clerical privilege—he had held minor orders in the church—Guido unsuccessfully appealed to Pope Innocent XII to set aside the judgment. On February 22 Guido and his men were publicly executed.

Such was the raw "gold" of fact which, Browning tells us in Book I, would be combined with the "alloy" of the poetic imagination and then "wrought into a shapely ring," a work to be symbolically entitled *The Ring and the Book* and to contain Browning's mature reading of life. At first, however, Browning seems to have regarded the Old Yellow Book as material for a novel, not a poem; he tried—fortunately without success—to give the document away. His interest in the case grew, partly because of his penchant for history, and he sought further documents. In 1862 he obtained another pamphlet relating to the execution of Guido, now called the "Secondary Source." But not until 1864, owing to other commitments, did the actual composition begin; soon he was working at top speed, and by November 1865 he had three-fourths of the poem in hand. Thereafter he worked sporadically; three more years were needed to complete the task.

Though that gold of "pure crude fact" lay in rich profusion in the two sources, arriving at the whole truth as to the apportionment of guilt and innocence, praise and blame, was problematic in the extreme. Latent in the very argumentative nature of the material—the advocacy, the strong partisanship incident to such a trial—was an important theme: the elusive nature of truth itself. Is truth ascertainable in this sublunary world? To what extent is it relative to—and therefore vitiated by—individual human perspectives? The "plague of squint" seems universal; men accept for truth what they wish to believe. Judgment is at best impure, warped by private biases and prejudices; and language itself, in addition to possessing such inherent weaknesses as ambiguity, is notoriously liable to distortion or artful manipulation.

To embody his theme of the relation of truth to human perspective and belief, Browning daringly chose to tell his "Roman murder story" ten times over from as many distinct points of view. The risk of boredom through repetition was minimized by having each character emphasize, suppress, and distort various elements of the case according to his own interests and motives. These ten dramatic monologues are "framed"—introduced and concluded—by Browning himself in Books I and XII. Book I tells how the strange old volume took hold of the poet's imagination as he "mastered the contents, knew the whole truth / Gathered together, bound up in this book . . ." (I.115–16). His role as artist, he explains, is to "resuscitate" that body of inert historical matter by means of an inspiriting art. He goes on to impart much information on the case, and gives previews of each monologuist's performance. In the concluding book (XII) Browning gives glimpses of the trial's aftermath, then reaffirms his belief "That Art remains the one way possible / Of speaking truth, to mouths like mine at least" (XII.839–40). Books II through X are arranged in triads, the first composed of gossips called "Half-Rome," "The Other Half-Rome," and "Tertium Quid." Each speaker "swerves" from the truth because of private biases that are eventually betrayed. In the next triad, the three principals—Guido, Caponsacchi, and Pompilia—give their versions, Guido's being artful and self-serving, but those of the priest and his "Donna Angelicata" being as truthful as passionate, subjective involvement in the matter allows. The final triad begins with the ridiculous—two buffoonish lawyers interested solely in professional advancement—and concludes

with the sublime: the magisterial judgment of the wise old Pope Inno-
cent XII, who alone among the speakers possesses the insight and intu-
ition necessary to approximate the whole truth. Though the poem could
well have ended with that natural climax, Browning adds another mono-
logue, in many ways the most remarkable of the ten: Guido speaks a sec-
ond time, now as a desperate condemned man who discovers belatedly
both his real identity as a naturally amoral being and the full extent of his
loathing for the vapid purity he sees in Pompilia—whom nonetheless he
implores to save him from extinction at the end.

This colossal aggregation of dramatic monologues—each of major
length—is a *tour de force*, one of the boldest literary experiments ever un-
dertaken. It is one that could easily have failed, had it not been for Brown-
ing's deft, inventive treatment, his use, for example, of devices from the
epic, the novel, and the drama. Instead of mere talk about the events,
there is vivid portrayal, with gesture and dialogue. Browning's dramatic
evocation of manners and morals in seventeenth-century Italy is Chaucer-
ian in its cumulative power. Further, Browning imposes a remarkable
unity on the work by paralleling and contrasting both theme and charac-
ter, and by weaving a dense, richly varied metaphorical pattern through-
out. The final effect is not unlike that produced by the reading of Balzac
or Dickens: the impression of a crowded, lively canvas depicting the
comédie humaine in all its infinite variety.

THE RING AND THE BOOK

Book V

Count Guido Franceschini[1]

Thanks, Sir, but, should it please the reverend Court,
I feel I can stand somehow, half sit down
Without help, make shift to even speak, you see,[2]
Fortified by the sip of . . . why, 't is wine,
Velletri,[3]—and not vinegar and gall,[4]   5
So changed and good the times grow! Thanks, kind Sir!
Oh, but one sip's enough! I want my head
To save my neck, there's work awaits me still.
How cautious and considerate . . . aie, aie, aie,
Nor your fault, sweet Sir! Come, you take to heart   10
An ordinary matter. Law is law.
Noblemen were exempt, the vulgar thought,
From racking; but, since law thinks otherwise,

---

1. Book V presents the first of three "inside" accounts, that of Guido, who addresses the judges
   a few days after the murders. His defense is followed by the testimony of Caponsacchi (Book
   VI) and the dying confession of Pompilia (Book VII). Much of the interest of Guido's mono-
   logue lies in his resourceful use of rhetoric and special pleading.
2. Guido is to make the most of the fact that he still suffers after-effects of the torture. This
   means of extracting a confession was once standard for grave crimes in Roman court pro-
   ceedings. On the use of judicial torture see A. K. Cook's *A Commentary upon Browning's
   "The Ring and the Book"* (New York: Oxford Univ. Press, 1920), App. VII.
3. Town near Rome, where a full-bodied wine is made.
4. Bitter drink offered to Christ on the cross (Matthew 27:34).

I have been put to the rack: all's over now,
And neither wrist—what men style, out of joint: 15
If any harm be, 't is the shoulder-blade,
The left one, that seems wrong i' the socket,—Sirs,
Much could not happen, I was quick to faint,
Being past my prime of life, and out of health.
In short, I thank you,—yes, and mean the word.   20
Needs must the Court be slow to understand
How this quite novel form of taking pain,
This getting tortured merely in the flesh,
Amounts to almost an agreeable change
In my case, me fastidious, plied too much   25
With opposite treatment, used (forgive the joke)
To the rasp-tooth toying with this brain of mine,
And, in and out my heart, the play o' the probe.
Four years have I been operated on
I' the soul, do you see—its tense or tremulous part—   30
My self-respect, my care for a good name,
Pride in an old one, love of kindred—just
A mother, brothers, sisters, and the like,
That looked up to my face when days were dim,
And fancied they found light there—no one spot,   35
Foppishly sensitive, but has paid its pang.
That, and not this you now oblige me with,
That was the Vigil-torment,[5] if you please!
The poor old noble House that drew the rags
O' the Franceschini's once superb array   40
Close round her, hoped to slink unchallenged by,—
Pluck off these! Turn the drapery inside out
And teach the tittering town how scarlet[6] wears!
Show men the lucklessness, the improvidence
Of the easy-natured Count before this Count,   45
The father I have some slight feeling for,
Who let the world slide, nor foresaw that friends
Then proud to cap[7] and kiss their patron's shoe,
Would, when the purse he left held spider-webs,
Properly push his child to wall one day!   50
Mimic the tetchy[8] humour, furtive glance,
And brow where half was furious, half fatigued,
O' the same son got to be of middle age,
Sour, saturnine,—your humble servant here,—
When things go cross and the young wife, he finds   55
Take to the window at a whistle's bid,
And yet demurs thereon, preposterous fool!—
Whereat the worthies judge he wants advice
And beg to civilly ask what's evil here,

---

5. The worse torture. The victim was seated on a bench, his bound arms wrenched upwards
   behind his back by a pulley for hours at a time.
6. Rich cloth signifying nobility.
7. Remove one's hat out of respect.
8. Touchy.

Perhaps remonstrate on the habit they deem   60
He's given unduly to, of beating her:
. . . Oh, sure he beats her—why says John so else,
Who is cousin to George who is sib[9] to Tecla's self
Who cooks the meal and combs the lady's hair?
What! 'T is my wrist you merely dislocate   65
For the future when you mean me martyrdom?
—Let the old mother's economy alone,
How the brocade-strips saved o' the seamy side
O' the wedding-gown buy raiment for a year?
—How she can dress and dish up—lordly dish   70
Fit for a duke, lamb's head and purtenance[1]—
With her proud hands, feast household so a week?
No word o' the wine rejoicing God and man
The less when three-parts water? Then, I say,
A trifle of torture to the flesh, like yours,   75
While soul is spared such foretaste of hell-fire,
Is naught. But I curtail the catalogue
Through policy,—a rhetorician's trick,—
Because I would reserve some choicer points
O' the practice, more exactly parallel   80
(Having an eye to climax) with what gift,
Eventual grace the Court may have in store
I' the way of plague—what crown of punishments.
When I am hanged or headed, time enough
To prove the tenderness of only that,   85
Mere heading, hanging,—not their counterpart,
Not demonstration public and precise
That I, having married the mongrel of a drab,[2]
Am bound to grant that mongrel-brat, my wife,
Her mother's birthright-license as is just,—   90
Let her sleep undisturbed, i' the family style,
Her sleep out in the embraces of a priest,
Nor disallow their bastard[3] as my heir!
Your sole mistake,—dare I submit so much
To the reverend Court?—has been in all this pains   95
To make a stone roll down hill,—rack and wrench
And rend a man to pieces, all for what?
Why—make him ope mouth in his own defence,
Show cause for what he has done, the irregular deed,
(Since that he did it, scarce dispute can be)   100
And clear his fame a little, beside the luck
Of stopping even yet, if possible,
Discomfort to his flesh from noose or axe—
For that, out come the implements of law!
May it content my lords the gracious Court   105

9. Kinsman.
1. Entrails, echoing Exodus 12:9.
2. Harlot. See headnote for Pompilia's background.
3. After his conviction, Guido acknowledges that he is really Gaetano's father (XI.1842ff.). Here, however, he must convince the judges that the murders were done to avenge his injured honor.

To listen only half so patient-long
As I will in that sense profusely speak,
And—fie, they shall not call in screws to help!
I killed Pompilia Franceschini, Sirs;
Killed too the Comparini, husband, wife,   110
Who called themselves, by a notorious lie,[4]
Her father and her mother to ruin me.
There's the irregular deed: you want no more
Than right interpretation of the same,
And truth so far—am I to understand?   115
To that then, with convenient speed,—because
Now I consider,—yes, despite my boast,
There is an ailing in this omoplat[5]
May clip my speech all too abruptly short,
Whatever the good-will in me. Now for truth!   120

I' the name of the indivisible Trinity!
Will my lords, in the plenitude of their light,
Weigh well that all this trouble has come on me
Through my persistent treading in the paths
Where I was trained to go,—wearing that yoke   125
My shoulder was predestined to receive,
Born to the hereditary stoop and crease?
Noble, I recognized my nobler still,
The Church, my suzerain; no mock-mistress, she;
The secular owned[6] the spiritual: mates of mine   130
Have thrown their careless hoofs up at her call
"Forsake the clover and come drag my wain!"
There they go cropping: I protruded nose
To halter, bent my back of docile beast,
And now am whealed,[7] one wide wound all of me,   135
For being found at the eleventh hour o' the day
Padding the mill-track, not neck-deep in grass:
—My one fault, I am stiffened by my work,
—My one reward, I help the Court to smile!

I am representative of a great line,   140
One of the first of the old families
In Arezzo, ancientest of Tuscan towns.
When my worst foe is fain to challenge this,
His worst exception runs—not first in rank
But second, noble in the next degree   145
Only; not malice' self maligns me more.
So, my lord opposite has composed, we know,
A marvel of a book, sustains the point

4. Pompilia's putative parents, the Comparini (Pietro and Violante) filed suit the year after the
   marriage to declare Pompilia illegitimate in the hope of recovering her dowry from Guido
   (who filed a countersuit).
5. Shoulder blade.
6. Admitted the claims of.
7. Flogged.

That Francis boasts the primacy 'mid saints;[8]
Yet not inaptly hath his argument   150
Obtained response from yon my other lord
In thesis published with the world's applause
—Rather 't is Dominic such post befits:
Why, at the worst, Francis stays a Francis still,
Second in rank to Dominic it may be,   155
Still, very saintly, very like our Lord;
And I at least descend from Guido once
Homager to the Empire,[9] nought below—
Of which account as proof that, none o' the line
Having a single gift beyond brave blood,   160
Or able to do aught but give, give, give
In blood and brain, in house and land and cash,
Not get and garner as the vulgar may,
We became poor as Francis[1] or our Lord.
Be that as it likes you, Sirs,—whenever it chanced   165
Myself grew capable anyway of remark,[2]
(Which was soon—penury makes wit premature)
This struck me, I was poor who should be rich
Or pay that fault[3] to the world which trifles not
When lineage lacks the flag yet lifts the pole:[4]   170
On, therefore, I must move forthwith, transfer
My stranded self, born fish with gill and fin
Fit for the deep sea, now left flap bare-backed
In slush and sand, a show to crawlers vile
Reared of the low-tide and aright therein.   175
The enviable youth with the old name,
Wide chest, stout arms, sound brow and pricking veins,
A heartful of desire, man's natural load,
A brainful of belief, the noble's lot,—
All this life, cramped and gasping, high and dry   180
I' the wave's retreat,—the misery, good my lords,
Which made you merriment at Rome of late,—
It made me reason, rather—muse, demand
—Why our bare dropping palace, in the street
Where such-an-one whose grandfather sold tripe   185
Was adding to his purchased pile a fourth
Tall tower, could hardly show a turret sound?
Why Countess Beatrice, whose son I am,
Cowered in the winter-time as she spun flax,
Blew on the earthen basket of live ash,   190
Instead of jaunting forth in coach and six
Like such-another widow who ne'er was wed?[5]
I asked my fellows, how came this about?

8. Guido alludes to the rivalry between two orders of friars, Franciscans and Dominicans.
9. Holder of a fief under the Emperor.
1. St. Francis (ca. 1182–1226), son of a wealthy merchant, devoted himself to a life of poverty.
2. Mockery.
3. Pay the penalty (of being poor).
4. When nobility fails to make proper display yet claims its rights.
5. I.e., an unwed mother, here the mistress of the dishonest priest in lines 200–208.

"Why, Jack, the suttler's[6] child, perhaps the camp's,
Went to the wars, fought sturdily, took a town   195
And got rewarded as was natural.
She of the coach and six—excuse me there!
Why, don't you know the story of her friend?
A clown dressed vines on somebody's estate,
His boy recoiled from muck, liked Latin more,   200
Stuck to his pen and got to be a priest,
Till one day . . . don't you mind that telling tract
Against Molinos,[7] the old Cardinal wrote?
He penned and dropped it in the patron's desk
Who, deep in thought and absent much of mind,   205
Licensed the thing, allowed it for his own;
Quick came promotion,—*suum cuique*,[8] Count!
Oh, he can pay for coach and six, be sure!"
"—Well, let me go, do likewise:[9] war's the word—
That way the Franceschini worked at first,   210
I'll take my turn, try soldiership."—"What, you?
The eldest son and heir and prop o' the house,
So do you see your duty? Here's your post,
Hard by the hearth and altar. (Roam from roof,
This youngster, play the gipsy out of doors,   215
And who keeps kith and kin that fall on us?)
Stand fast, stick tight, conserve your gods at home!"
"—Well then, the quiet course, the contrary trade!
We had a cousin amongst us once was Pope,
And minor glories manifold. Try the Church,   220
The tonsure,[1] and,—since heresy's but half-slain
Even by the Cardinal's tract he thought he wrote,—
Have at Molinos!"—"Have at a fool's head!
You a priest? How were marriage possible?
There must be Franceschini till time ends—   225
That's your vocation. Make your brothers priests,
Paul shall be porporate,[2] and Girolamo step
Red-stockinged[3] in the presence when you choose,
But save one Franceschini for the age!
Be not the vine but dig and dung its root,[4]   230
Be not a priest but gird up priesthood's loins,
With one foot in Arezzo stride to Rome,

6. Camp follower who peddles provisions to an army. Guido speculates that Jack's mother was a prostitute, and that he is a child of the whole camp of soldiers.
7. Spanish divine Miguel de Molinos (1627–96), who preached the concept of Quietism, the final stage of which entailed a rejection of all hindrances to direct union with God, including the church. Arrested by the Inquisition, Molinos was secretly tried, and his doctrines were condemned as heretical. He died in a prison at Rome in 1697. For the Pope's attitude to Molinism, see X.1863ff.
8. "To each his own."
9. Luke 10:37.
1. I.e., the taking of holy orders. The tonsure is the monk's or priest's shaven crown.
2. Wear the cardinal's royal purple. Guido is represented as the first-born son; hence his responsibility to perpetuate the family name. The younger sons were free to seek preferment in the church.
3. The dress of a monsignor, a member of the papal court.
4. Luke 13:6–9. In effect, serve the church, but take no vows of celibacy.

Spend yourself there and bring the purchase[5] back!
Go hence to Rome, be guided!"

               So I was.
I turned alike from the hill-side zig-zag thread   235
Of way to the table-land a soldier takes,
Alike from the low-lying pasture-place
Where churchmen graze, recline and ruminate,
—Ventured to mount no platform like my lords
Who judge the world, bear brain I dare not brag—   240
But stationed me, might thus the expression serve,
As who should fetch and carry, come and go,
Meddle and make i' the cause my lords love most—
The public weal, which hangs to the law, which holds
By the Church, which happens to be through God himself.   245
Humbly I helped the Church till here I stand,—
Or would stand but for the omoplat, you see!
Bidden qualify for Rome, I, having a field,
Went, sold it, laid the sum at Peter's foot:[6]
Which means—I settled home-accounts with speed,   250
Set apart just a modicum should suffice
To hold the villa's head above the waves
Of weed inundating its oil and wine,
And prop roof, stanchion wall o' the palace so
As to keep breath i' the body, out of heart   255
Amid the advance of neighbouring loftiness—
(People like building where they used to beg)—
Till succoured one day,—shared the residue
Between my mother and brothers and sisters there,
Black-eyed babe Donna This and Donna That,   260
As near to starving as might decently be,
—Left myself journey-charges, change of suit,
A purse to put i' the pocket of the Groom
O' the Chamber of the patron, and a glove
With a ring to it for the digits of the niece   265
Sure to be helpful in his household,—then
Started for Rome, and led the life prescribed.
Close to the Church, though clean of it, I assumed
Three or four orders of no consequence,[7]
—They cast out evil spirits and exorcise,   270
For example; bind a man to nothing more,
Give clerical savour to his layman's-salt,
Facilitate his claim to loaf and fish
Should miracle leave, beyond what feeds the flock,
Fragments to brim the basket of a friend[8]—   275

---

5. Reward for service to the church.
6. That of the church. See Acts 4:36–37. (Barnabas, having sold his land "brought the money, and laid it at the apostles' feet.")
7. What orders these were the records do not say. It is known that he served a Cardinal Nerli, and that his sojourn at Rome was unsuccessful.
8. Matthew 14:17–20.

While, for the world's sake, I rode, danced and gamed,
Quitted me[9] like a courtier, measured mine
With whatsoever blade had fame in fence,
—Ready to let the basket go its round
Even though my turn was come to help myself,   280
Should Dives[1] count on me at dinner-time
As just the understander of a joke
And not immoderate in repartee.
Utrique sic paratus,[2] Sirs, I said,
"Here," (in the fortitude of years fifteen,   285
So good a pedagogue is penury)
"Here wait, do service,—serving and to serve!
And, in due time, I nowise doubt at all,
The recognition of my service comes.
Next year I'm only sixteen. I can wait."   290

I waited thirty years, may it please the Court:
Saw meanwhile many a denizen o' the dung
Hop, skip, jump o'er my shoulder, make him wings
And fly aloft,—succeed, in the usual phrase.
Everyone soon or late comes round by Rome: 295
Stand still here, you'll see all in turn succeed.
Why, look you, so and so, the physician here,
My father's lacquey's son we sent to school,
Doctored and dosed this Eminence and that,
Salved the last Pope his certain obstinate sore,   300
Soon bought land as became him, names it now:
I grasp bell at his griffin-guarded gate,
Traverse the half-mile avenue,—a term,[3]
A cypress, and a statue, three and three,—
Deliver message from my Monsignor,   305
With varletry[4] at lounge i' the vestibule
I'm barred from who bear mud upon my shoe.
My father's chaplain's nephew, Chamberlain,[5]—
Nothing less, please you!—courteous all the same,
—He does not see me though I wait an hour   310
At his staircase-landing 'twixt the brace of busts,
A noseless Sylla, Marius[6] maimed to match,
My father gave him for a hexastich[7]
Made on my birthday,—but he sends me down,
To make amends, that relic I prize most—   315
The unburnt end o' the very candle, Sirs,
Purfled[8] with paint so prettily round and round,

9. Conducted myself.
1. The rich man of the parable (Luke 16:19–31).
2. "Thus prepared for either," i.e., for immediate or deferred advancement.
3. Bust on a pillar, such as those honoring Terminus, god of boundaries.
4. Crowd of attendants or menials.
5. Highest ranking cardinal.
6. Lucius Sulla (138–78 B.C.E.) and Gaius Marius (157–86 B.C.E.), Roman generals who became bitter political rivals.
7. Epigram of six lines.
8. Here, decorated.

He carried in such state last Peter's-day,—
In token I, his gentleman and squire,
Had held the bridle, walked his managed mule   320
Without a tittup[9] the procession through.
Nay, the official,—one you know, sweet lords!—
Who drew the warrant for my transfer late
To the New Prisons from Tordinona,[1]—he
Graciously had remembrance—"Francesc . . . ha?   325
His sire, now—how a thing shall come about!—
Paid me a dozen florins[2] above the fee,
For drawing deftly up a deed of sale
When troubles fell so thick on him, good heart,
And I was prompt and pushing! By all means!   330
At the New Prisons be it his son shall lie,—
Anything for an old friend!" and thereat
Signed name with triple flourish underneath.
These were my fellows, such their fortunes now,
While I—kept fasts and feasts innumerable,   335
Matins and vespers, functions to no end
I' the train of Monsignor and Eminence,
As gentleman-squire, and for my zeal's reward
Have rarely missed a place at the table-foot
Except when some Ambassador, or such like,   340
Brought his own people. Brief, one day I felt
The tick of time inside me, turning-point
And slight sense there was now enough of this:
That I was near my seventh climacteric,[3]
Hard upon, if not over, the middle life,   345
And, although fed by the east-wind,[4] fulsome-fine
With foretaste of the Land of Promise, still
My gorge gave symptom it might play me false;
Better not press it further,—be content
With living and dying only a nobleman,   350
Who merely had a father great and rich,
Who simply had one greater and richer yet,
And so on back and back till first and best
Began i' the night; I finish in the day.
"The mother must be getting old," I said;   355
"The sisters are well wedded away, our name
Can manage to pass a sister off, at need,
And do for dowry: both my brothers thrive—
Regular priests they are, nor, bat-like, 'bide
'Twixt flesh and fowl with neither privilege.   360
My spare revenue must keep me and mine.
I am tired: Arezzo's air is good to breathe;

---

9. Frisking, prancing movement.
1. The Carceri Nuove, or New Prisons, were built in the mid-seventeenth century by Innocent
   X; the older papal prison was the Torre di Nona or Tordinona, a tower in the city walls.
2. Gold coins named for Florence.
3. I.e., nearly forty-nine years old, an exaggeration, since Browning has him married at forty-
   five. (The actual Guido, ten years younger, was executed at forty.)
4. Job 15:2: "Should a wise man . . . fill his belly with the east wind?"

Vittiano,—one limes[5] flocks of thrushes there;
A leathern coat costs little and lasts long:
Let me bid hope good-bye, content at home!"   365
Thus, one day, I disbosomed me and bowed.
Whereat began the little buzz and thrill
O' the gazers round me; each face brightened up:
As when at your Casino, deep in dawn,
A gamester says at last, "I play no more,   370
Forego gain, acquiesce in loss, withdraw
Anyhow:" and the watchers of his ways,
A trifle struck compunctious at the word,
Yet sensible of relief, breathe free once more,
Break up the ring, venture polite advice—   375
"How, Sir? So scant of heart and hope indeed?
Retire with neither cross nor pile[6] from play?—
So incurious, so short-casting?[7]—give your chance
To a younger, stronger, bolder spirit belike,
Just when luck turns and the fine throw sweeps all?"   380
Such was the chorus: and its goodwill meant—
"See that the loser leave door handsomely!
There's an ill look,—it's sinister, spoils sport,
When an old bruised and battered year-by-year
Fighter with fortune, not a penny in poke,   385
Reels down the steps of our establishment
And staggers on broad daylight and the world,
In shagrag beard and doleful doublet, drops
And breaks his heart on the outside: people prate
'Such is the profit of a trip upstairs!'   390
Contrive he sidle forth, baulked of[8] the blow
Best dealt by way of moral, bidding down
No curse but blessings rather on our heads
For some poor prize he bears at tattered breast,
Some palpable sort of kind of good to set   395
Over and against the grievance: give him quick!"
Whereon protested Paul, "Go hang yourselves!
Leave him to me. Count Guido and brother of mine,
A word in your ear! Take courage, since faint heart
Ne'er won . . . aha, fair lady, don't men say?   400
There's a sors,[9] there's a right Virgilian dip!
Do you see the happiness o' the hint? At worst,
If the Church want no more of you, the Court
No more, and the Camp as little, the ingrates,—come,
Count you are counted:[1] still you've coat to back,   405
Not cloth of gold and tissue, as we hoped,

---

5. Catches with birdlime, a sticky substance smeared on branches.
6. Two sides of a coin (cf. "head nor tail"); hence penniless.
7. Throwing dice in a cautious, timid manner.
8. Spared from.
9. The sors Virgiliana was the Roman practice of opening Virgil at random in the hope of find-
   ing guidance.
1. A pun: "As a Count, you count for something (in the marriage market)."

But cloth with sparks and spangles on its frieze[2]
From Camp, Court, Church, enough to make a shine,
Entitle you to carry home a wife
With the proper dowry, let the worst betide!   410
Why, it was just a wife you meant to take!"

Now, Paul's advice was weighty: priests should know:[3]
And Paul apprised me, ere the week was out,
That Pietro and Violante, the easy pair,
The cits[4] enough, with stomach to be more,   415
Had just the daughter and exact the sum
To truck[5] for the quality of myself: "She's young,
Pretty and rich: you're noble, classic, choice.
Is it to be a match?" "A match," said I.
Done! He proposed all, I accepted all,   420
And we performed all. So I said and did
Simply. As simply followed, not at first
But with the outbreak of misfortune, still
One comment on the saying and doing—"What?
No blush at the avowal you dared buy   425
A girl of age beseems your granddaughter,[6]
Like ox or ass? Are flesh and blood a ware?
Are heart and soul a chattel?"
                            Softly, Sirs!
Will the Court of its charity teach poor me
Anxious to learn, of any way i' the world,   430
Allowed by custom and convenience, save
This same which, taught from my youth up, I trod?
Take me along with you; where was the wrong step?
If what I gave in barter, style and state
And all that hangs to Franceschinihood,   435
Were worthless,—why, society goes to ground,
Its rules are idiot's-rambling. Honour of birth,—
If that thing has no value, cannot buy
Something with value of another sort,
You've no reward nor punishment to give   440
I' the giving or the taking honour; straight
Your social fabric, pinnacle to base,
Comes down a-clatter like a house of cards.
Get honour, and keep honour free from flaw,
Aim at still higher honour,—gabble o' the goose!   445
Go bid a second blockhead like myself
Spend fifty years in guarding bubbles of breath,
Soapsuds with air i' the belly, gilded brave,
Guarded and guided, all to break at touch

2. Coarse wool.
3. Guido alludes to the words of St. Paul, who after advising celibacy says, "But if they cannot
   contain, let them marry: for it is better to marry than to burn" (1 Corinthians 7:9).
4. Citizens, i.e., prosperous bourgeois.
5. Barter.
6. Pompilla was thirteen when she married the forty-five-year-old Guido.

O' the first young girl's hand and first old fool's purse!   450
All my privation and endurance, all
Love, loyalty and labour dared and did,
Fiddle-de-dee!—why, doer and darer both,—
Count Guido Franceschini had hit the mark
Far better, spent his life with more effect,   455
As a dancer or a prizer,[7] trades that pay!
On the other hand, bid this buffoonery cease,
Admit that honour is a privilege,
The question follows, privilege worth what?
Why, worth the market-price,—now up, now down,   460
Just so with this as with all other ware:
Therefore essay the market, sell your name,
Style and condition to who buys them best!
"Does my name purchase," had I dared inquire,
"Your niece, my lord?" there would have been rebuff   465
Though courtesy, your Lordship cannot else—
"Not altogether! Rank for rank may stand:
But I have wealth beside, you—poverty;
Your scale flies up there: bid a second bid
Rank too and wealth too!" Reasoned like yourself!   470
But was it to you I went with goods to sell?
This time 't was my scale quietly kissed the ground,
Mere rank against mere wealth—some youth beside,
Some beauty too, thrown into the bargain, just
As the buyer likes or lets alone. I thought   475
To deal o' the square: others find fault, it seems:
The thing is, those my offer most concerned,
Pietro, Violante, cried they fair or foul?
What did they make o' the terms? Preposterous terms?
Why then accede so promptly, close with such   480
Nor take a minute to chaffer? Bargain struck,
They straight grew bilious,[8] wished their money back,
Repented them, no doubt: why, so did I,
So did your Lordship, if town-talk be true,
Of paying a full farm's worth for that piece   485
By Pietro of Cortona[9]—probably
His scholar Ciro Ferri may have retouched—
You caring more for colour than design—
Getting a little tired of cupids too.
That's incident[1] to all the folk who buy!   490
I am charged, I know, with gilding fact by fraud;
I falsified and fabricated, wrote
Myself down roughly richer than I prove,
Rendered a wrong revenue,—grant it all!
Mere grace, mere coquetry such fraud, I say: 495
A flourish round the figures of a sum

7. Prize-fighter.
8. Irate.
9. Baroque painter (1596–1669); Ferri (1634–89) was his chief pupil.
1. Likely to occur.

For fashion's sake, that deceives nobody.
The veritable back-bone, understood
Essence of this same bargain, blank and bare,
Being the exchange of quality for wealth,—   500
What may such fancy-flights be? Flecks of oil
Flirted by chapmen[2] where plain dealing grates.
I may have dripped a drop—"My name I sell;
Not but that I too boast my wealth"—as they,
"—We bring you riches; still our ancestor   505
Was hardly the rapscallion folk saw flogged,
But heir to we know who, were rights of force!"[3]
They knew and I knew where the backbone lurked
I' the writhings of the bargain, lords, believe!
I paid down all engaged for, to a doit,[4]   510
Delivered them just that which, their life long,
They hungered in the hearts of them to gain—
Incorporation with nobility thus
In word and deed: for that they gave me wealth.
But when they came to try their gain, my gift,   515
Quit Rome and qualify for Arezzo, take
The tone o' the new sphere that absorbed the old,
Put away gossip Jack and goody Joan
And go become familiar with the Great,
Greatness to touch and taste and handle now,[5]—   520
Why then,—they found that all was vanity,
Vexation, and what Solomon describes![6]
The old abundant city-fare was best,
The kindly warmth o' the commons, the glad clap
Of the equal on the shoulder, the frank grin   525
Of the underling at all so many spoons
Fire-new at neighbourly treat,—best, best and best
Beyond compare!—down to the loll itself
O' the pot-house[7] settle,—better such a bench
Than the stiff crucifixion by my dais   530
Under the piecemeal damask canopy
With the coroneted coat of arms a-top!
Poverty and privation for pride's sake,
All they engaged to easily brave and bear,—
With the fit upon them and their brains a-work,—   535
Proved unendurable to the sobered sots.
A banished prince, now, will exude a juice
And salamander-like[8] support the flame:
He dines on chestnuts, chucks the husks to help
The broil o' the brazier, pays the due baioc,[9]   540

2. Smooth talk sprinkled by merchants.
3. If justice were done.
4. Penny.
5. Cf. Colossians 2:21.
6. In Ecclesiastes.
7. Tavern.
8. Like the salamander of myth, a lizard-like creature who could live in the midst of flame.
9. *Baiocco*, papal coin of small value.

Goes off light-hearted: his grimace begins
At the funny humours of the christening-feast
Of friend the money-lender,—then he's touched
By the flame and frizzles[1] at the babe to kiss!
Here was the converse trial, opposite mind: 545
Here did a petty nature split on rock
Of vulgar wants predestinate for such—
One dish at supper and weak wine to boot!
The prince had grinned and borne: the citizen[2] shrieked,
Summoned the neighbourhood to attest the wrong,   550
Made noisy protest he was murdered,—stoned
And burned and drowned and hanged,—then broke away,
He and his wife, to tell their Rome the rest.
And this you admire, you men o' the world, my lords?
This moves compassion, makes you doubt my faith?   555
Why, I appeal to . . . sun and moon? Not I!
Rather to Plautus, Terence, Boccaccio's Book,
My townsman, frank Ser Franco's merry Tales,[3]—
To all who strip a vizard[4] from a face,
A body from its padding, and a soul   560
From froth and ignorance it styles itself,—
If this be other than the daily hap
Of purblind[5] greed that dog-like still drops bone,
Grasps shadow, and then howls the case is hard![6]

So much for them so far: now for myself,   565
My profit or loss i' the matter: married am I:
Text whereon friendly censors burst to preach.
Ay, at Rome even, long ere I was left
To regulate her life for my young bride
Alone at Arezzo, friendliness outbroke   570
(Sifting my future to predict its fault)
"Purchase and sale being thus so plain a point,
How of a certain soul bound up, may-be,
I' the barter with the body and money-bags?
From the bride's soul what is it you expect?"   575
Why, loyalty and obedience,—wish and will
To settle and suit her fresh and plastic mind
To the novel, not disadvantageous mould!
Father and mother shall the woman leave,
Cleave to the husband, be it for weal or woe:[7]   580
There is the law: what sets this law aside

1. Burns up: i.e., cannot endure.
2. Pietro (and Violante) Comparini, who left Arezzo for Rome after four months, bearing tales of poor treatment at Guido's house (see 762ff.).
3. Guido refers the judges to classics of comedy for analogues of the Comparini's greed. Plautus and Terence were Roman playwrights; "Boccaccio's Book" is the *Decameron* (1358), a collection of *novelle*; "Ser Franco" is Boccaccio's younger contemporary Franco Sacchetti, who also wrote *novelle*.
4. Mask.
5. Stupid.
6. Alluding to Aesop's fable of a dog who encounters his own reflection in a stream and, in trying to grab the bone of the "other" dog, drops his own into the water and loses it.
7. Genesis 2:24.

In my particular case? My friends submit
"Guide, guardian, benefactor,—fee, faw, fum,
The fact is you are forty-five years old,
Nor very comely even for that age: 585
Girls must have boys." Why, let girls say so then,
Nor call the boys and men, who say the same,
Brute this and beast the other as they do!
Come, cards on table! When you chaunt us next
Epithalamium[8] full to overflow   590
With praise and glory of white womanhood,
The chaste and pure—troll[9] no such lies o'er lip!
Put in their stead a crudity or two,
Such short and simple statement of the case
As youth chalks on our walls at spring of year!   595
No! I shall still think nobler of the sex,
Believe a woman still may take a man
For the short period that his soul wears flesh,
And, for the soul's sake, understand the fault
Of armour frayed by fighting. Tush, it tempts   600
One's tongue too much! I'll say—the law's the law:
With a wife I look to find all wifeliness,
As when I buy, timber and twig, a tree—
I buy the song o' the nightingale inside.

Such was the pact: Pompilia from the first   605
Broke it, refused from the beginning day
Either in body or soul to cleave to mine,
And published it forthwith to all the world.
No rupture,—you must join ere you can break,—
Before we had cohabited a month   610
She found I was a devil and no man,—
Made common cause with those who found as much,
Her parents, Pietro and Violante,—moved
Heaven and earth to the rescue of all three.
In four months' time, the time o' the parents' stay,   615
Arezzo was a-ringing, bells in a blaze,
With the unimaginable story rife
I' the mouth of man, woman and child—to-wit
My misdemeanour. First the lighter side,
Ludicrous face of things,—how very poor   620
The Franceschini had become at last,
The meanness and the misery of each shift
To save a soldo,[1] stretch and make ends meet.
Next, the more hateful aspect,—how myself
With cruelty beyond Caligula's[2]   625
Had stripped and beaten, robbed and murdered them,
The good old couple, I decoyed, abused,

8. Wedding song.
9. Sing.
1. Small Tuscan coin.
2. Roman emperor who was exceedingly cruel and probably mad (c.e. 12–41).

Plundered and then cast out, and happily so,
Since,—in due course the abominable comes,—
Woe worth[3] the poor young wife left lonely here!   630
Repugnant in my person as my mind,
I sought,—was ever heard of such revenge?
—To lure and bind her to so cursed a couch,
Such co-embrace with sulphur, snake and toad,
That she was fain to rush forth, call the stones   635
O' the common street to save her, not from hate
Of mine merely, but . . . must I burn my lips
With the blister of the lie? . . . the satyr-love
Of who but my own brother,[4] the young priest,
Too long enforced to lenten fare belike,   640
Now tempted by the morsel tossed him full
I' the trencher[5] where lay bread and herbs at best.
Mark, this yourselves say!—this, none disallows,
Was charged to me by the universal voice
At the instigation of my four-months' wife!—   645
And then you ask "Such charges so preferred,
(Truly or falsely, here concerns us not)
Pricked you to punish now if not before?—
Did not the harshness double itself, the hate
Harden?" I answer "Have it your way and will!"   650
Say my resentment grew apace: what then?
Do you cry out on the marvel? When I find
That pure smooth egg which, laid within my nest,
Could not but hatch a comfort to us all,
Issues a cockatrice[6] for me and mine,   655
Do you stare to see me stamp on it? Swans are soft:
Is it not clear that she you call my wife,
That any wife of any husband, caught
Whetting a sting like this against his breast,—
Speckled with fragments of the fresh-broke shell,   660
Married a month and making outcry thus,—
Proves a plague-prodigy to God and man?
She married: what was it she married for,
Counted upon and meant to meet thereby?
"Love" suggests some one, "love, a little word   665
Whereof we have not heard one syllable."
So, the Pompilia, child, girl, wife, in one,
Wanted the beating pulse, the rolling eye,
The frantic gesture, the devotion due
From Thyrsis to Neæra![7] Guido's love—   670
Why not Provençal roses[8] in his shoe,

---

3. Woe be to.
4. Girolamo, who like Caponsacchi was a canon of the Pieve church at Arezzo. He was accused
   of making improper advances to Pompilla and of maltreating the Comparini.
5. Plate or platter.
6. Mythical serpent hatched by a reptile from a cock's egg. Supposed to have the power of
   killing by its glance; hence, a treacherous person.
7. Stock names of lovers in pastoral poetry.
8. Ribbon rosettes, alluding to romantic troubadours from Provence in France.

Plume to his cap, and trio of guitars
At casement, with a bravo[9] close beside?
Good things all these are, clearly claimable
When the fit price is paid the proper way.   675
Had it been some friend's wife, now, threw her fan
At my foot, with just this pretty scrap attached,
"Shame, death, damnation—fall these as they may,
So I find you, for a minute! Come this eve!"
—Why, at such sweet self-sacrifice,—who knows?   680
I might have fired up, found me at my post,
Ardent from head to heel, nor feared catch cough.
Nay, had some other friend's . . . say, daughter, tripped
Upstairs and tumbled flat and frank on me,
Bareheaded and barefooted, with loose hair   685
And garments all at large,—cried " 'Take me thus!
Duke So-and-So, the greatest man in Rome—
To escape his hand and heart have I broke bounds,
Traversed the town and reached you!"—then, indeed,
The lady had not reached a man of ice!   690
I would have rummaged, ransacked at the word
Those old odd corners of an empty heart
For remnants of dim love the long disused,
And dusty crumblings of romance! But here,
We talk of just a marriage, if you please—   695
The every-day conditions and no more;
Where do these bind me to bestow one drop
Of blood shall dye my wife's true-love-knot[1] pink?
Pompilia was no pigeon, Venus' pet,
That shuffled from between her pressing paps   700
To sit on my rough shoulder,—but a hawk,
I bought at a hawk's price and carried home
To do hawk's service[2]—at the Rotunda,[3] say,
Where, six o' the callow nestlings in a row,
You pick and choose and pay the price for such.   705
I have paid my pound, await my penny's worth,
So, hoodwink,[4] starve and properly train my bird,
And, should she prove a haggard,[5]—twist her neck!
Did I not pay my name and style, my hope
And trust, my all? Through spending these amiss   710
I am here! 'T is scarce the gravity of the Court
Will blame me that I never piped a tune,
Treated my falcon-gentle[6] like my finch.
The obligation I incurred was just
To practise mastery, prove my mastership:—   715
Pompilia's duty was—submit herself,

9. Bodyguard or assassin.
1. Complicated double knot, symbol of love.
2. I.e., to obey its master.
3. The Piazza of the Pantheon, where birds are sold.
4. Blindfold. (The imagery is that of falconry.)
5. Here, an untrainable wild hawk. (Cf. *Othello*, III.iii.260–63 for a parallel metaphor.)
6. Goshawk, large brownish female hawk.

Afford me pleasure, perhaps cure my bile.
Am I to teach my lords what marriage means,
What God ordains thereby and man fulfils
Who, docile to the dictate, treads the house?   720
My lords have chosen the happier part with Paul
And neither marry nor burn,[7]—yet priestliness
Can find a parallel to the marriage-bond
In its own blessed special ordinance
Whereof indeed was marriage made the type:[8]   725
The Church may show her insubordinate,
As marriage her refractory. How of the Monk
Who finds the claustral[9] regimen too sharp
After the first month's essay? What's the mode
With the Deacon who supports indifferently[1]   730
The rod o' the Bishop when he tastes its smart
Full four weeks? Do you straightway slacken hold
Of the innocents, the all-unwary ones
Who, eager to profess,[2] mistook their mind?—
Remit a fast-day's rigour to the Monk   735
Who fancied Francis' manna meant roast quails,[3]—
Concede the Deacon sweet society,
He never thought the Levite-rule[4] renounced,—
Or rather prescribe short chain and sharp scourge
Corrective of such peccant humours?[5] This—   740
I take to be the Church's mode, and mine.
If I was over-harsh,—the worse i' the wife
Who did not win[6] from harshness as she ought,
Wanted the patience and persuasion, lore
Of love, should cure me and console herself.   745
Put case that I mishandle, flurry and fright
My hawk through clumsiness in sportsmanship,
Twitch out five pens[7] where plucking one would serve—
What, shall she bite and claw to mend the case?
And, if you find I pluck five more for that,   750
Shall you weep "How he roughs the turtle[8] there"?

Such was the starting; now of the further step.
In lieu of taking penance in good part,
The Monk, with hue and cry, summons a mob
To make a bonfire of the convent, say,—   755

---

7. See note to V.412.
8. In Ephesians 5:22–25, St. Paul makes this analogy: husband is to wife as Christ is to church. "Therefore as the church is subject unto Christ, so let the wives be to their own husbands in every thing."
9. Monastic.
1. Can hardly endure.
2. Take religious vows.
3. Cf. Numbers 11: 31–33.
4. Rules governing deacons.
5. Errant behavior.
6. Gain, improve.
7. Feathers.
8. Turtledove.

And the Deacon's pretty piece of virtue[9] (save
The ears o' the Court! I try to save my head)
Instructed by the ingenuous postulant,[1]
Taxes the Bishop with adultery, (mud
Needs must pair off with mud, and filth with filth)—   760
Such being my next experience. Who knows not—
The couple, father and mother of my wife,
Returned to Rome, published before my lords,
Put into print, made circulate far and wide
That they had cheated me who cheated them?   765
Pompilia, I supposed their daughter, drew
Breath first 'mid Rome's worst rankness, through the deed
Of a drab and a rogue, was by-blow bastard-babe
Of a nameless strumpet, passed off, palmed on me
As the daughter with the dowry. Daughter? Dirt   770
O' the kennel![2] Dowry? Dust o' the street! Nought more,
Nought less, nought else but—oh—ah—assuredly
A Franceschini and my very wife!
Now take this charge as you will, for false or true,—
This charge, preferred before your very selves   775
Who judge me now,—I pray you, adjudge again,
Classing it with the cheats or with the lies,
By which category I suffer most!
But of their reckoning, theirs who dealt with me
In either fashion,—I reserve my word,   780
Justify that in its place; I am now to say,
Whichever point o' the charge might poison most,
Pompilia's duty was no doubtful one.
You put the protestation in her mouth
"Henceforward and forevermore, avaunt   785
Ye fiends, who drop disguise and glare revealed
In your own shape, no longer father mine
Nor mother mine! Too nakedly you hate
Me whom you looked as if you loved once,—me
Whom, whether true or false, your tale now damns,   790
Divulged thus to my public infamy,
Private perdition, absolute overthrow.
For, hate my husband to your hearts' content,
I, spoil and prey of you from first to last,
I who have done you the blind service, lured   795
The lion to your pitfall,—I, thus left
To answer for my ignorant bleating there,
I should have been remembered and withdrawn
From the first o' the natural fury, not flung loose
A proverb and a by-word men will mouth   800
At the cross-way, in the corner, up and down
Rome and Arezzo,—there, full in my face,
If my lord, missing them and finding me,

9. I.e., his mistress.
1. Candidate for admission into a religious order, referring here to the Deacon.
2. Street drain, gutter.

Content himself with casting his reproach
To drop i' the street where such impostors die.   805
Ah, but—that husband, what the wonder were!—
If, far from casting thus away the rag
Smeared with the plague his hand had chanced upon,
Sewn to his pillow by Locusta's[3] wile,—
Far from abolishing, root, stem and branch,   810
The misgrowth of infectious mistletoe
Foisted into his stock for honest graft,[4]—
If he repudiate not, renounce nowise,
But, guarding, guiding me, maintain my cause
By making it his own, (what other way?)   815
—To keep my name for me, he call it his,
Claim it of who would take it by their lie,—
To save my wealth for me—or babe of mine
Their lie was framed to beggar at the birth—
He bid them loose grasp, give our gold again: 820
If he become no partner with the pair
Even in a game which, played adroitly, gives
Its winner life's great wonderful new chance,—
Of marrying, to-wit, a second time,—
Ah, if he did thus, what a friend were he!   825
Anger he might show,—who can stamp out flame
Yet spread no black o' the brand?—yet, rough albeit
In the act, as whose bare feet feel embers scorch,
What grace were his, what gratitude were mine!"
Such protestation should have been my wife's.   830
Looking for this, do I exact too much?
Why, here's the,—word for word, so much, no more,—
Avowal she made, her pure spontaneous speech
To my brother the Abate at first blush,
Ere the good impulse had begun to fade: 835
So did she make confession for the pair,
So pour forth praises in her own behalf.
"Ay, the false letter,"[5] interpose my lords—
"The simulated writing,—'t was a trick:
You traced the signs, she merely marked the same,   840
The product was not hers but yours." Alack,
I want no more impulsion to tell truth
From the other trick, the torture inside there!
I confess all—let it be understood—
And deny nothing! If I baffle you so,   845
Can so fence, in the plenitude of right,
That my poor lathen[6] dagger puts aside
Each pass o' the Bilboa,[7] beats you all the same,—

3. Female poisoner in the reigns of Claudius and Nero.
4. Passed off as a viable graft onto the Franceschini family tree.
5. Pompilia's letter of June 14, 1694, to Paolo (allegedly forged), in which she thanked him for
having married her to Guido, and affirmed that life was peaceful since her parents' departure.
6. Wooden, used of a counterfeit weapon.
7. Sword made in Bilbao, Spanish town famed for its steel.

What matters inefficiency of blade?
Mine and not hers the letter,—conceded, lords!   850
Impute to me that practice!—take as proved
I taught my wife her duty, made her see
What it behoved her see and say and do,
Feel in her heart and with her tongue declare,
And, whether sluggish or recalcitrant,   855
Forced her to take the right step, I myself
Was marching in marital rectitude!
Why who finds fault here, say the tale be true?
Would not my lords commend the priest whose zeal
Seized on the sick, morose or moribund,   860
By the palsy-smitten finger, made it cross
His brow correctly at the critical time?
—Or answered for the inarticulate babe
At baptism, in its stead declared the faith,
And saved what else would perish unprofessed?   865
True, the incapable hand may rally yet,
Renounce the sign with renovated strength,—
The babe may grow up man and Molinist,—
And so Pompilia, set in the good path
And left to go alone there, soon might see   870
That too frank-forward, all too simple-straight
Her step was, and decline to tread the rough,
When here lay, tempting foot, the meadow-side,
And there the coppice rang with singing-birds!
Soon she discovered she was young and fair,   875
That many in Arezzo knew as much.[8]
Yes, this next cup of bitterness, my lords,
Had to begin go filling, drop by drop,
Its measure up of full disgust for me,
Filtered into by every noisome[9] drain—   880
Society's sink toward which all moisture runs.
Would not you prophesy—"She on whose brow is stamped
The note of the imputation that we know,—
Rightly or wrongly mothered with a whore,—
Such an one, to disprove the frightful charge,   885
What will she but exaggerate chastity,
Err in excess of wifehood, as it were,
Renounce even levities permitted youth,
Though not youth struck to age by a thunderbolt?
Cry 'wolf' i' the sheepfold, where's the sheep dares bleat,   890
Knowing the shepherd listens for a growl?"
So you expect. How did the devil decree?
Why, my lords, just the contrary of course!
It was in the house from the window, at the church
From the hassock,—where the theatre lent its lodge,[1]   895

---

8. In Guido's suit against Pompilia and Caponsacchi for flight and adultery (called the "Process
  of Flight," or *processus fugae*) it was alleged that Pompilia had many lovers in Arezzo. The al-
  legation was quoted at the murder trial.
9. Filthy.
1. Loge or box.

Or staging for the public show left space,—
That still Pompilia needs must find herself
Launching her looks forth, letting looks reply
As arrows to a challenge; on all sides
Ever new contribution to her lap,   900
Till one day, what is it knocks at my clenched teeth
But the cup full, curse-collected all for me?
And I must needs drink, drink this gallant's praise,
That minion's prayer, the other fop's reproach,
And come at the dregs to—Caponsacchi! Sirs,   905
I,—chin-deep in a marsh of misery,
Struggling to extricate my name and fame
And fortune from the marsh would drown them all,
My face the sole unstrangled part of me,—
I must have this new gad-fly in that face,   910
Must free me from the attacking lover too!
Men say I battled ungracefully enough—
Was harsh, uncouth and ludicrous beyond
The proper part o' the husband: have it so!
Your lordships are considerate at least—   915
You order me to speak in my defence
Plainly, expect no quavering tuneful trills
As when you bid a singer solace you,—
Nor look that I shall give it, for a grace,
Stans pede in uno:[2]—you remember well   920
In the one case, 't is a plainsong too severe,[3]
This story of my wrongs,—and that I ache
And need a chair, in the other. Ask you me
Why, when I felt this trouble flap my face,
Already pricked with every shame could perch,—   925
When, with her parents, my wife plagued me too,—
Why I enforced not exhortation mild
To leave whore's-tricks and let my brows alone,[4]
With mulct of comfits, promise of perfume?

"Far from that! No, you took the opposite course,   930
Breathed threatenings, rage and slaughter!" What you will!
And the end has come, the doom is verily here,
Unhindered by the threatening. See fate's flare
Full on each face of the dead guilty three!
Look at them well, and now, lords, look at this!   935
Tell me: if on that day when I found first
That Caponsacchi thought the nearest way
To his church was some half-mile round by my door,
And that he so admired, shall I suppose,
The manner of the swallows' come-and-go   940
Between the props o' the window over-head—
That window happening to be my wife's,—

2. "Done standing on one foot"; i.e., an easy thing (Horace. *Satires*, I.iv.10).
3. Liturgical chant too austere in style.
4. Remain faithful; the proverbial cuckold grows horns on his forehead.

As to stand gazing by the hour on high,
Of May-eves, while she sat and let him smile,—
If I,—instead of threatening, talking big,   945
Showing hair-powder, a prodigious pinch,
For poison in a bottle,—making believe
At desperate doings with a bauble-sword,
And other bugaboo-and-baby-work,[5]—
Had, with the vulgarest household implement,   950
Calmly and quietly cut off, clean thro' bone
But one joint of one finger of my wife,
Saying "For listening to the serenade,
Here's your ring-finger shorter a full third:
Be certain I will slice away next joint,   955
Next time that anybody underneath
Seems somehow to be sauntering as he hoped
A flower would eddy out of your hand to his
While you please fidget with the branch above
O' the rose-tree in the terrace!"—had I done so,   960
Why, there had followed a quick sharp scream, some pain,
Much calling for plaister, damage to the dress,
A somewhat sulky countenance next day,
Perhaps reproaches,—but reflections too!
I don't hear much of harm that Malchus did   965
After the incident of the ear, my lords!
Saint Peter took the efficacious way;
Malchus was sore but silenced for his life:[6]
He did not hang himself i' the Potter's Field
Like Judas, who was trusted with the bag   970
And treated to sops after he proved a thief.[7]
So, by this time, my true and obedient wife
Might have been telling beads with a gloved hand;
Awkward a little at pricking hearts and darts
On sampler possibly, but well otherwise: 975
Not where Rome shudders now to see her lie.
I give that for the course a wise man takes;
I took the other however, tried the fool's,
The lighter remedy, brandished rapier dread
With cork-ball at the tip, boxed Malchus' ear   980
Instead of severing the cartilage,
Called her a terrible nickname, and the like,
And there an end: and what was the end of that?
What was the good effect o' the gentle course?
Why, one night I went drowsily to bed,   985
Dropped asleep suddenly, not suddenly woke,
But did wake with rough rousing and loud cry,
To find noon in my face, a crowd in my room,
Fumes in my brain, fire in my throat, my wife

---

5. In her actual deposition Pompilia alleged that Guido threatened to dispatch her by poison-
ing or stabbing.
6. Guido suppresses the fact that Peter was rebuked by Christ for this act (John 18:10–11).
7. John 13:26–30.

Gone God knows whither,—rifled vesture-chest,   990
And ransacked money-coffer. "What does it mean?"
The servants had been drugged too, stared and yawned
"It must be that our lady has eloped!"
—"Whither and with whom?"—"With whom but
     the Canon's self?
One recognizes Caponsacchi there!"—   995
(By this time the admiring neighbourhood
Joined chorus round me while I rubbed my eyes)
" 'T is months since their intelligence began,—
A comedy the town was privy to,—
He wrote and she wrote, she spoke, he replied,   1000
And going in and out your house last night
Was easy work for one . . . to be plain with you . . .
Accustomed to do both, at dusk and dawn
When you were absent,—at the villa, you know,
Where husbandry required the master-mind.   1005
Did not you know? Why, we all knew, you see!"
And presently, bit by bit, the full and true
Particulars of the tale were volunteered
With all the breathless zeal of friendship—"Thus
Matters were managed: at the seventh hour of night" . . .   1010
—"Later, at daybreak" . . . "Caponsacchi came" . . .
—"While you and all your household slept like death,
Drugged as your supper was with drowsy stuff" . . .
—"And your own cousin Guillichini[8] too—
Either or both entered your dwelling-place,   1015
Plundered it at their pleasure, made prize of all,
Including your wife . . ."—"Oh, your wife led the way,
Out of doors, on to the gate . . ."—"But gates are shut,
In a decent town, to darkness and such deeds:
They climbed the wall—your lady must be lithe—   1020
At the gap, the broken bit . . ."—"Torrione,[9] true!
To escape the questioning guard at the proper gate,
Clemente, where at the inn, hard by, 'the Horse,'
Just outside, a calash[1] in readiness
Took the two principals, all alone at last,   1025
To gate San Spirito, which o'erlooks the road,
Leads to Perugia, Rome and liberty."
Bit by bit thus made-up mosaic-wise,
Flat lay my fortune,—tesselated floor,
Imperishable tracery devils should foot   1030
And frolic it on, around my broken gods,
Over my desecrated hearth.   So much
For the terrible effect of threatening, Sirs!

---

8. A relative of Guido's accused, before the Arezzo court, of complicity in the elopement; Pom-
   pilia, in a letter to the Comparini, says he was to have accompanied her in the flight.
9. Bastion at northwest corner of Arezzo, adjacent to San Clemente gate. The evidence con-
   flicted as to when and by what means Pompilia fled, and Browning in this passage seizes on
   that fact to underscore his theme of "our human testimony false."
1. Carriage.

Well, this way I was shaken wide awake,
Doctored and drenched,[2] somewhat unpoisoned so.   1035
Then, set on horseback and bid seek the lost,
I started alone, head of me, heart of me
Fire, and each limb as languid . . . ah, sweet lords,
Bethink you!—poison-torture, try persuade
The next refractory Molinist with that! . . .   1040
Floundered thro' day and night, another day
And yet another night, and so at last,
As Lucifer kept falling to find hell,
Tumbled into the court-yard of an inn
At the end, and fell on whom I thought to find,   1045
Even Caponsacchi,—what part once was priest,
Cast to the winds now with the cassock-rags.
In cape and sword a cavalier confessed,
There stood he chiding dilatory grooms,
Chafing that only horseflesh and no team   1050
Of eagles would supply the last relay,
Whirl him along the league, the one post more
Between the couple and Rome and liberty.
'T was dawn, the couple were rested in a sort,
And though the lady, tired,—the tenderer sex,—   1055
Still lingered in her chamber,—to adjust
The limp hair, look for any blush astray,—
She would descend in a twinkling,—"Have you out
The horses therefore!"
              So did I find my wife.
Is the case complete? Do your eyes here see with mine?   1060
Even the parties dared deny no one
Point out of all these points
                 What follows next?
"Why, that then was the time," you interpose,
"Or then or never, while the fact was fresh,
To take the natural vengeance: there and thus   1065
They and you,—somebody had stuck a sword
Beside you while he pushed you on your horse,—
'T was requisite to slay the couple, Count!"
Just so my friends say. "Kill!" they cry in a breath,
Who presently, when matters grow to a head   1070
And I do kill the offending ones indeed,—
When crime of theirs, only surmised before,
Is patent, proved indisputably now,—
When remedy for wrong,[3] untried at the time,
Which law professes shall not fail a friend,   1075
Is thrice tried[4] now, found threefold worse than null,—
When what might turn to transient shade, who knows?
Solidifies into a blot which breaks
Hell's black off in pale flakes for fear of mine,—

2. Given antidote to the sleeping potion Pompilia administered.
3. Immediate revenge by manslaughter, excusable as a crime of passion.
4. In the three murders (with malice aforethought, hence inexcusable).

Then, when I claim and take revenge—"So rash?"   1080
They cry—"so little reverence for the law?"

Listen, my masters, and distinguish here!
At first, I called in law to act and help:
Seeing I did so, "Why, 't is clear," they cry,
"You shrank from gallant readiness and risk,   1085
Were coward: the thing's inexplicable else."
Sweet my lords, let the thing be! I fall flat,
Play the reed, not the oak, to breath of man.
Only inform my ignorance! Say I stand
Convicted of the having been afraid,   1090
Proved a poltroon, no lion but a lamb,—
Does that deprive me of my right of lamb
And give my fleece and flesh to the first wolf?
Are eunuchs, women, children, shieldless quite
Against attack their own timidity tempts?   1095
Cowardice were misfortune and no crime!
—Take it that way, since I am fallen so low
I scarce dare brush the fly that blows my face,
And thank the man who simply spits not there,—
Unless the Court be generous, comprehend   1100
How one brought up at the very feet of law
As I, awaits the grave Gamaliel's[5] nod
Ere he clench fist at outrage,—much less, stab!
—How, ready enough to rise at the right time,
I still could recognise no time mature   1105
Unsanctioned by a move o' the judgment-seat,
So, mute in misery, eyed my masters here
Motionless till the authoritative word
Pronounced amercement.[6] There's the riddle solved:
This is just why I slew nor her nor him,   1110
But called in law, law's delegate in the place,
And bade arrest the guilty couple, Sirs!
We had some trouble to do so—you have heard
They braved me,—he with arrogance and scorn,
She, with a volubility of curse,   1115
A conversancy in the skill of tooth
And claw to make suspicion seem absurd,
Nay, an alacrity to put to proof
At my own throat my own sword, teach me so
To try conclusions better the next time,—   1120
Which did the proper service with the mob.
They never tried to put on mask at all:
Two avowed lovers forcibly torn apart,
Upbraid the tyrant as in a playhouse scene,
Ay, and with proper clapping and applause   1125
From the audience that enjoys the bold and free.

5. Teacher of the "law of the fathers" to St. Paul (Acts 22:3).
6. Penalty.

I kept still, said to myself, "There's law!" Anon
We searched the chamber where they passed the night,
Found what confirmed the worst was feared before,
However needless confirmation now—   1130
The witches' circle intact, charms undisturbed
That raised the spirit and succubus,[7]—letters,[8] to-wit,
Love-laden, each the bag o' the bee that bore
Honey from lily and rose to Cupid's hive,—
Now, poetry in some rank blossom-burst,   1135
Now, prose,—"Come here, go there, wait such a while,
He's at the villa, now he's back again:
We are saved, we are lost, we are lovers all the same!"
All in order, all complete,—even to a clue
To the drowsiness that happed so opportune—   1140
No mystery, when I read "Of all things, find
What wine Sir Jealousy decides to drink—
Red wine? Because a sleeping-potion, dust
Dropped into white, discolours wine and shows."

—"Oh, but we did not write a single word!   1145
Somebody forged the letters in our name!—"
Both in a breath protested presently.
Aha, Sacchetti[9] again!—"Dame,"—quoth the Duke,
"What meaneth this epistle, counsel me,
I pick from out thy placket[1] and peruse,   1150
Wherein my page averreth thou art white
And warm and wonderful 'twixt pap and pap?"
"Sir," laughed the Lady, " 't is a counterfeit!
Thy page did never stroke but Dian's breast,
The pretty hound I nurture for thy sake: 1155
To lie were losel,[2]—by my fay, no more!"
And no more say I too, and spare the Court.

Ah, the Court! yes, I come to the Court's self;
Such the case, so complete in fact and proof,
I laid at the feet of law,—there sat my lords,   1160
Here sit they now, so may they ever sit
In easier attitude than suits my haunch!
In this same chamber did I bare my sores
O' the soul and not the body,—shun no shame,
Shrink from no probing of the ulcerous part,   1165
Since confident in Nature,—which is God,—
That she who, for wise ends, concocts a plague,
Curbs, at the right time, the plague's virulence too:
Law renovates even Lazarus,[3]—cures me!

---

7. Female demon supposed to have sexual intercourse with a man while he sleeps.
8. The most damaging evidence against the pair. In her deposition of May 1697 (in the so-called "Process of Flight") Pompilia stated she could neither read nor write.
9. Guido here mimics the elegant style of Sacchetti's *Novelle*.
1. Skirt pocket.
2. No good.
3. Man raised from the dead by Jesus (John 11:1–46).

Cæsar thou seekest? To Cæsar thou shalt go![4]   1170
Cæsar's at Rome: to Rome accordingly!

The case was soon decided: both weights, cast
I' the balance, vibrate, neither kicks the beam,
Here away, there away, this now and now that.
To every one o'my grievances law gave   1175
Redress, could purblind eye but see the point.
The wife stood a convicted runagate
From house and husband,—driven to such a course
By what she somehow took for cruelty,
Oppression and imperilment of life—   1180
Not that such things were, but that so they seemed:
Therefore, the end conceded lawful, (since
To save life there's no risk should stay our leap)
It follows that all means to the lawful end
Are lawful likewise,—poison, theft and flight.   1185
As for the priest's part, did he meddle or make,
Enough that he too thought life jeopardized;
Concede him then the colour charity
Casts on a doubtful course,—if blackish white
Or whitish black, will charity hesitate?   1190
What did he else but act the precept out,
Leave, like a provident shepherd, his safe flock
To follow the single lamb and strayaway?[5]
Best hope so and think so,—that the ticklish time
I' the carriage, the tempting privacy, the last   1195
Somewhat ambiguous accident at the inn,
—All may bear explanation: may? then, must!
The letters,—do they so incriminate?
But what if the whole prove a prank o' the pen,
Flight of the fancy, none of theirs at all,   1200
Bred of the vapours of my brain belike,
Or at worst mere exercise of scholar's-wit
In the courtly Caponsacchi: verse, convict?
Did not Catullus[6] write less seemly once?
Yet *doctus* and unblemished he abides.   1205
Wherefore so ready to infer the worst?
Still, I did righteously in bringing doubts
For the law to solve,—take the solution now!
"Seeing that the said associates, wife and priest,
Bear themselves not without some touch of blame   1210
—Else why the pother, scandal and outcry
Which trouble our peace and require chastisement?
We, for complicity in Pompilia's flight
And deviation, and carnal intercourse

---

4. Acts 25:12; this is the answer to Paul's request to be judged by Caesar.
5. Matthew 18:12–13.
6. Greatest Roman lyricist (84?–54? B.C.E.), famed for his passionate love poems and scur-
rilous lampoons. On the strength of several longer works he was given the title of *doctus*
("learned").

With the same, do set aside and relegate   1215
The Canon Caponsacchi for three years
At Civita[7] in the neighbourhood of Rome:
And we consign Pompilia to the care
Of a certain Sisterhood of penitents[8]
I' the city's self, expert to deal with such."   1220
Word for word, there's your judgment! Read it, lords,
Re-utter your deliberate penalty
For the crime yourselves establish! Your award—
Who chop a man's right-hand off at the wrist
For tracing with forefinger words in wine   1225
O' the table of a drinking-booth that bear
Interpretation as they mocked the Church!
—Who brand a woman black between the breasts
For sinning by connection[9] with a Jew:
While for the Jew's self—pudency[1] be dumb!   1230
You mete out punishment such and such, yet so
Punish the adultery of wife and priest!
Take note of that, before the Molinists do,
And read me right the riddle, since right must be!
While I stood rapt away with wonderment,   1235
Voices broke in upon my mood and muse.
"Do you sleep?" began the friends at either ear,
"The case is settled,—you willed it should be so—
None of our counsel, always recollect!
With law's award, budge! Back into your place!   1240
Your betters shall arrange the rest for you.
We'll enter a new action, claim divorce:
Your marriage was a cheat themselves allow:
You erred i' the person,—might have married thus
Your sister or your daughter unaware.   1245
We'll gain you, that way, liberty at least,
Sure of so much by law's own showing. Up
And off with you and your unluckiness—
Leave us to bury the blunder, sweep things smooth!"
I was in humble frame of mind, be sure!   1250
I bowed, betook me to my place again.
Station by station I retraced the road,
Touched at this hostel, passed this post-house by,
Where, fresh-remembered yet, the fugitives
Had risen to the heroic stature: still—   1255
"That was the bench they sat on,—there's the board
They took the meal at,—yonder garden-ground
They leaned across the gate of,"—ever a word
O' the Helen and the Paris, with "Ha! you're he,
The . . . much-commiserated husband?"[2] Step   1260

7. Civita Vecchia, about thirty-five miles northwest of Rome.
8. In actuality the Scalette Convent, but all Browning's speakers mistakenly place her in the
   convent of the Convertites.
9. Sexual intercourse.
1. Modesty.
2. Menelaus, husband of the faithless Helen of Troy.

By step, across the pelting, did I reach
Arezzo, underwent the archway's grin,
Traversed the length of sarcasm in the street,
Found myself in my horrible house once more,
And after a colloquy . . . no word assists!   1265
With the mother and the brothers, stiffened me
Straight out from head to foot as dead man does,
And, thus prepared for life as he for hell,
Marched to the public Square and met the world.
Apologize for the pincers, palliate screws?   1270
Ply me with such toy-trifles, I entreat!
Trust who has tried both sulphur and sops-in-wine!³

I played the man as I best might, bade friends
Put non-essentials by and face the fact.
"What need to hang myself as you advise?   1275
The paramour is banished,—the ocean's width,
Or the suburb's length,—to Ultima Thule,⁴ say,
Or Proxima Civitas,⁵ what's the odds of name
And place? He's banished, and the fact's the thing.
Why should law banish innocence an inch?   1280
Here's guilt then, what else do I care to know?
The adulteress lies imprisoned,—whether in a well
With bricks above and a snake for company,
Or tied by a garter to a bed-post,—much
I mind what's little,—least's enough and to spare!   1285
The little fillip on the coward's cheek
Serves as though crab-tree cudgel broke his pate.
Law has pronounced there's punishment, less or more:
And I take note o' the fact and use it thus—
For the first flaw in the original bond,   1290
I claim release. My contract was to wed
The daughter of Pietro and Violante. Both
Protest they never had a child at all.
Then I have never made a contract: good!
Cancel me quick the thing pretended one.   1295
I shall be free.⁶ What matter if hurried over
The harbour-boom⁷ by a great favouring tide,
Or the last of a spent ripple that lifts and leaves?
The Abate is about it. Laugh who wins!
You shall not laugh me out of faith in law!   1300
I listen, through all your noise, to Rome!"
                                      Rome spoke.
In three months letters thence admonished me,
"Your plan for the divorce is all mistake.
It would hold, now, had you, taking thought to wed

---

3. I.e., both extremely unpleasant (sulphur) and pleasant (sops-in-wine) experiences.
4. Northernmost region of the habitable world to ancient geographers.
5. Nearby city: i.e., Civita Vecchia, to which Caponsacchi was "relegated."
6. According to the records, no divorce proceeding was initiated by the Franceschini, even
though earlier (in 1694) such a suit had been contemplated (Cook).
7. Floating barrier across a harbor mouth.

Rachel of the blue eye and golden hair,   1305
Found swarth-skinned Leah cumber couch next day:[8]
But Rachel, blue-eyed golden-haired aright,
Proving to be only Laban's child, not Lot's,[9]
Remains yours all the same for ever more.
No whit to the purpose is your plea: you err   1310
I' the person and the quality—nowise
In the individual,—that's the case in point!
You go to the ground,—are met by a cross-suit
For separation, of the Rachel here,
From bed and board,—she is the injured one,   1315
You did the wrong and have to answer it.
As for the circumstance of imprisonment
And colour it lends to this your new attack,
Never fear, that point is considered too!
The durance[1] is already at an end;   1320
The convent-quiet preyed upon her health,
She is transferred now to her parents' house
—No-parents, when that cheats and plunders you,
But parentage again confessed in full,
When such confession pricks and plagues you more—   1325
As now—for, this their house is not the house
In Via Vittoria wherein neighbours' watch
Might incommode the freedom of your wife,
But a certain villa smothered up in vines
At the town's edge by the gate i' the Pauline Way,   1330
Out of eye-reach, out of ear-shot, little and lone,
Whither a friend,—at Civita, we hope,
A good half-dozen-hours' ride off,—might, some eve,
Betake himself, and whence ride back, some morn,
Nobody the wiser: but be that as it may,   1335
Do not afflict your brains with trifles now.
You have still three suits to manage,[2] all and each
Ruinous truly should the event play false.
It is indeed the likelier so to do,
That brother Paul, your single prop and stay,   1340
After a vain attempt to bring the Pope
To set aside procedures, sit himself
And summarily use prerogative,
Afford us the infallible[3] finger's tact
To disentwine your tangle of affairs,   1345

8. I.e., a divorce is possible only on the ground of a mistake as to the identity of the spouse. Cf. V.1242–45. (Jacob, who loved Rachel, was tricked into marrying Leah instead; see Genesis 29:15–30.)
9. Lot, made drunk by his two daughters, conceived a son with each; he was unaware of his incestuous acts (Genesis 19:30–35).
1. Forced confinement.
2. The three pending suits were: (1) Guido's countersuit (against the Comparini's claim of Pompilia's illegitimacy) to secure Pompilia's dowry; (2) Pompilia's suit for legal separation; and (3) Guido's suit against Pompilia for flight and adultery, brought at Arezzo. Paolo tried to have all three cases adjudicated simultaneously in a special session appointed by the pope, claiming that Guido, on the basis of having held holy orders, enjoyed ecclesiastical privilege. The pope, however, refused to intervene in the matter.
3. Allusion to the doctrine of papal infallibility; see note to X.150.

Paul,—finding it moreover past his strength
To stem the irruption,[4] bear Rome's ridicule
Of . . . since friends must speak . . . to be round with you . . .
Of the old outwitted husband, wronged and wroth,
Pitted against a brace of juveniles—   1350
A brisk priest who is versed in Ovid's art[5]
More than his Summa,[6] and a gamesome wife
Able to act Corinna[7] without book,
Beside the waggish parents who played dupes
To dupe the duper—(and truly divers scenes   1355
Of the Arezzo palace, tickle rib
And tease eye till the tears come, so we laugh;
Nor wants the shock at the inn its comic force,
And then the letters and poetry—*merum sal!*)[8]
—Paul, finally, in such a state of things,   1360
After a brief temptation to go jump
And join the fishes in the Tiber, drowns
Sorrow another and a wiser way:
House and goods, he has sold all off, is gone,
Leaves Rome,—whether for France or Spain, who knows?   1365
Or Britain almost divided from our orb.[9]
You have lost him anyhow."
                        Now,—I see my lords
Shift in their seat,—would I could do the same!
They probably please expect my bile was moved
To purpose, nor much blame me: now, they judge,   1370
The fiery titillation urged my flesh
Break through the bonds. By your pardon, no, sweet Sirs!
I got such missives in the public place;
When I sought home,—with such news, mounted stair
And sat at last in the sombre gallery,   1375
('T was Autumn, the old mother in bed betimes,
Having to bear that cold, the finer frame
Of her daughter-in-law had found intolerable—
The brother, walking misery away
O' the mountain-side with dog and gun belike)   1380
As I supped, ate the coarse bread, drank the wine
Weak once, now acrid with the toad's-head-squeeze,[1]
My wife's bestowment,—I broke silence thus:
"Let me, a man, manfully meet the fact,
Confront the worst o' the truth, end, and have peace!   1385
I am irremediably beaten here,—
The gross illiterate vulgar couple,—bah!
Why, they have measured forces, mastered mine,

4. Invasion.
5. The *Art of Love* (*Ars Amatoria*).
6. The *Summa Theologica* of St. Thomas Aquinas, important in the development of Roman
   Catholic theology.
7. Ovid's mistress, celebrated in *Amores*.
8. Latin for "pure salt," here meaning something like "brilliantly spicy."
9. Phrase is borrowed from Virgil, *Eclogues*, I.66.
1. Toads were supposedly poisonous.

Made me their spoil and prey from first to last.
They have got my name,—'t is nailed now fast to theirs,   1390
The child or changeling is anyway my wife;
Point by point as they plan they execute,
They gain all, and I lose all—even to the lure
That led to loss,—they have the wealth again
They hazarded awhile to hook me with,   1395
Have caught the fish and find the bait entire:
They even have their child or changeling back
To trade with, turn to account a second time.
The brother presumably might tell a tale
Or give a warning,—he, too, flies the field,[2]   1400
And with him vanish help and hope of help.
They have caught me in the cavern where I fell,
Covered my loudest cry for human aid
With this enormous paving-stone of shame.
Well, are we demigods or merely clay?   1405
Is success still attendant on desert?
Is this, we live on, heaven and the final state,
Or earth which means probation to the end?
Why claim escape from man's predestined lot
Of being beaten and baffled?—God's decree,   1410
In which I, bowing bruised head, acquiesce.
One of us Franceschini fell long since
I' the Holy Land, betrayed, tradition runs,
To Paynims[3] by the feigning of a girl
He rushed to free from ravisher, and found   1415
Lay safe enough with friends in ambuscade
Who flayed him while she clapped her hands and laughed:
Let me end, falling by a like device.
It will not be so hard. I am the last
O' my line which will not suffer any more.   1420
I have attained to my full fifty years,
(About the average of us all, 't is said,
Though it seems longer to the unlucky man)
—Lived through my share of life; let all end here,
Me and the house and grief and shame at once.   1425
Friends my informants,—I can bear your blow!"
And I believe 't was in no unmeet match
For the stoic's mood,[4] with something like a smile,
That, when morose December roused me next,
I took into my hand, broke seal to read   1430
The new epistle from Rome. "All to no use!
Whate'er the turn next injury take," smiled I,
"Here's one has chosen his part and knows his cue.
I am done with, dead now; strike away, good friends!
Are the three suits decided in a trice?   1435
Against me,—there's no question! How does it go?

2. Paolo had left Rome in 1697.
3. Infidels; a reference to the Crusades.
4. Insensibility to pain.

Is the parentage of my wife demonstrated
Infamous to her wish? Parades she now
Loosed of the cincture that so irked the loin?
Is the last penny extracted from my purse   1440
To mulct me for demanding the first pound
Was promised in return for value paid?
Has the priest, with nobody to court beside,
Courted the Muse in exile, hitched my hap⁵
Into a rattling ballad-rhyme which, bawled   1445
At tavern-doors, wakes rapture everywhere,
And helps cheap wine down throat this Christmas time,
Beating the bagpipes? Any or all of these!
As well, good friends, you cursed my palace here
To its old cold stone face,—stuck your cap for crest   1450
Over the shield that's extant in the Square,—
Or spat on the statue's cheek, the impatient world
Sees cumber tomb-top in our family church:
Let him creep under covert as I shall do,
Half below-ground already indeed. Good-bye!   1455
My brothers are priests, and childless so; that's well—
And, thank God most for this, no child leave I—
None after me to bear till his heart break
The being a Franceschini and my son!"

"Nay," said the letter, "but you have just that!   1460
A babe, your veritable son and heir—
Lawful,—'t is only eight months since your wife
Left you,—so, son and heir, your babe was born
Last Wednesday in the villa,—you see the cause
For quitting Convent without beat of drum,   1465
Stealing a hurried march to this retreat
That's not so savage as the Sisterhood
To slips and stumbles: Pietro's heart is soft,
Violante leans to pity's side,—the pair
Ushered you into life a bouncing boy: 1470
And he's already hidden away and safe
From any claim on him you mean to make—
They need him for themselves,—don't fear, they know
The use o' the bantling,⁶—the nerve thus laid bare
To nip at, new and nice, with finger-nail!"   1475

Then I rose up like fire, and fire-like roared.
What, all is only beginning not ending now?
The worm which wormed its way from skin through flesh
To the bone and there lay biting, did its best,—
What, it goes on to scrape at the bone's self,   1480
Will wind to inmost marrow and madden me?
There's to be yet my representative,
Another of the name shall keep displayed

5. Story.
6. Brat (and bastard).

The flag with the ordure on it, brandish still
The broken sword has served to stir a jakes?[7]   1485
Who will he be, how will you call the man?
A Franceschini,—when who cut my purse,
Filched my name, hemmed me round, hustled me hard
As rogues at a fair some fool they strip i' the midst,
When these count gains, vaunt pillage presently:—   1490
But a Caponsacchi, oh, be very sure!
When what demands its tribute of applause
Is the cunning and impudence o' the pair of cheats,
The lies and lust o' the mother, and the brave
Bold carriage of the priest, worthily crowned   1495
By a witness to his feat i' the following age,—
And how this three-fold cord[8] could hook and fetch
And land leviathan that king of pride![9]
Or say, by some mad miracle of chance,
Is he indeed my flesh and blood, this babe?   1500
Was it because fate forged a link at last
Betwixt my wife and me, and both alike
Found we had henceforth some one thing to love,
Was it when she could damn my soul indeed
She unlatched door, let all the devils o' the dark   1505
Dance in on me to cover her escape?
Why then, the surplusage of disgrace, the spilth
Over and above the measure of infamy,
Failing to take effect on my coarse flesh
Seasoned with scorn now, saturate with shame,—   1510
Is saved to instil on and corrode the brow,
The baby-softness of my first-born child—
The child I had died to see though in a dream,
The child I was bid strike out for, beat the wave
And baffle the tide of troubles where I swam,   1515
So I might touch shore, lay down life at last
At the feet so dim and distant and divine
Of the apparition, as 't were Mary's Babe
Had held, through night and storm, the torch aloft,—
Born now in very deed to bear this brand   1520
On forehead and curse me who could not save!
Rather be the town talk true, square's jest, street's jeer
True, my own inmost heart's confession true,
And he the priest's bastard and none of mine!
Ay, there was cause for flight, swift flight and sure!   1525
The husband gets unruly, breaks all bounds
When he encounters some familiar face,
Fashion of feature, brow and eyes and lips
Where he least looked to find them,—time to fly!
This bastard then, a nest for him is made,   1530

7. Privy.
8. Comprised of Pompilia, Caponsacchi, and Gaetano, whom Guido assumes is their son. Cf.
   Ecclesiastes 4:12.
9. Sea monster (Job 41); cf. the pope's treatment of leviathan (X.1096–1106).

As the manner is of vermin, in my flesh:
Shall I let the filthy pest buzz, flap and sting,
Busy at my vitals and, nor hand nor foot
Lift, but let be, lie still and rot resigned?
No, I appeal to God,—what says Himself,   1535
How lessons Nature when I look to learn?
Why, that I am alive, am still a man
With brain and heart and tongue and right-hand too—
Nay, even with friends, in such a cause as this,
To right me if I fail to take my right.   1540
No more of law; a voice beyond the law
Enters my heart, *Quis est pro Domino?*[1]

Myself, in my own Vittiano, told the tale
To my own serving-people summoned there:
Told the first half of it, scarce heard to end   1545
By judges who got done with judgment quick
And clamoured to go execute her 'hest—
Who cried "Not one of us that dig your soil
And dress your vineyard, prune your olive-trees,
But would have brained the man debauched our wife,   1550
And staked the wife whose lust allured the man,
And paunched[2] the Duke, had it been possible,
Who ruled the land yet barred us such revenge!"
I fixed on the first whose eyes caught mine, some four
Resolute youngsters with the heart still fresh,   1555
Filled my purse with the residue o' the coin
Uncaught-up by my wife whom haste made blind,
Donned the first rough and rural garb I found,
Took whatsoever weapon came to hand,
And out we flung and on we ran or reeled   1560
Romeward. I have no memory of our way,
Only that, when at intervals the cloud
Of horror about me opened to let in life,
I listened to some song in the ear, some snatch
Of a legend, relic of religion, stray   1565
Fragment of record very strong and old
Of the first conscience, the anterior right,
The God's-gift to mankind, impulse to quench
The antagonistic spark of hell and tread
Satan and all his malice into dust,   1570
Declare to the world the one law, right is right.
Then the cloud re-encompassed me, and so
I found myself, as on the wings of winds,
Arrived: I was at Rome on Christmas Eve.

Festive bells—everywhere the Feast o' the Babe,   1575
Joy upon earth, peace and good will to man!

1. "Who is on the Lord's side?" Having uttered this rallying cry, Moses, with "all the sons of
Levi," killed 3,000 calf-idolaters (Exodus 32:26).
2. Stabbed in the belly.

I am baptized. I started and let drop
The dagger. "Where is it, His promised peace?"
Nine days o' the Birth-Feast did I pause and pray
To enter into no temptation more.   1580
I bore the hateful house, my brother's once,
Deserted,—let the ghost of social joy
Mock and make mouths at me from empty room
And idle door that missed the master's step,—
Bore the frank wonder of incredulous eyes,   1585
As my own people watched without a word,
Waited, from where they huddled round the hearth
Black like all else, that nod so slow to come.
I stopped my ears even to the inner call
Of the dread duty, only heard the song   1590
"Peace upon earth," saw nothing but the face
O' the Holy Infant and the halo there
Able to cover yet another face
Behind it, Satan's which I else should see.
But, day by day, joy waned and withered off: 1595
The Babe's face; premature with peak and pine,[3]
Sank into wrinkled ruinous old age,
Suffering and death, then mist-like disappeared,
And showed only the Cross at end of all,
Left nothing more to interpose 'twixt me   1600
And the dread duty: for the angels' song,
"Peace upon earth," louder and louder pealed
"O Lord, how long, how long be unavenged?"[4]
On the ninth day, this grew too much for man.
I started up—"Some end must be!" At once,   1605
Silence: then, scratching like a death-watch-tick,[5]
Slowly within my brain was syllabled,
"One more concession, one decisive way
And but one, to determine thee the truth,—
This way, in fine, I whisper in thy ear: 1610
Now doubt, anon decide, thereupon act!"

"That is a way, thou whisperest in my ear!
I doubt, I will decide, then act," said I—
Then beckoned my companions: "Time is come!"

And so, all yet uncertain save the will   1615
To do right, and the daring aught save leave
Right undone, I did find myself at last
I' the dark before the villa with my friends,
And made the experiment, the final test,
Ultimate chance that ever was to be   1620
For the wretchedness inside. I knocked, pronounced
The name, the predetermined touch for truth,

3. Withering and grief.
4. Paraphrase of Revelation 6:10.
5. The sound of a death-watch beetle supposed to foretell the death of an inmate of the house.

"What welcome for the wanderer? Open straight—"
To the friend, physician, friar upon his rounds,
Traveller belated, beggar lame and blind?   1625
No, but—"to Caponsacchi!" And the door
Opened.
        And then,—why, even then, I think,
I' the minute that confirmed my worst of fears,
Surely,—I pray God that I think aright!—
Had but Pompilia's self, the tender thing   1630
Who once was good and pure, was once my lamb
And lay in my bosom, had the well-known shape
Fronted me in the door-way,—stood there faint
With the recent pang perhaps of giving birth
To what might, though by miracle, seem my child,—   1635
Nay more, I will say, had even the aged fool
Pietro, the dotard, in whom folly and age
Wrought, more than enmity or malevolence,
To practise and conspire against my peace,—
Had either of these but opened, I had paused.   1640
But it was she the hag, she that brought hell
For a dowry with her to her husband's house,
She the mock-mother, she that made the match
And married me to perdition, spring and source
O' the fire inside me that boiled up from heart   1645
To brain and hailed the Fury gave it birth,[6]—
Violante Comparini, she it was,
With the old grin amid the wrinkles yet,
Opened: as if in turning from the Cross,
With trust to keep the sight and save my soul,   1650
I had stumbled, first thing, on the serpent's head
Coiled with a leer at foot of it.
                There was the end!
Then was I rapt away by the impulse, one
Immeasurable everlasting wave of a need
To abolish that detested life. 'T was done: 1655
You know the rest and how the folds o' the thing,
Twisting for help, involved the other two
More or less serpent-like: how I was mad,
Blind, stamped on all, the earth-worms with the asp,
And ended so.
        You came on me that night,   1660
Your officers of justice,—caught the crime
In the first natural frenzy of remorse?
Twenty miles off, sound sleeping as a child
On a cloak i' the straw which promised shelter first,
With the bloody arms beside me,—was it not so?   1665
Wherefore not? Why, how else should I be found?
I was my own self, had my sense again,
My soul safe from the serpents. I could sleep:

---

6. Guido is attempting to diminish the force of the argument, urged repeatedly by the prosecution, that the murders were done in cold blood.

Indeed and, dear my lords, I shall sleep now,
Spite of my shoulder, in five minutes' space,   1670
When you dismiss me, having truth enough!
It is but a few days are passed, I find,
Since this adventure. Do you tell me, four?
Then the dead are scarce quiet where they lie,
Old Pietro, old Violante, side by side   1675
At the church Lorenzo,—oh, they know it well!
So do I. But my wife is still alive,
Has breath enough to tell her story yet,
Her way, which is not mine, no doubt at all.
And Caponsacchi, you have summoned him,—   1680
Was he so far to send for? Not at hand?
I thought some few o' the stabs were in his heart,
Or had not been so lavish: less had served.[7]
Well, he too tells his story,—florid prose
As smooth as mine is rough. You see, my lords,   1685
There will be a lying intoxicating smoke
Born of the blood,—confusion probably,—
For lies breed lies—but all that rests with you!
The trial is no concern of mine; with me
The main of the care is over: I at least   1690
Recognize who took that huge burthen off,
Let me begin to live again. I did
God's bidding and man's duty, so, breathe free;
Look you to the rest! I heard Himself prescribe,
That great Physician, and dared lance the core   1695
Of the bad ulcer; and the rage abates,
I am myself and whole now: I prove cured
By the eyes that see, the ears that hear again,
The limbs that have relearned their youthful play,
The healthy taste of food and feel of clothes   1700
And taking to our common life once more,
All that now urges my defence from death.
The willingness to live, what means it else?
Before,—but let the very action speak!
Judge for yourselves, what life seemed worth to me   1705
Who, not by proxy but in person, pitched
Head-foremost into danger as a fool
That never cares if he can swim or no—
So he but find the bottom, braves the brook.
No man omits precaution, quite neglects   1710
Secresy, safety, schemes not how retreat,
Having schemed he might advance. Did I so scheme?
Why, with a warrant which 't is ask and have,[8]
With horse thereby made mine without a word,
I had gained the frontier and slept safe that night.   1715
Then, my companions,—call them what you please,

---

7. Pompilla sustained twenty-two stab wounds.
8. Guido had improvidently failed to obtain a pass through the city gates. The pope muses
upon this "oversight" in X.810–41.

Slave or stipendiary,[9]—what need of one
To me whose right-hand did its owner's work?
Hire an assassin yet expose yourself?
As well buy glove and then thrust naked hand   1720
I' the thorn-bush. No, the wise man stays at home,
Sends only agents out, with pay to earn:
At home, when they come back,—he straight discards
Or else disowns. Why use such tools at all
When a man's foes are of his house, like mine,   1725
Sit at his board, sleep in his bed? Why noise,
When there's the *acquetta* and the silent way?[1]
Clearly my life was valueless.

                           But now
Health is returned, and sanity of soul
Nowise indifferent to the body's harm.   1730
I find the instinct bids me save my life;
My wits, too, rally round me; I pick up
And use the arms that strewed the ground before,
Unnoticed or spurned aside: I take my stand,
Make my defence. God shall not lose a life   1735
May do Him further service, while I speak
And you hear, you my judges and last hope!
You are the law: 't is to the law I look.
I began life by hanging to the law,
To the law it is I hang till life shall end.   1740
My brother made appeal to the Pope, 't is true,
To say proceedings, judge my cause himself
Nor trouble law,—some fondness of conceit[2]
That rectitude, sagacity sufficed
The investigator in a case like mine,   1745
Dispensed with the machine of law. The Pope
Knew better, set aside my brother's plea
And put me back to law,—referred the cause
Ad judices meos,[3]—doubtlessly did well.
Here, then, I clutch my judges,—I claim law—   1750
Cry, by the higher law whereof your law
O' the land is humbly representative,—
Cry, on what point is it, where either accuse,
I fail to furnish you defence? I stand
Acquitted, actually or virtually,   1755
By every intermediate kind of court
That takes account of right or wrong in man,
Each unit in the series that begins
With God's throne, ends with the tribunal here.
God breathes, not speaks, his verdicts, felt not heard,   1760
Passed on successively to each court I call

9. Hireling.
1. I.e., poison.
2. Foolish conception.
3. "To my panel of jurors."

Man's conscience, custom, manners, all that make
More and more effort to promulgate, mark
God's verdict in determinable words,
Till last come human jurists—solidify   1765
Fluid result,—what's fixable lies forged,
Statute,—the residue escapes in fume,
Yet hangs aloft, a cloud, as palpable
To the finer sense as word the legist[4] welds.
Justinian's Pandects[5] only make precise   1770
What simply sparkled in men's eyes before,
Twitched in their brow or quivered on their lip,
Waited the speech they called but would not come.
These courts then, whose decree your own confirms,—
Take my whole life, not this last act alone,   1775
Look on it by the light reflected thence!
What has Society to charge me with?
Come, unreservedly,—favour none nor fear,—
I am Guido Franceschini, am I not?
You know the courses I was free to take?   1780
I took just that which let me serve the Church,
I gave it all my labour in body and soul
Till these broke down i' the service. "Specify?"
Well, my last patron was a Cardinal.
I left him unconvicted of a fault—   1785
Was even helped, by way of gratitude,
Into the new life that I left him for,[6]
This very misery of the marriage,—he
Made it, kind soul, so far as in him lay—
Signed the deed where you yet may see his name.   1790
He is gone to his reward,—dead, being my friend
Who could have helped here also,—that, of course!
So far, there's my acquittal, I suppose.
Then comes the marriage itself—no question, lords,
Of the entire validity of that!   1795
In the extremity of distress, 't is true,
For after-reasons, furnished abundantly,
I wished the thing invalid,[7] went to you
Only some months since, set you duly forth
My wrong and prayed your remedy, that a cheat   1800
Should not have force to cheat my whole life long.
"Annul a marriage? 'T is impossible!
Though ring about your neck be brass not gold,
Needs must it clasp, gangrene you all the same!"
Well, let me have the benefit, just so far,   1805
O' the fact announced,—my wife then is my wife,
I have allowance for a husband's right.

4. Lawyer.
5. Also known as the *Digest*, a compilation of juristic codes and decisions commissioned by Byzantine emperor Justinian the Great (483–565). The *Digest* was still the foundation of Roman law in 1698.
6. The patron, Cardinal Nerli, had rather dismissed Guido (Cook).
7. See note to line 1296.

I am charged with passing right's due bound,—such acts
As I thought just, my wife called cruelty,
Complained of in due form,—convoked no court   1810
Of common gossipry, but took her wrongs—
And not once but so long as patience served—
To the town's[8] top, jurisdiction's pride of place,
To the Archbishop and Governor.
These heard her charge with my reply, and found   1815
That futile, this sufficient: they dismissed
The hysteric querulous rebel, and confirmed
Authority in its wholesome exercise,
They, with directest access to the facts.
"—Ay, for it was their friendship favoured you,   1820
Hereditary alliance against a breach
I' the social order: prejudice for the name
Of Franceschini!"—So I hear it said:
But not here. You, lords, never will you say
"Such is the nullity of grace and truth,   1825
Such the corruption of the faith, such lapse
Of law, such warrant have the Molinists
For daring reprehend us as they do,—
That we pronounce it just a common case,
Two dignitaries, each in his degree   1830
First, foremost, this the spiritual head, and that
The secular arm o' the body politic,
Should, for mere wrongs' love and injustice' sake,
Side with, aid and abet in cruelty
This broken beggarly noble,—bribed perhaps   1835
By his watered wine and mouldy crust of bread—
Rather than that sweet tremulous flower-like wife
Who kissed their hands and curled about their feet
Looking the irresistible loveliness
In tears that takes man captive, turns" . . . enough!   1840
Do you blast your predecessors? What forbids
Posterity to trebly blast yourselves
Who set the example and instruct their tongue?
You dreaded the crowd, succumbed to the popular cry,
Or else, would nowise seem defer thereto   1845
And yield to public clamour though i' the right!
You ridded your eye of my unseemliness,
The noble whose misfortune wearied you,—
Or, what's more probable, made common cause
With the cleric section, punished in myself   1850
Maladroit uncomplaisant laity,
Defective in behaviour to a priest
Who claimed the customary partnership
I' the house and the wife. Lords, any lie will serve![9]
Look to it,—or allow me freed so far!   1855

8. Arezzo.
9. i.e., to sway the people against this court.

Then I proceed a step, come with clean hands
Thus far, re-tell the tale told eight months since.
The wife, you allow so far, I have not wronged,
Has fled my roof, plundered me and decamped
In company with the priest her paramour: 1860
And I gave chase, came up with, caught the two
At the wayside inn where both had spent the night,
Found them in flagrant fault, and found as well,
By documents with name and plan and date,
The fault was furtive then that's flagrant now,   1865
Their intercourse a long established crime.
I did not take the license law's self gives
To slay both criminals o' the spot at the time,
But held my hand,—preferred play prodigy
Of patience which the world calls cowardice,   1870
Rather than seem anticipate the law
And cast discredit on its organs,—you.
So, to your bar I brought both criminals,
And made my statement: heard their counter-charge,
Nay,—their corroboration of my tale,   1875
Nowise disputing its allegements, not
I' the main, not more than nature's decency
Compels men to keep silence in this kind,—
Only contending that the deeds avowed
Would take another colour and bear excuse.   1880
You were to judge between us; so you did.
You disregard the excuse, you breathe away
The colour of innocence and leave guilt black,
"Guilty" is the decision of the court,
And that I stand in consequence untouched,   1885
One white integrity from head to heel.
Not guilty? Why then did you punish them?
True, punishment has been inadequate—
'T is not I only, not my friends that joke,
My foes that jeer, who echo "inadequate"—   1890
For, by a chance that comes to help for once,
The same case simultaneously was judged
At Arezzo, in the province of the Court
Where the crime had its beginning but not end.
They then, deciding on but half o' the crime,   1895
The effraction,[1] robbery,—features of the fault
I never cared to dwell upon at Rome,—
What was it they adjudged as penalty
To Pompilia,—the one criminal o' the pair
Amenable to their judgment, not the priest   1900
Who is Rome's?[2] Why, just imprisonment for life
I' the Stinche.[3] There was Tuscany's award[4]

1. Forcible entry.
2. As an ecclesiastic, Caponsacchi was immune from prosecution in a civil court.
3. Prison at Florence.
4. Cf. the pope's assessment of "that strange shameful judgment" (X.830–40).

To a wife that robs her husband: you at Rome—
Having to deal with adultery in a wife
And, in a priest, breach of the priestly vow[5]—   1905
Give gentle sequestration for a month
In a manageable Convent, then release,
You call imprisonment, in the very house
O' the very couple, which the aim and end
Of the culprits' crime was—just to reach and rest   1910
And there take solace and defy me: well,—
This difference 'twixt their penalty and yours
Is immaterial: make your penalty less—
Merely that she should henceforth wear black gloves
And white fan, she who wore the opposite—   1915
Why, all the same the fact o' the thing subsists.
Reconcile to your conscience as you may,
Be it on your own heads, you pronounced but half
O' the penalty for heinousness like hers
And his, that pays a fault at Carnival   1920
Of comfit-pelting past discretion's law,
Or accident to handkerchief in Lent
Which falls perversely as a lady kneels
Abruptly, and but half conceals her neck![6]
I acquiesce for my part: punished, though   1925
By a pin-point scratch, means guilty: guilty means
—What have I been but innocent hitherto?
Anyhow, here the offence, being punished, ends.

Ends?—for you deemed so, did you not, sweet lords?
That was throughout the veritable aim   1930
O' the sentence light or heavy,—to redress
Recognized wrong? You righted me, I think?
Well then,—what if I, at this last of all,
Demonstrate you, as my whole pleading proves,
No particle of wrong received thereby   1935
One atom of right?—that cure grew worse disease?
That in the process you call "justice done"
All along you have nipped away just inch
By inch the creeping climbing length of plague
Breaking my tree of life from root to branch,   1940
And left me, after all and every act
Of your interference,—lightened of what load?
At liberty wherein? Mere words and wind!
"Now I was saved, now I should feel no more
The hot breath, find a respite from fixed eye   1945
And vibrant tongue!" Why, scarce your back was turned,
There was the reptile, that feigned death at first,
Renewing its detested spire and spire
Around me, rising to such heights of hate

5. Though often called a priest, Caponsacchi was actually a subdeacon, a member of the low-
  est of the four major orders of clergy. He was bound by vows of celibacy, however.
6. Euphemism for bosom.

That, so far from mere purpose now to crush   1950
And coil itself on the remains of me,
Body and mind, and there flesh fang content,
Its aim is now to evoke life from death,
Make me anew, satisfy in my son
The hunger[7] I may feed but never sate,   1955
Tormented on to perpetuity,—
My son, whom, dead, I shall know, understand,
Feel, hear, see, never more escape the sight
In heaven that's turned to hell, or hell returned
(So rather say) to this same earth again,—   1960
Moulded into the image and made one,
Fashioned of soul as featured like in face,
First taught to laugh and lisp and stand and go
By that thief, poisoner and adulteress
I call Pompilia, he calls . . . sacred name,   1965
Be unpronounced, be unpolluted here!
And last led up to the glory and prize of hate
By his . . . foster-father, Caponsacchi's self,
The perjured priest, pink[8] of conspirators,
Tricksters and knaves, yet polished, superfine,   1970
Manhood to model adolescence by!
Lords, look on me, declare,—when, what I show,
Is nothing more nor less than what you deemed
And doled me out for justice,—what did you say?
For reparation, restitution and more,—   1975
Will you not thank, praise, bid me to your breasts
For having done the thing you thought to do,
And thoroughly trampled out sin's life at last?
I have heightened phrase to make your soft speech serve,
Doubled the blow you but essayed to strike,   1980
Carried into effect your mandate here
That else had fallen to ground: mere duty done,
Oversight of the master just supplied
By zeal i' the servant. I, being used to serve,
Have simply . . . what is it they charge me with?   1985
Blackened again, made legible once more
Your own decree, not permanently writ,
Rightly conceived but all too faintly traced.
It reads efficient, now, comminatory,[9]
A terror to the wicked, answers so   1990
The mood o' the magistrate, the mind of law.
Absolve, then, me, law's mere executant!
Protect your own defender,—save me, Sirs!
Give me my life, give me my liberty,
My good name and my civic rights again!   1995
It would be too fond, too complacent play
Into the hands o' the devil, should we lose

7. For vengeance.
8. The flower, or perfection.
9. Damning.

The game here, I for God: a soldier-bee
That yields his life, exenterate[1] with the stroke
O' the sting that saves the hive. I need that life.　　　2000
Oh, never fear! I'll find life plenty use
Though it should last five years more, aches and all!
For, first thing, there's the mother's age to help—
Let her come break her heart upon my breast,
Not on the blank stone of my nameless tomb!　　　2005
The fugitive brother[2] has to be bidden back
To the old routine, repugnant to the tread,
Of daily suit and service to the Church,—
Thro' gibe and jest, those stones that Shimei flung![3]
Ay, and the spirit-broken youth at home,[4]　　　2010
The awe-struck altar-ministrant, shall make
Amends for faith now palsied at the source,
Shall see truth yet triumphant, justice yet
A victor in the battle of this world!
Give me—for last, best gift—my son again,　　　2015
Whom law makes mine,—I take him at your word,
Mine be he, by miraculous mercy, lords!
Let me lift up his youth and innocence
To purify my palace, room by room
Purged of the memories, lend from his bright brow　　　2020
Light to the old proud paladin[5] my sire
Shrunk now for shame into the darkest shade
O' the tapestry, showed him once and shrouds him now!
Then may we,—strong from that rekindled smile,—
Go forward, face new times, the better day.　　　2025
And when, in times made better through your brave
Decision now,—might but Utopia be!—
Rome rife with honest women and strong men,
Manners reformed, old habits back once more,
Customs that recognize the standard worth,—　　　2030
The wholesome household rule in force again,
Husbands once more God's representative,
Wives like the typical Spouse[6] once more, and Priests
No longer men of Belial,[7] with no aim
At leading silly women captive, but　　　2035
Of rising to such duties as yours now,—
Then will I set my son at my right-hand
And tell his father's story to this point,
Adding "The task seemed superhuman, still
I dared and did it, trusting God and law:　　　2040
And they approved of me: give praise to both!"
And if, for answer, he shall stoop to kiss

1. Disemboweled.
2. Paolo.
3. 2 Samuel 16:5–13. The stones were cast at David and his servants.
4. Girolamo.
5. Paragon of chivalry.
6. See note to V.725.
7. Licentious people, sons of Satan.

My hand, and peradventure start thereat,—
I engage to smile "That was an accident
I' the necessary process,—just a trip   2045
O' the torture-irons in their search for truth,—
Hardly misfortune, and no fault at all."

Book VII

Pompilia[1]

I am just seventeen years and five months old,
And, if I lived one day more, three full weeks;[2]
'T is writ so in the church's register,
Lorenzo in Lucina, all my names
At length, so many names for one poor child,   5
—Francesca Camilla Vittoria Angela
Pompilia Comparini,—laughable!
Also 't is writ that I was married there
Four years ago: and they will add, I hope,[3]
When they insert my death, a word or two,—   10
Omitting all about the mode of death,—
This, in its place, this which one cares to know,
That I had been a mother of a son
Exactly two weeks. It will be through grace[4]
O' the Curate, not through any claim I have;   15
Because the boy was born at, so baptized
Close to, the Villa, in the proper church:
A pretty church, I say no word against,
Yet stranger-like,—while this Lorenzo seems
My own particular place, I always say.   20
I used to wonder, when I stood scarce high
As the bed here, what the marble lion meant,[5]
With half his body rushing from the wall,
Eating the figure of a prostrate man—
(To the right, it is, of entry by the door)   25
An ominous sign to one baptized like me,
Married, and to be buried there, I hope.
And they should add, to have my life complete,
He is a boy and Gaetan by name—
Gaetano, for a reason,[6]—if the friar   30

---

1. Pompilia's monologue takes place on the fourth day after the murders; simultaneously, Caponsacchi testifies before the court. Browning introduces her speech in Book I: 1076–1104. See Susan Brown's essay in this volume, pp. 659–78, for more on Pompilia in *The Ring and the Book*.
2. Pompilia's precise dating of her dying speech means it was given on January 6, 1698, the Feast of the Epiphany.
3. Browning's source said Pompilia and Guido were wed in San Lorenzo, Lucina, in December 1693.
4. Gaetano was born on December 18, 1697, fifteen days before the murders (January 2, 1698).
5. Lion statues (one of which is fierce) in the portico of the church of San Lorenzo, Lucina.
6. There is a St. Gaetano, canonized 1671.

Don Celestine[7] will ask this grace for me
Of Curate Ottoboni: he it was
Baptized me: he remembers my whole life
As I do his grey hair.
                        All these few things
I know are true,—will you remember them?   35
Because time flies. The surgeon cared for me,
To count my wounds,—twenty-two dagger-wounds,
Five deadly, but I do not suffer much—
Or too much pain,—and am to die to-night.

Oh how good God is that my babe was born,   40
—Better than born, baptized and hid away
Before this happened, safe from being hurt!
That had been sin God could not well forgive:
He was too young to smile and save himself.
When they took, two days after he was born,   45
My babe away from me to be baptized
And hidden awhile, for fear his foe should find,—
The country-woman, used to nursing babes,
Said "Why take on so? where is the great loss?
These next three weeks he will but sleep and feed,   50
Only begin to smile at the month's end;
He would not know you, if you kept him here,
Sooner than that; so, spend three merry weeks
Snug in the Villa, getting strong and stout,
And then I bring him back to be your own,   55
And both of you may steal to—we know where!"
The month—there wants of it two weeks this day!
Still, I half fancied when I heard the knock
At the Villa in the dusk, it might prove she—
Come to say "Since he smiles before the time,   60
Why should I cheat you out of one good hour?
Back I have brought him; speak to him and judge!"
Now I shall never see him; what is worse,
When he grows up and gets to be my age,
He will seem hardly more than a great boy;   65
And if he asks "What was my mother like?"
People may answer "Like girls of seventeen"—
And how can he but think of this and that,
Lucias, Marias, Sofias, who titter or blush
When he regards them as such boys may do?   70
Therefore I wish someone will please to say
I looked already old though I was young;
Do I not . . . say, if you are by to speak . . .
Look nearer twenty? No more like, at least,
Girls who look arch or redden when boys laugh,   75
Than the poor Virgin that I used to know
At our street-corner in a lonely niche,—

7. Augustinian friar, Pompilia's confessor, who later testified as to her saintly conduct during her dying hours.

The babe, that sat upon her knees, broke off,—
Thin white glazed clay, you pitied her the more:
She, not the gay ones, always got my rose.   80

How happy those are who know how to write![8]
Such could write what their son should read in time,
Had they a whole day to live out like me.
Also my name is not a common name,
"Pompilia," and may help to keep apart   85
A little the thing I am from what girls are.
But then how far away, how hard to find
Will anything about me have become,
Even if the boy bethink himself and ask!
No father that he ever knew at all,   90
Nor ever had—no, never had, I say!
That is the truth,—nor any mother left,
Out of the little two weeks that she lived,
Fit for such memory as might assist:
As good too as no family, no name,   95
Not even poor old Pietro's name, nor hers,
Poor kind unwise Violante, since it seems
They must not be my parents any more.
That is why something put it in my head
To call the boy "Gaetano"—no old name   100
For sorrow's sake; I looked up to the sky
And took a new saint to begin anew.
One who has only been made saint—how long?
Twenty-five years: so, carefuller, perhaps,
To guard a namesake than those old saints grow,   105
Tired out by this time,—see my own five saints![9]

On second thoughts, I hope he will regard
The history of me as what someone dreamed,
And get to disbelieve it at the last:
Since to myself it dwindles fast to that,   110
Sheer dreaming and impossibility,—
Just in four days too! All the seventeen years,
Not once did a suspicion visit me
How very different a lot is mine
From any other woman's in the world.   115
The reason must be, 't was by step and step
It got to grow so terrible and strange.
These strange woes stole on tiptoe, as it were,
Into my neighbourhood and privacy,
Sat down where I sat, laid them where I lay;   120
And I was found familiarised with fear,
When friends broke in, held up a torch and cried
"Why, you Pompilia in the cavern thus,

8. Pompilia's literacy was debated in court, but Browning depicts her as illiterate, thus resolving the issue of whether she wrote love letters to her rescuer, Caponsacchi.
9. The saints are named in lines 6–7.

How comes that arm of yours about a wolf?
And the soft length,—lies in and out your feet   125
And laps you round the knee,—a snake it is!"
And so on.
                    Well, and they are right enough,
By the torch they hold up now: for first, observe,
I never had a father,—no, nor yet
A mother: my own boy can say at least   130
"I had a mother whom I kept two weeks!"
Not I, who little used to doubt . . . I doubt
Good Pietro, kind Violante, gave me birth?
They loved me always as I love my babe
(—Nearly so, that is—quite so could not be—)   135
Did for me all I meant to do for him,
Till one surprising day, three years ago,
They both declared, at Rome, before some judge
In some Court where the people flocked to hear,
That really I had never been their child,   140
Was a mere castaway, the careless crime
Of an unknown man, the crime and care too much
Of a woman known too well,—little to these,
Therefore, of whom I was the flesh and blood:
What then to Pietro and Violante, both   145
No more my relatives than you or you?
Nothing to them! You know what they declared.

So with my husband,—just such a surprise,
Such a mistake, in that relationship!
Everyone says that husbands love their wives,   150
Guard them and guide them, give them happiness;
'T is duty, law, pleasure, religion: well,
You see how much of this comes true in mine!
People indeed would fain have somehow proved
He was no husband: but he did not hear,   155
Or would not wait, and so has killed us all.

Then there is . . . only let me name one more!
There is the friend,—men will not ask about,
But tell untruths of, and give nicknames to,
And think my lover, most surprise of all!   160
Do only hear, it is the priest they mean,
Giuseppe Caponsacchi: a priest—love,
And love me! Well, yet people think he did.
I am married, he has taken priestly vows,
They know that, and yet go on, say, the same,   165
"Yes, how he loves you!" "That was love"—they say,
When anything is answered that they ask:
Or else "No wonder you love him"—they say.
Then they shake heads, pity much, scarcely blame—
As if we neither of us lacked excuse,   170
And anyhow are punished to the full,

And downright love atones for everything!
Nay, I heard read out in the public Court
Before the judge, in presence of my friends,
Letters 't was said the priest had sent to me,   175
And other letters sent him by myself,
We being lovers!
              Listen what this is like!
When I was a mere child, my mother . . . that's
Violante, you must let me call her so
Nor waste time, trying to unlearn the word . . .   180
She brought a neighbour's child of my own age
To play with me of rainy afternoons;
And, since there hung a tapestry on the wall,
We two agreed to find each other out
Among the figures. "Tisbe, that is you,[1]   185
With half-moon on your hair-knot, spear in hand,
Flying, but no wings, only the great scarf
Blown to a bluish rainbow at your back:
Call off your hound and leave the stag alone!"
"—And there are you, Pompilia, such green leaves[2]   190
Flourishing out of your five finger-ends,
And all the rest of you so brown and rough:
Why is it you are turned a sort of tree?"
You know the figures never were ourselves
Though we nicknamed them so. Thus, all my life,—   195
As well what was, as what, like this, was not,—
Looks old, fantastic and impossible:
I touch a fairy thing that fades and fades.
—Even to my babe! I thought, when he was born,
Something began for once that would not end,   200
Nor change into a laugh at me, but stay
For evermore, eternally quite mine.
Well, so he is,—but yet they bore him off,
The third day, lest my husband should lay traps
And catch him, and by means of him catch me.   205
Since they have saved him so, it was well done:
Yet thence comes such confusion of what was
With what will be,—that late seems long ago,
And, what years should bring round, already come,
Till even he withdraws into a dream   210
As the rest do: I fancy him grown great,
Strong, stern, a tall young man who tutors me,
Frowns with the others "Poor imprudent child!
Why did you venture out of the safe street?
Why go so far from help to that lone house?   215
Why open at the whisper and the knock?"

---

1. Diana, goddess of the moon and hunting, pursued Actaeon with one of his hounds (Ovid, *Metamorphoses* 3.138–252).
2. Leaves of the bay (laurel) tree, into which Daphne was transformed when pursued by Apollo (*Metamorphoses* 1.452–567).

Six days ago when it was New Year's-day,
We bent above the fire and talked of him,
What he should do when he was grown and great.
Violante, Pietro, each had given the arm   220
I leant on, to walk by, from couch to chair
And fireside,—laughed, as I lay safe at last,
"Pompilia's march from bed to board is made,
Pompilia back again and with a babe,
Shall one day lend his arm and help her walk!"   225
Then we all wished each other more New Years.
Pietro began to scheme—"Our cause is gained;
The law is stronger than a wicked man:
Let him henceforth go his way, leave us ours!
We will avoid the city, tempt no more   230
The greedy ones by feasting and parade,—
Live at the other villa,[3] we know where,
Still farther off, and we can watch the babe
Grow fast in the good air; and wood is cheap
And wine sincere[4] outside the city gate.   235
I still have two or three old friends will grope
Their way along the mere half-mile of road,
With staff and lantern on a moonless night
When one needs talk: they'll find me, never fear,
And I'll find them a flask of the old sort yet!"   240
Violante said "You chatter like a crow:
Pompilia tires o' the tattle, and shall to bed:
Do not too much the first day,—somewhat more
To-morrow, and, the next, begin the cape
And hood and coat! I have spun wool enough."   245
Oh what a happy friendly eve was that!

And, next day, about noon, out Pietro went—
He was so happy and would talk so much,
Until Violante pushed and laughed him forth
Sight-seeing in the cold,—"So much to see   250
I' the churches! Swathe your throat three times!" she cried,
"And, above all, beware the slippery ways,
And bring us all the news by supper-time!"
He came back late, laid by cloak, staff and hat,
Powdered so thick with snow it made us laugh,   255
Rolled a great log upon the ash o' the hearth,
And bade Violante treat us to a flask,
Because he had obeyed her faithfully,
Gone sight-see through the seven, and found no church
To his mind like San Giovanni[5]—"There's the fold,   260
And all the sheep together, big as cats!
And such a shepherd, half the size of life,

---

3. Pompilia's parents, the Comparini, owned a single villa in Rome, but Browning thought they
   had two.
4. Not adulterated.
5. The church of St. John Lateran, one of seven major basilicas in Rome, boasting an elaborate
   Nativity scene.

Starts up and hears the angel"—when, at the door,
A tap: we started up: you know the rest.

Pietro at least had done no harm, I know;   265
Nor even Violante, so much harm as makes
Such revenge lawful. Certainly she erred—
Did wrong, how shall I dare say otherwise?—
In telling that first falsehood, buying me
From my poor faulty⁶ mother at a price,   270
To pass off upon Pietro as his child.
If one should take my babe, give him a name,
Say he was not Gaetano and my own,
But that some other woman made his mouth
And hands and feet,—how very false were that!   275
No good could come of that; and all harm did.
Yet if a stranger were to represent
"Needs must you either give your babe to me
And let me call him mine for evermore,
Or let your husband get him"—ah, my God,   280
That were a trial I refuse to face!
Well, just so here: it proved wrong but seemed right
To poor Violante—for there lay, she said,
My poor real dying mother in her rags,
Who put me from her with the life and all,   285
Poverty, pain, shame and disease at once,
To die the easier by what price I fetched—
Also (I hope) because I should be spared
Sorrow and sin,—why may not that have helped?
My father,—he was no one, any one,—   290
The worse, the likelier,—call him—he who came,
Was wicked for his pleasure, went his way,
And left no trace to track by; there remained
Nothing but me, the unnecessary life,
To catch up or let fall,—and yet a thing   295
She could make happy, be made happy with,
This poor Violante,—who would frown thereat?

Well, God, you see! God plants us where we grow.
It is not that because a bud is born
At a wild briar's end, full i' the wild beast's way,   300
We ought to pluck and put it out of reach
On the oak-tree top,—say "There the bud belongs!"
She thought, moreover, real lies were lies told
For harm's sake; whereas this had good at heart,
Good for my mother, good for me, and good   305
For Pietro who was meant to love a babe,
And needed one to make his life of use,
Receive his house and land when he should die.
Wrong, wrong and always wrong! how plainly wrong:

6. Sinful.

For see, this fault kept pricking, as faults do,   310
All the same at her heart: this falsehood hatched,
She could not let it go nor keep it fast.
She told me so,—the first time I was found
Locked in her arms once more after the pain,
When the nuns let me leave them and go home,   315
And both of us cried all the cares away,—
This it was set her on to make amends,
This brought about the marriage—simply this!
Do let me speak for her you blame so much!
When Paul, my husband's brother, found me out,   320
Heard there was wealth for who should marry me,
So, came and made a speech to ask my hand
For Guido,—she, instead of piercing straight
Through the pretence to the ignoble truth,
Fancied she saw God's very finger point,   325
Designate just the time for planting me
(The wild-briar slip[7] she plucked to love and wear)
In soil where I could strike real root, and grow,
And get to be the thing I called myself:
For, wife and husband are one flesh, God says,[8]   330
And I, whose parents seemed such and were none,
Should in a husband have a husband now,
Find nothing, this time, but was what it seemed,
—All truth and no confusion any more.
I know she meant all good to me, all pain   335
To herself,—since how could it be aught but pain
To give me up, so, from her very breast,
The wilding flower-tree-branch that, all those years,
She had got used to feel for and find fixed?
She meant well: has it been so ill i' the main?   340
That is but fair to ask: one cannot judge
Of what has been the ill or well of life,
The day that one is dying,—sorrows change
Into not altogether sorrow-like;
I do see strangeness but scarce misery,   345
Now it is over, and no danger more.
My child is safe; there seems not so much pain.
It comes, most like, that I am just absolved,
Purged of the past, the foul in me, washed fair,[9]—
One cannot both have and not have, you know,—   350
Being right now, I am happy and colour things.
Yes, everybody that leaves life sees all
Softened and bettered: so with other sights:
To me at least was never evening yet
But seemed far beautifuller than its day,   355
For past is past.
                    There was a fancy came,

7. Cutting.
8. Genesis 2.24; Mark 10.8.
9. She has just confessed to and received absolution from Don Celestine.

When somewhere, in the journey with my friend,
We stepped into a hovel to get food;
And there began a yelp here, a bark there,—
Misunderstanding creatures that were wroth   360
And vexed themselves and us till we retired.
The hovel is life: no matter what dogs bit
Or cats scratched in the hovel I break from,
All outside is lone field, moon and such peace—
Flowing in, filling up as with a sea   365
Whereon comes Someone, walks fast on the white,
Jesus Christ's self, Don Celestine declares,
To meet me and calm all things back again.[1]

Beside, up to my marriage, thirteen years
Were, each day, happy as the day was long: 370
This may have made the change too terrible.
I know that when Violante told me first
The cavalier—she meant to bring next morn,
Whom I must also let take, kiss my hand—
Would be at San Lorenzo the same eve   375
And marry me,—which over, we should go
Home both of us without him as before,
And, till she bade speak, I must hold my tongue,
Such being the correct way with girl-brides,
From whom one word would make a father blush,—   380
I know, I say, that when she told me this,
—Well, I no more saw sense in what she said
Than a lamb does in people clipping wool;
Only lay down and let myself be clipped.
And when next day the cavalier who came—   385
(Tisbe had told me that the slim young man
With wings at head, and wings at feet, and sword
Threatening a monster, in our tapestry,
Would eat a girl else,—was a cavalier)[2]
When he proved Guido Franceschini,—old   390
And nothing like so tall as I myself,
Hook-nosed and yellow in a bush of beard,
Much like a thing I saw on a boy's wrist,
He called an owl and used for catching birds,—
And when he took my hand and made a smile—   395
Why, the uncomfortableness of it all
Seemed hardly more important in the case
Than,—when one gives you, say, a coin to spend,—
Its newness or its oldness; if the piece
Weigh properly and buy you what you wish,   400
No matter whether you get grime or glare!
Men take the coin, return you grapes and figs.
Here, marriage was the coin, a dirty piece

1. Matthew 14:25–32.
2. Perseus, who slew the dragon to rescue Andromeda (*Metamorphoses* 4.663–752).

Would purchase me the praise of those I loved:
About what else should I concern myself?   405

So, hardly knowing what a husband meant,
I supposed this or any man would serve,
No whit the worse for being so uncouth:
For I was ill once and a doctor came
With a great ugly hat, no plume thereto,   410
Black jerkin[3] and black buckles and black sword,
And white sharp beard over the ruff in front,
And oh so lean, so sour-faced and austere!—
Who felt my pulse, made me put out my tongue,
Then oped a phial, dripped a drop or two   415
Of a black bitter something,—I was cured!
What mattered the fierce beard or the grim face?
It was the physic[4] beautified the man,
Master Malpichi,[5]—never met his match
In Rome, they said,—so ugly all the same!   420

However, I was hurried through a storm,
Next dark eve of December's deadest day—
How it rained!—through our street and the Lion's-mouth[6]
And the bit of Corso,—cloaked round, covered close,
I was like something strange or contraband,—   425
Into blank San Lorenzo, up the aisle,
My mother keeping hold of me so tight,
I fancied we were come to see a corpse
Before the altar which she pulled me toward.
There we found waiting an unpleasant priest   430
Who proved the brother, not our parish friend,[7]
But one with mischief-making mouth and eye,
Paul, whom I know since to my cost. And then
I heard the heavy church-door lock out help
Behind us: for the customary warmth,   435
Two tapers shivered on the altar. "Quick—
Lose no time!" cried the priest. And straightway down
From . . . what's behind the altar where he hid—
Hawk-nose and yellowness and bush and all,
Stepped Guido, caught my hand, and there was I   440
O' the chancel, and the priest had opened book,
Read here and there, made me say that and this,
And after, told me I was now a wife,
Honoured indeed, since Christ thus weds the Church,
And therefore turned he water into wine,[8]   445

---

3. Tight-fitting jacket, or doublet.
4. Medicine or medical skill.
5. Marcello Malpighi (1628–94) biologist and the Pope's personal physician 1691–94.
6. The Via della Bocca di Leone; the [Via del] Corso of line 428 is the main north-south thoroughfare in Rome.
7. Abate Paolo, whom Browning names as the officiating priest at the wedding; his sources did not specify who performed the ceremony.
8. The miracle of the wedding at Cana (John 2:1–10).

To show I should obey my spouse like Christ.
Then the two slipped aside and talked apart,
And I, silent and scared, got down again
And joined my mother who was weeping now.
Nobody seemed to mind us any more,   450
And both of us on tiptoe found our way
To the door which was unlocked by this, and wide.
When we were in the street, the rain had stopped,
All things looked better. At our own house-door,
Violante whispered "No one syllable   455
To Pietro! Girl-brides never breathe a word!"
"—Well treated to a wetting, draggle-tails!"
Laughed Pietro as he opened—"Very near
You made me brave the gutter's roaring sea
To carry off from roost old dove and young,   460
Trussed up in church, the cote, by me, the kite![9]
What do these priests mean, praying folk to death
On stormy afternoons, with Christmas close
To wash our sins off nor require the rain?"
Violante gave my hand a timely squeeze,   465
Madonna saved me from immodest speech,
I kissed him and was quiet, being a bride.

When I saw nothing more, the next three weeks,
Of Guido—"Nor the Church sees Christ" thought I:
"Nothing is changed however, wine is wine   470
And water only water in our house.
Nor did I see that ugly doctor since
That cure of the illness: just as I was cured,
I am married,—neither scarecrow will return."

Three weeks, I chuckled—"How would Giulia stare,   475
And Tecla smile and Tisbe laugh outright,
Were it not impudent[1] for brides to talk!"—
Until one morning, as I sat and sang
At the broidery-frame alone i' the chamber,—loud
Voices, two, three together, sobbings too,   480
And my name, "Guido," "Paolo," flung like stones
From each to the other! In I ran to see.
There stood the very Guido and the priest
With sly face,—formal but nowise afraid,—
While Pietro seemed all red and angry, scarce   485
Able to stutter out his wrath in words;
And this it was that made my mother sob,
As he reproached her—"You have murdered us,
Me and yourself and this our child beside!"
Then Guido interposed "Murdered or not,   490
Be it enough your child is now my wife!
I claim and come to take her." Paul put in,

9. Hawklike predator.
1. Immodest.

"Consider—kinsman, dare I term you so?—
What is the good of your sagacity
Except to counsel in a strait like this?   495
I guarantee the parties man and wife
Whether you like or loathe it, bless or ban.
May spilt milk be put back within the bowl—
The done thing, undone? You, it is, we look
For counsel to, you fitliest will advise!   500
Since milk, though spilt and spoilt, does marble good,
Better we down on knees and scrub the floor,
Than sigh, 'the waste would make a syllabub!'[2]
Help us so turn disaster to account,
So predispose the groom, he needs shall grace   505
The bride with favour from the very first,
Not begin marriage an embittered man!"
He smiled,—the game so wholly in his hands!
While fast and faster sobbed Violante—"Ay,
All of us murdered, past averting now!   510
O my sin, O my secret!" and such like.[3]

Then I began to half surmise the truth;
Something had happened, low, mean, underhand,
False, and my mother was to blame, and I
To pity, whom all spoke of, none addressed: 515
I was the chattel that had caused a crime.
I stood mute,—those who tangled must untie
The embroilment. Pietro cried "Withdraw, my child!
She is not helpful to the sacrifice
At this stage,—do you want the victim by   520
While you discuss the value of her blood?
For her sake, I consent to hear you talk:
Go, child, and pray God help the innocent!"

I did go and was praying God, when came
Violante, with eyes swollen and red enough,   525
But movement on her mouth for make-believe
Matters were somehow getting right again.
She bade me sit down by her side and hear.
"You are too young and cannot understand,
Nor did your father understand at first.   530
I wished to benefit all three of us,
And when he failed to take my meaning,—why,
I tried to have my way at unaware—
Obtained him the advantage he refused.
As if I put before him wholesome food   535
Instead of broken victual,[4]—he finds change

2. Luxurious cold dessert made with sweetened cream thickened with gelatin and beaten with wine, spirits, or fruit juice.
3. The secret of Pompilia's birth, not that of the clandestine marriage. Violante agreed to the marriage partly to erase Pompilia's tainted origin and to raise Pompilia (and her family) in the social scale.
4. Leftovers.

I' the viands, never cares to reason why,
But falls to blaming me, would fling the plate
From window, scandalize the neighbourhood,
Even while he smacks his lips,—men's way, my child!   540
But either you have prayed him unperverse
Or I have talked him back into his wits:
And Paolo was a help in time of need,—
Guido, not much—my child, the way of men!
A priest is more a woman than a man,   545
And Paul did wonders to persuade. In short,
Yes, he was wrong, your father sees and says;
My scheme was worth attempting: and bears fruit,
Gives you a husband and a noble name,
A palace and no end of pleasant things.   550
What do you care about a handsome youth?
They are so volatile, and tease their wives!
This is the kind of man to keep the house.
We lose no daughter,—gain a son, that's all:
For 't is arranged we never separate,   555
Nor miss, in our grey time of life, the tints
Of you that colour eve to match with morn.
In good or ill, we share and share alike,
And cast our lots into a common lap,
And all three die together as we lived!   560
Only, at Arezzo,—that's a Tuscan town,
Not so large as this noisy Rome, no doubt,
But older far and finer much, say folk,—
In a great palace where you will be queen,
Know the Archbishop and the Governor,   565
And we see homage done you ere we die.
Therefore, be good and pardon!"—"Pardon what?
You know things, I am very ignorant:
All is right if you only will not cry!"

And so an end! Because a blank begins[5]   570
From when, at the word, she kissed me hard and hot,
And took me back to where my father leaned
Opposite Guido—who stood eyeing him,
As eyes the butcher the cast panting ox[6]
That feels his fate is come, nor struggles more,—   575
While Paul looked archly on, pricked brow at whiles
With the pen-point as to punish triumph there,—
And said "Count Guido, take your lawful wife
Until death part you!"
            All since is one blank,
Over and ended; a terrific dream.   580
It is the good of dreams—so soon they go!
Wake in a horror of heart-beats, you may—
Cry "The dread thing will never from my thoughts!"

5. Psalm 46:1.
6. Thrown on its side preparatory to slaughter.

Still, a few daylight doses of plain life,
Cock-crow and sparrow-chirp, or bleat and bell   585
Of goats that trot by, tinkling, to be milked;
And when you rub your eyes awake and wide,
Where is the harm o' the horror? Gone! So here.
I know I wake,—but from what? Blank, I say!
This is the note of evil: for good lasts.   590
Even when Don Celestine bade "Search and find!
For your soul's sake, remember what is past,
The better to forgive it,"—all in vain!
What was fast getting indistinct before,
Vanished outright. By special grace perhaps,   595
Between that first calm and this last, four years
Vanish,—one quarter of my life, you know.
I am held up, amid the nothingness,
By one or two truths only—thence I hang,
And there I live,—the rest is death or dream,   600
All but those points of my support. I think
Of what I saw at Rome once in the Square
O' the Spaniards, opposite the Spanish House:[7]
There was a foreigner had trained a goat,
A shuddering white woman of a beast,   605
To climb up, stand straight on a pile of sticks
Put close, which gave the creature room enough:
When she was settled there he, one by one,
Took away all the sticks, left just the four
Whereon the little hoofs did really rest,   610
There she kept firm, all underneath was air.
So, what I hold by, are my prayer to God,
My hope, that came in answer to the prayer,
Some hand would interpose and save me—hand
Which proved to be my friend's hand: and,—blest bliss,—   615
That fancy which began so faint at first,
That thrill of dawn's suffusion through my dark,
Which I perceive was promise of my child,
The light his unborn face sent long before,—
God's way of breaking the good news to flesh.   620
That is all left now of those four bad years.
Don Celestine urged "But remember more!
Other men's faults may help me find your own.
I need the cruelty exposed, explained,
Or how can I advise you to forgive?"   625
He thought I could not properly forgive
Unless I ceased forgetting,—which is true:
For, bringing back reluctantly to mind
My husband's treatment of me,—by a light
That's later than my life-time, I review   630
And comprehend much and imagine more,
And have but little to forgive at last.

---

7. Spanish embassy, facing the Piazza di Spagna and the "Spanish steps."

For now,—be fair and say,—is it not true
He was ill-used and cheated of his hope
To get enriched by marriage? Marriage gave   635
Me and no money, broke the compact so:
He had a right to ask me on those terms,
As Pietro and Violante to declare
They would not give me: so the bargain stood:
They broke it, and he felt himself aggrieved,   640
Became unkind with me to punish them.
They said 't was he began deception first,
Nor, in one point whereto he pledged himself,
Kept promise: what of that, suppose it were?
Echoes die off, scarcely reverberate   645
For ever,—why should ill keep echoing ill
And never let our ears have done with noise?
Then my poor parents took the violent way
To thwart him,—he must needs retaliate,—wrong,
Wrong, and all wrong,—better say, all blind!   650
As I myself was, that is sure, who else
Had understood the mystery: for his wife
Was bound in some sort to help somehow there.
It seems as if I might have interposed,
Blunted the edge of their resentment so,   655
Since he vexed me because they first vexed him;
"I will entreat them to desist, submit,
Give him the money and be poor in peace,—
Certainly not go tell the world: perhaps
He will grow quiet with his gains."
                                 Yes, say   660
Something to this effect and you do well!
But then you have to see first: I was blind.
That is the fruit of all such wormy ways,
The indirect, the unapproved of God:
You cannot find their author's end and aim,   665
Not even to substitute your good for bad,
Your straight for the irregular; you stand
Stupefied, profitless, as cow or sheep
That miss a man's mind, anger him just twice
By trial at repairing the first fault.   670
Thus, when he blamed me, "You are a coquette,
A lure-owl posturing to attract birds,[8]
You look love-lures at theatre and church,
In walk, at window!"—that, I knew, was false:
But why he charged me falsely, whither sought   675
To drive me by such charge,—how could I know?
So, unaware, I only made things worse.
I tried to soothe him by abjuring walk,
Window, church, theatre, for good and all,

---

8. An owl, often placed on a pole with a mirror beneath, used to attract birds into the hunter's range.

As if he had been in earnest: that, you know,   680
Was nothing like the object of his charge.
Yes, when I got my maid to supplicate
The priest, whose name she read when she would read
Those feigned false letters I was forced to hear
Though I could read no word of,—he should cease   685
Writing,—nay, if he minded prayer of mine,
Cease from so much as even pass the street
Whereon our house looked,—in my ignorance
I was just thwarting Guido's true intent;
Which was, to bring about a wicked change   690
Of sport to earnest, tempt a thoughtless man
To write indeed, and pass the house, and more,
Till both of us were taken in a crime.
He ought not to have wished me thus act lies,
Simulate folly: but,—wrong or right, the wish,—   695
I failed to apprehend its drift. How plain
It follows,—if I fell into such fault,
He also may have overreached the mark,
Made mistake, by perversity of brain,
I' the whole sad strange plot, the grotesque intrigue   700
To make me and my friend unself ourselves,
Be other man and woman than we were!
Think it out, you who have the time! for me,—
I cannot say less; more I will not say.
Leave it to God to cover and undo!   705
Only, my dulness should not prove too much!
—Not prove that in a certain other point
Wherein my husband blamed me,—and you blame,
If I interpret smiles and shakes of head,—
I was dull too. Oh, if I dared but speak!   710
Must I speak? I am blamed that I forwent
A way to make my husband's favour come.
That is true: I was firm, withstood, refused . . .
—Women[9] as you are, how can I find the words?

I felt there was just one thing Guido claimed   715
I had no right to give nor he to take;
We being in estrangement, soul from soul:
Till, when I sought help, the Archbishop smiled,
Inquiring into privacies of life,
—Said I was blameable—(he stands for God)   720
Nowise entitled to exemption there.
Then I obeyed,—as surely had obeyed
Were the injunction "Since your husband bids,
Swallow the burning coal he proffers you!"
But I did wrong, and he gave wrong advice   725
Though he were thrice Archbishop,—that, I know!—
Now I have got to die and see things clear.

---

9. Nuns around her deathbed.

Remember I was barely twelve years old—
A child at marriage: I was let alone
For weeks, I told you, lived my child-life still   730
Even at Arezzo, when I woke and found
First . . . but I need not think of that again—
Over and ended! Try and take the sense
Of what I signify, if it must be so.
After the first, my husband, for hate's sake,   735
Said one eve, when the simpler cruelty
Seemed somewhat dull at edge and fit to bear,
"We have been man and wife six months almost:
How long is this your comedy to last?
Go this night to my chamber, not your own!"   740
At which word, I did rush—most true the charge—
And gain the Archbishop's house—he stands for God—
And fall upon my knees and clasp his feet,
Praying him hinder what my estranged soul
Refused to bear, though patient of the rest: 745
"Place me within a convent," I implored—
"Let me henceforward lead the virgin life
You praise in Her you bid me imitate!"
What did he answer? "Folly of ignorance!
Know, daughter, circumstances make or mar   750
Virginity,—'t is virtue or 't is vice.
That which was glory in the Mother of God
Had been, for instance, damnable in Eve
Created to be mother of mankind.
Had Eve, in answer to her Maker's speech   755
'Be fruitful, multiply, replenish earth'[1]—
Pouted 'But I choose rather to remain
Single'—why, she had spared herself forthwith
Further probation by the apple and snake,
Been pushed straight out of Paradise! For see—   760
If motherhood be qualified impure,
I catch you making God command Eve sin!
—A blasphemy so like these Molinists',
I must suspect you dip into their books."
Then he pursued "'T was in your covenant!"   765

No! There my husband never used deceit.
He never did by speech nor act imply
"Because of our souls' yearning that we meet
And mix in soul through flesh, which yours and mine
Wear and impress, and make their visible selves,   770
—All which means, for the love of you and me,
Let us become one flesh, being one soul!"
He only stipulated for the wealth;
Honest so far. But when he spoke as plain—
Dreadfully honest also—"Since our souls   775

1. Genesis 1:28.

Stand each from each, a whole world's width between,
Give me the fleshly vesture I can reach
And rend and leave just fit for hell to burn!"—
Why, in God's name, for Guido's soul's own sake
Imperilled by polluting mine,—I say,   780
I did resist; would I had overcome!

My heart died out at the Archbishop's smile;
—It seemed so stale and worn a way o' the world,
As though 't were nature frowning—"Here is Spring,
The sun shines as he shone at Adam's fall,   785
The earth requires that warmth reach everywhere:
What, must your patch of snow be saved forsooth
Because you rather fancy snow than flowers?"
Something in this style he began with me.
Last he said, savagely for a good man,   790
"This explains why you call your husband harsh,
Harsh to you, harsh to whom you love. God's Bread!²
The poor Count has to manage a mere child
Whose parents leave untaught the simplest things
Their duty was and privilege to teach,—   795
Goodwives' instruction, gossips' lore: they laugh
And leave the Count the task,—or leave it me!"
Then I resolved to tell a frightful thing.
"I am not ignorant,—know what I say,
Declaring this is sought for hate, not love.   800
Sir, you may hear things like almighty God.
I tell you that my housemate, yes—the priest
My husband's brother, Canon Girolamo—
Has taught me what depraved and misnamed love
Means, and what outward signs denote the sin,   805
For he solicits me and says he loves,
The idle young priest with nought else to do.
My husband sees this, knows this, and lets be.
Is it your counsel I bear this beside?"
"—More scandal, and against a priest this time!   810
What, 't is the Canon now?"—less snappishly—
Rise up, my child, for such a child you are,
The rod were too advanced a punishment!
Let's try the honeyed cake. A parable!
'Without a parable spake He not to them.'³   815
There was a ripe round long black toothsome fruit,
Even a flower-fig, the prime boast of May:
And, to the tree, said . . . either the spirit o' the fig,
Or, if we bring in men, the gardener,
Archbishop of the orchard—had I time   820
To try o' the two which fits in best: indeed
It might be the Creator's self, but then

2. Oath alluding to the Eucharist.
3. Matthew 13:34.

The tree should bear an apple, I suppose,—
Well, anyhow, one with authority said
'Ripe fig, burst skin, regale the fig-pecker[4]—   825
The bird whereof thou art a perquisite!'[5]
'Nay,' with a flounce, replied the restif fig,
'I much prefer to keep my pulp myself:
He may go breakfastless and dinnerless,
Supperless of one crimson seed, for me!'   830
So, back she flopped into her bunch of leaves.
He flew off, left her,—did the natural lord,—
And lo, three hundred thousand bees and wasps
Found her out, feasted on her to the shuck:
Such gain the fig's that gave its bird no bite!   835
The moral,—fools elude their proper lot,
Tempt other fools, get ruined all alike.
Therefore go home, embrace your husband quick!
Which if his Canon brother chance to see,
He will the sooner back to book again."   840

So, home I did go; so, the worst befell:
So, I had proof the Archbishop was just man,
And hardly that, and certainly no more.
For, miserable consequence to me,
My husband's hatred waxed nor waned at all,   845
His brother's boldness grew effrontery soon,
And my last stay and comfort in myself
Was forced from me: henceforth I looked to God
Only, nor cared my desecrated soul
Should have fair walls, gay windows for the world.   850
God's glimmer, that came through the ruin-top,
Was witness why all lights were quenched inside:
Henceforth I asked God counsel, not mankind.

So, when I made the effort, freed myself,
They said—"No care to save appearance here!   855
How cynic,—when, how wanton, were enough!"
—Adding, it all came of my mother's life—
My own real mother, whom I never knew,
Who did wrong (if she needs must have done wrong)
Through being all her life, not my four years,   860
At mercy of the hateful: every beast
O' the field was wont to break that fountain-fence,
Trample the silver into mud so murk
Heaven could not find itself reflected there.
Now they cry "Out on her, who, plashy pool,   865
Bequeathed turbidity and bitterness
To the daughter-stream where Guido dipt and drank!"

---

4. *Beccafico,* small bird whose delicate flesh is esteemed by gourmets; eaten after it has fat-
tened on figs and other fruits.
5. Sole property; reward; "restif" in the next line: perverse; rebellious.

Well, since she had to bear this brand—let me!
The rather do I understand her now,
From my experience of what hate calls love,—   870
Much love might be in what their love called hate.
If she sold . . . what they call, sold . . . me her child—
I shall believe she hoped in her poor heart
That I at least might try be good and pure,
Begin to live untempted, not go doomed   875
And done with ere once found in fault, as she.
Oh and, my mother, it all came to this?
Why should I trust those that speak ill of you,
When I mistrust who speaks even well of them?
Why, since all bound to do me good, did harm,   880
May not you, seeming as you harmed me most,
Have meant to do most good—and feed your child
From bramble-bush, whom not one orchard-tree
But drew bough back from, nor let one fruit fall?
This it was for you sacrificed your babe?   885
Gained just this, giving your heart's hope away
As I might give mine, loving it as you,
If . . . but that never could be asked of me!

There, enough! I have my support again,
Again the knowledge that my babe was, is,   890
Will be mine only. Him, by death, I give
Outright to God, without a further care,—
But not to any parent in the world,—
So to be safe: why is it we repine?
What guardianship were safer could we choose?   895
All human plans and projects come to nought:
My life, and what I know of other lives,
Prove that: no plan nor project! God shall care!

And now you are not tired? How patient then
All of you,—Oh yes, patient this long while   900
Listening, and understanding, I am sure!
Four days ago, when I was sound and well
And like to live, no one would understand.
People were kind, but smiled "And what of him,
Your friend, whose tonsure the rich dark-brown hides?   905
There, there!—your lover, do we dream he was?
A priest too—never were such naughtiness!
Still, he thinks many a long think, never fear,
After the shy pale lady,—lay so light
For a moment in his arms, the lucky one!"   910
And so on: wherefore should I blame you much?
So we are made, such difference in minds,
Such difference too in eyes that see the minds!
That man, you misinterpret and misprise[6]—

6. Undervalue.

The glory of his nature, I had thought,   915
Shot itself out in white light, blazed the truth
Through every atom of his act with me:
Yet where I point you, through the crystal shrine,
Purity in quintessence, one dew-drop,
You all descry a spider in the midst.   920
One says "The head of it is plain to see,"
And one, "They are the feet by which I judge,"
All say, "Those films were spun by nothing else."

Then, I must lay my babe away with God,
Nor think of him again, for gratitude.   925
Yes, my last breath shall wholly spend itself
In one attempt more to disperse the stain,
The mist from other breath fond[7] mouths have made,
About a lustrous and pellucid soul:
So that, when I am gone but sorrow stays,   930
And people need assurance in their doubt
If God yet have a servant, man a friend,
The weak a saviour and the vile a foe,—
Let him be present, by the name invoked,
Giuseppe-Maria Caponsacchi!
                                    There,   935
Strength comes already with the utterance!
I will remember once more for his sake
The sorrow: for he lives and is belied.
Could he be here, how he would speak for me!

I had been miserable three drear years   940
In that dread palace and lay passive now,
When I first learned there could be such a man.
Thus it fell: I was at a public play,
In the last days of Carnival last March,
Brought there I knew not why, but now know well.   945
My husband put me where I sat, in front;
Then crouched down, breathed cold through me from behind,
Stationed i' the shadow,—none in front could see,—
I, it was, faced the stranger-throng beneath,
The crowd with upturned faces, eyes one stare,   950
Voices one buzz. I looked but to the stage,
Whereon two lovers sang and interchanged
"True life is only love, love only bliss:
I love thee—thee I love!" then they embraced.
I looked thence to the ceiling and the walls,—   955
Over the crowd, those voices and those eyes,—
My thoughts went through the roof and out, to Rome
On wings of music, waft of measured words,—
Set me down there, a happy child again
Sure that to-morrow would be festa-day,   960

7. Foolish.

Hearing my parents praise past festas more,
And seeing they were old if I was young,
Yet wondering why they still would end discourse
With "We must soon go, you abide your time,
And,—might we haply see the proper friend   965
Throw his arm over you and make you safe!"

Sudden I saw him; into my lap there fell
A foolish twist of comfits,[8] broke my dream
And brought me from the air and laid me low,
As ruined as the soaring bee that's reached   970
(So Pietro told me at the Villa once)
By the dust-handful. There the comfits lay:
I looked to see who flung them, and I faced
This Caponsacchi, looking up in turn.
Ere I could reason out why, I felt sure,   975
Whoever flung them, his was not the hand,—
Up rose the round face and good-natured grin
Of one who, in effect, had played the prank,
From covert close beside the earnest face,—
Fat waggish Conti, friend of all the world.   980
He was my husband's cousin, privileged
To throw the thing: the other, silent, grave,
Solemn almost, saw me, as I saw him.

There is a psalm Don Celestine recites,
"Had I a dove's wings, how I fain would flee!"[9]   985
The psalm runs not "I hope, I pray for wings,"—
Not "If wings fall from heaven, I fix them fast,"—
Simply "How good it were to fly and rest,
Have hope now, and one day expect content!
How well to do what I shall never do!"   990
So I said "Had there been a man like that,
To lift me with his strength out of all strife
Into the calm, how I could fly and rest!
I have a keeper in the garden here
Whose sole employment is to strike me low   995
If ever I, for solace, seek the sun.
Life means with me successful feigning death,
Lying stone-like, eluding notice so,
Forgoing here the turf and there the sky.
Suppose that man had been instead of this!"   1000

Presently Conti laughed into my ear,
—Had tripped up to the raised place where I sat—
"Cousin, I flung them brutishly and hard!
Because you must be hurt, to look austere
As Caponsacchi yonder, my tall friend   1005
A-gazing now. Ah, Guido, you so close?

8. Pack of sweets in a roll of paper twisted at both ends.
9. Psalm 55:6.

Keep on your knees, do! Beg her to forgive!
My cornet battered like a cannon-ball.[1]
Good-bye, I'm gone!"—nor waited the reply.

That night at supper, out my husband broke,   1010
"Why was that throwing, that buffoonery?
Do you think I am your dupe? What man would dare
Throw comfits in a stranger lady's lap?
'T was knowledge of you bred such insolence
In Caponsacchi; he dared shoot the bolt,   1015
Using that Conti for his stalking-horse.
How could you see him this once and no more,
When he is always haunting hereabout
At the street-corner or the palace-side,
Publishing my shame and your impudence?   1020
You are a wanton,—I a dupe, you think?
O Christ, what hinders that I kill her quick?"
Whereat he drew his sword and feigned a thrust.

All this, now,—being not so strange to me,
Used to such misconception day by day   1025
And broken-in to bear,—I bore, this time,
More quietly than woman should perhaps;
Repeated the mere truth and held my tongue.

Then he said, "Since you play the ignorant,
I shall instruct you. This amour,—commenced   1030
Or finished or midway in act, all's one,—
'T is the town-talk; so my revenge shall be.
Does he presume because he is a priest?
I warn him that the sword I wear shall pink[2]
His lily-scented cassock through and through,   1035
Next time I catch him underneath your eaves!"

But he had threatened with the sword so oft
And, after all, not kept his promise. All
I said was "Let God save the innocent!
Moreover death is far from a bad fate.   1040
I shall go pray for you and me, not him;
And then I look to sleep, come death or, worse,
Life." So, I slept.
                        There may have elapsed a week,
When Margherita,—called my waiting-maid,
Whom it is said my husband found too fair—   1045
Who stood and heard the charge and the reply,
Who never once would let the matter rest
From that night forward, but rang changes still
On this the thrust and that the shame,[3] and how

___

1. Here, a conical twist of paper.
2. Stab.
3. Hardship.

Good cause for jealousy cures jealous fools,   1050
And what a paragon was this same priest
She talked about until I stopped my ears,—
She said, "A week is gone; you comb your hair,
Then go mope in a corner, cheek on palm,
Till night comes round again,—so, waste a week   1055
As if your husband menaced you in sport.
Have not I some acquaintance with his tricks?
Oh no, he did not stab the serving-man
Who made and sang the rhymes about me once!
For why? They sent him to the wars next day.   1060
Nor poisoned he the foreigner, my friend
Who wagered on the whiteness of my breast,—
The swarth skins of our city in dispute:
For, though he paid me proper compliment,
The Count well knew he was besotted with   1065
Somebody else, a skin as black as ink,
(As all the town knew save my foreigner)
He found and wedded presently,—'Why need
Better revenge?'—the Count asked. But what's here?
A priest that does not fight, and cannot wed,   1070
Yet must be dealt with! If the Count took fire
For the poor pastime of a minute,—me—
What were the conflagration for yourself,
Countess and lady-wife and all the rest?
The priest will perish; you will grieve too late: 1075
So shall the city-ladies' handsomest[4]
Frankest and liberalest[5] gentleman
Die for you, to appease a scurvy dog
Hanging's too good for. Is there no escape?
Were it not simple Christian charity   1080
To warn the priest be on his guard,—save him
Assured death, save yourself from causing it?
I meet him in the street. Give me a glove,
A ring to show for token! Mum's the word!"

I answered "If you were, as styled, my maid,   1085
I would command you: as you are, you say,
My husband's intimate,—assist his wife
Who can do nothing but entreat 'Be still!'
Even if you speak truth and a crime is planned,
Leave help to God as I am forced to do!   1090
There is no other help, or we should craze,
Seeing such evil with no human cure.
Reflect that God, who makes the storm desist,
Can make an angry violent heart subside.
Why should we venture teach Him governance?   1095
Never address me on this subject more!"

4. Women of fashion.
5. Freest.

Next night she said "But I went, all the same,
—Ay, saw your Caponsacchi in his house,
And come back stuffed with news I must outpour.
I told him 'Sir, my mistress is a stone: 1100
Why should you harm her for no good you get?
For you do harm her—prowl about our place
With the Count never distant half the street,
Lurking at every corner, would you look!
'T is certain she has witched you with a spell.   1105
Are there not other beauties at your beck?
We all know, Donna This and Monna That
Die for a glance of yours, yet here you gaze!
Go make them grateful, leave the stone its cold!'
And he—oh, he turned first white and then red,   1110
And then—'To her behest I bow myself,
Whom I love with my body and my soul:
Only a word i' the bowing! See, I write
One little word, no harm to see or hear!
Then, fear no further!' This is what he wrote.   1115
I know you cannot read,—therefore, let me!
'My idol!' " . . .
            But I took it from her hand
And tore it into shreds. "Why, join the rest
Who harm me? Have I ever done you wrong?
People have told me 't is you wrong myself: 1120
Let it suffice I either feel no wrong
Or else forgive it,—yet you turn my foe!
The others hunt me and you throw a noose!"

She muttered "Have your wilful way!" I slept.

Whereupon . . . no, I leave my husband out   1125
It is not to do him more hurt, I speak.
Let it suffice, when misery was most,
One day, I swooned and got a respite so.
She stooped as I was slowly coming to,
This Margherita, ever on my trace,   1130
And whispered—"Caponsacchi!"

                        If I drowned,
But woke afloat i' the wave with upturned eyes,
And found their first sight was a star! I turned—
For the first time, I let her have her will,
Heard passively,—"The imposthume[6] at such head,   1135
One touch, one lancet-puncture would relieve,—
And still no glance the good physician's way
Who rids you of the torment in a trice!
Still he writes letters you refuse to hear.
He may prevent[7] your husband, kill himself,   1140

6. Swelling or abscess.
7. Anticipate.

So desperate and all fordone is he!
Just hear the pretty verse he made to-day!
A sonnet from Mirtillo. '*Peerless fair* . . .'
All poetry is difficult to read,
—The sense of it is, anyhow, he seeks   1145
Leave to contrive you an escape from hell,
And for that purpose asks an interview.
I can write, I can grant it in your name,
Or, what is better, lead you to his house.
Your husband dashes you against the stones;   1150
This man would place each fragment in a shrine:
You hate him, love your husband!"
                              I returned
"It is not true I love my husband,—no,
Nor hate this man. I listen while you speak,
—Assured that what you say is false, the same: 1155
Much as when once, to me a little child,
A rough gaunt man in rags, with eyes on fire,
A crowd of boys and idlers at his heels,
Rushed as I crossed the Square, and held my head
In his two hands, 'Here's she will let me speak!   1160
You little girl, whose eyes do good to mine,
I am the Pope, am Sextus, now the Sixth;[8]
And that Twelfth Innocent, proclaimed to-day,[9]
Is Lucifer disguised in human flesh!
The angels, met in conclave, crowned me!'—thus   1165
He gibbered and I listened; but I knew
All was delusion, ere folk interposed
'Unfasten him, the maniac!' Thus I know
All your report of Caponsacchi false,
Folly or dreaming; I have seen so much   1170
By that adventure at the spectacle,
The face I fronted that one first, last time:
He would belie it by such words and thoughts.
Therefore while you profess to show him me,
I ever see his own face. Get you gone!"   1175

"—That will I, nor once open mouth again,—
No, by Saint Joseph and the Holy Ghost!
On your head be the damage, so adieu!"

And so more days, more deeds I must forget,
Till . . . what a strange thing now is to declare!   1180
Since I say anything, say all if true!
And how my life seems lengthened as to serve!
It may be idle or inopportune,
But, true?—why, what was all I said but truth,
Even when I found that such as are untrue   1185
Could only take the truth in through a lie?

8. There was no Pope Sextus the Sixth.
9. The date was July 12, 1691.

Now—I am speaking truth to the Truth's self:[1]
God will lend credit to my words this time.

It had got half through April. I arose
One vivid daybreak,—who had gone to bed   1190
In the old way my wont those last three years,
Careless until, the cup drained, I should die.
The last sound in my ear, the over-night,
Had been a something let drop on the sly
In prattle by Margherita, "Soon enough   1195
Gaieties end, now Easter's past: a week,
And the Archbishop gets him back to Rome,—
Everyone leaves the town for Rome, this Spring,—
Even Caponsacchi, out of heart and hope,
Resigns himself and follows with the flock."   1200
I heard this drop and drop like rain outside
Fast-falling through the darkness while she spoke:
So had I heard with like indifference,
"And Michael's pair of wings will arrive first[2]
At Rome, to introduce the company,   1205
And bear him from our picture where he fights
Satan,—expect to have that dragon loose
And never a defender!"—my sole thought
Being still, as night came, "Done, another day!
How good to sleep and so get nearer death!"—   1210
When, what, first thing at daybreak, pierced the sleep
With a summons to me? Up I sprang alive,
Light in me, light without me, everywhere
Change! A broad yellow sunbeam was let fall
From heaven to earth,—a sudden drawbridge lay,   1215
Along which marched a myriad merry motes,
Mocking the flies that crossed them and recrossed
In rival dance, companions new-born too.
On the house-eaves, a dripping shag of weed
Shook diamonds on each dull grey lattice-square,   1220
As first one, then another bird leapt by,
And light was off, and lo was back again,
Always with one voice,—where are two such joys?—
The blessed building-sparrow! I stepped forth,
Stood on the terrace,—o'er the roofs, such sky!   1225
My heart sang, "I too am to go away,
I too have something I must care about,
Carry away with me to Rome, to Rome!
The bird brings hither sticks and hairs and wool,
And nowhere else i' the world; what fly breaks rank,   1230
Falls out of the procession that befits,
From window here to window there, with all
The world to choose,—so well he knows his course?

---

1. God, as in John 14:6.
2. Aretino's fresco of St. Michael fighting a dragon (Satan), in the church of San Francesco in Arezzo.

I have my purpose and my motive too,
My march to Rome, like any bird or fly!   1235
Had I been dead! How right to be alive!
Last night I almost prayed for leave to die,
Wished Guido all his pleasure with the sword
Or the poison,—poison, sword, was but a trick,
Harmless, may God forgive him the poor jest!   1240
My life is charmed, will last till I reach Rome!
Yesterday, but for the sin,—ah, nameless be
The deed I could have dared against myself!
Now—see if I will touch an unripe fruit³
And risk the health I want to have and use!   1245
Not to live, now, would be the wickedness,—
For life means to make haste and go to Rome
And leave Arezzo, leave all woes at once!"

Now, understand here, by no means mistake!
Long ago had I tried to leave that house   1250
When it seemed such procedure would stop sin;
And still failed more the more I tried—at first
The Archbishop, as I told you,—next, our lord
The Governor,—indeed I found my way,
I went to the great palace where he rules,   1255
Though I knew well 't was he who,—when I gave
A jewel or two, themselves had given me,
Back to my parents,—since they wanted bread,
They who had never let me want a nosegay,—he
Spoke of the jail for felons, if they kept   1260
What was first theirs, then mine, so doubly theirs,
Though all the while my husband's most of all!
I knew well who had spoke the word wrought this:
Yet, being in extremity, I fled
To the Governor, as I say,—scarce opened lip   1265
When—the cold cruel snicker close behind—
Guido was on my trace, already there,
Exchanging nod and wink for shrug and smile,
And I—pushed back to him and, for my pains
Paid with . . . but why remember what is past?   1270
I sought out a poor friar the people call
The Roman, and confessed my sin which came
Of their sin,—that fact could not be repressed,—
The frightfulness of my despair in God:
And, feeling, through the grate, his horror shake,   1275
Implored him, "Write for me who cannot write,
Apprise my parents, make them rescue me!
You bid me be courageous and trust God:
Do you in turn dare somewhat, trust and write
'Dear friends, who used to be my parents once,   1280
And now declare you have no part in me,

---

3. Unripe fruit was supposed to bring on premature labor.

This is some riddle I want wit to solve,
Since you must love me with no difference.
Even suppose you altered,—there's your hate,
To ask for: hate of you two dearest ones   1285
I shall find liker love than love found here,
If husbands love their wives. Take me away
And hate me as you do the gnats and fleas,
Even the scorpions! How I shall rejoice!'
Write that and save me!" And he promised—wrote 1290
Or did not write; things never changed at all:
He was not like the Augustinian here![4]
Last, in a desperation I appealed
To friends, whoever wished me better days,
To Guillichini, that's of kin,[5]—"What, I—   1295
Travel to Rome with you? A flying gout[6]
Bids me deny my heart and mind my leg!"
Then I tried Conti, used to brave—laugh back
The louring thunder when his cousin scowled
At me protected by his presence: "You—   1300
Who well know what you cannot save me from,—
Carry me off! What frightens you, a priest?"
He shook his head, looked grave—"Above my strength!
Guido has claws that scratch, shows feline teeth;
A formidabler foe than I dare fret: 1305
Give me a dog to deal with, twice the size!
Of course I am a priest and Canon too,
But . . . by the bye . . . though both, not quite so bold
As he, my fellow-Canon, brother-priest,
The personage in such ill odour here   1310
Because of the reports—pure birth o' the brain!
Our Caponsacchi, he 's your true Saint George[7]
To slay the monster, set the Princess free,
And have the whole High-Altar to himself:
I always think so when I see that piece   1315
I' the Pieve, that 's his church and mine, you know:
Though you drop eyes at mention of his name!"

That name had got to take a half-grotesque
Half-ominous, wholly enigmatic sense,
Like any by-word, broken bit of song   1320
Born with a meaning, changed by mouth and mouth
That mix it in a sneer or smile, as chance
Bids, till it now means nought but ugliness
And perhaps shame.
     —All this intends to say,
That, over-night, the notion of escape   1325

---

4. Don Celestine.
5. Relative of Guido, charged with complicity in the elopement and adultery with Pompilia;
Browning saw both as false charges.
6. Gouty inflammation moving into different joints in the body.
7. Vasari's painting of St. George and the Dragon, in the church of St. Maria della Pieve.

Had seemed distemper, dreaming; and the name,—
Not the man, but the name of him, thus made
Into a mockery and disgrace,—why, she
Who uttered it persistently, had laughed,
"I name his name, and there you start and wince   1330
As criminal from the red tongs' touch!"—yet now,
Now, as I stood letting morn bathe me bright,
Choosing which butterfly should bear my news,—
The white, the brown one, or that tinier blue,—
The Margherita, I detested so,   1335
In she came—"The fine day, the good Spring time!
What, up and out at window? That is best.
No thought of Caponsacchi?—who stood there
All night on one leg, like the sentry crane,
Under the pelting of your water-spout—   1340
Looked last look at your lattice ere he leave
Our city, bury his dead hope at Rome.
Ay, go to looking-glass and make you fine,
While he may die ere touch one least loose hair
You drag at with the comb in such a rage!"   1345

I turned—"Tell Caponsacchi he may come!"

"Tell him to come? Ah, but, for charity,
A truce to fooling! Come? What,—come this eve?
Peter and Paul! But I see through the trick!
Yes, come, and take a flower-pot on his head,   1350
Flung from your terrace! No joke, sincere truth?"

How plainly I perceived hell flash and fade
O' the face of her,—the doubt that first paled joy,
Then, final reassurance I indeed
Was caught now, never to be free again!   1355
What did I care?—who felt myself of force[8]
To play with silk, and spurn the horsehair-springe.[9]

"But—do you know that I have bade him come,
And in your own name? I presumed so much,
Knowing the thing you needed in your heart.   1360
But somehow—what had I to show in proof?
He would not come: half-promised, that was all,
And wrote the letters you refused to read.
What is the message that shall move him now?"

"After the Ave Maria, at first dark,[1]   1365
I will be standing on the terrace, say!"

---

8. Required.
9. Playing with the bright silk bait of a trap (springe) while avoiding entrapment.
1. After the Angelus bell at 6 P.M.

"I would I had a good long lock of hair
Should prove I was not lying! Never mind!"

Off she went—"May he not refuse, that's all—
Fearing a trick!"
                    I answered, "He will come."   1370
And, all day, I sent prayer like incense up[2]
To God the strong, God the beneficent,
God ever mindful in all strife and strait,
Who, for our own good, makes the need extreme,
Till at the last He puts forth might and saves.   1375
An old rhyme came into my head and rang
Of how a virgin, for the faith of God,
Hid herself, from the Paynims that pursued,
In a cave's heart; until a thunderstone,[3]
Wrapped in a flame, revealed the couch and prey   1380
And they laughed—"Thanks to lightning, ours at last!"
And she cried "Wrath of God, assert His love!
Servant of God, thou fire, befriend His child!"
And lo, the fire she grasped at, fixed its flash,
Lay in her hand a calm cold dreadful sword   1385
She brandished till pursuers strewed the ground,
So did the souls within them die away,
As o'er the prostrate bodies, sworded, safe,
She walked forth to the solitudes and Christ:
So should I grasp the lightning and be saved!   1390

And still, as the day wore, the trouble grew
Whereby I guessed there would be born a star,
Until at an intense throe of the dusk,[4]
I started up, was pushed, I dare to say,
Out on the terrace, leaned and looked at last   1395
Where the deliverer waited me: the same
Silent and solemn face, I first descried
At the spectacle, confronted mine once more.

So was that minute twice vouchsafed me, so
The manhood, wasted then, was still at watch   1400
To save me yet a second time: no change
Here, though all else changed in the changing world!

I spoke on the instant, as my duty bade,
In some such sense as this, whatever the phrase.

"Friend, foolish words were borne from you to me;   1405
Your soul behind them is the pure strong wind,
Not dust and feathers which its breath may bear:

---

2. Psalm 141:2.
3. Meteorite ("thunderbolt" in the original manuscript), with reference to the old belief that
lightning came as a solid dart with destructive force.
4. Birth-pang.

These to the witless seem the wind itself,
Since proving thus the first of it they feel.
If by mischance you blew offence my way,   1410
The straws are dropt, the wind desists no whit,
And how such strays were caught up in the street
And took a motion from you, why inquire?
I speak to the strong soul, no weak disguise.
If it be truth,—why should I doubt it truth?—   1415
You serve God specially, as priests are bound,
And care about me, stranger as I am,
So far as wish my good,—that miracle
I take to intimate He wills you serve
By saving me,—what else can He direct?   1420
Here is the service. Since a long while now,
I am in course of being put to death:
While death concerned nothing but me, I bowed
The head and bade, in heart, my husband strike.
Now I imperil something more, it seems,   1425
Something that's truelier me than this myself,
Something I trust in God and you to save.
You go to Rome, they tell me: take me there,
Put me back with my people!"
                                    He replied—
The first word I heard ever from his lips,   1430
All himself in it,—an eternity
Of speech, to match the immeasurable depth
O' the soul that then broke silence—"I am yours."

So did the star rise, soon to lead my step,
Lead on, nor pause before it should stand still   1435
Above the House o' the Babe,⁵—my babe to be,
That knew me first and thus made me know him,
That had his right of life and claim on mine,
And would not let me die till he was born,
But pricked me at the heart to save us both,   1440
Saying "Have you the will? Leave God the way!"
And the way was Caponsacchi—"mine," thank God!
He was mine, he is mine, he will be mine.

No pause i' the leading and the light! I know,
Next night there was a cloud came, and not he: 1445
But I prayed through the darkness till it broke
And let him shine. The second night, he came.

"The plan is rash; the project desperate:
In such a flight needs must I risk your life,
Give food for falsehood, folly or mistake,   1450
Ground for your husband's rancour and revenge"—
So he began again, with the same face.

5. Cf. the star of Bethlehem (Matthew 2:9–11).

I felt that, the same loyalty—one star
Turning now red that was so white before—
One service apprehended newly: just   1455
A word of mine and there the white was back!

"No, friend, for you will take me! 'T is yourself
Risk all, not I,—who let you, for I trust
In the compensating great God: enough!
I know you: when is it that you will come?"   1460

"To-morrow at the day's dawn." Then I heard
What I should do: how to prepare for flight
And where to fly.

                              That night my husband bade
"—You, whom I loathe, beware you break my sleep
This whole night! Couch beside me like the corpse   1465
I would you were!" The rest you know, I think—
How I found Caponsacchi and escaped.

And this man, men call sinner? Jesus Christ!
Of whom men said, with mouths Thyself mad'st once,
"He hath a devil"—say he was Thy saint,[6]   1470
My Caponsacchi! Shield and show—unshroud
In Thine own time the glory of the soul
If aught obscure,—if ink-spot, from vile pens
Scribbling a charge against him—(I was glad
Then, for the first time, that I could not write)—   1475
Flirted his way, have flecked the blaze!

                                        For me,
'T is otherwise: let men take, sift my thoughts
—Thoughts I throw like the flax for sun to bleach!
I did pray, do pray, in the prayer shall die,
"Oh, to have Caponsacchi for my guide!"   1480
Ever the face upturned to mine, the hand
Holding my hand across the world,—a sense
That reads, as only such can read, the mark
God sets on woman, signifying so[7]
She should—shall peradventure—be divine;   1485
Yet 'ware, the while, how weakness mars the print
And makes confusion, leaves the thing men see,
—Not this man sees,—who from his soul, re-writes
The obliterated charter,—love and strength
Mending what's marred. "So kneels a votarist,[8]   1490
Weeds some poor waste traditionary plot
Where shrine once was, where temple yet may be,

6. John 7:20; 8:48.
7. In Genesis 3:16, this is the sign of woman's fallen state; also the promise of redemption
through the birth of Christ.
8. Worshipper.

Purging the place but worshipping the while,
By faith and not by sight, sight clearest so,[9]—
Such way the saints work,"—says Don Celestine.   1495
But I, not privileged to see a saint
Of old when such walked earth with crown and palm,[1]
If I call "saint" what saints call something else—
The saints must bear with me, impute the fault
To a soul i' the bud, so starved by ignorance,   1500
Stinted of warmth, it will not blow this year
Nor recognize the orb[2] which Spring-flowers know.
But if meanwhile some insect with a heart
Worth floods of lazy music, spendthrift joy—
Some fire-fly renounced Spring for my dwarfed cup,   1505
Crept close to me, brought lustre for the dark,
Comfort against the cold,—what though excess
Of comfort should miscall the creature—sun?
What did the sun to hinder while harsh hands
Petal by petal, crude and colourless,   1510
Tore me? This one heart gave me all the Spring!

Is all told? There's the journey: and where's time
To tell you how that heart burst out in shine?
Yet certain points do press on me too hard.
Each place must have a name, though I forget: 1515
How strange it was—there where the plain begins
And the small river mitigates its flow—
When eve was fading fast, and my soul sank,
And he divined what surge of bitterness,
In overtaking me, would float me back   1520
Whence I was carried by the striding day—
So,—"This grey place was famous once," said he—
And he began that legend of the place
As if in answer to the unspoken fear,
And told me all about a brave man dead,   1525
Which lifted me and let my soul go on!
How did he know too,—at that town's approach
By the rock-side,—that in coming near the signs
Of life, the house-roofs and the church and tower,
I saw the old boundary and wall o' the world   1530
Rise plain as ever round me, hard and cold,
As if the broken circlet joined again,
Tightened itself about me with no break,—
As if the town would turn Arezzo's self,—
The husband there,—the friends my enemies,   1535
All ranged against me, not an avenue
To try, but would be blocked and drive me back
On him,—this other, . . . oh the heart in that!
Did not he find, bring, put into my arms

9. 2 Corinthians 5:7; also John 20:29.
1. Iconographic symbols of martyrdom.
2. The sun.

A new-born babe?—and I saw faces beam 1540
Of the young mother proud to teach me joy,
And gossips round expecting my surprise
At the sudden hole through earth that lets in heaven.
I could believe himself by his strong will
Had woven around me what I thought the world 1545
We went along in, every circumstance,
Towns, flowers and faces, all things helped so well!
For, through the journey, was it natural
Such comfort should arise from first to last?
As I look back, all is one milky way; 1450
Still bettered more, the more remembered, so
Do new stars bud while I but search for old,
And fill all gaps i' the glory, and grow him—
Him I now see make the shine everywhere.
Even at the last when the bewildered flesh, 1455
The cloud of weariness about my soul
Clogging too heavily, sucked down all sense,—
Still its last voice was, "He will watch and care;
Let the strength go, I am content: he stays!"
I doubt not he did stay and care for all— 1560
From that sick minute when the head swam round,
And the eyes looked their last and died on him,
As in his arms be caught me, and, you say,
Carried me in, that tragical red eve,
And laid me where I next returned to life 1565
In the other red of morning, two red plates
That crushed together, crushed the time between,
And are since then a solid fire to me,—
When in, my dreadful husband and the world
Broke,—and I saw him, master, by hell's right, 1570
And saw my angel helplessly held back
By guards that helped the malice—the lamb prone,
The serpent towering and triumphant—then
Came all the strength back in a sudden swell,
I did for once see right, do right, give tongue 1575
The adequate protest: for a worm must turn
If it would have its wrong observed by God.
I did spring up, attempt to thrust aside
That ice-block 'twixt the sun and me, lay low
The neutralizer of all good and truth. 1580
If I sinned so,—never obey voice more
O' the Just and Terrible, who bids us—"Bear!"
Not—"Stand by, bear to see my angels bear!"
I am clear it was on impulse to serve God
Not save myself,—no—nor my child unborn! 1585
Had I else waited patiently till now?—
Who saw my old kind parents, silly-sooth
And too much trustful,[3] for their worst of faults,

3. Naïve.

Cheated, brow-beaten, stripped and starved, cast out
Into the kennel:[4] I remonstrated,   1590
Then sank to silence, for,—their woes at end,
Themselves gone,—only I was left to plague.
If only I was threatened and belied,
What matter? I could bear it and did bear;
It was a comfort, still one lot for all: 1595
They were not persecuted for my sake
And I, estranged, the single happy one.
But when at last, all by myself I stood
Obeying the clear voice which bade me rise,
Not for my own sake but my babe unborn,   1600
And take the angel's hand was sent to help—
And found the old adversary athwart[5] the path—
Not my hand simply struck from the angel's, but
The very angel's self made foul i' the face
By the fiend who struck there,—that I would not bear,   1605
That only I resisted! So, my first
And last resistance was invincible.
Prayers move God; threats, and nothing else, move men!
I must have prayed a man as he were God
When I implored the Governor to right   1610
My parents' wrongs: the answer was a smile.
The Archbishop,—did I clasp his feet enough,
Hide my face hotly on them, while I told
More than I dared make my own mother know?
The profit was—compassion and a jest.   1615
This time, the foolish prayers were done with, right
Used might, and solemnized the sport at once.
All was against the combat: vantage, mine?
The runaway avowed, the accomplice-wife,
In company with the plan-contriving priest?   1620
Yet, shame thus rank and patent, I struck, bare,
At foe from head to foot in magic mail,[6]
And off it withered, cobweb-armoury
Against the lightning! 'T was truth singed the lies
And saved me, not the vain sword nor weak speech!   1625

You see, I will not have the service fail!
I say, the angel saved me: I am safe!
Others may want and wish, I wish nor want
One point o' the circle plainer, where I stand
Traced round about with white to front the world.   1630
What of the calumny I came across,
What o' the way to the end?—the end crowns all.
The judges judged aright i' the main, gave me
The uttermost of my heart's desire, a truce

4. Gutter.
5. Across.
6. Armor.

From torture and Arezzo, balm for hurt,   1635
With the quiet nuns,—God recompense the good!
Who said and sang away the ugly past.
And, when my final fortune was revealed,
What safety while, amid my parents' arms,
My babe was given me! Yes he saved my babe: 1640
It would not have peeped forth, the bird-like thing,
Through that Arezzo noise and trouble: back
Had it returned nor ever let me see!
But the sweet peace cured all, and let me live
And give my bird the life among the leaves   1645
God meant him! Weeks and months of quietude,
I could lie in such peace and learn so much—
Begin the task, I see how needful now,
Of understanding somewhat of my past,—
Know life a little, I should leave so soon.   1650
Therefore, because this man restored my soul,
All has been right; I have gained my gain, enjoyed
As well as suffered,—nay, got foretaste too
Of better life beginning where this ends—
All through the breathing-while allowed me thus,   1655
Which let good premonitions reach my soul
Unthwarted, and benignant influence flow
And interpenetrate and change my heart,
Uncrossed by what was wicked,—nay, unkind.
For, as the weakness of my time drew nigh,   1660
Nobody did me one disservice more,
Spoke coldly or looked strangely, broke the love
I lay in the arms of, till my boy was born,
Born all in love, with nought to spoil the bliss
A whole long fortnight: in a life like mine   1665
A fortnight filled with bliss is long and much.
All women are not mothers of a boy,
Though they live twice the length of my whole life,
And, as they fancy happily all the same.
There I lay, then, all my great fortnight long,   1670
As if it would continue, broaden out
Happily more and more, and lead to heaven:
Christmas before me,—was not that a chance?
I never realized God's birth before—
How He grew likest God in being born.   1675
This time I felt like Mary, had my babe
Lying a little on my breast like hers.
So all went on till, just four days ago—
The night and the tap.

                    Oh it shall be success
To the whole of our poor family! My friends   1680
. . . Nay, father and mother,—give me back my word!
They have been rudely stripped of life, disgraced

Like children who must needs go clothed too fine,
Carry the garb of Carnival in Lent.
If they too much affected frippery,[7]   1685
They have been punished and submit themselves,
Say no word; all is over, they see God
Who will not be extreme to mark their fault
Or He had granted respite:[8] they are safe.

For that most woeful man my husband once,   1690
Who, needing respite, still draws vital breath,
I—pardon him? So far as lies in me,
I give him for his good the life he takes,
Praying the world will therefore acquiesce.
Let him make God amends,—none, none to me   1695
Who thank him rather that, whereas strange fate
Mockingly styled him husband and me wife,
Himself this way at least pronounced divorce,
Blotted the marriage-bond: this blood of mine
Flies forth exultingly at any door,   1700
Washes the parchment white,[9] and thanks the blow.
We shall not meet in this world nor the next,
But where will God be absent? In His face
Is light, but in His shadow healing too:
Let Guido touch the shadow and be healed![1]   1705
And as my presence was importunate,[2]—
My earthly good, temptation and a snare,—
Nothing about me but drew somehow down
His hate upon me,—somewhat so excused
Therefore, since hate was thus the truth of him,—   1710
May my evanishment for evermore
Help further to relieve the heart that cast
Such object of its natural loathing forth!
So he was made; he nowise made himself:
I could not love him, but his mother did.   1715
His soul has never lain beside my soul:
But for the unresisting body,—thanks!
He burned that garment spotted by the flesh.
Whatever he touched is rightly ruined: plague
It caught, and disinfection it had craved   1720
Still but for Guido; I am saved through him
So as by fire; to him—thanks and farewell![3]

Even for my babe, my boy, there's safety thence—
From the sudden death of me, I mean: we poor

---

7. Put on airs; relied on superficial show.
8. Time in which to confess their sins and receive absolution.
9. The marriage contract.
1. A melding of Luke 8:43–48, 2 Corinthians 4:6, and Acts 5:15; the idea is that the merest touch of Christ's garment, or even the shadow of God [actually, St. Peter in the latter two passages cited] has the power to save Guido.
2. Troublesome.
3. 1 Corinthians 3:15.

Weak souls, how we endeavour to be strong!   1725
I was already using up my life,—
This portion, now, should do him such a good,
This other go to keep off such an ill!
The great life; see, a breath and it is gone!
So is detached, so left all by itself   1730
The little life, the fact which means so much.[4]
Shall not God stoop the kindlier to His work,
His marvel of creation, foot would crush,
Now that the hand He trusted to receive
And hold it, lets the treasure fall perforce?   1735
The better; He shall have in orphanage
His own way all the clearlier: if my babe
Outlived the hour—and he has lived two weeks—
It is through God who knows I am not by.
Who is it makes the soft gold hair turn black,   1740
And sets the tongue, might lie so long at rest,
Trying to talk? Let us leave God alone!
Why should I doubt He will explain in time
What I feel now, but fail to find the words?
My babe nor was, nor is, nor yet shall be   1745
Count Guido Franceschini's child at all—
Only his mother's, born of love not hate!
So shall I have my rights in after-time.
It seems absurd, impossible to-day;
So seems so much else, not explained but known!   1750

Ah! Friends, I thank and bless you every one!
No more now: I withdraw from earth and man
To my own soul, compose myself for God.

Well, and there is more! Yes, my end of breath
Shall bear away my soul in being true!   1755
He is still here, not outside with the world,
Here, here, I have him in his rightful place!
'T is now, when I am most upon the move,
I feel for what I verily find—again
The face, again the eyes, again, through all,   1760
The heart and its immeasurable love
Of my one friend, my only, all my own,
Who put his breast between the spears and me.
Ever with Caponsacchi! Otherwise
Here alone would be failure, loss to me—   1765
How much more loss to him, with life debarred
From giving life, love locked from love's display,
The day-star stopped its task that makes night morn!
O lover of my life, O soldier-saint,
No work begun shall ever pause for death!   1770
Love will be helpful to me more and more

---

4. The life of the baby Gaetano.

I' the coming course, the new path I must tread—
My weak hand in thy strong hand, strong for that!
Tell him that if I seem without him now,
That's the world's insight! Oh, he understands!   1775
He is at Civita—do I once doubt[5]
The world again is holding us apart?
He had been here, displayed in my behalf
The broad brow that reverberates the truth,
And flashed the word God gave him, back to man!   1780
I know where the free soul is flown! My fate
Will have been hard for even him to bear:
Let it confirm him in the trust of God,
Showing how holily he dared the deed!
And, for the rest,—say, from the deed, no touch   1785
Of harm came, but all good, all happiness,
Not one faint fleck of failure! Why explain?
What I see, oh, he sees and how much more!
Tell him,—I know not wherefore the true word
Should fade and fall unuttered at the last—   1790
It was the name of him I sprang to meet
When came the knock, the summons and the end.
"My great heart, my strong hand are back again!"
I would have sprung to these, beckoning across
Murder and hell gigantic and distinct   1795
O' the threshold, posted to exclude me heaven:
He is ordained to call and I to come!
Do not the dead wear flowers when dressed for God?
Say,—I am all in flowers from head to foot!
Say,—not one flower of all he said and did,   1800
Might seem to flit unnoticed, fade unknown,
But dropped a seed, has grown a balsam-tree
Whereof the blossoming perfumes the place
At this supreme of moments! He is a priest;
He cannot marry therefore, which is right: 1805
I think he would not marry if he could.
Marriage on earth seems such a counterfeit,
Mere imitation of the inimitable:
In heaven we have the real and true and sure.
'T is there they neither marry nor are given   1810
In marriage but are as the angels:[6] right,
Oh how right that is, how like Jesus Christ
To say that! Marriage-making for the earth,
With gold so much,—birth, power, repute so much,
Or beauty, youth so much, in lack of these!   1815
Be as the angels rather, who, apart,
Know themselves into one, are found at length
Married, but marry never, no, nor give
In marriage; they are man and wife at once
When the true time is: here we have to wait   1820

5. Pompilia is unaware that Caponsacchi is in Rome.
6. Matthew 22:29–30.

Not so long neither! Could we by a wish
Have what we will and get the future now,
Would we wish aught done undone in the past?
So, let him wait God's instant men call years;
Meantime hold hard by truth and his great soul,   1825
Do out the duty! Through such souls alone
God stooping shows sufficient of His light
For us i' the dark to rise by. And I rise.

Book X

The Pope[1]

Like to Ahasuerus, that shrewd prince,[2]
I will begin,—as is, these seven years now,
My daily wont,—and read a History[3]
(Written by one whose deft right hand was dust
To the last digit, ages ere my birth)   5
Of all my predecessors, Popes of Rome:
For though mine ancient early dropped the pen,
Yet others picked it up and wrote it dry,
Since of the making books there is no end.[4]
And so I have the Papacy complete   10
From Peter first to Alexander last;
Can question each and take instruction so.
Have I to dare?—I ask, how dared this Pope?
To suffer?—Suchanone, how suffered he?
Being about to judge, as now, I seek   15
How judged once, well or ill, some other Pope;
Study some signal judgment that subsists
To blaze on, or else blot, the page which seals
The sum up of what gain or loss to God
Came of His one more Vicar in the world.   20

1. Antonio Pignatelli (1615–1700), a Neapolitan, was elected pope in 1691 to succeed Alexander VIII. He took the name of Innocent XII as a sign that he wished to emulate the papacy of Innocent XI, a vigorous reformer. Pignatelli had been vice-legate of Urbino, governor of Perugia, and nuncio to Tuscany, to Poland, and to Austria; he had been created cardinal and archbishop of Naples by Innocent XI. Pignatelli as Innocent XII put an end to nepotism and the sale of offices. He was benevolent, charitable, and frugal, and called the poor his relations; the Roman nobles, on the other hand, he severely punished for all violations of the law.
    The soliloquy of Browning's pope is set on February 21, 1698, the day before Guido and his accomplices are to be executed. Pleading ecclesiastical privilege—he had taken minor orders in the church—Guido has appealed his case to the pope. The pope is represented as an aged man aware that his own death cannot be far off, and anxious therefore that this possibly final act of judgment be right in the eyes of God. Meditating somberly on the Franceschini case, he finds in it the deepest human concerns: truth and falsehood, good and evil, faith and doubt. His speculations on these issues amount to an anatomy of the world as it stands at the close of the seventeenth century. Inevitably arises the question of the future of Western culture—with particular reference to religious faith—in the coming Age of Reason. The pope voices Browning's own creed, rather than that of orthodox Roman Catholicism; but he is no mere mouthpiece for the poet, who has created in the pope a fully realized dramatic character, one of the great philosophic heroes in literature.
2. Persian king who, one sleepless night, read of an abortive plot against him (Esther 6:1–3).
3. No single History has been identified.
4. Ecclesiastes 12:12.

So, do I find example, rule of life;
So, square and set in order the next page,
Shall be stretched smooth o'er my own funeral cyst.[5]

Eight hundred years exact before the year
I was made Pope, men made Formosus[6] Pope,   25
Say Sigebert[7] and other chroniclers.
Ere I confirm or quash the Trial here
Of Guido Franceschini and his friends,
Read,—How there was a ghastly Trial once
Of a dead man by a live man, and both, Popes: 30
Thus—in the antique penman's very phrase.

"Then Stephen, Pope and seventh of the name,[8]
Cried out, in synod as he sat in state,
While choler quivered on his brow and beard,
'Come into court, Formosus, thou lost wretch,   35
That claimedst to be late Pope as even I!'

"And at the word the great door of the church
Flew wide, and in they brought Formosus' self,
The body of him, dead, even as embalmed
And buried duly in the Vatican   40
Eight months before, exhumed thus for the nonce.
They set it, that dead body of a Pope,
Clothed in pontific vesture now again,
Upright on Peter's chair as if alive.

"And Stephen, springing up, cried furiously   45
'Bishop of Porto, wherefore didst presume
To leave that see and take this Roman see,
Exchange the lesser for the greater see,
—A thing against the canons of the Church?'

"Then one—(a Deacon who, observing forms,   50
Was placed by Stephen to repel the charge,
Be advocate and mouthpiece of the corpse)—
Spoke as he dared, set stammeringly forth
With white lips and dry tongue,—as but a youth,
For frightful was the corpse-face to behold,—   55
How nowise lacked there precedent for this.

"But when, for his last precedent of all,
Emboldened by the Spirit, out he blurts

5. Coffin.
6. Pope from 891–896, he sided with Arnulf, king of Germany, against the princes of Spoleto, and in 895 crowned Arnulf emperor. After his death the validity of his acts was contested, and Stephen VI, treating him as a usurper, disinterred his body in 897. Theodore II restored it to Christian burial, and John IX declared Formosus' pontificate valid. The violence described by Innocent in lines 32–149 was typical of the period.
7. Medieval chronicler Sigebert of Gembloux (ca. 1030–1112).
8. Actually the sixth, pope from 896–897. The other papacies named are: Romanus (897), Theodore II (897), John IX (898–900), and Sergius III (904–911) (lines 105–41).

'And, Holy Father, didst not thou thyself
Vacate the lesser for the greater see,   60
Half a year since change Arago for Rome?'
'—Ye have the sin's defence now, Synod mine!'
Shrieks Stephen in a beastly froth of rage:
'Judge now betwixt him dead and me alive!
Hath he intruded, or do I pretend?   65
Judge, judge!'—breaks wavelike one whole foam of wrath.

"Whereupon they, being friends and followers,
Said 'Ay, thou art Christ's Vicar, and not he!
Away with what is frightful to behold!
This act was uncanonic and a fault.'   70

"Then, swallowed up in rage, Stephen exclaimed
'So, guilty! So, remains I punish guilt!
He is unpoped, and all he did I damn:
The Bishop, that ordained him, I degrade:
Depose to laics[9] those he raised to priests: 75
What they have wrought is mischief nor shall stand,
It is confusion, let it vex no more!
Since I revoke, annul and abrogate
All his decrees in all kinds: they are void!
In token whereof and warning to the world,   80
Strip me yon miscreant of those robes usurped,
And clothe him with vile serge[1] befitting such!
Then hale the carrion to the market-place:
Let the town-hangman chop from his right hand
Those same three fingers which he blessed withal;   85
Next cut the head off once was crowned forsooth:
And last go fling them, fingers, head and trunk,
To Tiber[2] that my Christian fish may sup!'
—Either because of $IX\theta Y\Sigma$ which means Fish[3]
And very aptly symbolizes Christ,   90
Or else because the Pope is Fisherman,[4]
And seals with Fisher's-signet.

                              "Anyway,
So said, so done: himself, to see it done,
Followed the corpse they trailed from street to street
Till into Tiber wave they threw the thing.   95
The people, crowded on the banks to see,
Were loud or mute, wept or laughed, cursed or jeered,
According as the deed addressed their sense;
A scandal verily: and out spake a Jew
'Wot ye your Christ had vexed our Herod thus?'   100

9. Laypersons, not members of the clergy.
1. Garment of coarse wool worn by the poorer classes.
2. River flowing through Rome.
3. Initial letters of the phrase "Jesus Christ, son of God, Savior," which comprise the Greek word for "fish," an early symbol of Christianity.
4. Christ said to Peter and Andrew: "Follow me, and I will make you fishers of men" (Matthew 4:19). The pope's signet ring represents St. Peter fishing from a boat.

"Now when, Formosus being dead a year,
His judge Pope Stephen tasted death in turn,
Made captive by the mob and strangled straight,
Romanus, his successor for a month,
Did make protest Formosus was with God,   105
Holy, just, true in thought and word and deed.
Next Theodore, who reigned but twenty days,
Therein convoked a synod, whose decree
Did reinstate, repope the late unpoped,
And do away with Stephen as accursed.   110
So that when presently certain fisher-folk
(As if the queasy river could not hold
Its swallowed Jonas, but discharged the meal)
Produced the timely product of their nets,
The mutilated man, Formosus,—saved   115
From putrefaction by the embalmer's spice,
Or, as some said, by sanctity of flesh,—
'Why, lay the body again,' bade Theodore,
'Among his predecessors, in the church
And burial-place of Peter!' which was done.   120
'And,' addeth Luitprand,[5] 'many of repute,
Pious and still alive, avouch to me
That, as they bore the body up the aisle,
The saints in imaged row bowed each his head
For welcome to a brother-saint come back.'   125
As for Romanus and this Theodore,
These two Popes, through the brief reign granted each,
Could but initiate what John came to close
And give the final stamp to: he it was
Ninth of the name, (I follow the best guides)   130
Who,—in full synod at Ravenna held
With Bishops seventy-four, and present too
Eude[6] King of France with his Archbishopry,—
Did condemn Stephen, anathematize[7]
The disinterment, and make all blots blank,   135
'For,' argueth here Auxilius[8] in a place
De Ordinationibus, 'precedents
Had been, no lack, before Formosus long,
Of Bishops so transferred from see to see,—
Marinus,[9] for example:' read the tract.   140

"But, after John, came Sergius,[1] reaffirmed
The right of Stephen, cursed Formosus, nay
Cast out, some say, his corpse a second time.
And here,—because the matter went to ground,

5. Or Liudprand (ca. 922–972), Italian historian and bishop of Cremona.
6. Eudes (or Odo, d. 898), king of the Franks.
7. Condemn.
8. Frankish priest of the tenth century, who defended the papacy of Formosus.
9. Marinus I (or Martin II), pope from 882–884. He restored Formosus, then in exile, to his
   see as cardinal-bishop of Porto.
1. Between the two were Benedict IV (900–903) and Leo V (903).

Fretted by new griefs, other cares of the age,—   145
Here is the last pronouncing of the Church,
Her sentence that subsists unto this day.
Yet constantly opinion hath prevailed
I' the Church, Formosus was a holy man."

Which of the judgments was infallible?[2]   150
Which of my predecessors spoke for God?
And what availed Formosus that this cursed,
That blessed, and then this other cursed again?
"Fear ye not those whose power can kill the body
And not the soul," saith Christ, "but rather those   155
Can cast both soul and body into hell!"[3]

John judged thus in Eight Hundred Ninety Eight,
Exact eight hundred years ago to-day
When, sitting in his stead, Vice-gerent here,
I must give judgment on my own behoof.   160
So worked the predecessor: now, my turn!

In God's name! Once more on this earth of God's,
While twilight lasts and time wherein to work,
I take His staff with my uncertain hand,
And stay my six and fourscore years, my due   165
Labour and sorrow, on His judgment-seat,
And forthwith think, speak, act, in place of Him—
The Pope for Christ. Once more appeal is made
From man's assize[4] to mine: I sit and see
Another poor weak trembling human wretch   170
Pushed by his fellows, who pretend the right,
Up to the gulf which, where I gaze, begins
From this world to the next,—gives way and way,
Just on the edge over the awful dark:
With nothing to arrest him but my feet.   175
He catches at me with convulsive face,
Cries "Leave to live the natural minute more!"
While hollowly the avengers echo "Leave?
None! So has he exceeded man's due share
In man's fit license, wrung by Adam's fall,   180
To sin and yet not surely die,[5]—that we,
All of us sinful, all with need of grace,
All chary of our life,—the minute more
Or minute less of grace which saves a soul,—
Bound to make common cause with who craves time,   185
—We yet protest against the exorbitance
Of sin in this one sinner, and demand

2. Allusion to the controversial issue (in the 1860s) of papal infallibility, which was made an
   article of faith by the Vatican Council of 1870.
3. Matthew 10:28.
4. Superior civil court.
5. Genesis 3:4: "And the serpent said unto the woman, Ye shall not surely die."

That his poor sole remaining piece of time
Be plucked from out his clutch: put him to death!
Punish him now! As for the weal or woe   190
Hereafter, God grant mercy! Man be just,
Nor let the felon boast he went scot-free!"
And I am bound, the solitary judge,
To weigh the worth, decide upon the plea,
And either hold a hand out, or withdraw   195
A foot and let the wretch drift to the fall.
Ay, and while thus I dally, dare perchance
Put fancies for a comfort 'twixt this calm
And yonder passion that I have to bear,—
As if reprieve were possible for both   200
Prisoner and Pope,—how easy were reprieve!
A touch o' the hand-bell here, a hasty word
To those who wait, and wonder they wait long,
I' the passage there, and I should gain the life!—
Yea, though I flatter me with fancy thus,   205
I know it is but nature's craven-trick.
The case is over, judgment at an end,
And all things done now and irrevocable:
A mere dead man is Franceschini here,
Even as Formosus centuries ago.   210
I have worn through this sombre wintry day,
With winter in my soul beyond the world's,
Over these dismalest of documents
Which drew night down on me ere eve befell,—
Pleadings and counter-pleadings, figure of fact   215
Beside fact's self, these summaries to-wit,—
How certain three were slain by certain five:
I read here why it was, and how it went,
And how the chief o' the five preferred excuse,
And how law rather chose defence should lie,—   220
What argument he urged by wary word
When free to play off wile, start subterfuge,
And what the unguarded groan told, torture's feat
When law grew brutal, outbroke, overbore
And glutted hunger on the truth, at last,—   225
No matter for the flesh and blood between.
All's a clear rede[6] and no more riddle now.
Truth, nowhere, lies yet everywhere in these—
Not absolutely in a portion, yet
Evolvible from the whole: evolved at last   230
Painfully, held tenaciously by me.
Therefore there is not any doubt to clear
When I shall write the brief word presently
And chink the hand-bell, which I pause to do.
Irresolute? Not I, more than the mound   235
With the pine-trees on it yonder! Some surmise,

---

6. Account.

Perchance, that since man's wit is fallible,
Mine may fail here? Suppose it so,—what then?
Say,—Guido, I count guilty, there's no babe
So guiltless, for I misconceive the man!   240
What's in the chance should move me from my mind?
If, as I walk in a rough country-side,
Peasants of mine cry "Thou art he can help,
Lord of the land and counted wise to boot:
Look at our brother, strangling in his foam,   245
He fell so where we find him,—prove thy worth!"
I may presume, pronounce, "A frenzy-fit,
A falling-sickness or a fever-stroke!
Breathe a vein, copiously let blood at once!"
So perishes the patient, and anon   250
I hear my peasants—"All was error, lord!
Our story, thy prescription: for there crawled
In due time from our hapless brother's breast
The serpent which had stung him: bleeding slew
Whom a prompt cordial had restored to health."   255
What other should I say than "God so willed:
Mankind is ignorant, a man am I:
Call ignorance my sorrow, not my sin!"
So and not otherwise, in after-time,
If some acuter wit, fresh probing, sound   260
This multifarious mass of words and deeds
Deeper, and reach through guilt to innocence,
I shall face Guido's ghost nor blench a jot.
"God who set me to judge thee, meted out
So much of judging faculty, no more: 265
Ask Him if I was slack in use thereof!"
I hold a heavier fault imputable
Inasmuch as I changed a chaplain once,
For no cause,—no, if I must bare my heart,—
Save that he snuffled somewhat saying mass.   270
For I am ware it is the seed of act,
God holds appraising in His hollow palm,
Not act grown great thence on the world below,
Leafage and branchage, vulgar eyes admire.
Therefore I stand on my integrity,   275
Nor fear at all: and if I hesitate,
It is because I need to breathe awhile,
Rest, as the human right allows, review
Intent the little seeds of act, my tree,—
The thought, which, clothed in deed, I give the world   280
At chink of bell and push of arrased door.

O pale departure, dim disgrace of day!
Winter's in wane, his vengeful worst art thou,
To dash the boldness of advancing March!
Thy chill persistent rain has purged our streets   285
Of gossipry; pert tongue and idle ear

By this, consort 'neath archway, portico.
But wheresoe'er Rome gathers in the grey,
Two names now snap and flash from mouth to mouth—
(Sparks, flint and steel strike) Guido and the Pope.   290
By this same hour to-morrow eve—aha,
How do they call him?—the sagacious Swede[7]
Who finds by figures how the chances prove,
Why one comes rather than another thing,
As, say, such dots turn up by throw of dice,   295
Or, if we dip in Virgil[8] here and there
And prick for such a verse, when such shall point.
Take this Swede, tell him, hiding name and rank,
Two men are in our city this dull eve;
One doomed to death,—but hundreds in such plight   300
Slip aside, clean escape by leave of law
Which leans to mercy in this latter time;
Moreover in the plenitude of life
Is he, with strength of limb and brain adroit,
Presumably of service here: beside,   305
The man is noble, backed by nobler friends:
Nay, they so wish him well, the city's self
Makes common cause with who—house-magistrate,
Patron of hearth and home, domestic lord—
But ruled his own, let aliens cavil. Die?   310
He'll bribe a gaoler or break prison first!
Nay, a sedition may be helpful, give
Hint to the mob to batter wall, burn gate,
And bid the favourite malefactor march.
Calculate now these chances of escape!   315
"It is not probable, but well may be."
Again, there is another man, weighed now
By twice eight years beyond the seven-times-ten,
Appointed overweight to break our branch.
And this man's loaded branch lifts, more than snow,   320
All the world's cark and care, though a bird's nest
Were a superfluous burthen: notably
Hath he been pressed, as if his age were youth,
From to-day's dawn till now that day departs,
Trying one question with true sweat of soul   325
"Shall the said doomed man fitlier die or live?"
When a straw swallowed in his posset,[9] stool
Stumbled on where his path lies, any puff
That's incident to such a smoking flax,[1]
Hurries the natural end and quenches him!   330
Now calculate, thou sage, the chances here,

7. Still unidentified. It is possible Browning had in mind Swedish mathematician, scientist, and (late in life) mystic, Emanuel Swedenborg (1688–1772), whom Elizabeth Barrett Browning deeply admired. Swedenborg would have been only a boy in 1698, however.
8. See note to V.401.
9. Hot drink.
1. Isaiah 42:3: ". . . the smoking flax shall he [Christ] not quench: he shall bring forth judgment unto truth."

Say, which shall die the sooner, this or that?
"That, possibly, this in all likelihood."
I thought so: yet thou tripp'st, my foreign friend!
No, it will be quite otherwise,—to-day   335
Is Guido's last: my term is yet to run.

But say the Swede were right, and I forthwith
Acknowledge a prompt summons and lie dead:
Why, then I stand already in God's face
And hear "Since by its fruit a tree is judged,[2]   340
Show me thy fruit, the latest act of thine!
For in the last is summed the first and all,—
What thy life last put heart and soul into,
There shall I taste thy product." I must plead
This condemnation of a man to-day.   345

Not so! Expect nor question nor reply
At what we figure as God's judgment-bar!
None of this vile way by the barren words
Which, more than any deed, characterize
Man as made subject to a curse: no speech—   350
That still bursts o'er some lie which lurks inside,
As the split skin across the coppery snake,
And most denotes man! since, in all beside,
In hate or lust or guile or unbelief,
Out of some core of truth the excrescence comes,   355
And, in the last resort, the man may urge
"So was I made, a weak thing that gave way
To truth, to impulse only strong since true,
And hated, lusted, used guile, forwent faith."
But when man walks the garden of this world   360
For his own solace, and, unchecked by law,
Speaks or keeps silence as himself sees fit,
Without the least incumbency to lie,
—Why, can he tell you what a rose is like,
Or how the birds fly, and not slip to false   365
Though truth serve better? Man must tell his mate
Of you, me and himself, knowing he lies,
Knowing his fellow knows the same,—will think
"He lies, it is the method of a man!"
And yet will speak for answer "It is truth"   370
To him who shall rejoin "Again a lie!"
Therefore these filthy rags of speech, this coil
Of statement, comment, query and response,
Tatters all too contaminate for use,
Have no renewing: He, the Truth, is, too,   375
The Word.[3] We men, in our degree, may know
There, simply, instantaneously, as here
After long time and amid many lies,

2. Matthew 12:33.
3. John 14:6 and 1:14.

Whatever we dare think we know indeed
—That I am I, as He is He,—what else?   380
But be man's method for man's life at least!
Wherefore, Antonio Pignatelli, thou
My ancient self, who wast no Pope so long
But studiedst God and man, the many years
I' the school, i' the cloister, in the diocese   385
Domestic, legate-rule in foreign lands,[4]—
Thou other force in those old busy days
Than this grey ultimate decrepitude,—
Yet sensible of fires that more and more
Visit a soul, in passage to the sky,   390
Left nakeder than when flesh-robe was new—
Thou, not Pope but the mere old man o' the world,
Supposed inquisitive and dispassionate,
Wilt thou, the one whose speech I somewhat trust,
Question the after-me, this self now Pope,   395
Hear his procedure, criticize his work?
Wise in its generation is the world.[5]

This is why Guido is found reprobate.
I see him furnished forth for his career,
On starting for the life-chance in our world,   400
With nearly all we count sufficient help:
Body and mind in balance, a sound frame,
A solid intellect: the wit to seek,
Wisdom to choose, and courage wherewithal
To deal in whatsoever circumstance   405
Should minister to man, make life succeed.
Oh, and much drawback! what were earth without?
Is this our ultimate stage, or starting-place
To try man's foot, if it will creep or climb,
'Mid obstacles in seeming, points that prove   410
Advantage for who vaults from low to high
And makes the stumbling-block a stepping-stone?
So, Guido, born with appetite, lacks food:
Is poor, who yet could deftly play-off[6] wealth:
Straitened, whose limbs are restless till at large.   415
He, as he eyes each outlet of the cirque[7]
And narrow penfold for probation, pines
After the good things just outside its grate,
With less monition, fainter conscience-twitch,
Rarer instinctive qualm at the first feel   420
Of greed unseemly, prompting grasp undue,
Than nature furnishes her main mankind,—
Making it harder to do wrong than right
The first time, careful lest the common ear

4. Innocent had been bishop in Italy and had represented the pope in Poland and Germany.
5. Luke 16:8.
6. Feign.
7. Arena.

Break measure, miss the outstep of life's march.   425
Wherein I see a trial fair and fit
For one else too unfairly fenced about,
Set above sin, beyond his fellows here:
Guarded from the arch-tempter all must fight,
By a great birth, traditionary name,   430
Diligent culture, choice companionship,
Above all, conversancy with the faith
Which puts forth for its base of doctrine just
"Man is born nowise to content himself,
But please God."[8] He accepted such a rule,   435
Recognized man's obedience; and the Church,
Which simply is such rule's embodiment,
He clave to, he held on by,—nay, indeed,
Near pushed inside of, deep as layman durst,
Professed so much of priesthood as might sue   440
For priest's-exemption where the layman sinned,—
Got his arm frocked which, bare, the law would bruise.
Hence, at this moment, what's his last resource,
His extreme stay and utmost stretch of hope
But that,—convicted of such crime as law   445
Wipes not away save with a worldling's blood,—
Guido, the three-parts consecrate, may 'scape?
Nay, the portentous[9] brothers of the man
Are veritably priests, protected each
May do his murder in the Church's pale,   450
Abate Paul, Canon Girolamo!
This is the man proves irreligiousest
Of all mankind, religion's parasite!
This may forsooth plead dinned ear, jaded sense,
The vice o' the watcher who bides near the bell,   455
Sleeps sound because the clock is vigilant,
And cares not whether it be shade or shine,
Doling out day and night to all men else!
Why was the choice o' the man to niche himself
Perversely 'neath the tower where Time's own tongue   460
Thus undertakes to sermonize the world?
Why, but because the solemn is safe too,
The belfry proves a fortress of a sort,
Has other uses than to teach the hour:
Turns sunscreen, paravent and ombrifuge[1]   465
To whoso seeks a shelter in its pale,
—Ay, and attractive to unwary folk
Who gaze at storied portal, statued spire,
And go home with full head but empty purse,
Nor dare suspect the sacristan[2] the thief!   470
Shall Judas,—hard upon the donor's heel,

8. Romans 15:1 and 1 Thessalonians 4:1.
9. Sinister.
1. Refuge from wind and rain; i.e., from the world's buffeting.
2. Custodian of church's sacred vessels.

To filch the fragments of the basket,—plead
He was too near the preacher's mouth, nor sat
Attent with fifties in a company?
No,—closer to promulgated decree,   475
Clearer the censure of default. Proceed!

I find him bound, then, to begin life well;
Fortified by propitious circumstance,
Great birth, good breeding, with the Church for guide,
How lives he? Cased thus in a coat of proof,   480
Mailed like a man-at-arms, though all the while
A puny starveling,—does the breast pant big,
The limb swell to the limit, emptiness
Strive to become solidity indeed?
Rather, he shrinks up like the ambiguous fish,   485
Detaches flesh from shell and outside show,
And steals by moonlight (I have seen the thing)
In and out, now to prey and now to skulk.
Armour he boasts when a wave breaks on beach,
Or bird stoops for the prize: with peril nigh,—   490
The man of rank, the much-befriended-man,
The man almost affiliate to the Church,·
Such is to deal with, let the world beware!
Does the world recognize, pass prudently?
Do tides abate and sea-fowl hunt i' the deep?   495
Already is the slug from out its mew,
Ignobly faring with all loose and free,
Sand-fly and slush-worm at their garbage-feast,
A naked blotch no better than they all:
Guido has dropped nobility, slipped the Church,   500
Plays trickster if not cut-purse, body and soul
Prostrate among the filthy feeders—faugh!
And when Law takes him by surprise at last,
Catches the foul thing on its carrion-prey,
Behold, he points to shell left high and dry,   505
Pleads "But the case out yonder is myself!"
Nay, it is thou, Law prongs amid thy peers,
Congenial vermin; that was none of thee,
Thine outside,—give it to the soldier-crab![3]

For I find this black mark impinge the man,   510
That he believes in just the vile of life.
Low instinct, base pretension, are these truth?
Then, that aforesaid armour, probity
He figures in,[4] is falsehood scale on scale;
Honour and faith,—a lie and a disguise,   515
Probably for all livers in this world,
Certainly for himself! All say good words
To who will hear, all do thereby bad deeds

3. Hermit crab, which lives in empty shells.
4. Cf. Ephesians 6:13–14: "the whole armour of God . . . the breastplate of righteousness."

To who must undergo; so thrive mankind!
See this habitual creed exemplified   520
Most in the last deliberate act; as last,
So, very sum and substance of the soul
Of him that planned and leaves one perfect piece,
The sin brought under jurisdiction now,
Even the marriage of the man: this act   525
I sever from his life as sample, show
For Guido's self, intend to test him by,
As, from a cup filled fairly at the fount,
By the components we decide enough
Or to let flow as late, or staunch the source.   530

He purposes this marriage, I remark,
On no one motive that should prompt thereto—
Farthest, by consequence, from ends alleged
Appropriate to the action; so they were:
The best, he knew and feigned, the worst he took.   535
Not one permissible impulse moves the man,
From the mere liking of the eye and ear,
To the true longing of the heart that loves,
No trace of these: but all to instigate,
Is what sinks man past level of the brute   540
Whose appetite if brutish is a truth.
All is the lust for money: to get gold,—
Why, lie, rob, if it must be, murder! Make
Body and soul wring gold out, lured within
The clutch of hate by love, the trap's pretence!   545
What good else get from bodies and from souls?
This got, there were some life to lead thereby,
—What, where or how, appreciate those who tell
How the toad lives: it lives,—enough for me!
To get this good,—with but a groan or so,   550
Then, silence of the victims,—were the feat.
He foresaw, made a picture in his mind,—
Of father and mother stunned and echoless
To the blow, as they lie staring at fate's jaws
Their folly danced into, till the woe fell;   555
Edged in a month by strenuous cruelty
From even the poor nook whence they watched the wolf
Feast on their heart, the lamb-like child his prey;
Plundered to the last remnant of their wealth,
(What daily pittance pleased the plunderer dole)   560
Hunted forth to go hide head, starve and die,
And leave the pale awe-stricken wife, past hope
Of help i' the world now, mute and motionless,
His slave, his chattel, to first use, then destroy.
All this, he bent mind how to bring about,   565
Put plain in act and life, as painted plain,
So have success, reach crown of earthly good,
In this particular enterprise of man,

By marriage—undertaken in God's face
With all these lies so opposite God's truth,   570
For end so other than man's end.

                                        Thus schemes
Guido, and thus would carry out his scheme:
But when an obstacle first blocks the path,
When he finds none may boast monopoly
Of lies and tricks i' the tricking lying world,—   575
That sorry timid natures, even this sort
O' the Comparini, want nor trick nor lie
Proper to the kind,—that as the gor-crow⁵ treats
The bramble-finch so treats the finch the moth,
And the great Guido is minutely matched   580
By this same couple,—whether true or false
The revelation of Pompilia's birth,
Which in a moment brings his scheme to nought,—
Then, he is piqued, advances yet a stage,
Leaves the low region to the finch and fly,   585
Soars to the zenith whence the fiercer fowl
May dare the inimitable swoop. I see.
He draws now on the curious⁶ crime, the fine
Felicity and flower of wickedness;
Determines, by the utmost exercise   590
Of violence, made safe and sure by craft,
To satiate malice, pluck one last arch-pang
From the parents, else would triumph out of reach,
By punishing their child, within reach yet,
Who, by thought, word or deed, could nowise wrong   595
I' the matter that now moves him. So plans he,
Always subordinating (note the point!)
Revenge, the manlier sin, to interest
The meaner,—would pluck pang forth, but unclench
No gripe in the act, let fall no money-piece.   600
Hence a plan for so plaguing, body and soul,
His wife, so putting, day by day, hour by hour,
The untried torture to the untouched place,
As must precipitate an end foreseen,
Goad her into some plain revolt, most like   605
Plunge upon patent suicidal shame,
Death to herself, damnation by rebound
To those whose hearts he, holding hers, holds still:
Such plan as, in its bad completeness, shall
Ruin the three together and alike,   610
Yet leave himself in luck and liberty,
No claim renounced, no right a forfeiture,
His person unendangered, his good fame
Without a flaw, his pristine worth intact,—
While they, with all their claims and rights that cling,   615

5. Carrion crow.
6. Singular, cunning.

Shall forthwith crumble off him every side,
Scorched into dust, a plaything for the winds.
As when, in our Campagna,[7] there is fired
The nest-like work that overruns a hut;
And, as the thatch burns here, there, everywhere, 620
Even to the ivy and wild vine, that bound
And blessed the home where men were happy once,
There rises gradual, black amid the blaze,
Some grim and unscathed nucleus of the nest,—
Some old malicious tower, some obscene tomb 625
They thought a temple in their ignorance,
And clung about and thought to lean upon—
There laughs it o'er their ravage,—where are they?
So did his cruelty burn life about,
And lay the ruin bare in dreadfulness, 630
Try the persistency of torment so
Upon the wife, that, at extremity,
Some crisis brought about by fire and flame,
The patient frenzy-stung must needs break loose,
Fly anyhow, find refuge anywhere, 635
Even in the arms of who should front her first,
No monster but a man—while nature shrieked
"Or thus escape, or die!" The spasm arrived,
Not the escape by way of sin,—O God,
Who shall pluck sheep Thou holdest, from Thy hand?[8] 640
Therefore she lay resigned to die,—so far
The simple cruelty was foiled. Why then,
Craft to the rescue, let craft supplement
Cruelty and show hell a masterpiece!
Hence this consummate lie, this love-intrigue, 645
Unmanly simulation of a sin,
With place and time and circumstance to suit—
These letters false beyond all forgery—
Not just handwriting and mere authorship,
But false to body and soul they figure forth— 650
As though the man had cut out shape and shape
From fancies of that other Aretine,[9]
To paste below—incorporate the filth
With cherub faces on a missal-page!

Whereby the man so far attains his end 655
That strange temptation is permitted,—see!
Pompilia wife, and Caponsacchi priest,
Are brought together as nor priest nor wife
Should stand, and there is passion in the place,
Power in the air for evil as for good, 660
Promptings from heaven and hell, as if the stars
Fought in their courses for a fate to be.

7. The ruin-dotted plain surrounding Rome.
8. John 10:28.
9. Pietro Aretino (1492–1556), author of satires and obscene sonnets.

Thus stand the wife and priest, a spectacle,
I doubt not, to unseen assemblage there.
No lamp will mark that window for a shrine,   665
No tablet signalize the terrace, teach
New generations which succeed the old
The pavement of the street is holy ground;
No bard describe in verse how Christ prevailed
And Satan fell like lightning![1] Why repine?   670
What does the world, told truth, but lie the more?

A second time the plot is foiled; nor, now,
By corresponding sin for countercheck,
No wile and trick that baffle trick and wile,—
The play o' the parents! Here the blot is blanched   675
By God's gift of a purity of soul
That will not take pollution, ermine-like
Armed from dishonour by its own soft snow.
Such was this gift of God who showed for once
How He would have the world go white: it seems   680
As a new attribute were born of each
Champion of truth, the priest and wife I praise,—
As a new safeguard sprang up in defence
Of their new noble nature: so a thorn
Comes to the aid of and completes the rose—   685
Courage to-wit, no woman's gift nor priest's,
I' the crisis; might leaps vindicating right.
See how the strong aggressor, bad and bold,
With every vantage, preconcerts[2] surprise,
Leaps of a sudden at his victim's throat   690
In a byeway,—how fares he when face to face
With Caponsacchi? Who fights, who fears now?
There quails Count Guido armed to the chattering teeth,
Cowers at the steadfast eye and quiet word
O' the Canon of the Pieve![3] There skulks crime   695
Behind law called in to back cowardice:
While out of the poor trampled worm the wife,
Springs up a serpent![4]

                   But anon of these.
Him I judge now,—of him proceed to note,
Failing the first, a second chance befriends   700
Guido, gives pause ere punishment arrive.
The law he called, comes, hears, adjudicates,
Nor does amiss i' the main,—secludes the wife
From the husband, respites the oppressed one, grants
Probation to the oppressor, could he know   705
The mercy of a minute's fiery purge!
The furnace-coals alike of public scorn,

1. Luke 10:18.
2. Plans.
3. Caponsacchi's church at Arezzo.
4. Pompilia drew a sword and brandished it when Guido caught the pair at Castelnuovo.

Private remorse, heaped glowing on his head,
What if,—the force and guile, the ore's alloy,
Eliminate, his baser soul refined—   710
The lost be saved even yet, so as by fire?[5]
Let him, rebuked, go softly all his days[6]
And, when no graver musings claim their due,
Meditate on a man's immense mistake
Who, fashioned to use feet and walk, deigns crawl—   715
Takes the unmanly means—ay, though to ends
Man scarce should make for, would but reach thro' wrong,—
May sin, but nowise needs shame manhood so:
Since fowlers hawk, shoot, nay and snare the game,
And yet eschew vile practice, nor find sport   720
In torch-light treachery or the luring owl.

But how hunts Guido? Why, the fraudful trap—
Late spurned to ruin by the indignant feet
Of fellows in the chase who loved fair play—
Here he picks up its fragments to the least,   725
Lades him and hies to the old lurking-place
Where haply he may patch again, refit
The mischief, file its blunted teeth anew,
Make sure, next time, first snap shall break the bone.
Craft, greed and violence complot revenge: 730
Craft, for its quota, schemes to bring about
And seize occasion and be safe withal:
Greed craves its act may work both far and near,
Crush the tree, branch and trunk and root, beside.
Whichever twig or leaf arrests a streak   735
Of possible sunshine else would coin itself,
And drop down one more gold piece in the path:
Violence stipulates "Advantage proved
And safety sure, be pain the overplus!
Murder with jagged knife![7] Cut but tear too!   740
Foiled oft, starved long, glut malice for amends!"
And what, craft's scheme? scheme sorrowful and strange
As though the elements, whom mercy checked,
Had mustered hate for one eruption more,
One final deluge to surprise the Ark   745
Cradled and sleeping on its mountain-top:
Their outbreak-signal—what but the dove's coo,
Back with the olive in her bill for news
Sorrow was over?[8] 'T is an infant's birth,
Guido's first born, his son and heir, that gives   750
The occasion:[9] other men cut free their souls

5. 1 Corinthians 3:15.
6. Isaiah 38:15.
7. Guido's dagger had "little hook-teeth on the edge" (II.147).
8. Genesis 8:6–11.
9. The pope accepts the argument of Pompilia's lawyer Bottini that Guido had a strong motive
   to withhold revenge until Pompilia was delivered of a baby: if Guido had remained childless,
   the estate (to which Pietro had only the "usufruct," or temporary use) would revert to the
   kinsmen of the Comparini.

From care in such a case, fly up in thanks
To God, reach, recognize His love for once:
Guido cries "Soul, at last the mire is thine!
Lie there in likeness of a money-bag   755
My babe's birth so pins down past moving now,
That I dare cut adrift the lives I late
Scrupled to touch lest thou escape with them!
These parents and their child my wife,—touch one,
Lose all! Their rights determined on[1] a head   760
I could but hate, not harm, since from each hair
Dangled a hope for me: now—chance and change!
No right was in their child but passes plain
To that child's child and through such child to me.
I am a father now,—come what, come will,   765
I represent my child; he comes between—
Cuts sudden off the sunshine of this life
From those three: why, the gold is in his curls!
Not with old Pietro's, Violante's head,
Not his grey horror, her more hideous black—   770
Go these, devoted to the knife!"
                          'T is done:
Wherefore should mind misgive, heart hesitate?
He calls to counsel, fashions certain four
Colourless natures counted clean till now,
—Rustic simplicity, uncorrupted youth,   775
Ignorant virtue! Here's the gold o' the prime[2]
When Saturn ruled, shall shock our leaden day—
The clown abash the courtier! Mark it, bards!
The courtier tries his hand on clownship here,
Speaks a word, names a crime, appoints a price,—   780
Just breathes on what, suffused with all himself,
Is red-hot henceforth past distinction now
I' the common glow of hell. And thus they break
And blaze on us at Rome, Christ's birthnight-eve![3]
Oh angels that sang erst "On the earth, peace!   785
To man, good will!"—such peace finds earth to-day!
After the seventeen hundred years, so man
Wills good to man, so Guido makes complete
His murder! what is it I said?—cuts loose
Three lives that hitherto he suffered cling,   790
Simply because each served to nail secure,
By a corner of the money-bag, his soul,—
Therefore, lives sacred till the babe's first breath
O'erweights them in the balance,—off they fly!

---

1. Settled upon.
2. The mythical Golden Age, when Saturn (Cronus) ruled the world. This age of rural simplic-
   ity and happiness was followed by the Silver, Bronze, Heroic, and Iron Ages, i.e., by almost
   unrelieved decline.
3. Gaetano was born December 18; Guido arrived in Rome December 24, but waited until Jan-
   uary 2 to commit the crime. (See V.1561–1652 for Guido's version.)

So is the murder managed, sin conceived   795
To the full: and why not crowned with triumph too?
Why must the sin, conceived thus, bring forth death?
I note how, within hair's-breadth of escape,
Impunity and the thing supposed success,
Guido is found when the check comes, the change,   800
The monitory touch o' the tether—felt
By few, not marked by many, named by none
At the moment, only recognized aright
I' the fulness of the days, for God's, lest sin
Exceed the service, leap the line: such check—   805
A secret which this life finds hard to keep,
And, often guessed, is never quite revealed—
Needs must trip Guido on a stumbling-block
Too vulgar, too absurdly plain i' the path!
Study this single oversight of care,   810
This hebetude[4] that marred sagacity,
Forgetfulness of all the man best knew,—
How any stranger having need to fly,
Needs but to ask and have the means of flight.
Why, the first urchin tells you, to leave Rome,   815
Get horses, you must show the warrant, just
The banal scrap, clerk's scribble, a fair word buys,
Or foul one, if a ducat[5] sweeten word,—
And straight authority will back demand,
Give you the pick o' the post-house![6]—how should he,   820
Then, resident at Rome for thirty years,
Guido, instruct a stranger! And himself
Forgets just this poor paper scrap, wherewith
Armed, every door he knocks at opens wide
To save him: horsed and manned, with such advance   825
O' the hunt behind, why, 't were the easy task
Of hours told on the fingers of one hand,
To reach the Tuscan frontier, laugh at-home,
Light-hearted with his fellows of the place,—
Prepared by that strange shameful judgment, that   830
Satire upon a sentence just pronounced
By the Rota[7] and confirmed by the Granduke,—
Ready in a circle to receive their peer,
Appreciate his good story how, when Rome,
The Pope-King and the populace of priests   835
Made common cause with their confederate
The other priestling who seduced his wife,
He, all unaided, wiped out the affront

---

4. Stupidity.
5. Gold coin.
6. I.e., the fastest horses, which Guido could not use for escape to Tuscany because of his fail-
   ure to obtain a pass through the city gates.
7. The Criminal Rota of Florence, the court of last appeal, which had confirmed the sentence
   of the Commissary of Arezzo in the case of Pompilia's flight. Pompilia's "trial" at Arezzo, re-
   sulting in her being sentenced to life imprisonment, was nugatory since she was then under
   Roman jurisdiction.

With decent bloodshed and could face his friends,
Frolic it in the world's eye. Ay, such tale   840
Missed such applause, and by such oversight!
So, tired and footsore, those blood-flustered five
Went reeling on the road through dark and cold,
The few permissible miles, to sink at length,
Wallow and sleep in the first wayside straw,   845
As the other herd quenched, i' the wash o' the wave,
—Each swine, the devil inside him: so slept they,
And so were caught and caged—all through one trip,
One touch of fool in Guido the astute!
He curses the omission, I surmise,   850
More than the murder. Why, thou fool and blind,
It is the mercy-stroke that stops thy fate,
Hamstrings and holds thee to thy hurt,—but how?
On the edge o' the precipice! One minute more,
Thou hadst gone farther and fared worse, my son,   855
Fathoms down on the flint and fire beneath!
Thy comrades each and all were of one mind,
Thy murder done, to straightway murder thee
In turn, because of promised pay withheld.
So, to the last, greed found itself at odds   860
With craft in thee, and, proving conqueror,
Had sent thee, the same night that crowned thy hope,
Thither where, this same day, I see thee not,
Nor, through God's mercy, need, to-morrow, see.

Such I find Guido, midmost blotch of black   865
Discernible in this group of clustered crimes
Huddling together in the cave they call
Their palace outraged day thus penetrates.
Around him ranged, now close and now remote,
Prominent or obscure to meet the needs   870
O' the mage and master, I detect each shape
Subsidiary i' the scene nor loathed the less,
All alike coloured, all descried akin
By one and the same pitchy furnace stirred
At the centre: see, they lick the master's hand,—   875
This fox-faced horrible priest, this brother-brute
The Abate,—why, mere wolfishness looks well,
Guido stands honest in the red o' the flame,
Beside this yellow that would pass for white,
Twice Guido, all craft but no violence,   880
This copier of the mien and gait and garb
Of Peter and Paul, that he may go disguised,
Rob halt and lame, sick folk i' the temple-porch![8]
Armed with religion, fortified by law,
A man of peace, who trims the midnight lamp   885
And turns the classic page—and all for craft,

8. Acts 3:1–11.

All to work harm with, yet incur no scratch!
While Guido brings the struggle to a close,
Paul steps back the due distance, clear o' the trap
He builds and baits.[9] Guido I catch and judge;   890
Paul is past reach in this world and my time:
That is a case reserved. Pass to the next,
The boy of the brood, the young Girolamo[1]
Priest, Canon, and what more? nor wolf nor fox,
But hybrid, neither craft nor violence   895
Wholly, part violence part craft: such cross
Tempts speculation—will both blend one day,
And prove hell's better product? Or subside
And let the simple quality emerge,
Go on with Satan's service the old way?   900
Meanwhile, what promise,—what performance too!
For there's a new distinctive touch, I see,
Lust—lacking in the two—hell's own blue tint
That gives a character and marks the man
More than a match for yellow and red. Once more,   905
A case reserved: why should I doubt? Then comes
The gaunt grey nightmare in the furthest smoke,
The hag that gave these three abortions birth,
Unmotherly mother and unwomanly
Woman, that near turns motherhood to shame,   910
Womanliness to loathing: no one word,
No gesture to curb cruelty a whit
More than the she-pard thwarts her playsome whelps
Trying their milk-teeth on the soft o' the throat
O' the first fawn, flung, with those beseeching eyes,   915
Flat in the covert! How should she but couch,
Lick the dry lips, unsheath the blunted claw,
Catch 'twixt her placid eyewinks at what chance
Old bloody half-forgotten dream may flit,
Born when herself was novice to the taste,   920
The while she lets youth take its pleasure. Last,
These God-abandoned wretched lumps of life,
These four companions,—country-folk this time,
Not tainted by the unwholesome civic breath,
Much less the curse o' the Court! Mere striplings too,   925
Fit to do human nature justice still!
Surely when impudence in Guido's shape
Shall propose crime and proffer money's-worth
To these stout tall rough bright-eyed black-haired boys,
The blood shall bound in answer to each cheek   930
Before the indignant outcry break from lip!
Are these i' the mood to murder, hardly loosed
From healthy autumn-finish of ploughed glebe,[2]
Grapes in the barrel, work at happy end,

9. See note to V.1400.
1. Pompilia had charged Girolamo with making "dishonorable advances" to her.
2. Field.

And winter near with rest and Christmas play?   935
How greet they Guido with his final task—
(As if he but proposed "One vineyard more
To dig, ere frost come, then relax indeed!")
"Anywhere, anyhow and anywhy,
Murder me some three people, old and young,   940
Ye never heard the names of,—and be paid
So much!" And the whole four accede at once.
Demur? Do cattle bidden march or halt?
Is it some lingering habit, old fond faith
I' the lord o' the land, instructs them,—birthright badge   945
Of feudal tenure claims its slaves again?
Not so at all, thou noble human heart!
All is done purely for the pay,—which, earned,
And not forthcoming at the instant, makes
Religion heresy, and the lord o' the land   950
Fit subject for a murder in his turn.
The patron with cut throat and rifled purse,
Deposited i' the roadside-ditch, his due,
Nought hinders each good fellow trudging home,
The heavier by a piece or two in poke,   955
And so with new zest to the common life,
Mattock and spade, plough-tail and waggon-shaft,
Till some such other piece of luck betide,
Who knows? Since this is a mere start in life,
And none of them exceeds the twentieth year.   960
Nay, more i' the background yet? Unnoticed forms
Claim to be classed, subordinately vile?
Complacent lookers-on that laugh,—perchance
Shake head as their friend's horse-play grows too rough
With the mere child he manages amiss—   965
But would not interfere and make bad worse
For twice the fractious tears and prayers: thou know'st
Civility better, Marzi-Medici,[3]
Governor for thy kinsman the Granduke!
Fit representative of law, man's lamp   970
I' the magistrate's grasp full-flare, no rushlight-end
Sputtering 'twixt thumb and finger of the priest!
Whose answer to the couple's cry for help
Is a threat,—whose remedy of Pompilia's wrong,
A shrug o' the shoulder, and facetious word   975
Or wink, traditional with Tuscan wits,
To Guido in the doorway. Laud to law!
The wife is pushed back to the husband, he
Who knows how these home-squabblings persecute
People who have the public good to mind,   980
And work best with a silence in the court!

---

3. Governor of Arezzo, no kin to the Medici, as Innocent supposes.

Ah, but I save my word at least for thee,
Archbishop,[4] who art under, i' the Church,
As I am under God,—thou, chosen by both
To do the shepherd's office, feed the sheep—   985
How of this lamb that panted at thy foot
While the wolf pressed on her within crook's[5] reach?
Wast thou the hireling that did turn and flee?[6]
With thee at least anon the little word!

Such denizens o' the cave now cluster round   990
And heat the furnace sevenfold: time indeed
A bolt from heaven should cleave roof and clear place,
Transfix and show the world, suspiring[7] flame,
The main offender, scar and brand the rest
Hurrying, each miscreant to his hole: then flood   995
And purify the scene with outside day—
Which yet, in the absolutest drench of dark,
Ne'er wants a witness, some stray beauty-beam
To the despair of hell.

            First of the first,
Such I pronounce Pompilia, then as now   1000
Perfect in whiteness: stoop thou down, my child,
Give one good moment to the poor old Pope
Heart-sick at having all his world to blame—
Let me look at thee in the flesh as erst,
Let me enjoy the old clean linen garb,   1005
Not the new splendid vesture! Armed and crowned,
Would Michael, yonder,[8] be, nor crowned nor armed,
The less pre-eminent angel? Everywhere
I see in the world the intellect of man,
That sword, the energy his subtle spear,   1010
The knowledge which defends him like a shield—
Everywhere; but they make not up, I think,
The marvel of a soul like thine, earth's flower
She holds up to the softened gaze of God!
It was not given Pompilia to know much,   1015
Speak much, to write a book, to move mankind,
Be memorized by who records my time.
Yet if in purity and patience, if
In faith held fast despite the plucking fiend,
Safe like the signet stone with the new name   1020
That saints are known by,—if in right returned
For wrong, most pardon for worst injury,
If there be any virtue, any praise,[9]—
Then will this woman-child have proved—who knows?—

---

4. Bishop of Arezzo.
5. The crook or crozier symbolizes a bishop's office as spiritual shepherd.
6. John 10:12–13.
7. Breathing.
8. St. Michael's statue atop the Mausoleum of Hadrian.
9. Philippians 4:8.

Just the one prize vouchsafed unworthy me,   1025
Seven years a gardener of the untoward ground,
I till,—this earth, my sweat and blood manure
All the long day that barrenly grows dusk:
At least one blossom makes me proud at eve
Born 'mid the briers of my enclosure! Still   1030
(Oh, here as elsewhere, nothingness of man!)
Those be the plants, imbedded yonder South
To mellow in the morning, those made fat
By the master's eye, that yield such timid leaf,
Uncertain bud, as product of his pains!   1035
While—see how this mere chance-sown cleft-nursed seed
That sprang up by the wayside 'neath the foot
Of the enemy, this breaks all into blaze,
Spreads itself, one wide glory of desire
To incorporate the whole great sun it loves   1040
From the inch-height whence it looks and longs! My flower,
My rose, I gather for the breast of God,
This I praise most in thee, where all I praise,
That having been obedient to the end
According to the light allotted, law   1045
Prescribed thy life, still tried, still standing test,—
Dutiful to the foolish parents first,
Submissive next to the bad husband,—nay,
Tolerant of those meaner miserable
That did his hests, eked out the dole of pain,—   1050
Thou, patient thus, couldst rise from law to law,
The old to the new, promoted at one cry
O' the trump of God to the new service, not
To longer bear, but henceforth fight, be found
Sublime in new impatience with the foe!   1055
Endure man and obey God: plant firm foot
On neck of man, tread man into the hell
Meet for him, and obey God all the more!
Oh child that didst despise thy life so much
When it seemed only thine to keep or lose,   1060
How the fine ear felt fall the first low word
"Value life, and preserve life for My sake!"
Thou didst . . . how shall I say? . . . receive so long
The standing ordinance of God on earth,
What wonder if the novel claim had clashed   1065
With old requirement, seemed to supersede
Too much the customary law? But, brave,
Thou at first prompting of what I call God,
And fools call Nature, didst hear, comprehend,
Accept the obligation laid on thee,   1070
Mother elect, to save the unborn child,
As brute and bird do, reptile and the fly,
Ay and, I nothing doubt, even tree, shrub, plant
And flower o' the field, all in a common pact
To worthily defend the trust of trusts,   1075

Life from the Ever Living:—didst resist—
Anticipate the office that is mine—
And with his own sword stay the upraised arm,
The endeavour of the wicked, and defend
Him[1] who,—again in my default,—was there   1080
For visible providence: one less true than thou
To touch, i' the past, less practised in the right,
Approved less far in all docility
To all instruction,—how had such an one
Made scruple "Is this motion a decree?"   1085
It was authentic to the experienced ear
O' the good and faithful servant. Go past me
And get thy praise,—and be not far to seek
Presently when I follow if I may!

And surely not so very much apart   1090
Need I place thee, my warrior-priest,—in whom
What if I gain the other rose, the gold,[2]
We grave to imitate God's miracle,
Greet monarchs with, good rose in its degree?
Irregular noble 'scapegrace—son the same!   1095
Faulty—and peradventure ours the fault
Who still misteach, mislead, throw hook and line,
Thinking to land leviathan[3] forsooth,
Tame the scaled neck, play with him as a bird,
And bind him for our maidens! Better bear   1100
The King of Pride go wantoning awhile,
Unplagued by cord in nose and thorn in jaw,
Through deep to deep, followed by all that shine,
Churning the blackness hoary: He who made
The comely terror, He shall make the sword   1105
To match that piece of netherstone his heart,
Ay, nor miss praise thereby; who else shut fire
I' the stone, to leap from mouth at sword's first stroke,
In lamps of love and faith, the chivalry
That dares the right and disregards alike   1110
The yea and nay o' the world? Self-sacrifice,—
What if an idol took it? Ask the Church
Why she was wont to turn each Venus here,—
Poor Rome perversely lingered round, despite
Instruction, for the sake of purblind love,—   1115
Into Madonna's shape,[4] and waste no whit
Of aught so rare on earth as gratitude!
All this sweet savour was not ours but thine,

---

1. Caponsacchi.
2. The pope's gift of a golden rose, annually given a king or notable person to whom the Holy
See was obliged.
3. Sea monster. Lines 1096–1107 loosely paraphrase several verses from Job 41. Cf.
V.1497–98.
4. "After a period of merciless destruction, some classical monuments were spared by the
Popes; temples were converted into churches, and statues of pagan gods were occasionally
made to do duty as Christian images" (Alexander Pope, note to The Dunciad, III.101).

Nard[5] of the rock, a natural wealth we name
Incense, and treasure up as food for saints,   1120
When flung to us—whose function was to give
Not find the costly perfume. Do I smile?
Nay, Caponsacchi, much I find amiss,
Blameworthy, punishable in this freak
Of thine, this youth prolonged, though age was ripe,   1125
This masquerade in sober day, with change
Of motley too,—now hypocrite's disguise,
Now fool's costume:[6] which lie was least like truth,
Which the ungainlier, more discordant garb
With that symmetric soul inside my son,   1130
The churchman's or the worldling's,—let him judge,
Our adversary who enjoys the task!
I rather chronicle the healthy rage,—
When the first moan broke from the martyr-maid
At that uncaging of the beasts,—made bare   1135
My athlete on the instant, gave such good
Great undisguised leap over post and pale
Right into the mid-cirque, free fighting-place.
There may have been rash stripping—every rag
Went to the winds,—infringement manifold   1140
Of law's prescribed pudicity,[7] I fear,
In this impulsive and prompt self-display!
Ever such tax comes of the foolish youth;
Men mulct[8] the wiser manhood, and suspect
No veritable star swims out of cloud.   1145
Bear thou such imputation, undergo
The penalty I nowise dare relax,—
Conventional chastisement and rebuke.
But for the outcome, the brave starry birth
Conciliating earth with all that cloud,   1150
Thank heaven as I do! Ay, such championship
Of God at first blush, such prompt cheery thud
Of glove on ground that answers ringingly
The challenge of the false knight,—watch we long,
And wait we vainly for its gallant like   1155
From those appointed to the service, sworn
His body-guard with pay and privilege—
White-cinct,[9] because in white walks sanctity,
Red-socked, how else proclaim fine scorn of flesh,
Unchariness of blood[1] when blood faith begs!   1160
Where are the men-at-arms with cross on coat?
Aloof, bewraying their attire: whilst thou
In mask and motley, pledged to dance not fight,[2]

5. Or spikenard, aromatic herb.
6. I.e., the garb of a layman, worn to help Pompilia escape from Arezzo.
7. Modesty prescribed by law.
8. Punish, as by a fine.
9. With a belt of white. The pope describes a cardinal's garb.
1. I.e., willingness to shed blood.
2. Caponsacchi's superior had urged him to pay court to the ladies of Arezzo.

Sprang'st forth the hero! In thought, word and deed,
How throughout all thy warfare thou wast pure,   1165
I find it easy to believe: and if
At any fateful moment of the strange
Adventure, the strong passion of that strait,
Fear and surprise, may have revealed too much,—
As when a thundrous midnight, with black air   1170
That burns, rain-drops that blister, breaks a spell,
Draws out the excessive virtue of some sheathed
Shut unsuspected flower that hoards and hides
Immensity of sweetness,—so, perchance,
Might the surprise and fear release too much   1175
The perfect beauty of the body and soul
Thou savedst in thy passion for God's sake,
He who is Pity. Was the trial sore?
Temptation sharp? Thank God a second time!
Why comes temptation but for man to meet   1180
And master and make crouch beneath his foot,
And so be pedestaled in triumph? Pray
"Lead us into no such temptations, Lord!"
Yea, but, O Thou whose servants are the bold,
Lead such temptations by the head and hair,   1185
Reluctant dragons,[3] up to who dares fight,
That so he may do battle and have praise!
Do I not see the praise?—that while thy mates
Bound to deserve i' the matter, prove at need
Unprofitable through the very pains   1190
We gave to train them well and start them fair,—
Are found too stiff, with standing ranked and ranged,
For onset in good earnest, too obtuse
Of ear, through iteration of command,
For catching quick the sense of the real cry,—   1195
Thou, whose sword-hand was used to strike the lute,
Whose sentry-station graced some wanton's gate,
Thou didst push forward and show mettle, shame
The laggards, and retrieve the day. Well done!
Be glad thou hast let light into the world   1200
Through that irregular breach o' the boundary,—see
The same upon thy path and march assured,
Learning anew the use of soldiership,
Self-abnegation, freedom from all fear,
Loyalty to the life's end! Ruminate,   1205
Deserve the initiatory spasm,[4]—once more
Work, be unhappy but bear life, my son!

And troop you, somewhere 'twixt the best and worst,
Where crowd the indifferent product, all too poor
Makeshift, starved samples of humanity!   1210

---

3. Echo of Horace's phrase *reluctantes dracones* in *Odes*, IV.iv.11. For Horace, however, *reluctantes* meant "struggling, resisting," not "battle-shy."
4. I.e., "rebirth" into a life of selfless service.

Father and mother, huddle there and hide!
A gracious eye may find you! Foul and fair,
Sadly mixed natures: self-indulgent,—yet
Self-sacrificing too: how the love soars,
How the craft, avarice, vanity and spite   1215
Sink again! So they keep the middle course,
Slide into silly crime at unaware,
Slip back upon the stupid virtue, stay
Nowhere enough for being classed, I hope
And fear. Accept the swift and rueful death,   1220
Taught, somewhat sternlier than is wont, what waits
The ambiguous creature,—how the one black tuft
Steadies the aim of the arrow just as well
As the wide faultless white on the bird's breast!
Nay, you were punished in the very part   1225
That looked most pure of speck,—'t was honest love
Betrayed you,—did love seem most worthy pains,
Challenge such purging, since ordained survive
When all the rest of you was done with? Go!
Never again elude the choice of tints!   1230
White shall not neutralize the black, nor good
Compensate bad in man, absolve him so:
Life's business being just the terrible choice.

So do I see, pronounce on all and some
Grouped for my judgment now,—profess no doubt   1235
While I pronounce: dark, difficult enough
The human sphere, yet eyes grow sharp by use,
I find the truth, dispart the shine from shade,
As a mere man may, with no special touch
O' the lynx-gift[5] in each ordinary orb: 1240
Nay, if the popular notion class me right,
One of well-nigh decayed intelligence,—
What of that? Through hard labour and good will,
And habitude that gives a blind man sight
At the practised finger-ends of him, I do   1245
Discern, and dare decree in consequence,
Whatever prove the peril of mistake.
Whence, then, this quite new quick cold thrill,—cloudlike,
This keen dread creeping from a quarter scarce
Suspected in the skies I nightly scan?   1250
What slacks the tense nerve, saps the wound-up spring
Of the act that should and shall be, sends the mount
And mass o' the whole man's-strength,—conglobed so late—
Shudderingly into dust, a moment's work?
While I stand firm, go fearless, in this world,   1255
For this life recognize and arbitrate,
Touch and let stay, or else remove a thing,
Judge "This is right, this object out of place,"

5. Piercing eyesight possessed by the fabulous lynx, half dog and half panther.

Candle in hand that helps me and to spare—
What if a voice deride me, "Perk and pry!⁶   1260
Brighten each nook with thine intelligence!
Play the good householder, ply man and maid
With tasks prolonged into the midnight, test
Their work and nowise stint of the due wage
Each worthy worker: but with gyves⁷ and whip   1265
Pay thou misprision of a single point
Plain to thy happy self who lift'st the light,
Lament'st the darkling,—bold to all beneath!
What if thyself adventure, now the place
Is purged so well? Leave pavement and mount roof,   1270
Look round thee for the light of the upper sky,
The fire which lit thy fire which finds default
In Guido Franceschini to his cost!
What if, above in the domain of light,
Thou miss the accustomed signs, remark eclipse?   1275
Shalt thou still gaze on ground nor lift a lid,—
Steady in thy superb prerogative,
Thy inch of inkling,—nor once face the doubt
I' the sphere above thee, darkness to be felt?"

Yet my poor spark had for its source, the sun;⁸   1280
Thither I sent the great looks which compel
Light from its fount: all that I do and am
Comes from the truth, or seen or else surmised,
Remembered or divined, as mere man may:
I know just so, nor otherwise. As I know,   1285
I speak,—what should I know, then, and how speak
Were there a wild mistake of eye or brain
As to recorded governance above?
If my own breath, only, blew coal alight
I styled celestial and the morning-star?   1290
I, who in this world act resolvedly,
Dispose of men, their bodies and their souls,
As they acknowledge or gainsay the light
I show them,—shall I too lack courage?—leave
I, too, the post of me, like those I blame?   1295
Refuse, with kindred inconsistency,
To grapple danger whereby souls grow strong?
I am near the end; but still not at the end;
All to the very end is trial in life:
At this stage is the trial of my soul   1300
Danger to face, or danger to refuse?
Shall I dare try the doubt now, or not dare?

O Thou,—as represented here to me
In such conception as my soul allows,—

6. Pry: inquire into (OED); perk: carry oneself smartly.
7. Shackles.
8. Here Browning gives his own interpretation of Christianity, emphasizing the Incarnation.

Under Thy measureless, my atom width!—   1305
Man's mind, what is it but a convex glass
Wherein are gathered all the scattered points
Picked out of the immensity of sky,
To re-unite there, be our heaven for earth,
Our known unknown, our God revealed to man?   1310
Existent somewhere, somehow, as a whole;
Here, as a whole proportioned to our sense,—
There, (which is nowhere, speech must babble thus!)
In the absolute immensity, the whole
Appreciable solely by Thyself,—   1315
Here, by the little mind of man, reduced
To littleness that suits his faculty,
In the degree appreciable too;
Between Thee and ourselves—nay even, again,
Below us, to the extreme of the minute,   1320
Appreciable by how many and what diverse
Modes of the life Thou madest be! (why live
Except for love,—how love unless they know?)
Each of them, only filling to the edge,
Insect or angel, his just length and breadth,   1325
Due facet of reflection,—full, no less,
Angel or insect, as Thou framedst things.
I it is who have been appointed here
To represent Thee, in my turn, on earth,
Just as, if new philosophy[9] know aught,   1330
This one earth, out of all the multitude
Of peopled worlds, as stars are now supposed,—
Was chosen, and no sun-star of the swarm,
For stage and scene of Thy transcendent act[1]
Beside which even the creation fades   1335
Into a puny exercise of power.
Choice of the world, choice of the thing I am,
Both emanate alike from Thy dread play
Of operation outside this our sphere
Where things are classed and counted small or great,—   1340
Incomprehensibly the choice is Thine!
I therefore bow my head and take Thy place.
There is, beside the works, a tale of Thee
In the world's mouth, which I find credible:
I love it with my heart: unsatisfied,   1345
I try it with my reason, nor discept
From any point I probe and pronounce sound.
Mind is not matter nor from matter, but
Above,—leave matter then, proceed with mind!
Man's be the mind recognized at the height,—   1350
Leave the inferior minds and look at man!
Is he the strong, intelligent and good
Up to his own conceivable height? Nowise.

9. I.e., science, especially the new astronomy of Copernicus.
1. The Incarnation, ultimate proof of God's love.

Enough o' the low,—soar the conceivable height,
Find cause to match the effect in evidence,   1355
The work i' the world, not man's but God's; leave man!
Conjecture of the worker by the work:
Is there strength there?—enough: intelligence?
Ample: but goodness in a like degree?
Not to the human eye in the present state,   1360
An isoscele[2] deficient in the base.
What lacks, then, of perfection fit for God
But just the instance which this tale supplies
Of love without a limit? So is strength,
So is intelligence; let love be so,   1365
Unlimited in its self-sacrifice,
Then is the tale true and God shows complete.
Beyond the tale, I reach into the dark,
Feel what I cannot see, and still faith stands:
I can believe this dread machinery   1370
Of sin and sorrow, would confound me else,
Devised,—all pain, at most expenditure
Of pain by Who devised pain,—to evolve,
By new machinery in counterpart,
The moral qualities of man—how else?—   1375
To make him love in turn and be beloved,
Creative and self-sacrificing too,
And thus eventually God-like, (ay,
"I have said ye are Gods,"[3]—shall it be said for nought?)
Enable man to wring, from out all pain,   1380
All pleasure for a common heritage
To all eternity: this may be surmised,
The other is revealed,—whether a fact,
Absolute, abstract, independent truth,
Historic, not reduced to suit man's mind,—   1385
Or only truth reverberate, changed, made pass
A spectrum into mind, the narrow eye,—
The same and not the same, else unconceived—
Though quite conceivable to the next grade
Above it in intelligence,—as truth   1390
Easy to man were blindness to the beast
By parity of procedure,—the same truth
In a new form, but changed in either case:
What matter so intelligence be filled?
To a child, the sea is angry, for it roars: 1395
Frost bites, else why the tooth-like fret[4] on face?
Man makes acoustics deal with the sea's wrath,
Explains the choppy cheek by chymic[5] law,—
To man and child remains the same effect
On drum of ear and root of nose, change cause   1400

2. Here, triangle with two equal sides, representing strength and intelligence; the base is good-
ness.
3. Psalms 82:6; John 10:34.
4. Chapped spot.
5. Chymic: related to the digestive process. Choppy: chapped.

Never so thoroughly: so my heart be struck,
What care I,—by God's gloved hand or the bare?[6]
Nor do I much perplex me with aught hard,
Dubious in the transmitting of the tale,—
No, nor with certain riddles set to solve.   1405
This life is training and a passage; pass,—
Still, we march over some flat obstacle
We made give way before us; solid truth
In front of it, what motion for the world?[7]
The moral sense grows but by exercise.   1410
'T is even as man grew probatively
Initiated in Godship, set to make
A fairer moral world than this he finds,
Guess now what shall be known hereafter. Deal
Thus with the present problem: as we see,   1415
A faultless creature is destroyed, and sin
Has had its way i' the world where God should rule.
Ay, but for this irrelevant circumstance
Of inquisition after blood, we see
Pompilia lost and Guido saved: how long?   1420
For his whole life: how much is that whole life?
We are not babes, but know the minute's worth,
And feel that life is large and the world small,
So, wait till life have passed from out the world.
Neither does this astonish at the end,   1425
That whereas I can so receive and trust,
Other men, made with hearts and souls the same,
Reject and disbelieve,—subordinate
The future to the present,—sin, nor fear.
This I refer still to the foremost fact,   1430
Life is probation and the earth no goal
But starting-point of man: compel him strive,
Which means, in man, as good as reach the goal,—
Why institute that race, his life, at all?
But this does overwhelm me with surprise,   1435
Touch me to terror,—not that faith, the pearl,
Should be let lie by fishers wanting food,—
Nor, seen and handled by a certain few
Critical and contemptuous, straight consigned
To shore and shingle for the pebble it proves,—   1440
But that, when haply found and known and named
By the residue made rich for evermore,
These,—that these favoured ones, should in a trice
Turn, and with double zest go dredge for whelks,[8]
Mud-worms that make the savoury soup! Enough   1445
O' the disbelievers, see the faithful few!
How do the Christians here deport them, keep

6. I.e., by myths or by facts.
7. I.e., absolute ("solid") truth, if presented to man at once, would be an obstacle to his moral
   growth, since there would be no need for him to search onward.
8. Marine snails.

Their robes of white unspotted by the world?
What is this Aretine Archbishop, this
Man under me as I am under God,   1450
This champion of the faith, I armed and decked,
Pushed forward, put upon a pinnacle,
To show the enemy his victor,—see!
What's the best fighting when the couple close?
Pompilia cries, "Protect me from the wolf!"   1455
He—"No, thy Guido is rough, heady, strong,
Dangerous to disquiet: let him bide!
He needs some bone to mumble, help amuse
The darkness of his den with: so, the fawn
Which limps up bleeding to my foot and lies,   1460
—Come to me, daughter!—thus I throw him back!"
Have we misjudged here, over-armed our knight,
Given gold and silk where plain hard steel serves best,
Enfeebled whom we sought to fortify,
Made an archbishop and undone a saint?   1465
Well, then, descend these heights, this pride of life,
Sit in the ashes with a barefoot monk
Who long ago stamped out the worldly sparks,
By fasting, watching, stone cell and wire scourge,
—No such indulgence as unknits the strength—   1470
These breed the tight nerve and tough cuticle,[9]
And the world's praise or blame runs rillet-wise
Off the broad back and brawny breast, we know!
He meets the first cold sprinkle of the world,
And shudders to the marrow. "Save this child?   1475
Oh, my superiors, oh, the Archbishop's self!
Who was it dared lay hand upon the ark
His betters saw fall nor put finger forth?[1]
Great ones could help yet help not: why should small?
I break my promise: let her break her heart!"   1480
These are the Christians not the worldlings, not
The sceptics, who thus battle for the faith!
If foolish virgins disobey and sleep,[2]
What wonder? But, this time, the wise that watch,
Sell lamps and buy lutes, exchange oil for wine,   1485
The mystic Spouse betrays the Bridegroom here.[3]
To our last resource, then! Since all flesh is weak,
Bind weaknesses together, we get strength:
The individual weighed, found wanting, try
Some institution, honest artifice   1490
Whereby the units grow compact and firm!
Each props the other, and so stand is made

---

9. Skin.
1. It was the hapless Uzzah who sacrilegiously touched the ark of God when it tottered. God killed him for his error (2 Samuel 6:6–7).
2. Their error, rather, was failure to get oil for their lamps before sleeping. They were thus unready for the arrival of the Bridegroom (Matthew 25:1–13).
3. The church (Spouse) betrays Christ (Bridegroom). The symbolism is that of St. Paul (Ephesians 5:23–24).

By our embodied cowards that grow brave.
The Monastery called of Convertites,[4]
Meant to help women because these helped Christ,—   1495
A thing existent only while it acts,
Does as designed, else a nonentity,—
For what is an idea unrealized?—
Pompilia is consigned to these for help.
They do help: they are prompt to testify   1500
To her pure life and saintly dying days.
She dies, and lo, who seemed so poor, proves rich.
What does the body[5] that lives through helpfulness
To women for Christ's sake? The kiss turns bite,
The dove's note changes to the crow's cry: judge!   1505
"Seeing that this our Convent claims of right
What goods belong to those we succour, be
The same proved women of dishonest life,—
And seeing that this Trial made appear
Pompilia was in such predicament,—   1510
The Convent hereupon pretends to said
Succession of Pompilia, issues writ,
And takes possession by the Fisc's[6] advice."
Such is their attestation to the cause
Of Christ, who had one saint at least, they hoped: 1515
But, is a title-deed to filch, a corpse
To slander, and an infant-heir to cheat?
Christ must give up his gains then! They unsay
All the fine speeches,—who was saint is whore.
Why, scripture yields no parallel for this!   1520
The soldiers only threw dice for Christ's coat;[7]
We want another legend of the Twelve
Disputing if it was Christ's coat at all,
Claiming as prize the woof of price[8]—for why?
The Master was a thief, purloined the same,   1525
Or paid for it out of the common bag!
Can it be this is end and outcome, all
I take with me to show as stewardship's fruit,
The best yield of the latest time, this year
The seventeen-hundredth since God died for man?   1530
Is such effect proportionate to cause?
And still the terror keeps on the increase
When I perceive . . . how can I blink the fact?
That the fault, the obduracy to good,
Lies not with the impracticable stuff   1535

4. The convent of Santa Maria Maddalena della Convertite, founded to save immoral women.
   After Pompilia's death, the Convertites, who had a legal right to claim the property of loose
   women, attempted to defame her in order to acquire her estate. But the court, declaring her
   innocent of adultery, rejected the convent's suit.
5. The convent.
6. The Fisc is Bottini, prosecutor at Guido's trial. His associate Gambi made application to the
   court on behalf of the Convertites. Bottini's cynical "defense" of Pompilia (Book IX)
   amounts to an attack upon her innocence.
7. Matthew 27:35.
8. Costly fabric.

Whence man is made, his very nature's fault,
As if it were of ice the moon may gild
Not melt, or stone 't was meant the sun should warm
Not make bear flowers,—nor ice nor stone to blame:
But it can melt, that ice, can bloom, that stone,   1540
Impassible to rule of day and night!
This terrifies me, thus compelled perceive,
Whatever love and faith we looked should spring
At advent of the authoritative star,
Which yet lie sluggish, curdled at the source,—   1545
These have leapt forth profusely in old time,
These still respond with promptitude to-day,
At challenge of—what unacknowledged powers
O' the air, what uncommissioned meteors, warmth
By law, and light by rule should supersede?   1550
For see this priest, this Caponsacchi, stung
At the first summons,—"Help for honour's sake,
Play the man, pity the oppressed!"—no pause,
How does he lay about him in the midst,
Strike any foe, right wrong at any risk,   1555
All blindness, bravery and obedience!—blind?
Ay, as a man would be inside the sun,
Delirious with the plenitude of light
Should interfuse him to the finger-ends—
Let him rush straight, and how shall he go wrong?   1560
Where are the Christians in their panoply?
The loins we girt about with truth, the breasts
Righteousness plated round, the shield of faith,
The helmet of salvation, and that sword
O' the Spirit, even the word of God,[9]—where these?   1565
Slunk into corners! Oh, I hear at once
Hubbub of protestation! "What, we monks,
We friars, of such an order, such a rule,
Have not we fought, bled, left our martyr-mark
At every point along the boundary-line   1570
'Twixt true and false, religion and the world,
Where this or the other dogma of our Church
Called for defence?" And I, despite myself,
How can I but speak loud what truth speaks low,
"Or better than the best, or nothing serves!   1575
What boots deed, I can cap and cover straight
With such another doughtiness to match,
Done at an instinct of the natural man?"
Immolate body, sacrifice soul too,—
Do not these publicans the same?[1] Outstrip!   1580
Or else stop race you boast runs neck and neck,
You with the wings, they with the feet,—for shame!
O, I remark your diligence and zeal![2]

9. Ephesians 6:14–17.
1. Matthew 5:46–47. In the Gospels, the publican or tax-collector is a symbol of corruption.
2. That the zeal of the church is often misplaced is illustrated by the following true narrative of

Five years long, now, rounds faith into my ears,
"Help thou, or Christendom is done to death!"   1585
Five years since, in the Province of To-kien,[3]
Which is in China as some people know,
Maigrot, my Vicar Apostolic there,
Having a great qualm, issues a decree.
Alack, the converts use as God's name, not   1590
Tien-chu but plain *Tien* or else mere *Shang-ti*,
As Jesuits please to fancy politic,
While, say Dominicans, it calls down fire,—
For *Tien* means heaven, and *Shang-ti*, supreme prince,
While *Tien-chu* means the lord of heaven: all cry,   1595
"There is no business urgent for despatch
As that thou send a legate, specially
Cardinal Tournon, straight to Pekin, there
To settle and compose the difference!"
So have I seen a potentate all fume   1600
For some infringement of his realm's just right,
Some menace to a mud-built straw-thatched farm
O' the frontier; while inside the mainland lie,
Quite undisputed-for in solitude,
Whole cities plague may waste or famine sap: 1605
What if the sun crumble, the sands encroach,
While he looks on sublimely at his ease?
How does their ruin touch the empire's bound?

And is this little all that was to be?
Where is the gloriously-decisive change,   1610
Metamorphosis the immeasurable
Of human clay to divine gold, we looked
Should, in some poor sort, justify its price?
Had an adept of the mere Rosy Cross[4]
Spent his life to consummate the Great Work,   1615
Would not we start to see the stuff it touched
Yield not a grain more than the vulgar got
By the old smelting-process years ago?
If this were sad to see in just the sage
Who should profess so much, perform no more,   1620
What is it when suspected in that Power
Who undertook to make and made the world,
Devised and did effect man, body and soul,
Ordained salvation for them both, and yet . . .
Well, is the thing we see, salvation?

                              I   1625

---

a semantic controversy in China. The resolution of the quarrel was left to Innocent's suc-
cessor, Clement XI.
3. Actually Fukien.
4. A Rosicrucian, adherent of seventeenth- and eighteenth-century religious movement de-
   voted to esoteric wisdom. Their "Great Work" was the alchemical transmutation of base
   metal into gold.

Put no such dreadful question to myself,
Within whose circle of experience burns
The central truth, Power, Wisdom, Goodness,—God:
I must outlive a thing ere know it dead:
When I outlive the faith there is a sun,   1630
When I lie, ashes to the very soul,—
Someone, not I, must wail above the heap,
"He⁵ died in dark whence never morn arose."
While I see day succeed the deepest night—
How can I speak but as I know?—my speech   1635
Must be, throughout the darkness, "It will end:
The light that did burn, will burn!" Clouds obscure—
But for which obscuration all were bright?
Too hastily concluded! Sun-suffused,
A cloud may soothe the eye made blind by blaze,—   1640
Better the very clarity of heaven:
The soft streaks are the beautiful and dear.
What but the weakness in a faith supplies
The incentive to humanity, no strength
Absolute, irresistible, comports?⁶   1645
How can man love but what he yearns to help?
And that which men think weakness within strength,
But angels know for strength and stronger yet—
What were it else but the first things made new,
But repetition of the miracle,   1650
The divine instance of self-sacrifice
That never ends and aye begins for man?
So, never I miss footing in the maze,
No,—I have light nor fear the dark at all.

But are mankind not real, who pace outside   1655
My petty circle, world that's measured me?
And when they stumble even as I stand,
Have I a right to stop ear when they cry,
As they were phantoms who took clouds for crags,
Tripped and fell, where man's march might safely move?   1660
Beside, the cry is other than a ghost's,
When out of the old time there pleads some bard,
Philosopher, or both,⁷ and—whispers not,
But words it boldly. "The inward work and worth
Of any mind, what other mind may judge   1665
Save God who only knows the thing He made,
The veritable service He exacts?
It is the outward product men appraise.
Behold, an engine hoists a tower aloft:
'I looked that it should move the mountain too!'   1670

---

5. Jesus (see Matthew 27:45).
6. I.e., an incentive which absolute strength does not bring with it (Cook).
7. Euripides, Greek dramatist (ca. 484–407 B.C.E.) who is the imagined speaker in lines 1664–1784.

Or else 'Had just a turret toppled down,
Success enough!'—may say the Machinist[8]
Who knows what less or more result might be:
But we, who see that done we cannot do,
'A feat beyond man's force,' we men must say.   1675
Regard me and that shake I gave the world!
I was born, not so long before Christ's birth
As Christ's birth haply did precede thy day,—
But many a watch before the star of dawn:
Therefore I lived,—it is thy creed affirms,   1680
Pope Innocent, who art to answer me!—
Under conditions, nowise to escape,
Whereby salvation was impossible.
Each impulse to achieve the good and fair,
Each aspiration to the pure and true,   1685
Being without a warrant or an aim,
Was just as sterile a felicity
As if the insect, born to spend his life
Soaring his circles, stopped them to describe
(Painfully motionless in the mid-air)   1690
Some word of weighty counsel for man's sake,
Some 'Know thyself' or 'Take the golden mean!'
—Forwent his happy dance and the glad ray,
Died half an hour the sooner and was dust.
I, born to perish like the brutes, or worse,   1695
Why not live brutishly, obey brutes' law?
But I, of body as of soul complete,
A gymnast at the games, philosopher
I' the schools, who painted, and made music,—all
Glories that met upon the tragic stage   1700
When the Third Poet's tread surprised the Two,[9]—
Whose lot fell in a land where life was great
And sense went free and beauty lay profuse,
I, untouched by one adverse circumstance,
Adopted virtue as my rule of life,   1705
Waived all reward, loved but for loving's sake,
And, what my heart taught me, I taught the world,
And have been teaching now two thousand years.
Witness my work,—plays that should please, forsooth!
'They might please, they may displease, they shall teach,   1710
For truth's sake,' so I said, and did, and do.
Five hundred years ere Paul spoke, Felix heard,[1]—
How much of temperance and righteousness,
Judgment to come, did I find reason for,
Corroborate with my strong style[2] that spared   1715
No sin, nor swerved the more from branding brow
Because the sinner was called Zeus and God?

8. Zeus.
9. When Euripides began to rival the older Aeschylus and Sophocles.
1. Acts 24:22–27.
2. Stylus or pen.

How nearly did I guess at that Paul knew?
How closely come, in what I represent
As duty, to his doctrine yet a blank?   1720
And as that limner not untruly limns
Who draws an object round or square, which square
Or round seems to the unassisted eye,
Though Galileo's tube display the same
Oval or oblong,—so, who controverts   1725
I rendered rightly what proves wrongly wrought
Beside Paul's picture? Mine was true for me.
I saw that there are, first and above all,
The hidden forces, blind necessities,
Named Nature, but the thing's self unconceived: 1730
Then follow,—how dependent upon these,
We know not, how imposed above ourselves,
We well know,—what I name the gods, a power
Various or one: for great and strong and good
Is there, and little, weak and bad there too,   1735
Wisdom and folly: say, these make no God,—
What is it else that rules outside man's self?
A fact then,—always, to the naked eye,—
And so, the one revealment possible
Of what were unimagined else by man.   1740
Therefore, what gods do, man may criticize,
Applaud, condemn,—how should he fear the truth?—
But likewise have in awe because of power,
Venerate for the main munificence,
And give the doubtful deed its due excuse   1745
From the acknowledged creature of a day
To the Eternal and Divine. Thus, bold
Yet self-mistrusting, should man bear himself,
Most assured on what now concerns him most—
The law of his own life, the path he prints,—   1750
Which law is virtue and not vice, I say,—
And least inquisitive where search least skills,
I' the nature we best give the clouds to keep.
What could I paint beyond a scheme like this
Out of the fragmentary truths where light   1755
Lay fitful in a tenebrific[3] time?
You have the sunrise now, joins truth to truth,
Shoots life and substance into death and void;
Themselves compose the whole we made before:
The forces and necessity grow God,—   1760
The beings so contrarious that seemed gods,
Prove just His operation manifold
And multiform, translated, as must be,
Into intelligible shape so far
As suits our sense and sets us free to feel.   1765
What if I let a child think, childhood-long,

3. Dark.

That lightning, I would have him spare his eye,
Is a real arrow shot at naked orb?
The man knows more, but shuts his lids the same:
Lightning's cause comprehends nor man nor child.   1770
Why then, my scheme, your better knowledge broke,
Presently re-adjusts itself, the small
Proportioned largelier, parts and whole named new:
So much, no more two thousand years have done!
Pope, dost thou dare pretend to punish me,   1775
For not descrying sunshine at midnight,
Me who crept all-fours, found my way so far—
While thou rewardest teachers of the truth,
Who miss the plain way in the blaze of noon,—
Though just a word from that strong style of mine,   1780
Grasped honestly in hand as guiding-staff,
Had pricked them a sure path across the bog,
That mire of cowardice and slush of lies
Wherein I find them wallow in wide day!"

How should I answer this Euripides?   1785
Paul,—'t is a legend,—answered Seneca,[4]
But that was in the day-spring; noon is now:
We have got too familiar with the light.
Shall I wish back once more that thrill of dawn?
When the whole truth-touched man burned up, one fire?   1790
—Assured the trial, fiery, fierce, but fleet,
Would, from his little heap of ashes, lend
Wings to that conflagration of the world
Which Christ awaits ere He makes all things new:
So should the frail become the perfect, rapt   1795
From glory of pain to glory of joy; and so,
Even in the end,—the act renouncing earth,
Lands, houses, husbands, wives and children here,—
Being that other act which finds all, lost,
Regained, in this time even, a hundredfold,   1800
And, in the next time, feels the finite love
Blent and embalmed with the eternal life.
So does the sun ghastlily seem to sink
In those north parts, lean all but out of life,
Desist a dread mere breathing-stop, then slow   1805
Re-assert day, begin the endless rise.
Was this too easy for our after-stage?
Was such a lighting-up of faith, in life,
Only allowed initiate, set man's step
In the true way by help of the great glow?   1810
A way wherein it is ordained he walk,
Bearing to see the light from heaven still more
And more encroached on by the light of earth,

4. Roman philosopher and tragedian (42? B.C.E.–C.E. 65). In the fourth century certain letters
were discovered, purporting to have passed between Seneca and St. Paul. They are univer-
sally regarded as a forgery.

Tentatives earth puts forth to rival heaven,
Earthly incitements that mankind serve God   1815
For man's sole sake, not God's and therefore man's.
Till at last, who distinguishes the sun
From a mere Druid[5] fire on a far mount?
More praise to him who with his subtle prism
Shall decompose both beams and name the true.   1820
In such sense, who is last proves first indeed;[6]
For how could saints and martyrs fail see truth
Streak the night's blackness? Who is faithful now?
Who untwists heaven's white from the yellow flare
O' the world's gross torch, without night's foil that helped 1825
Produce the Christian act so possible
When in the way stood Nero's cross and stake,[7]—
So hard now when the world smiles "Right and wise!
Faith points the politic, the thrifty way,
Will make who plods it in the end returns   1830
Beyond mere fool's-sport and improvidence.
We fools dance thro' the cornfield of this life,
Pluck ears to left and right and swallow raw,
—Nay, tread, at pleasure, a sheaf underfoot,
To get the better at some poppy-flower,—   1835
Well aware we shall have so much less wheat
In the eventual harvest: you meantime
Waste not a spike,—the richlier will you reap!
What then? There will be always garnered meal
Sufficient for our comfortable loaf,   1840
While you enjoy the undiminished sack!"
Is it not this ignoble confidence,
Cowardly hardihood, that dulls and damps,
Makes the old heroism impossible?

Unless . . . what whispers me of times to come?   1845
What if it be the mission of that age[8]
My death will usher into life, to shake
This torpor of assurance from our creed,
Re-introduce the doubt discarded, bring
That formidable danger back, we drove   1850
Long ago to the distance and the dark?
No wild beast now prowls round the infant camp:
We have built wall and sleep in city safe:
But if some earthquake try the towers that laugh
To think they once saw lions rule outside,   1855
And man stand out again, pale, resolute,
Prepare to die,—which means, alive at last?
As we broke up that old faith of the world,
Have we, next age, to break up this the new—

---

5. Druidism was the faith of the Celts of ancient Gaul and Britain.
6. Matthew 19:30.
7. For immolation of Christian martyrs.
8. The eighteenth century, often called the "Age of Reason."

Faith, in the thing, grown faith in the report—   1860
Whence need to bravely disbelieve report
Through increased faith i' the thing reports belie?
Must we deny,—do they, these Molinists,[9]
At peril of their body and their soul,—
Recognized truths, obedient to some truth   1865
Unrecognized yet, but perceptible?—
Correct the portrait by the living face,
Man's God, by God's God in the mind of man?—
Then, for the few that rise to the new height,
The many that must sink to the old depth,   1870
The multitude found fall away! A few,
E'en ere new law speak clear, may keep the old,
Preserve the Christian level, call good good
And evil evil, (even though razed and blank
The old titles,) helped by custom, habitude,   1875
And all else they mistake for finer sense
O' the fact that reason warrants,—as before,
They hope perhaps, fear not impossibly.
At least some one Pompilia left the world
Will say "I know the right place by foot's feel,   1880
I took it and tread firm there; wherefore change?"
But what a multitude will surely fall
Quite through the crumbling truth, late subjacent,
Sink to the next discoverable base,
Rest upon human nature, settle there   1885
On what is firm, the lust and pride of life!
A mass of men, whose very souls even now
Seem to need re-creating,—so they slink
Worm-like into the mud, light now lays bare,—
Whose future we dispose of with shut eyes   1890
And whisper—"They are grafted, barren twigs,
Into the living stock of Christ: may bear
One day, till when they lie death-like, not dead,"—
Those who with all the aid of Christ succumb,
How, without Christ, shall they, unaided, sink?   1895
Whither but to this gulf before my eyes?
Do not we end, the century and I?
The impatient antimasque treads close on kibe[1]
O' the very masque's self it will mock,—on me,
Last lingering personage, the impatient mime   1900
Pushes already,—will I block the way?
Will my slow trail of garments ne'er leave space
For pantaloon, sock, plume and castanet?
Here comes the first experimentalist
In the new order of things,—he plays a priest;   1905
Does he take inspiration from the Church,
Directly make her rule his law of life?

9. See note to V.203.
1. Kibe: Sore heel. Antimasque: interlude, often mocking, between the acts of a masque, an elaborately staged drama.

Not he: his own mere impulse guides the man—
Happily sometimes, since ourselves allow
He has danced, in gaiety of heart, i' the main   1910
The right step through the maze we bade him foot.
But if his heart had prompted him break loose
And mar the measure? Why, we must submit,
And thank the chance that brought him safe so far.
Will he repeat the prodigy? Perhaps.   1915
Can he teach others how to quit themselves,
Show why this step was right while that were wrong?
How should he? "Ask your hearts as I asked mine,
And get discreetly through the morrice[2] too;
If your hearts misdirect you,—quit the stage,   1920
And make amends,—be there amends to make!"
Such is, for the Augustin[3] that was once,
This Canon Caponsacchi we see now.
"But my heart answers to another tune,"
Puts in the Abate, second in the suite,[4]   1925
"I have my taste too, and tread no such step!
You choose the glorious life, and may, for me!
I like the lowest of life's appetites,—
So you judge,—but the very truth of joy
To my own apprehension which decides.   1930
Call me knave and you get yourself called fool!
I live for greed, ambition, lust, revenge;
Attain these ends by force, guile: hypocrite,
To-day, perchance to-morrow recognized
The rational man, the type of common sense."   1935
There's Loyola[5] adapted to our time!
Under such guidance Guido plays his part,
He also influencing in the due turn
These last clods where I track intelligence
By any glimmer, these four at his beck   1940
Ready to murder any, and, at their own,
As ready to murder him,—such make the world!
And, first effect of the new cause of things,
There they lie also duly,—the old pair
Of the weak head and not so wicked heart,   1945
With the one Christian mother, wife and girl,
—Which three gifts seem to make an angel up,—
The world's first foot o' the dance is on their heads!
Still, I stand here, not off the stage though close
On the exit: and my last act, as my first,   1950
I owe the scene, and Him who armed me thus
With Paul's sword[6] as with Peter's key. I smite

2. Or morris, English folk dance performed by costumed men.
3. St. Augustine (354–430), Bishop of Hippo, who here symbolizes the church as institution (cf. lines 1906–1907).
4. Procession.
5. St. Ignatius Loyola (1491–1556), founder of the Jesuit order.
6. Symbol of Paul's defence of Christianity; not mentioned of Paul in Scripture, but attributed to him in art from the eleventh century.

With my whole strength once more, ere end my part,
Ending, so far as man may, this offence.
And when I raise my arm, who plucks my sleeve?   1955
Who stops me in the righteous function,—foe
Or friend? Oh, still as ever, friends are they
Who, in the interest of outraged truth
Deprecate such rough handling of a lie!
The facts being proved and incontestable,   1960
What is the last word I must listen to?
Perchance—"Spare yet a term this barren stock
We pray thee dig about and dung and dress
Till he repent and bring forth fruit even yet!"[7]
Perchance——"So poor and swift a punishment   1965
Shall throw him out of life with all that sin:
Let mercy rather pile up pain on pain
Till the flesh expiate what the soul pays else!"
Nowise! Remonstrants on each side commence
Instructing, there's a new tribunal now   1970
Higher than God's—the educated man's!
Nice sense of honour in the human breast
Supersedes here the old coarse oracle—
Confirming none the less a point or so
Wherein blind predecessors worked aright   1975
By rule of thumb: as when Christ said,—when, where?
Enough, I find it pleaded in a place,[8]—
"All other wrongs done, patiently I take:
But touch my honour and the case is changed!
I feel the due resentment,—*nemini*   1980
Honorem trado[9] is my quick retort."
Right of Him, just as if pronounced to-day!
Still, should the old authority be mute
Or doubtful or in speaking clash with new,
The younger takes permission to decide.   1985
At last we have the instinct of the world
Ruling its household without tutelage:
And while the two laws, human and divine,
Having busied finger with this tangled case,
In pushes the brisk junior, cuts the knot,   1990
Pronounces for acquittal. How it trips
Silverly o'er the tongue! "Remit the death!
Forgive, . . . well, in the old way, if thou please,
Decency and the relics of routine
Respected,—let the Count go free as air!   1995
Since he may plead a priest's immunity,—
The minor orders help enough for that,
With Farinacci's[1] licence,—who decides

---

7. Parable of the fig tree (Luke 8:8–9).
8. By Guido's attorney, Arcangeli (VIII.658).
9. The pope is wrong, for the (misquoted) words are not Christ's but God's: *Gloriam meam alteri non dabo*, "My glory will I not give to another" (Isaiah 42:8, Vulgate).
1. Authority on canon law.

That the mere implication of such man,
So privileged, in any cause, before   2000
Whatever Court except the Spiritual,
Straight quashes law-procedure,—quash it, then!
Remains a pretty loophole of escape
Moreover, that, beside the patent fact
O' the law's allowance, there's involved the weal   2005
O' the Popedom: a son's privilege at stake,
Thou wilt pretend the Church's interest,
Ignore all finer reasons to forgive!
But herein lies the crowning cogency—
(Let thy friends teach thee while thou tellest beads)   2010
That in this case the spirit of culture speaks,
Civilization is imperative.
To her shall we remand all delicate points
Henceforth, nor take irregular advice
O' thy sly, as heretofore: she used to hint   2015
Remonstrances, when law was out of sorts
Because a saucy tongue was put to rest,
An eye that roved was cured of arrogance:
But why be forced to mumble under breath
What soon shall be acknowledged as plain fact,   2020
Outspoken, say, in thy successor's time?
Methinks we see the golden age return!
Civilization and the Emperor
Succeed to Christianity and Pope.
One Emperor then, as one Pope now: meanwhile,   2025
Anticipate a little! We tell thee 'Take
Guido's life, sapped society shall crash,
Whereof of the main prop was, is, and shall be
—Supremacy of husband over wife!'
Does the man rule i' the house, and may his mate   2030
Because of any plea dispute the same?
Oh, pleas of all sorts shall abound, be sure,
One but allowed validity,—for, harsh
And savage, for, inept and silly-sooth,
For, this and that, will the ingenious sex   2035
Demonstrate the best master e'er graced slave:
And there's but one short way to end the coil,[2]—
Acknowledge right and reason steadily
I' the man and master: then the wife submits
To plain truth broadly stated. Does the time   2040
Advise we shift—a pillar? nay, a stake
Out of its place i' the social tenement?[3]
One touch may send a shudder through the heap
And bring it toppling on our children's heads!
Moreover, if ours breed a qualm in thee,   2045
Give thine own better feeling play for once!
Thou, whose own life winks o'er the socket-edge,

2. Confusion.
3. Structure.

Wouldst thou it went out in such ugly snuff
As dooming sons dead, e'en though justice prompt?
Why, on a certain feast, Barabbas' self   2050
Was set free, not to cloud the general cheer:[4]
Neither shalt thou pollute thy Sabbath close![5]
Mercy is safe and graceful. How one hears
The howl begin, scarce the three little taps
O' the silver mallet[6] silent on thy brow,—   2055
'His last act was to sacrifice a Count
And thereby screen a scandal of the Church!
Guido condemned, the Canon justified
Of course,—delinquents of his cloth go free!'
And so the Luthers chuckle, Calvins scowl,   2060
So thy hand helps Molinos to the chair
Whence he may hold forth till doom's day on just
The *petit-maître*[7] priestlings,—in the choir
Sanctus et Benedictus, with a brush
Of soft guitar-strings that obey the thumb,   2065
Touched by the bedside, for accompaniment!
Does this give umbrage to a husband? Death
To the fool, and to the priest impunity!
But no impunity to any friend
So simply over-loyal as these four   2070
Who made religion of their patron's cause,
Believed in him and did his bidding straight,
Asked not one question but laid down the lives
This Pope took,—all four lives together make
Just his own length of days,—so, dead they lie,   2075
As these were times when loyalty's a drug,
And zeal in a subordinate too cheap
And common to be saved when we spend life!
Come, 't is too much good breath we waste in words:
The pardon, Holy Father! Spare grimace,   2080
Shrugs and reluctance! Are not we the world,
Art not thou Priam?[8] Let soft culture plead
Hecuba-like, '*non tali*' (Virgil serves)
'*Auxilio*' and the rest! Enough, it works!
The Pope relaxes, and the Prince is loth,   2085
The father's bowels yearn, the man's will bends,
Reply is apt. Our tears on tremble, hearts
Big with a benediction, wait the word
Shall circulate thro' the city in a trice,
Set every window flaring, give each man   2090

4. Acceding to the will of the people, Pilate released Barabbas and delivered Christ to be cru-
   cified (Matthew 27:15–26).
5. I.e., your final days.
6. Part of a ceremony performed at the death bed of a pope before formal announcement of his
   passing.
7. Foppish.
8. Aged king of Troy, who dressed for battle as Troy was falling, but was restrained by his wife
   Hecuba saying, "It is not aid like that, nor any armed defence, which is needed now"
   (*Aeneid*, II.521–22).

O' the mob his torch to wave for gratitude.
Pronounce then, for our breath and patience fail!"

I will, Sirs: but a voice other than yours
Quickens my spirit. "*Quis pro Domino?*
Who is upon the Lord's side?" asked the Count.[9]   2095
I, who write—
              "On receipt of this command,
Acquaint Count Guido and his fellows four
They die to-morrow: could it be to-night,
The better, but the work to do, takes time.
Set with all diligence a scaffold up,   2100
Not in the customary place, by Bridge
Saint Angelo, where die the common sort;
But since the man is noble, and his peers
By predilection haunt the People's Square,[1]
There let him be beheaded in the midst,   2105
And his companions hanged on either side:
So shall the quality see, fear and learn.
All which work takes time: till to-morrow, then,
Let there be prayer incessant for the five!"

For the main criminal I have no hope   2110
Except in such a suddenness of fate.
I stood at Naples once, a night so dark
I could have scarce conjectured there was earth
Anywhere, sky or sea or world at all:
But the night's black was burst through by a blaze—   2115
Thunder struck blow on blow, earth groaned and bore,
Through her whole length of mountain visible:
There lay the city thick and plain with spires,
And, like a ghost disshrouded, white the sea.
So may the truth be flashed out by one blow,   2120
And Guido see, one instant, and be saved.
Else I avert my face, nor follow him
Into that sad obscure sequestered state[2]
Where God unmakes but to remake the soul
He else made first in vain; which must not be.[3]   2125
Enough, for I may die this very night
And how should I dare die, this man let live?

Carry this forthwith to the Governor!

---

9. Guido has quoted Moses' words to justify his stepping "beyond the law" to commit the
   vengeful murders. (See note to V.1542.)
1. Piazza del Popolo, where the executions took place on February 22, 1698.
2. Purgatory.
3. For the pope it is unthinkable that any soul would be eternally damned; even Guido can be
   salvaged ultimately by an all-loving God.

The Later Achievement
(After 1870)

FROM *FIFINE AT THE FAIR* (1872)

Prologue

AMPHIBIAN[1]

I

The fancy I had to-day,
    Fancy which turned a fear!
I swam far out in the bay,
    Since waves laughed warm and clear.

II

I lay and looked at the sun,   5
    The noon-sun looked at me:
Between us two, no one
    Live creature, that I could see.

III

Yes! There came floating by
    Me, who lay floating too,   10
Such a strange butterfly![2]
    Creature as dear as new:

IV

Because the membraned wings
    So wonderful, so wide,
So sun-suffused, were things   15
    Like soul and nought beside.

---

1. This lyric serves as prologue to the long casuistical monologue *Fifine at the Fair* (1872), a latter-day Don Juan's defense of infidelity. Here swimming, a new pleasure for the aging poet, provides the vehicle for speculation upon the function of poetry. As in the main poem, the setting is the resort town of Pornic in Brittany.
2. In antiquity the butterfly symbolized the soul. In Christian art the life cycle of the caterpillar, chrysalis, and butterfly stood for life, death, and resurrection. (See lines 33–34, 39–40.)

V

A handbreadth over head!
    All of the sea my own,
It owned the sky instead;
    Both of us were alone.   20

VI

I never shall join its flight,
    For, nought buoys flesh in air.
If it touch the sea—good night!
    Death sure and swift waits there.

VII

Can the insect feel the better   25
    For watching the uncouth play
Of limbs that slip the fetter,
    Pretend as they were not clay?

VIII

Undoubtedly I rejoice
    That the air comports so well   30
With a creature which had the choice
    Of the land once. Who can tell?

IX

What if a certain soul[3]
    Which early slipped its sheath,
And has for its home the whole   35
    Of heaven, thus look beneath,

X

Thus watch one who, in the world,
    Both lives and likes life's way,
Nor wishes the wings unfurled
    That sleep in the worm, they say?   40

XI

But sometimes when the weather
    Is blue, and warm waves tempt
To free oneself of tether,
    And try a life exempt

---

3. The poet's dead wife.

XII

From worldly noise and dust,   45
   In the sphere which overbrims
With passion and thought,—why, just
   Unable to fly, one swims!

XIII

By passion and thought upborne,
   One smiles to oneself—"They fare   50
Scarce better, they need not scorn
   Our sea, who live in the air!"

XIV

Emancipate[4] through passion
   And thought, with sea for sky,
We substitute, in a fashion,   55
   For heaven—poetry:

XV

Which sea, to all intent,
   Gives flesh such noon-disport
As a finer element
   Affords the spirit-sort.   60

XVI

Whatever they are, we seem:
   Imagine the thing they know;
All deeds they do, we dream;
   Can heaven be else but so?

XVII

And meantime, yonder streak   65
   Meets the horizon's verge;
That is the land, to seek
   If we tire or dread the surge:

XVIII

Land the solid and safe—
   To welcome again (confess!)   70
When, high and dry, we chafe
   The body, and don the dress.

4. Emancipated.

XIX

Does she look, pity, wonder
    At one who mimics flight,
Swims—heaven above, sea under,   75
    Yet always earth in sight?

Epilogue

I

Savage I was sitting in my house, late, lone:
    Dreary, weary with the long day's work:[2]
Head of me, heart of me, stupid as a stone:
        Tongue-tied now, now blaspheming like a Turk;
When, in a moment, just a knock, call, cry,   5
    Half a pang and all a rapture, there again were we!—
"What, and is it really you again?" quoth I:
    "I again, what else did you expect?" quoth She.

II

"Never mind, hie away from this old house—
    Every crumbling brick embrowned[3] with sin and shame!   10
Quick, in its corners ere certain shapes arouse!
    Let them—every devil of the night—lay claim,
Make and mend, or rap and rend, for me! Good-bye!
    God be their guard from disturbance at their glee,
Till, crash, comes down the carcass in a heap!" quoth I: 15
    "Nay, but there's a decency required!" quoth She.

III

"Ah, but if you know how time has dragged, days, nights!
    All the neighbour-talk with man and maid—such men!
All the fuss and trouble of street-sounds, window-sights:
    All the worry of flapping door and echoing roof; and then,   20
All the fancies . . . Who were they had leave, dared try
    Darker arts that almost struck despair in me?
If you knew but how I dwelt down here!" quoth I:
    "And was I so better off up there?" quoth She.

---

1. Unmistakably autobiographical, this lyric serves as epilogue to *Fifine at the Fair*. The scene
   may be Browning's house in London.
2. Echoes of the situation and style of Poe's "The Raven" are evident ("Once upon a midnight
   dreary, while I pondered, weak and weary, . . . came a tapping . . .").
3. It is not difficult to detect here a pun on Browning's name.

IV

"Help and get it over! *Re-united to his wife*   25
(How draw up the paper lets the parish-people know?)
Lies M., or N., departed from this life,
  Day the this or that, month and year the so and so.
What i' the way of final flourish? Prose, verse? Try!
  Affliction sore long time he bore, or, what is it to be?   30
Till God did please to grant him ease.[4] Do end!" quoth I:
  "I end with—Love is all and Death is nought!" quoth She.

FROM *ARISTOPHANES' APOLOGY* (1875)

[Thamuris Marching][1]

* * *
                              "Once and only once, trod stage,
Sang and touched lyre in person, in his youth,
Our Sophokles,[2]—youth, beauty, dedicate
To Thamuris who named the tragedy.
The voice of him was weak; face, limbs and lyre,   5
These were worth saving: Thamuris stands yet
Perfect as painting helps in such a case.
At least you know the story, for 'best friend'[3]
Enriched his 'Rhesos' from the Blind Bard's store;[4]
So haste and see the work, and lay to heart   10
What it was struck me when I eyed the piece!
Here stands a poet punished for rash strife
With Powers above his power, who see with sight
Beyond his vision, sing accordingly
A song, which he must needs dare emulate.   15
Poet, remain the man nor ape the Muse!

"But—lend me the psalterion![5] Nay, for once—
Once let my hand fall where the other's lay!
I see it, just as I were Sophokles,
That sunrise and combustion of the east!"   20

And then he sang—are these unlike the words?

---

4. Alluding to an epitaph in Charles Kingsley's *The Water-Babies* (1863): "Instruction sore long
   time I bore, / And cramming was in vain; / Till heaven did please my woes to ease / With wa-
   ter on the brain."
1. This song is excerpted from *Aristophanes' Apology* (lines 5167–5264), an elaborate defense
   of the Greek tragedian Euripides, whom Browning deeply admired. Here Aristophanes sings
   of the legendary Thracian poet Thamyris, who marches exultantly to challenge the Muses to
   a poetic contest at Dorion in Messenia. Angered at his presumption, they are to blind
   Thamyris and deprive him of his gift of song (see *Iliad*, II.594ff., and *Paradise Lost*, III.35).
   Browning enjoyed reading these lines aloud.
2. Sophocles, preeminent Greek tragedian.
3. Euripides. The *Rhesos* (or *Rhesus*) (line 9) is a tragedy doubtfully attributed to Euripides.
4. Homer's *Iliad*, part of which is the basis for the *Rhesus*.
5. Psaltery, stringed instrument resembling the zither.

Thamuris marching,—lyre and song of Thrace—
(Perpend[6] the first, the worst of woes that were
Allotted lyre and song, ye poet-race!)

Thamuris from Oichalia, feasted there   25
By kingly Eurutos of late, now bound
For Dorion at the uprise broad and bare

Of Mount Pangaios[7] (ore with earth enwound
Glittered beneath his footstep)—marching gay
And glad, Thessalia[8] through, came, robed and crowned,   30

From triumph on to triumph, mid a ray
Of early morn,—came, saw and knew the spot
Assigned him for his worst of woes, that day.

Balura[9]—happier while its name was not—
Met him, but nowise menaced; slipt aside,   35
Obsequious river to pursue its lot

Of solacing the valley—say, some wide
Thick busy human cluster, house and home,
Embanked for peace, or thrift that thanks the tide.

Thamuris, marching, laughed "Each flake of foam"   40
(As sparklingly the ripple raced him by)
"Mocks slower clouds adrift in the blue dome!"

For Autumn was the season; red the sky
Held morn's conclusive signet of the sun
To break the mists up, bid them blaze and die.   45

Morn had the mastery as, one by one,
All pomps produced themselves along the tract
From earth's far ending to near heaven begun.

Was there a ravaged tree? it laughed compact
With gold, a leaf-ball crisp, high-brandished now,   50
Tempting to onset frost which late attacked.

Was there a wizened shrub, a starveling bough,
A fleecy thistle filched from by the wind,
A weed, Pan's[1] trampling hoof would disallow?

6. Ponder.
7. Mountain in Thrace containing deposits of gold and silver. (See Aeschylus, *Persae*, 494.)
8. Thessaly, region of eastern Greece between the Pindus mountains and the Aegean.
9. The river Balyra ("cast away"), so named because Thamyris after being blinded threw his lyre into it.
1. Greek god of flocks and shepherds, represented as goatlike. He is supposed to have invented the musical pipe of seven reeds.

Each, with a glory and a rapture twined   55
About it, joined the rush of air and light
And force: the world was of one joyous mind.

Say not the birds flew! they forebore their right—
Swam, revelling onward in the roll of things.
Say not the beasts' mirth bounded! that was flight—   60

How could the creatures leap, no lift of wings?
Such earth's community of purpose, such
The ease of earth's fulfilled imaginings,—

So did the near and far appear to touch
I' the moment's transport,—that an interchange   65
Of function, far with near, seemed scarce too much;

And had the rooted plant aspired to range
With the snake's license, while the insect yearned
To glow fixed as the flower, it were not strange—

No more than if the fluttery tree-top turned   70
To actual music, sang itself aloft;
Or if the wind, impassioned chantress, earned

The right to soar embodied in some soft
Fine form all fit for cloud-companionship,
And, blissful, once touch beauty chased so oft.   75

Thamuris, marching, let no fancy slip
Born of the fiery transport; lyre and song
Were his, to smite with hand and launch from lip—

Peerless recorded, since the list grew long
Of poets (saith Homeros) free to stand   80
Pedestalled mid the Muses' temple-throng,

A statued service, laurelled, lyre in hand,
(Ay, for we see them)—Thamuris of Thrace
Predominating foremost of the band.

Therefore the morn-ray that enriched his face,   85
If it gave lambent chill, took flame again
From flush of pride; he saw, he knew the place.

What wind arrived with all the rhythms from plain,
Hill, dale, and that rough wildwood interspersed?
Compounding these to one consummate strain,   90

It reached him, music; but his own outburst
Of victory concluded the account,
And that grew song which was mere music erst.

"Be my Parnassos,[2] thou Pangaian mount!
And turn thee, river, nameless hitherto!   95
Famed shalt thou vie with famed Pieria's[3] fount!

"Here I await the end of this ado:
Which wins—Earth's poet or the Heavenly Muse."[4] . . .

* * *

FROM *PACCHIAROTTO AND HOW HE WORKED IN DISTEMPER: WITH OTHER POEMS* (1876)

House[1]

I

Shall I sonnet-sing you about myself?
  Do I live in a house you would like to see?[2]
Is it scant of gear, has it store of pelf?[3]
  "Unlock my heart with a sonnet-key?"[4]

II

Invite the world, as my betters[5] have done?   5
  "Take notice: this building remains on view,
Its suites of reception every one,
  Its private apartment and bedroom too;

III

"For a ticket, apply to the Publisher."
  No: thanking the public, I must decline.   10
A peep through my window, if folk prefer;
  But, please you, no foot over threshold of mine!

2. Parnassus, mountain near Delphi, sacred to Apollo and the Muses.
3. District on northern slope of Mt. Olympus sacred to the Muses.
4. The song ends abruptly here. (Aristophanes adds: " 'Tell the rest, / Who may!' ")
1. This is the best-known poem in *Pacchiarotto* (1876), a volume largely devoted to castigating the poet's critics, chief among whom was Alfred Austin (1835–1913), who was to succeed Tennyson as poet laureate. "House" is a rather shrill defense of the author's right to privacy—a right which the reticent Browning went to extremes to protect, especially in the 1870s and 1880s, when he enjoyed lionization in London. During this period there developed two disparate Robert Brownings: the public self—sociable, talkative, and prosperous-looking—erected as a façade to mask the private self, revealed only to a select few. So intrigued was Henry James by this role-playing that he made Browning the model for his Clare Vawdrey, the enigmatic novelist *of The Private Life* (1893): "The poet and the 'member of society' were, in a word, dissociated in him as they can rarely elsewhere have been."
2. Browning's focusing on a house exposed catastrophically to public view may be a pointed reply to D. G. Rossetti's sonnet sequence *The House of Life* (1870).
3. Riches.
4. Loose paraphrase of Wordsworth's "Scorn not the sonnet" (1827), lines 2–3; the same lines are quoted (inaccurately) in lines 38–39. The "key" is of course the sonnet form, which enjoyed a notable revival in the nineteenth century. Browning himself wrote very few sonnets.
5. Browning has in mind the poets extolled as masters of the sonnet in "Scorn not the sonnet": Shakespeare, Petrarch, Tasso, Camoëns, Dante, Spenser, and Milton.

IV

I have mixed with a crowd and heard free talk
    In a foreign land where an earthquake chanced:
And a house stood gaping, nought to baulk   15
    Man's eye wherever he gazed or glanced.

V

The whole of the frontage shaven sheer,
    The inside gaped: exposed to day,
Right and wrong and common and queer,
    Bare, as the palm of your hand, it lay.   20

VI

The owner? Oh, he had been crushed, no doubt!
    "Odd tables and chairs for a man of wealth!
What a parcel of musty old books about!
    He smoked,—no wonder he lost his health!

VII

"I doubt if he bathed before he dressed.   25
    A brasier?—the pagan, he burned perfumes!
You see it is proved, what the neighbours guessed:
    His wife and himself had separate rooms."

VIII

Friends, the goodman of the house at least
    Kept house to himself till an earthquake came: 30
'T is the fall of its frontage permits you feast
    On the inside arrangement you praise or blame.

IX

Outside should suffice for evidence:
    And whoso desires to penetrate
Deeper, must dive by the spirit-sense—   35
    No optics like yours, at any rate!

X

"Hoity toity! A street to explore,
    Your house the exception! '*With this same key
Shakespeare unlocked his heart*,' once more!"[6]
    Did Shakespeare? If so, the less Shakespeare he![7]   40

1874   1876

6. Lines 2–3 of "Scorn not the sonnet"; Browning added the word "same."
7. I.e., insofar as he laid bare his private feelings, Shakespeare was acting uncharacteristically.
In his *Essay on Shelley*, Browning sees Shakespeare as a purely "objective" or dramatic poet;
the sonnets are not mentioned.

Fears and Scruples[1]

I

Here's my case. Of old I used to love him
   This same unseen friend, before I knew:
Dream there was none like him, none above him,—
   Wake to hope and trust my dream was true.

II

Loved I not his letters[2] full of beauty?   5
   Not his actions[3] famous far and wide?
Absent, he would know I vowed him duty;
   Present, he would find me at his side.

III

Pleasant fancy! for I had but letters,
   Only knew of actions by hearsay: 10
He himself was busied with my betters;
   What of that? My turn must come some day.

IV

"Some day" proving—no day! Here's the puzzle.
   Passed and passed my turn is. Why complain?
He's so busied! If I could but muzzle   15
   People's foolish mouths that give me pain!

V

"Letters?" (hear them!) "You a judge of writing?
   Ask the experts![4]—How they shake the head
O'er these characters, your friend's inditing—
   Call them forgery from A to Z!   20

VI

"Actions? Where's your certain proof" (they bother)
   "He, of all you find so great and good,
He, he only, claims this, that, the other
   Action—claimed by men, a multitude?"

---

1. The title alludes to *Macbeth* II.3.135–36: "Fears and scruples shake us: / In the great hand of God I stand. . . ." This parable of religious doubt foreshadows the long poem "La Saisiaz" (1878).
2. The Scriptures.
3. Miracles, now explained in purely human terms.
4. The "higher critics" of the Bible (Strauss, Renan, and others), who were questioning the authenticity of certain portions of Scripture.

VII

I can simply wish I might refute you,   25
    Wish my friend would,—by a word, a wink,—
Bid me stop that foolish mouth,—you brute you!
    He keeps absent,—why, I cannot think.

VIII

Never mind! Though foolishness may flout me,
    One thing's sure enough: 't is neither frost,   30
No, nor fire, shall freeze or burn from out me
    Thanks for truth—though falsehood, gained—though lost.

IX

All my days, I'll go the softlier,⁵ sadlier,
    For that dream's sake! How forget the thrill
Through and through me as I thought "The gladlier   35
    Lives my friend because I love him still!"

X

Ah, but there's a menace someone utters!
    "What and if your friend at home play tricks?
Peep at hide-and-seek behind the shutters?
    Mean your eyes should pierce through solid bricks?   40

XI

"What and if he, frowning, wake you, dreamy?
    Lay on you the blame that bricks—conceal?
Say 'At least I saw who did not see me,
    Does see now, and presently shall feel'?"

XII

"Why, that makes your friend a monster!" say you: 45
    "Had his house no window? At first nod,
Would you not have hailed him?" Hush, I pray you!
    What if this friend happen to be—God?

---

5. Isaiah 38:15: "I shall go softly all my years in the bitterness of my soul."

Numpholeptos[1]

Still you stand, still you listen, still you smile!
Still melts your moonbeam[2] through me, white awhile,
Softening, sweetening, till sweet and soft
Increase so round this heart of mine, that oft
I could believe your moonbeam-smile has past   5
The pallid limit, lies, transformed at last
To sunlight and salvation—warms the soul
It sweetens, softens! Would you pass that goal,
Gain love's birth at the limit's happier verge,
And, where an iridescence lurks, but urge   10
The hesitating pallor on to prime
Of dawn!—true blood-streaked, sun-warmth, action-time,
By heart-pulse ripened to a ruddy glow
Of gold above my clay—I scarce should know
From gold's self, thus suffused! For gold means love.   15
What means the sad slow silver smile above
My clay but pity, pardon?—at the best,
But acquiescence that I take my rest,
Contented to be clay, while in your heaven
The sun reserves love for the Spirit-Seven[3]   20
Companioning God's throne they lamp[4] before,
—Leaves earth a mute waste only wandered o'er
By that pale soft sweet disempassioned moon
Which smiles me slow forgiveness! Such the boon
I beg? Nay, dear, submit to this—just this   25
Supreme endeavour! As my lips now kiss
Your feet, my arms convulse your shrouding robe,
My eyes, acquainted with the dust, dare probe
Your eyes above for—what, if born, would blind
Mine with redundant bliss, as flash may find   30
The inert nerve, sting awake the palsied limb,
Bid with life's ecstasy sense overbrim
And suck back death in the resurging joy—
Love, the love whole and sole without alloy!

Vainly! The promise withers! I employ   35
Lips, arms, eyes, pray the prayer which finds the word,
Make the appeal which must be felt, not heard,

1. The poem has been interpreted autobiographically as Browning's expression of rebellion against the fifteen-year bondage to the memory of his dead wife (*Portrait*, pp. 259–61; De-Vane, pp. 405–06). But Browning said, "I had no particular woman in my mind," and called the poem "an allegory . . . of an impossible ideal object of love" held by a man sadly aware that the "being is imaginary, not real, a nymph and no woman" (DeVane, p. 405). The title, adapted from Plutarch, means "caught or entranced by a nymph." In Greek mythology nymphs were beautiful female personifications of natural objects. Though they evoked passion, they could feel none. "Numpholeptos" resembles Tennyson's early monologue "Tithonus" (1833) in subject, tone, and imagery.
2. Cf. Elizabeth Barrett Browning as "my moon of poets" in "One Word More," line 188.
3. See Revelation 4:5: "seven lamps of fire burning before the throne, which are the seven Spirits of God."
4. Shine.

And none the more is changed your calm regard:
Rather, its sweet and soft grow harsh and hard—
Forbearance, then repulsion, then disdain.   40
Avert the rest! I rise, see!—make, again
Once more, the old departure for some track
Untried yet through a world which brings me back
Ever thus fruitlessly to find your feet,
To fix your eyes, to pray the soft and sweet   45
Which smile there—take from his new pilgrimage
Your outcast, once your inmate, and assuage
With love—not placid pardon now—his thirst
For a mere drop from out the ocean erst
He drank at! Well, the quest shall be renewed.   50
Fear nothing! Though I linger, unembued
With any drop, my lips thus close. I go!
So did I leave you, I have found you so,
And doubtlessly, if fated to return,
So shall my pleading persevere and earn   55
Pardon—not love—in that same smile, I learn,
And lose the meaning of, to learn once more,
Vainly!

      What fairy track do I explore?
What magic hall return to, like the gem
Centuply-angled[5] o'er a diadem?   60
You dwell there, hearted; from your midmost home
Rays forth—through that fantastic world I roam
Ever—from centre to circumference,
Shaft upon coloured shaft: this crimsons thence,
That purples out its precinct through the waste.   65
Surely I had your sanction when I faced,
Fared forth upon that untried yellow ray
Whence I retrack my steps? They end to-day
Where they began—before your feet, beneath
Your eyes, your smile: the blade is shut in sheath,   70
Fire quenched in flint; irradiation, late
Trimphant through the distance, finds its fate,
Merged in your blank pure soul, alike the source
And tomb of that prismatic glow:[6] divorce
Absolute, all-conclusive! Forth I fared,   75
Treading the lambent flamelet: little cared
If now its flickering took the topaz tint,
If now my dull-caked path gave sulphury hint
Of subterranean rage—no stay nor stint
To yellow, since you sanctioned that I bathe,   80
Burnish me, soul and body, swim and swathe
In yellow license. Here I reek suffused
With crocus, saffron, orange, as I used

5. Possessing a hundred facets.
6. Cf. "My Star," where the soul-mate throws off color like a prism.

With scarlet, purple, every dye o' the bow
Born of the storm-cloud. As before, you show   85
Scarce recognition, no approval, some
Mistrust, more wonder at a man become
Monstrous in garb, nay—flesh disguised as well,
Through his adventure. Whatsoe'er befell,
I followed, whereso'er it wound, that vein   90
You authorized should leave your whiteness, stain
Earth's sombre stretch beyond your midmost place
Of vantage,—trode that tinct whereof the trace
On garb and flesh repel you! Yes, I plead
Your own permission—your command, indeed,   95
That who would worthily retain the love
Must share the knowledge shrined those eyes above,
Go boldly on adventure, break through bounds
O' the quintessential whiteness that surrounds
Your feet, obtain experience of each tinge   100
That bickers[7] forth to broaden out, impinge
Plainer his foot its pathway all distinct
From every other. Ah, the wonder, linked
With fear, as exploration manifests
What agency it was first tipped the crests   105
Of unnamed wildflower, soon protruding grew
Portentous mid the sands, as when his hue
Betrays him and the burrowing snake gleams through;
Till, last . . . but why parade more shame and pain?
Are not the proofs upon me? Here again   110
I pass into your presence, I receive
Your smile of pity, pardon, and I leave . . .
No, not this last of times I leave you, mute,
Submitted to my penance, so my foot
May yet again adventure, tread, from source   115
To issue, one more ray of rays which course
Each other, at your bidding, from the sphere
Silver and sweet, their birthplace, down that drear
Dark of the world,—you promise shall return
Your pilgrim jewelled as with drops o' the urn   120
The rainbow paints from, and no smatch[8] at all
Of ghastliness at edge of some cloud-pall
Heaven cowers before, as earth awaits the fall
O' the bolt and flash of doom. Who trusts your word
Tries the adventure: and returns—absurd   125
As frightful—in that sulphur-steeped disguise
Mocking the priestly cloth-of-gold, sole prize
The arch-heretic was wont to bear away
Until he reached the burning. No, I say:
No fresh adventure! No more seeking love   130
At end of toil, and finding, calm above

7. Flickers.
8. Slight trace.

My passion, the old statuesque regard,
The sad petrific[9] smile!

              O you—less hard
And hateful than mistaken and obtuse
Unreason of a she-intelligence!   135
You very woman with the pert pretence
To match the male achievement! Like enough!
Ay, you were easy victors, did the rough
Straightway efface itself to smooth, the gruff
Grind down and grow a whisper,—did man's truth   140
Subdue, for sake of chivalry and ruth,
Its rapier-edge to suit the bulrush-spear
Womanly falsehood fights with! O that ear
All fact pricks rudely, that thrice-superfine
Feminity of sense, with right divine   145
To waive all process, take result stain-free
From out the very muck wherein . . .

                  Ah me!
The true slave's querulous outbreak! All the rest
Be resignation! Forth at your behest
I fare. Who knows but this—the crimson-quest—   150
May deepen to a sunrise, not decay
To that cold sad sweet smile?—which I obey.

FROM *JOCOSERIA* (1883)

Adam, Lilith, and Eve[1]

One day it thundered and lightened.
Two women, fairly frightened,
Sank to their knees, transformed, transfixed,
At the feet of the man who sat betwixt;
And "Mercy!" cried each—"if I tell the truth   5
Of a passage in my youth!"

Said This:[2] "Do you mind the morning
I met your love with scorning?
As the worst of the venom left my lips,
I thought 'If, despite this lie, he strips   10

---

9. Able to petrify; ironic echo of "beatific."
1. Irritated by a friend's misinterpretation of this poem, Browning gave the following reading: ". . . the story is simply that a man once knew a woman who, while she loved him, pretended that she did not—which pretence, like a man and a fool, he believed, so of course was not married to her—but to a woman who did *not* love him but another though she said she did love him—which, like a man and a fool—he believed: one day as they sat together, each, on a sudden impulse, told him the truth—which, like a man and a fool, he disbelieved. Surely there is nothing so difficult here . . ." (*Learned Lady*, p. 156).
2. Lilith, important figure in Jewish legend. In rabbinic literature Lilith is a demon of the night and seducer of men. She was regarded as Adam's first wife; their union was marred by strife.

The mask from my soul with a kiss—I crawl
His slave,—soul, body and all!' "

Said That:[3] "We stood to be married;
The priest, or someone, tarried;
'If Paradise-door prove locked?' smiled you.   15
I thought, as I nodded, smiling too,
'Did one, that's away, arrive—nor late
Nor soon should unlock Hell's gate!' "

It ceased to lighten and thunder.
Up started both in wonder,   20
Looked round and saw that the sky was clear,
Then laughed "Confess you believed us, Dear!"
"I saw through the joke!" the man replied.
They re-seated themselves beside.

Never the Time and the Place

Never the time and the place
    And the loved one all together![1]
        This path—how soft to pace!
        This May—what magic weather!
    Where is the loved one's face?   5
In a dream that loved one's face meets mine,
    But the house is narrow, the place is bleak
Where, outside, rain and wind combine
    With a furtive ear, if I strive to speak,
    With a hostile eye at my flushing cheek,   10
With a malice that marks each word, each sign!
    O enemy sly and serpentine,
        Uncoil thee from the waking man!
            Do I hold the Past
                Thus firm and fast   15
        Yet doubt if the Future hold I can?
This path so soft to pace shall lead
Thro' the magic of May to herself indeed!
Or narrow if needs the house must be,
Outside are the storms and strangers: we—   20
Oh, close, safe, warm sleep I and she,
    —I and she!

3. Eve.
1. The "loved one" is Elizabeth Barrett Browning. Cf. "The Householder" ("Epilogue" to *Fifine at the Fair*).

FROM *PARLEYINGS WITH CERTAIN PEOPLE OF IMPORTANCE IN THEIR DAY* (1887)

Reticent in the extreme about his private life (see "House"), Browning held biographers suspect. To handicap any effort at chronicling his own life he burned many of his private papers in 1885. Believing that his poetry alone should represent him to the world, he wrote no memoirs—though rumors persisted that he would do so. Speculation was ended by the publication in 1887 of *Parleyings with Certain People of Importance in Their Day*, aptly characterized as "notes for Browning's mental autobiography" (DeVane, p. 491). Dropping entirely his usual dramatic mask, Browning speaks his mind to seven figures of importance to his own intellectual development. The seven—Bernard de Mandeville, Daniel Bartoli, Christopher Smart, George Bubb Dodington, Francis Furini, Gerard de Lairesse, and Charles Avison—represent seven lifelong interests: philosophy, history, poetry, politics, painting, the classics, and music. After airing his settled opinions, Browning contrasts them with those of several outstanding contemporaries. Thus in "Bernard de Mandeville" the always optimistic Browning deplores the cosmic pessimism of Thomas Carlyle; in "Gerard de Lairesse" he criticizes the "Hellenism" of Matthew Arnold; and in "Christopher Smart" he attacks the poetry of "Aesthetes" such as A. C. Swinburne. The *Parleyings* are thoroughly and admirably treated in William C. DeVane's *Browning's Parleyings: The Autobiography of a Mind*, 2nd ed. (New York, 1964).

The English poet Christopher Smart (1722–71), whose irregular habits did not prevent his becoming a fellow of Pembroke College, Cambridge, went to London about 1752 to take up the life of a writer. His forgotten *Poems on Several Occasions* (1752) proved him at best a mediocre versifier. His unhappy life, complicated by drink and ill health, was after 1751 marked by periods of insanity. By 1756 he had developed a religious mania, which, according to his friend Samuel Johnson, took the form of "falling upon his knees, and saying his prayers in the street, or in any other unusual place. . . ." In 1763 he was confined in a madhouse, where he wrote the ecstatic "Song to David," by far his greatest poem, and today the only one by which he is remembered. Neglected in the eighteenth century as the product of a deranged mind, it was greatly appreciated by the romantics. In this "Parleying," Browning perpetuates the legend that Smart, lacking writing materials, indented the poem with a key on the wainscot of his madhouse room.

With Christopher Smart

I

It seems as if . . . or did the actual chance
Startle me and perplex? Let truth be said!
How might this happen? Dreaming, blindfold led
By visionary hand, did soul's advance
Precede my body's, gain inheritance   5
Of fact by fancy—so that when I read
At length with waking eyes your Song, instead

Of mere bewilderment, with me first glance
Was but full recognition that in trance
Or merely thought's adventure some old day   10
Of dim and done-with boyishness, or—well,
Why might it not have been, the miracle
Broke on me as I took my sober way
Through veritable regions of our earth
And made discovery, many a wondrous one?   15

II

Anyhow, fact or fancy, such its birth:
I was exploring some huge house, had gone
Through room and room complacently, no dearth
Anywhere of the signs of decent taste,
Adequate culture: wealth had run to waste   20
Nowise, nor penury was proved by stint:
All showed the Golden Mean without a hint
Of brave extravagance that breaks the rule.
The master of the mansion was no fool
Assuredly, no genius just as sure!   25
Safe mediocrity had scorned the lure
Of now too much and now too little cost,
And satisfied me sight was never lost
Of moderate design's accomplishment
In calm completeness. On and on I went,   30
With no more hope than fear of what came next,
Till lo, I push a door, sudden uplift
A hanging, enter, chance upon a shift
Indeed of scene! So—thus it is thou deck'st,
High heaven, our low earth's brick-and-mortar work?   35

III

It was the Chapel. That a star, from murk
Which hid, should flashingly emerge at last,
Were small surprise: but from broad day I passed
Into a presence that turned shine to shade.
There fronted me the Rafael Mother-Maid,[1]   40
Never to whom knelt votarist in shrine
By Nature's bounty helped, By Art's divine
More varied—beauty with magnificence—
Than this: from floor to roof one evidence
Of how far earth may rival heaven. No niche   45
Where glory was not prisoned to enrich
Man's gaze with gold and gems, no space but glowed
With colour, gleamed with carving—hues which owed
Their outburst to a brush the painter fed
With rainbow-substance—rare shapes never wed   50

---

1. Raphael Sanzio (1483–1520) painted a number of famous Madonnas. It is not clear which of these Browning has in mind.

To actual flesh and blood, which, brain-born once,
Became the sculptor's dowry, Art's response
To earth's despair. And all seemed old yet new:
Youth,—in the marble's curve, the canvas' hue,
Apparent,—wanted not the crowning thrill   55
Of age the consecrator.[2] Hands long still
Had worked here—could it be, what lent them skill
Retained a power to supervise, protect,
Enforce new lessons with the old, connect
Our life with theirs? No merely modern touch   60
Told me that here the artist, doing much,
Elsewhere did more, perchance does better, lives—
So needs must learn.

IV

               Well, these provocatives
Having fulfilled their office, forth I went
Big with anticipation—well-nigh fear—   65
Of what next room and next for startled eyes
Might have in store, surprise beyond surprise.
Next room and next and next—what followed here?
Why, nothing! not one object to arrest
My passage—everywhere too manifest   70
The previous decent null and void of best
And worst, mere ordinary right and fit,
Calm commonplace which neither missed, nor hit
Inch-high, inch-low, the placid mark proposed.

V

Armed with this instance, have I diagnosed   75
Your case, my Christopher? The man was sound
And sane at starting: all at once the ground
Gave way beneath his step, a certain smoke
Curled up and caught him, or perhaps down broke
A fireball wrapping flesh and spirit both   80
In conflagration.[3] Then—as heaven were loth
To linger—let earth understand too well
How heaven at need can operate—off fell
The flame-robe, and the untransfigured man
Resumed sobriety,—as he began,   85
So did he end nor alter pace, not he!

VI

Now, what I fain would know is—could it be
That he—whoe'er he was that furnished forth

2. I.e., Raphael's painting, while reflecting the "new art" of the Italian Renaissance, did not
   lack a classical background. (The work of his Roman period [1508–20] was strongly influ-
   enced by his study of ancient sculpture.)
3. Cf. the transfiguration of Christ (Mark 9:1–8).

The Chapel, making thus, from South to North,[4]
Rafael touch Leighton,[5] Michelagnolo   90
Join Watts, was found but once combining so
The elder and the younger, taking stand
On Art's supreme,[6]—or that yourself who sang
A Song[7] where flute-breath silvers trumpet-clang,
And stations you for once on either hand   95
With Milton and with Keats,[8] empowered to claim
Affinity on just one point—(or blame
Or praise my judgment, thus it fronts you full)—
How came it you resume the void and null,
Subside to insignificance,—live, die   100
—Proved plainly two mere mortals who drew nigh
One moment—that,[9] to Art's best hierarchy,
This,[1] to the superhuman poet-pair?
What if, in one point only, then and there
The otherwise all-unapproachable   105
Allowed impingement? Does the sphere pretend
To span the cube's breadth, cover end to end
The plane with its embrace? No, surely! Still,
Contact is contact, sphere's touch no whit less
Than cube's superimposure. Such success   110
Befell Smart only out of throngs between
Milton and Keats that donned the singing-dress[2]—
Smart, solely of such songmen, pierced the screen
'Twixt thing and word, lit language straight from soul,—
Left no fine film-flake on the naked coal   115
Live from the censer—shapely or uncouth,
Fire-suffused through and through, one blaze of truth
Undeadened by a lie,—(you have my mind)—
For, think! this blaze outleapt with black behind
And blank before, when Hayley[3] and the rest . . .   120
But let the dead successors worst and best
Bury their dead: with life be my concern—
Yours with the fire-flame: what I fain would learn
Is just—(suppose me haply ignorant
Down to the common knowledge, doctors vaunt[4])   125

4. From Italy to England.
5. I.e., synthesizing old and new. The painters are: Sir Frederick Leighton (1830–96), English painter and sculptor, who had painted a portrait of Browning and had designed Elizabeth Barrett Browning's monument; Michelangelo (Michelagniolo Buonarroti, 1475–1564), greatest Florentine painter of the Renaissance; and George Frederic Watts (1817–1904), English painter and sculptor, who also had painted Browning's portrait.
6. Supreme height, summit.
7. "A Song to David."
8. John Milton (1608–74) and John Keats (1795–1821); the "flute-breath" is associated with the latter, the "trumpet-clang" with the former. Smart's poem synthesizes Miltonic grandeur and Keatsian sensuousness.
9. The one "that furnished forth / The chapel" (lines 88–89).
1. Christopher Smart.
2. Eighteenth-century poets.
3. William Hayley (1745–1820), English poet and biographer. He "and the rest" represent mediocrity.
4. I.e., assume that I am ignorant, possessing only the common sense the philosophers make so much of. (Browning perhaps alludes to the "Scottish common-sense philosophers" of the

Just this—why only once the fire-flame was:
No matter if the marvel came to pass
The way folk judged—if power too long suppressed
Broke loose and maddened, as the vulgar guessed,
Or simply brain-disorder (doctors said)   130
A turmoil of the particles disturbed
Brain's workaday performance in your head,
Spurred spirit to wild action health had curbed:
And so verse issued in a cataract
Whence prose, before and after, unperturbed   135
Was wont to wend its way. Concede the fact
That here a poet was who always could—
Never before did—never after would—
Achieve the feat: how were such fact explained?

VII

Was it that when, by rarest chance, there fell   140
Disguise from Nature, so that Truth remained
Naked, and whoso saw for once could tell
Us others of her majesty and might
In large, her lovelinesses infinite
In little,—straight you used the power wherewith   145
Sense, penetrating as through rind to pith
Each object, thoroughly revealed might view
And comprehend the old things thus made new,[5]
So that while eye saw, soul to tongue could trust
Thing which struck word out,[6] and once more adjust   150
Real vision to right language, till heaven's vault
Pompous with sunset, storm-stirred sea's assault
On the swilled[7] rock-ridge, earth's embosomed brood
Of tree and flower and weed, with all the life
That flies or swims or crawls, in peace or strife,   155
Above, below,—each had its note and name
For Man to know by,—Man who, now—the same
As erst in Eden, needs that all he sees
Be named him[8] ere he note by what degrees
Of strength and beauty to its end Design   160
Ever thus operates—(your thought and mine,
No matter for the many dissident[9])—
So did you sing your Song, so truth found vent
In words for once with you?

---

late eighteenth century. Thomas Reid, Dugald Stewart, and others hoped to counter exces-
sively metaphysical or skeptical points of view by appealing to common sense in philosophi-
cal disputes.)
5. Revelation 21:5 ". . . Behold, I make all things new."
6. Called the words forth.
7. Drenched.
8. For him. (Cf. Genesis 2:19–20; Adam's naming of creatures.) For Browning a main function
of art is awakening men to the wonders of nature; cf. "Fra Lippo Lippi," lines 300–302.
9. I.e., we share the same philosophy, regardless of the many who disagree with us. (Probably
Browning has poets like A. C. Swinburne in mind.)

VIII

Then—back was furled
The robe thus thrown aside, and straight the world   165
Darkened into the old oft-catalogued
Repository of things that sky, wave, land,
Or show or hide, clear late, accretion-clogged
Now, just as long ago, by tellings and
Re-telling to satiety, which strike   170
Muffled upon the ear's drum. Very like
None was so startled as yourself when friends
Came, hailed your fast-returning wits: "Health mends
Importantly, for—to be plain with you—
This scribble on the wall was done—in lieu   175
Of pen and paper—with—ha, ha!—your key
Denting it on the wainscot! Do you see
How wise our caution was? Thus much we stopped
Of babble that had else grown print: and lopped
From your trim bay-tree[1] this unsightly bough—   180
Smart's who translated Horace![2] Write us now" . . .
Why, what Smart did write—never afterward
One line to show that he, who paced the sward,[3]
Had reached the zenith from his madhouse cell.

IX

Was it because you judged (I know full well   185
You never had the fancy)—judged—as some—
That who makes poetry must reproduce
Thus ever and thus only, as they come,
Each strength, each beauty, everywhere diffuse
Throughout creation, so that eye and ear,   190
Seeing and hearing, straight shall recognize,
At touch of just a trait, the strength appear,—
Suggested by a line's lapse see arise
All evident the beauty,—fresh surprise
Startling at fresh achievement? "So, indeed,   195
Wallows the whale's bulk in the waste of brine,
Nor otherwise its feather-tufts make fine
Wild Virgin's Bower when stars faint off to seed!"[4]
(My prose—your poetry I dare not give,
Purpling too much my mere grey argument.)   200
—Was it because you judged—when fugitive

1. Tree sacred to Apollo, god of poetry, here a metaphor for poetic reputation.
2. Roman poet Horace (Quintus Horatius Flaccus, 65–8 B.C.E.) was widely imitated and translated by the English "neoclassical" writers. Smart's having translated him would have been evidence of sanity as well as good taste. (Skeptical of poetic inspiration through Dionsyiac frenzy, Horace concludes his Ars Poetica with a caricature of the mad poet who wanders about "spewing out verses.")
3. Grass, here symbolic of commonness or mediocrity.
4. The purple virgin's bower is a kind of wild clematis, a shrubby climber the fruits of which bear feathered seeds, often called "old man's beard." The plant's purple and gray are alluded to in line 200.

Was glory found, and wholly gone and spent
Such power of startling up deaf ear, blind eye,
At truth's appearance,—that you humbly bent
The head and, bidding vivid work good-bye,   205
Doffed lyric dress and trod the world once more
A drab-clothed decent proseman as before?
Strengths, beauties, by one word's flash thus laid bare
—That was effectual service: made aware
Of strengths and beauties, Man but hears the text,   210
Awaits your teaching.[5] Nature? What comes next?
Why all the strength and beauty?—to be shown
Thus in one word's flash, thenceforth let alone
By Man who needs must deal with aught that's known
Never so lately and so little? Friend,   215
First give us knowledge, then appoint its use!
Strength, beauty are the means: ignore their end?
As well you stopped at proving how profuse
Stones, sticks, nay stubble lie to left and right
Ready to help the builder,—careless quite   220
If he should take, or leave the same to strew
Earth idly,—as by word's flash bring in view
Strength, beauty, then bid who beholds the same
Go on beholding. Why gains unemployed?
Nature was made to be by Man enjoyed   225
First; followed duly by enjoyment's fruit,
Instruction—haply leaving joy behind:
And you, the instructor, would you slack pursuit
Of the main prize, as poet help mankind
Just to enjoy, there leave them? Play the fool,   230
Abjuring a superior privilege?
Please simply when your function is to rule—
By thought incite to deed?[6] From edge to edge
Of earth's round, strength and beauty everywhere
Pullulate[7]—and must you particularize   235
All, each and every apparition? Spare
Yourself and us the trouble! Ears and eyes
Want so much strength and beauty, and no less
Nor more, to learn life's lesson by. Oh, yes—
The other method's favoured in our day![8]   240
The end ere the beginning: as you may,
Master the heavens before you study earth,

5. The metaphor is that of a preacher who had read the Bible lesson but has yet to deliver his sermon based on that "text."
6. In his moral emphasis Browning recalls Sir Philip Sidney's "Apology for Poetry" (1595): Poetry must both "teach and delight" and must "draw us to as high a perfection as our degenerate souls . . . can be capable of"; at its noblest the art can move men to "virtuous action." Browning's statement, "your function is to rule" (line 232), paraphrases the last sentence of Shelley's "Defence of Poetry" (1821): "Poets are the unacknowledged legislators of the world."
7. Abound.
8. Under attack here is the English "Aesthetic Movement," led in poetry by A. C. Swinburne (1837–1909), whose "pagan" and sensual verse in *Atalanta in Calydon* (1865) and *Poems and Ballads* (1866) made him the literary sensation of the time.

Make you familiar with the meteor's birth
Ere you descend to scrutinize the rose!
I say, o'erstep no least one of the rows   245
That lead man from the bottom where he plants
Foot first of all, to life's last ladder-top:
Arrived there, vain enough will seem the vaunts
Of those who say—"We scale the skies, then drop
To earth—to find, how all things there are loth   250
To answer heavenly law: we understand
The meteor's course, and lo, the rose's growth—
How other than should be by law's command!"
Would not you tell such—"Friends, beware lest fume
Offuscate sense: learn earth first ere presume   255
To teach heaven legislation. Law must be
Active in earth or nowhere: earth you see,—
Or there or not at all, Will, Power and Love[9]
Admit discovery,—as below, above
Seek next law's confirmation! But reverse   260
The order, where's the wonder things grow worse
Than, by the law your fancy formulates,
They should be? Cease from anger at the fates
Which thwart themselves so madly. Live and learn,
Not first learn and then live, is our concern."   265

ca. 1885

FROM *ASOLANDO: FANCIES AND FACTS* (1889)

Prologue[1]

"The Poet's age is sad: for why?[2]
　　In youth, the natural world could show
No common object but his eye
　　At once involved with alien glow[3]—
His own soul's iris-bow.[4]   5

"And now a flower is just a flower:
　　Man, bird, beast are but beast, bird, man—

9. Browning often speaks of this triad of divine attributes; see for example *The Ring and the Book*, X.1350ff.
1. *Asolando: Fancies and Facts*, Browning's last volume of poetry, was published on December 12, 1889, the day of his death in Venice; in his final hours he heard of its enthusiastic reception by the British public. In September 1889 Browning had returned to Asolo, the Italian town that is the setting for *Pippa Passes* (1841), to compose or revise poems for *Asolando*. As Roma King has stated, "In spite of the audaciousness of the love lyrics, there is a solemnity about the volume. Browning writes with a finality which suggests that he knew it would perhaps be his last work" (*The Focusing Artifice* [1968], p. 234).
　　The "Prologue" recalls the poet's first visit to Asolo in June 1838.
2. The first two stanzas are spoken by an unreflective friend of the poet's.
3. Cf. Wordsworth's "Ode: Intimations of Immortality" (especially stanza 1).
4. Iris was goddess of rainbows.

Simply themselves, uncinct by dower
  Of dyes[5] which, when life's day began,
Round each in glory ran."   10

Friend, did you need an optic glass,
  Which were your choice? A lens to drape
In ruby, emerald, chrysopras,[6]
  Each object—or reveal its shape
Clear outlined, past escape,   15

The naked very thing?—so clear
  That, when you had the chance to gaze,
You found its inmost self appear
  Through outer seeming—truth ablaze,
Not falsehood's fancy-haze?   20

How many a year, my Asolo,
  Since—one step just from sea to land—
I found you, loved yet feared you so—
  For natural objects seemed to stand
Palpably fire-clothed! No—   25

No mastery of mine o'er these!
  Terror with beauty, like the Bush[7]
Burning but unconsumed. Bend knees,
  Drop eyes to earthward! Language? Tush!
Silence 't is awe decrees.   30

And now? The lambent flame is—where?
  Lost from the naked world: earth, sky,
Hill, vale, tree, flower,—Italia's rare
  O'er-running beauty crowds the eye—
But flame? The Bush is bare.   35

Hill, vale, tree, flower—they stand distinct,
  Nature to know and name. What then?
A Voice spoke thence which straight unlinked
  Fancy from fact: see, all's in ken:[8]
Has once my eyelid winked?   40

No, for the purged ear apprehends
  Earth's import, not the eye late dazed:
The Voice said "Call my works thy friends!
  At Nature dost thou shrink amazed?
God is it who transcends."   45

ASOLO: Sept. 6, 1889.

---

5. I.e., not enveloped by rich colors.
6. Apple-green silica which grows paler on exposure to light.
7. See Exodus 3, in which the Lord appears to Moses as a burning bush. Cf. lines 27ff.
8. View.

Bad Dreams. I[1]

Last night I saw you in my sleep:
  And how your charm of face was changed!
I asked "Some love, some faith you keep?"
  You answered "Faith gone, love estranged."

Whereat I woke—a twofold bliss: 5
  Waking was one, but next there came
This other: "Though I felt, for this,[2]
  My heart break, I loved on the same."

Bad Dreams. II

You in the flesh and here—
  Your very self! Now, wait!
One word! May I hope or fear?
  Must I speak in love or hate?
Stay while I ruminate!   5

The fact and each circumstance
  Dare you disown? Not you!
That vast dome, that huge dance,
  And the gloom which overgrew
A—possibly festive crew!   10

For why should men dance at all—
  Why women—a crowd of both—
Unless they are gay? Strange ball—
  Hands and feet plighting troth,
Yet partners enforced and loth!   15

Of who danced there, no shape
  Did I recognize: thwart, perverse,
Each grasped each, past escape
  In a whirl or weary or worse:
Man's sneer met woman's curse,   20

While he and she toiled as if
  Their guardian set galley-slaves
To supple chained limbs grown stiff:
  Unmanacled trulls and knaves—
The lash for who misbehaves!   25

1. This sequence of poems shares with "James Lee's Wife" (1864) and George Meredith's *Modern Love* (1862) the theme of the estrangement of a modern couple. The obscurity, partly due to the dream symbolism, is perhaps traceable to the autobiographical element. A close friend, the young and wealthy American widow, Mrs. Clara Bloomfield-Moore, insisted that "no one can understand ['Bad Dreams'] so well as myself" (*Portrait*, p. 268). Browning apparently had a painful emotional experience as her guest at St. Moritz, Switzerland, in the fall of 1888, of which this may be the esoteric and ambiguous psychological record.
2. I.e., "because of this," the dream lover's denial of love.

And a gloom was, all the while,
  Deeper and deeper yet
O'ergrowing the rank and file
  Of that army of haters—set
To mimic love's fever-fret.   30

By the wall-side close I crept,
  Avoiding the livid maze,
And, safely so far, outstepped
  On a chamber—a chapel, says
My memory or betrays—   35

Closet-like, kept aloof
  From unseemly witnessing
What sport made floor and roof
  Of the Devil's palace ring
While his Damned amused their king.   40

Ay, for a low lamp burned,
  And a silence lay about
What I, in the midst, discerned
  Though dimly till, past doubt,
'T was a sort of throne stood out—   45

High seat with steps, at least:
  And the topmost step was filled
By—whom? What vestured priest?
  A stranger to me,—his guild,
His cult, unreconciled   50

To my knowledge how guild and cult
  Are clothed in this world of ours:
I pondered, but no result
  Came to—unless that Giaours[3]
So worship the Lower Powers.   55

When suddenly who entered?
  Who knelt—did you guess I saw?
Who—raising that face where centred
  Allegiance to love and law
So lately—off-casting awe,   60

Down-treading reserve, away
  Thrusting respect . . . but mine
Stands firm—firm still shall stay!
  Ask Satan! for I decline
To tell—what I saw, in fine!   65

3. Infidels.

Yet here in the flesh you come—
     Your same self, form and face,—
In the eyes, mirth still at home!
     On the lips, that commonplace
Perfection of honest grace!   70

Yet your errand is—needs must be—
     To palliate—well, explain,
Expurgate in some degree
     Your soul of its ugly stain.
Oh, you—the good in grain—   75

How was it your white took tinge?
     "A mere dream"—never object!
Sleep leaves a door on hinge
     Whence soul, ere our flesh suspect,
Is off and away: detect   80

Her vagaries when loose, who can!
     Be she pranksome, be she prude,
Disguise with the day began:
     With the night—ah, what ensued
From draughts of a drink hell-brewed?   85

Then She: "What a queer wild dream!
     And perhaps the best fun is—
Myself had its fellow—I seem
     Scarce awake from yet. 'T was this—
Shall I tell you? First, a kiss!   90

"For the fault was just your own,—
     'T is myself expect apology:
You warned me to let alone
     (Since our studies were mere philology)
That ticklish⁴ (you said) Anthology.⁵   95

"So, I dreamed that I passed *exam*
     Till a question posed me sore:
'Who translated this epigram
     By—an author we best ignore?'⁶
And I answered 'Hannah More'!"⁷   100

---

4. Prurient, lewd.
5. Probably the Greek Anthology, a collection of epigrams, short elegiac poems composed be-
   tween the seventh century B.C.E., and the tenth century C.E. Some are humorous or satirical.
   But Browning may have had in mind the Latin Anthology (sixth century C.E.), which in-
   cludes the erotic poem *Pervigilium Veneris*, a song celebrating Venus Genetrix (mother of the
   Romans).
6. Possibly Martial (ca. C.E. 40–104), many of whose epigrams are spiced with obscenities. Her
   ludicrous answer (line 100) reflects the man's attempt to keep her sheltered intellectually.
7. Ethical and religious writer and reformer (1745–1833), a member of the Evangelical
   "Clapham Sect." Among her works is *Practical Piety* (1811).

Bad Dreams. III

This was my dream: I saw a Forest
　　Old as the earth, no track nor trace
Of unmade man. Thou, Soul, explorest—
　　Though in a trembling rapture—space
Immeasurable! Shrubs, turned trees,　　　　　5
Trees that touch heaven, support its frieze
Studded with sun and moon and star:
While—oh, the enormous growths that bar
Mine eye from penetrating past
　　Their tangled twine where lurks—nay, lives　　10
Royally lone, some brute-type cast
　　I' the rough, time cancels, man forgives.

On, Soul! I saw a lucid City[8]
　　Of architectural device
Every way perfect. Pause for pity,　　　　　15
　　Lightning! nor leave a cicatrice
On those bright marbles, dome and spire,
Structures palatial,—streets which mire
Dares not defile, paved all too fine
For human footstep's smirch, not thine—　　20
Proud solitary traverser,
　　My Soul, of silent lengths of way—
With what ecstatic dread, aver,
　　Lest life start sanctioned by thy stay!

Ah, but the last sight was the hideous!　　　25
　　A City, yes,—a Forest, true,—
But each devouring each. Perfidious
　　Snake-plants had strangled what I knew
Was a pavilion once: each oak
Held on his horns some spoil he broke　　　30
By surreptitiously beneath
Upthrusting: pavements, as with teeth,
Griped huge weed widening crack and split
　　In squares and circles stone-work erst.
Oh, Nature—good! Oh, Art—no whit　　　35
　　Less worthy! Both in one—accurst!

---

8. Cf. Tennyson's "The Palace of Art" (1832, 1842), an allegory of purely intellectual delights experienced by the Soul.

Bad Dreams. IV

It happened thus: my slab, though new,
    Was getting weather-stained,—beside,
Herbage, balm, peppermint o'ergrew
    Letter and letter: till you tried
Somewhat, the Name was scarce descried.   5

That strong stern man my lover came:
    —Was he my lover? Call him, pray,
My life's cold critic bent on blame
    Of all poor I could do or say
To make me worth his love one day—   10

One far day when, by diligent
    And dutiful amending faults,
Foibles, all weaknesses which went
    To challenge and excuse assaults
Of culture wronged by taste that halts[9]—   15

Discrepancies should mar no plan
    Symmetric of the qualities
Claiming respect from—say—a man
    That's strong and stern. "Once more he pries
Into me with those critic eyes!"   20

No question! so—"Conclude, condemn
    Each failure my poor self avows!
Leave to its fate all you contemn!
    There's Solomon's selected spouse:[1]
Earth needs must hold such maids—choose them!"   25

Why, he was weeping! Surely gone
    Sternness and strength: with eyes to ground
And voice a broken monotone—
    "Only be as you were! Abound
In foibles, faults,—laugh, robed and crowned   30

"As Folly's veriest queen,—care I
    One feather-fluff? Look pity, Love,
On prostrate me—your foot shall try
    This forehead's use—mount thence above,
And reach what Heaven you dignify!"   35

Now, what could bring such change about?
    The thought perplexed: till, following
His gaze upon the ground,—why, out
    Came all the secret! So, a thing
Thus simple has deposed my king!   40

9. Falters, wavers.
1. See Song of Solomon 4:9: "Thou hast ravished my heart, my sister, my spouse. . . ."

For, spite of weeds that strove to spoil
Plain reading on the lettered slab,
My name was clear enough—no soil
Effaced the date when one chance stab
Of scorn . . . if only ghosts might blab!   45

"Imperante Augusto Natus Est—"[1]

What it was struck the terror into me?
This, Publius: closer! while we wait our turn
I'll tell you. Water's warm (they ring inside)
At the eighth hour, till when no use to bathe.

Here in the vestibule where now we sit,   5
One scarce stood yesterday, the throng was such
Of loyal gapers, folk all eye and ear
While Lucius Varius Rufus[2] in their midst
Read out that long-planned late-completed piece,
His Panegyric on the Emperor.   10
"Nobody like him" little Flaccus[3] laughed
"At leading forth an Epos[4] with due pomp!
Only, when godlike Cæsar[5] swells the theme,
How should mere mortals hope to praise aright?
Tell me, thou offshoot of Etruscan kings!"   15
Whereat Mæcenas[6] smiling sighed assent.

I paid my quadrans, left the Thermæ's[7] roar
Of rapture as the poet asked "What place
Among the godships Jove, for Cæsar's sake,
Would bid its actual occupant vacate   20

---

1. Like "Karshish" and "Cleon," this monologue re-creates pagan antiquity on the verge of the Christian era. It is set during the thirteenth consulship of Augustus (ca. 2 B.C.E.) in Rome, where a senator and his friend Publius await their turn at the public bath. The senator's prophecy of Christ's coming (lines 158–59) is taken from *The Sibylline Oracles* (III.47–51, 55–60) hailing the advent of an "immortal" and "holy king" and from Virgil's *Fourth Eclogue* (Pollio), which celebrates a "boy's birth, in whom the iron race shall begin to cease, and the golden to arise over all the world." The title, meaning "He [Christ] was born in the reign of Augustus," is from St. Augustine's *The City of God*, XVIII. chap. 46.

   For the portrait of Augustus the poet drew upon Suetonius' *De vita Caesarum* (*The Lives of the Caesars*). "Augustus" ("Exalted One") was the title awarded Gaius Julius Caesar Octavianus (63 B.C.E.–C.E. 14) in 27 B.C.E. in recognition that he has brought peace and saved the Roman republic through the defeat of Antony and Cleopatra at Actium (31 B.C.E.) and through the restoration of order at home. As "first citizen," Octavian was invested with comprehensive authority, wielding domestic power through a series of consulships. He revived the Roman state religion, was named *Pontifex Maximus* (head of the council of priests), and arranged to have his "genius" deified. As patron of the arts and literature he has had few equals; in his reign flourished Ovid, Horace, and Virgil.
2. Esteemed epic and tragic poet (64 B.C.E.–C.E. 9); none of Varius' work is extant except for two lines of a panegyric on Augustus, quoted by Horace in *Epistle I*.
3. Horace, or Quintus Horatius Flaccus (65–8 B.C.E.), five years younger than Virgil; famous for his odes, epistles, and satires. Suetonius describes him as short and stout.
4. Heroic poem.
5. Augustus was widely regarded as divine. (See Virgil, *Aeneid*, VI.788–805.)
6. Died 8 B.C.E. Enlightened patron of a circle including Varius, Horace, and Virgil; also friend and counselor to Augustus.
7. *Thermae*: warm baths. Quadrans: Roman coin.

In favour of the new divinity?"
And got the expected answer "Yield thine own!"—
Jove thus dethroned, I somehow wanted air,
And found myself a-pacing street and street,
Letting the sunset, rosy over Rome,   25
Clear my head dizzy with the hubbub—say
As if thought's dance therein had kicked up dust
By trampling on all else: the world lay prone,
As—poet-propped, in brave hexameters[8]—
Their subject triumphed up from man to God.   30
Caius Octavius Cæsar the August—
Where was escape from his prepotency?
I judge I may have passed—how many piles
Of structure dropt like doles from his free hand
To Rome on every side? Why, right and left,   35
For temples you've the Thundering Jupiter,
Avenging Mars, Apollo Palatine:
How count Piazza, Forum—there's a third
All but completed. You've the Theatre
Named of Marcellus—all his work, such work!—   40
One thought still ending, dominating all—
With warrant Varius sang "Be Cæsar God!"
By what a hold arrests he Fortune's wheel,
Obtaining and retaining heaven and earth
Through Fortune, if you like, but favour—no!   45
For the great deeds flashed by me, fast and thick
As stars which storm the sky on autumn nights—
Those conquests! but peace crowned them,—so, of peace!
Count up his titles only—these, in few—
Ten years Triumvir, Consul thirteen times,   50
Emperor, nay—the glory topping all—
Hailed Father of his Country, last and best
Of titles, by himself accepted so:
And why not? See but feats achieved in Rome—
Not to say, Italy—he planted there   55
Some thirty colonies—but Rome itself
All new-built, "marble now, brick once," he boasts:
This Portico, that Circus. Would you sail?
He has drained Tiber for you: would you walk?
He straightened out the long Flaminian Way.[9]   60
Poor? Profit by his score of donatives!
Rich—that is, mirthful? Half-a-hundred games
Challenge your choice! There's Rome—for you and me
Only? The centre of the world besides!
For, look the wide world over, where ends Rome?   65
To sunrise? There's Euphrates—all between!
To sunset? Ocean and immensity:
North,—stare till Danube stops you: South, see Nile,

8. Classical six-measure line, primarily the meter of epic poetry.
9. Northern road of ancient Italy, leading from the Flaminian gate of Rome to Ariminium (Rimini).

The Desert and the earth-upholding Mount.[1]
Well may the poet-people each with each   70
Vie in his praise, our company of swans,
Virgil and Horace, singers—in their way—
Nearly as good as Varius, though less famed:
Well may they cry, "No mortal, plainly God!"

Thus to myself myself said, while I walked: 75
Or would have said, could thought attain to speech,
Clean baffled by enormity of bliss
The while I strove to scale its heights and sound
Its depths—this masterdom o'er all the world
Of one who was but born,—like you, like me,   80
Like all the world he owns,—of flesh and blood.
But he—how grasp, how gauge his own conceit
Of bliss to me near inconceivable?
Or—since such flight too much makes reel the brain—
Let's sink—and so take refuge, as it were,   85
From life's excessive altitude—to life's
Breathable wayside shelter at its base!
If looms thus large this Cæsar to myself
—Of senatorial rank and somebody—
How must he strike the vulgar nameless crowd,   90
Innumerous swarm that's nobody at all?
Why,—for an instance,—much as yon gold shape
Crowned, sceptred, on the temple opposite—
Fulgurant[2] Jupiter—must daze the sense
Of—say, yon outcast begging from its step!   95
What, anti-Cæsar, monarch in the mud,
As he is pinnacled above thy pate?[3]
Ay, beg away! thy lot contrasts full well
With his whose bounty yields thee this support—
Our Holy and Inviolable One,   100
Cæsar, whose bounty built the fane[4] above!
Dost read my thought? Thy garb, alack, displays
Sore usage truly in each rent and stain—
Faugh! Wash though in Suburra![5] 'Ware the dogs
Who may not so disdain a meal on thee!   105
What, stretchest forth a palm to catch my alms?
Aha, why yes: I must appear—who knows?—
I, in my toga, to thy rags and thee—
Quæstor—nay, Ædile, Censor—Pol![6] perhaps
The very City-Prætor's[7] noble self!   110

1. Mount Atlas (actually a mountain range in northwest Africa), where Atlas was supposed to
   have stood holding the earth on his shoulders. Lines 66–69 outline world geography as the
   Romans understood it in 2 B.C.E.
2. Emitting flashes of lightning.
3. Head.
4. Temple.
5. Low street in Rome.
6. An oath by Pollux, twin of Castor. Quæstor, Ædile, Censor: three municipal offices in as-
   cending order of importance.
7. The *prætor urbanus* was the highest magistrate in a Latin town.

As to me Cæsar, so to thee am I?
Good: nor in vain shall prove thy quest, poor rogue!
Hither—hold palm out—take this quarter-as![8]

And who did take it? As he raised his head,
(My gesture was a trifle—well, abrupt),   115
Back fell the broad flap of the peasant's-hat,
The homespun cloak that muffled half his cheek
Dropped somewhat, and I had a glimpse—just one!
One was enough. Whose—whose might be the face?
That unkempt careless hair—brown, yellowish—   120
Those sparkling eyes beneath their eyebrows' ridge
(Each meets each, and the hawk-nose rules between)
—That was enough, no glimpse was needed more!
And terrifying into my mind
Came that quick-hushed report was whispered us,   125
"They do say, once a year in sordid garb
He plays the mendicant, sits all day long,
Asking and taking alms of who may pass,
And so averting, if submission help,
Fate's envy, the dread chance and change of things   130
When Fortune—for a word, a look, a nought—
Turns spiteful and—the petted lioness—
Strikes with her sudden paw, and prone falls each
Who patted late her neck superiorly,
Or trifled with those claw-tips velvet-sheathed."   135
"He's God!" shouts Lucius Varius Rufus: "Man
And worms'-meat any moment!" mutters low
Some Power, admonishing the mortal-born.

Ay, do you mind? There's meaning in the fact
That whoso conquers, triumphs, enters Rome,   140
Climbing the Capitolian,[9] soaring thus
To glory's summit,—Publius, do you mark—
Ever the same attendant who, behind,
Above the Conqueror's head supports the crown
All-too-demonstrative for human wear,   145
—One hand's employment—all the while reserves
Its fellow, backward flung, to point how, close
Appended from the car, beneath the foot
Of the up-borne exulting Conqueror,
Frown—half-descried—the instruments of shame,   150
The malefactor's due. Crown, now—Cross, when?

Who stands secure? Are even Gods so safe?
Jupiter that just now is dominant—
Are not there ancient dismal tales how once
A predecessor[1] reigned ere Saturn came,   155

8. Very small coin.
9. Capitol on the hill.
1. Uranus, father of the race of Titans or Elder Gods, among whom was Saturn (Cronus). Ac-

And who can say if Jupiter be last?
Was it for nothing the grey Sibyl[2] wrote
"Cæsar Augustus regnant, shall be born
In blind Judæa"—one to master him,
Him and the universe? An old-wife's tale?   160

Bath-drudge! Here, slave! No cheating! Our turn next.
No loitering, or be sure you taste the lash!
Two strigils,[3] two oil-drippers, each a sponge!

Development[1]

My Father was a scholar and knew Greek.
When I was five years old, I asked him once
"What do you read about?"
                              "The siege of Troy."[2]
"What is a siege and what is Troy?"
                              Whereat
He piled up chairs and tables for a town,   5
Set me a-top for Priam,[3] called our cat
—Helen, enticed away from home (he said)
By wicked Paris,[4] who couched somewhere close
Under the footstool, being cowardly,
But whom—since she was worth the pains, poor puss—   10
Towzer and Tray,—our dogs, the Atreidai,[5]—sought
By taking Troy to get possession of
—Always when great Achilles ceased to sulk,[6]
(My pony in the stable)—forth would prance
And put to flight Hector—our page-boy's self.   15
This taught me who was who and what was what:
So far I rightly understood the case
At five years old: a huge delight it proved
And still proves—thanks to that instructor sage

---

cording to Hesiod (*Theogony*, 133–87), Saturn castrated Uranus with a sickle, then ruled over the other Titans until his son Zeus (Jupiter) dethroned him. Saturn fled to Italy, inaugurating the Golden Age; he was the Roman agricultural deity.
2. The Erythraean sibyl, credited by St. Augustine with having "sung many things about Christ more plainly than the other sibyls" (*City of God*, XVIII. chap. 23). Augustus, it is said, consulted the oracles at Delphi to learn of his successor. When told a Judean child was his enemy and lord, he built an altar on the Capitoline Hill with the inscription *Ara Primogeniti Dei* ("Altar of God's First-Born").
3. Scrapers used at the baths.
1. Temperamentally unsuited to systematic instruction, Browning never earned a university degree. From boyhood his unorthodox education consisted mainly of reading for pleasure in his father's excellent library, where he developed a lifelong interest in the Greek classics. See the early "Artemis Prologizes" (1842) and the late poems containing translations from Euripides: *Balaustion's Adventure* (1871) and *Aristophanes' Apology* (1875).
2. The *Iliad*.
3. King of Troy and father of Paris and Hector.
4. His carrying Helen off to Troy precipitated the Trojan War.
5. Sons of Atreus: Menelaus and Agamemnon.
6. Achilles sulked in his tent when Briseis, a beautiful captive, was taken from him by Agamemnon; he entered battle to avenge the death of his friend Patroclus, killing the Trojan leader Hector.

My Father, who knew better than turn straight   20
Learning's full flare on weak-eyed ignorance,
Or, worse yet, leave weak eyes to grow sand-blind,
Content with darkness and vacuity.

It happened, two or three years afterward,
That—I and playmates playing at Troy's Siege—   25
My Father came upon our make-believe.
"How would you like to read yourself the tale
Properly told, of which I gave you first
Merely such notion as a boy could bear?
Pope,[7] now, would give you the precise account   30
Of what, some day, by dint of scholarship,
You'll hear—who knows?—from Homer's very mouth.
Learn Greek by all means, read the 'Blind Old Man,
Sweetest of Singers'—*tuphlos* which means 'blind,'
Hedistos which means 'sweetest.' Time enough!   35
Try, anyhow, to master him some day;
Until when, take what serves for substitute,
Read Pope, by all means!"
                              So I ran through Pope,
Enjoyed the tale—what history so true?
Also attacked my Primer, duly drudged,   40
Grew fitter thus for what was promised next—
The very thing itself, the actual words,
When I could turn—say, Buttmann[8] to account.

Time passed, I ripened somewhat: one fine day,
"Quite ready for the Iliad, nothing less?   45
There's Heine,[9] where the big books block the shelf:
Don't skip a word, thumb well the Lexicon!"

I thumbed well and skipped nowise till I learned
Who was who, what was what, from Homer's tongue,
And there an end of learning. Had you asked   50
The all-accomplished scholar, twelve years old,
"Who was it wrote the Iliad?"—what a laugh!
"Why, Homer, all the world knows: of his life
Doubtless some facts exist: it's everywhere:
We have not settled, though, his place of birth: 55
He begged, for certain, and was blind beside:
Seven cities claimed him—Scio, with best right,
Thinks Byron.[1] What he wrote? Those Hymns[2] we have.
Then there's the 'Battle of the Frogs and Mice,'[3]

---

7. Alexander Pope (1688–1744), whose translation of the *Iliad* (1720) in heroic couplets was very popular.
8. Philipp Karl Buttman (1764–1829), author of a standard Greek grammar for schoolboys.
9. Christian Gottlob Heyne (1729–1812). editor of a standard text of the *Iliad*.
1. More than seven cities have claimed the honor. Modern scholars favor Smyrna or the island of Chios ("Scio"). Cf. Byron, *The Bride of Abydos* 2. 27.
2. The Homeric Hymns, collection of invocations and epic narratives of unknown authorship.
3. The *Batrachomyomachia*, burlesque epic attributed to Homer, but probably of much later date.

That's all—unless they dig 'Margites'[4] up   60
(I'd like that) nothing more remains to know."

Thus did youth spend a comfortable time;
Until—"What's this the Germans say is fact
That Wolf[5] found out first? It's unpleasant work
Their chop and change, unsettling one's belief: 65
All the same, while we live, we learn, that's sure."
So, I bent brow o'er *Prolegomena.*
And, after Wolf, a dozen of his like
Proved there was never any Troy at all,
Neither Besiegers nor Besieged,—nay, worse,—   70
No actual Homer, no authentic text,
No warrant for the fiction I, as fact,
Had treasured in my heart and soul so long—
Ay, mark you! and as fact held still, still hold,
Spite of new knowledge, in my heart of hearts   75
And soul of souls, fact's essence freed and fixed
From accidental fancy's guardian sheath.
Assuredly thenceforward—thank my stars!—
However it got there, deprive who could—
Wring from the shrine my precious tenantry,   80
Helen, Ulysses, Hector and his Spouse,[6]
Achilles and his Friend?—though Wolf—ah, Wolf!
Why must he needs come doubting, spoil a dream?

But then "No dream's worth waking"[7]—Browning says:
And here's the reason why I tell thus much.   85
I, now mature man, you anticipate,
May blame my Father justifiably
For letting me dream out my nonage[8] thus,
And only by such slow and sure degrees
Permitting me to sift the grain from chaff,   90
Get truth and falsehood known and named as such.
Why did he ever let me dream at all,
Not bid me taste the story in its strength?
Suppose my childhood was scarce qualified
To rightly understand mythology,   95
Silence at least was in his power to keep:
I might have—somehow—correspondingly—
Well, who knows by what method, gained my gains,
Been taught, by forthrights not meanderings,

---

4. Lost satirical poem, authorship unknown but attributed to Homer by Aristotle and Zeno.
5. Friedrich August Wolf (1759–1824), a founder of modern classical philology and author of
   the famous *Prolegomena in Homerum* (1795), which theorized that the *Iliad* and *Odyssey*
   were not by one author but were the blending of several poems handed down by oral recita-
   tion and unified by subsequent treatment. The analogy of modern Homeric scholarship to
   the work of the biblical critics is clear: as Wolf was to Homer, so were Strauss and Renan to
   the Gospels. See "Christmas-Eve," XV (1850) and "A Death in the Desert" (1864) for the
   poet's reply to the so-called "Higher Criticism."
6. Andromache. Achilles' friend is Patroclus (line 82).
7. The controlling idea of *Asolando*, which repeatedly states the poet's preference for fact over
   fancy, reality over "dreaming's vapour-wreath" ("Dubiety," line 12).
8. Youth.

My aim should be to loathe, like Peleus' son,[9]   100
A lie as Hell's Gate, love my wedded wife,
Like Hector, and so on with all the rest.
Could not I have excogitated this
Without believing such men really were?
That is—he might have put into my hand   105
The "Ethics"?[1] In translation, if you please,
Exact, no pretty lying that improves,
To suit the modern taste: no more, no less—
The "Ethics": 't is a treatise I find hard
To read aright now that my hair is grey,   110
And I can manage the original.
At five years old—how ill had fared its leaves!
Now, growing double o'er the Stagirite,[2]
At least I soil no page with bread and milk,
Nor crumple, dogsear and deface—boys' way.   115

Epilogue[1]

At the midnight in the silence of the sleep-time,
    When you set your fancies free,
Will they pass to where—by death, fools think, imprisoned—
Low he lies who once so loved you, whom you loved so,
        —Pity me?   5

Oh to love so, be so loved, yet so mistaken![2]
    What had I on earth to do
With the slothful, with the mawkish, the unmanly?
Like the aimless, helpless, hopeless, did I drivel
        —Being—who?   10

One who never turned his back but marched breast forward,
    Never doubted clouds would break,
Never dreamed, though right were worsted, wrong would triumph,
Held we fall to rise, are baffled to fight better,
        Sleep to wake.   15

No, at noonday in the bustle of man's work-time
    Greet the unseen with a cheer!
Bid him forward, breast and back as either should be,
"Strive and thrive!" cry "Speed—fight on, fare ever
        There as here!"   20

---

9. Achilles, whose resentment at Agamemnon's breach of faith is the theme of the *Iliad* (see Book I).
1. The *Nichomachean Ethics*, treatise on morals by Aristotle.
2. Aristotle (384–322 B.C.E.), born at Stagira, a Greek colonial town on the Aegean.
1. Of the poem Browning is reported to have said, "It almost looks like bragging to say this, and as if I ought to cancel it; but it's the simple truth; and as it's true, it shall stand." The "Epilogue" has traditionally concluded all editions of Browning's poetry. Cf. Tennyson's "Crossing the Bar."
2. You (the person addressed in line 2) are mistaken in pitying me.

Prose

FROM "INTRODUCTORY ESSAY" TO THE *LETTERS OF PERCY BYSSHE SHELLEY* (1852)

Browning published very little formal prose. His only signed critical work of importance is the "Introductory Essay" to the *Letters of Percy Bysshe Shelley* (1852), now called the *Essay on Shelley*. After touching briefly upon its ostensible subject, literary biography, the essay falls into two sections: in the first Browning advances the theory that successive literary periods are dominated by "objective" and "subjective" poetry in alternation; in the second he attempts to fix Shelley's unique place in this scheme of literary history and to vindicate the character of the poet, whom Browning then regarded as a maligned and neglected genius. After his momentous discovery of Shelley's poetry in 1826, Browning had undergone an intellectual conversion to Shelleyan principles, from which he was largely "unconverted" by 1833 (see notes to *Pauline*). Yet for two decades more Shelley was to remain a star of the first magnitude in Browning's firmament (see "Memorabilia" [1855]). When in 1851 he strove to formulate the reasons for his longstanding admiration of Shelley the poet, he as yet knew little (save fragmentary accounts) of Shelley the man. But disenchantment was not long in coming: as early as 1856 Browning was forcibly made aware of Shelley's desertion of his first wife, Harriet; thereafter his faith in Shelley's character remained badly shaken. Because the chasm between the poet and the man had widened unacceptably for Browning, he was to refuse in 1885 the presidency of the newly founded Shelley Society.

The *Essay on Shelley* was written in late 1851 at the request of Browning's friend and erstwhile publisher, Edward Moxon, who needed a preface to his newly acquired collection of twenty-five unpublished Shelley letters. The volume was printed in early 1852 but was suppressed forthwith, owing to the timely discovery that at least one of the letters was spurious. The essay was, however, reprinted in Browning's lifetime by both the Browning and the Shelley Societies. The extract here is from the opening paragraphs; the text is that of H. F. B. Brett-Smith (1921, 1923), a transcription of the 1852 Moxon volume in the Bodleian Library, Oxford.

An opportunity having presented itself for the acquisition of a series of unedited letters by Shelley, all more or less directly supplementary to and illustrative of the collection already published by Mr. Moxon,[1] that gentleman has decided on securing them. They will prove an acceptable addition to a body of correspondence, the value of which to-

---

1. *Essays, Letters from Abroad, Translations and Fragments*, ed. Mary W. Shelley, 2 vols. (1840, 1852). The Brownings owned a copy of the 1840 edition.

wards a right understanding of its author's purpose and work, may be said to exceed that of any similar contribution exhibiting the worldly relations of a poet whose genius has operated by a different law.

Doubtless we accept gladly the biography of an objective[2] poet, as the phrase now goes; one whose endeavour has been to reproduce things external (whether the phenomena of the scenic universe, or the manifested action of the human heart and brain) with an immediate reference in every case, to the common eye and apprehension of his fellow men, assumed capable of receiving and profiting by this reproduction. It has been obtained through the poet's double faculty of seeing external objects more clearly, widely, and deeply, than is possible to the average mind, at the same time that he is so acquainted and in sympathy with its narrower comprehension as to be careful to supply it with no other materials than it can combine into an intelligible whole. The auditory of such a poet will include, not only the intelligences which, save for such assistance, would have missed the deeper meaning and enjoyment of the original objects, but also the spirits of a like endowment with his own, who, by means of his abstract, can forthwith pass to the reality it was made from, and either corroborate their impressions of things known already, or supply themselves with new from whatever shows in the inexhaustible variety of existence may have hitherto escaped their knowledge. Such a poet is properly the ποιητης, the fashioner;[3] and the thing fashioned, his poetry, will of necessity be substantive, projected from himself and distinct. We are ignorant what the inventor of "Othello" conceived of that fact as he beheld it in completeness, how he accounted for it, under what known law he registered its nature, or to what unknown law he traced its coincidence. We learn only what he intended we should learn by that particular exercise of his power,—the fact itself,—which, with its infinite significances, each of us receives for the first time as a creation, and is hereafter left to deal with, as, in proportion to his own intelligence, he best may. We are ignorant, and would fain be otherwise.

Doubtless, with respect to such a poet, we covet his biography. We desire to look back upon the process of gathering together in a lifetime, the materials of the work we behold entire; of elaborating, perhaps under difficulty and with hindrance, all that is familiar to our admiration in the apparent facility of success. And the inner impulse of this effort and operation, what induced it? Did a soul's delight in its own extended sphere of vision set it, for the gratification of an insuppressible power, on labour, as other men are set on rest? Or did a sense of duty or of love lead it to communicate its own sensations to mankind? Did an irresistible sympathy with men compel it to bring down and suit its own provision of knowledge and beauty to their narrow scope? Did the personality of such an one stand like an open watch-tower in the midst of the territory it is erected to gaze on, and

2. The distinction between "objective" and "subjective" writing was appropriated from German thought in the 1820s by Coleridge and other English Romantic critics. Browning's use of the terms is typical.
3. Greek poiētēs, from poiein, "to make."

were the storms and calms, the stars and meteors, its watchman was wont to report of, the habitual variegation of his every-day life, as they glanced across its open roof or lay reflected on its four-square parapet? Or did some sunken and darkened chamber of imagery witness, in the artificial illumination of every storied compartment we are permitted to contemplate, how rare and precious were the outlooks through here and there an embrasure upon a world beyond, and how blankly would have pressed on the artificer the boundary of his daily life, except for the amorous diligence with which he had rendered permanent by art whatever came to diversify the gloom? Still, fraught with instruction and interest as such details undoubtedly are, we can, if needs be, dispense with them. The man passes, the work remains. The work speaks for itself, as we say: and the biography of the worker is no more necessary to an understanding or enjoyment of it, than is a model or anatomy of some tropical tree, to the right tasting of the fruit we are familiar with on the market-stall,—or a geologist's map and stratification, to the prompt recognition of the hill-top, our land-mark of every day.

We turn with stronger needs to the genius of an opposite tendency— the subjective poet of modern classification. He, gifted like the objective poet with the fuller perception of nature and man, is impelled to embody the thing he perceives, not so much with reference to the many below as to the One above him, the supreme Intelligence which apprehends all things in their absolute truth,—an ultimate view ever aspired to, if but partially attained, by the poet's own soul. Not what man sees, but what God sees—the *Ideas* of Plato,[4] seeds of creation lying burningly on the Divine Hand—it is toward these that he struggles. Not with the combination of humanity in action, but with the primal elements of humanity he has to do; and he digs where he stands,—preferring to seek them in his own soul as the nearest reflex of that absolute Mind, according to the intuitions of which he desires to perceive and speak. Such a poet does not deal habitually with the picturesque groupings and tempestuous tossings of the forest-trees, but with their roots and fibres naked to the chalk and stone. He does not paint pictures and hang them on the walls, but rather carries them on the retina of his own eyes: we must look deep into his human eyes, to see those pictures on them. He is rather a seer, accordingly, than a fashioner, and what he produces will be less a work than an effluence. That effluence cannot be easily considered in abstraction from his personality,—being indeed the very radiance and aroma of his personality, projected from it but not separated. Therefore, in our approach to the poetry, we necessarily approach the personality of the poet; in apprehending it we apprehend him, and certainly we cannot love it without loving him. Both for love's and for understanding's sake we desire to know him, and as readers of his poetry must be readers of his biography also.

4. The Platonic Idea is "a supposed eternally existing pattern or archetype of any class of things, of which the individual things in that class are imperfect copies, and from which they derive their existence" (*OED*).

I shall observe, in passing, that it seems not so much from any essential distinction in the faculty of the two poets or in the nature of the objects contemplated by either, as in the more immediate adaptability of these objects to the distinct purpose of each, that the objective poet, in his appeal to the aggregate human mind, chooses to deal with the doings of men, (the result of which dealing, in its pure form, when even description, as suggesting a describer, is dispensed with, is what we call dramatic poetry), while the subjective poet, whose study has been himself, appealing through himself to the absolute Divine mind, prefers to dwell upon those external scenic appearances which strike out most abundantly and uninterruptedly his inner light and power, selects that silence of the earth and sea in which he can best hear the beating of his individual heart, and leaves the noisy, complex, yet imperfect exhibitions of nature in the manifold experience of man around him, which serve only to distract and suppress the working of his brain. These opposite tendencies of genius will be more readily descried in their artistic effect than in their moral spring and cause. Pushed to an extreme and manifested as a deformity, they will be seen plainest of all in the fault of either artist, when subsidiarily to the human interest of his work his occasional illustrations from scenic nature are introduced as in the earlier works of the originative painters[5]—men and women filling the foreground with consummate mastery, while mountain, grove and rivulet show like an anticipatory revenge on that succeeding race of landscape-painters[6] whose "figures" disturb the perfection of their earth and sky. It would be idle to inquire, of these two kinds of poetic faculty in operation, which is the higher or even rarer endowment. If the subjective might seem to be the ultimate requirement of every age, the objective, in the strictest state, must still retain its original value. For it is with this world, as starting point and basis alike, that we shall always have to concern ourselves: the world is not to be learned and thrown aside, but reverted to and relearned.[7] The spiritual comprehension may be infinitely subtilised, but the raw material it operates upon, must remain. There may be no end of the poets who communicate to us what they see in an object with reference to their own individuality; what it was before they saw it, in reference to the aggregate human mind, will be as desirable to know as ever. Nor is there any reason why these two modes of poetic faculty may not issue hereafter from the same poet in successive perfect works, examples of which, according to what are now considered the exigences of art, we have hitherto possessed in distinct individuals only.[8] A mere running in of the one faculty upon the other, is, of course, the ordinary circumstance. Far more rarely it

5. Browning may have in mind such Italian Renaissance painters as Ghirlandaio, Botticelli, and Leonardo da Vinci, in whose work the natural setting is often a distant backdrop.
6. Perhaps the great English landscape painters John Constable (1776–1837) and J. M. W. Turner (1775–1851), who often placed their human figures in the middle distance or background and made them appear diminutive amid the grandeur of their surroundings.
7. This sentence fairly states the theme of "Fra Lippo Lippi"; see especially lines 282–315.
8. At this point it becomes clear that Browning's classification of poets is tripartite, the third class emerging from the fusion of the subjective and the objective elements.

happens that either is found so decidedly prominent and superior, as to be pronounced comparatively pure: while of the perfect shield, with the gold and the silver side set up for all comers to challenge,[9] there has yet been no instance. Either faculty in its eminent state is doubtless conceded by Providence as a best gift to men, according to their especial want. There is a time when the general eye has, so to speak, absorbed its fill of the phenomena around it, whether spiritual or material, and desires rather to learn the exacter significance of what it possesses, than to receive any augmentation of what is possessed. Then is the opportunity for the poet of loftier vision, to lift his fellows, with their half-apprehensions, up to his own sphere, by intensifying the import of details and rounding the universal meaning. The influence of such an achievement will not soon die out. A tribe of successors (Homerides)[1] working more or less in the same spirit, dwell on his discoveries and reinforce his doctrine; till, at unawares, the world is found to be subsisting wholly on the shadow of a reality, on sentiments diluted from passions, on the tradition of a fact, the convention of a moral, the straw of last year's harvest. Then is the imperative call for the appearance of another sort of poet,[2] who shall at once replace this intellectual rumination of food swallowed long ago, by a supply of the fresh and living swathe; getting at new substance by breaking up the assumed wholes into parts of independent and unclassed value, careless of the unknown laws for recombining them (it will be the business of yet another poet[3] to suggest those hereafter), prodigal of objects for men's outer and not inner sight, shaping for their uses a new and different creation from the last, which it displaces by the right of life over death,—to endure until, in the inevitable process, its very sufficiency to itself shall require, at length, an exposition of its affinity to something higher,—when the positive yet conflicting facts shall again precipitate themselves under a harmonising law, and one more degree will be apparent for a poet to climb in that mighty ladder, of which, however cloud-involved and undefined may glimmer the topmost step, the world dares no longer doubt that its gradations ascend.[4]

Such being the two kinds of artists, it is naturally, as I have shown, with the biography of the subjective poet that we have the deeper concern. Apart from his recorded life altogether, we might fail to determine with satisfactory precision to what class his productions belong, and what amount of praise is assignable to the producer. Certainly, in the face of any conspicuous achievement of genius, philosophy, no less than sympathetic instinct, warrants our belief in a great moral

9. According to a medieval allegory, two knights came from opposite directions upon a shield suspended from a tree. One side was gold, the other silver. The knights hotly disputed its metallic composition, their debate finally flaring into combat. Luckily a third knight rode up, settling the matter by informing the combatants that the shield was made of both metals.
1. The Homerides, or "clan of Homer," were a guild of professional poets and reciters living at ancient Chios in Asia Minor. They were dedicated to preserving the Homeric tradition.
2. The objective poet.
3. The subjective poet.
4. Browning's theory of literary history, while obviously cyclic, is also "progressivist" or transcendental, as the metaphor of the "mighty ladder" suggests. It is in keeping with that branch of Victorian evolutionary thought (Hegelian at base) which optimistically posited the continual upward progress of culture.

purpose having mainly inspired even where it does not visibly look out of the same. Greatness in a work suggests an adequate instrumentality; and none of the lower incitements, however they may avail to initiate or even effect many considerable displays of power, simulating the nobler inspiration to which they are mistakenly referred, have been found able, under the ordinary conditions of humanity, to task themselves to the end of so exacting a performance as a poet's complete work. As soon will the galvanism[5] that provokes to violent action the muscles of a corpse, induce it to cross the chamber steadily: sooner. The love of displaying power for the display's sake, the love of riches, of distinction, of notoriety,—the desire of a triumph over rivals, and the vanity in the applause of friends,—each and all of such whetted appetites grow intenser by exercise and increasingly sagacious as to the best and readiest means of self-appeasement,—while for any of their ends, whether the money or the pointed finger of the crowd, or the flattery and hate to heart's content, there are cheaper prices to pay, they will all find soon enough, than the bestowment of a life upon a labour, hard, slow, and not sure. Also, assuming the proper moral aim to have produced a work, there are many and various states of an aim: it may be more intense than clear-sighted, or too easily satisfied with a lower field of activity than a steadier aspiration would reach. All the bad poetry in the world (accounted poetry, that is, by its affinities) will be found to result from some one of the infinite degrees of discrepancy between the attributes of the poet's soul, occasioning a want of correspondency between his work and the verities of nature,—issuing in poetry, false under whatever form, which shows a thing not as it is to mankind generally, nor as it is to the particular describer, but as it is supposed to be for some unreal neutral mood, midway between both and of value to neither, and living its brief minute simply through the indolence of whoever accepts it or his incapacity to denounce a cheat. Although of such depths of failure there can be no question here, we must in every case betake ourselves to the review of a poet's life ere we determine some of the nicer questions concerning his poetry,—more especially if the performance we seek to estimate aright, has been obstructed and cut short of completion by circumstances,—a disastrous youth or a premature death. We may learn from the biography whether his spirit invariably saw and spoke from the last height to which it had attained. An absolute vision is not for this world, but we are permitted a continual approximation to it, every degree of which in the individual, provided it exceed the attainment of the masses, must procure him a clear advantage. Did the poet ever attain to a higher platform than where he rested and exhibited a result? Did he know more than he spoke of?

I concede however, in respect to the subject of our study as well as some few other illustrious examples, that the unmistakable quality of the verse would be evidence enough, under usual circumstances, not only of the kind and degree of the intellectual but of the moral consti-

5. Physiological stimulation by application of electricity.

tution of Shelley: the whole personality of the poet shining forward from the poems, without much need of going further to seek it. The "Remains"—produced within a period of ten years,[6] and at a season of life when other men of at all comparable genius have hardly done more than prepare the eye for future sight and the tongue for speech—present us with the complete enginery of a poet, as signal in the excellence of its several adaptitudes as transcendent in the combination of effects,—examples, in fact, of the whole poet's function of beholding with an understanding keenness the universe, nature and man, in their actual state of perfection in imperfection,[7]—of the whole poet's virtue of being untempted by the manifold partial developments of beauty and good on every side, into leaving them the ultimates he found them,—induced by the facility of the gratification of his own sense of those qualities, or by the pleasure of acquiescence in the short-comings of his predecessors in art, and the pain of disturbing their conventionalisms,—the whole poet's virtue, I repeat, of looking higher than any manifestation yet made of both beauty and good, in order to suggest from the utmost actual realisation of the one a corresponding capability in the other, and out of the calm, purity and energy of nature, to reconstitute and store up for the forthcoming stage of man's being, a gift in repayment of that former gift, in which man's own thought and passion had been lavished by the poet on the else-incompleted magnificence of the sunrise, the else-uninterpreted mystery of the lake,—so drawing out, lifting up, and assimilating this ideal of a future man, thus descried as possible, to the present reality of the poet's soul already arrived at the higher state of development, and still aspirant to elevate and extend itself in conformity with its still-improving perceptions of, no longer the eventual Human, but the actual Divine. In conjunction with which noble and rare powers, came the subordinate power of delivering these attained results to the world in an embodiment of verse more closely answering to and indicative of the process of the informing spirit, (failing as it occasionally does, in art, only to succeed in highest art),—with a diction more adequate to the task in its natural and acquired richness, its material colour and spiritual transparency,—the whole being moved by and suffused with a music at once of the soul and the sense, expressive both of an external might of sincere passion and an internal fitness and consonancy,—than can be attributed to any other writer whose record is among us. Such was the spheric poetical faculty of Shelley, as its own self-sufficing central light, radiating equally through immaturity and accomplishment, through many fragments and occasional completion, reveals it to a competent judgment.

* * *

1851

---

6. From 1813 (*Queen Mab*) to 1822 (*The Triumph of Life*, unfinished). Shelley died by drowning in 1822.
7. This paradox is developed in "Andrea del Sarto" (1855).

CRITICISM

Victorian Views

JOHN FORSTER

Evidences of a New Genius for Dramatic Poetry†

* * *

This is the simple and unaffected title of a small volume[1] which was published some half-dozen months ago, and which opens a deeper vein of thought, of feeling, and of passion, than any poet has attempted for years. Without the slightest hesitation we name Mr. Robert Browning at once with Shelley, Coleridge, Wordsworth. He has entitled himself to a place among the acknowledged poets of the age. This opinion will possibly startle many persons; but it is most sincere. It is no practice of ours to think nothing of an author because all the world have not pronounced in his favour, any more than we would care to offer him our sympathy and concern on the score of the world's indifference. A man of genius, we have already intimated, needs neither the one nor the other. He who is conscious of great powers can satisfy himself by their unwearied exercise alone. His day will come. He need never be afraid that truth and nature will wear out, or that Time will not eventually claim for its own all that is the handywork of Nature. Mr. Browning is a man of genius, he has in himself all the elements of a great poet, philosophical as well dramatic,—

> The youngest he
> That sits in shadow of Apollo's tree

—but he sits there, and with as much right to his place as the greatest of the men that are around him have to theirs. For the reception that his book has met with he was doubtless already well prepared,—as well for the wondering ignorance that has scouted it, as for the condescending patronage which has sought to bring it forward, as one brings forward a bashful child to make a doubtful display of its wit and learning. "We hope the best; put a good face on the matter; but are sadly afraid the thing cannot answer." We tell Mr. Browning, on the other hand, what we do not think *he* needs to be told, that the thing WILL answer. He has written a book that will live—he has scattered the seeds of much thought among his countrymen—he has communi-

† From his unsigned article in *The New Monthly Magazine and Literary Journal*, 46 (March 1836): 289–308.

1. *Paracelsus* (1835), which Forster had already favorably reviewed in *The Examiner* for Sept. 6, 1835 (pp. 563–65). Forster and W. J. Fox, editor of *The Monthly Repository*, were the unknown Browning's earliest champions. [*Editor.*]

cated an impulse and increased activity to reason and inquiry, as well as a pure and high delight to every cultivated mind;—and this is the little and scantily-noticed volume of *Paracelsus*!

Before going farther, it may be as well to come to some understanding with the reader respecting the course of this article. In sitting down to write, we confess we had intended to limit ourselves to the matters strictly embraced in our title, and we took up Mr. Browning's volume with the intention of waiving many new and striking points of philosophical suggestion contained in it, for the purpose of considering more emphatically the evidences it abundantly presents of a new genius for dramatic poetry. We find, however, on examination, that we cannot restrict ourselves to so narrow a view of the poem. Its subject-matter and treatment are both so startlingly original, and both so likely to be altogether misunderstood; it embraces in its development so many of the highest questions, and glances with such a masterly perception at some of the deepest problems, of man's existence; that we feel, while to touch upon these various topics will not interfere with the object we first proposed, it is only in this way that a proper and just appreciation of the singular power and beauty, even of the dramatic portions of this poem, can be conveyed to the reader. We venture to promise him, in accompanying us through our criticism, that if, in its course, we do not break even a wholly new ground of philosophical inquiry into character, we shall at least suggest to him some valuable and very interesting trains of thought. It is the greatest glory of such labours as those of Mr. Browning, that they open up, on every side of us in the actual world, new sources of understanding and sympathy. * * *

* * * Passion is invariably displayed, and never merely analysed. Even at those moments when we seem most of all to be listening to its results alone, we are made most vividly sensible of the presence of the very agents by which the results have been determined. Mr. Browning has the power of a great dramatic poet; we never think of Mr. Browning while we read his poem; we are not identified with him, but with the persons into whom he has flung his genius. The objections to a dialogue of the French school do not apply. We get beyond conjecture and reasoning, beyond a general impression of the situation of the speakers, beyond general reflections on their passions, and hints as to their rise, continuance, and fall. We are upon the scene ourselves,— we hear, feel, and see,—we are face to face with the actors,—we are a party to the tears that are shed, to the feelings and passions that are undergone, to the "flushed cheek and intensely sparkling eye." The same unrelaxing activity of thought and of emotion, by which the results of the poem are meant to be produced, is made to affect the reader in its progress; and he is as certain of the immediate presence of all that is going on, as in life he would be certain of any thing that made him laugh or weep. *In the agitation of the feelings, sight is given to the imagination.* This is an essential dramatic test, in which Mr. Browning is never found wanting.

* * *

THOMAS CARLYLE

[Letter to Browning]†

My dear Sir—Many months ago you were kind enough to send me your *Sordello*; and now this day I have been looking into your *Pippa Passes*, for which also I am your debtor. If I have made no answer hitherto, it was surely not for want of interest in you, for want of estimation of you: both Pieces have given rise to many reflexions in me, not without friendly hopes and anxieties in due measure. Alas, it is so seldom that any word one can speak is not worse than a word still unspoken;—seldom that one man, by his speaking or his silence, can, in great vital interests, help another at all!—

Unless I very greatly mistake, judging from these two works, you seem to possess a rare spiritual gift, poetical, pictorial, intellectual, by whatever name we may prefer calling it; to unfold which into articulate clearness is naturally the problem of all problems for you. This noble endowment, it seems to me farther, you are *not* at present on the best way for unfolding;—and if the world had loudly called itself content with these two Poems, my surmise is, the world could have rendered you no fataller disservice than that same! Believe me I speak with sincerity; and if I had not loved you well, I would not haver spoken at all.

A long battle, I could guess, lies before you, full of toil and pain, and all sorts of real *fighting*: a man attains to nothing here below without that. Is it not verily the highest prize you fight for? Fight on; that is to say, follow truly, with steadfast singleness of purpose, with valiant humbleness and openness of heart, what best light *you* can attain to; following truly so, better and ever better light will rise on you. The light we ourselves gain, by our very errors if not otherwise, is the only precious light. Victory, what I call victory, if well fought for, is sure to you.

If your own choice happened to point that way, I for one should hail it as a good omen that your next work were written in prose! Not that I deny you poetic faculty; far, very far from that. But unless poetic faculty mean a higher-power of common understanding, I know not what it means. One must first make a *true* intellectual representation of a thing, before any poetic interest that is true will supervene. All *cartoons* are geometrical withal; and cannot be made till we have fully learnt to make mere *diagrams* well. It is this that I mean by prose;—which hint of mine, most probably inapplicable at present, may perhaps at some future day come usefully to mind.

But enough of this: why have I written all this? Because I esteem yours no common case; and think such a man is not to be treated in the common way.

---

† From his letter dated June 21, 1841; in *New Letters of Thomas Carlyle*, ed. Alexander Carlyle (London: John Lane, 1904), I. 233–34.

And so persist in God's name, as you best see and can; and understand always that my true prayer for you is, Good Speed in the name of God!

*   *   *

GEORGE ELIOT

[Review of *Men and Women*] (1855)†

We never read Heinsius—a great admission for a reviewer—but we learn from M. Arago that the formidably erudite writer pronounces Aristotle's works to be characterized by a *majestic obscurity which repels the ignorant*.[1] We borrow these words to indicate what is likely to be the first impression of a reader who, without any previous familiarity with Browning, glances through his two new volumes of poems. The less acute he is, the more easily will he arrive at the undeniable criticism, that these poems have a 'majestic obscurity,' which repels not only the ignorant but the idle. To read poems is often a substitute for thought: fine-sounding conventional phrases and the sing-song of verse demand no co-operation in the reader; they glide over his mind with the agreeable unmeaningness of 'the compliments of the season,' or a speaker's exordium on 'feelings too deep for expression.' But let him expect no such drowsy passivity in reading Browning. Here he will find no conventionality, no melodious commonplace, but freshness, originality, sometimes eccentricity of expression; no didactic laying-out of a subject, but dramatic indication, which requires the reader to trace by his own mental activity the underground stream of thought that jets out in elliptical and pithy verse. To read Browning he must exert himself, but he will exert himself to some purpose. If he finds the meaning difficult of access, it is always worth his effort—if he has to dive deep, 'he rises with his pearl.' Indeed, in Browning's best poems he makes us feel that what we took for obscurity in him was superficiality in ourselves. We are far from meaning that all his obscurity is like the obscurity of the stars, dependent simply on the feebleness of men's vision. On the contrary, our admiration for his genius only makes us feel the more acutely that its inspirations are too often straitened by the garb of whimsical mannerism with which he clothes them. This mannerism is even irritating sometimes, and should at least be kept under restraint in *printed* poems, where the writer is not merely indulging his own vein, but is avowedly appealing to the mind of his reader.

Turning from the ordinary literature of the day to such a writer as Browning, is like turning from Flotow's music,[2] made up of well-

---

† From her unsigned review in *The Westminster Review* 65 (January 1856): 290–96. Footnotes are by the editors.
1. Daniel Heinsius (or Heins, 1580–1655), classical scholar of the Dutch Renaissance; Étienne Vincent Arago (1802–92), French dramatist.
2. Friedrich von Flotow (1812–83), German operatic composer.

pieced shreds and patches, to the distinct individuality of Chopin's Studies or Schubert's Songs. Here, at least, is a man who has something of his own to tell us, and who can tell it impressively, if not with faultless art. There is nothing sickly or dreamy in him: he has a clear eye, a vigorous grasp, and courage to utter what he sees and handles. His robust energy is informed by a subtle, penetrating spirit, and this blending of opposite qualities gives his mind a rough piquancy that reminds one of a russet apple. His keen glance pierces into all the secrets of human character, but, being as thoroughly alive to the outward as to the inward, he reveals those secrets, not by a process of dissection, but by dramatic painting. We fancy his own description of a poet applies to himself:

> He stood and watched the cobbler at his trade,
> The man who slices lemons into drink,
> The coffee-roaster's brazier, and the boys
> That volunteer to help him turn its winch.
> He glanced o'er books on stalls with half an eye,
> And fly-leaf ballads on the vendor's string.
> And broad-edge bold-print posters by the wall.
> *He took such cognizance of men and things,*
> *If any beat a horse, you felt he saw;*
> *If any cursed a woman, he took note;*
> *Yet stared at nobody,—they stared at him,*
> *And found, less to their pleasure than surprise,*
> *He seemed to know them and expect as much.*[3]

Browning has no soothing strains, no chants, no lullabys; he rarely gives voice to our melancholy, still less to our gaiety; he sets our thoughts at work rather than our emotions. But though eminently a thinker, he is as far as possible from prosaic; his mode of presentation is always concrete, artistic, and, where it is most felicitous, dramatic. Take, for example, 'Fra Lippo Lippi,' a poem at once original and perfect in its kind. The artist-monk, Fra Lippo, is supposed to be detected by the night-watch roaming the streets of Florence, and while sharing the wine with which he makes amends to the Dogberrys[4] for the roughness of his tongue, he pours forth the story of his life and his art with the racy conversational vigour of a brawny genius under the influence of the Care-dispeller.[5]

* * *

Extracts cannot do justice to the fine dramatic touches by which Fra Lippo is made present to us, while he throws out this instinctive Art-criticism. And extracts from 'Bishop Blougram's Apology,' an equally remarkable poem of what we may call the dramatic-psychological kind, would be still more ineffective. 'Sylvester Blougram, styled *in partibus Episcopus*,' is talking

3. "How It Strikes a Contemporary," lines 23–35; Eliot's emphasis.
4. Dogberry is a constable in Shakespeare's *Much Ado about Nothing*.
5. Eliot's extract of lines 81–306 of "Fra Lippo Lippi" is omitted.

> Over the glass's edge when dinner's done,
> And body gets its sop and holds its noise
> And leaves soul free a little,[6]

with 'Gigadibs the literary man,' to whom he is bent on proving by the most exasperatingly ingenious sophistry, that the theory of life on which he grounds his choice of being a bishop, though a doubting one is wiser in the moderation of its ideal, with the certainty of attainment, than the Gigadibs theory, which aspires after the highest and attains nothing. The way in which Blougram's motives are dug up from below the roots, and laid bare to the very last fibre, not by a process of hostile exposure, not by invective or sarcasm, but by making himself exhibit them with a self-complacent sense of supreme acuteness, and even with a crushing force of worldly common sense, has the effect of masterly satire. But the poem is too strictly consecutive for any fragments of it to be a fair specimen. Belonging to the same order of subtle yet vigorous writing are the 'Epistle of Karshish, the Arab physician,' 'Cleon,' and 'How it Strikes a Contemporary.' 'In a Balcony,' is so fine, that we regret it is not a complete drama instead of being merely the suggestion of a drama. One passage especially tempts us to extract.

> All women love great men
> If young or old—it is in all the tales—
> Young beauties love old poets who can love—
> Why should not he the poems in my soul,
> The love, the passionate faith, the sacrifice,
> The constancy? I throw them at his feet.
> Who cares to see the fountain's very shape
> And whether it be a Triton's or a Nymph's
> That pours the foam, makes rainbows all around?
> You could not praise indeed the empty conch;
> *But I'll pour floods of love and hide myself.*[7]

These lines are less rugged than is usual with Browning's blank verse; but generally, the greatest deficiency we feel in his poetry is its want of music. The worst poems in his new volumes are, in our opinion, his lyrical efforts; for in these, where he engrosses us less by his thought, we are more sensible of his obscurity and his want of melody. His lyrics, instead of tripping along with easy grace, or rolling with a torrent-like grandeur, seem to be struggling painfully under a burthen too heavy for them; and many of them have the disagreeable puzzling effect of a charade, rather than the touching or animating influence of song. We have said that he is never prosaic; and it is remarkable that in his blank verse, though it is often colloquial, we are never shocked by the sense of a sudden lapse into prose. Wordsworth is, on the whole, a far more musical poet than Browning, yet we remember no line in Browning so prosaic as many of Wordsworth's, which in some of his finest poems have the effect of bricks built into a rock. But we

6. Lines 18–20.
7. Lines 509–19; Eliot's emphasis.

must also say that though Browning never flounders helplessly on the plain, he rarely soars above a certain table-land—a footing between the level of prose and the topmost heights of poetry. He does not take possession of our souls and set them aglow, as the greatest poets—the greatest artists do. We admire his power, we are not subdued by it. Language with him does not seem spontaneously to link itself into song, as sounds link themselves into melody in the mind of the creative musician; he rather seems by his commanding powers to compel language into verse. He has *chosen* verse as his medium; but of our greatest poets we feel that they had no choice: Verse chose them. Still we are grateful that Browning chose this medium: we would rather have 'Fra Lippo Lippi' than an essay on Realism in Art; we would rather have 'The Statue and the Bust' than a three-volumed novel with the same moral; we would rather have 'Holy-Cross Day' than 'Strictures on the Society for the Emancipation of the Jews.'

* * *

WILLIAM MORRIS

[Browning's Alleged Carelessness]†

* * *

Yet a few words, and I have done. For, as I wrote this, many times angry indignant words came to my lips, which stopped my writing till I could be quieter. For I suppose, reader, that you see whereabouts among the poets I place Robert Browning; high among the poets of all time, and I scarce know whether first, or second, in our own: and, it is a bitter thing to me to see the way in which he has been received by almost everybody; many having formed a certain theory of their own about him, from reading, I suppose, some of the least finished poems among the "Dramatic Lyrics," make all the facts bend to this theory, after the fashion of theory-mongers: they think him, or say they think him, a careless man, writing down anyhow anything that comes into his head. Oh truly! "The Statue and the Bust" shows this! or the soft solemn flow of that poem, "By the Fireside!" "Paracelsus!"—that, with its wonderful rhythm, its tender sadness, its noble thoughts, must have been very easy to write, surely!

Then they say, too, that Browning is so obscure as not to be understood by any one. Now, I know well enough what they mean by "obscure," and I know also that they use the word wrongly; meaning difficult to understand fully at first reading, or, say at second reading, even: yet, taken so, in what a cloud of obscurity would "Hamlet" be! Do they think this to be the case? they daren't *say* so at all events, though I suspect some of them of thinking so.

Now I don't say that Robert Browning is not sometimes really ob-

---

† From his unsigned review of *Men and Women* in *Oxford and Cambridge Magazine* 1.3 (March 1856): 162–72. Footnotes are by the editors.

scure. He would be a perfect poet (of some calibre or other) if he were not; but I assert, fearlessly, that this obscurity is seldom so prominent as to make his poems hard to understand on this ground: while, as to that which they call obscurity, it results from depth of thought, and greatness of subject, on the poet's part, and on his readers' part, from their shallower brains and more bounded knowledge; nay, often I fear from mere wanton ignorance and idleness.

So I believe that, though this obscurity, so called, would indeed be very objectionable, if, as some seem to think, poetry is merely a department of "light literature"; yet, if it is rather one of the very grandest of all God's gifts to men, we must not think it hard if we have sometimes to exercise thought over a great poem, nay, even sometimes the utmost straining of all our thoughts, an agony almost equal to that of the poet who created the poem.

However, this accusation against Browning of carelessness, and consequent roughness in rhythm, and obscurity in language and thought, has come to be pretty generally believed; and people, as a rule, do not read him; this evil spreading so, that many, almost unconsciously, are kept from reading him, who, if they did read, would sympathize with him thoroughly.

But it was always so; it was so with Tennyson when he first published his poems; it was so last year with *Maud*; it is so with Ruskin; they petted him indeed at first; his wonderful eloquence having some effect even upon the critics; but, as his circle grew larger, and larger, embracing more and more truth, they more and more fell off from him; his firm faith in right they call arrogance and conceit now; his eager fighting with falsehood and wrong they call unfairness. I wonder what they will say to his new volume.[1]

The story of the Præ-Raphaelites[2]—we all know that, only here, thank Heaven! the public has chosen to judge for itself somewhat, though to this day their noblest pictures are the least popular.

Yes, I wonder what the critics would have said to "Hamlet Prince of Denmark," if it had been first published by Messrs. Chapman and Hall in the year 1855.

JOHN RUSKIN

[Browning and the Italian Renaissance]†

* * *

How far in these modern days, emptied of splendour, it may be necessary for great men having certain sympathies for those earlier ages, to act in this differently from all their predecessors; and how far they

1. *Modern Painters*, vols. III and IV (1856).
2. A group of contemporary artists (among whom were D. G. Rossetti and Morris himself), the Pre-Raphaelites praised Browning's work well before it was widely accepted.
† From *Modern Painters*, IV (1856); in *The Works of John Ruskin*, ed. E. T. Cook and Alexander Wedderburn (London: Allen, 1903–12), VI, 446–49. Footnotes are by the editors.

may succeed in the resuscitation of the past by habitually dwelling in all their thoughts among vanished generations, are questions, of all practical and present ones concerning art, the most difficult to decide; for already in poetry several of our truest men have set themselves to this task, and have indeed put more vitality into the shadows of the dead than most others can give the presences of the living. Thus Longfellow, in the *Golden Legend*, has entered more closely into the temper of the Monk, for good and for evil, than ever yet theological writer or historian, though they may have given their life's labour to the analysis; and, again, Robert Browning is unerring in every sentence he writes of the Middle Ages; always vital, right, and profound; so that in the matter of art, with which we have been specially concerned, there is hardly a principle connected with the mediæval temper, that he has not struck upon in those seemingly careless and too rugged rhymes of his. There is a curious instance, by the way, in a short poem referring to this very subject of tomb and image sculpture; and illustrating just one of those phases of local human character which, though belonging to Shakespere's own age, he never noticed, because it was specially Italian and un-English; connected also closely with the influence of mountains on the heart, and therefore with our immediate inquiries. I mean the kind of admiration with which a southern artist regarded the *stone* he worked in; and the pride which populace or priest took in the possession of precious mountain substance, worked into the pavements of their cathedrals, and the shafts of their tombs.

Observe, Shakespere, in the midst of architecture and tombs of wood, or freestone, or brass, naturally thinks of *gold* as the best enriching and ennobling substance for them;—in the midst also of the fever of the Renaissance he writes, as every one else did, in praise of precisely the most vicious master of that school—Giulio Romano;[1] but the modern poet, living much in Italy, and quit of the Renaissance influence, is able fully to enter into the Italian feeling, and to see the evil of the Renaissance tendency, not because he is greater than Shakespeare, but because he is in another element, and has *seen* other things.[2]

*   *   *

I know no other piece of modern English, prose or poetry, in which there is so much told, as in these lines, of the Renaissance spirit,—its worldliness, inconsistency, pride, hypocrisy, ignorance of itself, love of art, of luxury, and of good Latin. It is nearly all that I said of the central Renaissance in thirty pages of the *Stones of Venice* put into as many lines, Browning's being also the antecedent work. The worst of it is that this kind of concentrated writing needs so much *solution* before the reader can fairly get the good of it, that people's patience fails them, and they give the thing up as insoluble; though, truly, it ought to be to the current of common thought like Saladin's talisman,

1. Italian painter (ca. 1499–1546), praised in *The Winter's Tale*, V.ii.97.
2. Ruskin quotes forty-four lines of "The Bishop Orders His Tomb at St. Praxed's Church" (1845).

dipped in clear water, not soluble altogether, but making the element medicinal.

*   *   *

WALTER BAGEHOT

[Browning's Grotesque Art]†

*   *   *

There is . . . a third kind of art which differs from these [the pure and the ornate][1] on the point in which they most resemble one another. Ornate and pure art have this in common, that they paint the types of literature in as good perfection as they can. Ornate art, indeed, uses undue disguises and unreal enchancements; it does not confine itself to the best types; on the contrary it is its office to make the best of imperfect types and lame approximations; but ornate art, as much as pure art, catches its subject in the best light it can, takes the most developed aspect of it which it can find, and throws upon it the most congruous colours it can use. But grotesque art does just the contrary. It takes the type, so to say, *in difficulties*. It gives a representation of it in its minimum development, amid the circumstances least favourable to it, just while it is struggling with obstacles, just where it is encumbered with incongruities. It deals, to use the language of science, not with normal types but with abnormal specimens; to use the language of old philosophy, not with what nature is striving to be, but with what by some lapse she has happened to become.

This art works by contrast. It enables you to see, it makes you see, the perfect type by painting the opposite deviation. It shows you what ought to be by what ought not to be, when complete it reminds you of the perfect image, by showing you the distorted and imperfect image. Of this art we possess in the present generation one prolific master. Mr. Browning is an artist working by incongruity. Possibly hardly one of his most considerable efforts can be found which is not great because of its odd mixture. He puts together things which no one else would have put together, and produces on our minds a result which no one else would have produced, or tried to produce. His admirers may not like all we may have to say of him. But in our way we too are among his admirers. No one ever read him without seeing not only his great ability but his great *mind*. He not only possesses superficial useable talents, but the strong something, the inner secret something which uses them and controls them; he is great, not in mere accomplishments, but in himself. He has applied a hard strong intellect to real life; he has applied the same intellect to the problems of his age. He has striven to know what *is*: he has endeavoured not to be cheated

---

† From "Wordsworth, Tennyson, and Browning; or, Pure, Ornate, and Grotesque Art in English Poetry," *The National Review* 19 (Nov. 1864): 27–67. Footnotes are by the editors.
1. Exemplified by Wordsworth and Tennyson, respectively.

by counterfeits, to be infatuated with illusions. His heart is in what he says. He has battered his brain against his creed till he believes it. He has accomplishments too, the more effective because they are mixed. He is at once a student of mysticism, and a citizen of the world. He brings to the club sofa distinct visions of old creeds, intense images of strange thoughts: he takes to the bookish student tidings of wild Bohemia, and little traces of the *demi-monde*. He puts down what is good for the naughty and what is naughty for the good. Over women his easier writings exercise that imperious power which belongs to the writings of a great man of the world upon such matters. He knows women, and therefore they wish to know him. If we blame many of Browning's efforts, it is in the interest of art, and not from a wish to hurt or degrade him.

If we wanted to illustrate the nature of grotesque art by an exaggerated instance we should have selected a poem which the chance of late publication brings us in this new volume. Mr. Browning has undertaken to describe what may be called *mind in difficulties*—mind set to make out the universe under the worst and hardest circumstances. He takes "Caliban," not perhaps exactly Shakespeare's Caliban, but an analogous and worse creature; a strong thinking power, but a nasty creature—a gross animal, uncontrolled and unelevated by any feeling of religion or duty. The delineation of him will show that Mr. Browning does not wish to take undue advantage of his readers by a choice of nice subjects.[2]

*   *   *

It may seem perhaps to most readers that these lines are very difficult, and that they are unpleasant. And so they are. We quote them to illustrate, not the *success* of grotesque art, but the *nature* of grotesque art. It shows the end at which this species of art aims, and if it fails it is from over-boldness in the choice of a subject by the artist, or from the defects of its execution. A thinking faculty more in difficulties—a great type,—an inquisitive, searching intellect under more disagreeable conditions, with worse helps, more likely to find falsehood, less likely to find truth, can scarcely be imagined. Nor is the mere description of the thought at all bad: on the contrary, if we closely examine it, it is very clever. Hardly anyone could have amassed so many ideas at once nasty and suitable. But scarcely any readers—any casual readers—who are not of the sect of Mr. Browning's admirers will be able to examine it enough to appreciate it. From a defect, partly of subject, and partly of style, many of Mr. Browning's works make a demand upon the reader's zeal and sense of duty to which the nature of most readers is unequal. They have on the turf the convenient expression "staying power": some horses can hold on and others cannot. But hardly any reader not of especial and peculiar nature can hold on through such composition. There is not enough of "staying power" in human nature. One of his greatest admirers once owned to us that he seldom or never began a new poem without looking on in advance,

2. Quotes "Caliban Upon Setebos," lines 1–11, 24–56.

and foreseeing with caution what length of intellectual adventure he was about to commence. Whoever will work hard at such poems will find much mind in them: they are a sort of quarry of ideas, but whoever goes there will find these ideas in such a jagged, ugly, useless shape that he can hardly bear them.

We are not judging Mr. Browning simply from a hasty recent production. All poets are liable to misconceptions, and if such a piece as "Caliban upon Setebos" were an isolated error, a venial and particular exception, we should have given it no prominence. We have put it forward because it just elucidates both our subject and the characteristics of Mr. Browning. But many other of his best known pieces do so almost equally; what several of his devotees think his best piece is quite enough illustrative for anything we want. It appears that on Holy Cross day at Rome the Jews were obliged to listen to a Christian sermon in the hope of their conversion, though this is, according to Mr. Browning, what they really said when they came away:[3]—

* * *

It is very natural that a poet whose wishes incline, or whose genius conducts him to a grotesque art, should be attracted towards mediæval subjects. There is no age whose legends are so full of grotesque subjects, and no age where real life was so fit to suggest them. Then, more than at any other time, good principles have been under great hardships. The vestiges of ancient civilisation, the germs of modern civilisation, the little remains of what had been, the small beginnings of what is, were buried under a cumbrous mass of barbarism and cruelty. Good elements hidden in horrid accompaniments are the special theme of grotesque art, and these mediæval life and legends afford more copiously than could have been furnished before Christianity gave its new elements of good, or since modern civilisation has removed some few at least of the old elements of destruction. A *buried* life like the spiritual mediæval was Mr. Browning's natural element, and he was right to be attracted by it. His mistake has been, that he has not made it pleasant; that he has forced his art to topics on which no one could charm, or on which he, at any rate, could not; that on these occasions and in these poems he has failed in fascinating men and women of sane taste.

We say "sane" because there is a most formidable and estimable *insane* taste. The will has great though indirect power over the taste, just as it has over the belief. There are some horrid beliefs from which human nature revolts, from which at first it shrinks, to which, at first, no effort can force it. But if we fix the mind upon them they have a power over us just because of their natural offensiveness. They are like the sight of human blood: experienced soldiers tell us that at first men are sickened by the smell and newness of blood almost to death and fainting, but that as soon as they harden their hearts and stiffen their minds, as soon as they *will* bear it, then comes an appetite for slaughter, a tendency to gloat on carnage, to love blood, at least for the mo-

3. Quotes "Holy-Cross Day," lines 1–18, 61–120.

ment, with a deep eager love. It is a principle that if we put down a healthy instinctive aversion, nature avenges herself by creating an unhealthy insane attraction. For this reason the most earnest truthseeking men fall into the worst delusions; they will not let their mind alone; they force it towards some ugly thing, which a crotchet of argument, a conceit of intellect recommends, and nature punishes their disregard of her warning by subjection to the holy one, by belief in it. Just so the most industrious critics get the most admiration. They think it unjust to rest in their instinctive natural horror: they overcome it, and angry nature gives them over to ugly poems and marries them to detestable stanzas.

Mr. Browning possibly, and some of the worst of Mr. Browning's admirers certainly, will say that these grotesque objects exist in real life, and therefore they ought to be, at least may be, described in art. But though pleasure is not the end of poetry, pleasing is a condition of poetry. An exceptional monstrosity of horrid ugliness cannot be made pleasing, except it be made to suggest—to recall—the perfection, the beauty, from which it is a deviation. Perhaps in extreme cases no art is equal to this; but then such self-imposed problems should not be worked by the artist; these out-of-the-way and detestable subjects should be let alone by him. It is rather characteristic of Mr. Browning to neglect this rule. He is the most of a realist, and the least of an idealist of any poet we know.

*   *   *

Something more we had to say of Mr. Browning, but we must stop. It is singularly characteristic of this age that the poems which rise to the surface, should be examples of ornate art, and grotesque art, not of pure art. We live in the realm of the half educated. The number of readers grows daily, but the quality of readers does not improve rapidly. The middle class is scattered, headless; it is well-meaning but aimless; wishing to be wise, but ignorant how to be wise. The aristocracy of England never was a literary aristocracy, never even in the days of its full power—of its unquestioned predominance did it guide—did it even seriously try to guide—the taste of England. Without guidance young men, and tired men are thrown amongst a mass of books; they have to choose which they like; many of them would much like to improve their culture, to chasten their taste, if they knew how. But left to themselves they take, not pure art, but showy art; not that which permanently relieves the eye and makes it happy whenever it looks, and as long as it looks, but *glaring* art which catches and arrests the eye for a moment, but which in the end fatigues it. But before the wholesome remedy of nature—the fatigue arrives—the hasty reader has passed on to some new excitement, which in its turn stimulates for an instant, and then is passed by for ever. These conditions are not favourable to the due appreciation of pure art—of that art which must be known before it is admired—which must have fastened irrevocably on the brain before you appreciate it—which you must love ere it will seem worthy of your love. Women too, whose voice in literature counts as well as that of men—and in a light literature counts for more than that of men—women, such as we know them, such as they are likely to be, ever prefer a delicate unreality to a true or firm art. A dressy literature, an exaggerated literature seem to be fated to us. These are our curses, as other times had theirs.

*   *   *

ROBERT W. BUCHANAN

[*The Ring and the Book*]†

At last, the *opus magnum* of our generation lies before the world—the "ring is rounded"; and we are left in doubt which to admire most, the supremely precious gold of the material or the wondrous beauty of the workmanship. The fascination of the work is still so strong upon us, our eyes are still so spell-bound by the immortal features of Pompilia (which shine through the troubled mists of the story with almost insufferable beauty), that we feel it difficult to write calmly and without exaggeration; yet we must record at once our conviction, not merely that *The Ring and the Book* is beyond all parallel the supremest poetical achievement of our time, but that it is the most precious and profound spiritual treasure that England has produced since the days of Shakspeare. Its intellectual greatness is as nothing compared with its transcendent spiritual teaching. Day after day it grows into the soul of the reader, until all the outlines of thought are brightened and every mystery of the world becomes more and more softened into human emotion. Once and for ever must critics dismiss the old stale charge that Browning is a mere intellectual giant, difficult of comprehension, hard of assimilation. This great book *is* difficult of comprehension, *is* hard of assimilation; not because it is obscure—every fibre of the thought is clear as day; not because it is intellectual,—and it is intellectual in the highest sense,—but because the capacity to comprehend such a book must be spiritual; because, although a child's brain might grasp the general features of the picture, only a purified nature could absorb and feel its profoundest meanings. The man who tosses it aside because it is "difficult" is simply adopting a subterfuge to hide his moral littleness, not his mental incapacity. It would be unsafe to predict anything concerning a production so many-sided; but we quite believe that its true public lies outside the literary circle, that men of inferior capacity will grow by the aid of it, and that feeble women, once fairly initiated into the mystery, will cling to it as a succour passing all succour save that which is purely religious.

*   *   *

We should be grossly exaggerating if we were to aver that Mr. Browning is likely to take equal rank with the supreme genius of the world; only a gallery of pictures like the Shakspearean group could en-

† From his unsigned review in *The Atheneum* (March 20, 1869): 399–400.

able him to do that; and, moreover, his very position as an educated modern must necessarily limit his field of workmanship. What we wish to convey is, that Mr. Browning exhibits—to a great extent in all his writings, but particularly in this great work—a wealth of nature and a perfection of spiritual insight which we have been accustomed to find in the pages of Shakspeare, and in those pages only. His fantastic intellectual feats, his verbosity, his power of quaint versification, are quite other matters. The one great and patent fact is, that, with a faculty in our own time at least unparalleled, he manages to create beings of thoroughly human fibre; he is just without judgment, without preoccupation, to every being so created; and he succeeds, without a single didactic note, in stirring the soul of the spectator with the concentrated emotion and spiritual exaltation which heighten the soul's stature in the finest moments of life itself.

*   *   *

ALFRED AUSTIN

The Poetry of the Period: Mr. Browning†

*   *   *

* * * Whether Mr. Browning keeps a Commonplace Book, we have no means of knowing; but we have every means of knowing that he thinks in prose, for the prose thoughts are there before us, gratuitiously turned by some arbitrary whim, which we confess completely puzzles us, into metre. Mr. Browning is, as we have said, a profound thinker, and nearly all his thoughts have the quality of depth. Now, probably all thoughts to which this quality of depth can be ascribed, arrive at the portals of the brain in this prose—their natural vesture; whilst, on the contrary, lofty thoughts, their antitheses, usually enter it in the subtle garb of music. Here we have a clear difference in kind; prose thoughts, so to speak, from below—poetical thoughts, so to speak, from above. If we suppose a permeable plane dividing these two regions of thought, we can easily understand how there comes to be what we may call a sliding scale of poets, and a sliding scale of philosophical thinkers; some of the latter, to whom the faculty of philosophising cannot be denied, being rather shallow—some of the former, whose claims to poetical status cannot fairly be questioned, not being very soaring; and we can further understand how the natural denizens of one sphere may ever and anon cross the permeable plane, invade the other sphere, and seem to belong to it in the sense in which foreigners belong to a country they are constantly visiting. But for all that there ever remains a substantial difference between the two spheres and between their respective native inhabitants, be-

---

† From "The Poetry of the Period," *Temple Bar* 26 (June 1869): 316–33. This article by Austin (1835–1913; poet laureate 1896–1913) is famous for having provoked Browning to reply with the peppery volume *Pacchiarotto and How He Worked in Distemper: With Other Poems* (1876). Footnotes are by the editors.

tween the country of poetry and the country of prose, between poetical power and instinct and philosophical power and proclivity. Accordingly, where a man talks the language of the sphere to which he properly belongs—in other words, when a philosophical thinker publishes his thoughts in prose, or a poetical thinker addresses us in verse—our task is comparatively simple. All we have got to do is to decide whether the former be profound or shallow, and whether the latter have a lofty or a lagging pinion. It is when a man affects to talk the language of the sphere to which he does not essentially belong, that he deceives some people, and puzzles us all. This is precisely what Mr. Browning has done. Hence most people scarcely know what to make of this poetico-philosophical hybrid, this claimant to the great inheritance of bardic fame, whose hands are the hands of Esau, but whose voice is the voice of Jacob. Several, whose eyes, like those of Isaac, are dim, and who therefore cannot see, admit the claim—hesitatingly, it is true, again like Isaac—of the hands,[1] and accept him as a poet. But it is the true resonant voice, not the made-up delusive hand, which is the test of the singer; and to those whose sight is not dim, Mr. Browning is not a poet at all—save in the sense that all cultivated men and women of sensitive feelings are poets—but a deep thinker, a profound philosopher, a keen analyser, and a biting wit. With this key to what to most persons is a riddle—for, despite the importunate attempts of certain critics who, as we have already said, having placed Mr. Tennyson on a poetical pedestal considerably too high for him, are now beginning to waver in their extravagant creed, and are disposed to put him on one a trifle lower, placing Mr. Browning there instead, the general public has not yet become quite reconciled to the operation—we think we shall be able to rid them of their perplexities.   *   *   *

*   *   *

But how about "Andrea del Sarto," "Fra Lippo Lippi," "A Death in the Desert," "Caliban on Setebos," and "Bishop Blougram's Apology?" What have we to say about these? This much. That, with the exception of "Caliban on Setebos"—which, on account of its rendering certain prevailing modes of thought on theological questions, has been very much over-estimated—they are productions betraying the possession of peculiar imagination, of mordant wit of almost the highest kind, of a delicious sense of humour, and, in "Andrea del Sarto," of deep tenderness. But neither tenderness, nor humour, nor wit, nor even imagination, nor indeed all these together, will constitute a man a poet. Laplace, Bacon, Copernicus, Newton, Mr. Darwin, all have immense imagination; and we might, of course, extend the list indefinitely. We think we have allowed it to be seen that we regard Mr. Browning's intellectual powers as very considerable indeed. "Bishop Blougram's Apology" is an astonishing production, which we invariably read almost throughout with unflagging zest. But it is not poetry. There is not a line of poetry in it from first to last, and we confess we

---

1. To obtain the blessing due his elder brother Esau, Jacob deceived his blind father Isaac by disguising his smooth hands with goatskins (Genesis 27:1–29).

prefer it to all Mr. Browning's compositions. Suppose he had never written anything else, would it have occurred to anybody that he was a poet, or even aspiring to be a poet? In order still further to illustrate our meaning, suppose Mr. Tennyson had never written anything but "The Northern Farmer"—a piece we chuckle over with inexpressible delight—again, would it have occurred to anybody that Mr. Tennyson was a poet, or was pretending to be such? Of course not; no more than it would have occurred to his contemporaries to have regarded Cowper as a poet if he had never written anything but "John Gilpin," whose pre-eminent success positively annoyed its author? So with "Bishop Blougram's Apology," and all of Mr. Browning's compositions, or passages in his compositions, which are *ejusdem generis*[2] with it. They are witty, wise, shrewd, deep, true, wonderful—anything or everything but poetry. It is the greatest, though apparently the commonest, mistake in the world to suppose that the quality of verse, provided the thoughts it expresses are excellent thoughts, involves for those thoughts and their expression the quality of poetry. This has been Mr. Browning's *ignis fatuus*[3] through life; and the absurd chase it has led him he in turn has led those who have not found out what it is he has all along been following. In a word, Mr. Browning's so-called Muse is a *lusus naturæ*,[4] a sport, to use gardeners' language; but certain sapient critics have been exulting over it, as though it were a new and finer specimen of the old true poetic stock. Moreover, Mr. Browning's undoubted faculty of depth has bewitched and bewrayed them. Despite their protestations of being perfectly content with Mr. Tennyson as the great poet who justifies the period, they are not content with him. They have all along more or less consciously felt what we insisted on in our article last month—his want of loftiness. Now, in Mr. Browning they have found something that unquestionably is not in Mr. Tennyson, and they have begun to fancy that that something may possibly supply Mr. Tennyson's shortcomings. That comes of not having thought the matter out with regard to either of these authors. They know Mr. Tennyson wants something or other: they know Mr. Browning has something or other. But from lack of patient reflection and investigation they fail to perceive for themselves that what Mr. Tennyson wants is height, and what Mr. Browning has is depth. This once clearly perceived, it is obvious that the latter characteristic cannot mend the imperfection of the former characteristic. You might just as well try to make a mountain higher by excavating round it, or make swallows fly more soaringly by yourself descending a coal-pit. We have already very explicitly given our estimate of Mr. Tennyson as a poet; and though it is such as thousands of men who have fancied themselves beloved of the Muses would have given anything to have honestly formed of them, it is far removed from that in which his more ardent admirers at times affect to indulge. One thing, however, is certain. They need be in no fear lest Mr. Tennyson should be displaced by

2. Of the same kind.
3. Literally, "foolish fire"; a delusive or impractical aim.
4. A freak of nature.

any critic in his sound senses to make way for Mr. Browning. When men desire to behold the flight of an eagle, and cannot get it, they do not usually regard the tramp of an elephant as a substitute.

We therefore beg of the general public to return to the bent of its own original judgment, and, unbewildered by those who would fain be its guides, to treat Mr. Browning's "Poetical Works" as it treated "Paracelsus," &c., on its first appearance—as though they were non-existent. We know it has now much to contend against. When the academy and the drawing-room, when pedantry and folly, combine to set a fashion, it requires more self-confidence than the meek public commonly possesses to laugh the silly innovation down. To Mr. Tennyson's credit be it spoken, he has never gone looking for fame. The ground we tread on is delicate; and we will, therefore, only add that we should have been better pleased if the author, who is now so ridiculously obtruded as his rival, had imitated him in that particular. Small London literary coteries, and large fashionable London salons, cannot crown a man with the bays of Apollo. They may stick their trumpery tinsel wreaths upon him, but these will last no longer than the locks they encircle. They may confer notoriety, but fame is not in their gift. All they can bestow is as transitory as themselves. Let the sane general public, therefore, we say, take heart, and bluntly forswear Mr. Browning and all his works. It is bad enough that there should be people, pretending to authority among us, who call a man a great poet when, though unquestionably a poet, he has no marks of greatness about him. But that is a venial error, and a trifling misfortune, compared to what would be the misery of living in an age which gibbetted itself beforehand for the pity of posterity, by deliberately calling a man a poet who—however remarkable his mental attributes and powers—is not specifically a poet at all. We hope we shall be spared this humiliation. At any rate, we must protest against being supposed willingly to participate in it.

P.S.—It will be observed that we have abstained from all mention of "The Ring and the Book." Our readers must not, however, suppose that the foregoing paper was written before that work appeared. Not at all. But "The Ring and the Book" throws no new light on the subject; and what we have said of Mr. Browning's aim, method, and manner, whilst examining his other compositions, holds equally good of his latest, wonderful but unpoetical, production. We have refrained from scrutinising it, only because conscientious criticism of art, like art itself, is long, and Magazine articles are short.

ALGERNON CHARLES SWINBURNE

[Browning's Obscurity]†

* * *

The charge of obscurity is perhaps of all charges the likeliest to impair the fame or to imperil the success of a rising or an established poet. It is as often misapplied by hasty or ignorant criticism as any other on the roll of accusations; and was never misapplied more persistently and perversely than to an eminent writer of our own time. The difficulty found by many in certain of Mr. Browning's works arises from a quality the very reverse of that which produces obscurity properly so called. Obscurity is the natural product of turbid forces and confused ideas; of a feeble and clouded or of a vigorous but unfixed and chaotic intellect. Such a poet as Lord Brooke, for example—and I take George Chapman and Fulke Greville[1] to be of all English poets the two most genuinely obscure in style upon whose works I have ever adventured to embark in search of treasure hidden beneath the dark gulfs and crossing currents of their rocky and weedy waters, at some risk of my understanding being swept away by the groundswell—such a poet, overcharged with overflowing thoughts, is not sufficiently possessed by any one leading idea, or attracted towards any one central point, to see with decision the proper end and use with resolution the proper instruments of his design. Now if there is any great quality more perceptible than another in Mr. Browning's intellect it is his decisive and incisive faculty of thought, his sureness and intensity of perception, his rapid and trenchant resolution of aim. To charge him with obscurity is about as accurate as to call Lynceus[2] purblind or complain of the sluggish action of the telegraphic wire. He is something too much the reverse of obscure; he is too brilliant and subtle for the ready reader of a ready writer to follow with any certainty the track of an intelligence which moves with such incessant rapidity, or even to realize with what spider-like swiftness and sagacity his building spirit leaps and lightens to and fro and backward and forward as it lives along the animated line of its labour, springs from thread to thread and darts from centre to circumference of the glittering and quivering web of living thought woven from the inexhaustible stores of his perception and kindled from the inexhaustible fire of his imagination. He never thinks but at full speed; and the rate of his thought is to that of another man's as the speed of a railway to that of a waggon or the speed of a telegraph to that of a railway. It is hopeless to enjoy the charm or to apprehend the gist of his writings except with a mind thoroughly alert, an attention awake at all points, a spirit open and ready to be kindled by the contact of the writer's. To do justice to any book which

---

† From Algernon Charles Swinburne, *George Chapman: A Critical Essay* (London: Chatto and Windus, 1875), pp. 15–24. Footnotes are by the editors.
1. George Chapman (ca. 1559–1634), English dramatist, best known for his translations of Homer; Sir Fulke Greville, Lord Brooke (1554–1628), English poet.
2. One of the Argonauts, whose sight was so keen that he could see through the earth.

deserves any other sort of justice than that of the fire or the wastepaper basket, it is necessary to read it in the fit frame of mind; and the proper mood in which to study for the first time a book of Mr. Browning's is the freshest, clearest, most active mood of the mind in its brightest and keenest hours of work. Read at such a time, and not "with half-shut eyes falling asleep in a half-dream,"[3] it will be found (in Chapman's phrase) "pervial" enough to any but a sluggish or a sandblind eye; but at no time and in no mood will a really obscure writer be found other than obscure. The difference between the two is the difference between smoke and lightning; and it is far more difficult to pitch the tone of your thought in harmony with that of a foggy thinker, than with that of one whose thought is electric in its motion. To the latter we have but to come with an open and pliant spirit, untired and undisturbed by the work or the idleness of the day, and we cannot but receive a vivid and active pleasure in following the swift and fine radiations, the subtle play and keen vibration of its sleepless fires; and the more steadily we trace their course the more surely do we see that these forked flashes of fancy and changing lights of thought move unerringly around one centre, and strike straight in the end to one point. Only random thinking and random writing produce obscurity; and these are the radical faults of Chapman's style of poetry. We find no obscurity in the lightning, whether it play about the heights of metaphysical speculation or the depths of character and motive; the mind derives as much of vigorous enjoyment from the study by such light of the one as of the other. The action of so bright and swift a spirit gives insight as it were to the eyes and wings to the feet of our own; the reader's apprehension takes fire from the writer's, and he catches from a subtler and more active mind the infection of spiritual interest; so that any candid and clear-headed student finds himself able to follow for the time in fancy the lead of such a thinker with equal satisfaction on any course of thought or argument; when he sets himself to refute Renan through the dying lips of St. John or to try conclusions with Strauss in his own person, and when he flashes at once the whole force of his illumination full upon the inmost thought and mind of the most infamous criminal, a Guido Franceschini or a Louis Bonaparte,[4] compelling the black and obscene abyss of such a spirit to yield up at last the secret of its profoundest sophistries, and let forth the serpent of a soul that lies coiled under the most intricate and supple reasonings of self-justified and self-conscious crime. And thanks to this very quality of vivid spiritual illumination, we are able to see by the light of the author's mind without being compelled to see with his eyes, or with the eyes of the living mask which he assumes for his momentary impersonation of saint or sophist, philosopher or malefactor; without accepting one conclusion, conceding one point, or condoning one crime. It is evident that to produce any such effect requires above all things brightness and decision as well as subtlety and

---

3. Adapted from Tennyson's "The Lotos-Eaters," lines 100–101.
4. Swinburne refers to "A Death in the Desert," "Christmas-Eve" (XVI), *The Ring and the Book*, and "Prince Hohenstiel-Schwangau, Saviour of Society."

pliancy of genius; and this is the supreme gift and distinctive faculty of
Mr. Browning's mind. If indeed there be ever any likelihood of error in
his exquisite analysis, he will doubtless be found to err rather through
excess of light than through any touch of darkness; we may doubt, not
without a sense that the fittest mood of criticism might be that of a
self-distrustful confidence in the deeper intuition of his finer and
more perfect knowledge, whether the perception of good or evil would
actually be so acute in the mind of the supposed reasoner; whether for
instance a veritable household assassin, a veritable saviour of society
or other incarnation of moral pestilence, would in effect see so clearly
and so far, with whatever perversion or distortion of view, into the re-
cesses of the pit of hell wherein he lives and moves and has his being;
recognising with quick and delicate apprehension what points of van-
tage he must strive to gain, what outposts of self-defence he may hope
to guard, in the explanation and vindication of the motive forces of his
nature and the latent mainspring of his deeds. This fineness of intel-
lect and dramatic sympathy which is ever on the watch to anticipate
and answer the unspoken imputations and prepossessions of his
hearer, the very movements of his mind, the very action of his in-
stincts, is perhaps a quality hardly compatible with a nature which we
might rather suppose, judging from public evidence and historic indi-
cation, to be sluggish and short-sighted, "a sly slow thing with circum-
spective eye"[5] that can see but a little way immediately around it, but
neither before it nor behind, above it nor beneath; and whose intro-
spection, if ever that eye were turned inward, would probably be tur-
bid, vacillating, cloudy and uncertain as the action of a spirit
incapable of self-knowledge but not incapable of self-distrust, timid
and impenitent, abased and unabashed, remorseless but not resolute,
shameless but not fearless. If such be in reality the public traitor and
murderer of a nation, we may fairly infer that his humbler but not
viler counterpart in private life will be unlikely to exhibit a finer qual-
ity of mind or a clearer faculty of reason. But this is a question of re-
alism which in no wise affects the spiritual value and interest of such
work as Mr. Browning's. What is important for our present purpose is
to observe that this work of exposition by soliloquy and apology by
analysis can only be accomplished or undertaken by the genius of a
great special pleader, able to fling himself with all his heart and all his
brain, with all the force of his intellect and all the strength of his
imagination, into the assumed part of his client; to concentrate on the
cause in hand his whole power of illustration and illumination, and
bring to bear upon one point at once all the rays of his thought in one
focus. Apart from his gift of moral imagination, Mr. Browning has in
the supreme degree the qualities of a great debater or an eminent
leading counsel; his finest reasoning has in its expression and develop-
ment something of the ardour of personal energy and active interest
which inflames the argument of a public speaker; we feel, without the
reverse regret of Pope, how many a firstrate barrister or parliamentary

5. Adapted from Pope's *Essay on Man,* IV.226.

tactician has been lost in this poet.[6] The enjoyment that his best and most characteristic work affords us is doubtless far other than the delight we derive from the purest and highest forms of lyric or dramatic art; there is a radical difference between the analyst and the dramatist, the pleader and the prophet. It would be clearly impossible for the subtle tongue which can undertake at once the apology and the anatomy of such motives as may be assumed to impel or to support a "Prince Hohenstiel-Schwangau" on his ways of thought and action, ever to be touched with the fire which turns to a sword or to a scourge the tongue of a poet[7] to whom it is given to utter as from Patmos or from Sinai the word that fills all the heaven of song with the lightnings and thunders of chastisement. But in place of lyric rapture or dramatic action we may profitably enjoy the unique and incomparable genius of analysis which gives to these special pleadings such marvellous life and interest as no other workman in that kind was ever or will ever again be able to give; we may pursue with the same sense of strenuous delight in a new exercise of intellect and interest the slender and luminous threads of speculation wound up into a clue with so fine a skill and such happy sleight of hand in *Fifine at the Fair* or the sixth book of *Sordello*, where the subtle secret of spiritual weakness in a soul of too various powers and too restless refinement is laid bare with such cunning strength of touch, condemned and consoled with such farsighted compassion and regret.

* * *

GERARD MANLEY HOPKINS

[Strictures on Browning]†

* * *

* * * Browning has, I think, many frigidities. Any untruth to nature, to human nature, is frigid. Now he has got a great deal of what came in with Kingsley and the Broad Church school,[1] a way of talking (and making his people talk) with the air and spirit of a man bouncing up from table with his mouth full of bread and cheese and saying that he meant to stand no blasted nonsense. There is a whole volume of Kingsley's essays which is all a kind of munch and a not standing of any blasted nonsense from cover to cover. Do you know what I mean? The *Flight of the Duchess*, with the repetition of "My friend," is in this

---

6. Allusion to *Dunciad*, IV.170: "How many Martials were in PULTENEY lost!" Martial was a Roman poet; William Pulteney, Earl of Bath (1684–1764), an English politician and pamphleteer.
7. Victor Hugo, whose *Les Châtiments* (1853), like "Prince Hohenstiel-Schwangau," satirizes Napoleon III.
† From a letter to R. W. Dixon (Oct. 12, 1881) in *The Correspondence of Gerard Manley Hopkins and Richard Watson Dixon*, ed. C. C. Abbott (London: Oxford University Press, 1935), pp. 74–75. Footnotes are by the editors.
1. Charles Kingsley (1819–75), novelist, clergyman, and leader of the "Broad Church" or liberal wing of the established church. He was an apostle of a "healthful and manly" religious outlook, dubbed "Muscular Christianity."

vein. Now this is *one* mood or vein of human nature, but they would have it all and look at all human nature through it. And Tennyson in his later works has been "carried away with their dissimulation."[2] The effect of this style is a frigid bluster. A true humanity of spirit, neither mawkish on the one hand nor blustering on the other, is the most precious of all qualities in style, and this I prize in your poems, as I do in Bridges'.[3] After all it is the breadth of his human nature that we admire in Shakespeare.

I read some, not much, of the *Ring and the Book*, but as the tale was not edifying and one of our people, who had been reviewing it, said that further on it was coarser, I did not see, without a particular object, sufficient reason for going on with it. So far as I read I was greatly struck with the skill in which he displayed the facts from different points of view: this is masterly, and to do it through three volumes more shews a great body of genius. I remember a good case of "the impotent collection of particulars" of which you speak in the description of the market place at Florence where he found the book of the trial: it is a pointless photograph of still life, such as I remember in Balzac, minute upholstery description; only that in Balzac, who besides is writing prose, all tells and is given with a reserve and simplicity of style which Browning has not got. Indeed I hold with the oldfashioned criticism[4] that Browning is not really a poet, that he has all the gifts but the one needful and the pearls without the string; rather one should say raw nuggets and rough diamonds. I suppose him to resemble Ben Jonson, only that Ben Jonson has more real poetry.

*   *   *

OSCAR WILDE

[Browning as "Writer of Fiction"]†

*   *   *

The members of the Browning Society,[1] like the theologians of the Broad Church Party, or the authors of Mr. Walter Scott's Great Writers' Series, seem to me to spend their time in trying to explain their divinity away. Where one had hoped that Browning was a mystic, they have sought to show that he was simply inarticulate. Where one had fancied that he had something to conceal, they have proved that he had but little to reveal. But I speak merely of his incoherent work. Taken as a whole, the man was great. He did not belong to the

2. Galatians 2:13.
3. Robert Bridges (1844–1930), poet laureate 1913–30.
4. Represented at its most negative by Alfred Austin's "The Poetry of the Period: Mr. Browning" (1869), an excerpt from which appears in this volume.
† From "The True Function and Value of Criticism," *Nineteenth Century* 28 (July 1890): 123–47. Footnotes are by the editors.
1. The London Browning Society, organized in 1881 by Frederick J. Furnivall and Miss Emily Hickey. Though much ridiculed during its eleven-year history, it helped establish Browning's reputation as a profound thinker.

Olympians, and had all the incompleteness of the Titan. He did not survey, and it was but rarely that he could sing. His work is marred by struggle, violence, and effort, and he passed not from emotion to form, but from thought to chaos. Still, he was great. He has been called a thinker, and was certainly a man who was always thinking, and always thinking aloud; but it was not thought that fascinated him, but rather the processes by which thought moves. It was the machine he loved, not what the machine makes. The method by which the fool arrives at his folly was so dear to him as the ultimate wisdom of the wise. So much, indeed, did the subtle mechanism of mind fascinate him that he despised language, or looked upon it as an incomplete instrument of expression. Rhyme, that exquisite echo which in the Muse's hollow hill creates and answers its own voice; rhyme, which in the hands of a real artist becomes not merely a material element of metrical beauty, but a spiritual element of thought and passion also, waking a new mood, it may be, or stirring a fresh train of ideas, or opening by mere sweetness and suggestion of sound some golden door at which the Imagination itself had knocked in vain; rhyme, which can turn man's utterance to the speech of gods; rhyme, the one chord we have added to the Greek lyre, became in Robert Browning's hands a grotesque, misshapen thing, which made him at times masquerade in poetry as a low comedian, and ride Pegasus too often with his tongue in his cheek. There are moments when he wounds us by monstrous music. Nay, if he can only get his music by breaking the strings of his lute, he breaks them, and they snap in discord, and no Athenian tettix,[2] making melody from tremulous wings, lights on the ivory horn to make the movement perfect or the interval less harsh. Yet, he was great: and though he turned language into ignoble clay, he made from it men and women that live. He is the most Shakespearian creature since Shakespeare. If Shakespeare could sing with myriad lips, Browning could stammer through a thousand mouths. Even now, as I am speaking, and speaking not against him but for him, there glides through the room the pageant of his persons. There, creeps Fra Lippo Lippi with his cheeks still burning from some girl's hot kiss. There, stands dread Saul with the lordly male-sapphires gleaming in his turban. Mildred Tresham[3] is there, and the Spanish monk, yellow with hatred, and Blougram, and the Rabbi Ben Ezra, and the Bishop of St. Praxed's. The spawn of Setebos gibbers in the corner, and Sebald, hearing Pippa pass by, looks on Ottima's haggard face, and loathes her and his own sin and himself. Pale as the white satin of his doublet, the melancholy king watches with dreamy treacherous eyes too loyal Strafford[4] pass to his doom, and Andrea shudders as he hears the cousin's whistle in the garden, and bids his perfect wife go down. Yes, Browning was great. And as what will he be remembered? As a poet? Ah, not as a poet! He will be remembered as a writer of fiction, as the most supreme writer of fiction, it may be, that we have ever had. His

2. Or tetrix, genus of grouse locusts.
3. Young heroine of Browning's tragedy A Blot in the 'Scutcheon (1843).
4. Hero of Browning's drama Strafford (1837).

sense of dramatic situation was unrivalled, and, if he could not answer his own problems, he could at least put problems forth. Considered from the point of view of a creator of character he ranks next to him who made Hamlet. Had he been articulate he might have sat beside him. The only man living who can touch the hem of his garment is George Meredith. Meredith is a prose-Browning, and so is Browning. He used poetry as a medium for writing in prose.

* * *

HENRY JAMES

Browning in Westminster Abbey†

The lovers of a great poet are the people in the world who are most to be forgiven a little wanton fancy about him, for they have before them, in his genius and work, an irresistible example of the application of the imaginative method to a thousand subjects. Certainly, therefore, there are many confirmed admirers of Robert Browning to whom it will not have failed to occur that the consignment of his ashes to the great temple of fame of the English race was exactly one of those occasions in which his own analytic spirit would have rejoiced and his irrepressible faculty for looking at human events in all sorts of slanting coloured lights have found a signal opportunity. If he had been taken with it as a subject, if it had moved him to the confused yet comprehensive utterance of which he was the great professor, we can immediately guess at some of the sparks he would have scraped from it, guess how splendidly, in the case, the pictorial sense would have intertwined itself with the metaphysical. For such an occasion would have lacked, for the author of "The Ring and the Book," none of the complexity and convertibility that were dear to him. Passion and ingenuity, irony and solemnity, the impressive and the unexpected, would each have forced their way through; in a word the author would have been sure to take the special, circumstantial view (the inveterate mark of all his speculation) even of so foregone a conclusion as that England should pay her greatest honour to one of her greatest poets. As they stood in the Abbey, at any rate, on Tuesday last, those of his admirers and mourners who were disposed to profit by his warrant for enquiring curiously may well have let their fancy range, with its muffled step, in the direction which *his* fancy would probably not have shrunk from following, even perhaps to the dim corners where humour and the whimsical lurk. Only, we hasten to add, it would have taken Robert Browning himself to render the multifold impression.

One part of it on such occasion is of course irresistible—the sense that these honours are the greatest that a generous nation has to confer and that the emotion that accompanies them is one of the high

† First published in *The Speaker* 1 (Jan. 4, 1891): 11–12; reprinted in *English Hours* (Boston: Houghton Mifflin, 1905), pp. 51–59.

moments of a nation's life. The attitude of the public, of the multi-
tude, at such hours, is a great expansion, a great openness to ideas of
aspiration and achievement; the pride of possession and of bestowal,
especially in the case of a career so complete as Mr. Browning's, is so
present as to make regret a minor matter. We possess a great man
most when we begin to look at him through the glass plate of death;
and it is a simple truth, though containing an apparent contradiction,
that the Abbey never takes us so benignantly as when we have a valued
voice to commit to silence there. For the silence is articulate after all,
and in worthy instances the preservation great. It is the other side of
the question that would pull most the strings of irresponsible reflec-
tion—all those conceivable postulates and hypotheses of the poetic
and satiric mind to which we owe the picture of how the bishop or-
dered his tomb in St. Praxed's. Macaulay's "temple of silence and rec-
onciliation"—and none the less perhaps because he himself is now a
presence there—strikes us, as we stand in it, not only as local but as
social, a sort of corporate company; so thick, under its high arches, its
dim transepts and chapels, is the population of its historic names and
figures. They are a company in possession, with a high standard of dis-
tinction, of immortality, as it were; for there is something serenely in-
expugnable even in the position of the interlopers. As they look out, in
the rich dusk, from the cold eyes of statues and the careful identity of
tablets, they seem, with their converging faces, to scrutinise deco-
rously the claims of each new recumbent glory, to ask each other how
he is to be judged as an accession. How difficult to banish the idea
that Robert Browning would have enjoyed prefiguring and playing
with the mystifications, the reservations, even perhaps the slight buzz
of scandal, in the Poets' Corner, to which his own obsequies might
give rise! Would not his great relish, in so characteristic an interview
with his crucible, have been his perception of the bewildering mod-
ernness, to much of the society, of the new candidate for a niche?
That is the interest and the fascination, from what may be termed the
inside point of view, of Mr. Browning's having received, in this direc-
tion of becoming a classic, the only official assistance that is ever con-
ferred upon English writers.

It is as classics on one ground and another—some members of it
perhaps on that of not being anything else—that the numerous as-
sembly in the Abbey holds together, and it is as a tremendous and in-
comparable modern that the author of "Men and Women" takes his
place in it. He introduces to his predecessors a kind of contemporary
individualism which surely for many a year they had not been re-
minded of with any such force. The tradition of the poetic character
as something high, detached, and simple, which may be assumed to
have prevailed among them for a good while, is one that Browning has
broken at every turn; so that we can imagine his new associates to
stand about him, till they have got used to him, with rather a sense of
failing measures. A good many oddities and a good many great writers
have been entombed in the Abbey; but none of the odd ones have

been so great and none of the great ones so odd. There are plenty of
poets whose right to the title may be contested, but there is no poetic
head of equal power—crowned and recrowned by almost importunate
hands—from which so many people would withhold the distinctive
wreath. All this will give the marble phantoms at the base of the great
pillars, and the definite personalities of the honorary slabs something
to puzzle out until, by the quick operation of time, the mere fact of his
lying there among the classified and protected makes even Robert
Browning lose a portion of the bristling surface of his actuality.

For the rest, judging from the outside and with his contemporaries,
we of the public can only feel that his very modernness—by which we
mean the all-touching, all-trying spirit of his work, permeated with ac-
cumulations and playing with knowledge—achieves a kind of con-
quest, or at least of extension, of the rigid pale. We cannot enter here
upon any account either of that or of any other element of his genius,
though surely no literary figure of our day seems to sit more uncon-
sciously for the painter. The very imperfections of this original are fas-
cinating, for they never present themselves as weaknesses; they are
boldnesses and overgrowths, rich roughnesses and humours, and the
patient critic need not despair of digging to the primary soil from
which so many disparities and contradictions spring. He may finally
even put his finger on some explanation of the great mystery, the im-
perfect conquest of the poetic form by a genius in which the poetic
passion had such volume and range. He may successfully say how it
was that a poet without a lyre—for that is practically Browning's defi-
ciency: he had the scroll, but not often the sounding strings—was nev-
ertheless, in his best hours, wonderfully rich in the magic of his art, a
magnificent master of poetic emotion. He will justify on behalf of a
multitude of devotees the great position assigned to a writer of verse of
which the nature or the fortune has been (in proportion to its value
and quantity) to be treated rarely as quotable. He will do all this and a
great deal more besides; but we need not wait for it to feel that some-
thing of our latest sympathies, our latest and most restless selves,
passed the other day into the high part—the show-part, to speak
vulgarly—of our literature. To speak of Mr. Browning only as he was in
the last twenty years of his life, how quick such an imagination as his
would have been to recognise all the latent or mystical suitabilities
that, in the last resort, might link to the great Valhalla by the Thames
a figure that had become so conspicuously a figure of London! He had
grown to be intimately and inveterately of the London world; he was
so familiar and recurrent, so responsive to all its solicitations, that,
given the endless incarnations he stands for to-day, he would have
been missed from the congregation of worthies whose memorials are
the special pride of the Londoner. Just as his great sign to those who
knew him was that he was a force of health, of temperament, of tone,
so what he takes into the Abbey is an immense expression of life—of
life rendered with large liberty and free experiment, with an unpreju-
diced intellectual eagerness to put himself in other people's place, to

participate in complications and consequences; a restlessness of psychological research that might well alarm any pale company for their formal orthodoxies.

But the illustrious whom he rejoins may be reassured, as they will not fail to discover: in so far as they are representative it will clear itself up that, in spite of a surface unsuggestive of marble and a reckless individualism of form, he is quite as representative as any of them. For the great value of Browning is that at bottom, in all the deep spiritual and human essentials, he is unmistakably in the great tradition—is, with all his Italianisms and cosmopolitanisms, all his victimisation by societies organised to talk about him, a magnificent example of the best and least dilettantish English spirit. That constitutes indeed the main chance for his eventual critic, who will have to solve the refreshing problem of how, if subtleties be not what the English spirit most delights in, the author of, for instance, "Any Wife to Any Husband" made them his perpetual pasture, and yet remained typically of his race. He was indeed a wonderful mixture of the universal and the alembicated. But he played with the curious and the special, they never submerged him, and it was a sign of his robustness that he could play to the end. His voice sounds loudest, and also clearest, for the things that, as a race, we like best—the fascination of faith, the acceptance of life, the respect for its mysteries, the endurance of its charges, the vitality of the will, the validity of character, the beauty of action, the seriousness, above all, of the great human passion. If Browning had spoken for us in no other way, he ought to have been made sure of, tamed and chained as a classic, on account of the extraordinary beauty of his treatment of the special relation between man and woman. It is a complete and splendid picture of the matter, which somehow places it at the same time in the region of conduct and responsibility. But when we talk of Robert Browning's speaking "for us," we go to the end of our privilege, we say all. With a sense of security, perhaps even a certain complacency, we leave our sophisticated modern conscience, and perhaps even our heterogeneous modern vocabulary, in his charge among the illustrious. There will possibly be moments in which these things will seem to us to have widened the allowance, made the high abode more comfortable, for some of those who are yet to enter it.

Modern Essays in Criticism

ROBERT LANGBAUM

The Dramatic Monologue:
Sympathy versus Judgment†

Writers on the dramatic monologue never fail to remark how little has been written on the subject—and I shall be no exception. The reason for the neglect is, I think, that no one has quite known what to do with the dramatic monologue except to classify it, to distinguish kinds of dramatic monologues and to distinguish the dramatic monologue from both the lyrical and the dramatic or narrative genres. Such classifications are all too easily made and have a way of killing off further interest in the subject. For they too often mean little beyond themselves, they close doors where they ought to open them.

The usual procedure in discussing the dramatic monologue is to find precedents for the form in the poetry of all periods, and then to establish, on the model of a handful of poems by Browning and Tennyson, objective criteria by which the form is henceforth to be recognized and judged. The procedure combines, I think, opposite mistakes; it is at once too restrictive and not restrictive enough, and in either case tells us too little. For once we decide to treat the dramatic monologue as a traditional genre, then every lyric in which the speaker seems to be someone other than the poet, almost all love-songs and laments in fact (*Lycidas*, *The Song of Songs*, *Polyphemus' Complaint* by Theocritus, the Anglo-Saxon *Banished Wife's Complaint*) become dramatic monologues; as do all imaginary epistles and orations and all kinds of excerpts from plays and narratives—e.g. all long speeches and soliloquies, those portions of epics in which the hero recounts the events that occurred before the opening of the poem, Chaucer's prologues to the *Canterbury Tales* and the tales themselves since they are told by fictitious persons: almost all first person narratives, in fact, become dramatic monologues. While such a classification is *true* enough, what does it accomplish except to identify a certain mechanical resemblance?—since the poems retain more affinity to the lyric, the drama, the narrative than to each other.

† From *The Poetry of Experience: The Dramatic Monologue in Literary Tradition*. Reprinted by permission of the University of Chicago Press. Copyright © Robert Langbaum 1957, 1985. Originally published 1957 by Random House. W. W. Norton & Company paperback edition 1963, 1971. Reprinted by permission of the author.

But if we are, on the other hand, too restrictive, we do little more than describe the handful of Browning and Tennyson poems we are using as models. We come out with the idea that dramatic monologues are more or less like Browning's *My Last Duchess*, and that most dramatic monologues being rather less like it are not nearly so good. We are told, for example, that the dramatic monologue must have not only a speaker other than the poet but also a listener, an occasion, and some interplay between speaker and listener. But since a classification of this sort does not even cover all the dramatic monologues of Browning and Tennyson, let alone those of other poets, it inevitably leads to quarrels about which poems are to be admitted into the canon; and worse, it leads to sub-classifications, to a distinction between what one writer calls "formal" dramatic monologues, which have only three of the necessary criteria, and "typical" dramatic monologues, which have all four. As for poems with only the dramatized speaker and perhaps the occasion—poems like Tennyson's *St Simeon Stylites* and Browning's *Childe Roland* and *Caliban*, which are among the best and most famous of all dramatic monologues—this writer, in order to salvage her classification, calls them "approximation."[1]

The trouble with so narrow a criterion is that it suggests a decline of the dramatic monologue since Browning's time. It blinds us to the developing life of the form, to the importance of dramatic monologues in the work of such twentieth-century poets as Yeats, Eliot, Pound, Frost, Masters, Robinson and both Lowells, Amy and Robert (the form is particularly favoured by American poets). Robert Lowell's latest volume (*The Mills of the Kavanaughs*, 1951) consists entirely of dramatic monologues; while Pound, who in many places acknowledges his debt to Browning, has said of the dramatic monologues of Browning's *Men and Women* that "the form of these poems is the most vital form of that period,"[2] and has called a volume of his own *Personae*. Although Eliot has little to say in favour of Browning, the dramatic monologue has been the main form in his work until he assumed what appears to be a personal voice in the series of religious meditations beginning with *Ash Wednesday*. The dramatic monologue is proportionately as important in Eliot's work as in Browning's, Eliot having contributed more to the development of the form than any poet since Browning[3] Certainly *Prufrock*, *Portrait of a Lady*, *Gerontion*, *Journey of the Magi*,

---

1. Ina Beth Sessions in her book, *A Study of the Dramatic Monologue in American and Continental Literature* (San Antonio, Texas: Alamo Printing Co., 1933). An extract with revisions appears as "The Dramatic Monologue," *PMLA*, June 1947. For other examples of this approach, see another book-length study: S. S. Curry, *Browning and the Dramatic Monologue* (Boston: Expression Co., 1908); and papers by Claud Howard, "The Dramatic Monologue: Its Origin and Development," *Studies in Philology*, IV (Chapel Hill, N.C.: University of North Carolina Press, 1910), and R. H. Fletcher, "Browning's Dramatic Monologs [sic]," *Modern Language Notes*, April 1908.

2. Reviewing Eliot's *Prufrock and Other Observations* in 1917. Reprinted as "T. S. Eliot," *Literary Essays*, edited with an introduction by T. S. Eliot (Norfolk, Conn: New Directions; London: Faber and Faber, 1954), p. 419.

3. "For the eventual writer of the literary history of the twentieth century, Eliot's development of the dramatic soliloquy, a form that has been called 'the most flexible and characteristic genre of English verse,' cannot be divorced from the impetus furnished by 'Men and Women' to 'Personae.'" (Matthiessen, *Achievement of Eliot*, p. 73, London: Oxford Univ. Press, 1935.)

A Song for Simeon and *Marina* do as much credit to the dramatic monologue as anything of Browning's; while in *The Waste Land* Eliot has opened new possibilities for the form by constructing a kind of *collage* of dramatic monologues as perceived by Tiresias, whose dramatic monologue the poem is.[4]

To understand the continuing life of the dramatic monologue, we must abandon the exclusive concern with objective criteria by which poems are either combined when they lack any effect in common, or else are separated when they have a common effect but lack the necessary mechanical resemblance. It is when we look inside the dramatic monologue, when we consider its effect, its *way* of meaning, that we see its connection with the poetry that precedes and follows Browning. We see, on the one hand, that the dramatic monologue is unprecedented in its effect, that its effect distinguishes it, in spite of mechanical resemblance, from the monologues of traditional poetry; and on the other hand, we welcome as particularly illuminating just those "approximations" that distress the classifiers. We welcome them because, having without the mechanical resemblance the same effect as the so-called "typical" dramatic monologues, they show us what the form is essentially doing.

One writer on the dramatic monologue has managed to suggest what it is essentially doing; and he has done this at just the point where he abandons objective criteria to make an intuitive leap inside the form. In a Warton Lecture of 1925 which remains the best study of the dramatic monologue, M. W. MacCallum sees sympathy as its way of meaning:

> But in every instance . . . the object [of the dramatic monologue] is to give facts from within. A certain dramatic understanding of the person speaking, which implies a certain dramatic sympathy with him, is not only the essential condition, but the final cause of the whole species.[5]

Unfortunately, MacCallum does not pursue the implications of this insight. If he had, he would not be so disposed to isolate the dramatic monologue within the Victorian period, and he would not confine his consideration to its quality as a monologue. Although the fact that a poem is a monologue helps to determine our sympathy for the speaker,

4. "Tiresias, although a mere spectator and not indeed a 'character,' is yet the most important personage in the poem, uniting all the rest. Just as the one-eyed merchant, seller of currants, melts into the Phoenician Sailor, and the latter is not wholly distinct from Ferdinand Prince of Naples, so all the women are one woman, and the two sexes meet in Tiresias. What Tiresias *sees*, in fact, is the substance of the poem." (Eliot's Notes on *The Waste Land*, III, p. 218.)

5. "The Dramatic Monologue in the Victorian Period," *Proceedings of the British Academy 1924–1925*, p. 276. See also an earlier paper which moves in the same direction, though not nearly so far: G. H. Palmer, "The Monologue of Browning," *Harvard Theological Review*, April 1918; and the three pages Bliss Perry devotes to the subject in *A Study of Poetry* (Boston: Houghton Mifflin, 1920), pp. 267–70. Stopford Brooke makes the pioneering remarks on the dramatic monologue in Chap. XIII of *Tennyson: His Art and Relation to Modern Life* (London: Isbister, 1895). But Brooke in his *Tennyson* and William Lyon Phelps in Chap. V of *Robert Browning, How To Know Him* (Indianapolis: Bobbs-Merrill, 1915), are more concerned with the content of individual dramatic monologues than with generic characteristics.

since we must adopt his viewpoint as our entry into the poem, the monologue quality remains nevertheless a means, and not the only means, to the end—the end being to establish the reader's sympathetic relation to the poem, to give him "facts from within."

The distinction may seem niggling unless we see that, by subordinating the dramatic monologue's quality as a monologue to the larger question of the reader's relation to it, we are able to understand the wider connections of the form. For to give facts from within, to derive meaning that is from the poetic material itself rather than from an external standard of judgment, is the specifically romantic contribution to literature; while sympathy or projectiveness, what the Germans call *Einfühlung*, is the specifically romantic way of knowing. Once we consider the dramatic monologue as a poetry of sympathy, we are in a position to see the connection not only between the dramatic monologues of the nineteenth and twentieth centuries but between the dramatic monologue and all that is unprecedented in poetry since the latter eighteenth century. We can see in the differences between the dramatic monologue on the one hand, and the dramatic lyric and lyrical drama of the romanticists on the other, the articulation of a form potential in romantic poetry from the start.

The standard account of the dramatic monologue is that Browning and Tennyson conceived it as a reaction against the romantic confessional style. This is probably true. Both poets had been stung by unfriendly criticism of certain early poems in which they had too much revealed themselves; and both poets published, in 1842, volumes which were a new departure in their careers and which contained dramatic monologues. The personal sting was probably responsible for Tennyson's decade of silence before 1842; it was almost certainly responsible for the disclaimer attached by Browning to his 1842 *Dramatic Lyrics*: "so many utterances of so many imaginary persons, not mine." Yet the reserve of the two poets cannot explain the coincidence that, working independently, they both arrived at the same form and produced at first try dramatic monologues so perfect (Browning's *My Last Duchess* and Tennyson's *Ulysses* and *St Simeon Stylites*) that they were never themselves to surpass them. We must look for precedents; we must suspect that they inherited a form which required only one more step in its development to achieve the objectivity they desired.

Browning's poetry before 1842 suggests by the manner of its failure the kind of precedent that lay behind the dramatic monologue, and the kind of problem that remained for the dramatic monologue to solve. His first published work, *Pauline* (1833), is the poem in which he too much revealed himself. It is transparently autobiographical (although the fictitious identity of the lady addressed provides a disguise of a sort), tracing the poet's intellectual development up to the age of twenty, the time of writing. It was of *Pauline* that John Stuart Mill said: "The writer seems to me possessed with a more intense and morbid self-consciousness than I ever knew in any sane human being"—a criticism Browning took so to heart that he would not allow *Pauline* to be published again until 1867; and then with an apologetic preface which repeats the disclaimer of 1842: "The thing was my earliest attempt at 'poetry always dramatic in principle, and so many utterances of so many imaginary persons, not mine.' " In spite of which disclaimer, he is reported to have said in his old age that "his early poems were so transparent in their meaning as to draw down upon him the ridicule of the critics, and that, boy as he was, this ridicule and censure stung him into quite another style of writing."[6]

We can follow his attempts at "another style" in *Paracelsus* (1835), a dramatic poem, and *Sordello* (1833–40), an historical narrative. There is, however, little enough drama in *Paracelsus*, and the narrative line is at best intermittent in *Sordello*; in both poems the style that takes over is the introspective, transparently autobiographical history of a soul in the manner of *Pauline*—the soul being in all three recognizable as the same passionately idealistic and endlessly ambitious, endlessly self-absorbed disciple of Shelley. In the preface to the first edition of *Paracelsus*, Browning says that he has reversed the usual method of drama:

> Instead of having recourse to an external machinery of incidents to create and evolve the crisis I desire to produce, I have ventured to display somewhat minutely the mood itself in its rise and progress, and have suffered the agency by which it is influenced and determined to be generally discernible in its effects alone, and subordinate throughout, if not altogether excluded.

And reflecting in 1863 on the failure of *Sordello*, he says in the preface dedicating the new edition of the poem to his friend, the French critic Milsand: "My stress lay on the incidents in the development of a soul: little else is worth study. I, at least, always thought so—you, with many known and unknown to me, think so—others may one day think so."

Did Browning forget that the romantic poets had thought so, that even Arnold, who disagreed, could hardly help but write poetry as though he too thought so, and that the enormous popularity of the "spasmodic"[7] poets gave evidence that by mid-century almost everyone thought so? The question is perhaps answered by Milsand, who, in reviewing *Men and Women* for the *Revue Contemporaine* of September 1856, describes Browning's dramatic monologues in terms applicable to the whole of what I have been calling the poetry of experience. "What Mr Browning has attempted," says Milsand, "is the fusion of two kinds of poetry into one." And after citing Browning's remarks in the *Essay on Shelley* on the distinction between subjective and objective poetry:

6. Quoted in W. C. DeVane, *A Browning Handbook* (New York: Appleton-Century-Crofts, 1955), pp. 46–47; (London: John Murray, 1937), p. 44. Just as the failure of *Pauline* is considered responsible for Browning's reluctance to speak in his own voice, so Tennyson seems to have been similarly wounded by the failure of his 1832 volume, especially by Lockhart's personally insulting review of it in the *Quarterly*. Harold Nicolson gives an amusing account of this review, considering it as "undoubtedly one of the main causes of the silent and morose decade which was to follow." (*Tennyson*, London: Constable, 1949, pp. 112–17.)
7. Term applied to English poets of the 1840s and 1850s (Sydney Dobell, P. J. Bailey, Alexander Smith, and others) whose verse was often uneven in style and exaggerated in emphasis. [*Editor.*]

This alone indicates that he sympathizes equally with both kinds of inspiration, and I am inclined to think that from the beginning, and partly without his knowing it, his constant effort has been to reconcile and combine them, in order to find a way of being, not in turn but simultaneously, lyric and dramatic, subjective and pictorial. . . . [His poetry] would have us conceive the inner significance of things by making us see their exteriors.[8]

Compare these remarks of Milsand and Browning with Wordsworth's: "the feeling therein developed gives importance to the action and situation, and not the action and situation to the feeling," and with Pound's description of his own poetry:

To me the short so-called dramatic lyric—at any rate the sort of thing I do—is the poetic part of a drama the rest of which (to me the prose part) is left to the reader's imagination or implied or set in a short note. I catch the character I happen to be interested in at the moment he interests me, usually a moment of song, self-analysis, or sudden understanding or revelation. And the rest of the play would bore me and presumably the reader.[9]

Add to the comparison Pound's idea that drama is less poetic than other kinds of poetry because "the maximum charge of verbal meaning cannot be used on the stage,"[1] and Virginia Woolf's aim "to saturate" in her novels "every atom":

I mean to eliminate all waste, deadness, superfluity: to give the moment whole; whatever it includes. . . . Waste, deadness, come from the inclusion of things that don't belong to the moment; this appalling narrative business of the realist: getting on from lunch to dinner: it is false, unreal, merely conventional. Why admit anything to literature that is not poetry—by which I mean saturated?[2]

And we see Browning's innovations as part of a general change of sensibility—a demand that all literature yield much the same effect, an effect of lyrical intensity.

When we have said all the objective things about Browning's *My Last Duchess*, we will not have arrived at the meaning until we point out what can only be substantiated by an appeal to effect—that moral judgment does not figure importantly in our response to the duke, that we even identify ourselves with him. But how is such an effect produced in a poem about a cruel Italian duke of the Renaissance who out of unreasonable jealousy has had his last duchess put to death, and is now about to contract a second marriage for the sake of dowry? Certainly, no summary or paraphrase would indicate that condemna-

8. pp. 545–46.
9. To William Carlos Williams, 21 October 1908, *Letters 1907–1941*, ed. D. D. Paige (New York: Harcourt, Brace, 1950), pp. 3–4; (London, Faber and Faber, 1951), p. 36.
1. *ABC of Reading* (New Haven: Yale University Press, 1934), p. 33; (London: Routledge, 1934), p. 31.
2. *A Writer's Diary*, ed. Leonard Woolf (London: The Hogarth Press, 1953), p. 139.

tion is not our principal response. The difference must be laid to form, to that extra quantity which makes the difference in artistic discourse between content and meaning.

The objective fact that the poem is made up entirely of the duke's utterance has of course much to do with the final meaning, and it is important to say that the poem is in form a monologue. But much more remains to be said about the way in which the content is laid out, before we can come near accounting for the whole meaning. It is important that the duke tells the story of his kind and generous last duchess to, of all people, the envoy from his prospective duchess. It is important that he tells his story while showing off to the envoy the artistic merits of a portrait of the last duchess. It is above all important that the duke carries off his outrageous indiscretion, proceeding triumphantly in the end downstairs to conclude arrangements for the dowry. All this is important not only as content but also as form, because it establishes a relation between the duke on the one hand, and the portrait and the envoy on the other, which determines the reader's relation to the duke and therefore to the poem—which determines, in other words, the poem's meaning.

The utter outrageousness of the duke's behaviour makes condemnation the least interesting response, certainly not the response that can account for the poem's success. What interests us more than the duke's wickedness is his immense attractiveness. His conviction of matchless superiority, his intelligence and bland amorality, his poise, his taste for art, his manners—high-handed aristocratic manners that break the ordinary rules and assert the duke's superiority when he is being most solicitous of the envoy, waiving their difference of rank ("Nay, we'll go / Together down, sir"); these qualities overwhelm the envoy, causing him apparently to suspend judgment of the duke, for he raises no demur. The reader is no less overwhelmed. We suspend moral judgment because we prefer to participate in the duke's power and freedom, in his hard core of character fiercely loyal to itself. Moral judgment is in fact important as the thing to be suspended, as a measure of the price we pay for the privilege of appreciating to the full this extraordinary man.

It is because the duke determines the arrangement and relative subordination of the parts that the poem means what it does. The duchess's goodness shines through the duke's utterance; he makes no attempt to conceal it, so preoccupied is he with his own standard of judgment and so oblivious of the world's. Thus the duchess's case is subordinated to the duke's, the novelty and complexity of which engages our attention. We are busy trying to understand the man who can combine the connoisseur's pride in the lady's beauty with a pride that caused him to murder the lady rather than tell her in what way she displeased him, for in that

> would be some stooping; and I choose
> Never to stoop.

The duke's paradoxical nature is fully revealed when, having boasted how at his command the duchess's life was extinguished, he turns back to the portrait to admire of all things its life-likeness:

> There she stands
> As if alive.

This occurs ten lines from the end, and we might suppose we have by now taken the duke's measure. But the next ten lines produce a series of shocks that outstrip each time our understanding of the duke, and keep us panting after revelation with no opportunity to consolidate our impression of him for moral judgment. For it is at this point that we learn to whom he has been talking; and he goes on to talk about dowry, even allowing himself to murmur the hypocritical assurance that the new bride's self and not the dowry is of course his object. It seems to me that one side of the duke's nature is here stretched as far as it will go; the dazzling figure threatens to decline into paltriness admitting moral judgment, when Browning retrieves it with two brilliant strokes. First, there is the lordly waiving of rank's privilege as the duke and the envoy are about to proceed downstairs, and then there is the perfect all-revealing gesture of the last two and a half lines when the duke stops to show off yet another object in his collection:

> Notice Neptune, though,
> Taming a sea-horse, thought a rarity,
> Which Claus of Innsbruck cast in bronze for me!

The lines bring all the parts of the poem into final combination, with just the relative values that constitute the poem's meaning. The nobleman does not hurry on his way to business, the connoisseur cannot resist showing off yet another precious object, the possessive egotist counts up his possessions even as he moves toward the acquirement of a new possession, a well-dowered bride; and most important, the last duchess is seen in final perspective. She takes her place as one of a line of objects in an art collection; her sad story becomes the *cicerone's* anecdote lending piquancy to the portrait. The duke has taken from her what he wants, her beauty, and thrown the life away; and we watch with awe as he proceeds to take what he wants from the envoy and by implication from the new duchess. He carries all before him by sheer force of will so undeflected by ordinary compunctions as even, I think, to call into question—the question rushes into place behind the startling illumination of the last lines, and lingers as the poem's haunting afternote—the duke's sanity.

The duke reveals all this about himself, grows to his full stature, because we allow him to have his way with us; we subordinate all other considerations to the business of understanding him. If we allowed indignation, or pity for the duchess, to take over when the duke moves from his account of the murder to admire the life-likeness of the portrait, the poem could hold no further surprises for us; it could not even go on to reinforce our judgment as to the duke's wickedness, since the duke does not grow in wickedness after the account of the murder. He grows in strength of character, and in the arrogance and poise which enable him to continue command of the situation after his confession of murder has threatened to turn it against him. To take the full measure of the duke's distinction we must be less concerned to condemn than to appreciate the triumphant transition by which he ignores clean out of existence any judgment of his story that the envoy might have presumed to invent. We must be concerned to appreciate the exquisite timing of the duke's delay over Neptune, to appreciate its fidelity to the duke's own inner rhythm as he tries once more the envoy's already sorely tried patience, and as he teases the reader too by delaying for a lordly whim the poem's conclusion. This willingness of the reader to understand the duke, even to sympathize with him as a necessary condition of reading the poem, is the key to the poem's form. It alone is responsible for a meaning not inherent in the content itself but determined peculiarly by the treatment.

I have chosen *My Last Duchess* to illustrate the working of sympathy, just because the duke's egregious villainy makes especially apparent the split between moral judgment and our actual feeling for him. The poem carries to the limit an effect peculiarly the genius of the dramatic monologue—I mean the effect created by the tension between sympathy and moral judgment. Although we seldom meet again such an unmitigated villain as the duke, it is safe to say that most successful dramatic monologues deal with speakers who are in some way reprehensible.

Browning delighted in making a case for the apparently immoral position; and the dramatic monologue, since it requires sympathy for the speaker as a condition of reading the poem, is an excellent vehicle for the "impossible" case. Mr Sludge and Bishop Blougram in matters of the spirit, Prince Hohenstiel-Schwangau in politics, and in love Don Juan of *Fifine*, are all Machiavellians who defend themselves by an amoral casuistry. The combination of villain and aesthete creates an especially strong tension, and Browning exploits the combination not only in *My Last Duchess* but again in *The Bishop Orders His Tomb*, where the dying Renaissance bishop reveals his venality and shocking perversion of Christianity together with his undeniable taste for magnificence:

> Some lump, ah God, of *lapis lazuli*,
> Big as a Jew's head cut off at the nape,
> Blue as a vein o'er the Madonna's breast . . .

and again in *The Laboratory* where the Rococo court lady is much concerned with the colour of the poison she buys and would like

> To carry pure death in an earring, a casket,
> A signet, a fan-mount, a filigree basket!

To the extent that these poems are successful, we admire the speaker for his power of intellect (as in *Blougram*) or for his aesthetic passion and sheer passion for living (as in *The Bishop Orders His Tomb*). *Hohenstiel-Schwangau* and *Fifine* are not successful because no outline of character emerges from the intricacy of the argument, there is no one to sympathize with and we are therefore not convinced even though the arguments are every bit as good as in the successful poems. Arguments cannot make the case in the dramatic monologue but only passion, power, strength of will and intellect, just those existential virtues which are independent of logical and moral correctness and are therefore best made out through sympathy and when clearly separated from, even opposed to, the other virtues. Browning's contemporaries accused him of "perversity" because they found it necessary to sympathize with his reprehensible characters.

But Browning's perversity is intellectual and moral in the sense that most of his characters have taken up their extraordinary positions through a perfectly normal act of will. Tennyson, on the other hand, although less interested in novel moral positions, goes much farther than Browning in dealing in his successful dramatic monologues with an emotional perversity that verges on the pathological. Morally, Tennyson's *St Simeon Stylites* is a conventional liberal Protestant attack upon asceticism. But the poem is unusual because the saint's passion for a heavenly crown is shown as essentially demonic; his hallucinations, self-loathing and insatiable lust for self-punishment suggest a psyche as diseased (we should nowadays call it sado-masochistic) as the ulcerous flesh he boasts of. St Simeon conceives himself in both body and soul as one disgusting sore:

> Altho' I be the basest of mankind,
> From scalp to sole one slough and crust of sin,

and there is in his advice to his disciples a certain obscene zest:

> Mortify
> Your flesh, like me, with scourges and with thorns;
> Smite, shrink not, spare not.

Browning would have complicated the case against asceticism, he might have emphasized the moral ambiguity presented by the saintly ambition which does not differ in quality from the ambition for money or empire; or if he did simplify, it would be to present the case against ascetic ritualism satirically as in *The Spanish Cloister*. Tennyson, however, is more interested in the psychological ambiguity, pursuing the saint's passion to its obscurely sexual recesses.

Treating a similar example of religious buccaneering, Browning has written in *Johannes Agricola in Meditation* a dramatic monologue of sheer lyric exultation. Johannes is, like St Simeon, on a rampage for salvation and confident of attaining it. But compare with St Simeon's the beauty of Johannes' conception of his own spiritual position:

> There's heaven above, and night by night
> I look right through its gorgeous roof;
> No suns and moons though e'er so bright
> Avail to stop me; splendour-proof
> I keep the broods of stars aloof:

For I intend to get to God,
  For 'tis to God I speed so fast,
For in God's breast, my own abode,
  Those shoals of dazzling glory passed,
  I lay my spirit down at last.

Although Browning clearly intends us to disapprove of Johannes' Antinomianism, he complicates the issue by showing the lofty passion that can proceed from the immoral doctrine. Nevertheless, the passion is rationally accounted for by the doctrine; Johannes is a fanatic, one who has gone to a philosophical extreme. A moral and philosophical term like *fanatic* will not suffice, however, to characterize St Simeon; we need also a term out of abnormal psychology. It is interesting to note in this connection that *Johannes Agricola* originally appeared together with *Porphyria's Lover* under the common heading of *Madhouse Cells*, but the poems were later separated and the heading abandoned. Without the heading, there is nothing in *Johannes Agricola* to make us suppose that the speaker is mad, that he is anything more than fanatically devoted to his Antinomian principles. That is because Browning does not, like Tennyson in *St Simeon*, pursue the passion downward to those subrational depths where lurk unsuspected motives.

In *Porphyria's Lover*, the speaker is undoubtedly mad. He strangles Porphyria with her own hair, as a culminating expression of his love and in order to preserve unchanged the perfect moment of her surrender to him. But even here, Browning is relying upon an extraordinary complication of what still remains a rationally understandable motive. The motive and action are no more unreasonable than in *A Forgiveness*, where we do not consider the speaker or his wife mad. She is unfaithful because of her great love for him, and he eventually forgives her by awarding her hate instead of contempt; she allows the life blood to flow out of her to help his hate pass away in vengeance. The motives in both poems are likely to demonstrate for us rather more ingenuity than madness; and it is generally true that extraordinary motives in Browning come not from disordered subconscious urges but, as in Henry James, from the highest moral and intellectual refinement.

* * *

* * * Since the past is understood in the same way that we understand the speaker of the dramatic monologue, the dramatic monologue is an excellent instrument for projecting an historical point of view. For the modern sense of the past involves, on the one hand, a sympathy for the past, a willingness to understand it in its own terms as different from the present; and on the other hand it involves a critical awareness of our own modernity. In the same way, we understand the speaker of the dramatic monologue by sympathizing with him, and yet by remaining aware of the moral judgment we have suspended for the sake of understanding. The combination of sympathy and judgment makes the dramatic monologue suitable for expressing all kinds of extraordinary points of view, whether moral, emotional or historical—since sympathy frees us for the widest possible range of experience, while the critical reservation keeps us aware of how far we are departing. The extraordinary point of view is characteristic of all the best dramatic monologues, the pursuit of experience in all its remotest extensions being the genius of the form.

We are dealing, in other words, with empiricism in literature. The pursuit of all experience corresponds to the scientific pursuit of all knowledge; while the sympathy that is a condition of the dramatic monologue corresponds to the scientific attitude of mind, the willingness to understand everything for its own sake and without consideration of practical or moral value. We might even say that the dramatic monologue takes toward its material the literary equivalent of the scientific attitude—the equivalent being, where men and women are the subject of investigation, the historicizing and psychologizing of judgment.

Certainly the Italian Renaissance setting of *My Last Duchess* helps us to suspend moral judgment of the duke, since we partly at least take an historical view; we accept the combination of villainy with taste and manners as a phenomenon of the Renaissance and of the old aristocratic order generally. The extraordinary combination pleases us the way it would the historian, since it impresses upon us the difference of the past from the present. We cannot, however, entirely historicize our moral judgment in this poem, because the duke's crime is too egregious to support historical generalization. More important, therefore, for the suspension of moral judgment is our psychologizing attitude—our willingness to take up the duke's view of events purely for the sake of understanding him, the more outrageous his view the more illuminating for us the psychological revelation.

In *The Bishop Orders His Tomb*, however, our judgment is mainly historicized, because the bishop's sins are not extraordinary but the universally human venalities couched, significantly for the historian, in the predilections of the Italian Renaissance. Thus, the bishop gives vent to materialism and snobbery by planning a bigger and better tomb than his clerical rival's. This poem can be read as a portrait of the age, our moral judgment of the bishop depending upon our moral judgment of the age. Ruskin praised the poem for its historical validity: "It is nearly all that I said of the Central Renaissance in thirty pages of *The Stones of Venice* put into as many lines"; but being no friend of the Renaissance, this is the spirit of the age he conceived Browning to have caught: "its worldliness, inconsistency, pride, hypocrisy, ignorance of itself, love of art, of luxury, and of good Latin."[3] Browning, who admired the Renaissance, would have admitted all this but he would have insisted, too, upon the enterprise and robust aliveness of the age. What matters, however, is that Browning has presented an historical image the validity of which we can all agree upon, even if our moral judgments differ as they do about the past itself.

In the same way, our understanding of the duke in *My Last Duchess* has a primary validity which is not disturbed by our differing moral

---

3. *Modern Painters* (London: Routledge; New York: Dutton, 1907), iv, 370.

judgments after we have finished reading the poem—it being charac-
teristically the style of the dramatic monologue to present its material
empirically, as a fact existing before and apart from moral judgment
which remains always secondary and problematical. Even where the
speaker is specifically concerned with a moral question, he arrives at
his answer empirically, as a necessary outcome of conditions within
the poem and not through appeal to an outside moral code. Since
these conditions are always psychological and sometimes historical as
well—since the answer is determined, in other words, by the speaker's
nature and the time he inhabits—the moral meaning is of limited ap-
plication but enjoys within the limiting conditions of the poem a valid-
ity which no subsequent differences in judgment can disturb.

Take as an example Browning's dramatic monologues in defence of
Christianity. Although the poet has undoubtedly an axe to grind, he
maintains a distinction between the undeniable fact of the speaker's
response to the conditions of the poem and the general Christian for-
mulation which the reader may or may not draw for himself. The
speaker starts with a blank slate as regards Christianity, and is brought
by the conditions of the poem to a perception of need for the kind of
answer provided by Christianity. Nevertheless, the perception is not
expressed in the vocabulary of Christian dogma and the speaker does
not himself arrive at a Christian formulation.

The speakers of the two epistolary monologues, *Karshish* and *Cleon*,
are first-century pagans brought by the historical moment and their
own psychological requirements to perceive the need for a God of
Love (*Karshish*) and a promise of personal immortality (*Cleon*). But
they arrive at the perception through secular concepts, and are pre-
vented by these same concepts from embracing the Christian answer
that lies before them. Karshish is an Arab physician travelling in Judea
who reports the case of the risen Lazarus as a medical curiosity, re-
garding Jesus as some master physician with the cure for a disease
that simulates death. He is ashamed, writing to his medical teacher, of
the story's mystical suggestions and purposely mixes it up with, and
even tries to subordinate it to, reports of cures and medicinal herbs.
Yet it is clear throughout that the story haunts him, and he has already
apologized for taking up so much space with it when he interrupts
himself in a magnificent final outburst that reveals the story's impact
upon his deepest feelings:

> The very God! think, Abib; dost thou think?
> So, the All-Great, were the All-Loving too—.

Nevertheless, he returns in the last line to the scientific judgment,
calling Lazarus a madman and using to characterize the story the
same words he has used to characterize other medical curiosities: "it is
strange."

Cleon is a Greek of the last period; master of poetry, painting,
sculpture, music, philosophy, he sums up within himself the whole
Greek cultural accomplishment. Yet writing to a Greek Tyrant who

possesses all that Greek material culture can afford, he encourages the Tyrant's despair by describing his own. The fruits of culture—self-consciousness and the increased capacity for joy—are curses, he says, since they only heighten our awareness that we must die without ever having tasted the joy our refinement has taught us to conceive. He demonstrates conclusively, in the manner of the Greek dialectic, that life without hope of immortality is unbearable. "It is so horrible," he says,

> I dare at times imagine to my need
> Some future state revealed to us by Zeus,
> Unlimited in capability
> For joy, as this is in desire for joy,
> —To seek which, the joy-hunger forces us.

He despairs because Zeus has not revealed this. Nevertheless, he dismisses in a hasty postscript the pretensions of "one called Paulus," "a mere barbarian Jew," to have "access to a secret shut from us."

The need for Christianity stands as empiric fact in these poems, just because it appears in spite of intellectual and cultural objections. In *Saul* there are no objections, but the need is still empiric in that it appears before the Christian formulation of it. The young David sings to Saul of God's love, of His sacrifice for man, and His gift of eternal life, because he needs to sing of the highest conceivable joy, his songs about lesser joys having failed to dispel Saul's depression. David "induces" God's love for Saul from his own, God's willingness to suffer for Saul from his own willingness, and God's gift of eternal life from his own desire to offer Saul the most precious gift possible.

> "O Saul,
> it shall be
> A Face like my face that receives thee; a Man
> like to me,
> Thou shalt love and be loved by, for ever:
> a Hand like this hand
> Shall throw open the gates of new life to thee!
> See the Christ stand!"

The speaker of *A Death in the Desert* is a Christian—St. John, the beloved disciple and author of the Fourth Gospel, conceived as speaking his last words before dying at a very old age. He has outlived the generation that witnessed the miracles of Christ and the apostles, and has lived to see a generation that questions the promise of Christ's coming and even His existence. As the last living eye-witness, John has been able to reassure this generation; but dying, he leaves a kind of Fifth Gospel for the skeptical generations to follow, generations that will question the existence of John himself. It is an empiricist gospel. "I say, to test man, the proofs shift," says John. But this is well, since belief in God would have no moral effect were it as inevitable as belief in the facts of nature. Myth, man's apprehension of truth, changes; but the Truth remains for each generation to rediscover for itself. The later generations will have sufficiently profited from the moral effect of Christianity, so as not to require proof by miracle or direct revelation. They will be able to "induce" God's love from their own and from their need to conceive a love higher than theirs. Thus, Browning invests with dogmatic authority his own anti-dogmatic line of Christian apologetics.

In *Bishop Blougram's Apology*, the case is complicated by the inappropriateness of the speaker and his argument to the Christian principles being defended. Blougram, we are told in an epilogue, "said true things, but called them by wrong names." A Roman Catholic bishop, he has achieved by way of the Church the good things of this world and he points to his success as a sign that he has made the right choice. For his relatively unsuccessful opponent, the agnostic literary man, Gigadibs, the bishop is guilty of hypocrisy, a vice Gigadibs cannot be accused of since he has made no commitments. Since the bishop admits to religious doubt (Gigadibs lives "a life of doubt diversified by faith," the bishop "one of faith diversified by doubt"), Gigadibs can even take pride in a superior respect for religion, he for one not having compromised with belief. Thus, we have the paradox of the compromising worldly Christian against the uncompromising unwordly infidel—a conception demonstrating again Browning's idea that the proofs do not much matter, that there are many proofs better and worse for the same Truth. For if Blougram is right with the wrong reasons, Gigadibs with admirable reasons or at least sentiments is quite wrong.

The point of the poem is that Blougram makes his case, even if on inappropriate grounds. He knows his argument is not the best ("he believed," according to the epilogue, "say, half he spoke"), for the grounds are his opponent's; it is Blougram's achievement that he makes Gigadibs see what the agnostic's proper grounds are. He is doing what Browning does in all the dramatic monologues on religion—making the empiricist argument, starting without any assumptions as to faith and transcendental values. Granting that belief and unbelief are equally problematical, Blougram proceeds to show that even in terms of this world only belief bears fruit while unbelief does not. This is indicated by Blougram's material success, but also by the fact that his moral behaviour, however imperfect, is at least in the direction of his professed principles; whereas Gigadibs' equally moral behaviour is inconsistent with his principles. Who, then, is the hypocrite? "I live my life here," says Blougram, "yours you dare not live."

But the fact remains—and this is the dramatic ambiguity matching the intellectual—that the bishop is no better than his argument, though he can conceive a better argument and a better kind of person. He cannot convert Gigadibs because his argument, for all its suggestion of a Truth higher than itself, must be understood dramatically as rationalizing a selfish worldly existence. What Gigadibs apparently does learn is that he is no better than the bishop, that he has been the same kind of person after the same kind of rewards only not succeeding so well, and that he has been as intellectually and morally dishonest with his sentimental liberalism as the bishop with his casuistry. All this is suggested indirectly by the last few lines of the epilogue, where we are told that Gigadibs has gone off as a settler to Australia. Rid of false intellectual baggage (the bishop's as well as his own), he will presumably start again from the beginning, "inducing" the Truth for himself. "I hope," says Browning,

> By this time he has tested his first plough,
> And studied his last chapter of St John.

St John, note, who makes the empiricist argument in *A Death in the Desert*, and whose Gospel Browning admired because of its philosophical rather than thaumaturgic treatment of Christianity.

Although *Blougram* and *A Death in the Desert* are too discursive to communicate their religious perceptions in the manner of *Karshish, Cleon* and *Saul*, as the speaker's immediate experience, they make their case empirically because in non-Christian terms. They might be considered as setting forth the rhetorical method of the more dramatic poems, a method for being taken seriously as intelligent and modern when broaching religion to the skeptical post-Enlightenment mind. The reader is assumed to be Gigadibs (it is because the bishop is so intelligent that Gigadibs finds it difficult to understand how he can believe), and the poet makes for his benefit a kind of "minimum argument," taking off from his grounds and obtruding no dogmatic assertions.

Eliot addresses his religious poetry to the same kind of reader, communicating his religious perceptions in terms that fall short of Christian dogma. This is especially interesting in Eliot since his concern has been with dogmatic religion, whereas Browning was always anti-dogmatic. Of course, the method is in both poets not merely a deliberate rhetorical device but the necessary outcome of their own religious uncertainties, and a sign that they share like Blougram the post-Enlightenment mind. This is again especially apparent in Eliot, who has dramatized in his poetry his movement from skepticism to orthodoxy, whereas Browning's poetry shows no significant religious *development*. Nevertheless, there is something of the obtuseness of Karshish and Cleon in those speakers of Eliot's dramatic monologues whose religious perceptions fall short of the Christian truth—and with the same effect as in Browning, that the reader can give assent to the speaker's experience without having to agree on doctrine.

In *Journey of the Magi*, one of the Magi describes with great clarity and detail the hardships of the journey to Bethlehem, but cannot say for certain what he saw there or what it meant. The Magi returned to their Kingdoms, like Karshish and Cleon "no longer at ease here, in the old dispensation," but still without light. The old Jew Simeon, in *A Song for Simeon*, is somewhat in the position of Browning's David in *Saul*; he sees clearly the glory of Christianity, but is too old to embrace it—not for him "the ultimate vision," the new dispensation is ahead of his time. In *Marina*, the speaker apparently finds the ultimate vision in the face of his newly recovered daughter and in the woodthrush song through the fog, but the vision is still not intelligible, not translated into Christian terms.

In the earlier skeptical poems, the fog is even thicker and no song of revelation comes through it. But Eliot uses idolatrous or "minimum" analogues to the Christian myth to indicate the groping for meaning, his own groping and that of the characters within the poem. The characters in *Gerontion* and *The Waste Land* practise idolatries, aesthetic and occultist. *Gerontion* ends with an occultist vision of the modern, cosmopolitan, unbelieving dead whirled around the universe on a meaningless wind:

> De Bailhache, Fresca, Mrs Cammel, whirled
> Beyond the circuit of the shuddering Bear
> In fractured atoms.

Yet seen in the subsequent lines as a natural phenomenon, the wind has a certain meaning in that it unites the parts of nature, north and south, into a single living whole:

> Gull against the wind, in the windy straits
> Of Belle Isle, or running on the Horn,
> White feathers in the snow, the Gulf claims,

and there is, I think, the suggestion that the wind may be a cleansing wind, one which may bring the rain the aged speaker has been waiting for. The same wind that carries off the dead may bring renewal to the depleted living; that is as much meaning and as much hope as the speaker can achieve.

It is as much meaning as our pagan ancestors achieved in the primitive vegetation myths of death and renewal, and Eliot uses the analogy of these myths to give at least that much meaning to the jumbled fragments of *The Waste Land*. Just as the vegetation gods were slain so they might rise renewed and restore the fertility of the land; so the longing for death, which pervades the modern waste land, is a longing for renewal and, if the reader wants to carry the analogy a step farther, a longing for redemption through the blood of Christ, the slain God.

The analogy with the vegetation myths is maintained even in the *Four Quartets*, which are written from a solidly orthodox position. The religious perceptions of these poems are couched less in Christian terms than in terms of that mystical fusion of anthropology and psychology, of myth and the unconscious, that Jung effected.[4] One wonders if the *Four Quartets* are not, for all their orthodoxy, more satisfying to the skeptical than to the orthodox, since the latter might well prefer an articulation of religious truth no less explicit than their own convictions. Post-Enlightenment minds, on the other hand, are particularly fascinated by the mystique of myth and the unconscious as a way back, I think, to a kind of religious speculation which commits them to nothing while preserving intact their status as intelligent,

---

4. For a discussion of Eliot's use of Jungian ideas and symbols, see Elizabeth Drew, *T. S. Eliot: The Design of His Poetry* (New York: Scribner's, 1949; London: Eyre and Spottiswoode, 1950).

scientific and modern. Myth and the unconscious are contemporary equivalents of Browning's pragmatism in making the "minimum" argument for Christianity.

Although not the only way to talk religion empirically, the dramatic monologue offers certain advantages to the poet who is not committed to a religious position, or who is addressing readers not committed and not wanting to be. The use of the speaker enables him to dramatize a position the possibilities of which he may want to explore as Browning explores the "impossible" case. The speaker also enables him to dramatize an emotional apprehension in advance of or in conflict with his intellectual convictions—a disequilibrium perhaps inevitable to that mind which I have been calling post-Enlightenment or romantic because, having been intellectually through the Enlightenment, it tries to re-establish some spiritual possibility. Browning's St John, in *A Death in the Desert*, defends religious myth as the expression of just this disequilibrium, of the emotional apprehension that exceeds formulated knowledge:

> "man knows partly but conceives beside,
> Creeps ever on from fancies to the fact,
> And in this striving, this converting air
> Into a solid he may grasp and use,
> Finds progress, man's distinctive mark alone,
> Not God's, and not the beasts'."

Even Eliot who professes to be against this "dissociation" of emotional apprehension from its formulated articulation (which for him is dogma), even in Eliot's poetry emotion is always a step ahead of reason—as for example the dim adumbrations of Christianity provided by the vegetation mythology of *The Waste Land*, or the disturbance of the Magi that exceeds their understanding, or that ultimate vision in *Marina* the articulation of which is obscured by the fog.

Not only can the speaker of the dramatic monologue dramatize a position to which the poet is not ready to commit himself intellectually, but the sympathy which we give the speaker for the sake of the poem and apart from judgment makes it possible for the reader to participate in a position, to see what it feels like to believe that way, without having finally to agree. There is, in other words, the same split between sympathy and judgment that we saw at work in our relation to the duke of *My Last Duchess*. The split is naturally most apparent in those dramatic monologues where the speaker is in some way reprehensible, where sympathy is in conflict with judgment, but it is also at work where sympathy is congruent with judgment although a step ahead of it. The split must in fact be at work to some degree, if the poem is to generate the effect which makes it a dramatic monologue.

Browning's *Rabbi Ben Ezra* is a dramatic monologue by virtue of its title only; otherwise it is a direct statement of a philosophical idea, because there is no characterization or setting. Because the statement is not conditioned by a speaker and a situation, there is no way of apprehending it other than intellectually; there is no split between its validity as somebody's apprehension and its objective validity as an idea. But in *Abt Vogler*, where the statement is also approved of, it is conditioned by the speaker's ecstasy as he extemporizes on the organ. His sublime vision of his music as annihilating the distinction between heaven and earth has validity as part of the ecstatic experience of extemporizing, but becomes a matter of philosophical conjecture as the ecstasy subsides and the music modulates back into the "C Major of this life." The disequilibrium between the empiric vision that lasts as long as the ecstasy and the music, and its philosophical implication, makes sympathy operative; and the tension between what is known through sympathy and what is only hypothesized through judgment generates the effect characteristic of the dramatic monologue.

Since sympathy is the primary law of the dramatic monologue, how does judgment get established at all? How does the poet make clear what we are to think of the speaker and his statement? Sometimes it is not clear. The Catholic reader might well consider Tennyson's St Simeon admirable and holy. Readers still try to decide whether Browning is for or against Bishop Blougram. Browning was surprised at accusations of anti-Catholicism that followed the publication of the poem, but he was even more surprised when Cardinal Wiseman (the model for Blougram) wrote in reviewing the poem for a Catholic journal: "*we should never feel surprise at his* [Browning's] *conversion.*"[5] We now know, at least from external evidence if not from more careful reading, that Browning's final judgment is against Don Juan of *Fifine* and Prince Hohenstiel-Schwangau (representing Napoleon III). But the reviewers considered that he was defending the incontinent Don Juan and accused him of perversity; while of *Hohenstiel-Schwangau*, one reviewer said that it was a "eulogism on the Second Empire," and another called it "a scandalous attack on the old constant friend of England."[6]

But these are exceptional cases, occurring mainly in Browning and the result partly of Browning's sometimes excessive ingenuity, partly of a judgment more complex than the reader is expecting, partly of careless reading. Certainly Don Juan's desertion of his wife and return to the gipsy girl in the end—even though he says it is for five minutes and "to clear the matter up"—ought for the careful reader to show up his argument as rationalizing a weak character, although the argument contains in itself much that is valid. In the same way, the final reference to Gigadibs as starting from the beginning with a plough and the Gospel of St John ought to indicate that he is getting closer to the truth than Blougram. I have tried to indicate that more is involved in our judgment of the bishop than the simple alternatives of *for* and *against*. As the bishop himself says of the modern interest in character, which interest is precisely the material of the dramatic monologue:

5. E. R. Houghton has established that Wiseman was not the reviewer after all. [*Editor.*]
6. Quoted in De Vane, *Browning Handbook*, (New York: Appleton-Century-Crofts), pp. 243, 369, 363; (London: John Murray), pp. 216, 327, 321.

Our interest's on the dangerous edge of things.
The honest thief, the tender murderer,
The superstitious atheist, demirep
That loves and saves her soul in new French books—
We watch while these in equilibrium keep
The giddy line midway: one step aside,
They're classed and done with. I, then, keep the line
Before your sages,—just the men to shrink
From the gross weights, coarse scales and labels broad
You offer their refinement. Fool or knave?
Why needs a bishop be a fool or knave
When there's a thousand diamond weights between?

There is judgment all right among modern empiricists, but it follows understanding and remains tentative and subordinate to it. In trying to take into account as many facts as possible and to be as supple and complex as the facts themselves, judgment cuts across the conventional categories, often dealing in paradoxes—the honest thief, the tender murderer. Above all, it brings no ready-made yardstick; but allows the case to establish itself in all its particularity, and to be judged according to criteria generated by its particularity.

In other words, judgment is largely psychologized and historicized. We adopt a man's point of view and the point of view of his age in order to judge him—which makes the judgment relative, limited in applicability to the particular conditions of the case. This is the kind of judgment we get in the dramatic monologue, which is for this reason an appropriate form for an empiricist and relativist age, an age which has come to consider value as an evolving thing dependent upon the changing individual and social requirements of the historical process. For such an age judgment can never be final, it has changed and will change again; it must be perpetually checked against fact, which comes before judgment and remains always more certain.

HERBERT F. TUCKER

Dramatic Monologue and the Overhearing of Lyric†

His muse made increment of anything,
From the high lyric down to the low rational.
(*Don Juan* III.lxxxv.5–6)

I would say, quoting Mill, "Oratory is heard, poetry is overheard." And he would answer, his voice full of contempt, that there was always an audience; and yet, in his moments of lofty speech, he himself was alone no matter what the crowd.
(*The Autobiography of William Butler Yeats*)

† From *Lyric Poetry: Beyond New Criticism*, ed. Chaviva Hošek and Patricia Parker (Ithaca: Cornell UP, 1985), pp. 226–43. Copyright © 1985 by Cornell University. Reprinted by permission of Cornell University Press.

I

"Eloquence is *heard*, poetry is *overheard*. Eloquence supposes an audience; the peculiarity of poetry appears to us to lie in the poet's utter unconsciousness of a listener. Poetry is feeling confessing itself to itself, in moments of solitude." "Lyric poetry, as it was the earliest kind, is also, if the view we are now taking of poetry be correct, more eminently and peculiarly poetry than any other."[1] Thus wrote John Stuart Mill in 1833, with the wild surmise of a man who had lately nursed himself through a severe depression, thanks to published poetry and its capacity to excite intimate feeling in forms uncontaminated by rhetorical or dramatic posturing. One listener Mill's characteristically analytic eloquence is likely to have found at once was Robert Browning, who moved in London among liberal circles that touched Mill's and who in the same year published his first work, the problematically dramatic *Pauline: A Fragment of a Confession*, to which Mill drafted a response Browning saw in manuscript. Browning's entire career—most notably the generic innovation for which he is widely remembered today, the dramatic monologue—would affirm his resistance to the ideas about poetry contained in Mill's essays. Indeed, as early as *Pauline* Browning was confessing to the open secret of spontaneous lyricism, but in ways that disowned it. What follows is emphatically the depiction of a bygone state:

> And first I sang as I in dream have seen
> Music wait on a lyrist for some thought,
> Yet singing to herself until it came.
> (II. 377–79)

In this complex but typical retrospect the poet of *Pauline* figures as an eavesdropper on his own Shelleyan juvenilia, themselves relics of a dream of disengaged and thoughtless youth from which the sadder but wiser poet has on balance done well to awaken. Browning's enfolding of a lyrical interval into a narrative history sets the pattern for the establishment of character throughout his subsequent work, a pattern knowingly at odds with the subjectivist convention that governed the reading of English poetry circa 1830 and to which Mill's essay gave memorable but by no means unique voice.[2]

To the most ambitious and original young poets of the day, Brown-

---

1. John Stuart Mill, *Essays on Poetry*, ed. F. Parvin Sharpless (Columbia, S.C., 1976), pp. 12, 36. The quotations come from two essays of 1833, "What is Poetry?" and "The Two Kinds of Poetry."
2. Ideas like Mill's abound, for example, in Macaulay's 1825 essay "Milton," in *Critical and Historical Essays* (London, 1883): "Analysis is not the business of the poet" (p. 3); "It is the part of the lyric poet to abandon himself, without reserve, to his own emotions" (p. 6); "It is just when Milton escapes from the shackles of the dialogue, when he is discharged from the labour of uniting two incongruous styles, when he is at liberty to indulge his choral raptures without reserve, that he rises even above himself" (p. 8). Comparing Mill's writings with T. S. Eliot's "The Three Voices of Poetry" (1953), Elder Olson, *American Lyric Poems* (New York, 1964), p. 2, concludes that "the study of the question has not advanced much in over a hundred years." Olson's conclusion retains its force after two decades. See Barbara Hardy, *The Advantage of Lyric* (Bloomington and London, 1977), p. 2: "Lyric poetry thrives, then, on exclusions. It is more than usually opaque because it leaves out so much of the accustomed context and consequences of feeling that it can speak in a pure, lucid, and intense voice."

ing and Alfred Tennyson, the sort of lyricism Mill admired must have seemed "overheard" in a sense quite other than Mill intended: heard overmuch, overdone, and thus in need of being done over in fresh forms. Among their other generic experiments in the lyrical drama (*Paracelsus*, *Pippa Passes*), the idyll ("Dora," "Morte d'Arthur"), and the sui generis historical epic form of *Sordello*, during the 1830s Tennyson and Browning arrived independently at the first recognizably modern dramatic monologues: "St. Simeon Stylites" (1842; written in 1833) and the paired poems of 1837 that we now know as "Johannes Agricola in Meditation" and "Porphyria's Lover." These early monologues were not only highly accomplished pieces; within the lyrical climate of the day they were implicitly polemical as well. The ascetic St. Simeon atop his pillar, exposed to the merciless assault of the elements, stands for an exalted subjectivity ironically demystified by the historical contextualization that is the generic privilege of the dramatic monologue and, I shall argue, one of its indispensable props in the construction of character. Browning's imagination was less symbolically brooding than Tennyson's and more historically alert, and he launched his dramatic monologues with speakers whose insanities were perversions, but recognizably versions, of the twin wellheads of the lyrical current that had come down to the nineteenth century from the Reformation and the Renaissance. The historical figure Johannes Agricola is an antinomian protestant lying against time as if his soul depended on it; and Porphyria's lover, though fictive, may be regarded as a gruesomely literal-minded Petrarch bent on possessing the object of his desire. Each of Browning's speakers, like St. Simeon Stylites, utters a monomaniacal manifesto that shows subjectivity up by betraying its situation in a history. The utterance of each stands revealed not as poetry, in Mill's terms, but as eloquence, a desperately concentric rhetoric whereby, to adapt Yeats's formulation from "Ego Dominus Tuus," the sentimentalist deceives himself.

What gets "overheard" in these inaugural Victorian monologues is history dramatically replayed. The charmed circle of lyric finds itself included by the kind of historical particularity that lyric genres exclude by design, and in the process readers find themselves unsettlingly historicized and contextualized as well. The extremity of each monologist's authoritative assertion awakens in us with great force the counter-authority of communal norms, through a *reductio ad absurdum* of the very lyric premises staked out in Mill's essays, most remarkably in a sentence that Mill deleted when republishing "What is Poetry?": "That song has always seemed to us like the lament of a prisoner in a solitary cell, ourselves listening, unseen in the next."[3] ("Ourselves"? How many of us in that next cell? Does one eavesdrop in company? Or is that not called going to the theater, and is Mill's overheard poetry not dramatic eloquence after all?) Tennyson's and Browning's first monologues imply that Mill's position was already its own absurd reduction—a reduction not just of the options for poetry

3. *Essays on Poetry*, p. 14.

but of the prerogatives of the unimprisoned self, which ideas like Mill's have been underwriting, as teachers of undergraduate poetry classes can attest, for the better part of two centuries. Tennyson and Browning wanted to safeguard the self's prerogatives, and to that extent they shared the aims of contemporary lyrical devotees. But both poets' earliest dramatic monologues compassed those aims through a more subtle and eloquent design than the prevailing creed would admit: a design that might preserve the self on the far side of, and as a result of, a contextual dismissal of attenuated Romantic lyricism and its merely soulful claims; a design that might, as Browning was to put it in the peroration to *The Ring and the Book* (1869), "Suffice the eye and save the soul beside" (XII.863). St. Simeon, Johannes, and Porphyria's lover emerge through their monologues as characters: poorer souls than they like to fancy themselves but selves for all that, de- and re-constructed selves strung on the tensions of their texts.

II

Both Tennyson and Browning proceeded at once to refine their generic discoveries, though they proceeded in quite different directions. While Tennyson kept the dramatic monologue in his repertoire, he turned to it relatively seldom; and with such memorable ventures as "Ulysses" and "Tithonus" he in effect relyricized the genre, running its contextualizing devices in reverse and stripping his speakers of personality in order to facilitate a lyric drive. Browning, on the other hand, moved his dramatic monologues in the direction of mimetic particularity, and the poems he went on to write continued to incorporate or "overhear" lyric in the interests of character-formation. "Johannes Agricola" and "Porphyria's Lover" had been blockbusters, comparatively single-minded exercises in the construction of a lurid character through the fissuring of an apparently monolithic ego. The gain in verisimilitude of Browning's later monologues is a function of the nerve with which he learned to reticulate the sort of pattern these strong but simple monologues had first knit. The degree of intricacy varies widely, but the generic design remains the same. Character in the Browningesque dramatic monologue emerges as an interference effect between opposed yet mutually informative discourses: between an historical, narrative, metonymic text and a symbolic, lyrical, metaphoric text that adjoins it and jockeys with it for authority. While each text urges its own priority, the ensemble works according to the paradoxical logic of the originary supplement: the alien voices of history and of feeling come to constitute and direct one another. Typically Browning's monologists tell the story of a yearning after the condition of lyric, a condition that is itself in turn unimaginable except as the object of, or pretext for, the yearning that impels the story plotted against it.[4]

4. Genre theorists have often observed this distinction, though usually in honoring the exclusivity of lyric. For Babette Deutsch, *Potable Gold* (New York, 1929), p. 21, the essential distinction lies between prose and poetry: "The one resembles a man walking toward a definite

What we acknowledge as the "life" of a dramatic monologue thus emerges through the interdependence of its fictive autobiography and its *élan vital*, each of which stands as the other's reason for being, and neither of which can stand alone without succumbing to one of two deconstructive ordeals that beset character in this genre (and that arguably first beset the self during the century in which this genre arose). The first ordeal lies through history and threatens to resolve the speaking self into its constituent influences, to unravel character by exposing it as merely a tissue of affiliations. At the same time, character in the dramatic monologue runs an equal but opposite risk from what certain Romantic poetics and hermeneutics would assert to be the self's very place of strength and what we have been calling, after Mill, the privacy of lyric. A kind of sublime idiocy, lyric isolation from context distempers character and robs it of contour, as Socrates said long ago in the *Ion* (lyric poets are out of their minds), and as Sharon Cameron, with an eye on Greek and earlier origins of lyric, has said again more recently: "the lyric is a departure not only from temporality but also from the finite constrictions of identity."[5] We find this lyric departure superbly dramatized in the valediction of Tennyson's Ulysses, that most marginal of characters, whose discourse poises itself at "the utmost bound of human thought" (l. 32). Insofar as we find Ulysses transgressing that bound—as for me he does in the final paragraph, with its address to a bewilderingly mythical crew of Ithacan mariners and with the concomitant evanescence of its "I"—we find Tennyson transgressing the generic boundary of dramatic monologue as well.

One good reason why the dramatic monologue is associated with Browning's name rather than with Tennyson's, who technically got to it first, is that in Browning the lyrical flight from narrative, temporality, and identity appears through a characteristic, and characterizing, resistance to its allure. Browning's Ulysses, had he invented one, would speak while bound to the mast of a ship bound elsewhere; his life would take its bearing from what he heard the Sirens sing, and their music would remain an unheard melody suffusing his monologue without rising to the surface of utterance.[6] Such a plot of lyri-

---

goal; the other is like a man surrendering himself to contemplation, or to the experience of walking for its own sake. Prose has intention; poetry has intensity." According to Kenneth Burke, *A Grammar of Motives* (1945; Berkeley and Los Angeles, 1969), p. 475, "The *state of arrest* in which we would situate the essence of lyric is not analogous to dramatic action at all, but is the dialectical counterpart of action." Olson, "The Lyric," *BMMLA*, 1 (1969), 65, says of lyrics that "while they may contain within themselves a considerable narrative or dramatic portion, that portion is subordinate to the lyrical whole. . . . Once expression and address and colloquy become subservient to a further end as affecting their form as complete and whole in themselves, we have gone beyond the bounds of the lyric." For a recent view of Browning opposed to that of the present essay see David Bergman, "Browning's Monologues and the Development of the Soul," *ELH*, 47 (1980), 774: "For Browning, historicity only prettifies a work. . . . History, the creation of a concrete setting, has never been a major focus for Browning." I would reply that history is indeed a major focus for Browning—one of the two foci, to speak geometrically, that define his notoriously elliptical procedures.

5. *Ion* 534; Sharon Cameron, *Lyric Time* (Baltimore and London, 1979), p. 208. See also the quirky Victorian theorist E. S. Dallas, *Poetics* (London, 1852), p. 83: "The outpourings of the lyric should spring from the law of unconsciousness. Personality or selfhood triumphs in the drama; the divine and all that is not Me triumphs in the lyric."

6. Although Browning never wrote such a monologue, he glanced at its possibility in "The Englishman in Italy" (1845), with its vision of "Those isles of the siren" (l. 199) and its audition

cism resisted would mark his poem as a dramatic monologue, which we should be justified in reading as yet another allegory of the distinctive turn on Romantic lyricism that perennially recreated Browning's poetical character. "R. B. a poem" was the title he gave in advance to this allegorical testament, in the fine letter, virtually an epistolary monologue, that he addressed on the subject to Elizabeth Barrett; and by the time of "One Word More" (1855) he could proudly affirm his wife's lyricism as the privately silencing otherness his public character was to be known by.[7]

Dramatic monologue in the Browning tradition is, in a word, anything but monological. It represents modern character as a quotient, a ratio of history and desire, a function of the division of the modern mind against itself. Our apprehension of character as thus constituted is a Romantic affair; in Jerome Christensen's apt phrase for the processing of the "lyrical drama" in Romanticism, it is a matter of learning to "read the differentials." As a sampling of the dozens of poetry textbooks published in recent decades will confirm, the dramatic monologue is our genre of genres for training in how to read between the lines—a hackneyed but valuable phrase that deserves a fresh hearing.[8] In the reading of a dramatic monologue we do not so much scrutinize the ellipses and blank spaces of the text as we people those openings by attending to the overtones of the different discourses that flank them. Between the lines, we read in a no-man's-land the notes whose intervals engender character. Perhaps the poet of the dramatic monologue gave a thought to the generic framing of his own art when he had the musician Abt Vogler (1864) marvel "That out of three sounds he frame, not a fourth sound, but a star" (l. 52). The quantum leap from text to fictive persona (the dramatic "star" of a monologue) is no less miraculous for being, like Abt Vogler's structured improvisation, "framed," defined and sustained as a put-up job. That such a process of character-construction tends to elude our received means of exegesis is a contributing cause for the depression of Browning's stock among the New Critics. But one way to begin explicating a dramatic monologue in the Browning tradition is to identify a discursive shift, a moment at which either of the genre's constitu-

---

of a song "that tells us / What life is, so clear"; "The secret they sang to Ulysses / When, ages ago, / He heard and he knew this life's secret / I hear and I know" (ll. 223–27). Life's secret, needless to add, goes untold in Browning's text.

7. Letter of 11 February 1845, in *Letters of Robert Browning and Elizabeth Barrett Barrett, 1845–1846*, ed. Elvan Kintner, 2 vols (Cambridge, Mass., 1969), 1:17.

8. Jerome Christensen, " 'Thoughts That Do Often Lie Too Deep for Tears': Toward a Romantic Concept of Lyrical Drama," *Wordsworth Circle*, 12:1 (1981), 61. For an appropriately genealogical testimonial to the pedagogical virtues of the dramatic monologue see Ina Beth Sessions's postscript to "The Dramatic Monologue," *PMLA*, 62 (1947), 516n.: "One of the most interesting comments concerning the dramatic monologue was made by Dr. J. B. Wharey of the University of Texas in a letter to the writer on January 17, 1935: 'The dramatic monologue is, I think, one of the best forms of disciplinary reading—that is, to use the words of the late Professor Genung, "reading pursued with the express purpose of feeding and stimulating inventive power." ' " Among the earliest systematic students of the genre in our century were elocution teachers; their professional pedigree broadly conceived goes back at least to Quintilian, who recommended exercises in impersonation (*prosopopoeia*) as a means of imaginative discipline. See A. Dwight Culler, "Monodrama and the Dramatic Monologue," *PMLA*, 90 (1975), 368.

tive modes—historical line or punctual lyric spot—breaks into the other.

III

Since the premier writer of dramatic monologues was, as usual in such matters, the most ingenious, it is difficult to find uncomplicated instances in Browning that are also representative. We might sample first a passage from "Fra Lippo Lippi" (1855), a sizeable blank-verse monologue that happens to contain lyric literally in the form of *stornelli*, lyrical catches Englished in italics that Browning's artist monk emits at odd intervals during the autobiography he is improvising for the night watch. In the following lines Lippo is taking off those critics whom his new painterly realism has disturbed:

> "It's art's decline, my son!
> You're not of the true painters, great and old;
> Brother Angelico's the man, you'll find;
> Brother Lorenzo stands his single peer:
> Fag on at flesh, you'll never make the third!"
> *Flower o' the pine,*
> *You keep your mistr . . . manners, and I'll stick to mine!*
> I'm not the third, then: bless us, they must know!
> Don't you think they're the likeliest to know,
> They with their Latin?
>
> (ll. 233–42)

The gap for interpretation to enter is, of course, the middle of the second italicized line, marked typographically by ellipsis and prosodically by the wreckage of the embedded snatch of song. Amid Lippo's tale of the modern artist's oppression by his superiors, by religious and representational traditions, and by the Latin learning that backs up both (poetry as overseen?), the apparently spontaneous individual talent bursts forth in a rebellious chant—which is then itself interrupted by a reminder, also apparently spontaneous, of Lippo's answerability to the authorities right in front of him. Lippo's lyric flower breeds a canker: the poetry we and the police thought we were overhearing turns out to be, through versatile revision or instant overdubbing, a rhetorically canny performance. Or, if we take a larger view, it turns out to have been rhetoric all along, Lippo's premeditated means of affirming solidarity with the unlettered night watch by ruefully policing his own speech in advance and incorporating this police action into the larger speech act that is his monologue.

The passage is intensely artificial yet intensely realistic, and we should note that its success does not rely on our deciding whether the monologist has forecast his occasion or stumbled upon it. The twist of the lyrical line against itself nets a speaking subject who is tethered to circumstances and, for that very reason, is anything but tongue-tied. Here as throughout the Browningesque monologue, character is not unfolded to comprehension but enfolded in a text that draws us in.

Even after nearly four hundred lines we do not grasp Lippo's character as an essence and know what he is; but if we have negotiated the text we know how he does. In the terms of the passage in question, we know his *manners*, not least his manner of covering up his *mistr* . . . Lippo's character arises, in the differentials between vitality and circumstances, as a way of life, a mazing text, a finely realized, idiosyncratic instance of a generic method.

A similarly punctuated digression from story, or transgression into lyric, occurs at the center of Browning's most famous monologue, "My Last Duchess" (1842):

> She had
> A heart—how shall I say?—too soon made glad,
> Too easily impressed; she liked whate'er
> She looked on, and her looks went everywhere.
> Sir, 't was all one! My favour at her breast,
> The dropping of the daylight in the West,
> The bough of cherries some officious fool
> Broke in the orchard for her, the white mule
> She rode with round the terrace—all and each
> Would draw from her alike the approving speech,
> Or blush, at least. She thanked men,—good! but thanked
> Somehow—I know not how—as if she ranked
> My gift of a nine-hundred-years-old name
> With anybody's gift.
>
> (ll. 21–34)

The framing hesitations of "How shall I say?" and "I know not how" may or may not come under the Duke's rhetorical control; but a comparable tic or stammer invades his discourse more subtly with the appositional style of the middle lines, which do here with syntax the work done otherwise in Fra Lippo's *stornelli*. Halfway through the monologue, these lines constitute a lyrical interlude around which the Duke's despotic narrative may be seen to circle, with a predatory envy that escapes his posture of condescension. Anaphora and grammatical suspension, time-honored refuges of lyric, harbor recurrent images of the daily and seasonal cycle, of natural affection, and of sexual generation that not only contradict the Duke's potent affiliation with art, culture, and domination but show these contradictions within the text to be contradictions within the Duke. Or rather, to discard the figuration of inside and outside that dramatic monologue at its best asks us to do without, it is these textual contradictions that constitute the Duke's character. The polymorphous perversity he here attributes to his last Duchess is as much an attribute of his own character as is the different, monomaniacal perversity with which he has put a stop to her egalitarian smiles. Each perversity so turns on the other as to knot the text up into that essential illusion we call character. Hence the Duke's characteristic inconsistency in objecting to the "officious fool" who, in breaking cherries for the Duchess, was not breaking ranks at all but merely executing his proper "office" in the

Duke's hierarchical world. Hence, too, the undecidable ambiguity of "My favour at her breast": the phrase oscillates between suggestions of a caress naturally given and of an heirloom possessively bestowed, and its oscillation is what makes the star of dramatic character shine. Such a semantic forking of the ways, like the plotting of spontaneity against calculation in Fra Lippo's "*mistr . . . manners*" revision, blocks reference in one direction, in order to refer us to the textual production of character instead.

Because in grammatical terms it is a paratactic pocket, an insulated deviation from the syntax of narrative line, the Duke's recounting of his Duchess's easy pleasures wanders from the aims of the raconteur and foregrounds the speech impediments that make her story his monologue.[9] Moreover, the Duke's listing is also a listening, a harkening after the kind of spontaneous lyric voice that he, like the writer of dramatic monologues, comes into his own by imperfectly renouncing. Lyric, in the dramatic monologue, is what you cannot have and what you cannot forget—think of the arresting trope Browning invented for his aging poet Cleon (1855), "One lyric woman, in her crocus vest" (l. 15)—and as an organizing principle for the genre, lyric becomes present through a recurrent and partial overruling. This resisted generic nostalgia receives further figuration intertextually, in "My Last Duchess" and many another monologue, with the clustering of allusions at moments of lyric release. Here "The dropping of the daylight in the West" falls into Browning's text from major elegies, or refusals to mourn, by Milton ("Lycidas"), Wordsworth ("Tintern Abbey," "Intimations" ode), and Keats ("To Autumn"); and the Duchess on her white mule so recalls Spenser's lyrically selfless Una from the opening of *The Faerie Queene* as to cast the Duke as an archimage dubiously empowered.

Amid the Duke's eloquence the overhearing of poetry, in this literary-historical sense of allusion to prior poems, underscores the choral dissolution that lurks in lyric voice. Furthermore, it reinstates the checking of such dissolution as the mark of the individual self—of the dramatic speaker and also of the poet who, in writing him up, defines himself in opposition to lyrical orthodoxy and emerges as a distinct "I," a name to conjure with against the ominous: "This grew; I gave commands" (1.45). Toward the end of his career, in "House" (1876) Browning would in his own voice make more explicit this engagement with the literary past and would defend literary personality, against Wordsworth on the sonnet, as just the antithesis of unmediated sincerity: " ' *"With this same key / Shakespeare unlocked his heart,"* once

9. David I. Masson, "Vowel and Consonant Patterns in Poetry," in *Essays on the Language of Literature*, ed. Seymour Chatman and Samuel R. Levin (Boston, 1967), p. 3, observes that "where lyrical feeling or sensuous description occurs in European poetry, there will usually be found patterns of vowels and consonants." For more general consideration of the linguistics of lyric, see Edward Stankiewicz, "Poetic and Non-poetic Language in Their Interrelation," in *Poetics*, ed. D. Davie et al. (Gravenhage, 1961), p. 17: "Lyrical poetry presents the most interiorized form of poetic language, in which the linguistic elements are most closely related and internally motivated." Note that Stankiewicz, following the Russian Formalists, here refers not to psychological inwardness but to the nonreferential, auto-mimetic interiority of language itself.

more!' / Did Shakespeare? If so, the less Shakespeare he!" (ll. 38–40). Poetry of the unlocked heart, far from displaying character in Browning's terms, undoes it: Browning reads his chief precursor in the English dramatic line as a type of the objective poet, the poetical character known through a career-long objection to the sealed intimacies of the poem à clef.

IV

In 1831 Arthur Hallam gave a promising description of the best of Tennyson's *Poems, Chiefly Lyrical* (1830) as "a graft of the lyric on the dramatic." The Victorian dramatic monologue that soon ensued from these beginnings was likewise a hybrid genre, a hardy offshoot of the earlier hybrid genre in which the first Romantics had addressed the problem of how to write the long modern poem by making modern civilization and its discontents, or longing and its impediments, into the conditions for the prolonging and further hearing of poetry: the "greater Romantic lyric." The genre M. H. Abrams thus christened some years ago has by now achieved canonical status, but a reconsideration of its given name from the standpoint of the dramatic monologue may help us save it from assimilation to orthodox lyricism by reminding us that the genre Abrams called "greater" was not more-lyrical-than-lyric but rather more-than-lyrical. Despite a still high tide of assertions to the contrary, the works of the first generations of Romantic poets were on the whole much less lyrical than otherwise.[1] Once we conceive the Romantic tradition accordingly as a perennial intermarriage, which is to say infighting, of poetic kinds, we can situate the Victorian dramatic monologue as an eminently Romantic form. In correcting the literary-historical picture we can begin, too, to see how fin-de-siècle and modernist reactions to the Browningesque monologue have conditioned the writing, reading, and teaching of poetry, literary theory, and literary history in our own time.

At the beginning of Browning's century Coleridge remarked, "A poem of any length neither can be, nor ought to be, all poetry." By the end of the century Oscar Wilde, looking askance at Browning's achievement, took up Coleridge's distinction, but with a difference: "If he can only get his music by breaking the strings of his lute, he breaks them, and they snap in discord. . . . Meredith is a prose Browning, and so is Browning. He used poetry as a medium for writing in prose."[2]

---

1. Arthur Hallam, "On Some of the Characteristics of Modern Poetry, and on the Lyrical Poems of Alfred Tennyson," in *The Writings of Arthur Hallam*, ed. T. Vail Motter (New York, 1943), p. 197; M. H. Abrams, "Structure and Style in the Greater Romantic Lyric," in *From Sensibility to Romanticism*, ed. Frederick W. Hilles and Harold Bloom (New York, 1965), pp. 527–60. On the Romantic mixture of lyric with other genres see Cameron, *Lyric Time*, p. 217; Christensen, "'Thoughts,'" pp. 60–62; Robert Langbaum, "Wordsworth's Lyrical Characterizations," *Studies in Romanticism*, 21 (1982), 319–39. Langbaum's earlier book *The Poetry of Experience* (1957; rpt. New York, 1963), which places the dramatic monologue within Romantic tradition, should be consulted, as should two responses that appeared, almost concurrently, two decades later; Culler, "Monodrama," and Ralph W. Rader, "The Dramatic Monologue and Related Lyric Forms," *Critical Inquiry*, 3 (1976), 131–51.
2. Coleridge is quoted in Frederick A. Pottle, *The Idiom of Poetry* (Ithaca, 1941), p. 82. Wilde's comments occur in "The Critic as Artist" (1890), in *Literary Criticism of Oscar Wilde*, ed. Stanley Weintraub (Lincoln, Neb., 1968), p. 202.

The difference between Coleridge's and Wilde's ideas of what a poem should be is in large part a difference that the dramatic monologue had made in nineteenth-century poetry, a difference Browning inscribed into literary history by inscribing it into the characteristic ratios of his texts. Wilde and others at the threshold of modernism wanted Mill's pure lyricism but wanted it even purer. And through an irony of literary history that has had far-reaching consequences for our century, the Browningesque dramatic monologue gave them what they wanted. Symbolist and imagist writers could extract from such texts as *Pauline* and "Fra Lippo Lippi"—and also, to sketch in the fuller picture, from the Tennysonian idyll and most sophisticated Victorian novels—lyrical gems as finely cut as anything from the allegedly naive eras, Romantic or Elizabethan, upon which they bestowed such sentimental if creative regard. The hybrid dramatic monologue, as a result of its aim to make the world and subjectivity safe for each other in the interests of character, had proved a sturdy grafting stock for flowers of lyricism; and the governing pressures of the genre, just because they governed so firmly, had bred hothouse lyric varieties of unsurpassed intensity. These lyrical implants it was left to a new generation of rhymers, scholars, and anthologists to imitate, defend, and excerpt in a newly chastened lyric poetry, a severely purist poetics, and a surprisingly revisionist history of poetry.[3]

The fin-de-siècle purism of Wilde, Yeats, Arthur Symons, and others was polemically canted against the example of Browning; yet it remained curiously, even poignantly, in his debt. Consider, for example, Symons's resumption of a rhetoric very like Mill's, as he praises Verlaine in *The Symbolist Movement* (1899) for "getting back to nature itself": "From the moment when his inner life may be said to have begun, he was occupied with the task of an unceasing confession, in which one seems to overhear him talking to himself."[4] The pivotally wishful "unceasing," which distinguishes Symons's formulation from Mill's, also betrays a kind of elegiac overcompensation. Mill had dissolved audience in order to overhear poetry as if from an adjacent cell; Symons, writing at an appreciable historical remove from the achievements of Verlaine, is by contrast trapped in time. Symons's overhearing of poetry resembles less Mill's eavesdropping than the belated

3. Victorian writers were divided as to the chronological priority of lyric over other genres. For Dallas, as for Mill, "Lyrics are the first-fruits of art" (p. 245), while Walter Bagehot contends that "poetry begins in Impersonality" and that lyric represents a later refinement ("Hartley Coleridge" [1852], in *Collected Works*, ed. Norman St. John-Stevas, I [Cambridge, Mass., 1965], pp. 159–60). As to the normative status of lyric, however, the later nineteenth century had little doubt. Summaries and bibliographical aids may be found in Francis B. Gummere, *The Beginnings of Poetry* (New York, 1901), p. 147; Charles Mill Gayley and Benjamin Putnam Kurtz, *Methods and Materials of Literary Criticism* (Boston, 1920), p. 122: W. K. Wimsatt, Jr., and Cleanth Brooks, *Literary Criticism: A Short History* (New York, 1966), pp. 433, 751–52. For representative belletristic histories of poetry from a nostalgic, fin-de-siècle perspective see John Aldington Symonds, *Essays Speculative and Suggestive* (London, 1893), pp. 393 ff.; Edmund Gosse, "Introduction" to *Victorian Songs: Lyrics of the Affections and Nature*, ed. E. H. Garrett (Boston, 1895); and Arthur Symons, *The Symbolist Movement in Literature* (1899; rpt. New York, 1958) and *The Romantic Movement in English Poetry* (New York, 1909). On the influence of F. T. Palgrave's *Golden Treasury* (1861; rev. 1981), an anthology that "established, retroactively and for the future, the tradition of the English lyric," see Christopher Clausen, *The Place of Poetry* (Lexington, 1981), p. 67.

4. Symons, *The Symbolist Movement*, p. 49.

Browningesque audition of a poignant echo, and the symbolist movement he hopes to propel is fed by an overwhelming nostalgia that creates from its own wreck the thing it contemplates. The nostalgia for lyric that throbs through the influential versions of the poetic past Symons and his contemporaries assembled sprang from a range of cultural causes we are only beginning to understand adequately.[5] But we can observe here that the rhetorical pattern into which their lyrically normed historiography fell was precisely that of the poetic genre that had preeminently confronted lyricism with history in their century: the dramatic monologue. It is as if what Symons championed as the "revolt against exteriority, against rhetoric,"[6] having repudiated the "impure" Browning tradition in principle, was condemned to reiterate its designs in writing. The symbolist and imagist schools wanted to read in their French and English antecedents an expurgated lyric that never was on page or lip. It was, rather, a generic back-formation, a textual constituent they isolated from the dramatic monologue and related nineteenth-century forms; and the featureless poems the fin-de-siècle purists produced by factoring out the historical impurities that had ballasted these forms are now fittingly, with rare exceptions, works of little more than historical interest.

Virtually each important modernist poet in English wrote such poems for a time; each became an important poet by learning to write otherwise and to exploit the internal otherness of the dramatic monologue. When the lyrical bubble burst within its bell jar, poetry became modern once again in its return to the historically responsive and dialogical mode that Browning, Tennyson, and others had brought forward from the Romantics.[7] And upon the establishment of Yeats's mask, Pound's personae, Frost's monologues and idylls, and Eliot's impersonal poetry, it became a point of dogma among sophisticated readers that every poem dramatized a speaker who was not the poet. "Once we have dissociated the speaker of the lyric from the personality of the poet, even the tiniest lyric reveals itself as drama."[8] We recognize this

5. Marxian approaches now offer the most promising and comprehensive explanations of the fortunes of lyric as a product of industrial culture, yet recently published Marxian analyses evaluate the social functions of lyric very differently. For Theodor W. Adorno, "Lyric Poetry and Society" (1957: trans. Bruce Mayo, *Telos*, 20 [Summer 1974], 56–71), "The subjective being that makes itself heard in lyric poetry is one which defines and expresses itself as something opposed to the collective and the realm of objectivity" (p. 59); in contrast, Hugh N. Grady, "Marxism and the Lyric," *Contemporary Literature*, 22 (1981), 555, argues that "the lyric has become a specialized, though not exclusive, genre of Utopian vision in the modern era."

6. Symons, *The Symbolist Movement*, p. 65.

7. Olson, "The Lyric," p. 65, in distinguishing the "verbal acts" of lyric from those of more elaborated forms, himself acts fatally on the strength of a simile: "The difference, if I may use a somewhat homely comparison, is that between a balloon inflated to its proper shape, nothing affecting it but the internal forces of the gas, and a balloon subjected to the pressure of external forces which counteract the internal." But a balloon affected only by internal forces (i.e., a balloon in a vacuum) would not inflate but explode. That the "proper shape" of a poem, as of a balloon, arises not from sheer afflatus but as a compromise between "internal" and "external" forces is precisely my point about the framing of the dramatic monologue—as it is, I think, the dramatic monologue's (deflationary) point about the lyric.

8. Wimsatt and Brooks, *Literary Criticism*, p. 675; see also Cleanth Brooks and Robert Penn Warren, *Understanding Poetry* (1938; rev. ed. New York, 1950), p. liv. Don Geiger. *The Dramatic Impulse in Modern Poetics* (Baton Rouge, 1967), pp. 85–95, provides a capable overview of the persona poetics of the New Criticism.

declaration as dogma by the simple fact that we—at least most of us—had to learn it, and had to trade for it older presuppositions about lyric sincerity that we had picked up in corners to which New Critical light had not yet pierced. The new dogma took (and in my teaching experience it takes still) with such ease that it is worth asking why it did (and does), and whether as professors of poetry we should not have second thoughts about promulgating an approach that requires so painless an adjustment of the subjectivist norms we profess to think outmoded.

The conversion educated readers now routinely undergo from lyrical to dramatic expectations about the poems they study recapitulates the history of Anglo-American literary pedagogy during our century, the middle two decades of which witnessed a great awakening from which we in our turn are trying to awaken again. Until about 1940 teachers promoted poetry appreciation in handbooks and anthologies that exalted lyric as "the supreme expression of strong emotion . . . the very real but inexplicable essence of poetry," and that throned this essential emotion in the equally essential person of the poet: "Lyrical poetry arouses emotion because it expresses the author's feeling."[9] By 1960 the end of instruction had shifted from appreciating to understanding poetry, and to this end a host of experts marched readers past the author of a poem to its dramatic speaker. John Crowe Ransom's dictum that the dramatic situation is "almost the first head under which it is advisable to approach a poem for understanding" had by the 1960s advanced from advice to prescription. In Laurence Perrine's widely adopted *Sound and Sense* the first order of business is "to assume always that the speaker is someone other than the poet himself." For Robert Scholes in *Elements of Poetry* the speaker is the most elementary of assumptions: "In beginning our approach to a poem we must make some sort of tentative decision about who the speaker is, what his situation is, and who he seems to be addressing."[1]

That such forthright declarations conceal inconsistencies appears in the instructions of Robert W. Boynton and Maynard Mack, whose *Introduction to the Poem* promotes the familiar dramatic principle but pursues its issues to the verge of a puzzling conclusion. The authors begin dogmatically enough: "When we start looking closely at the dramatic character of poetry, we find that we have to allow for a more immediate speaker than the poet himself, one whom the poet has imagined speaking the poem, as an actor speaks a part written for him by a playwright." But then Boynton and Mack, with a candor unusual in the handbook genre, proceed to a damaging concession that dissolves the insubstantial pageant of the dramatic enterprise into thin air: "In some instances this imagined speaker is in no way definite or

9. Oswald Doughty, *English Lyric in the Age of Reason* (London, 1922), p. xv; Walter Blair and W. K. Chandler, eds., *Approaches to Poetry* (New York, 1935), p. 250.
1. Ransom is quoted in William Elton, *A Glossary of the New Criticism* (Chicago, 1949), p. 38. *Sound and Sense*, 2nd ed. (New York, 1963), p. 21; *Elements of Poetry* (New York, 1969), pp. 11–12.

distinctive; he is simply a voice." (When is a speaker not a speaker? When he is a "voice," nay, an Arnoldian "lyric cry.") With this last sentence Boynton and Mack offer an all but lyrical intimation of the mystification inherent in the critical fiction of the speaker and suggest its collusion with the mysteries of the subjectivist norm it was designed to supplant.[2] It may well be easier to indicate these mysteries than to solve them; what matters is that with our New Critical guides we seem to have experienced as little difficulty in negotiating the confusions entailed by the fiction of the speaker as we have experienced in converting ourselves and our students from lyrically expressive to dramatically objective norms for reading.

Why should we have made this conversion, and why do we continue to encourage it? Why should our attempts at understanding poetry through a New Criticism rely on a fiction that baffles the understanding? These are related questions, and their answers probably lie in considerations of pedagogical expediency. One such consideration must be the sheer hard work of bringing culturally stranded students into contact with the historical particularities from which a given poem arises. Life (and courses) being short, art being long, and history being longer still, the fiction of the speaker at least brackets the larger problem of context so as to define a manageable classroom task for literary studies. To such institutional considerations as these, which have been attracting needed attention of late, I would add a consideration more metaphysical in kind. The fiction of the speaker, if it removes from the study of poetry the burden, and the dignity, of establishing contact with history, puts us in compensatory contact with the myth of unconditioned subjectivity we have inherited from Mill and Symons in spite of ourselves. Through that late ceremony of critical innocence, the readerly imagination of a self, we modern readers have abolished the poet and set up the fictive speaker; and we have done so in order to boost the higher gains of an intersubjective recognition for which, in an increasingly mechanical age that can make Mill's look positively idyllic, we seem to suffer insatiable cultural thirst. The mastery of New Critical tools may offer in this light a sort of homeopathic salve, the application of a humanistic technology to technologically induced ills.

The thirst for intersubjective confirmation of the self, which has made the overhearing of a persona our principal means of understanding a poem, would I suspect be less strong if it did not involve a kind of bad faith about which Browning's Bishop Blougram (1855) had

2. Robert W. Boynton and Maynard Mack, *Introduction to the Poem* (New York, 1965), p. 24. On p. 45, to complete the circuit, the authors equate the "voice with "the poet." They thus return us through a backstage exit to Clement Wood's definition of lyric in *The Craft of Poetry* (New York, 1929), p. 189, as "the form in which the poet utters his own dramatic monolog." Compare the dramatic metaphor in Benedetto Croce's 1937 *Encyclopedia Britannica* article on "Aesthetic": "The lyric . . . is an objectification in which the ego sees itself on the stage, narrates itself, and dramatizes itself" (quoted in Wimsatt and Brooks, *Literary Criticism*, p. 510). For Geoffrey Crump, *Speaking Poetry* (London, 1953), p. 59, the reverse seems true: "an element of the dramatic is present in all lyrical poetry, because the speaker is to some extent impersonating the poet."

much to say: "With me, faith means perpetual unbelief / Kept quiet like the snake 'neath Michael's foot / Who stands calm just because he feels it writhe" (ll. 666–68). The New Criticism of lyric poetry introduced into literary study an anxiety of textuality that was its legacy from the Higher Criticism of scripture a century before: anxiety over the tendency of texts to come loose from their origins into an anarchy that the New Critics half acknowledged and half sought to curb under the regime of a now avowedly fictive self, from whom a language on parole from its author might nonetheless issue as speech. What is poetry? Textuality a speaker owns. The old king of self-expressive lyricism is dead: Long live the Speaker King! At a king's ransom we thus secure our reading against the subversive textuality of what we read; or as another handbook from the 1960s puts it with clarity: "So strong is the oral convention in poetry that, in the absence of contrary indications, we infer a voice and, though we know we are reading words on a page, create for and of ourselves an imaginary listener."[3] Imaginative recreation "for and of ourselves" here depends upon our suppressing the play of the signifier beneath the hand of a convention "so strong" as to decree the "contrary indications" of textuality absent most of the time.

Deconstructive theory and practice in the last decade have so directed our attention to the persistence of "contrary indications" that the doctrine espoused in my last citation no longer appears tenable. It seems incumbent upon us now to choose between intersubjective and intertextual modes of reading, between vindicating the self and saving the text. Worse, I fear, those of us who are both teachers and critics may have to make different choices according to the different positions in which we find ourselves—becoming by turns intertextual readers in the study and intersubjective readers in the classroom—in ways that not very fruitfully perpetuate a professional divide some latter-day Browning might well monologize upon. I wonder whether it must be so; and I am fortified in my doubts by the stubborn survival of the dramatic monologue, which began as a response to lyric isolationism, and which remains to mediate the rivalry between intersubjective appeal and intertextual rigor by situating the claims of each within the limiting context the other provides.

In its charactered life the dramatic monologue can help us put in their places critical reductions of opposite but complementary and perhaps even cognate kinds: on one hand, the transcendentally face-saving misprisions that poetry has received from Victorian romanticizers, Decadent purists, and New Critical impersonalists alike; on the other hand, the abysmal disfigurements of a deconstruction that would convert poetry's most beautiful illusion—the speaking presence—into a uniform textuality that is quite as "purist," in its own way, as anything the nineteenth century could imagine. An exemplary teaching genre, the dramatic monologue can teach us, among other things, that while texts do not absolutely lack speakers, they do not

---

3. Jerome Beaty and William H. Matchett, *Poetry: From Statement to Meaning* (New York, 1965), p. 103.

simply have them either; they invent them instead as they go. Texts do not come from speakers, speakers come from texts. *Persona fit non nascitur*. To assume in advance that a poetic text proceeds from a dramatically situated speaker is to risk missing the play of verbal implication whereby character is engendered in the first place through colliding modes of signification; it is to read so belatedly as to arrive only when the party is over. At the same time, however, the guest the party convenes to honor, the ghost conjured by the textual machine, remains the articulate phenomenon we call character: a literary effect we neglect at our peril. For to insist that textuality is all and that the play of the signifier usurps the recreative illusion of character is to turn back at the threshold of interpretation, stopping our ears to both lyric cries and historical imperatives, and from our studious cells overhearing nothing. Renewed stress upon textuality as the basis for the Western written character is a beginning as important to the study of poetry now as it has been for over a century to the writing of dramatic monologues and to the modern tradition they can illuminate in both backward and forward directions. But textuality is only the beginning.

ISOBEL ARMSTRONG

The Politics of Dramatic Form†

To begin with Mill, Browning's poems, 'Porphyria' and 'Johannes Agricola' constitute a running dialogue with his ideas. The two *Repository* monologues emerge as parodies of his aesthetics and their politics. They draw out and expose the implications of Mill's thought with devastating rigour and virtuosity. Mill's apologetics, 'What is poetry?' and 'The two kinds of poetry', make a fundamental distinction between two kinds of knowledge.[1] One is the knowledge granted by expressive feeling and psychological experience. The other is the knowledge granted by the scientist. The poet describes the lion affectively through the emotions, the scientist neutrally, abstractly and literally (the lion becomes a locus classicus of Utilitarian aesthetics, making an appearance in George Eliot's famous justification of realism in *Adam Bede*, 1859).[2] Hallam had granted knowledge to the poet of sensation as well as to the poet of reflection. In denying the poet knowledge Mill effectively removes poetic knowledge into the post-Kantian realm of the aesthetic, cut off from discursive rationality and instrumental activity. But, despite his emphasis on emotion, the representation of the poet's lion must take place without self-conscious displays of subjectivity. This was the ground of Mill's objection to

---

† From *Victorian Poetry: Poetry, Poetics, and Politics* (New York: Routledge, 1993), pp. 136–54. Copyright © 1993 by Isobel Armstrong. Reprinted by permission of Routledge / Taylor & Francis.
1. *Monthly Repository*, N.S., VII (1833), 60–70 ('What is poetry?'), 714–24 ('Two kinds of poetry').
2. 'What is poetry?', 63.

Pauline. His attack on its morbid self-consciousness this side of mad-
ness is perfectly consistent with his belief in expressive emotion. Like
Fox, he believed that the poet educates feeling, but unlike Fox he be-
lieved that poetry educates by belonging to the domain of private feel-
ing and not by negotiating the public world of power. His distinction
between the poet of nature (Shelley) and the poet of culture
(Wordsworth) rests on his belief that the drama of expressive presen-
tation actually transcends the immediate social order and has its own
form of truth. The poet of nature frees feeling and emotions, returning
a refreshed and purified experience to the society from which he has
escaped in order that the social can have access to a new aesthetic or-
der, a harmonised and healthy order, which becomes a form of control
on excesses of emotion.[3] Here is initiated the idea of poetry as therapy,
an alternative poetics which attempts to erase the political by propos-
ing to cure the neurosis of social division rather than to analyse it.
This view was to be influential in the nineteenth century, from Arnold
to the later Morris. Mill, borrowing from the ideas of Dugald Stewart,
preferred the lyric experience which was 'synchronous' (he speaks of
using the language of the philosophers) because it *orders* feeling.[4]
Random, sequential associations interfere with the pure experience,
whereas synchronous, instantaneous experience controls and shapes
emotion.

The purest form of expressive lyric is feeling *dramatised* as 'solilo-
quy', but this drama is not a public transaction between actor and
audience. The distinction between poetry and 'eloquence' follows.
Whereas the orator is the self-conscious scientist of feeling, publicly
manipulating emotion and using psychological states instrumentally in
the cause of action, or influence, the true poet is unself-conscious
and alone with his affective, emotional condition which never goes be-
yond itself. 'All poetry is of the nature of soliloquy'.[5] All poetry is a
construct, a representation, but the poet of soliloquy eliminates the
evidence of its own construction.

> [Poetry] is feeling confessing itself to itself, in moments of soli-
> tude, and embodying itself in symbols which are the nearest pos-
> sible representations of the feeling in the exact shape in which it
> exists in the poet's mind. Eloquence is feeling pouring itself out
> to other minds . . . poetry . . . is soliloquy in full dress, and on the
> stage. . . . But no trace of consciousness that any eyes are upon us
> must be visible in the work itself. The actor knows that there is an
> audience present; but if he acts as though he knew it, he acts ill
> . . . he [the poet] can succeed in excluding from his work every
> vestige of such lookings-forth into the outward and every-day
> world. . . . But when he turns around and addresses himself to
> another person; when the act of utterance is not itself the end,

3. 'Two kinds of poetry', 715.
4. Ibid., 716. Mill is deeply ambivalent about the two kinds of poetry. Though Wordsworth is
never 'ebullient' (718), Shelley lacks 'mental discipline' (719), even though ideally the poet
of nature such as Shelley should be superior to the poet of culture in whom thought domi-
nates.
5. 'What is poetry?', 65.

but a means to an end . . . then it ceases to be poetry and becomes eloquence.[6]

Poetry is 'heard', eloquence is 'overheard'. Inward-looking, private feeling, Mill says, apparently with enthusiasm, approaches almost to 'monotony',[7] and goes on to extend his distinction between poetry and eloquence to opera. With this formulation, constituting poetry as private production, Mill seals a distinction between poetry and the external world which, defining the poetic as the solitary work of the speaking subject over and against communality, was to have consequences for the rest of the century. It is a poetics of exclusion. We are back with the claustrophobia which *Pauline* struggles against. The poetics of exclusion generates a politics of exclusion or enclosure as the speaking subject in his or her private cell of subjectivity communicates if at all by accidental empathy. No audience is required, and the isolated lookers-on gain no knowledge except that of an equally isolated and dissociated psychological condition.

The two monologues, printed originally as 'Porphyria' and 'Johannes Agricola' (later their order was reversed and their titles extended), come into being as analytical experiments in the logic of Mill's closet poetics. Significantly they were later called 'Madhouse Cells'. They are a parody of the private utterance overheard rather than heard, the drama of soliloquy 'unconscious of being seen'. Nothing Browning had done before has their concentration and economy. Through them the fallacies of the poetics and politics of exclusion are explored. They achieve what was not achieved in *Pauline*, the poem which is simultaneously expressive utterance *and* reversed as objectified feeling, so that the speaking subject is at once self-analytical and capable of being the object of analysis which goes beyond the self. The parody of Mill's drama points up the central element of drama which is excluded in soliloquy: these poems are about acting and *taking action*, the construction of roles and their connection with volition and agency which relates people to the world. Browning takes those areas which were coming progressively to occupy the status of private experience of the self in his culture—sexuality and religion—as test cases. These were, in fact, the experiences which Mill was later to say were outside the jurisdiction of public morals.[8] The poems chart 'conditions of extremity'. 'Porphyria' narrates a fictional episode in which a sexual murder takes place as the woman named in the title arrives on an illicit visit to her lover. The title of 'Johannes Agricola' refers to the historical character who was an extreme Antinomian in believing himself to be one of the elect. Johannes Agricola is not required, so he argues, to act. Alone with an (almost certainly imaginary) lover, alone with one's God, this is the logical conclusion of Mill's solitude. The cold and greedy violence of these monologues establish a privacy in which the external world disappears. Where Tennyson depicts a self alienated

6. Ibid.
7. Ibid., 64.
8. J. S. Mill, *On Liberty*, 1859.

and excluded from the world of choice and action, Browning depicts its opposite but dialectically related experience, a condition in which the private encroaches on and absorbs the public world to the extent that the public world is non-existent. The ultimate action for Porphyria's lover becomes the choice to kill: 'surprise' / Made my heart swell, and still it grew / While I debated what to do. / . . . I found / A thing to do . . . / And strangled her' (33–41). Johannes Agricola lives in a world where to act is unnecessary because God has predestined all experience; 'I lie where I have always lain, / . . . God said / This head this hand should rest upon / Thus, ere he fashioned star or sun' (11–20): 'Be sure that thought and word and deed / All go to swell his love for me' (26–7). The self 'swells' in both poems, to exclude all else.

The critique of overheard drama raises a number of crucial problems. If the soliloquist is solipsist, speaking to himself, who is the addressee of private poetry? A relationship with a looker-on or an audience is excluded so that no space for dialogue can exist. Both monologues are remarkable for the silencing of the voice of the other as the speakers live in a world without reciprocity to the extent that their own speech is almost redundant, too. Porphyria 'called me', but 'no voice replied' (15): and the poem ends, 'And yet God has not said a word!' (60). God predetermines every word for Johannes Agricola, so that his own praise of God is unnecessary, for God is speaking to himself through him. The syntax here points two ways as the infinitive verb makes it unclear whether it is God or Agricola who engages in the act of blessing: 'ful-fed / By unexhausted power to bless' (41–2).

The solipsism of expressive emotion privately experienced leads to another consequence—mania, delusion, paranoia and visions of total power as the speaking subject relinquishes relationships. When Porphyria enters, dripping from a storm, and proceeds to undress and seduce her strangely passive lover, it is not clear whether or not she has been conjured by the fantasist's dream of a seduction which is at the same time a form of mothering. He watches his seduction as he watches the process of stripping.

> Withdrew the dripping cloak and shawl . . .
>   let the damp hair fall,
> And, last, she sat down by my side
> And called me. When no voice replied,
> She put my arm about her waist,
> And made her smooth white shoulder bare,
> And all her yellow hair displaced,
> And, stooping, made my cheek lie there,
> And spread, o'er all, her yellow hair,
> Murmuring how she loved me.
>   (11, 13–21)[9]

The enclosing curtain of hair recalls *Pauline*, but this poem explores power and mastery in sexual relations with far more intensity. If the

9. Quotations of Browning's poetry are from *Robert Browning: The Poems*, John Pettigrew and Thomas J. Collins, eds, 2 vols, Harmondsworth, 1981.

speaker is actually indulging in sexual fantasy he gains power and mastery over his seductress in imagination because she is his object. He does not speak, not from catatonic passivity, but because of a sense of control: the fantasist has no need to participate in human discourse with the productions of his fantasy. She is literally not there. Porphyria's voice is his ventriloquism. As he repeats but reverses her seduction by taking charge of the strangled woman, the depersonalised female body changes to 'it'.

> I propped her head up as before,
> Only, this time my shoulder bore
> Her head, which droops upon it still:
> The smiling rosy little head,
> So glad it has its utmost will,
> That all it scorned at once is fled,
> And I, its love, am gained instead!
> (49–55)

The ambiguity of the reversible possessive 'its' in 'its love' points up the blurring of subject and object in fantasy. The speaker is both possessor and possessed, for 'love' both owns and is owned by 'it'. The same process goes on in 'Johannes Agricola' where Johannes is an object of God's 'content' (30) by loving him and literally the 'content' of God's love itself. Logically he *is* God.

A second consequence of solipsist soliloquy is the emergence of private contracts which come about directly as a result of the speaker's belief that they are exempt from public contracts and institutional agreements. Their contracts become a parody of legal and socially agreed definition. Definition, in fact, becomes an entirely private matter. Porphyria is the sexual property of another man but desires another contract, to 'give herself to me forever' (25). Johannes Agricola places himself and his relationship with God outside the sordid bargaining process involved in the economics of praise and good works expressed essentially as an economics of *repayment*. He refuses to 'bargain' (59), 'paying a price' (60) of praise, but he can do this precisely because God has already made a prior bargain and invoked legality to ensure his election—a guarantee and a 'warrant' (33), 'irreversibly/Pledged' (29–30)—God 'pays him off' as Mill said of *Pauline*. The vulnerable and suspect status of public contracts, and the equally vulnerable status of identity when it deems itself exempt from them, is exposed in these negotiations. Johannes speaks of the non-elect forced to 'win' (47) God's love, thus turning contract into a wager and identifying God with arbitrary chance, or worse, with the idea of competition. So a further question emerges—what is a law if it applies to some people and not others, or if there are two kinds of law for different kinds of people?

Lastly, solipsist soliloquy carries in its train, following on from madness and the dissolving of the notion of contract, the abolition of time. The speakers exempt themselves from temporality and history because their actions need not take place as a causal sequence. Mill's objection to the successive experience is taken literally, and it becomes clear that the 'synchronous' experience is incoherent. Agricola speaks in the present tense, and the monologue is held together in simultaneity by the ironical reiteration of 'I lie': I stay in the same place and I am untruthful. The arrest of temporality occurs because there is no need for agency in a preordained world—'I lie where I have always lain' (11). God bade him 'grow/Guiltless forever' (22–3) (my emphasis) but growth depends on becoming, and becoming cannot occur if futurity has been attained already, as the beginning of the monologue implies—'For in God's breast, my own abode . . . I lay my spirit down at last' (8, 10). God's breast is his dwelling place, but as his abode and God are identical, again, logically, he is God. The intention ('For I intend to get to God' (6)) has already been pre-empted in the fact of predestination. Thus Agricola has no past, but his exemption from temporality actually depends on assuming that the rest of the world is not exempt. Temporality is there to define his freedom from it. The physical universe of suns, moons and stars which his mind cuts through to God is overcome as if it did not exist, transcended or 'passed' (9). But transcendence is only possible if the material world of process, capable of 'passing' into death, exists. The crowds of passionately believing men, women and children God has 'undone' (54) before the world began are ruthlessly condemned to 'striving' (50) in time, in order to be transcended by the elect Johannes Agricola. The incoherence of the doctrine of the elect, not to speak of its political implications, points remorselessly to the incoherence of Christian notions of heaven and hell.

'Porphyria' works as a successive narrative, but by the end of the poem the events have turned into the 'synchronous' totality of a retrospect—'And thus we sit together now' (58). If the poem is a memory, the speaker has a past. If it is a fantasy nothing has happened—'And all night long we have not stirred' (59). Delusions invent an illusory temporality which is quite independent of historical time. God cannot intervene in imaginary time and withdraws from it. Hence he 'has not said a word' (60). The monomaniac hubris of these two monologues works in contrary motion one to the other, but with the same result. In one, God and creation are indistinguishable because time has been abolished. In the other, God has disappeared because time is imaginary.

The derangement of these monologues comes from Browning's remorseless understanding of the structural problems which arise from the expressive poet's abolition of externality, of agency and action, time, and above all the obliteration of the reader. The characters obsessively read themselves, and if we understand the poems in terms of expressive psychological moments, they effectively suppress the fact that they are being read or 'heard'. They obliterate the active, critical presence of the reader because they obliterate their status as *texts*. So what of the politics of 'heard' poetry, or drama? Through Fox's alternative theory of drama as oratory, as an open, public transaction in which the work, like the actor who recognises the existence of his audience, declares itself as oratory and ideology, it is possible to turn these poems around and to see them as psychological texts rather than psychological expositions or expressions, a second poem created with exactly the same words as the first. This takes us some way into the extraordinary complexities opening out in Browning's work. But in these poems Browning took on a double debate with both Mill and Fox, and a reading of them is not complete without an understanding of the way in which they begin to reach towards another poetics. It is this which enabled Browning to become a political poet, not because he wrote directly of radical problems, but because it released him into the possibility of making a cultural critique in terms of the structure of the monologue itself. If a direct, working-class–based political poetry was closed to him by virtue of his middle-class status, he could write poetry which became cultural critique by presenting and dramatising a politics of poetics. For 'Porphyria' and 'Johannes Agricola' constitute a politics of Mill's poetics. They achieve this by engaging with further strategies which go beyond the tactics of the immediate lampoon. What these are can be derived from Fox's understanding of 'heard' poetry.

Fox's writing on literature constitutes a conscious and deliberate effort to develop a *Utilitarian* and radical aesthetics. While this rests on a fundamental politicising of all literature there is simultaneously, as has been said, a sustained effort to deepen, expand and enrich the Benthamite concept of pleasure through a less mechanistic reading of the process of association than was customarily identified with Benthamism. It is through dramatic poetry that the poet exercises 'one rich ministry of pleasure'. Where the legislator, philosopher and divine must postpone pleasure and fulfilment in different ways the poet 'seizes upon the soul' immediately.[1] Indeed, Fox vigorously defended Bentham from the charge of narrow mechanistic thought. Though Mill depoliticises his expressive poetics, and is otherwise very different from Fox in his aesthetic thought, he shares in Fox's project to explore a new, associationist theory of poetry. But Fox's theory of poetry was fully dramatic and public where Mill's interest was directed to private soliloquy and opera. Significantly, Horne describes opera as the concern of the élite and aristocratic in the impassioned call for the reform of contemporary drama and the economic stranglehold of patent monopoly which prefaces his translation of A. W. Schlegel's lectures on drama. Which class, he asks, responds most to drama? Opera is an aristocratic pursuit comparable to the fighting of mock medieval battles, as in the farcical revival of tournament by Eglinton.

> Is it the aristocracy? They prefer the opera, the scenery, the wardrobe, the heroic Eglintonian pageantry. Is it the middle classes? They are the very followers and only supporters of the true drama. Is it the working classes? The large minority delight in the impassioned drama, and humbly reverence its power: the majority flock to the external shows.[2]

1. *Westminster Review*, XII (1830), 5.
2. A. W. Schlegel, *A Course of Lectures on Dramatic Art and Literature*, trans. John Black, ed. R. H. Horne, 2 vols, 2nd edn, London 1840, xxx.

Fox's development of a Utilitarian poetics goes hand in hand with his attention to drama. If the prerequisite of the poetry which 'influences the associations of unnumbered minds' is that it is 'oratorial', open and 'heard' as a public transaction, then it must be rhetorically self-conscious and aware of itself as text and as ideology. In a remarkable passage on preaching, Fox speaks of the presentation of doctrine in preaching which must go on in detachment from the minister's subjectivity, which must go on, indeed, even when his own feelings are not identified with what he says. He compares his work to that of the actor, who deliberately manipulates and constructs a role and generates emotion through it.

> On certain days, nay, at certain hours, and even minutes, he is bound publicly and solemnly to tell his God that he is in a particular state of mind and feeling, when perhaps he is in a very different state of mind and feeling. He modulates his voice, as he reads the liturgy, to the emotions of reverence, contrition, supplication, thanksgiving, sympathy etc; but who is so totally ignorant of the human mind as to imagine that these emotions either do or can arise within him at his bidding, and in their prescribed order of succession?[3]

So though these poetics are based on a theory of emotion they are not based on complete psychological identification with feeling on the part of either author or reader but on an analytical, detached, dramatic rendering of feeling in which there is an active, critical participation on the part of the audience. Poetry tasks the 'intellect' as well as the 'senses' because it makes use of 'the science of mind', that is, the discoveries of associationist psychology. Such analytical poetry is democratic in three ways. In the first place, it is democratic because it either contains or is structured in terms of *dialogue*. Fox insists that all poetry is dramatic even when it is not dramatic in form. Mental phenomena are externalised as events so that they are the equivalent of a set of incidents which can be publicly examined and mediated. 'Then a poem, however short, should be a narrative, or a drama, and have something of that sort of interest, and consequently of pleasure, which we experience in being conducted through a chain of events to a catastrophe'.[4] The drama may be constructed out of the associative process itself, not 'the current of outward circumstances' but 'that of the phantoms which are ever passing in long procession through the brain'. A poem may be dramatic without the existence of literal dialogue, but there *will* be a dialogue constituted by opposition and conflict within thought and feeling. 'By dramatic we do not mean that the poet should have recourse to personae and dialogue; but he should at least employ those defined and contrasted feelings which will, in very narrow space, shadow forth the strivings of the external and literal drama'.[5] The radical aesthetics of drama turns on the existence of dia-

3. *Monthly Repository*, N.S., VIII (1834), 535.
4. *Westminster Review*, XII (1830), 4. Compare his analysis of Browning's *Pauline* in terms of 'scenery', 'agencies', 'events': *Monthly Repository*, N.S., VII (1833), 254.
5. *Westminster Review*, XII (1830), 5.

logue or its equivalent because it is in dialogue that there is space for debate within the text and between text and reader. Moreover, it is only through dialogue that there is the active possibility of *change*. Schlegel based his definition of drama not on the fact of conversation between characters where 'the poet does not speak in his own person', but on the presence of dialogue. 'It is dialogue', Schlegel says emphatically, which is the very foundation of drama, for this *changes* us as intellectual and moral beings.

> When the characters deliver thoughts and sentiments opposed to each other, but which operate no change, and which leave the minds of both in exactly the same state in which they were at the commencement; the conversation may indeed be deserving of attention, but can be productive of no dramatic interest.[6]

Drama, then, refuses to 'leave the mind . . . in exactly the same state' as it was at the start. That is its essence. And inherent in this is action, action as energetic, non-passive involvement, as well as literal action, for action is 'life itself'.

The second democratic aspect of analytical drama is consequent again on the poet's access to the 'science of man', associationist psychology. The dramatic poet, as Fox says in his essay on Tennyson, can project himself into the subjectivity and associative complexity of any psychological state. But he will be particularly concerned with analysing the 'modern' psychological condition. Hence he abrogates the epic of Troy as against the French Revolution as the materials of poetry. But it is important to see here that Fox is not simply asserting that the modern reader is given access to contemporary subjects. He includes the open inspection of political events within the provenance of the science of man, but such topics are the result of a deeper analytical purpose. This is the exploration of psychological conditions as historical entities, as the product of different forms of culture: 'the whole should be based upon a profound knowledge of human nature, its constitution and history, its strength and weaknesses, its capabilities and its destiny; and where there is this science of man in the poet's mind, its existence will be ever felt'.[7] The poet has access to a radical historical and cultural analysis in which particular associative configurations occur at particular moments in history. Poetry is critique. Here poetry becomes a form of knowledge reached through the emotions and the critical intellect. 'It is an essence distilled from the fine arts and liberal sciences; nectar for the gods. It tasks the senses, the fancy, the feelings, and the intellect, and employs the best powers of all in one rich ministry of pleasure'.[8] Where Mill made a distinction between poetry and science or knowledge, Fox puts the two together.

Lastly, dramatic poetry is democratic because it deals with objecti-

---

6. Schlegel, *Lectures*, 21. In reading unacted drama we are compelled, he writes, to read in a participatory way, 'to supply the representation ourselves' (24).
7. *The Westminster Review*, XII (1830), 5.
8. Ibid. The review begins with a defence of intellect in poetry, claiming Bentham as an imaginative poet, and Milton as thinker. The attributes associated with poetry and prose are deliberately disrupted to demonstrate that these are artificial, culturally made categories.

fied materials which are capable of eliciting a responsive associative train in readers, who can corroborate or dissent from its delineations by reference to their own experience and build new patterns of association from the poet's explorations. This is very different from the disruptive, subversive function that the poet's breaking of associative patterns achieves in Hallam's aesthetics. Fox's poet and reader proceed by negotiation, Hallam's poet–reader relationship proceeds by a series of non-rational ruptures. Mill, of course, does not make provision for a relationship at all. For Fox the objectified representations of poetry are to be as *material* as possible. The poet 'must give us pictures'. It is impossible for language to produce 'actual' pictures but the poet must enable the reader to come to an independent mental representation of external things and develop 'new combinations' by appealing to the physical experience of the senses. 'His words should be such as are associated with the most common and most vivid recollections of those external objects whose presence most gratifies the senses'.[9] Here is an attempt to formulate poetic realism at the same time as recognising that the world is mediated through representations, and the ever present possibility of new representations.

Fox's curious combination of Benthamite materialism and rational philosophy of pleasure with Coleridgean idealist passion is strange. He can say that the finest poetry 'almost identifies poetical with religious inspiration' and almost in the same breath speaks of the poet in terms of the crudest psychological and social engineering: 'A great master of the art can play upon the nervous system, and produce and control its vibrations as easily as the well-practised performer can try the compass and power of a musical instrument'.[1] Thus democratic negotiation and a preoccupation with power belong uneasily together.

What did Browning take from Fox and what did he reject? There is no doubt that he was experimenting with the dialogic drama of externalised psychological narrative in 'Porphyria' and 'Johannes Agricola'. There are times when he describes his analytical procedures almost in Fox's words. In the preface to *Paracelsus* (1835) he claims that his poem is an attempt to 'reverse' the usual procedures of writing so that the literal external conditions of action are displaced by an analysis of the subject's internal drama. In *Strafford* (1837) he speaks of analysing action in character rather than character in action. In fact in the process of dialogic objectification Mill's expressive poem becomes the anti-expressive poem. In 'Porphyria' and 'Johannes Agricola' Browning relies on the hermeneutic shock created by the absence of dialogue. Characters so patently talking to themselves force a conscious intervention, force the reader to be aware of his or her exclusion and simultaneously force that awareness into a consciousness of *reading*, understanding the poem as the object of analysis and thus as ideology. So the structural relationships set up in the poems themselves become a political paradigm of change through an evolving,

9. Ibid., 4.
1. Ibid.

participating dialogue with the protagonist. Subsequently Browning refined the dialogic process and made it more complex by introducing a silent listener within the monologue itself, so that the poem is doubly a text, but the rudiments of this structural politics are all here in these early poems. Dialogic action declares power relations and thus their presence becomes one of the factors included in the process of analysis. In these poems the very extremity of the speaking subject's will to power and possession—one speaker virtually worshipped by God, another by his lover—is enough to indicate the implications of the act of appropriating which conceives the world as that which harmoniously answers one's own needs. The storm at the start of 'Porphyria' both echoes the speaker's mood with its vexation and 'spite' and yet he enters into a kind of power struggle with the elements conceiving their very animation and aggression as turned against him. This is an example of the way in which acts of mind are seen as a drama of changing events in dynamic relation to the reader.

It is clear, too, that Fox's understanding of political poetry as cultural critique, in which psychological states are rooted in history, is at work in these poems. The de-institutionalised private union with God, the curious reversal in which the self as God worships the self, the translation of this in an economics of relationships which is both repudiated and exploited in a contradictory way by the speaker, all this is an analysis of cultural forms in which experience is implicated in ideas of payment. Similarly, in Porphyria', the displacement of sexuality outside the institution of marriage, as the illicit affair becomes the consequence, the mirror image of licit, contractual union, is a brilliant social analysis of the way in which marriage and adultery are bound together in bourgeois society. So, too, is the objectification of the woman's body. A. W. Schlegel thought of the modern, romantic drama as a drama about dividedness and about the distorted desire which emerges from such alienation. The division of labour and the objectification of commodity occur in psychological forms. Browning's poem is a study of alienated desire, literally the desire for an object, a dead object. It is a cultural fantasy produced by social organisation. Whereas in Mill's terms these would be the expression of diseased subjectivities, in Fox's terms the poems would be a commentary, a critique of constitutive modern structures, religious, economic and sexual, which create diseased subjectivity and the madness of individualism. The reader is forced from one kind of recognition to the other, from the perception of diseased subjectivity to an analysis of its cultural form, because the poems parody expressive lyric.

It is Fox's account of realism, and the attempt to account for representation, which is least developed in his theory. The 'mental reproduction' of reality in 'new and becoming combinations' leaves the poem unanchored in the material world and is in danger of returning representation to solipsist subjectivity. It endorses that curious split in Fox's work between an assent to imaginative construction and positivist, technological instrumentalism. Browning's work, on the other hand, seems to develop very arrestingly and agnostically the whole problem of representation. There was, however, a paradigm for the work of art as pure construct. It is Bentham's theory of fictions. Fox may be dealing tentatively with the paradigm when he talks of 'new' combinations, though the question of direct influence is much less important than the nature of this model of fiction, which was certainly available at the time. Bentham's theory of fictions grants the work of art the status of cultural construct. The possibility for conscious investigation of representation *as* fiction is built into his theory. At the same time it is a model which enables the artist to speculate on the nature of the kind of intervention an imaginative construction makes in the world. It invites more complex and problematical political questions than Fox asked. Above all, it provides for a theory of poetic language. So one can see Browning's poetry developing a Benthamite poetics beyond Fox's theories.

The Dramatic Poem and the Theory of Fictions

Browning never failed to acknowledge that the materials of art are the representation of 'external' objects, or objects where general cultural agreement about their representation exists. Thus the work of art is democratic because it is open to inspection and analysis, as Fox saw. To anticipate a prose work of 1851, Browning's prefatory essay to a collection of letters he supposed to be by Shelley, this is the ground on which the 'objective' poet is formed. There is, however, a more decisive and sophisticated shift from realism to representation than in Fox's work. The objective poet stays within the world of received and *experienced* representation. He can 'reproduce things external [either the scenic universe or the human heart and brain] . . . with an immediate reference, in every case, to the common eye and apprehension of his fellow men, assumed capable of receiving and profiting by this reproduction'.[2] Either he produces an 'intelligible whole' for inexperienced readers, or he provides material for 'corroboration' and amplification by more adventurous readers.[3] Readers, indeed, are in a position of critical awareness. They not only corroborate but actively bring their own imagination and intelligence to a reading and *develop* it. This must be the only guarantee of the real, and constitutes a democratic poetry which brings the active reader's interpretative power to the poem. Browning's account of the objective poet's work allows for access to the poem by Fox's uneducated readers. The poor for whom the middle-class poet cannot, according to Fox, write effectively, are granted a participatory role. The objective poet's art is Browning's attempt to ground poetry in common representations and to reclaim an area for the ideologically disabled middle-class poet. The objective poet is objective because he allows for his work to be a critique and become the object of a critique.

2. Browning's introductory essay, dated 1851, to twenty-five letters of Shelley, later discovered to be spurious, was first published in 1852. It was reprinted in 1881. See 'On the poet objective and subjective; On the latter's aim; On Shelley as man and poet', *Browning Society Papers*, F. J. Furnivall, ed., I, 1881, 5–19: 5.
3. 'On the poet objective and subjective', 5.

We 'covet' the objective poet's biography because he is necessarily detached from his material. The objective poem is 'substantive', 'projected from himself and distinct'.[4] Such distinctness is a way of precluding that appropriation of the external world from which Fox's account of psychological projection is not free. The coveted biography is eliminated. True to the *Repository*'s belief in drama as the only ideologically liberating form, Browning writes that objective poetry 'is what we call dramatic poetry', when 'even description, as suggesting a describer, is dispensed with'. Thus the reader is forced to hear, not overhear, a substantive and public poetry. The man passes, the work remains.'[5]

Having established the dramatic poetry which is available to critique, Browning seems to undo this work by reintroducing Mill's 'overheard' private *expressive* poet in his account of the 'subjective' writer. We 'necessarily approach the personality of the poet' and read biographically because such subjective poetry is the 'effluence' of unique vision. This move is baffling until we look again at the Platonic terms of this description. It is an attempt to look much more rigorously than Mill at the structural part played by the subject in the creation of a work of art. For of course it is not possible to eliminate the psychology of the writing subject in art, and nor is it desirable. But the utterance of the poet is precisely not the inward monody of pure feeling: 'the *Ideas* of Plato, seeds of creation lying burningly on the Divine Hand— it is towards these he struggles': 'Not what man sees, but what God sees'.[6] The objective poet sees and portrays what *man* sees and stays within the limits of the human subject. The subjective poet—and there is a Promethean impudence here—struggles to create as *God* creates. He is supremely external and analytical and deals with the constitutive elements of experience and not with superficial expressive forms. His art is a construct, one of 'the primal elements of humanity' and not a 'combination' of experiences.[7] The analogue of God's mind is the human mind and its *fictions*, pictures 'on the retina of his own eyes'.[8] The subjective poet is Browning's effort to allow for the existence of what Fox barely conceived, constitutive fictions.

The work of the subjective poet has always been seen by Browning's interpreters as the rendering of an inner life, of human essence over and against a history. As we shall see by turning again to the two *Repository* monologues, Browning was never free of casuistry and is prepared to run the risk of his theories by exposing them as casuistry. But here Browning claims that the subjective poet is immersed in history. Not only do the poet's imaginative fictions intervene in history but they must be constructed on the model of Plato's 'Ideas' out of the human mind and its experience which is 'the nearest reflex' of divine mind. Mind does not transcend itself because mind itself is the model

4. Ibid., 6, 5.
5. Ibid., 7, 6.
6. Ibid., 7.
7. Ibid.
8. Ibid.

for the creation of fictions. On the other hand, mind is not at the mercy of its own psychological experience either.

Browning is in a complex dialogue with Mill and Fox which involves him in both displacing and recentring the subject. Mill's unified expressive subject turns out to be the fragmented victim of psychological moments. If Fox's solid, analytical dramatic poetry is invoked to redress the privacy of Mill's poet, that drama is now displaced from the immediate external world to become a function of shared *representation*. What a representation can be is further sophisticated by the introduction of the idea of fictions. As Browning makes clear, objective and subjective forms are never produced as pure forms distinct from one another. But it is fiction, rather than the subject itself, which is at the centre of art. It is characteristic of Browning's restless deviance that the introduction of fictions makes a genuine political poetry at once harder to achieve and more possible. And it is absolutely typical of him that in the notion of the fiction as it is explored in the *Repository* poems, he chose the most politically disreputable and least credible model to hand in radical circles, the dangerous power of the legal fiction. For it is in the legal fiction that the concept of fiction was circulating at this time, the legal fictions which Bentham had condemned as despotic and tyrannical, the tools of power and injustice. And moreover he had associated legal fictions with the corruption of language. It is no accident that 'Porphyria' and 'Johannes Agricola' are obsessed with legality and the guarantee of contract which turns out to be exploited for private power, or that legalism and language are explored together.

As 'objective' poems, 'Porphyria' and 'Johannes Agricola' are immediately apprehendable as 'intelligible wholes', melodramatic and vivid representations of madness and psychosis. The *logic* of psychosis and its cultural significance is laid bare for the reader who wishes to develop and explore the nature of madness. Here Browning's readings are consonant with Fox. As 'subjective' poems, going further than Fox, they represent the fictions of madness and become explorations into the status and language of fictions themselves. And it is here that Browning places the fiction at the most dangerous edge of casuistry. The importance of this is that it is a casuistry from which Bentham himself was not free, for he recognised that human language finds it impossible to do without fictions. 'Porphyria' and 'Johannes Agricola' are experiments in the concepts he termed first-order fictions, love and God. Real entities are those things which have a correspondent image in experience. Fictional entities, love and God, are those things which do not have correspondent images in experience, and that is their problem at the same time as it can be their justification.[9]

In the review of Coleridge in which Fox developed his political aes-

<hr>

9. *Bentham's Theory of Fictions*, C. K. Ogden, ed., London, 1932, 12. 'A fictitious entity is an entity to which, though by the grammatical form of the discourse employed in speaking of it, existence by ascribed, yet in truth and reality existence is not meant to be ascribed. Every noun-substantive which is not the name of a real entity, perceptible and inferential, is the name of a fictitious entity' (12).

thetic, he refers to a radical Utilitarian defence of Bentham in the *Westminster Review* which disputes conservative readings of Bentham. The article quotes liberally from Bentham's writings and concentrates on his attack on legal language and fictions. It demonstrates conclusively that the law for Bentham was the crucial institution because it is where conservative oppression manifests itself openly and issues directly in action and control. Mill's famous defence of Bentham as a codifier, on the other hand, in the essay to which I have referred, weakens the violence and political intensity of Bentham's attack on despotism. The writer of the Bentham article is at pains to show, first that Bentham condemned legal language because its eloquence was *aesthetic*, and secondly that legal fictions are the product of this aesthetic language. Forms of words are substituted for arguments (one example is the speaker who, like Johannes, says 'I am of the number of the Elect') and forms of words begin to have an autonomous life of their own which depends on 'the music of the maxim, absorbing the whole imagination'.[1] They prevent the listener from perceiving 'the nothingness' of a statement. Nevertheless, this 'nothingness' perpetrates actions. For legal fictions are constructions of events which substantively effect people's lives, making the innocent guilty and the guilty innocent. The writer means not merely chicanery and quibble but the train of precedent and legalism which actually result in contradictions in the real world, such as the acquittal tax on the innocent.[2] So fictions *intervene* in the world however aesthetic they may seem. To fight them we have to behave as if they were true. The writer savagely derides as conservative a reading of Bentham which actually justifies legal fictions aesthetically on the grounds of their internal coherence, and characterises it as mere 'sport'—'the construction of an independent system artificially deduced out of its own technical principles etc.'[3]

'To be spoken of at all, every fictitious entity must be spoken of as if it were real', Bentham wrote elsewhere.[4] 'Nothingness' fictional entities might be, but they are essential to language and the process of conceptualisation. 'Every fictitious entity bears some relation to some real entity'.[5] Fictions are entities for this reason. They have an analogical base in physical and psychical experience but cannot be reduced to it. They cannot be translated or substituted for a real entity—words such as God, love, soul, are examples. But by exhaustive redescribing, metaphorising and *linguistic* substitution you can point to the fictional entity by reference to the real entity and demonstrate the structural relationship of the fictional to the real entity. This is a subtle route through the philosophical extremes of nominalism and realism, the independence of language from the world, and the referentiality which

---

1. *Westminster Review*, X (1829), 367–393: 387. For the discussion of 'nothingness' in language, see 386. For reference to the elect, 385. The author is at pains to demonstrate Bentham's intense and deeply considered attack on the despotism of the law.
2. Ibid., 391.
3. Ibid., 389–90, 390.
4. Ogden, *Bentham's Theory of Fictions*, 13.
5. Ibid., 12.

ties words to things. It neither consolidates pure representation nor identifies the sign and the thing signified. Curiously, its advantage to an artist is that it confirms the necessity of fictions and places them as central to the process of thinking, in spite of the discreditable purposes to which they may be put. Moreover, it asserts that fictional constructs intervene substantively in the world and affect choices and actions however fictional they may be. They are as enabling as they are disreputable. Lastly, the theory of fictions is a theory of language, which sanctions the ceaseless productions of language (as paraphrase, metaphor, metonymy) not as rhetoric but for the purpose of clarifying the structural relationships fictional entities bear to real entities. Bentham wrote:

> To language, then—to language alone—it is, that fictitious entities owe their existence; their impossible, yet indispensable, existence.[6]

It is a justification for a poetics. Ironically, this theory of 'nothingness', which evolved from an attack on the dishonesty and violent power of the law, *is* an aesthetic theory. It is a successful aesthetic theory. It is a successful aesthetic theory simply because it was an attempt to explain and understand the *effectiveness* of fictions. For Bentham it would be ineffectual idealism in the face of the law's fictions to assume they could be spoken of as if they were not real. The importance of the theory lies in Bentham's willingness to speak of a fiction 'as if it were real'. It is a flagrantly, almost perversely, paradoxical theory.

It is a short step from legal to aesthetic to psychological fictions. The importance of a theory of fictions to Browning is that it provides him with an account of the imaginative construct which is an intervention in the world and which escapes from solipsism and a subject-centred discourse. It also produces an account of poetic language in terms of definition and demonstration which depends for its being on abundance, on repetition and redescription in the public forum. The truly poetic language is a forensic language, is a product of legal debate. Both the form in which a fictitious intervention occurs in the world of choice and action and the way in which its language evolves secure a truly public, politically open situation in which questions can be investigated without mystification or the exploitation of power relationships. But more significant than all this, a theory of fictions is important because it is paradoxical. Browning's poems are not demonstrations of the nature of the fiction, but, like everything he did, a sceptical enquiry into it. Hence they are test cases of his own and Bentham's fictions, explorations of the casuistry which treats a fiction 'as if it were real'. At one and the same time this is firm political ground, and ground which gives under one's feet.

Agricola's fiction, that he is one of the elect, appears to concern only himself and God and yet it involves a ruthless rejection of other kinds of worshipper. Its exclusiveness has a substantive function in

6. Ibid., 15.

shaping his relations with the world. 'God' is a fictional entity at what Bentham calls 'the first remove', formed, presumably, on analogy with its noun 'man'.[7] Not only does God have human characteristics, such as anger and pride, but He is more human than Agricola, possessed of a past, planning and determining the future, exercising arbitrary power, expressing emotion, capable of the energy of thought and calculation. He performs all the functions Agricola has abrogated by resorting to passivity. This is the logic of treating God as if He were 'real', exactly like a human being. Agricola's mind creates God in his own image of despotism. Fictional entities, Bentham says, often control, dominate and organise our understanding of real entities, as if the fictitious body were a stake, and the real body a beast tied to it.[8] The connection between a word and its import is 'altogether arbitrary' but coercive. That is why war 'with all its miseries' emerges from language itself.[9] The blasphemous irony of this monologue is that Agricola is only doing what Christians ought to do in thinking of God as 'real'. The reader can only enter the complexity of the fiction by entering into the poem as if it were 'real'.

The remorseless process of sceptical exploration is directed to another problem in 'Porphyria'. What is the status of the 'murder'? If it is imaginary, what is the difference between a fiction and fantasy or delusion? And how does each materially intervene in the world? For they all seem to work in the same way. What is the status of an *imagined* or fictional action? Such 'actions' do not appear to impinge on the world and yet the conviction that something has 'happened' has to be dispelled by treating it 'as if it were real'—that is to say, to disprove anything, its possibility has to be taken seriously. The morbid violence, the intensity and extremity of feeling is substantive, produced by and producing the fiction. Porphyria's lover, however mad, has to be initially granted belief, and there is some strange sense in which the murder *is* in existence with the contemplation of its possibility, particularly as truth might be stranger than fiction. The pure idealism of the fiction is constantly shown to have material effects on the world in the most disturbing of contexts. In fact, fictions and the language of fictions, since they impinge on and create action, are crucial to political life, and indeed to all experience. Browning did not so much directly politicise his material in these two monologues as begin to write a politics of fictions.

In words which recall 'Porphyria' in an eloquent analysis of the contiguity of fiction and hallucination, Browning considers in the case of Shelley whether 'the idea of the enamoured lady following him to Naples, and of the "man in the cloak" who struck him in the Pisan post-office, were equally illusory,—the mere projection, in fact, from

7. Ibid., 9, 11. Bentham argues that ontological propositions such as God can be derived by inference and thus it is arguable that ultimately they are real entities. But it is also clear that *perceptible* experience alone, which has repercussions in the world of sense and in the immediate materiality of experience, produces the only securely non-fictional terms of existence. See also 44.
8. Ibid., lxviii.
9. Ibid., lii.

himself, of the image of his own love and hate'.[1] He quotes Shelley himself—'To nurse the image of *unfelt caresses* / Till dim imagination just possesses / The half-created shadow', and adds, 'of unfelt caresses,—and of unfelt blows as well?'[2] The 'unfelt caresses' of Porphyria and their problematical status reappear in this essay, written nearly fifteen years later. Porphyria may be a projection of 'his own [the lover's] love and hate', but before we can discover whether this is an 'entity' of fiction or a hallucination the poem has to be read seriously, and in this way it has already intervened in the world. The strange syntax of the later title, meaning the lover *of* Porphyria and the lover *possessed* by her, suggests how the 'fictitious' erotic 'body' ties meaning to the stake.

The discovery of the fiction and its potential for a new poetics and a new poetry was of critical importance to Browning. It also led to a politics which stems directly from an account of consciousness and human action, for paradoxically the idealism of the fiction may *determine* action. In the *Monthly Repository* of 1835, Horne spelled out the problematical relationship between consciousness and politics through a discussion of Hazlitt's *On the Principles of Human Action*. 'Mind is the only criterion of all things; the only type and proof of reality; the only measure of creation. . . . The only fixed datum for metaphysical speculations, is consciousness'.[3] Even though, as Hazlitt says, 'self' is a fiction, 'this fine illusion of the brain and forgery of language' grounds human action.[4] Consciousness is constructed from memory and memory is a series of constructs. It is through the fictions of memory that the fiction of the future is established. The future is a projection of memory.

> And in truth, it requires a considerable effort of abstraction clearly to distinguish and separate the objects we frame for the future, from those we have been conscious of in the past; so much are our imaginations mixed up with memory. In some cases this almost amounts, speaking abstractedly, to a solecism. I contemplate a statue or a figure, in imagination, having heard of it only: a few days after, I contemplate as near as possible the same idea, i.e. the memory of a former or past imagination. Is it not then a reasonable paradox, that the future is often unconsciously identified in the mind with the past?[5]

We can already see Browning's great epistemological lyrics of the 1850s in these speculations. Horne goes on to ask what '*real* interest' he could have had in the statue if he sees it in reality and discovers it to be quite different from his imagination. And yet knowledge of the existence of the 'real' statue makes possible his imaginary construction of it. Such epistemological speculation, he claims, is not ideal, for it affects the sphere of moral and practical action. For 'The Sun of hope

1. Browning, 'On the poet objective and subjective', 17.
2. Ibid.
3. *Monthly Repository*, N.S., IX (1835), 484.
4. Ibid.
5. Ibid.

is a fiction which the wisdom of the Creator has implanted in our minds with all the force of anticipated reality'.[6] All action is the product of the repetitions of the past in consciousness and a product of imagination. Belief in political action must depend on a projection in which the 'past wrongs' of a people are redressed through that mental process which identifies the past with the future. So action is based on a risk. This principle of action is at once utterly sceptical and completely affirmative. Consciousness only guarantees that 'Man stands like a speck upon a progressive point, between two eternities'.[7] And yet this negation of certitude must be the very ground on which action, and the future itself becomes possible. In 'Porphyria' and 'Johannes Agricola' Browning began a formative experiment, the exhaustive agnostic exploration of the risks of fiction.

The essays of Fox and Horne can be seen as markers for the formation of a new kind of Victorian poem. The different, oddly discrepant pressures of radical Utilitarian aesthetics, Shelleyan idealism and a Benthamite concern with fictions, combined to make possible the dramatic lyric or what has come to be known vaguely as the dramatic monologue. From Fox came a conviction of the ideological necessity of drama and a programme for drama as externalised conflict objectified as the materials for democratic participation. From Horne came a belief in the central structural importance of dialogue and an epistemological concern with the importance of the fiction or construct as the determinant of action. And behind both is the presence of Bentham. In Browning's work all these possibilities for a poetics and practice are opened up sceptically as problems. But his heard drama, originally in a parody of Mill's overheard drama, shifts the poem from psychology to epistemology and the textual complexity of the fiction. The possibility of agency and the structure of consciousness itself are at stake in the status of fictions. Browning's poetry becomes a dare with the status of the fiction, an analytical process which ceaselessly investigates the nature of utterance and its representations and their cultural meaning. Included in his poems is an understanding that they are made of language and that though they pretend to be speech, they are writing—not actually heard, but read. We read them self-consciously as texts. But it is through this process that they become forms of knowledge rather than the expressive emotion which Mill distinguished from truth. They belong to Benthamite science rather than liberal feeling.

* * *

6. Ibid., 485.
7. Ibid.

JENNIFER A. WAGNER-LAWLOR

The Pragmatics of Silence, and the Figuration of the Reader in Browning's Dramatic Monologues†

Alberto Schön has observed that silence is a concept rarely personified: "There scarcely exists a silence 'made man.' In the various myths it is the divine word that prevails and if anything it is the men who observe the silence (mystic) in an attempt to approach [the] gods."[1] Silence under such circumstances indicates consensus, and indeed more than consensus—absolute faith, awe, recognition of an ineffability before which there is no need to talk. The rarity of a silence "made man" makes its appearance the more noteworthy—and in this essay I would like to explore a sighting, as it were, that has been too little discussed.

The dramatic monologue is a genre that was not invented by nineteenth-century poets, but it was certainly taken up and fully exploited for the first time by them, particularly Robert Browning. Since then, the critical spotlight has been focused primarily upon the figure of the speaker, a typically eloquent rhetorician whose admirably complex manipulations of his auditor have been the study of literary critics. Browning critics have long noted that the typical speaker of a Browning monologue is aggressive, often threatening, nearly always superior, socially and/or intellectually, to the auditor. The auditor on the other hand cannot help but hear, as it were; he is, by generic definition, absolutely silent, a passive receptor of a verbal tour de force that leaves him no opportunity for response—indeed, that often actively discourages him from doing so.

The generically mandated silence of the auditor is not, therefore—to return to Schön's observation—a mystic silence, or even the silence of a faithful Moses receiving the Word. Far from being a silence of consensus, the auditor's is often a silence of intimidation. This is surely the intent of many a Browning speaker: by silencing his auditor, the speaker accomplishes his own typically narcissistic self-delineation, puts himself in the spotlight, keeps the body of the implied listener, the "you" of the poem, not only in shadow but as shadow. Foregrounding the aggression and rhetorical power of the speaker has thus tended to allow the effacement of the second-person addressee in favor of exploring the complex brush-work in the speaker's self-portrait.

Recent linguistic theories of silence, however, make possible closer attention to the shadowy figure of the second-person addressee. Viewed in terms of communicative acts, represented or otherwise, the silent listener is absolutely crucial; the dramatic situation itself is ob-

† From *Victorian Poetry* 35.3 (1997): 287–302. Reprinted by permission of the author.
1. "Silence in the Myth: Psychoanalytic Observations," in *The Regions of Silence: Studies on the Difficulty of Communicating*, ed. Maria Grazia Ciani (Amsterdam: J. C. Gieben, 1987), p. 9.

viously only created by the presence of the other, and he is necessary for the delineation of the speaker's self-portrait.[2] Recent work on the pragmatics of silence has outlined the many ways in which silence is clearly not mere absence of speech, but is itself heavy with communicative value; there is communication structured through silence, just as through speech.[3]

In particular, what Adam Jaworski calls the "bipolar valence of silence" provides an altogether different lens through which to view the dynamics of the dramatic monologue. Turning aside from the success with which the speaker controls his narcissistic self-delineation, this essay will explore how the pragmatic ambiguity of second-person silence in monologues highlights the tension between consensus and resistance. This tension is a central characteristic of the genre—what any dramatic monologue is "really about"—because it clarifies the genre's ultimate irony: dramatic monologue ends up spotlighting the silent auditor precisely by effacing him/her in shadow. Like a stage whisper intended for all to hear, the shadowy figure who is the auditor cannot help but be seen finally by the figure for whom that auditor is obviously a stand-in—the reader.

My argument is that dramatic monologue thus constructs the image of the audience through the very silence it enforces upon the textual auditor. The genre self-reflexively figures its own problems of interpretation, and of the freedom of the reader in the effaced, voiceless shadow of the implied listener, who emerges from obscurity as the figure of the reader. The reader too may be silent, at least at first—but as the nature of the speech act in which s/he vicariously participates becomes clearer, s/he will not likely remain so. Through the performance of interpretation, the reader distinguishes her/himself from both the speaker and the auditor; in doing so, the reader both fulfills, but also ironically undermines, the speaker's apparent tyranny over the communicative situation that makes up the discourse of the poem.

2. Psychoanalysts have explored the parallel therapeutic situation: Lacan, for example, asks this: "Then who is this *other* to whom I am more attached than myself, since, at the heart of my assent to my own identity, it is still he who wags me?" (Quoted by Paul Kugler, *The Alchemy of Discourse: An Archetypal Approach to Language* [Lewisburg: Bucknell Univ. Press, 1982], p. 98.) On the creation of "ego" or subjectivity through language—and the notion that it is only through language that we are conscious, are "subject" at all, see: Emile Benveniste, "Subjectivity in Language," chap. 21 in *Problems in General Linguistics*, trans. Mary Elizabeth Meek (1966; Coral Gables, Florida: Univ. of Miami Press, 1971), pp. 223–230; Ann Banfield, "Where Epistemology, Style, and Grammar Meet Literary History: The Development of Represented Speech and Thought," *NLH 9*, no. 3 (Autumn 1977): 415–454. For the relation of subject-construction and dramatic monologue, see Rosemary Huisman, "Who Speaks and For Whom? The Search for Subjectivity in Browning's Poetry," *AUMLA 71* (May 1989): 64–87; E. Warwick Slinn, *Browning and the Fictions of Identity* (Totowa: Barnes & Noble, 1982); Slinn, "Consciousness as Writing: Deconstruction and Reading Victorian Poetry," pp. 54–68 in *Critical Essays on Robert Browning*, ed. Mary Ellis Gibson (New York: G. K. Hall, 1992); Slinn, "Some Notes on Monologues as Speech Acts," *BSN 15* (Spring 1984): 1–9; and Herbert Tucker, "Dramatic Monologue and the Overhearing of Lyric," in *Lyric Poetry: Beyond New Criticism*, ed. Chaviva Hošek and Patricia Parker (Ithaca: Cornell Univ. Press, 1985), pp. 226–243.
3. See: Adam Jaworski's *The Power of Silence: Social and Pragmatic Perspectives* (Newbury Park: SAGE Publications, 1993); Wayne C. Anderson, "The Rhetoric of Silence in the Discourse of Coleridge and Carlyle," *South Atlantic Review* 49 (January 1984): 72–90; and articles by Muriel Saville-Troike, Anne Graffan Walker, and Deborah Tannen in *Perspectives on Silence*, ed. Deborah Tannen and Muriel Saville-Troike (Norwood: Ablex Publishing Corporation, 1985).

1

The landmark work on dramatic monologue appeared in 1957 from Robert Langbaum, whose book, *The Poetry of Experience*, outlines the tension in all dramatic monologues between what he called "sympathy" and "judgment." That is, the reader's own response to the speaker swings between a sympathetic identification with him, no matter how strange or disturbed that speaker may be, and a more objective, distanced judgment. Since Langbaum published his work, most criticism on dramatic monologue has concerned itself with that speaker and with his verbal self-delineation—how it is accomplished, how the textual auditor or we, the "real readers," are lured into the speaker's verbal webs, and how irony springs the verbal traps that have been set. It is the will of the speaker that dazzles and disturbs, and the last thirty years of criticism are right in following Langbaum by pronouncing that the dramatic monologue is a post-Romantic resistance to the dangers of Romantic subjectivity.[4]

The merits and impact of Langbaum's thesis have always been unquestionable; and yet in focusing upon our relation with the speaker, subsequent analyses of the form have tended to underplay the degree to which we are also sympathetic with the implied listener, who complicates the scheme that Langbaum sets forth. The body of that shadowy figure, the text's implied listener, that "you," is intentionally kept out of the spotlight by the speaker, whose sole purpose is an often narcissistic self-delineation. Two perfect examples of this are the infamous Duke of Browning's "My Last Duchess," and the charismatic title scoundrel of "Fra Lippo Lippi." But suppose one were to ask, rather than the usual "what does the speaker's rhetoric mean," a different question: "What does the auditor's silence 'mean'?"

From the perspective of linguistic pragmatics, the aggressive narcissism of the speaker, who does not let the auditor speak, sets up a violation of "access rights" to discourse. Mary Louise Pratt notes that in any such circumstance, having "agreed" to become an audience, we "at most . . . can indicate our displeasure by some nonverbal means, like facial expression or body posture." Indeed, we sometimes learn that despite their silence, the auditors of dramatic monologues do in fact communicate to the speaker: we occasionally discern this when the speaker—say the Duke or Lippi—corrects or modifies his remarks in evident response to some gesture or facial expression from the listener. But as Pratt goes on to point out, in such a case "audiences in

4. See Carol Christ, "Self-Concealment and Self-Expression in Eliot's and Pound's Dramatic Monologues," *VP* 22 (1984): 217–226; Lee Erickson, *Robert Browning: His Poetry and His Audiences* (Ithaca: Cornell Univ. Press, 1984); Constance W. Hassett, *The Elusive Self in the Poetry of Robert Browning* (Athens: Univ. of Ohio Press, 1982); Robert Langbaum, *The Poetry of Experience: The Dramatic Monologue in Modern Literary Tradition* (London: Chatto & Windus, 1957; repr. Norton, 1971); Loy D. Martin, *Browning's Dramatic Monologues and the Post-Romantic Subject* (Baltimore: Johns Hopkins Univ. Press, 1985); J. Hillis Miller, *The Disappearance of God: Five Nineteenth-Century Writers* (Cambridge: Harvard Univ. Press, 1963); E. Warwick Slinn, *Browning and the Fictions of Identity*; Herbert F. Tucker, Jr., *Browning's Beginnings: The Art of Disclosure* (Minneapolis: Univ. of Minnesota Press, 1980).

this sense are indeed captive, and speakers addressing audiences are obliged to make the captivity worthwhile."[5]

In most of Browning's monologues, however, this contract of pragmatic obligation and expectation is crucially not the voluntary one that Pratt most often discusses.[6] While the reader may be said to have "chosen" to "hear" a particular dramatic monologue, the textual listener often has not. The listener in the typical Browning monologue recognizes the speaker's superior position of power; given the latter's aggressive, sometimes even menacing nature, the apparent passivity of the silent listener seems at once the more remarkable, and yet the more understandable. Again, think of Browning's Duke of Ferrara. Who would dare to question or pose an objection to the behavior he is revealing to us? The silence of the auditor, a mere envoy, is not so surprising; he is quite simply in no position to dissent.

This leads to a second point: the auditor is participating not in a voluntary or "chosen" silence but in what linguists call "imposed" silence, which Paolo Scarpi defines as occurring "when one of the two [speakers] recognises the influence or supremacy of the other . . . *Choice* and *imposition* can express respectively assertion and recognition of leadership."[7] The imposed code of silence is grounded in fear, adds Scarpi, and while its pragmatic implication is "consensus," in actuality verbal communication has merely been "suspended" by the intimidated listener. Such an imposed silence is dangerous because, as Scarpi puts it, "it may coincide with oblivion, negation and the loss of the individual identity."[8] "Exactly so!" the narcissistic Browning speaker might agree, as he sets up, usually far from innocently, a system of imposed silence that is necessary for his own self-delineation. The listener's silence means either assent, or, at the very least, a recognition of and acquiescence in a system that places the speaker himself at the center; as Deborah Tannen points out, silence is always a "joint production" (p. 100). The silence of the addressee is a perceptibly oppressive one, particularly as by generic definition he is unable to break the situational silence, whether in agreement or disagreement, whether in comprehension or misunderstanding. And caught as we are in the same verbal web as we read, without any clearly discernible response from the textual auditor, we tend to turn always back toward the speaker, complicitous ourselves now in his self-portraiture.

The position of the addressee is therefore ambiguous, and in the silence that maintains that ambiguity, the speaker can impose what meaning he will. A remarkable acknowledgment of this ambiguity appears at the end of the strange poem "Porphyria's Lover"; having stran-

5. Mary Louise Pratt, *Toward A Speech Act Theory of Literary Discourse* (Bloomington: Indiana Univ. Press, 1977), pp. 106–107.
6. See Cynthia Goldin Bernstein, " 'My Last Duchess': A Pragmatic Approach to the Dramatic Monologue," *The SECOL Review* 14 (1990): 127–142.
7. Paolo Scarpi, "The Eloquence of Silence: Aspects of a Power Without Words," in Ciani, p. 23.
8. Ciani, p. 37. See also Maeterlink, who says that passive silence is "the shadow of sleep, of death, or non-existence" (quoted by John Auchard, in *Silence in Henry James: The Heritage of Symbolism and Decadence* [University Park: Pennsylvania State Univ. Press, 1986], p. 13).

gled his lady with a long strand of her own hair, the speaker wonders aloud that "yet God has not said a word!" It is unclear whether the lover expects to hear approval or disapproval from God. Even had God spoken, however, Porphyria's lover would most likely have heard nothing anyway, so maniacally, indeed criminally, extreme is his solipsism.

The ambiguity of the figure of the addressee is rooted in the ambiguity of silence itself—and in fact such bivalence is characteristic of the functions assigned to silence by linguists. Jaworski names at least five possible functions of silence in communication, each one bearing positive and negative values. As noted earlier, Jaworski calls this the "bipolar" nature of silence, and naturally the value can be assigned only by looking at the context of the speech act. So, for example, silence's "revelatory function" may either make something known to a person, or may hide information.

More relevant to the argument of this essay is the function Jaworski calls the judgmental: positively, silence can signal assent and favor; negatively, it signals dissent or disfavor. This function parallels Langbaum's description of the reader's relation to a monologue speaker as either "sympathetic" or "judgmental." But at the level of the poem itself, so tight is the speaker's control that it seems difficult to know which value is to be attributed to the silence of this particular communicative event. Tannen notes that "whether or not silence is uncomfortable in interaction hinges on whether or not participants feel something should be said, in which case silence is perceived as an omission" (p. 96). It is interesting to turn this remark back upon Porphyria's lover again, who clearly does see God's silence as an omission—and yet who does not recognize in his last line's repressed whisper of conscience the voice of God; the lover has effectively silenced even Him.

The same sort of ambiguity is present in "Andrea del Sarto," in which the silence of the painter's wife, Lucrezia, is motivated not by fear, as in "My Last Duchess," but by indifference. I can never imagine her listening to del Sarto's words, but rather for the whistle-signal of her "cousin" outside. Del Sarto's monologue is to some degree a delay tactic to keep her indoors with him for once. While, however, she is temporarily held captive by the painter's desire to speak—and perhaps by a momentary but shallow sense of politeness—the apparent irrelevance of his speech to her behavior or thoughts is thematized in the poem precisely as the painter's own, crushing fault. His irrelevance is in fact the gist of his self-portrait—for which he knows he will be judged as an artist, and for which he judges himself now as a man. The poem exploits the ambiguity of silence: Lucrezia at once humors and dismisses him, as he seems well aware, by sitting with him at all; he wonders, hopelessly, if her acquiescence is a mark of favor. And yet simultaneously, she rejects him by not disagreeing with his negative self-delineation. Her judgment of him, and her worst punishment as well, is implicit in her very silence.

2

While the relevance of the speaker's narrative to the auditor may be ambiguous, that ambiguity of silence in Browning's monologues is clarified when one acknowledges that what is in question here is not a "real" conversation, but a literary representation of one, or an imitation speech act. This communicative situation obviously changes everything, from the problem of relevance, to the problem of silence—and what I will be arguing in the remainder of this essay is that these two problems conflate within the figure of the reader.

While the implied auditor of the poem, the "you," remains generically imprisoned within the situational parameters defined by the speaker, and thus remains passively mute, the reader, though aligned with that auditor, is not so compelled. Jack Selzer points out that "real readers" may or may not identify with the implied reader of a text—here, the second-person addressee of a monologue—and he promotes Iser's "more flexible account" of the reading process, which "allows for an active reader who may well choose to remain quite distinct from the role suggested by the implied reader."[9] The sooner the reader, "active and yet text-based," as Selzer puts it, recalls his nonidentity with the poem's "you," the sooner the ambiguity of silence may clarify into the active silence of dissent, and the violation of H. P. Grice's maxim of relevance within the Cooperative Principle justified at the extratextual level.[1] As Pratt notes, we the actual readers assume in such circumstances that the narrative will be "relevant" and worth hearing. But within the context of the poem, even that will sometimes be unclear for the dramatic monologue's addressee. These narratives often seem directed by the speaker toward him/herself, and the dismissal of the relevance of his narrative for the auditor is matched by control of access rights to the implied "conversation."

Pratt also points out that the reader of a literary work may in theory always be "attending to at least two utterances at once—the author's display text and the fictional speaker's discourse, whatever it is." This duality "is not always exploited by the author" (p. 174)—but it is, I am arguing, essential to the very nature of the dramatic monologue. Pratt adds that all literary texts have "display-producing relevance" or "tellability," which we the audience, voluntarily reading such a text, will search for. And the distinction of the dramatic lyric is that its relevance may lie less in the particular narratives that make up the poems than in the pragmatic dynamics that these poems do—indeed must—highlight. In real speech, the auditor of a narrative will always have the opportunity to respond to the relevance of the speaker's discourse—even if not to his face. This is obviously impossible in the dramatic monologue,

9. Jack Selzer, "More Meanings of *Audience*," from *A Rhetoric of Doing: Essays on Written Discourse in Honor of James L. Kinneavy*, ed. Stephen P. Witte, Neil Nakadate, and Roger D. Cherry (Carbondale: Southern Illinois Univ. Press, 1992), pp. 166–167.
1. See H. P. Grice, *Studies in the Way of Words* (Cambridge: Harvard Univ. Press, 1989). Chap. 2, "Logic and Conversation," outlines Grice's concept of the Cooperative Principle, its several corollary maxims (such as "relevance"), and the many ways in which the "quasi-contractual basis" (p. 29) of any conversational situation may be disrupted or pushed aside.

which begins and ends with that discourse. The monologue must assume a relation of consent, a relation of assent as generically preestablished, and it forces the auditor into a position of passive receptivity, whether voluntary or not. The relevance of the speaker's narrative to anyone but himself need not be immediately apparent, and cannot necessarily be found within the poem itself. Sometimes the speaker is, within the context of the poem, nearly speaking to himself, as in "Porphyria's Lover," or, to cite another nineteenth-century masterpiece, in D. G. Rossetti's "Jenny," in which the auditor is the sleeping prostitute. There could be no greater sign of the "irrelevance" of speech than the silence of those recipients, one dead, the other asleep.

Dramatic monologue's generic demand for silence is, as suggested above, at least a pragmatic violation—an enforced listening—and from that source springs the prevailing sense of "danger" or threat to the auditor that characterizes so many of Browning's monologue situations. From this violation too may stem the negative response of actual contemporary readers to Browning's work; some readers supposed that the speaker's characteristic pragmatic hostility toward his auditor paralleled Browning's disdain toward the reader. While not accusing him of that exactly, John Ruskin did complain to Browning of the obscurity of his work. The great critic and others, in considering that obscurity willful, also thought it to be a kind of violation of the author-reader contract: "You are worse than the worst Alpine Glacier I ever crossed," groused Ruskin, "Bright, deep enough surely, but so full of clefts that half the journey has to be done with ladder and hatchet."[2] An excerpt from Browning's famous response points out how entirely that eminent critic had simply misread his work because they had different conceptions of that contract:

> We don't read poetry the same way, by the same law; it is too clear. I cannot begin writing poetry till my imaginary reader has conceded licences to me which you demur at altogether. I *know* that I don't make out my conception by my language; all poetry being a putting the infinite within the finite. You would have me paint it all plain out, which can't be; but by various artifices I try to make shift with touches and bits of outlines which *succeed* if they bear the conception from me to you.[3]

Browning expects, in other words, more cooperation from the reader in the bringing forth of meaning than Ruskin and other contemporaries were accustomed to grant. And while Browning's speakers characteristically "flout" or "exploit" (as Grice would put it) one or more maxims pertaining to the Cooperative Principle, the reader may well be forced to supply the "logic" of a monologue's implied conver-

2. December 2, 1855, published in David J. De Laura, "Ruskin and the Brownings: Twenty-five Unpublished Letters," *John Rylands Library Bulletin* 54 (1972): 326–327.
3. December 10, 1855, in W. G. Collingwood, *The Life and Work of John Ruskin*, 2 vols. (London: Methuen, 1893), 1:200. David E. Latané, Jr., outlines what he calls an "aesthetics of difficulty"; he discusses the relationship of this aesthetic to audiences and, consequently, market forces, that preferred simplicity, or at least "accessibility," in literature (see chap. 1 of *Browning's Sordello and the Aesthetics of Difficulty* [University of Victoria / English Literary Studies (No. 40 in the ELS Monograph Series, 1987)], pp. 15–39).

sation by stepping out of the conversational context of the poem. While the silence of the auditor in the poem represents a failure of language, it is a failure any responsible literary reader, searching for meaning or "tellability" as Pratt suggests, cannot abide.

Auditor and reader must, therefore, part ways, and the issue of silence is crucial here. For the auditor, silence signals a failure of language, but silence can also, according to Tannen, offer an alternative to the reader: "Personal exploration is the existence of cognitive activity underlying silence; the failure of language refers to its social function" (p. 100). Whereas the auditor's silence may represent an involuntary consensus, the silence of the actual reader, who is forced to step out of the place of the noninterpretive auditor, may signify the opposite. This silence is the space of the open resistance of the will of the speaker by the interpretive will of the reader. In pragmatic terms, the reader (unlike, for example, either the "next duchess"'s envoy or the languid Lucrezia) may become "impolite" in a manner that the textual listener, too intimidated or too acquiescent to challenge the speaker's superiority, dares not be.[4] In hermeneutical terms, the reader has become an interpreter.

An intratextual aesthetic communication between two fictional protagonists shifts into an extratextual public communication, or, I could also say, into an inter-textual public communication. These terms I borrow from Ernest W. B. Hess-Lüttich, whose article on the pragmatics of literary communication describes the kind of shift I want to mark:

> As soon as the recipient also takes over the role of an observer of the whole process, for instance as critic, linguist, or psychologist, another metacommunicative level has to be taken into account. . . . This second communicative relationship is by no means a mere addendum, but structurally implied within the text itself. And the role of the audience is by no means only that of passive perceivers: perception is a very active interpreting process.[5]

This is "a structural prerequisite of dramatic tension," adds Hess-Lüttich, as well as of "other classic dramatic devices," including irony (p. 237).

The aggressive monologuist would strategically discourage us from interpretation. But such aggression, while perhaps intimidating the auditor, may well provoke the reader to recall his difference from that auditor, and to disalign him- or herself from the shadowy textual stand-in.[6] In responding, in interpreting, the reader is transforming

---

4. The pragmatics of politeness, and particularly of the politeness of and in literary texts, are relevant here. See Roger D. Sell's article on this in the collection of essays he edited entitled *Literary Pragmatics* (London: Routledge, 1991). Tannen also discusses "silence and negative and positive politeness" in *Perspectives on Silence*, pp. 97ff.

5. Ernest W. B. Hess-Lüttich, "How Does the Writer of a Dramatic Text Interact With His Audience," in Sell, pp. 235–236.

6. For a parallel view from a Browning critic, see John Maynard: "Most of these generally too open fax receivers," says Maynard, "provoke our contempt. Hearing the silence audible of the listener, we break into our own noisy response. It is almost as if Browning has found a poetic gadget to provoke reader response" ("Reading the Reader in Robert Browning's Dra-

the monologue, at the metacommunicative level, into a kind of dialogue.[7] Pratt describes such a situation well:

> The fictional speaker thus produces a lack of consensus, and the author implicates that this lack of consensus is part of what he is displaying, part of what he wants us to experience, evaluate, and interpret. He may intend us to replace the speaker's version with a better one, question our own interpretive faculties, or simply delight in the imaginative exercise of calculating "what's really going on." (p. 199)[8]

Yuri Lotman concurs in this description, asserting that "between text and audience a relationship is formed which is characterized not as passive perception but rather as a dialogue. Dialogic speech is distinguished not only by the common code of two juxtaposed utterances, but also by the presence of a common memory shared by addresser and addressee" (p. 81).

If this is the case, a crucial irony emerges: by discontinuing the sympathetic identification that the reader shared with the listener, the reader does acknowledge the speaker's construction of himself through language; the self-portrait has been successfully completed. However, the textual status of the monologue ends up being crucial for the speaker—for it betrays him. The speaker, however narcissistic he may be, only exists through figuring himself in language. Only the real reader, distinct from that "you" in the poem, has the freedom, gained at the expense of the speaker himself, to realize the speaker's self-portrait fully—that is, to interpret.

There is no larger gap or indeterminacy in dramatic monologue than that passive, silent, listening figure. But his very silence is precisely what induces the reader to what Wolfgang Iser calls the "constitutive activity" that is interpretation—that is, indeed, the emergence of the aesthetic object.[9] This conforms to Robert Browning's remark concerning the role of what we would now call "the ideal reader":

---

matic Monologues," *Critical Essays on Robert Browning*, ed. Mary Ellis Gibson [New York: G. K. Hall, 1992], p. 74). Maynard concludes that we should read the reader "not to define the ideal interpretive position, but to explore the range of response—experiences—the poem generates. . . . If we begin with the listener in the poem in order to decide where to position the cameras of our various readers, we had better be prepared for a variety of listeners as well" (p. 76). Also see Latané, who explores the dynamics of the audience "in and out" of the text; Maynard, "Browning, Donne, and the Triangulation of the Dramatic Monologue," *John Donne Journal* 4, no. 2 (1985): 253–267; and John Woolford, who is one of the few Browning critics who recognizes the significance (both in the sense of "importance" and in the sense of "signifying") of silence. He anticipates my own argument in suggesting that it is the silence of the second-person consciousness that most severely complicates Langbaum's thesis (*Browning the Revisionary* [London: Macmillan, 1988]).

7. See Rosemary Huisman's "Who Speaks and For Whom? The Search for Subjectivity in Browning's Poetry," *AUMLA* 71 (May 1989) for her conclusion that the term "dramatic monologue" is a misnomer, given the dialogic relation between speaker and reader that emerges (p. 83).

8. Yuri Lotman is not talking about dramatic monologue specifically, but about literary texts generally when he remarks that "orientation toward a certain type of collective memory, and consequently toward a structure of the audience acquires a character that is different in principle. It ceases to be automatically implied in the text and becomes a signified (i.e. free) artistic element which can enter the text as part of a game." See Yuri Lotman, "The Text and the Structure of Its Audience," *NLH* 14, no. 1 (Autumn 1982): 84.

9. My description of the pragmatics of dramatic monologue parallels the reading process as described by Iser in his "Interaction between Text and Reader," in *The Reader in the Text: Es-*

It is certain . . . that a work like mine depends more immediately [than acted drama] on the intelligence and sympathy of the reader for its success—indeed were my scenes stars it must be his co-operating fancy which, supplying all chasms, shall connect the scattered lights into a constellation—a Lyre or a Crown. (Woolford, p. 27)

This same passage points at the very real influence of the author as well; he, after all, is putting the stars in their places, if not lighting the space between one and another well. It seems no wonder in this light that so many of Browning's monologues are self-reflexively about art itself: the poems are pointing as precisely toward the paradigmatic structure of their own "correct" interpretation as the extraordinary passage just quoted, and Browning indicates the way toward a "process aesthetics," rather than toward the more traditional "product aesthetics."[1]

To put it another way, while the potential effect or force of a dramatic monologue remains unfulfilled with respect to the auditor, who has been effaced through his own enforced silence, that force is effected at a different level; access is gained in the relation of that utterance to the real reader. The hierarchy set up by the speaker himself is thus undermined by the poem's own status as text, without which it would be difficult in some poems to know that anything had been "communicated" to the auditor at all.[2] The speaker has therefore both gained and lost, because his demand for identity is accomplished at his own expense, simultaneously undermined by something or someone not in his control, free of the system of silence the speaker has established—the subjectivity of the real reader. Jack Selzer would call such a figure the "resisting reader" (p. 171), a term that he borrows from feminist theorists (particularly Judith Fetterley) in an effort to

---

says on Audience and Interpretation, ed. Susan Suleiman and Inge Crosman (Princeton: Princeton Univ. Press, 1980), pp. 106–119. As Iser says, "If the blank is largely responsible for the activities described, then participation means that the reader is not simply called upon to 'internalize' the positions given in the text, but he is induced to make them act upon and so transform each other, as a result of which the aesthetic object begins to emerge. The structure of the blank organizes this participation, revealing simultaneously the intimate connection between this structure and the reading subject. This interconnection completely conforms to a remark made by Piaget: 'In a word, the subject is there and alive, because the basic quality of each structure is the structuring process itself.' The blank in the fictional text appears to be a paradigmatic structure; its function consists in initiating structured operations in the reader, the execution of which transmits the reciprocal interaction of textual positions into consciousness" (p. 119).

    There is a fascinating relationship here between the problem of intersubjectivity and recent game theory, as applied to pragmatic or hermeneutic processes. I noticed while researching this paper that the trope of "game-playing"—from "boxing" to "feint" (Maynard, Sinfield)—turned up both in discussions of dramatic monologue, and in abstract accounts of the reading process. See Elizabeth W. Bruss, "The Game of Literature and Some Literary Games," NLH 9, no. 1 (Autumn 1977): 153–172; John Maynard; Pia Teodorescu-Brînzeu, "The Monologue as Dramatic Sign," Poetics 13 (1984): 136; Yuri Lotman, "The Text and the Structure of Its Audience," p. 84; Christopher Collins, "The Poetics of Play: Reopening Jakobson's 'Closing Statement,' " chap. 3 in The Poetics of the Mind: Literature and the Psychology of Imagination (Philadelphia: Univ. of Pennsylvania Press, 1991), pp. 47–66.

1. I borrow these terms from Nils Erik Enkvist, "On the interpretability of texts in general and of literary texts in particular," in Sell, pp. 24–25.

2. See Wolfgang Iser, The Act of Reading: A Theory of Aesthetic Response (Baltimore: Johns Hopkins Univ. Press, 1978): "Only when the recipient shows by his responses that he has correctly received the speaker's intention are the conditions fulfilled for the success of the linguistic action" (p. 57).

connect this moment of disalignment from the textual auditor, implied or not, to a more general dialogism.[3] But this resistance is obviously gained only through the textual status of the poem itself.

Lotman concludes that the "collective memory" that textuality alone makes available to the real reader shifts the orientation of the "structure of the audience" such that it "acquires a character that is different in principle" (p. 84). In the context of dramatic monologue, Lotman's description of the audience's "character" acquires a force greater even than that of the pun: it pinpoints the figuration of the audience in and through the dynamics of reading a dramatic monologue. I mean "figuration" in two senses here: the emergence of the auditor/reader as a subjective figure standing in opposition to the speaker; and, the troping of audience generally through the emergence of a "you" that is not the textual auditor, but the reader outside the text.

The discernment of the reader rather than the speaker has been an implicit subject of such poems all along—certainly it has been one focus of the "drama" of dramatic monologue. "And what easy work these novelists have of it!" wrote Browning to Elizabeth Barrett in 1845:

> A Dramatic poet has to *make* you love or admire his men and women,—they must *do* and *say* all that you are to see and hear— really do it in your face, say it in your ears, and it is wholly for *you*, in *your* power, to *name*, characterize and so praise or blame, *what* is so said and done . . . <if you don't perceive of yourself,> there is no standing by, for the Author, and telling you: but with these novelists, a scrape of the pen—out blurting of a phrase, and the miracle is achieved.[4]

Note in this passage the ambiguity of the poet's admonition "if you don't perceive of yourself"; he certainly meant "by yourself"—and yet, in the context of my argument, I cannot help hearing also Browning's insistence on the reader's awareness of him/herself as a figure, both as a subjective self, and as a trope.

This figuration or troping of the reader is best illustrated by returning to the poem that has become the touchstone of so many discus-

3. For a fuller exploration of the "dialogic element" in dramatic monologue, see Ashton Nichols, "Dialogism in the Dramatic Monologue: Suppressed Voices in Browning," *VIJ* 18 (1990): 29–51. Here of course lie the full implications of ideology's insinuations through silence, for as Scarpi notes, "Silence . . . becomes a necessary condition for not being excluded from the 'centre.' The myestes who takes part in the celebration of the Mysteries in silence corresponds to the citizen who obeys the 'law' (and how else but in silence?). Indeed, silence is revealed to be one of the conditions necessary to be admitted to the 'centre.' . . . Silence . . . assumes the form of an adhesion to the 'law' which the initiate carries for ever depicted on his body [in tribal initiations]" (Ciani, pp. 30–31). Silence becomes, Scarpi concludes, a "discriminating tool with regard to those who are out. . . . It assumes the form of a type of 'discourse' of the order." In his *Marxism and Literary Criticism* (London: Basil Blackwell, 1990), Terry Eagleton also pinpoints the connection between ideology and silence: "It is in the significant *silences* of a text, in its gaps and absences, that the presence of ideology can be most positively felt. It is these silences which the critic must make 'speak.' The text is, as it were, ideologically forbidden to say certain things. . . . Far from constituting a rounded coherent whole, it displays a conflict and contradiction of meanings; and the significance of the work lies in the difference rather than unity between these meanings" (pp. 34–35).
4. </> indicate Browning's insertion of material in his own text; August 10, 1845, in *Letters of Robert Browning and Elizabeth Barrett Browning*, ed. Elvan Kintner, 2 vols. (Cambridge: Belknap Press of Harvard Univ. Press, 1969), 1:150.

sions of dramatic monologue, "My Last Duchess." I have touched down on this poem throughout the essay, and would like to make the implicit reading constructed over the course of these pages more explicit henceforth. So much attention is paid the Duke and his rhetorical manipulation of the envoy that little attention is paid the third figure present, the painted figure of the Duchess herself. Her "imposed silence," to recall Scarpi's terms, does "coincide with oblivion," since she is both silent and dead. And yet, is she truly oblivious? Literally, of course, the answer is yes. Figuratively, however, reports of her death may have been exaggerated. For what is most remarkable about this figure? That she looks "as if she were alive" (l. 2), so much so that "never read / Strangers like you that pictured countenance" without "[seeming] to want to ask, if they durst, / How such a glance came there" (ll. 6–12). The picture so accurately portrays the essential generosity of spirit that brought out the "half-flush" (l. 19) that animates her face in life and death alike, that the Duke realizes he has not, in fact, escaped his irritation at and by her at all.

This painted portrait powerfully provokes the desire for dialogue about its subject, and the reason for this is not simply because the Duchess is so strikingly "there" as if alive, but also because she is so silent in her very presence. Her image alone tells a story that strangers "read," and while the Duke would control the interpretation of this visual text, he betrays a recognition that the viewer's interpretation must already have begun. A man obsessed with possession, whether of property or persons, the Duke is finally possessed himself (in the other sense) by the life-like figure, with its immortalized "glance" over which he has no more control now than he did before; the sympathetic glance that "went everywhere" (l. 24) and the blush that favored all continue to do so. The resistance to the Duke's narcissistic self-delineation, to put it another way, comes from the "liveliness" of the painting itself; the Duchess' life-in-death acts upon the Duke as a ghostly provocation, and his acknowledgment of the beauty and candor of her painted face, epitomized by the heightened color of her blushing cheek, belies his story of her supposed betrayal of the Duke himself.

The constant play of interpretation that the reader requires is made possible, in other words, by the image of the Duchess herself; the glance that sees the joy of the world, and the "spot of joy" that marks the spirit that so animated her countenance, are continuously undermining the "authoritative version" of the story that would reduce her from subject to object. I argued earlier that it is textuality that betrays the Duke; that betrayal is clearly figured here in the visual text of the portrait, the very "truthfulness" of which exposes the need for, even demands, a (re)reading of her gaze. The painting is a textual trompe l'oeil, the subject and object shifting back and forth like figures in a carpet; it is also a figuration of the shifting relationship of reader to text. Far from being effaced, the Duchess is time and time again brought back to life by the Duke's pathological sensitivity to an unguided, and therefore free, reading of that face.

This portrait is finally an ironical figuration of none other than the actual reader, who like the Duchess is a presence, "alive" because s/he is ultimately beyond the control of the Duke's attempted rhetorical and, therefore, hermeneutical tyranny; we, like the Duchess, are at once inside and outside the frame of the Duke's own verbal self-portrait. On the one hand, the will of the interpreting subject, provoked by the silence of the envoy and portrait alike, is constantly reanimated, as resistant to the Duke as that now monumentally indeterminate spot of joy; on the other hand, the reader, like the Duchess, keeps the Duke alive, the dynamics of reading and interpretation in play. She tropes the event of interpretation; the Duke's mistake is to assert what is clearly not true—that his painting is "merely an object." He ignores what he himself senses in his own compulsion to talk: that the significance, the meaning of the painting, is determined by interpretive operations that are simply beyond his control. Through these operations, the figures of the Duchess and of the reader alike necessarily emerge as strongly as that of the Duke himself.

Perhaps what Browning was attempting to achieve was what Patrocinio Schweikart calls the caring reader, "absorbed in the text but not effaced by it," who "gains a dual perspective through reading both the self and the text in question, and enacts a reciprocal relationship—an 'interanimation'—among author, text, and reader that is mutually respectful and liberating."[5] The ironic freedom of the Duchess' gaze, preserved forever by the portrait's evidently uncanny likeness and "liveliness," thus tropes the actual reader's freedom as interpreter—a freedom that is, to go back to Pratt, rooted in the very textuality of this interpretive event: "Given such a guarantee [that the Cooperative Principle can be restored in any work of literature by the concept of implicature], the Audience is free to confront, explore, and interpret the communicative breakdown and to enjoy the display of the forbidden" (p. 215).

Such an achievement makes sense in the context of Browning scholarship that has established both Browning's Victorian fear of the self-imprisonment of the Romantic subject, and his active resistance to tyranny of any sort, whether political or domestic.[6] This proposed freedom of the reader through the text may be analogous to arguments from recent Whitman scholars, particularly Kerry C. Larson and C. Carroll Hollis, who have outlined the way in which Whitman's poetry highlights, rather than obscures, the rhetorical or persuasive nature of literature, and foregrounds what Larson calls the "achievement of assent as an active and indeed central feature of its drama."[7] Whitman's aim, argues Larson, is to override the mediations between "I" and "you."

Browning certainly does not attempt that kind of Whitmanian conflation. The reading offered here of "My Last Duchess" may well prompt

5. Quoted by Selzer, "More Meanings of *Audience*," p. 171.
6. See the early pages of Woolford's *Browning the Revisionary* on the dynamics of reading in Browning's monologues. Also interested in the reader's silence is Joseph A. Dupras; see his "'My Last Duchess': Paragon and Parergon," *PLL* 32, no. 1 (Winter 1996): 3–18.
7. Kerry C. Larson and C. Carroll Hollis, *Whitman's Drama of Consensus* (Chicago: Chicago Univ. Press, 1988); also see C. Carroll Hollis, *Language and Style in Leaves of Grass* (Baton Rouge: Louisiana State Univ. Press, 1983). I am grateful to my colleague Paul Naylor for pointing out this connection, and also for commenting on a draft of this essay.

one to ask whether then the figure for the author in this text must not be the Duke. But unlike the Duke, Browning is not demanding the "rhetoric of enthrallment," as David E. Latané puts it (p. 28), that goes along with political tyranny; rather, Browning is highlighting a rhetoric not only of obscurity, but also of indeterminacy, which may perplex (hence his "aesthetics of difficulty"), but carefully does not enthrall, does not tyrannically demand identity of speaker and listener, any more than of author and reader. His monologues do reinforce a cooperative (or what Schweikart would call "interanimating") model of reading by highlighting or even thematizing the inability of the actual reader to remain wholly sympathetic to either the text's speaker or, for that matter, to the text's auditor. And this is, once again, the reader's particular freedom, that s/he can exploit and explore with a variety of interpretive approaches the significant textual silences that s/he alone can make speak.

I began this essay by quoting Alberto Schön: "There scarcely exists a silence 'made man.' " What I am suggesting is that in the Browning dramatic monologue the figure of the silent auditor does emerge, in and through the shift from the passive to the active mode of silence, within the reader. The discernment of the second-person auditor is only possible through the reader's own more distant, objective, and possibly resistant response to the speaker. With the full force of irony, the self-image that the speaker would delineate is only achieved when the reader distinguishes her/himself from the shadowy passivity of the listener's silence, and pulls away from a sympathetic association with that manipulated figure. And in turn, the reader, while performing the action of constituting the speaker, will also delineate—in her own image—the form of the silent listener. In this kind of poem, silence is "made man," created in the image of the second-person "I" that refuses to be effaced, that is, the "you," the reader.[8]

CATHERINE MAXWELL

Browning's Pygmalion and the Revenge of Galatea†

> I will make an Eve, be the artist that began her,
> Shaped her to his mind!
> —"Women and Roses," 47–48[1]

In Browning's poetry, the creative act is epitomized by a male artist's desire to immortalize his feminine ideal. For these male artists, the

8. This essay is an expanded version of a paper presented at the 1993 Modern Language Association convention in Toronto. The panel, sponsored by the Linguistic Approaches to Literature division, was put together by Professor Cynthia Bernstein of Auburn, and I would like to thank her for her encouragement. I am also grateful to Professor David Herman of North Carolina State University, whose valuable and thorough comments on a draft of this essay helped direct revisions.
† From *ELH* 60.4 (1993): 989–1013. Reprinted by permission of the Johns Hopkins University Press.
1. I use throughout *Robert Browning: The Poems*, ed. John Pettigrew and Thomas J. Collins, 2 vols. (Harmondsworth: Penguin, 1981). Line numbers are included in parentheses within the text.

creation of woman represents the primal scene of aesthetic produc-
tion: it is not simply the human but the feminine subject who is the
image and end of creative endeavour: "I always see the garden and
God there / A-making man's wife" ("Fra Lippo Lippi," 266–67). Man,
succeeding to the position of the anthropomorphic and masculine de-
ity, becomes the maker of his own match. Woman, rather than being a
subject in her own right, functions as the device that completes man's
lack, simultaneously reflecting him back to himself in a reassuring
fullness. The poems' male actors, whether genuine or aspirant artists,
have constant recourse to a vocabulary that frames their female part-
ners as art-objects, and the repetition of this pattern raises the ques-
tion of whether Browning exposes or colludes with this identification.

U. C. Knoepflmacher opened this debate with the well-supported
contention that Browning ironizes the Romantic epipsyche in his po-
etry, revealing the extent to which woman as other is narcissistically
conceived as a prop, extension, or guarantor of male identity.[2] Carol
Christ's slightly later examination, "The Feminine Subject in Victorian
Poetry," adopts a more suspicious tone. Having made the entirely le-
gitimate claim that, "like Tennyson, Browning associates woman with
the poetical character," she proceeds to assert the significance of
woman in Browning's poetry as the focus of the male and frequently
murderous gaze—"Browning's . . . male characters seek to appropriate
a woman of their desire."[3] She suggests, however, that this appropria-
tion is part of the poet's own larger project: "Fearful of the feminiza-
tion of culture, the poet of the period strove to make the female
subject bear his name."[4] Thus she reads the struggle of Browning's
male protagonists to control, master, fix the women of their desire as a
reflection of his own creative anxiety: "Browning reveals and obscures
the erotic transgression of the artist by controlling the looks of oth-
ers."[5] The taming of the woman's own gaze, the control of her license
to survey, is as much the preoccupation of the poet as it is that of his
male monologuists. "The female subject satisfies the desire to look and
be looked at, while it shields the creator from direct regard."[6] This
view, a more sophisticated version of that critical rationale which
reads Browning's dramatis personae as masks for his own desires, is
problematic. Although Christ acknowledges Knoepflmacher, her per-
ceptions seem to jar with his judgment of ironization. If Browning is in
league with his male monologuists, to what extent can his project be
ironic? And *does* he endorse the views of his male protagonists; does
he really believe that the poetical character can be appropriated in this
way? Christ's alliance of poet with his monologuists makes her miss
the fact that the strategies of appropriation pictured in the poems are
severely flawed, fail even, that the poems stage the very impossibility

2. U. C. Knoepflmacher, "Projection and the Female Other: Romanticism, Browning, and the
   Victorian Dramatic Monologue," *Victorian Poetry* 22 (1984): 139–59.
3. Carol Christ, "The Feminine Subject in Victorian Poetry." *ELH* 54 (1987): 385–401; 396.
4. Christ (note 3), 400.
5. Christ, 399.
6. Christ, 399.

of appropriation. Isn't 'poetical character' something that exceeds man's grasp? Surely the ironization that Knoepflmacher remarks is most powerfully in force when Browning yokes sexuality and art, and thus emphasizes the very fabrication of male fantasy and its constituent role in a masculine myth of creativity?

Although critics have spoken of Browning's obsession with the myth of Andromeda's rescue by Perseus, this story seems to me to be a reaction to a larger mythic influence and one in which the poet shows that preservation by the male is not necessarily synonymous with rescue and liberation.[7] For Browning's real compulsion is Ovid's story of Pygmalion who, disgusted by the women he sees about him, sculpts his ideal woman, and then falls hopelessly in love with the statue he has created. The goddess Venus at last takes pity on him and animates the statue so that it can become his flesh and blood bride.[8] Browning lays bare the misogyny of Ovid's Pygmalion, for whom no living woman is good enough. His poems show how male subjects, threatened by woman's independent spirit, replace her with statues, pictures, prostheses, corpses, which seem to them more than acceptable substitutes for the real thing. Browning's male speakers typically invert Ovid's myth, reducing a woman, even through her death, to a composition of their own creating. They desire feminine simulacra, static art-objects, whose fixed value will reflect their self-estimation. Yet these attempts are always equivocally presented as, time and time again, Browning shows us their fatuity. We see exposed the confusion of values that allows these speakers their justifications. But not only is the error of judgment made plain; increasingly, as he explores the myth, Browning reveals how the speaker's plan goes askew. The female subject consistently eludes her captor, unmasks the poverty of his suppositions, or returns to haunt him. Allied spectres of memory and history cloud his presentations, while intermittent moments of vision and the recognition of the repressed disturb the reader's apprehensions. Art-objects cannot be fixed any more than human beings; contexts change them, and no artist or owner can control the divergent responses they may arouse in the viewer. Just so, Browning shows that what Christ calls "poetical character," and what I would call imaginative energy, cannot be subject to possession; can only be glimpsed, fleetingly experienced, not permanently stayed; that it is always in excess of prescription and delimitation.

"Porphyria's Lover," one of the earliest of Browning's monologues, is

7. William Clyde DeVane, "The Virgin and the Dragon," *Yale Review*, n.s. 37 (1947): 33–46. Adrienne Munich, *Andromeda's Chains: Gender and Interpretation in Victorian Literature and Art* (New York: Columbia Univ. Press, 1989).

8. Ovid, *Metamorphoses* 10.243–97. I use throughout the Loeb edition with English translation by Frank Justus Miller, 2 vols. (London and Cambridge: William Heinemann and Harvard Univ. Press, 1916). Ovid does not name Pygmalion's bride; later writers call her Galatea. J. Hillis Miller's recent study of the Pygmalion story as it impinges on various nineteenth-century novels has an excellent Proem—"Pygmalion's Prosopopoeia"—containing a detailed discussion of Ovid's myth. Miller writes: "For Pygmalion, the other is not really other. Pygmalion has himself made Galatea. She is the mirror image of his desire. . . . It is as if Narcissus' reflection in the pool had come alive and could return his love." *Versions of Pygmalion* (Cambridge: Harvard Univ. Press, 1990), 4–5.

an assured critique through myth, through literary revision, of a form of appropriation typified by a male speaker's narcissistic sexual mastery of a woman.[9] It accumulates its power by borrowing from the Pygmalion story not once but twice. Browning's parodic "good minute" (36) centers the poem whose second half macabrely reverses the action of the first in which Porphyria appears as actor. Porphyria enters the poem as the dominant partner, the maker and doer, while her sullen lover is silent and recalcitrantly passive. She composes the scene, even choreographing his posture, in order to rouse his response, to "bring him to life" again. All this is narrated, crucially and with a certain amount of implied criticism, by the lover, whose sudden inversion of the roles and attitudes might initially be seen to be a kind of rough justice: the woman has manipulated him, now he turns the tables on her. The problem with this neat symmetry is that he has produced it, and to accept it overlooks the fact that we see Porphyria only through his eyes. His picture of her as free agent is conditioned by his subliminal resentment of her autonomy: she is a rich girl selfishly indulging a whim at a poor man's expense, Marie Antoinette playing the cottager in her spare time, a seductress, an *agent provocateur*. Various identifiable oppositions—male and female, active and passive, rich and poor, socialite and solitary—are manipulated by the speaker in an attempt to upset more disturbing oppositions such as aggressor and victim, life and death, art and murder. In spite of the speaker's camouflage, the difference between himself and Porphyria is that however self-centered he may represent her behavior to be, her intent is to arouse and awaken and his is to fix and preserve. The lover's narrative impresses us with its linear recounting of events, but we need to remember the importance of reading backwards, and thus credit the speaker's retrospective reading of Porphyria as his attempt to rationalize, to recast her as a reflection of himself. Porphyria's lover is a Pygmalion who thus continues to work his designs on the body of his beloved long after he has achieved his end, not only by his projection of his desire as her "will" (53); for while she features as his dead Galatea, he makes her also a version of himself, a lesser Pygmalion.

As various critics have pointed out, the name "Porphyria" recalls Keat's Porphyro in *The Eve of St. Agnes*. Knoepflmacher's comments on this name are particularly suggestive in their reference both to status and statuary:

> Porphyro's name (as well as Porphyria's) is derived from the Greek word for purple (as Keats knows when he alludes to the "purple

9. "Porphyria's Lover" was first published as "Porphyria" with "Johannes Agricola" in the *Monthly Repository* for January 1836, and both were reprinted with slight revisions under the general title "Madhouse Cells" in the *Dramatic Lyrics* of 1842. A generative kernel for "Porphyria's Lover" can be found in Browning's earliest published work, *Pauline* (1833), where we encounter the image of the sculptor Pygmalion and the murderer-creator who imputes his own desire to his mistress (896–902). It seems likely that Browning, embarrassed by what he later regarded as the ingenuous self-exposure of that piece, then reflected critically upon some of the postures and impostures struck by its speaker. For the 1833 text, see *The Poetical Works of Robert Browning*, ed. Ian Jack, 4 vols. (Oxford: Clarendon Press, 1983–1991), 1:96.

riot" in Porphyro's heart); as such the name suggests a warm hue, as well as a high station. But the vermilion dye of porphyry is obtained by pulverizing ("porphyrizing") a hard red shell or equally hard red slab of rock (as Keats again suggests when he describes Porphyro as a "smooth-sculptured stone," a "throbbing star," a "vermeil dyed" shield for Madeline's beauty).[1]

When Keats names his lover, he stresses his nobility; the youth is a gentléman, who offers true love, not "ruffian passion" (K, 149), and it is important that his love-making is the fulfillment of Madeline's own private fantasy. Porphyro is seen to awaken her from sleep into the reality she desires. Keats's Porphyro *can* be read as correctly interpreting and enacting the dream of Madeline; the lover in Browning's poem imputes Porphyria's desire as part of his flawed self-justification.[2] If the story of Pygmalion or its Miltonic Biblical parallel touches upon *The Eve of St. Agnes*, Keats's revision represents both man and woman as achieving their dream.[3] Both lovers, with their elaborate rites and preparations show the tendency for composition and scene-play we associate with the figure of Pygmalion. Both, too, in either the deep repose of sleep or in pale immobile trance, enact the sculptured pathos of Galatea; and if Porphyro summons Madeline from her sleep, she implores his release from his frozen posture. It's possible to see Browning's poem either as a direct challenge to Keats's romantic vision or, as Knoepflmacher suggests, a revision exaggerating those latent ambiguities in *The Eve of St. Agnes* which suggest that the story is

---

1. Knoepflmacher (note 2), 151. Knoepflmacher's article makes some important connections between the two poems. The link was first recognized by Alice Chandler in "The Eve of St. Agnès' and 'Porphyria's Lover,' " *Victorian Poetry* 3 (1965): 272–74. While Michael Mason pointed out near sources for the poem in Bryan Proctor's *Marcian Colonna* and *Blackwood's Magazine*, these seem less important to me than Browning's examination of myth and his determining revision of a great precursor in Keats. See Michael Mason, "Browning and the Dramatic Monologue" in *Writers and their Background: Robert Browning*, ed. Isobel Armstrong (London: G. Bell & Sons, 1974), 231–66. For Keats's poems, I use throughout *The Poems of John Keats*, ed. Miriam Allott (London: Longman, 1970). Line numbers are included parenthetically in text and abbreviated *K*. The passages cited by Knoepflmacher come from "The Eve of St. Agnes," 297, 318, 336.
2. Various literary critics have seen Porphyro's behavior in a more equivocal light: Knoepflmacher, following Jack Stillinger, writes of "the hoodwinked Madeline" ([note 2], 146) and claims that "Porphyro played on Madeline's wishful and childish trust" (152). The problem with such a view is that it casts Madeline, stereotypically, as a wronged woman, and discounts the force of her own desire. If Madeline herself has recourse to the stereotype in stanza 37, it is because she momentarily fears that Porphyro will abandon her. Stillinger's seminal article saw Madeline not only as "hoodwinked," but "self-hoodwinked"—the gull of her own superstition. Space forbids discussion of Stillinger's essay with its curious description of Madeline's condition as "pitiful yet, . . . reprehensible," but one wonders if the author is not unduly disturbed by the heroine's desire. See the revised form of the essay in Jack Stillinger, "Skepticism in *The Eve of St. Agnes*," in *The Hoodwinking of Madeline and Other Essays on Keats's Poems* (Urbana: Univ. of Illinois Press, 1971), 67–93; 84, 86. Marjorie Levinson refers more frankly to Madeline's "masturbatory dreaming" in her *Keats's Life of Allegory* (Basil Blackwell: Oxford, 1988), 111. My own ensuing comments on Keats's poem in relation to Browning's try to indicate a difficulty present in the picturing of *both* lovers' desires.
3. The Biblical and Ovidian parallel evokes spontaneously Keats's pronouncement in his letter to Benjamin Bailey (22 November 1817) that: "The Imagination may be compared to Adam's dream—he awoke and found it truth." *The Letters of John Keats 1814–1821*, ed. Hyder E. Rollins, 2 vols. (Cambridge: Harvard Univ. Press, 1958), 1:185. One does not necessarily have to be what Stillinger ([note 11], 69–70) calls a "metaphysical" critic of the poem to see Porphyro and Madeline playing—turn and turn about—the Adam and the Eve of St. Agnes. See also Adam's dream in Milton's *Paradise Lost* 8.452–90.

less than ideal.[4] Another reading (and the most likely in my opinion)
results from a combination of these two responses: Browning under-
stands the seeming mutuality of two lovers who get what they want by
playing Pygmalion to be no real mutuality.

Hillis Miller indicates the strong auto-erotic element present in
Ovid's account of Pygmalion's fashioning of Galatea, and to the extent
that both lovers act out their fantasy without reference to the con-
scious desire of the other, their consummation could be said to derive
from auto-erotic impulses; desires coincide by happy fortuity not by
what one might term true consensuality.[5] It is this paradigm of desire
that I think troubled Browning, elements of which he transferred into
his own de-idealizing poem. The monologuist makes the lady Por-
phyria seem first like the heroic well-born Porphyro when she comes
to awaken her lover from his lassitude; she is also Madeline with
Madeline's sexual desire writ large.[6] Both are versions of Pygmalion;
both preserve the sense of an actor who sees herself as the source of
animation; but both versions are ultimately narcissistic reflections of
the speaker, this poem's true Pygmalion, an onanist in deed and word,
who in the second part of the poem reduces his woman to sculpture,
to the rosy-hued porphyry, or, within the less rose-colored connota-
tions of the poem, a doll with a painted face thenceforth represented
by a neuter pronoun: "the smiling rosy little head / So glad it has its
utmost will."[7] The final irony of this poem is the speaker's Pygmalion-
like wish to see the woman he has murdered as somehow animated,
perfected, achieved, one could also say "finished," through the force of
the desire he has imputed to her. Remade in his image, and in his eyes
reconciled to her better self (which is the self he has fixed and fash-
ioned for her), her life-likeness promotes the suggestion that she
is now, as refined essence, more alive for him than "dead," a word

4. These are, variously, depending on one's critical stance: Porphyro as voyeur and ravisher,
   Madeline as superstitious gull or overly voluptuous virgin, the storm, negative imagery,
   Keats's jokiness and parody.
5. For references to Pygmalion as onanist, see Miller (note 8), 6, 8, 10.
6. Knoepflmacher indicates the influence of various of Coleridge's poems on "Porphyria's
   Lover" ([note 2], 152), but doesn't cite the one that had the most determinable effect on
   Keats's poem—"Christabel." The erotic content of "Christabel" is admittedly blurred, but
   "The Eve of St. Agnes" picks up on the theme of a night-time visitation and tryst in a Gothic
   pile, and the strange fusion of nightmare with the reality of a possible sexual violation is
   transmuted by Keats into the more acceptable seduction as realized dream. "Porphyria's
   Lover," lifting the storm from the end of "St. Agnes" to its own beginning, reinstates the
   theme of sexual violence: Porphyria is the last in a line of blue-eyed maidens, not as saintly
   as Christabel, nor as ambiguously fortunate as Madeline.
7. Incidentally we might notice Browning's dark-humored reference to Ovid's text when he
   mentions the blush induced on the dead woman's cheek. In *Metamorphoses* 10, when the
   ivory statue becomes mortal, we are told she blushes at Pygmalion's kiss: "dataque oscula
   virgo/sensit et erubuit [The maiden felt the kisses and blushed]" (292–93). This blush seems
   significant in the light of the fact that Pygmalion abjures women because of the behavior of
   the Propoetides, who become so accustomed to a life of shame they lose the power to blush
   "sanguisque induruit oris [the blood of their faces hardened]" (241), and are eventually
   turned to stone by Venus. Pygmalion's successful animation of his ideal is, of course, a re-
   versal of this petrification. At the same time, as Alice Chandler (note 10) has pointed out
   (273), Browning also makes contact with Keats through the image of the "rosy little head"
   and "the shut bud that holds a bee," which remind one of Keats's (possibly sceptical) re-
   marks on Madeline, who falls blissfully into her St. Agnes' Eve dream-fantasy "blinded alike
   from sunshine and from rain, / As though a rose should shut, and be a bud again" (242–43).
   If Keats is sceptical, Browning's evocation of this line in the context of death is emphatically
   so.

Browning artfully suggests is repressed in the rhyming couplet "fled/instead" (54–55).[8]

Browning follows up "Porphyria's Lover" with another version of Pygmalion in the verse drama *Pippa Passes* (1841). This time the artistic motif is more overt as he examines the relationship between the young sculptor, Jules, and Phene, an artist's model.[9] Jules, a follower of Canova, becomes the jape of his fellow students who resent his supercilious airs and write him a love-letter purporting to come from the hand of Phene. A correspondence develops, the impressionable Jules falls in love and proposes marriage, and the students persuade Phene, the unfortunate pawn in this charade, to marry Jules on the condition that she will not speak to him until after the ceremony, then to reveal to him by means of a memorized poem the nature of the trick played upon him. During this scene, the reader cannot fail to notice the extent to which the unhappy girl, rendered speechless and thus even more statuesque, is addressed by the man in a language that situates her as art-object. Even as Jules claims that she outstrips his own artistic efforts and conceptions, that she is a "live truth" (23), the "real flesh" (82), his idealization, his total lack of real knowledge of her (represented most fully in his hypothetical pre-nuptial sculpture of her as Hippolyta), implies he regards her as a superlative work of art. Phene's affective revelation is followed by Jules's resolve to leave her and avenge himself but, true to the structure of the drama, this decision is reversed by the song of Pippa, heard as she passes by the house. The problem is that Jules's subsequent apprehension of Phene as person, freshly animated by the vitality of her speech, is still clouded by his appropriation of her as *objet d'art*, and the notion of himself as creator:

> Look at the woman here with the new soul,
> Like my own Psyche,—fresh upon her lips
> Alit, the visionary butterfly,
> Waiting my word to enter and make bright,
> Or flutter off and leave all blank as first.
>
> (288–92)

"This new soul," he declares, "is mine," (300). One version of Pygmalion and Galatea has thus given way to reveal another lurking beneath the surface. Browning shows that new-found soul, supposedly a deeper truth, is just another construct or obstruction to authentic love. Jules's (admittedly exquisite) verse makes Phene speak, though she departs both from his script and that of the jokers. But after Jules's conversion by Pippa's song. Phene is once more silent, a *tabula*

---

8. Miller's comments on Ovid's story are pertinent ([note 8], 7): It "embodies a male fantasy whereby a woman cannot be the object of sexual desire and cannot desire in return unless she has been made so by male effort." Commenting on Ovid's use of the phrase "ars adeo latet arte sua" (252)—so cleverly did his art conceal his art—Miller writes: "Pygmalion is so skillful an artist, skilled even in concealing his art from himself, that he is taken in by his own fabrication: it seems to him that Galatea must be a real girl" (9). This self-delusion is that also practiced by the lover in Browning's poem.

9. The Jules and Phene episode is heralded at the end of "Part I: Morning" of *Pippa Passes*, and is developed in "Part II: Noon." All references are to Part II.

rasa, awaiting Jule's shaping hand, and even her very soul is something he has bestowed or will bestow upon her. The Jules and Phene episode underlines the emphasis of "Porphyria's Lover," but it also provides a fascinating number of elements that Browning will use to very different effect in later work.

It would be easy to see "My Last Duchess" as simply another elegant variation in the same vein. This poem, written some six years after the publication of "Porphyria's Lover" and a year after *Pippa Passes*, has obvious affiliations to both pieces, and although the chronological gap between the two shorter works seems quite large, the later poem, which makes its first appearance with "Porphyria's Lover" in Browning's first published collection of poems, may still be reckoned as one of his earliest monologues. Nonetheless there are important advances made in "My Last Duchess," which is a more complex and troubled poem than the earlier monologue. Porphyria is deprived of her voice to be ventriloquized by her lover, and although the reader perceives the devious doublings and equivocations in his speech, the speaker himself, however doomed and fragile his attempt at constructing his own identity, retains his spurious voice of mastery. To date, Browning has shown us the hollow victory of the appropriating male, but "My Last Duchess" does something much more truly dramatic. The poem stages a confrontation in which the dead returns to challenge the living, and thereby empties and renders null the gesture of appropriation.

I have written elsewhere of how the Duke's language is fissured and disfigured by a latent power which I identify with that of the woman he has tried to suppress.[1] The poem writes the scene of the Duke's compulsive reviewing of a woman who disturbs him as much in her death as she did in life. As the Duchess's "looks" continue to break the boundaries of his self-definition with disrespect for his "nine-hundred-years-old name," the Duke is forced to admit that the passionate "glance," which discourses so eloquently with her beholders, has neither origin nor sanction in himself. The erosion of verbal control over meaning which signals the Duke's involuntary admission also admits the troubling presence of the Duchess. I suggest that in this revival Browning makes his elusive female subject complicit with the uncontainable power he ascribes to imaginative energy. As I return once more to the poem, I want to back my case for the Duchess's reanimation with specific reference to the myth of Pygmalion.

If in "Porphyria's Lover" Browning refers to Ovid's myth directly, and then indirectly through his meditation on Keats's *The Eve of St. Agnes*, he uses a similar approach in "My Last Duchess," save that here the intermediary text is even clearer in its Ovidian echoes. Readers of Shakespeare's *The Winter's Tale* can hardly fail to notice that the famous "statue scene" in which Hermione is returned to her contrite husband by Paulina borrows crucially from Ovid's narrative. Readers of Browning will be struck by the many echoes that find their way into

---

1. Catherine Maxwell, "Not the Whole Picture: Browning's 'unconquerable shade,'" *Word & Image* 8 (1992): 322–32.

"My Last Duchess."[2] In Shakespeare's play, Leontes and others are taken by Paulina through her "gallery," which, rather like that belonging to the Duke, possesses "many singularities" (*WT*, 5.3.10, 12), but whose *pièce de resistance* is said to be a statue of Leontes's deceased wife, Hermione, by the famous sculptor Julio Romano which is kept concealed behind a curtain.[3] Here are Paulina's words at the moment when she unveils the statue:

> As she lived peerless,
> So her dead likeness I do well believe
> Excels what ever yet you looked upon,
> Or hand of man hath done. Therefore I keep it
> Lonely, apart. But here it is. Prepare
> To see the life as lively mocked as ever
> Still sleep mocked death. Behold, and say 'tis well.
>
> *She draws a curtain and reveals the figure of Hermione, standing like a statue*
>
> I like your silence; it the more shows off
> Your wonder. But yet speak.
>
> (*WT*, 5.3.14–22)[4]

Leontes is moved by the resemblance to cry:

> O, thus she stood,
> Even with such life of majesty—warm life,
> As now it coldly stands—when first I wooed her.
> I am ashamed. Does not the stone rebuke me
> For being more stone than it?
>
> (*WT*, 5.3.34–38)

Browning's recall of both Shakespeare and Ovid is illustrated in his ingeniously layered recasting of the myth. The Duke replaces Paulina, Shakespeare's parodic Pygmalion. The actual painting of the Duchess is, of course, the handiwork of the artist Frà Pandolf, but, in his equation of the woman with her portrait, it is the Duke who plays Pygmalion in this drama. As in "Porphyria's Lover," the action seems at first to invert the myth: the woman may be read as reduced to her likeness. The portrait, made while the sitter lived, now after her death

---

2. The only reference I have found to the play in Browning criticism is an essay on sources in Victorian poetry entitled "The Pertinacious Victorian Poets" by L. C. Stevenson in *Victorian Literature: Modern Essays in Criticism*, ed. Austin Wright (New York: Oxford Univ. Press, 1960), 16–31; 26–27. The essay, slightly revised from its original publication in 1952, makes thematic links between play and poem, but does not cover the shared Ovidian source.

3. All Shakespearean references are to *William Shakespeare: The Complete Works*, ed. Stanley Wells and Gary Taylor (Oxford: Clarendon Press, 1986). References to *The Winter's Tale* are included parenthetically in text and abbreviated *WT*.

4. Ian Jack has posited that "My Last Duchess" echoes a moment in Tennyson's "The Gardener's Daughter; or, The Pictures" (1842), in which the elderly speaker tells his auditors to view a picture of his dead lover: "Raise thy soul; / Make thine heart ready with thine eyes: / the time / Is come to raise the veil. Behold her there, / As I beheld her ere she knew my heart." *The Poems of Tennyson*, 2nd ed., ed. Christopher Ricks, 3 vols. (London: Longman, 1987), 1:267–70. See Ian Jack, *Browning's Major Poetry* (Oxford: Clarendon Press, 1973), 92–93. It seems to me that while Browning's poem may take in this reminiscence of Tennyson's, both derive ultimately from Shakespeare's play.

takes on the symbolic status of mortal remains, a secret memorial curtained off for private view like a wife in purdah. It is in this guise that the work can be said to be of the Duke's execution.

At one level, as Lionel Stevenson has pointed out, Browning's revision "ironically controvert[s]" Shakespeare's play: it is the widowed husband, the Duke, who apparently unmoved, unveils an image and a history which seem to betoken death rather than life.[5] Yet the Duke is but "apparently unmoved." In actuality, he is moved not by pathos but the anxiety of experiencing the shifting grounds of his identity. The moments when he directly refers to the portrait show a confusion between the once-living woman and her painted image, yet this confusion is also one of the means by which he lets the Duchess revive. The Duke is Pygmalion in that he animates the portrait. Porphyria's lover tried the strategy of animator in his conclusion, but it was just a strategy and thus a failure. The difference with the Duke is that Browning plays the joke against him; this animation is unwilled and, as such, is the revenge of Galatea.

Echoes from the hidden script of *The Winter's Tale* and the vivification of Hermione thus function not only ironically but in complicity with the more cryptic maneuvers of the poem. Shakespeare gives the role of Pygmalion primarily to Paulina, who first "creates" the statue, and then, acting as Venus, animates it when she sees the penitent longing of Leontes. By placing the power of reanimation in the hands of Paulina and Hermione, Shakespeare revises the misogyny of the Pygmalion myth. The women reassert their own image and significance and so, too, does Browning's Duchess; for while she owes her revival to the Duke, she effectively steals his show. In *The Winter's Tale*, the wonder of the onlookers is provoked by the blurring of verisimilar art with vital reality. While Browning indicates the dehumanizing potential of such a combination, he is also able to invert, as Shakespeare does, the banal tendency to objectify, and thus contrives a movement from the mere mimicry of art to something altogether more troubling. In the following exchange with Paulina and Polixenes, Leontes is agonized by the signs of life that disturb the portrayal of his wife:

> *Paul.*   No longer shall you gaze on't, lest your fancy
>   May think anon it moves.
>
> *Leon.*   Let be, let be!
>   Would I were dead but that methinks already.
>   What was he that did make it? See, my lord,
>   Would you not deem it breathed, and that those veins
>   Did verily bear blood?

5. Instead of the penitence of Leontes, Browning seems to substitute the frantic mania of that other jealous husband Othello, hidden under the mannered tones of the Duke's speech. The Duke's repetition of the word "smile" reminds me of Othello's cruelly derisive reiteration of "turn" when he rebukes his wife in front of the scandalized Lodvico (*Othello*, 4.1.250–61). Other fragments of Othello's speech, such as "sir" and "command," find their way into Browning's poem, and the seminal phrase "O well painted passion!" bears a distinct fruit when it becomes "the depth and passion" seen in the "pictured countenance."

Pol.   Masterly done.
          The very life seems warm upon her lip.
  Leon. The fixture of her eye has motion in't,
          As we are mocked with art.

(*WT*, 5.3.60–67)

These voiced tributes to a perplexing vitalism can be heard echoing through "My Last Duchess," where they discompose the Duke's facility. This mocking by art of the boundaries of life and death confounds the strategist who would confuse them for his own shallow purposes. The blush, supposedly a sign of animation, is horribly faked by Porphyria's lover, but the Duchess's spot of joy, unelicited by the Duke, reverses the power relation. Although painted, the spot defies the Duke's control or suppression, betokening an uncanny animation. As with Hermione, in the Duchess's "dead likeness" we see "life as lively mocked as ever / Still sleep mocked death."[6] The Duchess's return, her intrusion on and distortion of the space of her husband's self-justification makes him into a mockery of his very self.

As we move into Browning's most famous single volume, *Men and Women* (1855), the poet continues to innovate upon the image of Pygmalion. "Women and Roses," which I cited in my opening, is Browning's magnificent rewrite of the meditation on the æsthetic object we find in Keats's "Ode on a Grecian Urn" and "Ode on Indolence." The poet-speaker in Keat's "Grecian Urn" is teased and thwarted by the cool impenetrability of the urn which he characterizes as an icy-hearted virgin—a "still unravished bride of quietness." The frozen scenes on the urn both attract and repel the viewer who is unable to effect the complete imaginative entry he desires. The "Ode on Indolence" presents a dream in which three female figures "like figures on a marble urn" (K, 5) circle about three times "as when the urn once more / Is shifted round" (K, 7–8), and the speaker subsequently identifies the figures as Love, Ambition, and Poesy—figures he eventually dismisses. In Browning's "Women and Roses," the speaker dreams of a red-rose tree around which circle three groups of women representing women of the past, the present, and the future. Each of these groups corresponds to one of the three roses on the rose-tree, but all three groups resist the poet speaker's attempt to arrest them. The speaker's address to these different women fuses amorous expression with that of the would-be artist who wishes to capture the moment forever:

> How shall I fix you, fire you, freeze you,
> Break my heart at your feet to please you?
> Oh, to possess and be possessed!

(18–20)

When the thwarted speaker at last turns to contemplate the "Beauties yet unborn," for a moment he believes that through his artistry he

---

6. The word "mocked" here carries the primary sense of "imitated," but it seems also to have the connotation of "made a nonsense of," "ironized" or "parodied."

can himself create the feminine models that will dominate the future. The motif of Pygmalion is recast in the image of the Christian God who creates the first woman:

> What shall arrive with the cycle's change?
> A novel grace and a beauty strange.
> I will make an Eve, be the artist that began her,
> Shaped her to his mind!
>
> (44–48)

However, this desire, like the speaker's previous desires, is also blocked by the realization that these women, once created, cannot be stayed or controlled even by their creator:

> —Alas! in like manner
> They circle their rose on my rose-tree
>
> (48–49)

Again, in this poem, the combined figure of woman with art conveys the elusiveness of what a male speaker vainly struggles to control and master.

The great monologue "Andrea del Sarto" recasts the language of "My Last Duchess." The painter, who seems so much more sympathetic a character than the Duke, has recourse to essentially the same ideas of encapsulating the feminine. He is unable to master his wife Lucrezia who, far from being contained, is a free agent, at liberty to take other lovers. Her implied promiscuity is made one with the freedom of her looks:

> My face, my moon, my everybody's moon,
> Which everybody looks on and calls his,
> And, I suppose, is looked on by in turn,
> While she looks—no-one's: very dear, no less.
> You smile? why, there's my picture read made
>
> (29–33)

In spite of what is presented as his beguilingly indulgent affection for her, there is no doubt that the painter holds his wife responsible for his artistic failure. She has not provided him with the "soul" (118) or "mind" (126) necessary for his inspiration. Her freedom, her defection from the enclosure of his work-room, has condemned him both to mediocrity and a lonely confinement "inside the melancholy little house" (212). Blind affection is pitted against single-minded genius. Appealingly tender though he seems, Andrea's rationalization of his unachieved success has its roots in a version of Pygmalion. Lucrezia is no epipsyche. Because she does not submit to his project, provide the reflection necessary to his self-determination, Andrea sees his work as lacking colour and verve: "A common greyness silvers everything,— / All in a twilight you and I alike" (35–36). At the same time, his famous credo of inspiration that "a man's reach should exceed his grasp" and his understanding that his technical skill is not matched by inventiveness does not fully cohere with this reckoning of his wife's ideal role.

Andrea's under-achievement is rehearsed in one of Browning's most acclaimed monologues. It seems that out of the striving to account for what animates conception, invigorates looking, and out of the failure to capture that which tantalizes, slips, eludes, exceeds, is born the strongest poetry; it is not only that Browning declares this failure in his poems, but that this "failure" becomes a way of presenting the imagination in its elusiveness, as he reaches and cannot grasp it. What we glimpse in his poems is that which eludes the speaker. The poet makes the site of this failure into the ground of the appearance and vanishing the drama, of the imagination. As Browning strategizes these scenes, as he modifies the myth of Pygmalion, he begins to effect an inversion which allows him to stage more directly the feminine subjects who express the uncontainable power of the imagination. He begins this innovation most forcibly in *Dramatis Personæ* (1864), the first collection published after his wife's death in June 1861.

"James Lee's Wife" is the monologue of a female speaker, and as such is cited by Knoepflmacher as the culmination in Browning's critique of male-female relations.[7] In the ninth section of the poem, the speaker, alienated from a husband who has tired of her,

understands that only by evading him can she ever hope to force him to grasp her true import. Her removal may cause James Lee to re-imagine—and re-image his own selfhood; only then will he be able to take the next step and recognize his wife's image as a speculary analogue or epipsyche of himself.[8]

Knoepflmacher then cites the following lines:

> Strange, if a face, when you thought of me,
>   Rose like your own face present now,
> With eyes as dear in their dear degree,
>   Much such a mouth, and as bright a brow,
> Till you saw yourself, while you cried "'Tis she!"
>
> (353–57)

When he quotes the poem's conclusion, however, Knoepflmacher makes no direct comment on its radical aggression in which the specular language a man traditionally uses to describe his female epipsyche is violently revised by the woman. Although apparently self-deprecating, the woman turns her husband into a version of herself, and the theme of appropriation signaled in yet another of Browning's "possessive" poem titles undergoes the strangest metamorphosis:

> Why, fade you might to a thing like me,
>   And your hair grow to these coarse hanks of hair,
> Your skin, this bark of a gnarled tree,—
>   You might turn myself!—should I know or care
> When I should be dead of joy, James Lee?
>
> (368–72)[9]

---

7. Knoepflmacher (note 2), 139–41.
8. Knoepflmacher, 140.
9. Cited in Knoepflmacher, 139. Browning originally called the poem "James Lee."

This theme of the man turning woman has already been launched in, of all places, Jules's first speech to Phene in *Pippa Passes*: "Nay, look ever / This one way till I change, grow you—I could / Change into you, beloved!" (2.8–10). Mixed in with the appropriative language of Pygmalion, a language devoid of any real acknowledgment of the woman's self, Jules's protestation carries no real challenge for its speaker. But in "James Lee's Wife," the sentiment is not a man's idealizing, but a woman's attempt to convert and disfigure a man who has deprived her of identity.

The same theme reoccurs more forcibly in an often overlooked lyric included in the second edition of *Dramatis Personæ* in 1868. "Eurydice to Orpheus" was written to accompany Frederic Leighton's painting in the Royal Academy exhibition in 1864. Leighton, and Browning after him, follow a variant of the Orpheus legend invented by Gluck and his librettist Calzabigi for the opera *Orfeo ed Euridice* (1762).[1] In Ovid's account, Orpheus is allowed to retrieve his wife from Hades on the condition that he does not turn to look at her as they make their long return to the world. However, Gluck includes the detail that not only is Orpheus not allowed to look, but that he is not allowed to tell Eurydice why he won't. Eurydice is naturally distressed by Orpheus's refusal to look at her, and it is on her insistence that he eventually looks round and thus forfeits her once more. Browning repeats the desire of Gluck's Euridice for "un sguardo solo [a single look]," but with the difference that his Eurydice seems to have an instinctive understanding that what she asks for may cancel out her redemption from the Underworld. Yet still she asks—her argument being that the moment of the look transcends the penalty it may incur.

> One look now
> Will lap me round for ever, not to pass
> Out of its light, though darkness lie beyond:
> Hold me but safe again within the bond
> Of one immortal look!
>
> (2–6)

Again it is the woman who speaks in her own voice, and again, in spite of the logic of the myth, it is her triumph. Although the lyric has a pictorial origin, picture is unformed and disintegrated in Eurydice's speech. "My Last Duchess" launched a process of subtle disfiguration whereby the man is compromised by a woman; the lyric accelerates this process. Its curiously ambivalent language implies the defacement of Orpheus; it is he that disappears and not Eurydice:

> But give them me, the mouth, the eyes, the brow!
> Let them once more absorb me!
>
> (1–2)

The listed features are dislocated, form no definite portrait, and sound at the same time personal and impersonal; lacking possessive pro-

---

1. A fuller account of the background to this poem can be found in my "Robert Browning and Frederic Leighton: 'Che farò senza Euridice?," in *The Review of English Studies* 44 (1993). For the myth, see Ovid *Metamorphoses* 10.1–77.

nouns, they could be attributed either to Eurydice or Orpheus. As Eurydice's, they might be the features she had in the world before she became a shade and which Orpheus has the power to restore by his reclaiming look of acknowledgment. But they can also be the features of Orpheus, his familiar look, from which Eurydice has been separated during her stay in the underworld, and which she now wants. But wants for what reason? To behold him? For him to see her? Is she to be reconstituted by his look or does she demand his features for her own self-recovery? How much Browning lets saturate into that world "absorb," meaning *entrance, fascinate, demand the whole attention of,* as well as *subsume* and *engulf.* Thus Eurydice may want not merely to study her husband's features, but to be wholly engaged by them, mentally and physically, as if her essence should blend into and combine with them. And in this process, Orpheus' dislocated features are given to his wife, become no longer his. Absorbing Eurydice necessitates Orpheus' own disfiguration.

The more orthodox telling of the Orpheus-Eurydice myth makes the male poet-singer the active role and gives Eurydice a passive dependency. Browning reverses these roles, and it is Eurydice who becomes the lyric speaker. What does this erasure and disfiguration of Orpheus portend? Does Browning's lyric anticipate the later dismemberment and decollation of Orpheus, torn apart by women who resent his apparent misogyny?[2] In a simple sense it might be viewed as the resolving correction of the Pygmalion theme that has been developing throughout Browning's work; the female victim, first suffering and then subversive, finally triumphs in her own voice.[3] The Pygmalion narrative occurs as an episode in the Ovidian Song of Orpheus—poetry's Song of Songs, but also the song that identifies poetry with a masculine point of view.[4] The violent revenge of the Ciconian women, so abhorred by Ovid, could be seen as an inevitable response, and Browning's lyric, involving the subtle incorporation of this violence into Eurydice's petition, a feminist revision of both classical and operatic myth. Browning could also be seen to propose or create a male epipsyche for his female speaker, who then appears to be engulfed by her just as countless feminine figures have been by male speakers. Certainly the language and style of the poem suggest a revision of Shelley's early narcissistic and epipsychic sonnet "To—" (1814/15), with its opening line "Yet look on me—take not thine eyes away" (as well as Phene's humble honorific to Jules: "You creature with the eyes! / If I could look for ever up to them. . . . Keep me so, / above the world"

2. *Metamorphoses* 11.1–43. For Orpheus's misogyny, see *Metamorphoses* 10.78–85. Orpheus, after the death of Eurydice, is said to have shunned women and turned his attention to boys. Ovid, who tends to take the male part, trivializes the reaction of the Ciconian women, and sees their revenge only as an outrage. There is evidence to support the idea that orphism was a predominantly misogynist cult.
3. One might note that the power relations inherent in the question of who speaks and who is deprived of voice are central to Browning, although resolving this question (as in "My Last Duchess") requires more than just a simple face reading.
4. The Ovidian narrative, the Song of Orpheus (*Metamorphoses* 10.148–739), which contains the story of Pygmalion, is indulgent towards its male and censorious of its female characters.

[129–40]).[5] But is the symmetry *that* simple, and what does Browning intend by this feminine subsumption?

The figure of woman and particularly the charged focus of her face thus seems to be identified in poems with the imagination, appearing not as a trite and conventional muse, but as a power that cannot be appropriated, a power which can, nonetheless, exceed, subvert, and break boundaries. It is projected as that which could overwhelm the rigidities of "masculine" identity, and even reconstruct it. Eurydice, like the Duchess, coalesces with the poet's own imaginative power, and the poetry pictures to the reader the imagination as it traverses the poem. Browning's representations of women are not attempts to embody "female consciousness" or stage "feminine experience," any more than one would expect his men to represent "male experience." Having said that, of course, the poet is beautifully observant of the ruses, strategies, and assumptions that contribute to the complexity of sexual politics, but these are given a poetic significance and become part of the symbolic fabric of the poem. Swinburne was right when he "denie[d] Browning the skill of impersonating a true woman," because I do not think impersonation and experiential truth was Browning's primary concern: "How does it fare with his Colombes, Constances, Mildreds, Phenes, who are visibly fleshless and senseless?"[6] To lack visible flesh and sense is proper when these phantasmal female forms upset regular pictorial and representational coordinates as something so peculiarly elusive and something so potentially disruptive; imaginative energy conceived as femininity exceeds and disturbs the strictures of more orthodox protocols conceived as masculinity: the artist Pygmalion is out-maneuvered by Galatea, the poet Orpheus is rendered speechless by Eurydice. Even when creativity is imaged as masculine appropriation, as in this extract from the "Parleying with Charles Avision," that control may be absorbed or blurred by an effect that shifts concentration from creator to creation and to the fortuities of pathos in the looks of the women represented:

> Give momentary feeling permanence,
> So that thy capture hold, a century hence,
> Truth's very heart of truth as, safe today,
> The Painter's Eve, the Poet's Helena,
> Still rapturously bend, afar still throw
> The wistful gaze!
>
> (243–48)

I would suggest that the tendency to represent woman as vitally disfiguring poetic energy, a conception subliminally present as far back as "My Last Duchess," becomes fully operative in Browning's later work. In this we may speculate that the death of Elizabeth Barrett played some considerable part. *Dramatis Personæ* (1864) is a volume as much

5. *Shelley: Poetical Works*, ed. Thomas Hutchinson, rev. ed. G. M. Matthews (New York: Oxford Univ. Press, 1970), 523.
6. Knoepflmacher (note 2), 158; Swinburne, "The Chaotic School," in *New Writings by Swinburne*, ed. Cecil Y. Lang (Syracuse: Syracuse Univ. Press, 1964), 53, cited by Knoepflmacher, 158.

touched by the death of Elizabeth Barrett as is Hardy's "Poems of 1912–13" touched by the death of his wife, and its contents are subsequently marked with loss and bereavement. Knoepflmacher tells us that "Barrett . . . furnished Browning with a further link to the Romantic idealization of a female complement who might restore an incomplete male self."[7] But if, after her death, Browning dwells upon the return of the woman who called him "my Orpheus," this works out in the poetry as something more extraordinary than Knoepflmacher's formula would imply; it is as if Browning comes to identify her with poetry itself, imagines himself as absorbed into her and thereby partially erased.[8] Whether this is an extension of Browning's self-effacing respect for his wife's work, as shown both during her life and after, the guilt of the survivor, a form of the introjection or incorporation that characterize mourning and melancholia, or a combination of all or part of these, is not my quarry here, though it seems necessary to indicate how force of circumstance could accentuate or catalyze a tendency already present in the writer's work.[9]

Carol Christ has made the interesting comment: "A feminized lyric, associated with his dead wife, comes to take the place of Shelley in his poetry as the unreachable and unspeakable ideal before which he claims his own poetic space."[1] Browning's "Eurydice to Orpheus" is, as I have indicated, a Shelleyan lyric which owes some of its inspiration to Elizabeth Barrett's death. But Christ also makes the claim that "Browning's absorption of the lyric within the dramatic effectively contains the feminine." Yet Browning does write straight lyrics— "Eurydice to Orpheus" included—and it is debatable whether the feminine-identified lyric moments one encounters in the dramatic verse *are* contained; rather they appear to arrest attention only to displace themselves and disrupt narrative continuity; produce the uncanny; modify the nature of the dramatic, deregulating notions of coherent persona and personality.

Browning himself thought "Beatrice Signorini" the best poem of his last volume, *Asolando: Facts and Fancies* (1889). This neglected but fascinating poem is a satirical comedy of sexual manners. Notable for its delineation of woman as artist, it may also be regarded as Browning's last use of the Pygmalion motif. In this poem, Browning maps the tensions which arise for a male protagonist when he deliberates

7. Knoepflmacher, 141.
8. *The Letters of Robert Browning and Elizabeth Barrett Browning*, ed. Elvan Kintner, 2 vols. (Cambridge: Harvard Univ. Press, 1969), 1:532 (12 March 1846).
9. "I *know*—that you are immeasurably my superior, . . . I know and could prove you are as much my Poet as my Mistress" (RB to EBB [19 April 1846]), in Kintner [note 35], 638); "how much my happiness would be disturbed by allying myself with a woman to whose intellect, as well as goodness, I could *not* look up?" (RB to EBB [13 August 1846], Kintner, 2.960; "But, NO, dearest Isa,—the simple truth is that *she* was the poet, and I the clever person by comparison" (*Dearest Isa: Robert Browning's Letters to Isabella Blagden*, ed. Edward C. McAleer [Austin: Univ. of Texas Press, 1951], 365 [19 August 187]). On mourning and melancholia, see Sigmund Freud "Mourning and Melancholia" (1917 [1915]), in *The Pelican Freud Library*, ed. Angela Richards and Albert Dickson, 15 vols. (Harmondsworth: Penguin, 1973–1986), 11:245–68. See also a remarkable paper "Introjection-Incorporation: *Mourning* or *Melancholia*" by Nicolas Abraham and Maria Torok, in *Psychoanalysis in France*, ed. S. Lebovici and D. Widlöcher (New York: International Univ. Press, 1980), 3–16.
1. Christ (note 3), 396.

between wife and mistress, a theme central to the earlier *Fifine at the Fair* (1872). Art, in particular painting, is subjoined to the plot, for not only is the male protagonist, Francesco, a painter (and, it would seem, a decidedly mediocre one), but his mistress, Artemisia, is a painter too, and one whose skills far exceed those of her lover.[2] Browning's mischievous treatment of Francesco's internal debate is an ironic variant on the old King's notorious apportioning of sex roles in Tennyson's *The Princess* (1842):

> Man for the field and woman for the hearth:
> Man for the sword and for the needle she:
> Man with the head and woman with the heart:
> Man to command and woman to obey;
> All else confusion.
>
> (*The Princess*, 5.437–41)[3]

This domestic pietism is translated with a comic and cynically realist tone into Francesco's understanding of sexual division:

> Man boasts mind:
> Woman, man's sport calls mistress, to the same
> Does body's suit and service.
>
> (135–37)

Francesco, whom the narrator calls sardonically "Our true male estimator," reflects anxiously on the possibility of submitting himself to Artemisia:

> If I crouch under proudly, lord turned slave,
> Were it not worthier both than if she gave
> Herself—in treason to herself—to me?
>
> (86–88)

The narrator then mocks the ratiocination that ensues when Francesco considers this espousal of what would be more conventionally "the woman's part."[4]

> And, all the while, he felt it could not be.
> Such love were true love: love that way who can!
> Someone that's born half woman not whole man:
> For man, prescribed man better or man worse,
> Why, whether microcosm or universe,
> What law prevails alike through great and small,

2. Artemisia is Artemisia Gentileschi (1593–1653?) and Francesco, Francesco Romanelli (1617–62). Browning's story is based on the factual narrative provided by Filippo Baldinucci in his *Notizie de' Professori del Disegno*, 6 vols. (Florence: S. Franchi, 1681–1728), 5:293–4. His recasting of the story is, in part, a reaction against Baldinucci's prudishness. For a part translation, see William Clyde DeVane, *A Browning Handbook*, 2nd ed. (New York: Appleton-Century-Crofts, 1955), 544.
3. Ricks (note 22), 2:185–296, 264.
4. The phrase comes from Elizabeth's teasing reproach to Robert: "In your ways towards me, you have acted throughout too much 'the woman's part,' as that is considered. . . . And now, you still go on—you persist—you will be the woman of the play, to the last; let the prompter prompt ever so against you. You are to do everything I like, instead of my doing what *you* like, . . . and to 'honour & obey' *me*, in spite of what was in the vows last saturday [sic]." (14 Sept. 1846), in Kintner (note 35), 2:1073.

> The world and man—world's miniature we call?
> Man is the master.
>
> (89–96)[5]

When Francesco and Artemisia end their affair, she dispatches him back to Viterbo, and marriage, with a gift intended for his wife, but properly a challenge to Francesco himself:

> She twitched aside a veiling cloth.
> "Here is my keepsake—frame and picture both:
> For see, the frame is all of flowers festooned
> About an empty space,—left thus, to wound
> No natural susceptibility:
> How can I guess? 'Tis you must fill, not I,
> The central space with—her whom you like best!
> That is your business, mine has been the rest.
> But judge!"
>
> (162–70)

In this teasing gesture, Artemisia shows she recognizes the limited terms of Francesco's sexual consciousness and the male desire for appropriation. Her request for Francesco to become Pygmalion seems to be as much a mocking framing of him as is the flowery border she has painted for the canvas.[6]

Overwhelmed with sudden passion for Atemisia, Francesco bids her turn model and produces a masterpiece—which we never see clearly but of whose "perfection" we are, perhaps ironically, assured: "That face was worthy of its frame, 'tis said— / Perfect, suppose!" (244–45).[7] The couple then part never to meet again. But the portrait resurfaces later, once more as challenge, this time to the woman Francesco patronizes as "my placid Beatricé-wife." Set upon the "whim" of confronting Beatrice with her rival's portrait, Francesco stages a second unveiling, and one might note that, unlike Artemisia's parodic gesture, this is an unveiling which the narrator hints is that of the onanistic *connoisseur*:

> He drew aside
> The veil, displayed the flower-framed portrait kept
> For private delectation.
>
> (291–93)

---

5. From the published version of *The Princess*, Tennyson omitted these disparaging lines: "if there be / Men-women, let them marry women-men / And make a proper marriage." Ricks (note 22), 2:290.

6. The image occurs also in the epigraph to *Jocoseria* (1883): "—Where is the blot? / Beamy the world, yet a blank all the same, / —Framework which waits for a picture to frame. / What of the leafage, what of the flower? / Roses embowering with naught they embower! / Come then, complete incompletion, O comer, / Pant through the blueness, perfect the summer!" (4–10).

7. In a rare article on the poem, John G. Rudy sees Francesco's preoccupation with artistic perfection as a substitute for a genuine relationship with a woman who is his superior: "He endeavours to capture her in his art and to hold her beauty in an eternal stasis divorced from earthly love and morality. . . . [He] hopes to acquire through art what he cannot have in life." See "Browning's 'Beatrice Signorini' and the Problems of Æsthetic Aspiration," in *Browning Society Notes* 7 (1977): 89.

This reminiscence of the Duke and the autoeroticism of Pygmalion is then violently assaulted by another challenger. Beatrice's unanticipated reaction is first to evaluate the flower-frame, and then "disengage" (303) it from the picture, in sum to cut the actual portrait to shreds with a dagger-like hair ornament—"woe to all inside the coronal!" (310). The effect this has on her surprised husband is to increase both his love and estimation of her; the marriage continues enriched and happy, and the narrator decides magnanimously that maybe Francesco wasn't such a mediocre painter after all.

The reader is left wondering over this strange passage of events: does Browning tame the poem and deprive it of its more radical aspects? It seems at first that Francesco gets off lightly as the clash is between the two female rivals with the image of the mistress being symbolically stabbed and disfigured:

> Stab followed stab,—cut, slash, she ruined all
> The masterpiece. Alack for eyes and mouth
> The dimples and endearment—North and South,
> East, West, the tatters in a fury flew:
> There yawned the circlet.
>
> (311–15)

And yet it is Artemisia's work, her frame, her original gift to Beatrice, that is left unscathed, and Francesco's fantasy that is destroyed. What is damaged, as the mastery contained in the "masterpiece" is abruptly emptied out, is not the woman but the epipsychic ideal created to gratify masculine voyeurism and corroborate Francesco's anxious male identity.[8] Artemisia starts and Beatrice finishes a process that implicates and exposes Francesco as Pygmalion. The disfiguration of the portrait is thus, in principle, a shift from ideal to reality, and as such represents the necessary disfiguration of Francesco himself; it demands a *volte face*, the need to face up and address neglected issues, to turn and see Beatrice as she really is—which is what in fact she seems to be demanding: "look at me; look at me again."[9] Browning's naming of the poem after Beatrice herself reemphasizes this new focus.

Browning is not so innocent as to suggest a complete transformation. There are a few equivocal notes. Francesco's words of acclamation, like those of Jules, still derive in part from the language of the artist, and it is hard to tell whether this is a redemption of that language or a residue of the former attitude. To Beatrice, who is shown "with mien defiant" of death (or worse), and yet "Passively statuesque" (317, 319), Francesco declares:

> Then you ever were, still are,
> And henceforth shall be—no occulted star
> But my resplendent Bicé, sun-revealed,

8. Rudy corroborates: "Beatrice, in preserving the flowers round the portrait, is not necessarily attacking art, nor even Artemisia. Rather, Beatrice is destroying perhaps unconsciously, her husband's delusion of perfection in the portrait" ([note 43], 91).

9. "Poetics," another poem from *Asolando*, is, in the tradition of Shakespeare's Sonnet 130, a denial of empty poeticisms in favor of the beloved's reality: "Be the moon the moon: my Love I place beside it: / What is she? Her human self,—no lower word will serve" (7–8).

Full rondure! Woman-glory unconcealed,
So front me.

(324–28)

Beatrice is not condemned to be locked up (or "kept for private de-
lectation"), but in calling her "full rondure" or "Woman-glory," is
this a correction or simple evocation of the painting's rondure and
Francesco's tentative question to Artemisia: "This glory-guarded mid-
dle space—is mine? / For me to fill?" (211–12). While Browning
leaves us pondering the blurrings of these words, we can see that
Francesco, for all his faults and lack of delicacy, is a far more interest-
ing character than Jules in that he has a self-questioning faculty and
some sense of his own limitations. The conclusion may be less than
perfect—perhaps because Browning is sceptical about perfection in
earthly relations—but Francesco's change of heart is certainly an ad-
vance on Jules's alarmingly empty conversion.

Moreover, as in *The Winter's Tale*, the women are responsible for
the turn of events and the control of their own identity. Beatrice's dis-
figuration of the portrait marks her own transformation: the demure
wife becomes critic, surprises her husband with her unforseen inter-
pretive skills, and avenges herself in an act of violence. Artemisia's gift
to her communicates a cryptic message that indicts Francesco.
Browning hints at the partnership involved in the shared framing and
disfiguration of Francesco as Pygmalion, Beatrice's vandalization of
her husband's work preserves Artemisia's flower-frame and "restores"
its central space. She abuses Francesco's ideal image of Artemisia as a
"serpent" (306), but immediately afterwards Browning describes her
own hair with a serpentine metaphor—"coils / On coils" (306–7)—
which suggests he sees a coidentity. After all, both women outstrip
the idealizing flower-imagery satirically offered by Artemisia to Fran-
cesco.[1] Furthermore, Beatrice's laceration of the portrait, whose un-
veiling she rightly regards as an act of sexual threat and aggression,
uncannily makes her an archetypal Gentileschi heroine. The historical
Artemisia's most famous painting is the superb *Judith beheading
Holofernes* in the Uffizi, in which two women, Judith and her maidser-
vant, mercilessly decapitate her would-be rapist.[2] The extreme vio-
lence of Beatrice's reaction is Browning's own invention; it represents
the uncontainable energy he associates with the feminine, and with
the imagination that destroys the "masculine" striving for possession,
capture, and completion.

This article has argued that Browning examines creativity through a
shrewdly observed dialectic of masculine and feminine types. Not only

---

1. In swapping an innocuous femininity for something more canny and redoubtable, Browning
   may recall Lady Macbeth's words: "Look like the innocent flower / But be the serpent
   under't" (*Macbeth*, 1.5.64–65).
2. For an illustration, see Germaine Greer, *The Obstacle Race: The Fortunes of Women Painters
   and their Work* (London: Secker & Warburg, 1979), 190. It has been suggested that Gen-
   tileschi's painting is informed by the experience of her own rape as a young woman. Brown-
   ing would have seen this painting—mentioned in Baldinucci (note 38), 5:293–then in the
   Palazzo Pitti. His friend, the art critic Anna Jameson, had commented on the painting in her
   Visits and Sketches at Home and Abroad, 4 vols. (London: Saunders and Otley, 1834), 2:119;
   3:252–53.

does feminine imaginative energy elude Browning's male speakers, but it splits and disfigures them. However, this gendered critique dramatizes a larger process that is at work in all of his attempts at portraiture where human identity is made up, as Pater claimed it was, of a perpetual weaving and unweaving of the self, and creativity is characterized by a continuing process of construction and dissolution.[3] One, if not the primary pleasure, of reading Browning is our sensation of a release of energy when the speaker disfigures; when an apparently solid core of identity is broken and begins to dissolve and evaporate. For this very moment of loss is also a moment of creation: in the gap or fissure, we glimpse the forces that underlie portraiture and which give it its appeal. In the time and space of the portrait, there is also the space of a radical decomposition vitally integral to the total picture. Again and again Browning's portraits radiate energy, but that illumination is not the high finish of a coherent speaking likeness, but the flash of brilliant disfiguration which momentarily irradiates the shifting imaginative terrain that grounds composition.

DANIEL KARLIN

Browning's Poetry of Intimacy†

Henry James thought Browning's writing on 'the great human passion', the 'extraordinary beauty of his treatment of the special relation between man and woman', to be the feature of his work which would, on its own, have ensured his classic status.[1] 'Special' is not a euphemism for 'sexual' (though it includes it). James is responding to Browning's sense of the relation as 'special' in its importance, its intensity, and—the quality which particularly concerns me here—its preoccupying nature. Love singles out Browning's men and women, as it singled him out in his own love for Elizabeth Barrett; the relation between lovers in his work passionately excludes other kinds of relation, seeing them as intrusion or threat. Love is all-encompassing and absolute in its claims: Browning's speakers recognize the claim even if they do not believe it can be fulfilled. 'If two lives join, there is oft a scar, / They are one and one, with a shadowy third; / One near one is too far', the speaker of 'By the Fire-Side' warns (ll. 228–30);[2] but he and his 'perfect wife' have achieved a union without the 'shadowy third': 'We two stood there, with never a third . . . we knew that a bar was broken between / Life and life: we were mixed at last / In spite of the mortal screen' (ll. 186, 233–5). For the speaker of 'Two in the

3. Walter Pater, *The Renaissance: Studies in Art and Poetry. The 1883 Text*, ed. Donald L. Hill (Berkeley: Univ. of California Press), 188.
† From *Essays in Criticism* 39.1 (1989): 47–64. Reprinted by permission of Oxford University Press. Newly revised by the author for this Norton Critical Edition.
1. 'Browning in Westminster Abbey' (1890), later reprinted in *English Hours* (1905).
2. All quotations, except for *The Ring and the Book*, from *Robert Browning: The Poems*, ed. J. Pettigrew and T. J. Collins, 2 vols. (New Haven and London, 1981). Quotations from *The Ring and the Book* from the edition by R. D. Altick (Harmondsworth, 1971).

Campagna' such a union is impossible: 'I would that you were all to me, / You that are just so much, no more . . . I yearn upward, touch you close, / Then stand away' (ll. 36–7, 46–7). Still what connects these poems is the lovers' isolation; their affair is their own affair; the same principle of exclusion operated in Browning's own marriage, most strikingly, as is to be expected, at its beginning. Elizabeth Barrett's famous flight from her family has perhaps drawn attention away from the fact that Browning, too, in marrying was leaving home for the first time.

Until *The Ring and the Book* it is rare for relations other than those between the lovers themselves to be acknowledged at all in Browning's love poetry. Where they are acknowledged, it is as the source of frustration, division, or even tragedy. The girl in 'The Confessional' who confides her lover's secret to a priest (aptly doubling as her 'Father') brings death to him and torment to herself; the lovers in 'The Statue and the Bust' fail because they take account of the world rather than their own passion, as do those in 'Dîs Aliter Visum' and 'Youth and Art'. 'Andrea del Sarto' has the characteristic situation of Browning's lovers, face to face, alone with each other; but the 'Cousin' shadows the intimate colloquy which Andrea wistfully wishes to have with Lucrezia, 'Both of one mind, as married people use' (l. 16). Browning's lovers are always striving to achieve this intimate isolation: Browning himself, as speaker in 'One Word More', turns away from his own 'fifty men and women' to his wife: 'I am mine and yours—the rest be all men's', he says, rejoicing that 'the meanest of [God's] creatures / Boasts two soul-sides, one to face the world with, / One to show a woman when he loves her!' (ll. 1, 135, 184–6). The speaker of 'Love Among the Ruins' (the first poem of *Men and Women*, as 'One Word More' is the last) dismisses 'whole centuries of folly, noise and sin'; the past is itself like a crowded city which fades into impalpability and leaves the lovers to 'rush . . . Each on each' (ll. 81, 71–2). The speaker of 'Cristina', too, imagines the moment when 'Mine and her souls rushed together' (l. 48), a moment the reader may suspect to be one of delusion rather than fulfilment; at any rate Browning's interest in these matters extends into regions of the mad and the morbid, as the lovers in 'Porphyria's Lover', 'Evelyn Hope', and 'Too Late' make evident. The poem I shall be discussing in detail, 'A Lovers' Quarrel', also registers a doubt as to what is implied by the exclusive and all-encompassing claims that lovers make.

The pressure of genre may have something to do with Browning's treatment of love: sexual passion, in its exclusive and obsessive mode, may be thought the province of poetry (even dramatic poetry); it is in the novel that we expect sexual love to be embedded in the family and in society. And although family and society certainly figure in the most novelistic of Browning's writings, *The Ring and the Book*, they do so in strikingly negative forms. Pompilia is sold into marriage with Guido by her putative parents; Guido's family in Arezzo appear as secondary persecutors and predators; 'Society' in Arezzo (in the persons of its secular and religious leaders, the Archbishop and the Governor) refuses

Pompilia the help she pleads for. With the family either weak and de-
fective, or monstrous, and society indifferent or colluding with the op-
pressor, the way is open for the romantically single and singular figure
of Pompilia's rescuer, Caponsacchi, who breaks through the con-
straints of his social identity in order to save her. Andromeda has,
after all, been chained to the rock by her own parents; Perseus's rec-
ommendation is not that of a stable family background. Whereas in
Middlemarch (to take a representative and contemporary example) the
whole action of the novel is concerned with the interplay between per-
sonal and social codes, the action of *The Ring and the Book* seems de-
signed to bring Pompilia and Caponsacchi, as passionate suffering
spirits, face to face in a communion which transcends their nominal
social identities:

> Yes, my end of breath
> Shall bear away my soul in being true!
> He is still here, not outside with the world,
> Here, here, I have him in his rightful place!
> 'Tis now, when I am most upon the move,
> I feel for what I verily find—again
> The face, again the eyes, again, through all,
> The heart and its immeasurable love
> Of my one friend, my only, all my own,
> Who put his breast between the spears and me.
> Ever with Caponsacchi!
>
> (vii 1771–81)

Pompilia's words are sexually ecstatic (orgasm is traditionally figured
as a death, the 'bearing away' of the soul out of the body) and also
masterful ('Here, here, I have him'); her visionary union with, and ap-
propriation of, Caponsacchi is the more powerful since she is actually,
not metaphorically, dying, 'most upon the move', her identity on the
point of being dissolved and yet, she affirms, most centered and self-
poised ('I feel for what I verily find'). The idea that a person's true self
is to be found in his or her transcedent union with another has a long
literary history, of course, from Plato's *Symposium* to the poetry of
Browning's 'revered and magisterial Donne' (at times Browning's love
poetry seems like an extended commentary on 'Lovers' Infiniteness',
especially the final lines),[3] and the idea that sexual love is connected
with power has an equally long lineage, but these are axioms which
Browning also proved upon his pulses.

The first months after Robert Browning and Elizabeth Barrett mar-
ried, in September 1846, were spent at Pisa. They were months of un-
interrupted and concentrated intimacy. The 'great storm of gossip'
which Elizabeth Barrett had anticipated was rumbling far away.
Browning was no longer dining out with 'Dickens and his set', or walk-

---

3. 'But we will have a way more liberal, / Than changing hearts, to join them, so we shall / Be
   one, and one another's all.' 'Revered and magisterial Donne' is from *The Two Poets of Croisic*,
   l. 912, one of many admiring allusions in Browning's poetry and letters. Compare also
   Shakespeare's *The Phoenix and the Turtle*: 'So they lov'd as love in twain / Had the essence
   but in one; / Two distincts, division none: / Number there in love was slain' (ll. 25–9).

ing over to Chelsea to hear Carlyle's 'divine philosophy'. The Brownings knew no-one in Italy, and, after their friend and travelling companion Mrs Jameson left them installed in their apartment in the
Collegio Fernandino, they were virtually cut off from their network of
family and friends. Marriage did not take Elizabeth Barrett from her
room in Wimpole Street and launch her into the brilliant social world
from which, as she saw it, Browning had 'condescended' to seek her
out. If anything it reduced, rather than expanded, her immediate social horizon. Wimpole Street was never the hermetically sealed cave of
legend; Elizabeth Barrett had been visited by (among others) Mrs
Jameson and Mary Russell Mitford, and news of the London literary
world had been brought to her almost daily by her devoted 'cousin' and
friend, John Kenyon. At Pisa it was as though the Brownings had
fallen into a social well. In fact they liked it there; they had not fallen,
they had jumped. Writing to her close friend Julia Martin, Elizabeth
Barrett Browning described the idyll of her new life:

> Everyday I am out walking while the golden oranges look at me
> over the walls, & when I am tired . . . & I sit down on a stone to
> watch the lizards . . . Also we have driven up to the foot of the
> mountains, & seen them reflected down in the little pure lake of
> Asciano—& we have seen the pine woods, & met the camels
> laden with faggots, all in a line. So now ask me again if I enjoy my
> liberty as you expect . . . The worst of Pisa is, or would be to some
> persons, that, socially speaking it has its dullnesses . . it is not
> lively like Florence . . not in that way—But we do not want soci
> ety—we shun it rather.[4]

'Society' here has two meanings. In the narrow sense it is the society
of people of the same nationality and class, English tourists or expatriates, to avoid whom was a major preoccupation of the lovers when
they were deciding where to live.[5] 'Rome is better than London, because it is other than London', says Claude in *Amours de Voyage*; but,
though like him the Brownings had gone to Italy to be 'rid, at least for
a time, of / All one's friends and relations', they did so not as an abandonment of relationship but a concentration and intensification of it.
'Yet, in despite of all, we turn like fools to the English', Claude goes
on; and the Trevellyn family to whom he turns are frank in their regret
that Rome is 'Not very gay' because 'the English are mostly at Naples'.[6]
The Brownings, however, were turning not to the English but to each
other. And in the wider sense the 'society' they were rejecting means
simply anyone else, other people, outsiders who might intrude into the
closed nuptial circle. This wider human 'society', literally absent from
Elizabeth Barrett Browning's description, is displaced in figurative

4. Letter of 5–9 November 1846; *The Brownings' Correspondence*, ed. P. Kelley and S. Lewis,
   vol. 14 (Winfield, Ks and London 1998), pp. 42–3; hereafter *Correspondence*. Both Elizabeth Barrett and Browning use a two-point ellipsis, as here, instead of a dash; my ellipses are
   indicated by three points.
5. Browning's comment in his letter of 10 July 1846 is typical: 'As for the travelling English,
   they are horrible and, at Florence, unbearable . . their voices in your ear at every turn . . and
   such voices!' (*Correspondence*, vol. 13 [1995], p. 147).
6. Arthur Hugh Clough, *Amours de Voyage*, Canto I, ll. 27–29, 32, 57.

terms onto the picturesque landscape, the oranges that look at her, the lizards she looks at in turn, the mountains she and Browning drive out to visit (natural aristocrats, preening themselves without vanity in a 'pure' mirror), the camels they meet. The oranges seem to have grown themselves for themselves, the camels are self-loading. Where human society subtracts from the economy of love, everything here adds to it. The world is stable, productive, ordered (the laden camels are 'all in a line'). 'I enjoy my liberty': a liberty born not of Romantic solitude, but of being bound to another: the 'I' of the passage is always entwined with, always becoming a 'we'. Isolation, the key to Romantic visionary experience, gives way to togetherness; the experience itself modulates from the Wordsworthian sublime to the domestic beautiful, smaller in scale (the foot, not the summit, of the mountains).

Still, the word 'shun' has something disturbing about it. The thing to be shunned may be repugnant or dangerous; but the person who shuns it may be guilty or ashamed. The *OED* cites another happy couple in *Paradise Lost*:

> So passed they naked on, nor shunned the sight
> Of God or angel, for they thought no ill;
> So hand in hand they passed, the loveliest pair
> That ever since in love's embraces met . . .
>
> (iv 319–22)

Adam and Eve, of course, have no human society to shun; they are all in all to each other, 'Imparadised in one another's arms, / The happier Eden' (iv 506–7), the words of Satan, let us remember, a visitor from that emblem of (especially urban) society, Pandemonium. Satan is determined to make an eternal triangle out of the nuptial pairing: 'League with you I seek, / And mutual amity so strait, so close, / That I with you must dwell, or you with me' (iv 374–6), an aim which, sinister in him, is laudable in Christ, the bridegroom of all saved souls; yet Milton insists, in his celebration of 'wedded Love', that it is the 'sole propriety / In Paradise of all things common else' (iv 750–2). The sexual union between two people, sanctified by marriage, reserves for them a private enclosed space, like the bower in which, though they do not 'shun' the angels, Adam and Eve nevertheless retire to make love.

The attitude to society which Elizabeth Barrett Browning expresses in her letter was perhaps not as natural to her as to Browning, given their respective histories. In an early letter to him, she denied holding 'the philosophy or affectation which beholds the world through darkness instead of light, & speaks of it wailingly', and spoke instead of the two 'lessons' she had learned from her 'course of bitter mental discipline & long bodily seclusion': 'the wisdom of cheerfulness—& the duty of social intercourse'.[7] Browning's reply caricatured this phrase for his own purposes:

> So you have got to like society, and would enjoy it, you think? For
> me, I always hated it,—have put up with it these six or seven

---

7. Letter of 5 March 1845; *Correspondence*, vol. 10 (1992), p. 112.

years past lest by foregoing it I should let some unknown good escape me, in the true time of it, and only discover my fault when too late,—and now, that I have done most of what is to be done, *any* lodge in a garden of cucumbers for me![8]

He will be content to join her in her seclusion, he means; but, replied Elizabeth Barrett, 'what you say of society draws me on to many comparative thoughts of your life & mine':

> You seem to have drunken of the cup of life full, with the sun shining on it. I have lived only inwardly,—or with *sorrow*, for a strong emotion. Before this seclusion of my illness, I was secluded still—& there are few of the youngest women in the world who have not seen more, heard more, known more, of society, than I, who am scarcely to be called young now. I grew up in the country . . had no social opportunities, . . had my heart in books & poetry, . . & my experience, in reveries . . . And so time passed, & passed—and afterwards, when my illness came . . . I turned to thinking with some bitterness . . . that I had stood blind in this temple I was about to leave, . . that I had seen no Human nature . . that my brothers & sisters of the earth were *names* to me . . . how willingly I would as a poet exchange some of this lumbering, ponderous helpless knowledge of books, for some experience of life & man . . .[9]

But as the correspondence, and the relationship, progressed, Elizabeth Barrett began to voice the same negative views about society as Browning. The love letters tell a story of increasing closeness, of a physical and mental drawing together of the two lovers.

> And now, my love—I am round you . . my whole life is wound up and down and over you . . I feel you stir everywhere: I am not conscious of thinking or feeling but *about* you, with some reference to you—so I will live, so may I die![1]

So Browning; and this is Elizabeth Barrett:

> For I have none in the world who will hold me to make me live in it, except only you—I have come back for you alone . . at your voice . . & because you have use for me! I have come back to live a little for you—I see *you*. My fault is . . not that I think too much of what people will say. I see you & hear you. 'People' did not make me live for *them* . . I am not theirs, but your's—I deserve that you should believe in me, beloved, because my love for you is '*Me*.'[2]

'You' and 'your's' occur eleven times in this short passage; as the caustic emphasis on 'People' suggests, such concentration on the single other inevitably expresses itself, in part, in the rhetoric of exclusion. 'Oh, why are you not here,—' Browning writes on one occasion,

8. Letter of 11 March 1845; *Correspondence*, vol. 10 (1992), pp. 120–1. The 'lodge in a garden of cucumbers' is from Isaiah 1: 8.
9. Letter of 20 March 1845; *Correspondence*, vol. 10 (1992), p. 133.
1. Letter of 16 November 1845; *Correspondence*, vol. 11 (1993), p. 174.
2. Letter of 29 July 1846; *Correspondence*, vol. 13 (1995), pp. 205–6.

where I sit writing,—whence, in a moment, I could get to know why the lambs are bleating so, in the field behind . . . I see a beautiful sunshine (2 ½ p.m.) and a chestnut tree leafy all over, in a faint trembling chilly way, to be sure—and a holly hedge I see, and shrubs, and blossomed trees over the garden wall,—were you but here, dearest, dearest—how we would go out, with Flush on before—for with a key I have, I lock out the world, and then look down on it,—for there is a vast view from our greatest hill . . .[3]

Marriage meant that Elizabeth Barrett was able to join Browning on such outings. As in the landscape she describes in her letter to Julia Martin, the landscape Browning describes here is domestic rather than wild, and paradisally unpeopled; not only that, but access to it is privileged and in itself exclusive. *I lock out the world, and then look down on it*: the literal 'looking down' is also a depreciation, for Browning is rejoicing in a kind of poet's (and lover's) snobbery.[4]

Since they excluded others from their excursions, we would expect the Brownings to exclude them from their hearth. 'We mean to cut everybody we ever knew,' wrote Elizabeth Barrett Browning to her sister Henrietta, 'so that nobody need be offended.' And, she went on,

> Robert works himself up into a fine frenzy in talking of the horrors of mixed society, and sometimes exhorts me just as if I wanted exhortation—"Those people will spoil all our happiness, if we once let them in, you will see! If you speak of your health & save yourself on that plea, they will seize upon *me*—oh, dont I know them?" He walks up and down the room, thoroughly worked up—"But, dearest," say I, with my remarkable placidity . . "*I* am not going to let anybody in . . . I desire it quite as little as you"—"There is that coarse, vulgar M.[rs] Trollope—I do hope, Ba, if you dont wish to give me the greatest pain, that you wont receive that vulgar, pushing, woman who is not fit to speak to you.'—'Well . . now we are at M.[rs] Trollope! you will have your headache in a minute—now do sit down, & let us talk of something else, & be quite sure that if we get into such scrapes, it wont be my fault."—I assure you I don't exaggerate his visionary fears of the 'the world,' & 'society'—What makes *him* perfectly happy is to draw his chair next mine & let the time slip away.[5]

In another letter to Henrietta she gives more details of the life without 'those people':

> Certainly we are apt to talk nonsense with ever so many inflections & varieties . . & sitting here tête à tête, are at times quite

---

3. Letter of 16 April 1846; *Correspondence*, vol. 12 (1994), p. 252.
4. The aesthetic may be termed anti-Romantic; immediately after the passage cited, Browning tells an anecdote in which Wordsworth puts him down, and by which Wordsworth himself is put down for being egotistically sublime: '. . . there is a vast view from our greatest hill—did I ever tell you that Wordsworth was shown that hill or its neighbour,—someone saying "RB lives over *there* by that HILL".—"Hill"? interposed Wordsworth—"*we* call that, such as that,— a *rise*"!'
5. Letter of 7 January 1847; *Correspondence*, vol. 14 (1998), p. 94. The Brownings did eventually get to know Fanny Trollope in Florence, and found her 'very agreeable, and kind, and good-natured'. Letter of 30 January 1851; *Letters of Elizabeth Barrett Browning*, ed. F. G. Kenyon, 2 vols. (1898), i 476.

merry—He amuses me & makes me laugh, till I refuse to laugh
any more—such spirits he has & power of jesting & amusing—
alternating with the serious feeling & thinking, . . & never of a
sort to incline him to leave <this> room for what is called "gai-
eties." Our gaieties are between the chesnuts & the fire . . . We
have been nowhere but into the churches, & have exchanged no
word with a creature . . . I saw many more people in my room in
Wimpole Street—And we both delight in the quietness, & give no
sign of being tired of one another . . which is the principal
thing—[6]

We are close, now, to the subject and tone of 'A Lovers' Quarrel'. The
relationship which the poem describes clearly alludes to the winter
months of 1846–7 which the Brownings spent at Pisa, though its ac-
tual setting, and the contemporary events to which it alludes, belong
to a different place and later time.[7]

The poem begins by reversing an old trope, that of spring as the
time of sexual awakening. Spring has come, indeed, but its promise is
empty for the poem's speaker:

> Oh, what a dawn of day!
> How the March sun feels like May!
>   All is blue again
>   After last night's rain,
> And the South dries the hawthorn-spray.
>   Only, my Love's away!
> I'd as lief that the blue were grey.
>
>   (ll. 1–7)

It was in winter—before the 'quarrel' of the title—that the lovers were
happy. The winter setting of this idyll symbolizes the coldness and hos-
tility of the outside world, the world of otherness which cannot (they
think) reach the lovers in their magically protected hearth:

> Dearest, three months ago!
> When we lived blocked-up with snow,—
>   When the wind would edge
>   In and in his wedge,
> In, as far as the point could go—
>   Not to our ingle, though,
> Where we loved each the other so!
>
>   (ll. 15–21)

The hearth-fire replaces the 'March sun' as the figure of sexual
warmth, because a hearth is indoors, enclosed, private, whereas the

---

6. Letter of 21–24 November 1846; *Correspondence*, vol. 14 (1998), pp. 50–1. See n. 18 be-
low.
7. The *terminus a quo* for composition of the poem is 30 January 1853, when Napoleon III was
married (an event alluded to in ll. 29–35). At the time the Brownings were living in Flo-
rence, and Elizabeth Barrett Browning was strongly interested in spiritualism (see l. 43). It
should be noted that, though the Brownings disagreed about both Napoleon III and spiritu-
alism, these are not the sources of the 'lovers' quarrel' in the poem, but on the contrary are
mentioned in the context of their happy life together before the quarrel happened. There is
no evidence that the Brownings ever had a quarrel like the one described in the poem, and
every reason to believe that no such quarrel took place.

Spring sunshine is open, unbounded, promiscuous. The lovers' rela-
tionship—its uninhibited, playful eroticism—depends on their being
'blocked-up', secure from intrusion.

> Laughs with so little cause!
> We devised games out of straws.
> 　　We would try and trace
> 　　One another's face
> In the ash, as an artist draws;
> 　　Free on each other's flaws,
> How we chattered like two church daws!
>
> 　　　　　　　　　　　　　　　　　　(ll. 22–8)

'One another's face . . . each other's flaws': in this private space, love is
obsessively reflexive, attentive only to itself. Even when the outside
world is referred to, its 'edge' is softened: a political event is mediated
as fairy-tale and aestheticised for the lovers' contemplation:

> What's in the 'Times'?—a scold
> At the Emperor deep and cold;
> 　　He has taken a bride
> 　　To his gruesome side,
> That's as fair as himself is bold:
> 　　There they sit ermine-stoled,
> And she powders her hair with gold.
>
> 　　　　　　　　　　　　　　　　　　(ll. 29–35)

　The lovers, safe in their bourgeois nook, can afford this child-like
wonder at a very different kind of couple; similarly, they can explore in
fantasy the exotic landscape of the Pampas and infuse it with erotic
suggestion (ll. 36–42), or hold a spiritualist séance which confirms
their 'mutual flame':

> Try, will our table turn?
> Lay your hands there light, and yearn
> 　　Till the yearning slips
> 　　Through the finger-tips
> In a fire which a few discern,
> 　　And a very few feel burn,
> And the rest, they may live and learn!
>
> 　　　　　　　　　　　　　　　　　(ll. 43–9)[8]

Such erotic elitism confers on the lovers a sense of invulnerability;
they play with danger and death, imagining themselves as 'seamen in
woeful case', embracing each other as they drown (ll. 50–6);[9] they are
confident enough to play, also, at exchanging genders:

8. The 'fire' refers to the 'odic' flame which was said to stream from the fingertips of a mes-
merist; see Browning's poem 'Mesmerism' (also published in *Men and Women*), in which the
hands of the speaker 'give vent / To my ardour and my aim / And break into very flame'
(ll. 63–5). Although Browning was sceptical, to say the least, about the claims made by spir-
itualism and mesmerism, his work in this period reflects his wife's advocacy of them, as well
as his own long-standing interest in the occult, dating back to the quotation from Cornelius
Agrippa which prefaces *Pauline*, and the subject of his first acknowledged poem, *Paracelsus*.
9. In 'James Lee's Wife' (the opening poem of *Dramatis Personae*) Browning returned to the
subject matter of 'A Lovers' Quarrel' in grimmer mood, and the image of drowning seamen is

Teach me to flirt a fan
As the Spanish ladies can,
　　Or I tint your lip
　　With a burnt stick's tip
And you turn into such a man!

(ll. 64–8)

It is at this point that the speaker, returning from the present tense of memory to the 'real' present in which the poem is spoken, describes the 'quarrel' which gives the poem its title. A lovers' quarrel is proverbially slight and short-lived, but for the lovers in the poem the exact opposite is the case. Having invested everything in their love's perfection, the least flaw in that perfection ruins the whole and ruins it for ever. Disaster comes

When a shaft from the devil's bow
　　Pierced to our ingle-glow,
And the friends were friend and foe!

(ll. 82–4)

What the wind edging in its wedge had failed to do, the devil succeeds in doing, reaching the lovers in their seemingly invulnerable refuge. Yet the devil comes not from outside, but from within. It is not the world which destroys the lovers' relationship, but the relationship itself which breaks under the strain of its perfection.

We are never told exactly what the quarrel was, only that the man was at fault, and that his fault consisted of 'a word', 'a bubble born of breath', 'a moment's spite / When a mere mote threats the white' (ll. 86, 89, 104–5). The speaker's attempt to mitigate his fault by belittling it only draws attention to its enormity, since what is being measured is not the material fact but its significance. The answer to his anguished question

Woman, and will you cast
For a word, quite off at last
　　Me, your own, your You[?]

(ll. 92–4)

is contained in the very form in which the question is put. Like the apple which is the occasion of the Fall, the speaker's 'hasty word' (l. 106) is trivial in itself but momentous in its result, because it symbolizes the undoing of love's cosmic order and blurs the division between the lovers and the world. The speaker's supreme indifference to the life of the world, which has been the terrain of his happiness, now becomes that of his suffering:

---

used as an emblem of division and disaster (see section II, entitled 'By the Fireside'—ironically recalling the poem of that name as well as 'A Lovers' Quarrel'). Browning said of the couple in 'James Lee's Wife' that they were people newly-married, trying to realize a dream of being sufficient to each other, in a foreign land (where you can try such an experiment) and finding it break up—the man being tired *first*,—and tired precisely of the love (*Robert Browning and Julia Wedgwood*, ed. R. Curle [1937], p. 123).

Foul be the world or fair
More or less, how can I care?
   'Tis the world the same
   For my praise or blame,
And endurance is easy there.
   Wrong in the one thing rare—
Oh, it is hard to bear!

Here's the spring back or close,
When the almond-blossom blows:
   We shall have the word
   In a minor third
There is none but the cuckoo knows:
   Heaps of the guelder-rose!
I must bear with it, I suppose.

(ll. 113–26)

The cuckoo, of course, is an intruder in the nest, an unwanted 'third'
(not a minor one, either); its 'word' tauntingly echoes the 'word' with
which the speaker started the 'quarrel'. 'Oh, it is hard to bear! . . . I
must bear with it, I suppose'; but in fact the speaker does not bear
with it, or not in the mode of resignation and acceptance; the ending
of the poem is a flight from the spring, a return to winter, a final and
decisive rejection of the world:

Could but November come,
Were the noisy birds struck dumb
   At the warning slash
   Of his driver's-lash—
I would laugh like the valiant Thumb
   Facing the castle glum
And the giant's fee-faw-fum!

(ll. 127–33)

The 'noisy birds' recall those which, at the end of Chaucer's *Parlia-
ment of Fowls*, celebrate the ending of winter and the spring which sig-
nifies collective joy and procreation. Against this image the speaker
opposes his resolutely singular vision, identifying himself with the
'valiant Thumb', a fairy-tale hero who metamorphoses, in a later
poem, into Childe Roland confronting the Dark Tower alone and
dauntless.[1] The jaunty desperation of this image may be set against
the poised opening of 'By the Fire-Side' (only a few pages away in *Men
and Women*):

How well I know what I mean to do
   When the long dark autumn-evenings come,
And where, my soul, is thy pleasant hue?

1. Tom Thumb should be Jack the Giant-killer; the connection between the latter story and
   'Childe Roland to the Dark Tower Came' is made by Edgar (as Poor Tom, hence perhaps
   Browning's error about Tom Thumb) in the lines from *King Lear* (III iv 178–80) to which
   Browning alludes in the epigraph to that poem: 'Childe Rowland to the dark tower came, /
   His word was still "Fie, foh, and fum, / I smell the blood of a British man".'

> With the music of all thy voices, dumb
> In life's November too!

(ll. 1–5)

Here too the speaker anticipates winter and silence, specifically the silencing of poetry; the 'noisy birds' become the soul's 'voices' (the voices, we may think, of the many speakers of *Men and Women*), but the tone is notably unanxious and the syntax, unlike that of 'A Lovers' Quarrel', is not conditional, but affirmative. 'Could but November come' . . . 'How well I know what I mean to do': the contrast is between the assurance of vision and the uneasy strain of fantasy.

Along with this unease, we should note that the speaker's image of winter has undergone a change. He no longer sees winter as 'the mesmerizer Snow' who 'Put the earth to sleep' and allowed the lovers their 'time when the heart could show / All' (ll. 72, 74–6); Lear-like, he now sees winter stripping away 'the gear wherein equipped / We can stand apart, / Heart dispense with heart' (ll. 135–7), compelling men and women to recognize their most primitive emotional need. Fire, the image earlier in the poem of a domesticated Eros, an Eros of the hearth, is now the most basic comfort that human beings, freezing in the 'bare-walled crypt' (l. 140) of a loveless world, can bring to each other. It seems that the lighted interior of the poem, the private space where the lovers were at play and at one, was a delusion, part of 'the world's hangings' which must be 'ripped' away (l. 139). And yet the scene he presents in the 'crypt' is only a further version of the separation of the lovers from the world, more intense perhaps, but in principle unaltered. The 'crypt' is like the snow-bound cottage, only more so; the final image of the lovers is that of corpses, turning to each other to exchange their 'fires' (l. 145). 'The grave's a fine and private place, / But none, I think, do there embrace', wrote Marvell; but for lovers, the speaker suggests, the privacy of the grave is, as the estate agents say, its most desirable feature. In the last stanza of the poem, the speaker exultingly lays out his fantasy of complete restoration, complete fulfilment, complete and eternal possession:

> So, she'd efface the score,
> And forgive me as before.
>   It is twelve o'clock:
>   I shall hear her knock
> In the worst of a storm's uproar,
>   I shall pull her through the door,
> I shall have her for evermore!

(ll. 148–54)

Wherever this is, cottage or crypt, we may be sure that there is room for no one else. Perhaps Browning intends us, as readers, to be glad of that.

Interpretations of Poems

STEFAN HAWLIN

Browning's 'A Toccata of Galuppi's': How Venice Once Was Dear†

The criticism of a 'A Toccata of Galuppi's' has not yet matched the subtly contrived nature of the poem. The reasons for this are hard to see. Certainly it is a difficult poem, but it is also obviously attractive, cunningly arranged around one dichotomy, with nothing superfluous to its final effect. Though it has something of the poise and economy of a Keats ode, criticism of it has often been rudimentary. Perhaps it is the fusion of the lyric and dramatic that has made it elusive, or perhaps critics used to the well-characterized personae in other poems have found the anonymous speaker here unsatisfying. One factor in retarding appreciation has been the arguments in relation to the musical references. Much has been written about the accuracy and appropriateness of these, but a lot of this, while admirable from a musical point of view, has tended to see the references in isolation from the themes of the poem. Only in the last decade has adequate criticism begun to emerge.[1]

The comparison with Keats here may seem strange. In 'A Toccata' Browning is as downright and robust as usual, both in terms of theme and in terms of manner: there are the forward-moving dipodic rhythms, the boldly rhymed triplets, the almost aggressive imitation of the gestures of a colloquial speaking voice. What these can disguise is the extent to which the poem renegotiates Romantic themes: it is the poem of a man who read Byron avidly as a child, and who in his teens owned a copy of Keats's 1820 *Lamia* volume.[2] Galuppi's music, we might say, is the speaker's Grecian Urn: he interrogates it, he enters into its meaning, and it lets him in to another world and time.

† From *Review of English Studies* 41 (1990): 496–509. Reprinted by permission of Oxford University Press.

1. See in particular Herbert Tucker, *Browning's Beginnings* (Minneapolis, 1980), 189–94; R. G. Hampson, 'Good Alike at Grave and Gay: "A Toccata of Galuppi's" ', *Browning Society Notes*, 13/1 (1983), 30–8; W. Craig Turner, 'Art, Artist, and Audience in "A Toccata of Galuppi's" ', *Browning Institute Studies*, 15 (1987), 123–9; and John E. Schwiebert, 'Meter, Form and Sound Patterning in Robert Browning's "A Toccata of Galuppi's" ', *Studies in Browning and His Circle*, 15 (1988), 11–23.
2. For Browning's ownership of Keats's 1820 *Lamia* volume see *Letters of Robert Browning*, ed. Thurman L. Hood (London, 1933), 246; and John Maynard, *Browning's Youth* (Cambridge, Mass., 1977), 432 nn. 6, 11.

Like the 'Grecian Urn' the poem hinges on the teasing and ambiguous interrelation of art and reality, and on the questions raised by a work of art surviving into an era remote from itself—particularly of course the question of human transience. Keat's urn and his nightingale speak of an eternality removed from the actual world, whereas the music in 'A Toccata' apparently speaks from the very start of transience and death. This difference can obscure the deeper similarities. Only to a limited extent does the speaker keep his mortality theme in view, and the music, as much as Keats's nightingale, is what lets him in to a warm and luxuriant fantasy, something far away from the matter-of-fact world he usually inhabits. The sensual loveliness of eighteenth-century Venice is an intense and self-forgetting experience, like Keat's bower, though like the bower it too contains hints of mortality. The poem follows through what Helen Vendler has called 'the characteristic Keatsian movement from inception through intensity to desolation[3] for, leaving behind the warmth of Venice, the speaker experiences a complex sense of loss. At this point, stanza 11, a different Keatsian opposition comes to the fore in the conflict the speaker experiences between feeling and reason, imagination and 'cold philosophy' (or science). Browning would probably have read 'Lamia' in the characteristic Victorian manner as showing 'the blighting effect of science and analytic philosophy on the poetry of either the sensuous or the visionary imagination',[4] and certainly the speaker here appears as Apollonius, the man who would 'conquer all mysteries by rule and line',[5] destroying with his withering stare the luxurious bower of the Venetians. All this of course suggests something else: that, in a disguised form, the poem is essentially a Romantic defence of the 'poetry of the imagination' against the 'poor matter-of-fact' philosophy.[6]

A second background to the poem is in the poetry and life of Byron. Byron was the first important poetic influence on Browning as a boy, and as he matured he retained, with some lapses, his 'first feeling for Byron'. Browning knew *Childe Harold* extremely well; he read Thomas Moore's *Letters and Journals of Lord Byron* sometime after it came out in 1830; and his friends Arnould and Domett were both admirers of the poet.[7] In 1846, rereading Moore's *Letters*, he admitted to Elizabeth that his early admiration had extended beyond the poetry to a kind of hero-worship, and to an interest in the places Byron had visited.[8] It is in Moore's *Letters*, in a context in which he was interested, that he would have learnt all about the reality of the world of 'balls and masks begun at midnight'. Moore quotes extensively from Byron's correspondence, and Browning would have read, for example, Byron's complaints at his tiredness during the day and night whirl of Carnival,

3. Vendler, *The Odes of John Keats* (Cambridge, Mass. and London, 1983), 86.
4. W. Jackson Bate, *John Keats* (Cambridge, Mass., 1963), 547–8.
5. 'Lamia', Part II, l. 235: *The Poems of John Keats*, ed. M. Allott (London, 1970), 646.
6. See Leigh Hunt's *Indicator* review of *Lamia . . . and Other Poems*, in G. M. Matthews (ed.), *Keats: The Critical Heritage* (London, 1971), 169–70.
7. For Browning and Byron see Maynard, *Browning's Youth*, pp. 169–70, 175–8, 219–20, 427 n. 33.
8. *The Letters of Robert Browning and Elizabeth Barrett Barrett 1845–1846*, ed. E. Kintner (Cambridge, Mass., 1969), ii. 986, 993, 994 n. 5.

his insinuations of amorous intrigues, and, of course, his vivid depiction of the lax sexual mores of the Venetians.[9] Moore takes a forgiving and cosmopolitan attitude towards Byron's affairs with Marianna Segati and Margarita Cogni and to his 'career of libertinism'.[1] One wonders, though, if Browning would have responded to the atmosphere that surrounded Byron in the same relatively untroubled way. Perhaps 'A Toccata of Galuppi's' is, in part, a mature *rapprochement* with an atmosphere that was vivid but disquieting to his imagination.

Byron arrived in Venice in 1816, nineteen years after the fall of the Republic. In 1797, of course, the first French occupation brought to an end the eleven-hundred year line of the doges. Before this date the doge used to be rowed out each Ascension Day in the golden barge, the *Bucentaur*, to 'wed the sea with rings', but then (as Browning would have known from *Childe Harold*) the French burnt the *Bucentaur* and the ceremony was discontinued. In the years that followed the city struggled economically, the population fell, some palaces were destroyed and others badly neglected. When Byron arrived—the city now being under Austrian rule—its general state of decay was a natural subject for his romantic melancholy. In *Childe Harold*, in *Beppo*, and in 'Venice. An Ode' he lamented the city's present state and threw an atmosphere of nostalgia and romance over eighteenth-century Venice, the last heyday of the Republic's gaiety. *Childe Harold* Canto IV expresses wistful sadness that 'the well known song of the gondoliers . . . from Tasso's *Jerusalem*, has almost died with the independence of Venice',[2] that the palaces are 'crumbling to the shore', and that 'music meets not always now the ear' (21, 22). 'Nature', though, will not forget:

> . . . how Venice once was dear,
> The pleasant place of all festivity,
> The revel of the earth, the masque of Italy!
>
> (iv. 25–7)

The poem continues in this vein: 'The spouseless Adriatric mourns her lord'; 'the long file' of the doges are 'declin'd to dust'; and the 'vast and sumptuous pile'—the Ducal Palace—bespeaks the pageant of their splendid trust' (91, 127–30). *Beppo*, subtitled 'A Venetian Story', is set during a masked ball in Carnival time in the 1770s and throws glamour over the sensual loveliness and 'dissoluteness' of that era. (From Moore's *Letters* Browning would have known how much Byron was drawing on the social life around him.) 'Venice. An Ode', however, begins by contrasting the festivities of the past with the sadness of the present under Austrian rule:

> And the harsh sound of the barbarian drum,
> With dull and daily dissonance, repeats
> The echo of thy tyrant's voice along

9. Thomas Moore, *Letters and Journals of Lord Byron: with Notices of His Life* (London, 1830), ii. 51, 60, 68, 160, 182–3.
1. Ibid. ii. 182.
2. *The Complete Poetical Works of Lord Byron*, ed. Jerome J. McGann (Oxford, 1980–6), ii. 219 (note to l. 19). References to Canto IV are in the text. For *Beppo* and 'Venice. An Ode' see iv. 129–60, 201–6.

The soft waves, once all musical to song,
That heaved beneath the moonlight with the throng
Of gondolas—and to the busy hum
Of cheerful creatures, whose most sinful deeds
Were but the overbeating of the heart,
And flow of too much happiness, which needs
The aid of age to turn its course apart
From the luxuriant and voluptuous flood
Of sweet sensations, battling with the blood.

(20–31)

This is the world of young people and music evoked in 'A Toccata', though there the 'happiness' of the young people is scrutinized from a different point of view. I would suggest that Browning's view of Venice was mediated through Byron, and that this is a necessary perspective on the tone of voice that he gives his speaker.

In this context it is worth looking briefly at another poem that Browning knew well and treasured, 'Venice' (1839), by his close friend Alfred Domett.[3] Domett visited Venice in the 1830s when the city was beginning to recover economically from the post-war depression, yet his response to it is strongly controlled by the mood of *Childe Harold*. Domett approaches the city half expecting to find it as it was in the Middle Ages, but 'Unpitying Day lays Desolation bare!' The stucco 'peels from every time-stained wall', 'the grass unheeded grows' on the bridges and quays, and each palace 'piecemeal drops'. Behind the present scene is the ghost of eighteenth-century gaiety: the 'sluggish' water lies below arched windows 'ne'er illumined now' and hangs seaweed on the stairs 'no festive footstep presses' (I. iv–v). The city is still of course immensely beautiful but Domett is intent on veiling it with Byronic melancholy. The city is 'A queenly beauty in a slow decline', and he repeats Byron's conceit about the absence of music in a city 'whose very voice so long / Was Music' (I. ix). Domett regards the Venetians as responsible for their own fate—he is aware, that is, of the moral laxity of eighteenth-century Venice, that 'indulgence' was not balanced by 'restraint', nor 'luxury' by 'labour', and that 'passion's lightenings' were not 'rightly used' (II. xvi)—but his sense of the romance of the city, his love for its beauty, and his 'warm pity' (II. i) for its present condition override his moral awareness:

Fair Magdalene of faded Cities! gay
And guilty once as sad, yet lovely now!
To hide thy crimes, thou hast but to display
That sorrowful sweet brow! . . .
Before thy death-struck loveliness,
We feel awhile our indignation fly,
Our loathing all forgot in lively sympathy!

(II. ii)

3. Alfred Domett, 'Venice' (London, 1839). References by Part and Stanza are in the text. For Browning's knowledge of the poem see *The Brownings' Correspondence*, ed. P. Kelley and R. Hudson (Winfield, Kansas, 1984–), iv. 261, v. 328; and *The Browning Collections: A Reconstruction*, compiled by P. Kelley and B. A. Coley (London, 1984), 71.

These poems set in perspective the speaker's manner in 'A Toccata'. He has apparently never thought of responding to Venice along these lines. He is aware of the romance associated with the city, but it is foreign to his mentality. In this respect he has a hint of Mr Gradgrind about him; he is a 'man of realities', 'accustomed to view everything from the strong dispassionate ground of reason and calculation'.[4] The unsettling experience he has is based on an imaginative and affective impulse which he would normally regard as irresponsible. As he is drawn into the atmosphere of eighteenth-century Venice, his usual patterns of thought are subverted despite himself, and he ends the poem with a sense of Venice's 'dearness', and with something of Byron and Domett's wistful and forgiving attitude towards the city and its people. With this background in mind we may turn to the poem.[5]

The opening lines catch the speaker's first gestures of response to the music. He has heard a toccata by the eighteenth-century Venetian composer Baldassaro Galuppi and this has suggested to him the world in which the music was composed. He describes the music as sounding 'old'. By this he may only mean that to his nineteenth-century ear, used perhaps to Beethoven and Schubert, the manner of Galuppi's music sounds dated. (If this is the right reading all Browning is doing is giving the speaker the same experience he describes having himself with regard to Charles Avison's music in 'A Parleying with Charles Avison'.[6]) I would suggest, however, that by 'old' here the speaker is implying that the music is 'old-fashioned' or 'irrelevant' to him. He is a man of science or, in other words, a man of the times, a man interested in progress and the future; he is not used to thinking about a subject like eighteenth-century Venice. To him Venice is a 'has been', a state of the past, and little 'good' can come in thinking of its decadence. If this is right, the tone here, which is sometimes read as strongly supercilious, may really be more matter-of-fact. There is also an ambiguity in the tone: what the speaker says seems desponding, yet the dipodic rhythm gives him a buoyant air. If the poem is read well this disparity acts only vaguely and not insistently on the ear. Apparently bored with the obvious 'meaning' of the music, the speaker is actually pleased with himself for finding that meaning out:

> Oh Galuppi, Baldassaro, this is very sad to find!
> I can hardly misconceive you; it would prove me deaf and blind;
> But although I take your meaning, 't is with such a heavy mind!
>
> Here you come with your old music, and here's all the good it brings.

The extempore feel continues as the speaker quickly ransacks his mind for information about historic Venice and improvises a collage of the city. At first he is not particularly successful. He has what Carlyle would call a 'dryasdust' air in the slightly querulous way that he picks

4. Dickens, *Hard Times*, ed. G. Ford and S. Monad (Norton Critical edn., New York, 1966), 2, 74.
5. The text of 'A Toccata of Galuppi's' is given from *The Poetical Works* (London, Smith, Elder & Co., 1888–9), vi. 72–6.
6. Ibid. xvi. 224–7.

up impressions from the music. He is satisfied in evoking the city in impressionistic terms because it is not a subject that he feels is important. He is hesitant because he is thinking spontaneously and also because he feels tentative. He 'was never out of England'—but this is not an admission to us of his provinciality but really an admission to himself, a man of science, that he is now engaged in an act of imagination:

What, they lived once thus at Venice where the merchants were the
    kings,
Where Saint Mark's is, where the Doges used to wed the sea with
    rings?

Ay, because the sea's the street there; and 't is arched by . . . what
    you call
    . . . Shylock's bridge with houses on it, where they kept the carnival:
        I was never out of England—it's as if I saw it all.

Now the speaker picks up on line 5 ('What, they lived once thus . . .'), for the romance of Venetian life was his first thought in relation to the music. The meaning he has taken from the music is a response to its particular form. A toccata is a virtuoso piece in a fast tempo and it has naturally suggested the glittering element in Venetian life—the ceremony, for example, of the Doge throwing a ring into the sea. He now imagines the young people of the city running extravagantly through their lives in a manner that is as fast and brilliant as the music. At this point he is only adapting Victorian commonplaces about life in eighteenth-century Venice. Samuel Rogers' *Italy*, for example, gives this picture:

> Yet what so gay as VENICE? Every gale
> Breathed music! and who flocked not, while she reigned,
> To celebrate her Nuptials with the Sea;
> To wear the mask, and mingle in the crowd
> With Greek, Armenian, Persian—night and day
> (There, and there only, did the hour stand still,)
> Pursuing through her thousand labyrinths
> The Enchantress Pleasure . . .[7]

Victorian readers would have felt that the speaker's thought was developing along ordinary lines. Only on rereading would it have been apparent to them how the commonplace material is shaped as part of a larger pattern. The balls and masks go on in a *renewable* cycle of pleasure against the backdrop of warm *spring* seas:

Did young people take their pleasure when the sea was warm in May?
Balls and masks begun at midnight, burning ever to mid-day,
When they made up fresh adventures for the morrow, do you say?

The picture of the Venetian lady takes further these images of warmth and liveliness. It appears overdone even before we understand

---

7. From 'St. Mark's Place' in Samuel Rogers, *Italy, A Poem* (London, 1830), 62.

its place in the whole poem. In the first line there is epistrophe and compar, and in the second alliteration on 'b' and 'f' which follows through into the richly vowelled alliteration of the third line. The delicacy of the bell-flower image plays against the robust voluptuousness of the picture that follows. The whole effect comes close to caricature. As emerges later, 'buoyant' and 'abundance' are important words here:

Was a lady such a lady, cheeks so round and lips so red,—
On her neck the small face buoyant, like a bell-flower on its bed,
O'er the breast's superb abundance where a man might base his head?

At this point the speaker concentrates his idea of Venetian society in an apparently casual vignette. (It seems appropriate to imagine the scene in some florid, baroque saloon.) Galuppi sits at the clavichord amid a group of fashionable Venetians and somewhere in his audience a young couple leave off talking to hear him play. The humour here lies in the difference in composure between Galuppi and the young Venetians—they are full of the restless sap of youth while he is 'stately' at the clavichord. Why do they bother to sit through the concert? Perhaps it is expected of them, perhaps it is the fashionable thing to do, or perhaps amidst the diversions of Carnival they have been trapped in the room accidentally. The lady bites upon her mask, the gentleman fingers on his sword. Both are impatient at the interruption to their amorous tête-à-tête, and would rather be alone to themselves than listening to the music. It is the placing of 'stately' after the caesura that gives the wry twist. It separates off the different worlds of Galuppi and the young couple and suggests how remote they are from each other:

Well, and it was graceful of them—they'd break talk off and afford
—She, to bite her mask's black velvet—he, to finger on his sword,
While you sat and played Toccatas, stately at the clavichord?

The next stanzas are the most condensed in the poem and contain the musical references that have proved such a critical problem.[8] I would like to suggest that the difficulties of these references have been exaggerated. It seems likely that Browning was thinking of the expressive effects of specific musical intervals (and to readers with musical knowledge these lines can be particularly resonant). However, Browning makes his meaning apparent with words which are manifestly untechnical, words which are confusing, to different degrees, from a strictly musical point of view. To complain that Browning is musically inaccurate is to fail to appreciate the offhand, oblique way in which he lets his speaker come to the point.

Now—deliberately as is soon clear—the speaker directs his ear back to the music in a more attentive way, and claims to hear various intervals, the first of which are lesser thirds. 'Lesser' is not a conventional musical designation, but, certainly in this case, Browning was thinking

8. See Herbert E. Greene, 'Browning's Knowledge of Music', PMLA 62 (1947), 1095–9; and for recent discussions Charles W. Johnson, 'Lost "Chord," Wrong Chord,' and Other Musical Anomalies in "A Toccata of Galuppi's" ', Studies in Browning and His Circle, 4/1 (1976), 30–40, and John J. Joyce, 'The Music Poems and Robert Browning's Knowledge of Music', ibid. 8/2 (1980), 75–87.

of 'minor' thirds. All that is being drawn on here is the most elementary emotional resonances of the different intervals. Minor thirds may be said to have a slightly depressed effect in that they fall back from the fuller, happier effect of major thirds; they hint at feelings of pain and grief. It seems appropriate to draw on a distinction that Browning would have learnt as a boy. His music teacher, John Relfe, described the different effects of major and minor in these terms: the major keys were 'Masculine, Majestic or Sprightly' and the minor keys 'Effeminate, Plaintive or Pathetic'.[9] Given the minor thirds, the music is in a minor key, with exactly the 'plaintive' resonance suggested in Relfe's distinction.

'Sixths diminished', as a whole line of critics have zealously pointed out, is musically anomalous, for they would not be discrete intervals, but really just 'perfect fifths'. It has been suggested, rightly I think, that Browning had in mind 'minor' sixths, acutely dissonant intervals with a painful and sometimes anguished effect. Really, though, he was not bothered with musical accuracy. 'Diminished', while musically ambiguous, extends the suggestion of 'lesser'—of things not being full or ripe, of things falling back upon themselves—and just hints, in the larger context, at the diminishments that come with age.

'Those suspensions, those solutions' have been well explained by Paul Turner: 'A suspension is the holding on of a note in one chord into the following chord. It produces a discord, which is only resolved (a solution) when the note falls a degree to a note appropriate to the second chord. The terms aptly symbolize reluctance to die, combined with the realization that in the harmony of things one cannot stay, after the time has come for one to go.'[1] These nuanced expressions of closure lead to the 'commiserating sevenths'. These are most likely 'minor sevenths' which would be 'commiserating' because they are mild dissonances and quite unlike the acutely dissonant minor sixths. In an independent context the minor seventh has been described as having 'a gentle mournful feeling, which is made the more woeful by its undermining of the normal joyful feeling of the major triad supporting it'.[2]

Explicating these lines carefully can distract from their true effect, for the speaker is not labouring his meaning, but rather throwing off the point that has struck him. His manner is supple and offhand, teasing and urbane. Before the poem began he caught this dying fall in the music, some vaguely elegiac strain seemingly out of keeping with the way 'they lived once thus at Venice'. How, he wonders, did Galuppi's contemporaries respond to that strain in the music, if, that is, they heard it at all. He lets the young couple answer for the Venetian world. His implication is that they do catch this note in the music but

---

9. John Relfe, *The Elements of Harmony, Illustrated by a Variety of Examples and Exercises* (60 Great Portland St., Printed and Sold by the Author, 1801), 14. It is reasonable to suppose that Relfe would have used this work to teach Browning. It also contains an excellent section on suspensions (pp. 79–85).
1. *Men and Women* 1855, ed. P. Turner (Oxford, 1972), 321.
2. Deryck Cooke, *The Language of Music* (London, 1959), 74. See p. 71 for an excellent view of 'sixths diminished'.

that, instinctively, their natural optimism tries to turn it around. One asks 'Must we die?' while the other takes up the suggestion of commiseration offered by the sevenths: 'Life might last! we can but try!':

> What? Those lesser thirds so plaintive, sixths diminished,
>   sigh on sigh,
> Told them something? Those suspensions, those solutions—
>   'Must we die?'
> Those commiserating sevenths—'Life might last! we can but try!'

The music has perhaps made the young couple feel guilty, or made them think of ending their love-affair. In some way it has disturbed their sense of the fullness of their lives, and they turn to each other for reassurance. Neither makes an actual pledge of love or a declaration of his or her contentment, for both are feeling insecure. Each, by questions, asks the other to confirm the sense of 'happiness' that has been disturbed in themselves.

Between stanzas 7 and 8 there is a contrapuntal movement as the lovers' exchange emerges from the music to which it responds. The music hints at the parts of life that are in a minor key, but the couple veer away from such things. The echo from Catullus—the 'million' kisses—brings into focus the significance of stanzas 4 and 5. The music, to the speaker's mind, is hinting at 'lesserness' and 'diminishment' *against* the renewable round of balls and masks and the warm, spring seas of stanza 4, and against the 'buoyancy' and 'abundance' of the sensuousness of stanza 5. The plangencies of its minor key disturb the happy major key in which the Venetians usually live their lives. In this light the couple's brief exchange appears pathetic. Half sensing the music's implications, they defend themselves by talking of an infinite love, an ever-extendable 'happiness'.

The tone of 'Hark, the dominant's persistence . . .' is ambivalent. It could be read as sombre and moralizing but this seems to me wrong, and I would suggest a quieter, more neutral tone. The speaker (though he has contrived the whole situation) is only reporting a matter of fact; the couple are avoiding the 'meaning' of the music, but the music is persistent in what it has to say. This point is expressed by the dominant chord. The dominant, sounded in the appropriate way, yearns to be resolved by the tonic, so forming a 'perfect' cadence, the most natural and resolute of musical endings. Here the dominant, being sounded repeatedly, is being 'persistent' in its need to be 'answered' by the tonic. It is speaking of the endings natural to the order of things just at the point where the lovers are teasing each other into continuing their lives of pleasure. The tone is full of complacency and triumph. The speaker believes he has understood the mood of the music; he is 'in tune' with it in a way that ironically the contemporary audience was not:

> 'Were you happy?'—'Yes.'—'And are you still as happy?'—'Yes.
>   And you?'
> —'Then, more kisses!'—'Did I stop them, when a million seemed
>   so few?'
> Hark, the dominant's persistence till it must be answered to!

The music ends and the young couple leap to their feet pouring out profuse and superficial compliment. The speaker is sarcastic. Their enthusiasm is just another way of shaking off the music's intimations. They have registered that it was 'grave' but they neutralize this by saying that Galuppi is 'good alike at grave and gay'—the gravity becoming part of a trite contrast and not something significant in itself:

> So, an octave struck the answer. Oh, they praised you, I dare say!
> 'Brave Galuppi! that was music! good alike at grave and gay!
> 'I can always leave off talking when I hear a master play!'

Now the speaker sees the young couple as representatives of their kind, his tone being both arch and pathetic. The young people that flourished together in the warm spring now die alone 'one by one'. They have lives that 'come to nothing'—they never thought, like the speaker, to concentrate on achieving things. Death comes to them like a figure in one of their own masked balls, stepping forward and leading each in turn from the room. There is a hint of relish in this description of death:

> Then they left you for their pleasure: till in due time, one by one,
> Some with lives that came to nothing, some with deeds as well
>   undone,
> Death stepped tacitly and took them where they never see the sun.

At this point the speaker tries to concentrate again. He has traced out the obvious 'meaning' of Galuppi's music, allowing his mind to wander through an unimportant era. In his own terms, he has been wasting time and he seeks to take up again his usual resolute habits. We may imagine him returning to his study, pouring over Lyell's *Geology*, or beginning on a mathematical calculation. His desire, as always in his life, is to 'triumph o'er a secret wrung from nature's close reserve', an expression strongly reminiscent of the attitude adopted by Paracelsus in Browning's early play.[3] In Part I Paracelsus resolves to work 'so that the earth shall yield her secrets up' (364), and in Part III 'to search, discover, & dissect & prove' and to 'hoard & heap & class all Truths' (682, 705). More relevant still is a typical statement in Part IV:

> . . . night comes,
> And I shall give myself to painful study
> And patient searching after hidden lore,
> Shall *wring* some bright truth from its prison; . . .
> I shall review my captured truth . . .
>
> (iv. 381–4, 390)

It is also worth noticing the beginning of the third note to the play: 'Inexplebilis illa aviditas naturæ perscrutandi secreta . . .'. These seem to me more than echoes, for they suggest that Browning was imagining again something of Paracelsus's approach to life. Like the speaker of 'A Toccata' Paracelsus despises 'youth's allurements' (iii. 78) and

---

3. References to *Paracelsus* are to *The Poetical Works of Robert Browning*, ed. I. Jack and M. Smith (Oxford, 1983–), i.

young people 'who squander every energy / Convertible to good on painted toys, / Breath-bubbles, gilded dust!' (i. 804–6). Paracelsus, despising the frivolous, went on to despise 'ordinary' life. Through his quest for scientific knowledge he wanted to take the world to himself, and to ignore love and beauty (things which cannot be 'captured' or 'dissected'), things which open out life and make it vulnerable and wondering. One point where he describes this failing is relevant here:

> . . . life, death, light & shadow,
> The shews of the world . . . were bare receptacles
> Or indices of truth to be *wrung* thence
> Not ministers of sorrow or delight . . .
>
> (ii. 156–9)

I would suggest that Browning was recalling the significance of Paracelsus's error and that to some extent this line draws into the background the whole question of the Prometheanism examined in *Paracelsus*. There is, though, an important difference in tone: Paracelsus tries to wring 'some bright truth from its prison', the speaker 'from nature's close reserve'. The mock-heroic note suggests that the speaker has already realized what becomes apparent in the last stanza; he has become aware, in the manner of Paracelsus, of the narrowness involved in his way of life. Already the music is haunting his inner ear and filling him with dread:

> But when I sit down to reason, think to take my stand nor swerve,
> While I triumph o'er a secret wrung from nature's close reserve,
> In you come with your cold music till I creep thro' every nerve.

The 'ghostly cricket' image that follows is strangely involved and desolate, subverting cheerful associations like the 'cricket on the hearth', and suggesting that though the music is a ghost from the past, it is itself unconscious or indifferent to the world in which it originated. Now, starting off in a relatively neutral vein, the music brings home its meaning to the speaker. Venice is 'dead and done with', it has reaped the rewards of sensuality and indulgence. The soul of its people was obscured by being rooted in the life of the senses. At this point the poem is again near to commonplaces about Venice. Alfred Domett, in the poem quoted earlier, could say this:

> Time saps a race by stealthy arts and slow!
> Close, social life—thought—luxury—weaken; air
> And soil outworn less stalwart nerves bestow,
> And then great hearts grow rare!
> From individuals to the whole
> First sinks the body, then the soul;
> No hope for men until they find
> How much the body makes the mind! (II. xv)

In Domett's terms we may say that the Venetians have unmade their souls by living too much for the body:

Yes, you, like a ghostly cricket, creaking where a house was
    burned:
'Dust and ashes, dead and done with, Venice spent what
    Venice earned.
'The soul, doubtless, is immortal—where a soul can be discerned.

The music now tells the speaker that though the Venetians have
gone the way of all flesh, his soul will rise in the 'degree' it deserves.
This is deliberately obscure, for the music that seems so coaxingly to
agree with the speaker is really bringing home to him the fact of his
own death—the fact that he, a man dedicated to the sciences, and
with, in miniature as it were, the Promethean ambitions of Paracelsus,
will die as surely as the Venetian 'butterflies'. The speaker is 'pinned
and wriggling on the wall'. He, like Paracelsus, has more in common
with humble mankind than he liked to think:

'Yours for instance: you know physics, something of geology,
 'Mathematics are your pastime; souls shall rise in their degree;
 'Butterflies may dread extinction,—you'll not die, it cannot be!

The speaker is displacing his own new understanding into the mu-
sic. He is parodying to himself the assumptions and tones of his ac-
cusing existence, an existence previously forfeit to self-complacency
and contempt. Like some mischievous parrot the music has become
for him the means by which he can hear the tones of his own voice:

'As for Venice and her people, merely born to bloom and drop,
'Here on earth they bore their fruitage, mirth and folly were
    the crop:
'What of soul was left, I wonder, when the kissing had to stop?

The last verse is the most moving of all. The rhythm of the poem
slows down and all the earlier supple irony vanishes from the tone.
Suddenly, in the most tactile manner, the speaker is overpowered by
the loveliness and warmth of the Venetian women who have peopled
his fantasy. 'With such hair, too' catches a note of wonder. The world
of Venice which at the beginning of the poem was skimmed through
like some frivolous book now holds him for a moment in a tender,
even solicitous mood. He is poised on the brink of a wider sympathy
and love before collapsing back upon his new realization of his own
mortality. The last lines focus one of the oppositions on which the
poem centres: the warmth and sensuousness of life on the one hand—
the major key—and the knowledge of transience on the other—the
'coldness' of the minor:

'Dust and ashes!' So you creak it, and I want the heart to scold.
Dear dead women, with such hair, too—what's become of all
    the gold
Used to hang and brush their bosoms? I feel chilly and grown old.

The music has acted as the speaker's 'Cold Pastoral', but it leaves him
without Keats's sense of consolation, only with the sad and humble
knowledge of 'how Venice once was dear'.

HAROLD BLOOM

Browning's "Childe Roland":
All Things Deformed and Broken†

"What in the midst lay but the Tower itself?" The quester, "after a life spent training for the sight," sees nothing but everything he has estranged from himself. Browning's poem, to me his finest, is a crucial test for any reader, but peculiarly so for a reader rendered aware of Romantic tradition, and the anxieties fostered by its influence. What happens in the poem, difficult to determine, perhaps impossible to know with final assurance, depends upon the reader's judgment of Roland, the poem's speaker. How far can he be trusted in recounting his own catastrophe?

On New Year's Day, 1852, in Paris, Browning strenuously resolved to write a poem a day, a resolution kept for a fortnight, producing successively in its first three days *Women and Roses*, "Childe Roland to the Dark Tower Came," and *Love Among the Ruins*.[1] *Women and Roses*, as William Clyde DeVane commented, is wholly uncharacteristic of its poet, and is far likelier to make current readers think of Yeats than of Browning. Its curious structure alternates tercets and nine-line stanzas, the tercets introducing the roses of a dream-vision, and the longer stanzas presenting the poet's almost frantic responses to the vision's sexual appeal. Past, present, and future women dance to one cadence, each circling their rose on the poet's rose tree, and each evading his attempts "to possess and be possessed." Even the prophetic vision, a kind of Yeatsian *antithetical* influx, refuses the maker's shapings:

> What is far conquers what is near.
> Roses will bloom nor want beholders,
> Spring from the dust where our flesh moulders,
> What shall arrive with the cycle's change?
> A novel grace and a beauty strange.
> I will make an Eve, be the artist that began her,
> Shaped her to his mind!—Alas! in like manner
> They circle the rose on my rose tree.

Browning's experience of what Blake called the Female Will had been confined largely to his mother and his wife, neither of whom he had shaped to his mind; rather he had yielded to both. If *Women and Roses* indeed was "the record of a vivid dream" DeVane), then the dream was of reality, and not a wish-fulfillment. A greater, though nightmare, vision of reality came the next day.

> My first thought was, he lied in every word,
> That hoary cripple, with malicious eye

---

† From *The Ringers in the Tower: Studies in Romantic Tradition* (Chicago and London: The University of Chicago Press, 1971), pp. 157–67. Reprinted by permission of Writers' Representatives LLC. Footnotes below are by the editor.
1. The order given by Browning's biographers is "Love Among the Ruins" (Jan. 1), "Women and Roses" (Jan. 2), and "Childe Roland" (Jan. 3); see *BRP*, p. 293.

> Askance to watch the working of his lie
> On mine, and mouth scarce able to afford
> Suppression of the glee, that pursed and scored
>   Its edge, at one more victim gained thereby.
>
> What else should he be set for, with his staff?
>   What, save to waylay with his lies, ensnare
>   All travellers who might find him posted there,
> And ask the road? I guessed what skull-like laugh
> Would break, what crutch 'gin write my epitaph
>   For pastime in the dusty thoroughfare,
>
> If at his counsel I should turn aside
>   Into that ominous tract which, all agree,
>   Hides the Dark Tower.

The cripple's motives, the actual look of him, even whether his mouth worked with suppressed glee or with terror, or compassion, or whatever, we will never know, for we have only Childe Roland's monologue, and it takes less than the first fifteen lines he speaks for us to suspect all his impressions. Whether, if we rode by his side, we too would see all things deformed and broken, would depend upon the degree to which we shared in his desperation, his hopelessness not only of his quest but of himself and of all questings and questers. Why not throw up the irksome charge at once? If Roland tempts us to this question, asked of Paracelsus by Festus in the second of Browning's Shelleyan quest-romances, we can be assuaged by the great charlatan's reply:

>   A task, a task!
>   But wherefore hide the whole
> Extent of degradation once engaged
> In the confessing vein? Despite of all
> My fine talk of obedience and repugnance,
> Docility and what not, 'tis yet to learn
> If when the task shall really be performed,
> My inclination free to choose once more,
> I shall do aught but slightly modify
> The nature of the hated task I quit.
> In plain words, I am spoiled . . .
>   . . . God! how I essayed
> To live like that mad poet, for a while,
> To love alone; and how I felt too warped
> And twisted and deformed! What should I do,
> Even though released from drudgery, but return
> Faint, as you see, and halting, blind and sore,
> To my old life and die as I began?
> I cannot feed on beauty for the sake
> Of beauty only, nor can drink in balm
> From lovely objects for their loveliness;
> My nature cannot lose her first imprint;

> I still must hoard and heap and class all truths
> With one ulterior purpose: I must know!
> . . . .
>   . . . alas,
> I have addressed a frock of heavy mail
> Yet may not join the troop of sacred knights;
> And now the forest-creatures fly from me,
> The grass-banks cool, the sunbeams warm no more,
> Best follow, dreaming that ere night arrive,
> I shall o'ertake the company and ride
> Glittering as they!

This company, in "*Childe Roland to the Dark Tower Came*," has become "The Band" of failures, who glitter only in the Yeatsian Condition of Fire that Roland enters also in his dying:

> There they stood, ranged along the hillsides, met
>   To view the last of me, a living frame
>   For one more picture! in a sheet of flame
> I saw them and I knew them all.

The company of Browning scholars, notably DeVane, F. A. Pottle, W. O. Raymond, and Betty Miller, have charted for us the complexities of Browning's Shelleyan heritage, and his equivocal denial of that heritage. Mrs. Miller in particular reads *Childe Roland* in the context of the denial, as a poem of retribution appropriate to Browning's own sin in murdering his earlier, Shelleyan self as a sacrifice to his Oedipal anxieties, to his love for his Evangelical mother. The poem, like Coleridge's three poems of natural magic, *Christabel, The Ancient Mariner, Kubla Khan*, becomes a ballad of the imagination's revenge against the poet's unpoetic nature, against his failure to rise out of the morass of family romance into the higher romance of the autonomous spirit questing for evidences of its own creative election. Mrs. Miller's view seems to me the indispensable entry into Browning's darkest and most powerful romance, and once within we will find the fullest phenomenology of a consciousness of creative failure available to us in our language, fuller even than in Coleridge, whose censorious and magnificent intellect fought back too effectively against romance, in the holy name of the Logos. Browning embraced that name also, but in *Childe Roland* happily the embrace is evaded, and a terrible opening to vision is made instead.

If we go a day past *Childe Roland's* composition, to 3 January 1852, we find the indefatigable Browning writing *Love Among The Ruins*, where fallen Babylon exposes only a ruined tower:

> Now,—the single little turret that remains
>   On the plains,
> By the caper overrooted, by the gourd
>   Overscored,
> While the patching houseleek's head of blossom winks
>   Through the chinks—
> Marks the basement whence a tower in ancient time

Sprang sublime,
And a burning ring. . . .

It is "the Tower itself," but a day later, still "the round squat turret,
blind as the fool's heart," but seen now in the mundane, nightmare
fallen away into ruin, and Browning, blind to the night's lessons, falls
back on: "Love is best." Doubtless it is, when the quester is free to find
it, or be found by it. Shelley, who knew more about love than Brown-
ing, or most men (before or since), had the capacity of a stronger vi-
sionary, to confront the image of nightmare in the mundane:

> —so, o'er the lagune
> We glided; and from that funeral bark
> I leaned, and saw the city, and could mark
> How from their many isles, in evening's gleam,
> Its temples and its palaces did seem
> Like fabrics of enchantment piled to Heaven.
> I was about to speak, when—"We are even
> Now at the point I meant," said Maddalo,
> And bade the gondolieri cease to row.
> "Look, Julian, on the west, and listen well
> If you hear not a deep and heavy bell."
> I looked, and saw between us and the sun
> A building on an island; such a one
> As age to age might add, for uses vile,
> A windowless, deformed and dreary pile;
> And on the top an open tower, where hung
> A bell, which in the radiance swayed and swung
> We could just hear its hoarse and iron tongue:
> The broad sun sunk behind it, and it tolled
> In strong and black relief.—
> . . . .
> "And such," he cried, "is our mortality,
> And this must be the emblem and the sign
> Of what should be eternal and divine!—
> And like that black and dreary bell, the soul,
> Hung in a heaven-illumined tower, must toll
> Our thoughts and our desires to meet below
> Round the rent heart and pray—as madmen do
> For what? they know not—till the night of death
> As sunset that strange vision, severeth
> Our memory from itself, and us from all
> We sought and yet were baffled."[2]

Though it is not traditional to find in this passage one of the
"sources" of *Childe Roland*, it seems to me the truest precursor to
Browning's poem, on evidence both internal and external. It lay deep
in his mind as he wrote his poem, and emerged in the emblem of the
commonplace yet unique tower where the quester is met by his ca-
reer's ambiguous truth, and triumphantly accepts destruction by that

2. *Julian and Maddalo* (1818), lines 87–106, 120–30.

truth. Externals can be postponed until Roland's truth meets us in the poem, but the internal evidence of Romantic tradition finds us even as we enter Roland's realm of appearances, and are accosted by his "hoary cripple," an amalgam of Spenser's Archimago, Spenser's Despair, Shakespeare's Gloucester from *Lear*, and perhaps Ahasuerus, the Wandering Jew of Shelley's *Queen Mab* and *Hellas*. Gloucester as seen by Cornwall, I should amend, for the verbal origins of *Childe Roland* are in the snatch of verse sung by Edgar before his father suffers Cornwall's version of the Dark Tower:

> "Child Rowland to the dark tower came.
> His word was still 'Fie, foh, and fum,
> I smell the blood of a British man.' "

But the Browning version of the ogre is a *daimon* of self-betrayal, and the reader needs to trace influence in the manner of Borges, rather than of Lowes,[3] if source-study is to help in reading this poem. Kafka and Yeats, Gnostic[4] visionaries, are closer to the poem than Spenser and Shakespeare, or even Shelley, who in a true sense is the poem's pervasive subject, the betrayed ideal whose spirit haunts Roland, whose love chastizes Roland's way of knowing until it becomes a knowing that deforms and breaks all things it lights upon, and finds "all dark and comfortless," the blinded Gloucester's answer to Cornwall's vile taunt: "Where is thy luster now?"

To recognize Childe Roland as a Gnostic quester is to begin reading his poem as if it were a Borges parable of self-entrapment, another labyrinth made by men that men must decipher. A Gnostic quester is necessarily a kind of Quietist, for whom every landscape is infernal, and every shrine a squalor. In Shelleyan quest the objects of desire tend to touch the vanishing point of the visual and auditory, but the field of quest remains attractive, though not benign. Childe Roland moves in the Gnostic nightmare, where all natural context even looks and sounds malevolent, and the only goal of desire is to fail.

The greatest power of Browning's romance inheres not in its landscape (in which we are too ready to believe) but in the extraordinary, negative intensity of Childe Roland's consciousness, which brings to defeat an energy of perception so exuberant as to mock defeat's limits. This energy is very close to the remorseless drive of Shelley's Poet in *Alastor*, or of Shelley himself in *Epipsychidion*. The landscape of "*Childe Roland to the Dark Tower Came*," like that of *Alastor*, is charged by the quester's own furious, self-frustrated energy, and cannot at last contain that energy. When Childe Roland burns through the context he has invented, in his closing epiphany, he sees and hears all things he has made and marred, or rather made by breaking, him-

---

3. I.e., the eclectic approach of the modern Argentinian writer and critic Jorge Luis Borges (who has traced his leading metaphors through wide-ranging research into recondite literature) rather than the more restrictive method of John Livingston Lowes in *The Road to Xanadu* (1927); Lowes demonstrated that images from Coleridge's reading were stored in his unconscious mind until fused imaginatively in the creative act.
4. Adherent of ancient cult which held matter to be evil; emancipation is reached through *gnosis*, immediate knowledge of spiritual truth.

self and his vision, everything finally except the landscape of estrange-
ment he has been seeing all through the poem. "Burningly it came on
me all at once," he says, and "it" is place imagined into full meaning,
an uncovering so complete as to be triumph whatever else comes to
him. The Roland who sets the slughorn to his lips does not accept a
Gnostic conclusion, but ranges himself with those who have sounded
the trumpet of a prophecy to unawakened earth. A poem that com-
menced in the spirit of *The Castle* or *Meditations in a Time of Civil
War*[5] concludes itself deliberately in the Orphic spirit of the *Ode to the
West Wind's* last stanza.

Browning dates his *Introductory Essay* on Shelley[6] as "Paris, Decem-
ber 4th, 1851," a month before the composition of *Childe Roland*.
The *Essay* on Shelley is, with one exception, Browning's only prose
work of consequence, the exception being the *Essay on Tasso and
Chatterton* done a decade before *Childe Roland*. In *Julian and Mad-
dalo* the "windowless, deformed and dreary pile" with its "open tower"
and "hoarse and iron tongue" of a tolling bell is the madhouse of
Tasso's confinement, and one can surmise that "the round squat tur-
ret, blind as the fool's heart" has some intimate relation to the mad-
ness of poets. Chatterton, coupled with Tasso by Browning as a
victimized mad poet, enters *Childe Roland* at the close with the slug-
horn, a nonexistent instrument that appears only in his works, by a
corruption of "slogan." As a cry-to-battle by a crazed, self-defeated
poet, its appropriateness is overwhelming at *Childe Roland's* end. The
Essay on Tasso and Chatterton is essentially a defense of Chatterton's
assumption of the mask of Rowley, anticipating Browning's extraordi-
nary essay on Shelley, with its implicit defense of Browning's assump-
tion of the many masks of his mature poetry. Contrasting Shakespeare
as the objective poet to Shelley as the subjective (and thus help-
ing Yeats to his antinomies of *primary* and *antithetical* in *A Vision*),
Browning asks an unanswerable question about the unknowable ob-
jective artist:

> Did the personality of such an one stand like an open watch-
> tower in the midst of the territory it is erected to gaze on, and
> were the storms and calms, the stars and meteors, its watchman
> was wont to report of, the habitual variegation of his everyday life,
> as they glanced across its open door or lay reflected on its four-
> square parapet?

No such question need be asked concerning the subjective poet,
who is a seer, not a fashioner, and so produces "less a work than an ef-
fluence." The open tower of Shelley radiates "its own self-sacrificing
central light," making possible what Browning calls "his noblest and
predominating characteristic":

> This I call his simultaneous perception of Power and Love in
> the absolute, and of Beauty and Good in the concrete, while he

5. I.e., exhibiting the abject yearning for order and grace that mark Kafka's novel *The Castle*
(1926) and Yeats' poem "Meditations in Time of Civil War" (1923). Orphic: prophetic.
6. See above, pp. 445–52.

throws, from his poet's station between both, swifter, subtler, and
more numerous films for the connection of each with each, than
have been thrown by any modern artificer of whom I have knowl-
edge . . .

Browning was thirty-nine when he wrote his Shelley essay, and then
its sequel in *Childe Roland*. At thirty-nine the imagination has learned
that no spring can flower past meridian, and in one sense we can re-
gard *Childe Roland* as a classical poem of the fortieth year. Shelley
had died in his thirtieth year, but his imagination might have declined
the lesson in any case, for no imagination was ever so impatient of our
staler realities, and Browning, who was a superb reader of Shelley,
would have known this. Reading Shakespeare for his Shelley essay,
Browning came upon Edgar's assumption of a mask, and his ballad-
lines of the Dark Tower, and yoked together in his creative mind
highly disparate towers. The *Essay on Shelley* twice names *Julian and
Maddalo* as a major example of the poet's art, once citing it among
"successful instances of objectivity" together with "the unrivalled
Cenci." Browning is critically acute, for the landscape of *Julian and
Maddalo* is not only marvelously rendered, but is one of the rare in-
stances in nineteenth-century poetry of a landscape *not* estranged
from the self, and so not seen merely as a portion of the self expelled:

> I rode one evening with Count Maddalo
> Upon the bank of land which breaks the flow
> Of Adria towards Venice: a bare strand
> Of hillocks, heaped from ever-shifting sand,
> Matted with thistles and amphibious weeds,
> Such as from earth's embrace the salt ooze breeds,
> Is this; an uninhabited sea-side,
> Which the lone fisher, when his nets are dried,
> Abandons; and no other object breaks
> The waste, but one dwarf tree and some few stakes
> Broken and unrepaired, and the tide makes
> A narrow space of level sand thereon,
> Where 'twas our wont to ride when day went down,
> This ride was my delight. I love all waste
> And solitary places; where we taste
> The pleasure of believing what we see
> Is boundless, as we wish our souls to be.[7]

This rider experiencing the Sublime is the polar contrary to Childe
Roland, and to the mad poet dwelling in the "windowless, deformed
and dreary pile; / And on the top an open tower," who in some sense is
Roland's *daimon* or true self. In the debate between Shelley (as Julian)
and Lord Byron (as Count Maddalo) it is Shelley who insists on the
quester's will as being central and capable, and Byron who maintains a
darker wisdom, to which Shelley, unlike Roland (or Browning), quietly
declines surrender:

7. *Julian and Maddalo*, lines 1–17.

> "—it is our will
> That thus enchains us to permitted ill—
> We might be otherwise—we might be all
> We dream of happy, high majestical.
> Where is the love, beauty, and truth we seek
> But in our mind? and if we were not weak
> Should we be less in deed than in desire?"
> "Ay, if we were not weak—and we aspire
> How vainly to be strong!" said Maddalo:
> "You talk Utopia." "It remains to know,"
> I then rejoined, "and those who try may find
> How strong the chains are which our spirit bind;
> Brittle perchance as straw . . . we are assured
> Much may be conquered, much may be endured,
> Of what degrades and crushes us. We know
> That we have power over ourselves to do
> And suffer—what, we know not till we try;
> But something nobler than to live and die—"

The passage might well be epigraph to *Childe Roland*. Shelley, the sun-treading spirit of imaginative reproach or true Apollo of *Pauline*, the "mad poet" who sought love as opposed to Paracelsus's quest for knowledge, the spirit still not exorcised in *Sordello*, gives to *Childe Roland* and its nightmare landscape a sense of a hidden god, a presence felt by the void of its total absence. Roland rides across a world without imagination, seeing everywhere "such starved ignoble nature," his own, as he follows "my darkening path" to its conclusion.

DeVane found much of the "source" material for Roland's landscape in Gerard de Lairesse's *The Art of Painting in All its Branches*, a book Browning remembered as having read "more often and with greater delight, when I was a child, than any other." Lairesse, celebrated by Browning in the late *Parleyings*, gathered together the horrible in painting, as he saw it, in his Chapter 17, *Of Things Deformed and Broken, Falsely called Painter-like*, and DeVane demonstrated how many details Browning took from the one chapter, probably unknowingly. Childe Roland, like Browning, is painter as well as poet, and dies as a living picture, framed by "all the lost adventurers my peers," who like him found all things deformed and broken.

All this is the living circumference of "*Childe Roland to the Dark Tower Came*"; we move to the central meaning when we ponder the sorrow of this quester, this *aware* solipsist whose self-recognition has ceased to be an avenue to freedom. When Roland ceased to imagine (before his poem opens) he made it inevitable that he should be *found by* his phantasmagoria. By marching into that land of his own terrible force of failed will, he compels himself to know the degradation of what it is to be illuminated while himself giving no light. For this is the anxiety of influence, in that variety of poetic melancholy that issues from the terrible strength of post-Enlightenment literary tradition. Where *Childe Roland* excels, and makes its greatness as a poem, is in its unique and appalling swerve, its twist or Lucretian *clinamen* away from its precursors, from the whole line of internalized romance, and from Shelley in particular. This swerve is the vision of the end, where *all* the poets of the Romantic tradition are seen as having failed, to the degree where they stand together, ranged in the living flame, the fire the Promethean quester could not steal but had to burn through.

Yet Childe Roland dies in the courage of knowing—he too sees, and he knows, and so dies with a full intelligence as what Keats called an atom of perception; at the close, he ceases to be a figure of romance, for he knows too much.

Thomas Greene, in a superb insight, speaks of "the mystery and melancholy of romance, which always accepts less than total knowledge," since total knowledge successfully resists enchantment. Romance in *Childe Roland* passes into what George Ridenour has called "the typical mode," which though allegoric is yet allegorically self-contained, as though Browning's poem were that odd conceit, an allegory of allegorizing. Ridenour, in the most illuminating critical remarks yet made about the poem, relates the knight's trial by landscape (his reduced *geste*) to Browning's obsessive investigations into the nature of purposeful human act, and finds the poem to be finally a celebration. All men are questers, and capable of rising into the Burkean Sublime, however purposeless or compulsive their acts as they blunder toward goals both commonplace and unique, like the Dark Tower. Whether this is entirely celebration, since Roland fails his trial by landscape, may be doubted, but the triumphant surge of the end gives Ridenour considerable sanction, making his reading of the poem closer to what must be presumed as Browning's also than my own or Mrs. Miller's is.

If we follow Mrs. Miller by returning to the passage from *Paracelsus* quoted earlier in this essay, we can say that Roland is being punished, by himself, for having quested after knowledge rather than love, the punishment being to see all things as deformed and broken. One of Wordsworth's central insights is that to see without love, to see by knowing, is to deform and break, and Roland would thus exemplify a terrible Romantic truth. But this is to read as reductively as Roland sees, and to miss the awful greatness of Roland's landscape. Browning took Roland from Edgar's song, but giving the name to a quester means to invoke also, in some way, the rich romance associations of the name. In the *Chanson de Roland* the knight's loyalty to his lord, Charlemagne, is exemplary, and the final blast of his trumpet is a supreme self-sacrifice. In Ariosto though, Orlando is insane and disloyal through love's madness, with the love being silly, wretched, and unrequitted at that. In contrast to Browning's Roland, we can say of Tasso, Chatterton, and Shelley, his precursors in the band of questers, what Yeats said of certain Irish poets and rebels who had confounded his expectations, that excess of love may have bewildered them until they died. But if the romance quest is, as Angus Fletcher suggests in his powerful study of allegory, an obsessive pattern of desire that becomes a compulsive act, then Browning's Roland too is journeying to rebeget himself, despite his conscious desire only to make an end, any end. Though he finds, and is annihilated in finding, an extraordinary if only partly communicable knowledge, the meaning of his quest was still in his search for love. Love of whom? Of his precursors, the band of brothers who, one by one, "failed" triumphantly at the Dark Tower. A poet's love for another poet is no more disinterested than any other variation upon family romance, but a final knowledge that it was indeed love may be the revelation that makes for a kind of triumph, though not a salvation, at a dark end.

ERIK GRAY

Andrea del Sarto's Modesty†

In speech the use of the first person is common, even universal; but problems arise the moment first-person discourse is frozen and fixed in a lyric. The use of the word "I," so usual as to pass almost unnoticed in conversation or in dramatic poetry, comes to seem distortedly egocentric in lyric poems, where we are presented with the words of only a single speaker. This egocentricity, which may be inconspicuous when a poem first appears, grows more and more obvious as time goes on. Like a smile frozen in a photograph, which may have looked natural enough to begin with but which comes to look false or uncanny when seen repeatedly over many years, a much-read lyric seems to become more egotistical with time.

It is the readers, therefore, rather than the author of a given poem who are likely to be troubled by "lyric egotism"—by the tendency of the speaker's voice and point of view to seem to drown out or pre-empt all others. Robert Browning and Alfred Tennyson were both great readers of Romantic lyrics, and both appear to have been particularly sensitive to this aspect of their predecessors' work. This sensibility is detectable in the dramatic monologue, the form which Browning and Tennyson independently developed in the 1830s and which has long been recognized to have derived from the Romantic lyric, and more particularly, as W. David Shaw points out, from the works we now refer to as "conversation poems."[1] The grotesquely exaggerated egotism

† Originally published as " 'Out of me, out of me!': Andrea, Ulysses, and Victorian Revisions of Egotistical Lyric," *Victorian Poetry* 36.4 (1998): 417–30. Newly revised by the author for this Norton Critical Edition and reprinted by permission of the author.
1. See Shaw, "Lyric Displacement in the Victorian Monologue: Naturalizing the Vocative," *Nineteenth-Century Literature* 52 (1997): 302–25, especially p. 304: "Coleridge's conversation poems naturalize the ode and lyric by substituting, for formal apostrophes to seasons, places, and natural phenomena, the dramatic monologue's vocatives of direct address to a person." The monologue's debt to Romantic poetry received its first full-length critical consideration in Robert Langbaum, *The Poetry of Experience* (New York: W. W. Norton & Company 1957); notable additions to the critical tradition since then have included, among many others, Harold Bloom, *Poetry and Repression* (New Haven: Yale University Press, 1976), and the essays in the special issue of *Victorian Poetry* on "The Dramatic 'I'," ed. Linda Shires (Vol. 22, no. 2; Summer 1984), especially those by Herbert F. Tucker and U. C. Knoepflmacher. See also Tucker's sustainedly brilliant discussion of "Tithonus" in *Tennyson and the Doom of Romanticism* (Cambridge, Mass: Harvard University Press, 1988), pp. 239–64.

that distinguishes the earliest dramatic monologues suggests that the
Victorian poets were more acutely conscious than their predecessors
of the difficulties that accompany the presence of a single lyric voice.
Although the Romantics recognized poetic egotism, they tended to see
it as an epic problem: Wordsworth was referring only to *The Prelude*
when he felt misgivings "that a man should talk so much about him-
self" in verse.[2] Wordsworth's contemporaries, when they complained
of his egotism, tended to refer to *The Excursion*, of which William Ha-
zlitt wrote that "an endless intellectual egotism swallows up every-
thing. Even the dialogues introduced . . . are soliloquies of the same
character, taking different views of the subject. The recluse, the pas-
tor, and the pedlar, are three persons in one poet."[3] Keats was likewise
reacting most probably to *The Excursion* when, not long after Hazlitt's
essay appeared, he distinguished his own sort of poetry from "the
Wordsworthian or egotistical sublime."[4] None of these writers seems
to have sensed a similar egotism in Wordsworth's lyric poems; as a re-
sult, despite his resolutions, Keats's own odes and lyrics are not
noticeably less self-centered than Wordsworth's. As Harold Bloom
comments, "Keats, I think, protested too much in his zeal to overcome
self-concern, and I think also that Keats has deceived his critics into
literalizing his figuration of destroying the self."[5] A glance at his odes
reveals that Keats's self-effacement was certainly selective.

The Victorian poets registered their discomfort with the Romantic
lyric in their dramatic monologues, which frequently make use of
comic allusions to ironize the egotistical speaker. Browning's "Andrea
del Sarto," for instance, implicitly equates Andrea with some of the
more self-absorbed and self-deluded characters of Shakespearean
comedy. Yet it is not only through such irony that these later poems
distance themselves from the "egotistical sublime." A comparison of
"Andrea del Sarto" with the conversation poem to which it seems most
closely related, Coleridge's "The Eolian Harp," reveals what appears to
be a distinctive characteristic of the dramatic monologue as a genre:
the speaker's very egotism causes him to refrain from making general
or prescriptive pronouncements. Unlike their Romantic precursors,
Victorian monologists are content to speak only for themselves.

*   *   *

Andrea del Sarto demands little enough of his wife Lucrezia; he
asks only that she smile at him and hold his hand. He had plenty of
such encouragement in France, he remembers:

> That Francis, that first time,
> And that long festal year at Fontainebleau!

2. Quoted in Wordsworth, *The Prelude*, ed. Ernest de Selincourt and Helen Darbishire (Ox-
ford: Clarendon Press, 1959), p. xl.
3. William Hazlitt, "On Mr. Wordsworth's Poem The Excursion," *Complete Works*, ed. P. P.
Howe, vol. IV (London: J. M. Dent, 1930), p. 113.
4. Keats to Richard Woodhouse, 27 October 1818. *The Letters of John Keats*, ed. Hyder E.
Rollins (Cambridge, Mass: Harvard University Press, 1958), I, 387.
5. Bloom, *Poetry and Repression*, p. 136. Compare John Bayley's essay, "Keats and Reality":
"Paradoxically, it is the renunciation of the self that strikes us as self-absorbed, even solip-
sistic" (*English Poets: British Academy Chatterton Lectures* [Oxford: Clarendon Press, 1988],
p. 189).

> I surely then could sometimes leave the ground,
> Put on the glory, Rafael's daily wear,
> In that humane great monarch's golden look,—
> One finger in his beard or twisted curl
> Over his mouth's good mark that made the smile,
> One arm about my shoulder, round my neck,
> The jingle of his gold chain in my ear,
> I painting proudly with his breath on me.
>
> (ll. 149–58)[6]

Whose finger is playing with Francis's "beard or twisted curl"? His own, of course, we reply; the lines that follow make that clear enough. Besides (we might add), the picture is so explicitly intimate that it seems unnecessary to insist upon the slight grammatical ambiguity that temporarily allows the "finger" to be Andrea's.

And yet there is precedent for such dalliance, though with the roles reversed. Armado, the ridiculous Spanish retainer of the king of Navarre in Love's Labour's Lost, boasts to Holofernes:

> I must tell thee it will please his grace, by the world, sometime to lean upon my poor shoulder, and with his royal finger, thus dally with my excrement, with my mustachio—. . . . By the world, I recount no fable! Some certain special honours it pleaseth his greatness to impart to Armado.
>
> (5.1.91–95)[7]

The similarity between Armado and Andrea does not end here. Both are southerners invited to the court of a French king to entertain him; both fall in love with women who are considered (and whom they consider) below them, and both break their oaths to the monarch on account of this love. More broadly, Shakespeare's Navarre resembles Andrea's image of Fontainebleau: a royal enclosure where one can supposedly escape from intercourse with women and dedicate oneself entirely to one's calling. The courtiers of Navarre, however, almost immediately forswear their high-minded intentions, and spend the rest of the play self-consciously rationalizing their broken faith. In this sense Andrea finds an even closer soul-mate in Biron than in Don Armado.[8]

The allusion to Love's Labour's Lost adds an important comic note to Andrea's description of France, ironizing and undercutting his profession of artistic selflessness at Fontainebleau and calling into question his representation of it as a locus of artistic integrity. Some critics are not so skeptical: Mario D'Avanzo, for instance, draws a strict distinction between Francis and Lucrezia, between the type of artist that Andrea is when abroad and when at home. Francis, he writes, is an "imparter of inspiration," a Shelleyan epipsyche, a "roi soleil."[9] Carefully noting recurrent figures in the poem, D'Avanzo remarks that

---

6. All quotations from "Andrea del Sarto" refer to *The Poetical Works of Robert Browning*, vol. V: *Men and Women*, ed. Ian Jack and Robert Inglesfield (Oxford: Clarendon Press, 1995).
7. William Shakespeare, *Love's Labour's Lost*, ed. G. R. Hibbard (Oxford: Clarendon Press, 1990).
8. Biron's ability to rationalize is so Browningesque that "Le Byron de Nos Jours," the subtitle of "Dis Aliter Visum," could almost as well refer to Biron as to Byron.

around Francis cluster images of gold, the sun, Apollo, and "subjective" poetry, while on the other hand Lucrezia is associated with silver, the moon, the python (Apollo's enemy), and mere craftwork. This dichotomy is undeniably present in the poem, and no doubt this is the way that Andrea views his life, or would like to view it: he would like to think that he really was an inspired, Apollonian artist back in France, and that he gave up everything for Lucrezia's sake.

But how different is France from Fiesole? The difference seems to be one of degree rather than of essence. In those days when Andrea "put on . . . Rafael's daily wear," his inspiration remained earthly:

> I painting proudly with his breath on me,
> All his court round him, seeing with his eyes,
> Such frank French eyes.
>
> (ll. 158–60)[1]

This is an echo of the description of Raphael when he was doing his best work—"Pouring his soul, with kings and popes to see, / Reaching, that heaven might so replenish him, / Above and through his art" (ll. 108–10). What Andrea imitates, however, is not Raphael's divine effort, but his worldly circumstance—working under the eyes of rich patrons ("kings and popes"), which Andrea takes as a substitute for inner vision. Francis is no more a true epipsyche than Lucrezia; no more than she does he urge Andrea, "God and the glory! never care for gain" (l. 128). Andrea's work in France is a better-paid, more happily and perhaps more perfectly executed version of his other work: it is done "proudly," self-interestedly, for the sake of the king and for those who allow their judgments to be swayed by his. Andrea at Fontainebleau not only falls short of Raphael (except in his outer appearance) but does not even approximate those failed Florentine painters in whom "there burns a truer light of God" than in himself (l. 79).

Fontainebleau is no nearer heaven than Italy is. All the mediocrity that characterizes Andrea's career at home—the "fetter" that he feels, the reduction of his art to "ware"—is equally present abroad; the only difference is that Francis's fetter and his payment are made of gold: "The jingle of his gold chain in my ear" (ll. 52, 225, 157). Again *Love's Labour's Lost* is relevant: although the four protagonists believe they have set themselves free from death and time by retreating to their court, in fact they accomplish nothing of the sort. They congratulate themselves on having escaped and transcended earthly limitations, but Princess Katherine quickly sets them right. When the king is forced by the terms of his oath to receive the princess in an open field outside his court, she lets him know that heaven is not part of his domain:

9. Mario L. D'Avanzo, "Francis, Lucrezia, and the Figurative Language of 'Andrea del Sarto'," *Texas Studies in Literature and Language* 9 (1968): 527.

1. The similarity between Fontainebleau and Fiesole is visible in the near-tautology of "*frank French eyes*." Andrea the mediocre, the draftsman, the corrector of outlines, loves to have all things called by their right names, just as he loves to have outlines correctly sketched. This is why he takes delight in being able to tell Lucrezia, "There's what we painters call our harmony!" (l. 34); even more, he finds comfort in the fact that "The cue-owls speak the name we call them by" (l. 210). It seems significant that his best memories of France should also involve such a pleasingly exact relation between signifier and signified.

King: Fair Princess, welcome to the court of Navarre.
Princess: 'Fair' I give you back again, and welcome I have not yet.
            The roof of this court is too high to be yours.

                                                    (2.1.90–92)

Andrea seems to be aware of such limitations without being told, and this consciousness both sets Andrea apart from the courtiers of Navarre and begins to suggest his peculiar characteristic. He speaks of how his "hand kept plying" its trade in France—clearly the same "craftsman's hand" that he earlier contrasted to the "brain, / Heart, or whate'er else" of the inspired artist (ll. 161, 80–82). Andrea needs no princess to reveal to him that he was in fact no greater abroad than at home; his brief attempt to convince himself otherwise ("I *surely* then could *sometimes* leave the ground" [l. 151, emphasis added]) is half hearted.

The essential similarity between the two imaginative loci of the poem becomes even more obvious if we compare "Andrea del Sarto" to the great Romantic lyric that it rewrites, "The Eolian Harp." The situation in Coleridge's poem is the same in miniature: the speaker, sitting at home with his wife in the evening, looking over the landscape, recalls a time when he too went off without her and was meekly recalled by her imperious voice. But the "random gales" of inspiration that Coleridge experienced on the hillside, the "intellectual breeze" that filled his soul, are reduced in Browning to Francis's breathing down Andrea's neck: "I painting proudly with his breath on me" (l. 158).

The relationship between "Andrea del Sarto" and "The Eolian Harp" is worth pursuing, not only because they are so closely related, but because each could be considered to stand as an approved representative of its genre, the dramatic monologue and the Romantic conversation poem.[2] Browning's poem takes up exactly where Coleridge's left off— "But do not let us quarrel anymore." If it is not obvious that "The Eolian Harp" ends with a quarrel between the young couple, that is because the nature of Coleridge's poem occludes the presence of a second voice. The supposed otherness of the voice we hear at the end is a transparent fiction: it is the speaker's own guilty conscience that prompts him to silence himself and his "vain Philosophy" (l. 57);[3] had "pensive Sara" not been present, he would have projected the remonstrance elsewhere. This is the prerogative of the pantheistic thinker: the world, after all, seems to the speaker to consist of "one Life within us and abroad" (l. 26), and therefore any conflict appears to be as much internal as external. The theory is attractive; but the effect of

2. Both these categories are critical constructions, but not the less useful for that. For Susan Eilenberg the term "conversation poem" is not only useful but strangely appropriate: "[T]here is something about the language of the poems that seems to license the category and acknowledge the incongruity between the style and situation. For each of the conversation poems is based on the thwarted desire for response" (*Strange Power of Speech: Wordsworth, Coleridge, and Literary Possession* [New York and Oxford: Oxford University Press, 1992], p. 22). The two categories often run into each other; although part of my aim in this essay is to define a distinguishing feature, certain borderline cases ("Two in the Campagna," for example) defy categorization.
3. All quotations from Coleridge's poetry refer to Samuel Taylor Coleridge, *Poetical Works*, ed. Ernest Hartley Coleridge (Oxford: Clarendon Press, 1912).

such high-minded, all-encompassing speculation is to permit the speaker to take on the role of spokesman for all of nature, including his wife. He feels free to interpret her glance, and to cut off any "reproof" that she was actually going to speak (l. 49). Coleridge, like Hazlitt, complained that Wordsworth in his "dramatic" poems (notably *The Excursion*) projected his own voice on more than one character, creating "a species of ventriloquism, where two are represented as talking, while in truth one man only speaks."[4] It might be retorted that in "The Eolian Harp," one man is represented as talking, while in truth there are two people quarreling. This is not to say, of course, that the "reproof" we hear is actually Sara's: Coleridge's permanently guilty and self-flagellating nature is more in evidence than his wife's evangelical piety. But it is important to keep in mind the possibility that Sara might really have objected to her husband's speculations, if he had not pre-empted her by silencing himself. For if we accept Coleridge as spokesman and exclude the possibility of a second voice, we fall into the trap of believing in the very unanimity—the oneness of souls—that the poem itself seems so reluctant to approve.

Browning was quick to recognize the self-serving nature of Coleridge's willingness to contradict himself before anyone else had the chance to do so. As Loy D. Martin writes, "To Browning, modern individuals, including the Romantic poet, *create* their alienation as a wish-fulfillment, as a division of labor, a contradictory self-reification. Their estrangement is not antithetical but identical to the metaphysical commodity that is the Romantic myth of wholeness."[5] It is important to Coleridge that the poem should end with consensus, even though the consensus is to renounce and alienate the speaker's most heartfelt ideas. Such agreement paradoxically confirms the speculations it dismisses: if Sara agrees with her husband in his self-disapproval, then he is confirmed in his right to speak on her behalf, and this in turn endorses the possibility of the existence of a shared transcendental soul. By beginning "Andrea del Sarto" (which might almost be called "The Eolian Harp Sixty Years After") with a quarrel, therefore, Browning radically reassesses the situation at the end of Coleridge's poem. From the point of view of an outsider who is not invested in seeing all things as animated by a single spirit, he suggests, the speaker and his wife do not really seem to be agreeing and perhaps are not even communicating at all. The speaker's communication with another person at home is revealed to be as much a fantasy as his communion with nature abroad.

Browning also exposes and rewrites other instances of "the Romantic myth of wholeness." Whereas Coleridge's cottage had become part of the natural landscape in which it appeared—"our Cot o'ergrown / With white-flowered Jasmin, and the broad-leav'd Myrtle" (ll. 3–4)— Andrea sees his own house as nightmarishly unnatural:

---

4. Samuel Taylor Coleridge, *Biographia Literaria*, ed. James Engell and W. Jackson Bate (Princeton: Princeton University Press, 1983), II, 135.
5. Loy D. Martin, *Browning's Dramatic Monologues and the Post-Romantic Subject* (Baltimore: Johns Hopkins University Press, 1985), p. 29.

When I look up from painting, eyes tired out,
The walls become illumined, brick from brick
Distinct, instead of mortar, fierce bright gold,
That gold of his I did cement them with!

                                                    (ll. 215–18)

Coleridge's peaceful and overgrown "Cot" becomes Andrea's "melan-
choly little house / We built to be so gay with" (ll. 212–13), in the same
way that the intellectual breeze, "At once the Soul of each and God of
all," is reduced to the approving breath of Francis and his court. The
totalizing view of the world disintegrates, until eventually everything
that Coleridge took to be an essential part of himself, an outright pos-
session, Andrea recognizes to be distinctly other. The grateful conclu-
sion to "The Eolian Harp," where the speaker thanks God who "gave
me to possess / Peace, and this Cot, and thee, heart-honour'd Maid!" is
reversed at the end of "Andrea del Sarto." "Peace" Andrea cannot pos-
sess—only feeble peacefulness ("I am as peaceful as old age tonight"
[l. 244]), bought at the expense of having to ignore the cousin, the
Paris lords, and the memory of his parents. His "Cot" is not his at all,
being given not by God, but (unwillingly) by Francis. And as for the
"Maid"—Andrea does call her "mine," but concludes the poem two
lines later with "Again the Cousin's whistle! Go, my love" (l. 267).

What Browning accomplishes by his rewriting of the earlier lyric is
not, however, merely a grotesque and heavy irony, but a type of mod-
esty. For all his egotism, Andrea never goes so far as to suggest that his
inability to reach beyond his limitations forbids anyone else's achiev-
ing transcendence. When Coleridge on the other hand calls himself
back from his speculations, his renunciation presupposes not only
Sara's approval, but everyone's. This does not mean that the reader is
necessarily supposed to agree or even to sympathize with the speaker's
renunciation; it only means that the poem and the speaker of the
poem end up saying two very different things. Of the two philosophies
voiced in "The Eolian Harp"—the pantheism of the middle section,
and the more orthodox renunciation of the conclusion—the former is
more appealing: it is described with rich, even erotic images, whereas
the conclusion relies on flat rhetoric and litotes ("never guiltless," "nor
. . . dost thou not reject"). But this bias belongs to the poem, and per-
haps to the poet. The speaker himself, on the other hand, fully
believes what he proclaims: his dismissal of "the shapings of the unre-
generate mind" (l. 55) is not a personal resolution based on the imme-
diate situation, but a universalizing conclusion. And herein lies a
major difference between the lyric and the monologue: the speaker of
a monologue may not always be aware that his viewpoint is limited—
Johannes Agricola presumably is not—but at least he has that possibil-
ity.[6] But the Romantic speaker, though what he says may be (and often

---

6. I use the masculine pronoun because the speakers of the poems I discuss here happen to be
   male. I do not mean, however, to exclude lyrics or monologues written in a female voice; for
   an informative discussion of the latter, see Cynthia Scheinberg, "Recasting 'sympathy and
   judgment': Amy Levy, Women Poets, and the Victorian Dramatic Monologue," *Victorian Po-
   etry* 35 (1997): 173–91.

is) ironized in the context of the poem, and though he may only question or vacillate, claims to speak for all.[7]

Although Andrea may seem "modest" in contrast with a Romantic speaker like the one in "The Eolian Harp," he is not therefore a liberal humanist. If his conclusions are meant to apply only to himself, this is not because Andrea has an innate understanding of others, but quite contrarily because his viewpoint is so limited. Andrea has, for instance, a predilection for enclosure,[8] and he imputes this particular preference of his to everything around him: because he himself feels "safer" (l. 142) in his limited mediocrity, he assumes that the trees he sees feel "safer" (l. 43) inside the convent wall. Even the "ruff" he is so anxious to give his wife as a gift is probably not her idea but his, because it will frame her, just as he himself has already done—"Let my hands frame your face in your hair's gold" (ll. 241, 175).[9] And yet, for all that he submits everything he sees to this process of containment, at least it can be said that he never puts words in his wife's mouth.

Nor is Andrea's comparative modesty in this respect a function only of his weakness: the disinclination to impose one's views on others is characteristic of the genre. Sometimes the speaker of a dramatic monologue is convinced of what he says, and sometimes he feels the need to convince a listener (usually of something practical, as when Fra Lippo resists arrest). But generally his egotism is such that he does not much care what others think. Even Johannes Agricola, already mentioned as an example of a dramatic speaker who believes what he says to be absolutely true, could not care less whether other people share his view.

This claim may seem problematic: the shrilly insistent tone of many monologues would appear to suggest that monologists do care what their auditors believe. We might take as a prime example Tennyson's St. Simeon, who surely seems to require affirmation from his audience, whether human or divine. Yet a comparison of "St Simeon Stylites" to Coleridge's "Frost at Midnight" reveals that the distinction between Victorian monologist and Romantic lyricist holds true even here. Tennyson's poem may well be a conscious response to Coleridge's: "[A]ll my beard / Was tagged with icy fringes to the moon" reads like a grotesque and ironic rewriting of the final lines of "Frost at Midnight." Similarly, Simeon's paranoid recollection of his earlier, studious life, when demons "flapped my light out as I read: I saw / Their

---

7. In saying that the speaker of a Romantic lyric speaks universally, I am not disagreeing with, for instance, Jerome McGann, when he writes, "Shelley's ideology [in 'Adonais'] is time and place specific. . . . Shelley's futurism is not a model for human life, then, it is an example of human life" (*The Romantic Ideology* [Chicago: University of Chicago Press, 1983], p. 123). But what is true of Shelley is not true of the speaker of "Adonais," who, like the speaker of "The Eolian Harp," is torn in different directions, but believes that he speaks truly and timelessly when he concludes on a note of what McGann calls "futurism."

8. This predilection has often been noted; see for example Eleanor Cook, *Browning's Lyrics* (Toronto: University of Toronto Press, 1974), pp. 126–7, and Lee Erickson, "The Self and Others in Browning's *Men and Women*," *Victorian Poetry* 21 (1983): 53.

9. As mentioned at the start, Andrea asks nothing of his wife but smiles and hand-holding. This is appropriate, since the face and the hands are the two parts of the body that are visible in paintings of the Madonna—so that for Andrea, who views Lucrezia as a model, they are the only parts that need exist at all.

faces grow between me and my book," parodies Coleridge's schoolboy memories—"Awed by the stern preceptor's face, mine eye / Fixed with mock study on my swimming book."[1] More generally, Tennyson's poem picks up from Coleridge's the discourse of a man who has suffered in his youth and who bequeaths the benefits of his experience to others. These similarities encourage a comparison of the two speakers, and such a comparison reveals that Simeon, for all his monomania, is less inclined to impose his own views on others. Unlike Coleridge's speaker, he does not conclude by dictating what his audience shall think and feel and does not seem particularly concerned with the universal applicability of what he has learnt. Simeon is a rhetorician, not a philosopher; he seeks approval and worshippers, not agreement and disciples. So long as his listeners respond as he wishes, they may think as they like.

In this respect Simeon, like Andrea and other monologists, is distinguished from the typical speaker of a Romantic lyric, who feels a compulsion to hear his own thoughts echoed by other people or things. That is why Coleridge puts the voice of his conscience in Sara's mouth (or eye), why Wordsworth tells Dorothy how she will feel, why Keats causes even the "foster-child of silence" to speak out. These Romantic speakers are examples of the egotistical sublime, projecting and imposing themselves on others and then demanding assent. Andrea, on the other hand, although he too projects his desires, lacks this universalizing impulse. The speakers of Victorian dramatic monologues are no less egotistical than their predecessors, perhaps, but their egotism is less sublime, more modest.

ISOBEL ARMSTRONG

Browning's "Caliban" and Primitive Language†

"Caliban is so far from being a prototype of modern Jacobinism, that he is strictly the legitimate sovereign of the isle, and Prospero and the rest are usurpers" (Bate, p. 26). Hazlitt's response to Coleridge's identification of Caliban with lawless revolutionary violence, the response of dissenting radicalism to conservative readings of *The Tempest*, would have been familiar to RB, since he inherited the dissenting culture in whose traditions Hazlitt was one of the major figures.[1] But by 1864, when the poem appeared in *Dramatis Personae*, as Gillian Beer has demonstrated in her writings on Browning's "Caliban," things had become more complicated.[2] Ethnography and linguistics, anthro-

---

1. "St Simeon Stylites," ll. 30–32, 172–73; "Frost at Midnight," ll. 37–38; quotations from Tennyson refer to *The Poems of Tennyson*, ed. Christopher Ricks, 2nd ed. (Berkeley: University of California Press, 1987). Simeon's claim that his "bald brows in silent hours become / Unnaturally hoar with rime" (ll. 162–63) likewise suggests a parody of Coleridge.
† From *Robert Browning in Contexts*, ed. John Woolford (Winfield: Wedgestone Press, 1998), pp. 76–85. Reprinted by permission of the author.
1. See Armstrong, chap. 1.
2. See Beer, *The Missing Link*.

pology and philology, were new and newly intertwined disciplines. Through a common concern with the origins of consciousness and language in what was seen as the primal, intuitive, mythic imagination of natural magic and anthropomorphism, arising from the savage's incomplete separation of his own physiological experience from the world, linguists such as Richard Chenevix Trench and Max Müller shared ground explored by anthropological researchers such as Edward Tylor and August Schleicher. And behind them all, of course, was the Enlightenment enquiry into the origins of language pursued by Humboldt, Herder and Rousseau. How did the "first man" arrive at language—and what did he speak—if we are not to accept the premise of God-given speech?

The atrocities committed by Governor Eyre on black workers in Jamaica in 1862 raised the question of language and the nature of a fully human consciousness all over again, and with terrible sharpness. It was the decade when James Hunt and the Anthropological Society argued that the different racial origins of blacks and whites necessitated a hierarchy of power. In *Daniel Deronda* (1874–76) set in the 1860s, George Eliot has Grandcourt speak of the inferior nature of the slave mentality in Jamaica as that of the "beastly Baptist Caliban." So Shakespeare's Caliban could signify Jacobin revolutionary and half-human slave, a degenerate consciousness imposed upon by the irrational ideology of nonconformity.

What kind of thought and language is Caliban capable of and on which side of the antithesis between brute and human does he fall? Partly a visceral imagining of a fantasy of "primitive" consciousness, partly a rigorous unwinding of the contradictions of Victorian theories of race and language, "Caliban" is a test case for the argument that the slave is incapable of reason and therefore without entitlement to recognition as a fully human being.

Caliban *does* argue and verbalise: in a joke against the natural theologians, who believed, as against revealed religion, that evidence of divinity was to be rationally deduced from the operation of the natural, material world, and yielded up by a process of analogy, Caliban's reasoning process takes him into analogies which are by no means reassuring. But, with RB's characteristic way of releasing ironies signifying instantaneously multiple and sometimes contradictory possibilities, Caliban's thought represents a momentous effort of intellect. His attempt to work out the nature of Setebos, his God, takes place just before Prospero's storm hits the island, the beginning of *The Tempest*, and before he has seen any human beings other than Prospero and Miranda. These figures of domination, threatening but absent, are strangely remote from him. His argument is shaped round seven theses or propositions, each ending in analogy with "So He." I am concerned with the first two theses (ll. 26–97).

In one sense this is a movement from mythic thinking, that "disease of language," as Müller called it, to abstraction (Fraser, p. 14). There is a parody of the solar mythology Müller himself popularised as Caliban posits that Setebos made the moon and sun, "But not the stars;

the stars came otherwise" (l. 27). In another sense, that seemingly progressive movement to "science" is called into question. To be caught in the meshes of analogy is not to be sure which side of the analogy is dependent on the other: Caliban positing the deity Setebos in his own image (or deducing him from experience), positing Caliban, positing Setebos, constantly reverses a hierarchy of power depending on who is the originary figure in the comparison.

Caliban first posits a thinking principle and then agency. Each of the first four theses begins with "Thinketh." This hovers indeterminately between self-externalisation as third person, "he thinketh," an object which "thinketh," a reflexive autonomous "it thinks itself," and a command to *think*. And since the upper case "He," meaning Setebos, follows hard upon the demonstration of primitive objectified thought, there is an incipient confusion between the implied lower case, "he," meaning Caliban, and his God. But not for long. God is supremely uncomfortable with his changelessness (thesis one). His only resort is to exercise power by creating, "in spite," things weaker than he. And yet this weakness, true to the dialectic of master and slave, calls out Caliban's own sense of identity. It is while formulating the second thesis that he begins to use the pronoun "I" and to detach himself from the world, as Gillian Beer notices, separating out subject and object.

God makes Caliban rather as Caliban imagines making a fetish, his bird-mankin. As powerful being, there is no point in God making a replication of Himself: He makes what He *can't* be like; but this means a compromising and ultimately exasperating *identification* with weakness. With the need to "plague" (l. 67) weakness a reversal occurs. As Caliban to God, as the fetish to Caliban, the weaker, imperfect object experiences lack and desire and with it his own agency, and so paradoxically grows in a way God cannot. The more he grows, the more violent God becomes in the effort to retain His power, in the effort not to become inferior to His creation. It is an omnipotence on analogy with intoxication (Caliban has already learned to ferment "gourd-fruit" to "bladdery," ll. 68–71, froth before the advent of Stephano and Trinculo), and the transfer of power from self to fetish is regarded with superstitious hatred as well as with delight. The "live bird out of clay" (l. 76) can be a Caliban with wings, able to perform the feats he cannot. But as it takes on independent life—the artificial leg takes on the uncanny power to "grow again" (l. 89)—the need to torment is compulsive.

Implicitly the sadism of the slave owner is being analysed. It is irrational but not without its terrible logic. This leads on to the third thesis, the arbitrary universe of a God of pure power. But there is more to be said about the second thesis: a moment of violence for the powerful, it is a moment of supreme creativity for the powerless (the Hegelian dialectic works differently for each participant in the power relation). A fetish is a not quite achieved symbol, or an incompletely realised substitution. It involves a magical transfer of power on to the object but not quite a separation from self. It *is* a self, half way between a representation and the replica of a literal object. It is this rage with the literal and the *effort* of symbol-making which induces the rage which would tear the world to pieces and twist off the pincer of the crab—thwarted epistemophilia. Nevertheless the world of myth, language, and consciousness is radically altered with the interposition of the third term, manifested by the fetish. For Romantic theorists of language it marks the primal scene of the moment of the origin of language, when the self no longer exists in a condition of undifferentiated sensation. It was for this reason, possibly, that Freud took over the idea of the fetish from anthropologists to mark the importance of the third term which can accomplish a transfer of signification from one object to another.

Herder, arguing that language is not God-made, but man-made, presupposed a primal experience of virtually interchangeable sensation— "in nature all the threads are one single tissue. The darker the senses, the more they commingle" (Herder, pp. 140–41). (One thinks of Caliban's "meshes of fire," l. 14) "With what effort did he [man] learn to differentiate! to recognize his senses!" The mass of amorphous sensation can gradually be separated out: "The sense of vision is the coldest sense, and if it had always been so cold, [one thinks of Setebos fixed in "the cold"] . . . I do not see how one could make audible what one sees" (Herder, p. 141). Experience is separated out through an exercise in substitution: "The soul, caught in the throng of such converging sensations and needing to create a word, reached out and grasped possibly the word of an adjacent sense whose feeling flowed together with the first" (Herder, p. 141). Caliban appears to be in this synaesthetic condition of perception. "And feels about his spine small eft-things course" (l. 5). Eft-things course, "race" about his spine, and course, "flow," as blood flows. Language, self, and world are fused indistinguishably, the puns which will create verbal possibilities only latent in experience.

But it takes something more than substitution, or rather, a prior move, before this primordial condition can issue in language. The separating out of sensation is a self-conscious act which requires a distinguishing mark—inner language—to come into being. Thus language and self-consciousness spring into being simultaneously, and the mark is marked again and completed in sound—external language—which is not an equivalent of but indivisible from the signifying mark. Consciousness and signification are interdependent. This is the beginning of abstraction. Man is simultaneously a creature of reflection and language (Herder, pp. 144–47).

The capacity for abstraction, the ultimate achievement of language for so many nineteenth-century commentators, who often thought of a progressive, evolutionary move through figural and sense-based language of poetry or magic through religion or the social order to maturity in "science" and pure thought—a sequence endorsed by both Herder and Comte—is part of the poem's project. Yet there is also a careful gesture towards the concretions of primordial language. "The older and more original languages are, the more is this analogy of the senses noticeable in their roots," Herder said (p. 148). He commented on the proliferation of synonyms in primitive language. Primordial languages were thought to have no grammar, to be monosyllabic and holophrastic. RB brilliantly doubles monosyllables and drives compounds together, fusing words of synonyms which are redundant and tautologous—"eft-things" (l. 5), "pompion plant" (l. 7)—or constructing them out of multiple sensations—"green-dense" (l. 40), "sleek-wet" (l. 46).[3] Rousseau insisted that all language was figural to begin with, as if it knows no prior literal term and is trope in its originary moment.[4] The quiet which transcends Setebos becomes "the Quiet" (l. 137), an abstraction or general concept constructed out of the immediacy of sensation—or *lack* of the sense of hearing, which was the sharpest of all sense experiences for Herder. If abstraction, evolving beyond sensation and metaphor, is not possible, it is not possible to conceptualise God. In spite of his atavistic love of the swarming sensation at the origin of language, Herder admits that the concretions of figural language have their limitations: "Among all savages the same holds true according to their level of culture. In the language of the Barantola no word for sacred and in the Hottentots no word for spirit could be found" (Herder, p. 156). For Müller the words for spirit were fundamental to higher forms of language.

But where is Caliban to be placed in the linguistic spectrum? The poem withholds an answer. The signs are that he is caught inside his linguistic limits. It is hinted that Sycorax, his "dam," conceptualises the world differently, envisaging experience where power relations are not necessarily intrinsic, and this relativism means that Caliban's theories must be seen provisionally. From Herder to Frazer, the existence of gendered dialects spoken by the Caribs, a men's and a women's language structuring thought, was a matter of note.[5] Do the ancient structures of Caliban's language designate him as a being at the origins of the human race? His speech could represent the roots of Aryan language, the pure Indo-European language which was the construct of philologists. A blow would be struck at the hierarchical formulations of separate racial origin of white and black "families" of men if that were to be the case. On the other hand, he might be an ostensive definition of degeneration theory. Schleicher believed that language *must* degenerate from an original perfection and purity, just as the organic decay of the flower is inevitable.[6] The savage does not belong to a primal but a degenerate culture.

The question, what is Caliban's anthropological status? asks for a more complicated decision than a simple choice between alternatives, pure or degenerate. But first, what does each imply?

3. For a discussion of the characteristics thought to be typical of primitive language, see David Richards, "A Tour of Babel," in Fraser, pp. 89–91. Whether the theorist is Schelling, Comte, or lesser known figures such as Payne and Hyde Clark, the assumption was that the evolution of language involves a progressive growth of complexity and analytical sophistication from a simplicity which is characterised by redundance and unfunctional prolixity.
4. Rousseau, p. 12, "As man's first motives for speaking were of the passions, his first expressions were tropes. Figurative language was the first to be born."
5. Herder, p. 155: "the most common objects—bed, moon, sun, bow,—are named differently in the two" (languages). See also Fraser, p. 93.
6. Fraser, p. 87. The descent was from human to sub-human.

If Caliban is primal man, peer of Adam and Eve, his language exists in a state of pristine figurality. Moving through ritual and magic to abstraction, abandoning a libidinal existence of the body for the concept, his language is rich in developmental and progressive possibility. He is ready to achieve self-externalisation in the Feurerbachian I-thou relationship in which achieved self-consciousness enables man to speak to himself. The cognitive possibility of projection and the movement to new categories, the movement, as Caliban puts it, from grub to butterfly, is an inevitability.

If Caliban belongs to the culture of barbarism, on the other hand, he will be capable of a rudimentary self-externalisation only, swamped in the sensation which has subsumed thought and prey to the residual magic and superstition retained even in higher developmental states. The degenerate races drop out of history, Richard Chenevix Trench said, because their language retains nothing of the "fossil history" inherent to high cultures. "Even most degraded people have language," he said, but not the God-given Adamic language which has endowed us with the power of naming which complex civilisations retain because they need to replenish their store of words. The language of savages is a mere remnant of a better and nobler past—"a people who has gone the downward way," debasing personal and national life. The "brutal poverty" of savage language cannot conceptualise God (Trench, pp. 4, 11, 15). A tribe in New Holland has no word for God but one for abortion: another has many words for murder but makes no distinction between murder and killing (perhaps a problem for Western society rather than for Trench's savage). Words are not arbitrary signs but meaningfully assert the continuity of race and nation, demonstrating kinship and affiliation from which the savage has lapsed.

The many locations suggested for the origin of Aryan and Indo-European languages (West Turkestan, Bactria and Scandinavia among them) never included the West Indies, where we assume Caliban to be. But the circularity of the monologue seemingly prevents us from determining whether Caliban is a degenerate savage or whether civilisation is latent in his consciousness. The idea of the Quiet could be reaching for the conceptualisation of a pure non-anthropomorphic God. But this principle could also be derived from Caliban's need to keep "quiet" in the face of Prospero's violence, the nadir of oppressed consciousness for whom resistance is no longer possible (a form of the master/slave relationship contemplated by Hegel, and, for plantation workers, a dire passivity).[7] In Frazer's formulation, the "Quiet" could be the mistaken explanation of mythic consciousness.

But RB was never prone to easy relativism and facile scepticism. What matters is not that one can or cannot decide on Caliban's status, but that according to the position we choose for him his ethnographic status changes, and correspondingly changes the status of Prospero and Miranda, who occupy different stages in a temporal sequence.

If Caliban is originary man, Prospero is his product. He is part of a

7. Hegel, pp. 118–119.

progressive linear sequence in which Caliban, whose experience coexists with but is logically prior to his, actually has greater potential. On his belly like Satan, Caliban is nevertheless the pure origin determining Prospero's ascent. Prospero is the intermediary between Caliban and the God Caliban has produced, Setebos. Prospero has ascended *from* Caliban, perhaps, but his violence suggests the possibility of "degeneracy." If, therefore, Caliban is degenerate, then on a linear scale Prospero has "produced" Caliban (and Setebos), degrading them. The situation is reversed. Caliban is the product of Prospero's violent culture (a point made by Gillian Beer). He does not produce it. Each form of ethnographic status guarantees a different analogical relationship. If Prospero is created in Caliban's image, representations of him emerging from Caliban's projections, he is a creature of weakness and abject dependency. If, on the other hand, Caliban's fantasies are the product of Prospero's, Caliban is the creature of human violence. God is different in either case, weak on the one hand, cruel on the other. Arguably, if we accept this linear scale, Caliban can never conceptualise God, coming too early or too late in the evolutionary process.

But this impasse shows up the fallacy of mapping hierarchies determined by *descent* and origin on to a social order where Caliban and Prospero actually coexist. To justify hierarchy and power different histories have to be attributed to Caliban and Prospero, for which there is no intellectual justification. For the difference between Prospero and Caliban we have to search for other less implausible explanations. Tylor found one, remarking that if the urban working classes were termed savages, then their degradation was culturally made. The savage theoretically in a state of nature could not be conditioned in the same way (Fraser, p. 50).

The process of arguing by analogy and typologising through likeness turns out to be oppressive because its diachronic movement almost always implies the necessity of hierarchy. Similarly, a diachronic movement from concretion and figurality to abstraction is also likely to result in oppressively hierarchical thinking. There was a different model of language and its origins available to RB and I think it was hovering in "Caliban." He would have found it in Godwin's *Political Justice* (1793), a radical text to which, given his background in dissident thinking, we can reasonably expect him to have had access. Discussing the capacity of human institutions to develop, Godwin speaks of the institution of language. While he admits that abstraction "was necessary to the first existence of language," he refuses to admit that abstraction occurs through a movement from primitive origins in sensation and figurality.[8] Abstraction may well be "one of the sublimest operations of mind," but it is *always* within reach of *all* human beings because it is "coeval with and inseparable from the existence of mind," which, by definition, all human beings possess (Godwin, 3, 28). Thus he avoids the hierarchy of "ascent" which is implicit in both Herder and Rousseau. Moreover, he asserts, in later editions, *all* language is

8. See Godwin, vol. 3, p. 28; vol. 4, p. 53.

general, working through and with categories and classifications rather than with mimetic particularities. That words are to do with concepts *and not resemblances* has misled Burke into believing that there are "words without ideas"—a dangerously irrational position for Godwin, and one which asks for a connection between language and violence.[9] It is with the general idea of sheep and not with particular sheep or the particularities of sheep with which we are concerned. But this is not to assert, with Burke, that words are independent of meaning, for this opens the way to oppression through language as words are given any meaning we like and used for effects of pure sound.

For Godwin abstraction and *comparison*, another necessity for both thought and action, are bound up with one another. Abstraction, he argues, enables comparison, but this does not mean the perception of *likeness* to which analogy is tied. Comparison, which gives us our sense of preference and therefore of voluntary "action" and its possibilities, depends on a perception of both likeness and "differences." Analogy, suppressing "differences," paves the way for hierarchies based on similarity.[1] The recognition of differences, on the other hand, preserves thought from the tyranny of the same.

Is it the case that Caliban is most self-reflexive, most "fully human," when he recognises difference? It is difficult to say. But arguably what *analogy* enables him to do is to conceive of a world of violence alone— a world in which to imitate a jay screaming in pain gives pleasure to the birds who hate it, in which it is necessary to appease a violent God by cutting one's finger off. Analogy confirms the circle of violence, despite Caliban's rudimentary efforts to liberate himself from it. What one *can* say, however, is that violence is an attribute of human nature at whatever point in the evolutionary "scale" a person might be. Caliban's contemplation of torment and cruelty is the legacy of Prospero as much as it belongs to his own impulse. At the end of the poem a storm, the locus classicus for writers from Vico to Herder through to Frazer of the origins of language, when primitive man contemplates a powerful anthropomorphic God through figural comparison of the violence of the storm and the violence of a person, breaks over Caliban's head. The language here is a near paraphrase of Herder, who saw lightning and thunder as an example of the way "adjacent sense" (sight and sound) comes together. Herder quotes: "And ere a man finds time to say 'Look there!'." thunder comes (Herder, p. 141). RB's "Caliban," consummately reproduces Herder's concept in its rendering of the "adjacent" sensations of vision and sound, as thunder is pointed at after the white blaze of lightning asserts the dominant perception of sight: "White blaze— / A tree's head snaps—and there, there, there, there, there, / His thunder follows!" (ll. 289–91).

The thunder reduces Caliban to subjugation. But, so coercive is the context of Shakespeare's *The Tempest* in spite of RB's refusal to confirm this time scheme, that we are likely to suppose that this is the

---

9. Godwin, 4, 54. Material added to the second (1796) and third (1798) eds.
1. Godwin, 3, 28. "Comparison immediately leads to imperfect abstraction" (1798).

hurricane which begins the play. Thus it is neither "natural" thunder nor God's thunder. It is Prospero's thunder—the product of thoroughly human violence for all its magical power. Thunder, far from being at the origin of language as a figural moment, follows it. Consciousness and language existed before the originating moment.

WORKS CITED

Armstrong, Isobel. *Victorian Poetry: Poetry, Poetics and Politics.* London: Routledge, 1993.
Bate, Jonathan. "Shakespeare and the Literary Police." *London Review of Books*, 29 September 1988.
Beer, Gillian. *Forging the Missing Link: Interdisciplinary Stories.* Cambridge: Cambridge University Press, 1993.
Fraser, Robert, ed. *Sir James Frazer and the Literary Imagination.* London: Macmillan, 1990.
Godwin, William. *An Enquiry Concerning Political Justice.* In Mark Philp, ed., *Political and Philosophical Writings of William Godwin.* 7 vols. London, 1993.
Hegel, Georg W. F. *Phenomenology of Spirit.* Trans. A. V. Miller. Oxford: Clarendon Press, 1977.
Herder, Johann Gottfried. "Essay on the Origin of Language." Trans. Alexander Gode. John H. Moran and A. Gode, eds., *Two Essays on the Origin of Language.* Chicago: University of Chicago Press, 1966, pp. 86–166.
Rousseau, Jean-Jacques. "Essay On the Origin of Languages." Trans. John H. Moran. John H. Moran and A. Gode, eds., *Two Essays on the Origin of Language.* Chicago: University of Chicago Press, 1966, pp. 5–74.
Trench, Richard Chenevix. *On the Study of Words.* 4th ed. London: John W. Parker and Sons, 1853.

SUSAN BROWN

"Pompilia": The Woman (in) Question†

Robert Browning's *The Ring and the Book*, central as it is to the Victorian poetic canon, presents an ideal means of addressing the significance of gender in both Victorian poetry and its literary history. On its publication in 1869, Robert Buchanan immediately heralded it as "the supremest poetical achievement" of the Victorian age, and numerous critics have since concurred.[1] This stature is associated with a degree of formal experimentation that, in the view of Bernard Richards, "amounts to the creation of what is virtually a new genre."[2] And in spite of a broad range of emphasis and interpretation, there exists a critical consensus linking this generic innovation to the exploration of questions of epistemology, aesthetics, and language.

This assessment of *The Ring and the Book's* generic experimentation contrasts sharply with that of Elizabeth Barrett Browning's *Aurora Leigh*, whose innovative form is attributed to an explicitly feminist poetics resulting from engagement with what the Victorians referred to as "The Woman Question."[3] This debate over what we would now call

† From *Victorian Poetry* 34.1 (1996): 15–37. Copyright © West Virginia University. Reprinted by permission of the publisher.
1. Review of *The Ring and the Book, Athenaeum*, March 20, 1869, p. 399.
2. Bernard Richards, *English Poetry of the Victorian Period 1830–1890* (New York: Longman, 1988), p. 95.
3. See Dorothy Mermin, "Genre and Gender in Aurora Leigh," *VN* 69 (1986): 7–11; Marjorie Stone, "Gender Inversion and Genre Subversion: Aurora Leigh and The Princess," *VP* 25 (1987): 101–127; and Susan Stanford Friedman, "Gender and Genre Anxiety: Elizabeth Barrett Browning and H. D. as Epic Poets," *TSWL* 5 (1896): 203–28.

gender definitions, roles, and practices was one of the Victorian pe-
riod's most multifaceted, pervasive, and sustained series of contesta-
tions, affecting practically every aspect of public and private life and
impacting profoundly on both literary and non-literary discourses.[4]
Despite the relative inattention to such issues even in much recent
critical work, poetic discourse was as thoroughly implicated as fiction
in the ongoing construction of gender. The Woman Question had not
simply a thematic but an aesthetic impact on the course of Victorian
poetry and, as the following discussion of *The Ring and the Book* seeks
to demonstrate, is crucial to a revisionary account of such apparently
unrelated matters as generic innovation and development.

   Pompilia is the seventh book of *The Ring and the Book*, and with the
preceding *Giuseppe Caponsacchi* occupies the center of the text. Its
protagonist plays a crucial role in the events recounted by the speakers
in the poem. Yet *Pompilia* has not received the lion's share of critical
attention given to *The Ring and the Book*, its speaker having been
noted by critics from the outset for her "simplicity."[5] Most critics have
structured their inquiries around the issues of truth and artistry fore-
grounded in the framing books, *The Ring and the Book* and *The Book
and the Ring*; in so doing they have also, as William Walker has
pointed out, tended to "exempt" Pompilia's monologue "from those el-
ements which are claimed to distort the accounts given by other
speakers in the poem."[6] Pompilia has been represented almost univer-
sally, by feminist and non-feminist critics alike, as a passive victim
who pours forth on her deathbed an ingenuous testimony to her own
innocence. The assumption of Pompilia's innocence raises another re-
gion of broad critical consensus: the central action of the work is
taken to be the trial of Pompilia's husband Guido—is he guilty or in-
nocent? damned or saved?—so much so that critics such as Walker or
Ann P. Brady are exceptional in remembering that Pompilia is also on
trial, or at least conducting a defense of herself. Her trial has signifi-
cance as great and implications as far-reaching as Guido's, despite the
fact that she does not face formal legal charges.

   Pompilia is on trial as a fallen woman: she left her abusive husband

   4. A good introduction to many facets of the debate and its literature is Elizabeth K. Helsinger,
   Robin Lauterbach Sheets, and William Veeder, eds., *The Woman Question: Society and Lit-
   erature in Britain and America, 1837–1883*, 3 vols. (New York: Garland, 1983). For a
   demonstration of the significance and pervasiveness of gender in Victorian culture see Mary
   Poovey, *Uneven Developments: The Ideological Work of Gender in Mid-Victorian England*
   (Chicago: Univ. of Chicago Press, 1988). Studies of Victorian poetry which consider the
   Woman Question include Kathleen Blake, *Love and the Woman Question in Victorian Liter-
   ature: The Art of Self-Postponement* (Totowa, New Jersey: Barnes and Noble, 1983); Kath-
   leen Hickok, *Representations of Women: Nineteenth-Century British Women's Poetry*
   (Westport: Greenwood Press, 1984); and Rod Edmond, *Affairs of the Hearth: Victorian Po-
   etry and Domestic Narrative* (New York: Routledge, 1988). More generally, Alan Sinfield, *Al-
   fred Tennyson* (New York: Blackwell, 1986); Thaïs Morgan, "Mixed Metaphor, Mixed
   Gender: Swinburne and the Victorian Critics," *VN* 73 (Spring 1988): 16–19; Carol Christ,
   "The Feminine Subject in Victorian Poetry," *ELH* 54 (1987): 385–401; and Patricia O'Neill,
   "The Painting of Nudes and Evolutionary Theory: Parleyings on Victorian Constructions of
   Woman," *TSLL* 34 (1992): 541–567, all represent important discussions of the gendered
   field of Victorian poetics.
   5. Ezzat Abdulmajeed Khattab, The Critical Reception of Browning's *The Ring and the Book*
   (Salzburg: Institut für Englische Sprache und Litertur, Universität Salzburg, 1977), p. 45.
   6. William Walker, "Pompilia and Pompilia," *VP* 22 (1984): 47.

and escaped in the company of a priest toward Rome.[7] Although some
legal niceties are at stake, not to mention the murder of her adoptive
parents, the outcome of Pompilia's trial for adultery determines that of
her husband's trial for murder, for under seventeenth-century Roman
law a husband could kill an adulterous wife to restore his "honour."[8]
Guido's mistake, he claims, was in not killing Pompilia and Caponsac-
chi after overtaking them on the road to Rome:

> I did not take the license law's self gives
> To slay both criminals o' the spot at the time,
> But held my hand,—preferred play prodigy
> Of patience which the world calls cowardice,
> Rather than seem anticipate the law
> And cast discredit on its organs.
>
> (5.1878–83)[9]

Guido argues that the ecclesiastical court had in fact found them
guilty of adultery, hence Caponsacchi's banishment to Civita Vecchia,
and that he was therefore within his rights to kill his wife nine months
later with the help of four hired assassins.

More abstractly, Pompilia is on trial for asserting herself and at-
tempting self-determination in the face of directives to the contrary
from the authorities of husband, church, and state. Guido appears
more perturbed by her insubordination than by her alleged adultery.
She has broken the contract of marriage which gave him possession of
her, body and soul:

> —the law's the law:
> With a wife I look to find all wifeliness,
> As when I buy, timber and twig, a tree—
> I buy the song o' the nightingale inside.
>
> Such was the pact: Pompilia from the first
> Broke it, refused from the beginning day
> Either in body or soul to cleave to mine,
> And published it forthwith to all the world.
>
> (5.603–610)[1]

---

7. Robert Buchanan, reviewing *The Ring and the Book*, suggests that Pompilia will be a com-
fort and inspiration to "feeble" women (p. 399). In her deep distrust of representation
(ll. 884–885), Pompilia identifies herself and her plight with that of her prostitute mother:
"Well, since she had to bear this brand—let me!" (l. 874).

8. By "trial" I do not refer to the formal trials which predate the time-frame of *The Ring and
the Book*, either the ecclesiastical trial which makes no finding as regards Pompilia, or the
trial held in Guido's home town of Arezzo which finds her guilty. As Ann P. Brady argues: "It
is Pompilia who is on trial for her decisions and values which go contrary to cultural mores.
The final judgment of the court on her behalf is a moral victory for her and a reversal of so-
cietal norms" (*Pompilia: A Feminist Reading of Robert Browning's* The Ring and the Book
[Athens: Ohio Univ. Press, 1988], p. 15). The Pope pronounces her "perfect fame" in the
"definitive verdict" of the court (12.753, 750).

9. Robert Browning, *The Ring and the Book*, ed. Richard D. Altick (New York Penguin, 1971).
All parenthetical references are to this edition; references without a book number are to
Book 7, *Pompilia*.

1. The allusion to a nightingale in this passage suggests what is elsewhere confirmed: Guido's
sexual violation of his wife though marital rape was not in itself a crime under either seven-
teenth century Roman or nineteenth-century English law.

The articulation of Pompilia's offense in this passage reveals that, far from beginning with a real or imagined cuckoldry, Pompilia's wrong-doing as Guido sees it is quite independent of male agency. As E. War-wick Slinn remarks, "Pompilia refuses to submit, or rather submits in an act of such overt passivity that it parodies and undercuts the sub-mission he needs for his identity as strong male."[2] Pompilia's assertion of independent subjectivity is at the crux of the offense; this is why Pompilia, rather than Caponsacchi, is the object of Guido's revenge. Furthermore, Guido claims that he acted for the good of society; that Pompilia's insurrection represents a fatal inversion of the established social order and hierarchies; that in murdering his wife he was setting right the natural order; and that by acquitting him they can create a "Utopia":

> Rome rife with honest women and strong men,
> Manners reformed, old habits back once more,
> Customs that recognize the standard worth,—
> The wholesome household rule in force again,
> Husbands once more God's representative,
> Wives like the typical Spouse once more, and Priests
> No longer men of Belial.
>
> (5.2039–45)

The association between Guido and the society of *The Ring and the Book* is crucial to feminist readings such as Brady's, which argues that the patriarchal order is also tried and condemned through its agent, Guido. According to Brady, "every monologue" in Browning's "novel" "reveals how completely aware he is of the sexual cynicism emanating from the core of a patriarchal society. He forthrightly addresses these issues with their destructive effects on women, and exposes them to an equally patriarchal society in his own Victorian England." She calls the work "a powerfully incisive feminist judgment on the androcentric mores of patriarchy, and on its concomitant subjugation of women (pp. 125–26). *The Ring and the Book* is certainly a text which empha-sizes the interweaving of the personal and the political. Pompilia's is the story of a battered and sexually abused woman who finds, in turn-ing to the authorities of church and state for help, that her abuse is sanctioned, even encouraged, by them. Guido continuously asserts in his defense that his behavior is permitted by and indeed essential to the social order which he, as a male aristocrat, upholds: "Absolve, then, me, law's mere executant! / Protect your own defender,—save me, Sirs!" (5.2003–4).

As Brady's remarks imply, the internal topicality of *The Ring and the Book*, its emphasis on the details and debates of seventeenth-century Rome, on the social fabric into which its story is woven, paradoxically accentuates the sense of continuity between that world and the world in which the poem was written and published. This emphasis on the social, particularly the relations between individuals and the institu-

---

2. E. Warwick Slinn, *The Discourse of Self in Victorian Poetry* (Charlottesville: Univ. Press of Virginia, 1991), p. 176.

tions of the family, marriage, law, church, and state, is what distinguishes Browning's text from many other Victorian poems set in the past, for the complexity of the life depicted resembles more the texture of "modern," "civilized" life than a past, or pastoral, age marked primarily by nostalgic difference from the present.[3] The insistence on the social also goes some distance toward exonerating *The Ring and the Book* from the charges made by Nina Auerbach, among others, that it ignores Barrett Browning's critique of backward-looking verse.[4]

Aurora Leigh asserts as part of her poetic manifesto:

> I do distrust a poet who discerns
> No character or glory in his times,
> And trundles back his soul five hundred years,
> Past moat and drawbridge, into a castle-court,
> To sing—oh, not of lizard or of toad
> Alive i' the ditch there,—'twere excusable,
> But of some black chief, half knight, half sheep-lifter,
> Some beauteous dame, half chattel and half queen.
>
> *(Aurora Leigh* 5.189–96)

It is true that *The Ring and the Book* portrays a wife in a society which treats wives as chattels. Guido refers to the word in discussing his marriage to Pompilia, implying that the marriage trade is woven into the "social fabric" (5.429), while Pompilia describes her predicament as that of "the chattel that had caused a crime" (7.520). Yet, far from depicting such treatment of women as universal and natural, the poem emphasizes that the conditions it represents are historically specific and socially produced. Such treatment brings these issues into alignment with Victorian debate over precisely the same matters. Julia Wedgwood illustrates in a letter to Browning the case with which *The Ring and the Book* could be inserted into the debate over the Woman Question: "The speech about the *pain of womanliness* is to me a wonderful revelation of apprehension of *our* side of the question."[5]

There are many points of continuity between the concerns of *The Ring and the Book* and the Victorian Woman Question; my focus here is on the debates over domestic violence.[6] Although the Act of Charles the Second which had permitted a man "to chastise his wife with any reasonable instrument" was erased in 1829, the assumption that a

---

3. Roma King makes a similar point when he observes that Browning's "awareness of the limits of human reason and his distrust of those values codified in social customs and institutions . . . reflect more nearly the skeptical mood of the nineteenth than of the seventeenth century" (*The Focusing Artifice: The Poetry of Robert Browning* [Athens: Ohio Univ. Press, 1968], p. 133).

4. Nina Auerbach, "Robert Browning's Last Word," *Romantic Imprisonment* (New York: Columbia Univ. Press, 1986), p. 94ff.

5. *Robert Browning and Julia Wedgwood: A Broken Friendship as Revealed in Their Letters*, ed. Richard Curle (New York, 1937), p. 142.

6. The most comprehensive discussion of wife assault and debates surrounding it in the nineteenth century is A. James Hammerton, *Cruelty and Companionship: Conflict in Nineteenth-Century Married Life* (New York: Routledge, 1992). See also Anna Clark, "Humanity or Justice? Wifebeating and the Law in the Eighteenth and Nineteenth Centuries," *Regulating Womanhood: Historical Essays on Marriage, Motherhood and Sexuality*, ed. Carol Smart (New York: Routledge, 1992); Nancy Tomes, "A Torrent of Abuse: Crimes of Violence between Working-Class Men and Women in London, 1840–1875, *Journal of Social History* II (1977–78): 328–45.

man could assault his wife persisted both in legal practices and in the minds of many.[7] Part of the rationale for condoning wife assault came from the principle of coverture, which held that husband and wife were one in law. According to this principle, in the words of eighteenth-century jurist William Blackstone, a man "might give his wife moderate correction . . . as he is to answer for her misbehavior."[8] Thus, despite the nominal repeal of the "ancient privilege," "a husband's repeated abuse of his wife, no matter how severe, was not considered as serious an offense against marriage as a single instance of a wife's infidelity."[9] Detailed reports of trials for domestic violence or for separation or divorce on the grounds of cruelty appeared daily in Victorian newspapers and prompted numerous editorials and periodical articles on the subject of the prevention and legal redress of the crime. The 1850s witnessed a "moral panic" about the issue, and although flogging, which many advocated as an appropriate deterrent to the crime, was never instituted, a series of legislative measures was enacted during the remainder of the century to increase penalties, encourage prosecution, and help survivors of domestic violence.

Victorian debates over wifebeating were inextricable from the discourse of class. Many commentators assumed that such behavior was natural and exclusive to the working classes, who were likened to brutes or savages, but non-existent or intolerable in the middle and upper classes. As Anna Clark argues,

> by attributing wifebeating solely to working class brutes, newspapers and Parliamentary debate displaced the problem of male violence onto class. In an era when feminism was just beginning to be heard, the intense publicity over wifebeating potentially undermined the legitimacy of the patriarchal sexual contract, in which men's dominance was justified by their protection of their wives. (p. 201)

Yet not all Victorians displaced the problem entirely onto class. Evidence in the widely reported divorce court cases of both physical and sexual abuse of wives by middle- or upper-class husbands was there to be seen in the papers. In reviewing the aristocratic Caroline Norton's letter to the Queen about her inability to obtain redress from an abusive husband, John William Kaye stated that Norton's case was "an exceptional one in degree, we believe, but *only* in degree. Even in degree, though exceptional, it is not solitary; and in kind we are afraid it is common."[1] Here and in his 1856 essay "Outrages on Women," Kaye explicitly relates the problem of domestic violence to the broader parameters of the Woman Question. Anticipating Frances Power Cobbe's critique of the Victorian gender system in "The Final Cause of

7. As quoted by Frances Power Cobbe, "Wife Torture in England," *Contemporary Review* 32 (1878): 64.
8. William Blackstone, *Commentaries on the Laws of England*. Vol. 1: *The Rights Of Persons* (1765; Chicago: Univ. of Chicago Press, 1979), p. 420.
9. Blackstone, p. 421; Mary Lyndon Shanley, *Feminism, Marriage and the Law in Victorian England* (Princeton: Princeton Univ. Press, 1989), p. 170.
1. John William Kaye, "The Non-Existence of Women," *North British Review* 23 (1855): 537.

Woman," he remarks:

> Marriage is looked upon as the aim and end of woman's life.
> What else, it is said, can she do? What but misery, it would be
> better to ask, can result from such a system—what but wife-
> beatings or slow-torturings can be the growth of such ill-sorted
> marriages as this fatal necessity involves? Let us make women
> more independent—let us open out to them sure sources of hon-
> est employment—and it will not be long before wife-beating and
> other outrages on women sensibly diminish.[2]

Caroline Norton's case was a highly publicized illustration of the
fact that marriage might become a "fatal necessity" for women belong-
ing to the upper as well as the working classes. George Norton's phys-
ical abuse of his wife included throwing an inkstand at her head,
kicking her, burning her, and choking her. On leaving him, she found
she had no claim to the custody of her children. Although he was
guilty not only of cruelty but also infidelity, and thus liable to be sued
for divorce on the grounds of aggravated adultery, his wife found that
because she had once forgiven his abuse she was legally considered to
have condoned it and could not seek redress in the courts. He, how-
ever, attempted to sue her friend Prime Minister Melbourne for "crim-
inal conversation" or adultery with his wife, in hopes of obtaining
substantial damages, even though he had so little evidence to support
his charge that the jury pronounced it spurious without even hearing
the defense. Caroline Norton's problems were intrinsically bound up
with the legal "non-existence" of married women under Victorian com-
mon law, and particularly with the inability of wives to contract with
their husbands or retain their own earnings and property. Her pub-
lished accounts suggest that George Norton's brutality was motivated
by two complementary motives which he as a magistrate believed
would be well served by English law of the time: first, by a desire to
dominate his wife, mind and body, and second, by financial greed.

Pompilia's predicament and, I shall argue, the rhetorical strategy
she adopts, recall in numerous ways the plight of Norton, who called
hers a " 'Story of Real Life;' taking place among the English aristoc-
racy; with perfect impunity on the part of the wrong-doer!"[3] The most
obvious parallels include Guido's motivation by greed, his privilege as
a member of the gentry, and his confident reliance on the judicial sys-
tem to uphold his patriarchal privilege. His intellectual, moral, and
spiritual inferiority to Pompilia parallels the contrast between husband
and wife in Caroline Norton's representation of her relationship with
George. The distance between the opposing opinions of the two repre-
sentatives of the "public" in The Ring and the Book also finds its par-
allel in the larger Victorian debate over wife assault; Sergeant-at-Law
Edward Cox believed with many others that the abused woman in
most cases was "an angel of the fallen class, who has made her hus-

2. John William Kaye, "Outrages on Women," *North British Review* 25 (1856): 256.
3. *Caroline Norton's Defense: English Laws for Women in the Nineteenth Century*, intro. Joan
Huddleston (Chicago: Academy Chicago, 1982), p. 141.

band's home an earthly hell" while some feminists argued that the excuse of "provocation" was rarely if ever warranted, and if so was the result of vicious husbands wearing and dragging down decent wives.[4] The point is not that these positions precisely replicate those of the characters Half-Rome and The Other Half-Rome, but rather the similarity in texture between *The Ring and the Book* and the contested terrain of gender in Victorian Britain. Yet Browning's text also intensifies the horrors of Guido's violence by implying marital rape and sexual abuse. Both topics surface rarely in Victorian discussions of domestic violence, perhaps as a result of the combined force of "delicacy" and the "guarded language" in which such matters received public notice.[5] John Stuart Mill's objection to the prerogative of conjugal rights is an exception which serves well as a synopsis of Guido's abuse of his authority over Pompilia: "He can claim from her and enforce the lowest degradation of a human being, that of being made the instrument of an animal function contrary to her inclinations."[6] The continuities with the Woman Question in general and the case of Caroline Norton in particular indicate that, although *The Ring and the Book* is set in the seventeenth century, it nonetheless seriously engages with Victorian gender politics. In *The Ring and the Book* a property-based marriage system which makes women their husband's chattels, denies them the status of persons, and sanctions the sexual double standard comes under one of the most sustained attacks in Victorian literature.

At this point, I want to move on to the critique of Browning's representation of Pompilia offered by feminist critics from Ethel Mayne in 1913 to Elisabeth Bronfen in 1992.[7] For such critics, the depiction of Pompilia as a victim, and a dying one at that, marks a conservative representational gender politics. Nina Auerbach, in fact, drawing on the oft-noted similarities between Pompilia and Barrett Browning, considers Browning's portrayal of *The Ring and the Book's* only female speaker as an illiterate "victim/queen" in terms of a very adversarial artistic relationship: "It may be Robert Browning's ultimate victory over his celebrated wife that he robs Pompilia of a public voice" (p. 103). I want to suggest a more complex relation between voice and agency and a more productive relation, if not between Robert Browning and Elizabeth Barrett Browning, who are not my focus here, then between *The Ring and the Book* and *Aurora Leigh*, the period's most sustained marriage of feminist aesthetics and generic experimentation.

In her assessment of the general moral alignment of *The Ring and the Book*, Auerbach would seem to concur with the summary provided

---

4. Edward Cox, *The Principles of Punishment, as Applied in the Administration of the Criminal Law, by Judges and Magistrates* (London, 1877), p. 101. On nineteenth-century femnist arguments and positions, see Hammerton, Shanley, and Carol Bauer and Lawrence Ritt, " 'A Husband is a Beating Animal': Frances Power Cobbe Confronts the Wife-Abuse Problem in Victorian England" and "Wife-Abuse, Late Victorian English Feminists, and the Legacy of Frances Power Cobbe," *International Journal of Women's Studies* 6 (1983): 99–118, 195–207.
5. Hammerton, p. 109; see also Shanley on marital rape.
6. *The Subjection of Women in John Stuart Mill and Harriet Taylor Mill, Essays on Sex Equality*, ed. Alice S. Rossi (Chicago: Univ. of Chicago Press, 1970), p. 160.
7. Ethel Mayne, *Browning's Heroines* (London: Chatto and Windus, 1913) and Elisabeth Bronfen, *Over Her Dead Body: Death, Femininity and the Aesthetic* (New York: Routledge, 1992).

by Paul Turner: "For Browning . . . Guido was absolutely evil, and Pompilia (despite documentary evidence to the contrary) was absolutely good."[8] Auerbach simply opposes as anti-feminist the terms in which she understands Pompilia to be constructed as "good." Along with Turner and many other critics, she also highlights the discrepancy between the poem and Browning's source material, the Old Yellow Book, which suggests that the historical Pompilia was literate and hence at least capable of writing the love letters adduced at the trial as proof of her infidelity. Thus, Auerbach's indignation that Browning "blessed" Pompilia with illiteracy accepts unquestioningly Pompilia's own repeated assertions that she cannot read. Auerbach also implicitly endorses the prevalent critical view, expressed by the early commentator A. K. Cook, that she is "transparently truthful," a view which persists in Turner's assertion that "Pompilia talks with a touching simplicity that seems entirely her own."[9] Feminist objections to the representation of Pompilia and standard critical readings of *Pompilia* thus converge in an assessment of her as utterly passive in her relation to language and the world around her.

However, it seems rather surprising that any speaker of a dramatic monologue by Robert Browning should simply be taken at his or, less often, her word. Only recently have several critics, most notably William Walker, challenged the view that Pompilia's speech is transparent, unreflective self-expression and a disinterested expression of the "truth." Walker argues that "Pompilia's account shares the characteristics of the other monologues which make their relation to truth problematical." Many of the rhetorical aims and devices he highlights—her use of sarcasm and irony, her "sophisticated discourse of shifting tone," her employment of rhetorical strategies similar to Guido's—suggest that Pompilia and her monologue are more complex than most critics have assumed (pp. 47, 52). As critics such as Walker and Slinn demonstrate, her monologue is "not exempt from the subversive power of what the Pope calls the 'filthy rags of speech.' "[1] In fact, she may be a less passive, more sophisticated, and more effective speaker than even these critics contemplate.

Pompilia is on trial, and she knows it. Her narrative works, as many have observed, to exonerate Caponsacchi, but she also speaks on her own behalf. The narrator in *The Ring and the Book* says that it was thought she took so miraculously long to die "Just that Pompilia might defend herself" (I. 1080).[2] Although Pompilia is not testifying in a court of law as Guido is in his first monologue, according to Book I she does have a body of listeners, which includes the nuns who are caring for her, as well as "leech and man of law" (I. 1087). A defense

8. Paul Turner, *English Literature 1832–1890: Excluding the Novel* (New York: Oxford Univ. Press, 1989), p. 50.
9. A. K. Cook, *A Commentary upon Browning's* The Ring and the Book (New York: Oxford Univ. Press, 1920), p. 138; Turner, p. 51. For example, Auerbach makes reference to "the authenticity of Pompilia's truth," accepting that the text constructs it as truth, though objecting to its means of doing so ("Robert Browning's Last Word," p. 103).
1. Walker, p. 60; Slinn, p. 164.
2. This is a view which is encouraged by Pompilia herself, who exclaims, "And how my life seems lengthened as to served" (I. 1193).

also suggests persuasive rhetorical strategy, which Pompilia's mono-
logue amply exhibits. Her defense is so effective that generations of
critics have believed it implicitly.

One instance of a common rhetorical strategy in Pompilia's defense
is her refusal to specify the acts of abuse committed by Guido, claim-
ing in places amnesia—"All since [her marriage] is one blank"
(l. 583)—and in places a reluctance to incriminate him:

> Whereupon . . . no, I leave my husband out!
> It is not to do him more hurt, I speak.
> Let it suffice, when misery was most,
> One day, I swooned and got a respite so.
>
> (ll. 1134–37)

The repeated innuendo of lines such as "pushed back to him and, for
my pains, / Paid with . . . but why remember what is past?" effectively
leaves the form of abuse to the audience's imagination, while empha-
sizing its brutal effects by her very refusal to recall: "And so more days,
more deeds I must forget, / Till . . ." (ll. 1280–81, 1190–91; ellipses in
original). This strategy is similar to the one Walker notes in Pompilia's
"displacement from herself to others of imagery which would, as
[Park] Honan claims, bespeak bitterness or hatred on her part"
(p. 59). This is the case in the powerful passage early in her mono-
logue in which she indirectly vilifies Guido:

> All the seventeen years,
> Not once did a suspicion visit me
> How very different a lot is mine
> From any other woman's in the world.
> The reason must be, 't was by step and step
> It got to grow so terrible and strange:
> These strange woes stole on tiptoe, as it were,
> Into my neighbourhood and privacy,
> Sat down where I sat, laid them where I lay;
> And I was found familiarized with fear,
> When friends broke in, held up a torch and cried
> 'Why, you Pompilia in the cavern thus,
> How comes that arm of yours about a wolf?
> And the soft length,—lies in and out your feet
> And laps you round the knee,—a snake it is!'
> And so on.
>
> (ll. 113–28)

The passage is indicative of how Pompilia transmutes her life into an
elaborate representation of passivity and victimization, for her asser-
tions in this passage directly conflict with the events of her life. Far
from being naively ignorant of the wrongs done to her during the four
years of her marriage, Pompilia has been outraged by and actively op-
posed to them from the start. She decided independently that her hus-
band's treatment was unacceptable and attempted every institutional
recourse and avenue of escape possible to her in Arezzo: priests and
archbishops, the Governor, her adoptive parents, even the cousin-in-

law who was attempting to seduce her. And far from waiting in a cavern with her folk-tale wolf and Biblical serpent, one to be discovered by "friends," she takes the initiative to escape from her husband. Pompilia thus represents herself as passive when, to judge from what we know of her behavior, she was decidedly active.

What we know of Pompilia, just as what we know of all the other characters in *The Ring and the Book*, is entirely based on interpretation of the textual material. Given her attempt throughout her monologue to exonerate herself by portraying herself as passive and powerless, it seems to me less than clear that Pompilia is illiterate. It is of course impossible to prove that one is illiterate; one can only assert it and have that assertion corroborated by others, which Pompilia does. But what would one suspect in a different Browning monologue of a speaker who repeatedly makes such an unprovable but exculpatory claim? Pompilia reiterates her inability to read throughout her monologue, asserting it directly at least five times, once in the reported speech of her maid, and alluding to it often. However, she exhibits an unusual conceptual command of writing as well as a strange tendency to privilege writing in her own speech, which casts doubt on her claim to ignorance. It is interesting, for example, that when she opens her monologue by stating that her age is seventeen she immediately provides a source of official corroboration, saying it is "writ so . . . in the church's register, / Lorenzo in Lucina, all my names" (ll. 3–4). She adds that "Also 't is writ that I was married there / Four years ago," and expresses the hope that "a word or two" will be added regarding the birth and name of her son when they record her death (ll. 8–9). Such primary emphasis on written correlatives of her identity and history, rather than, for example, on witnesses, suggests a literate rather than an illiterate construction of identity.

This impression that Pompilia's thought-processes are literate rather than oral is borne out by some of the key images in her monologue. As Slinn has noted, Pompilia exhibits a sophisticated "subjectivity that is alert to the ironies of representation," from the "laughable" fact of the six names for "one poor child," to the figures in a tapestry that Pompilia and her friend Tisbe name after themselves: "You know the figures never were ourselves / Though we nicknamed them so."[3] Yet her speech reveals not simply the potential separation of external fact from internal representation" that Slinn emphasizes, but an understanding of language in particular, and written language at that. She distinguishes Caponsacchi, for example, from the way that her maid has represented him, in terms of the linguistic tag attached to him: "the name, / —Not the man, but the name of him, thus made / Into a mockery and disgrace" (ll. 1338–40). Pompilia expresses indignation throughout at the corruption of representational practices and the divorce between the order of discourse and the order of reality, whether that corruption is manifest in the incongruity of the grand names which she does not actually possess to the "nicknames" people give to

3. Slinn, p. 164; 7.7, 5, 197–198.

Caponsacchi in supposing him or her lover (l. 160). Even more strik-
ing is her image of Caponsacchi saving her by reading her correctly, by
affirming her understanding of herself by recovering the palimpsest
and reinscribing the true, divine text which has been distorted and
overwritten by the human and the social:

> Ever the face upturned to mine, the hand
> Holding my hand across the world,—a sense
> That reads, as only such can read, the mark
> God sets on woman, signifying so
> She should—shall peradventure—be divine;
> Yet, 'ware, the while, how weakness mars the print
> And makes confusion, leaves the thing men see,
> —Not this man,—who from his soul, re-writes
> The obliterated charter.

(ll. 1497–1505).

This passage strikingly parallels Aurora's description of her soul as
palimpsest in Book One of *Aurora Leigh*, indeed the passage in which
Aurora discovers the world of books. It is difficult to believe that such
an elaborate metaphor of textual corruption could issue from illiteracy.
   In his poststructuralist analysis of Pompilia as split subject, Slinn
argues that

> while Pompilia's role as victim governs her character as the prod-
> uct of her narrative (the person-as-thing), what dominates her
> consciousness as the speaking subject (the person-as-process) is
> the crisis brought about when the external certainties of her exis-
> tence prove to be illusions, when the objective facts of her world
> dissolve. (p. 164)

Yet Slinn, while countering earlier readings of the monologue as
static and transparent, nevertheless considers Pompilia's monologue
that of one held by the language which reflects her unacknowledged
desire: "Her perception of Caponsacchi's responses, therefore, as veri-
fying the sign of her divinity is crucial to the consummation of her dis-
course—to the confirmation of her spiritual identity" (p. 168). Thus,
although he stresses the sophistication of the monologue, Slinn attrib-
utes it to psychic rather than rhetorical complexity on the part of the
speaker.[4] Slinn makes the rather weak pronouncement that his analy-
sis "is not to suggest that she is a spiritual fraud, but . . . that her
monologue is open to reading ambiguous intentions," including hid-
den intentions which are apparently unacknowledged by the speaker
herself (p. 167). However, the representation of herself as person-as-
thing is fundamental to her rhetorical strategy; even what Slinn de-
scribes as person-as-process is often the product of rhetoric: in de-
scribing how the world has failed her, Pompilia makes her case.

---

4. Joseph Bristow, in also turning his attention to 7.1494–1506, likewise accepts Pompilia's il-
literacy but argues that she nevertheless "knows only too clearly the power invested in read-
ing and writing. Her apprehension of literacy . . . has extraordinary resonance. For she, as a
woman, is the most vulnerable sign to circulate in a signifying economy dominated by men"
(*Robert Browning* [New York: St. Martin's Press 1991], p. 155).

Walker's reading at least raises the possibility of Pompilia's guilt, noting that the time-frame of *The Ring and the Book* makes it conceivable that Pompilia's son Gaetano, if born slightly prematurely, was conceived on the flight to Rome. In favor of this possibility is the doubt that Pompilia could have known, as she claims to have, that she was pregnant less than two weeks after conception; she gives this as her reason for deciding to flee. Walker notes her insistence that Guido is not the father, that Gaetano was conceived in love rather than hate, and that she shows no ambivalence towards the offspring of a man she hates and fears. There is, however, an obvious precedent for such mother-love in *Aurora Leigh's* Marian, a figure who is associated, as Pompilia associates herself, with the Virgin Mary, as well as the fact that, Guido, in attempting to obtain custody of the child, seems certain that it is his (Walker, p. 60).

While one can conclude that Browning did, as critics have contended, ignore the historical evidence that Pompilia was literate and unconsciously imbued her speech with the thought-patterns of his own literate mind, there remains the alternate possibility that Browning represented a character who is literate and possibility guilty, but suppresses the fact to strengthen her case. Whatever his intention the possibility of her literacy is available from the text, which does not completely erase the inconsistency of evidence from The Old Yellow Book.[5] Placing Pompilia's monologue in question has the virtue of destabilizing its privileged position within the Browning canon and according it the same complexity and sophistication attached to the other monologues. The corollary to this revised view of *Pompilia* is that Pompilia is extraordinarily successful in her attempts to represent herself as passive, innocent, and illiterate, and that Pompilia's critics, as well as her society, have read out the agency that is evident in the narrative of *The Ring and the Book* and that underlies the rhetorical maneuvers of her monologue within it. Pompilia can thus be read as replicating the rhetorical strategy adopted by Victorian feminists in a variety of contexts: she actively asserts herself as passive, a social victim, in order to justify her assertive actions. As the object of her discourse she is social victim; as speaker she is linguistic and social agent. This closely resembles the strategy that Mary Poovey identifies in Caroline Norton's writings: "Norton justifies publicizing her private story by rhetorically splitting herself into two persons: the long-suffering victim of social injustice and the vindicating polemical writer."[6] The similarity is strengthened by the fact that Pompilia's defiance is understood by Guido and Half-Rome as a rebellion with radical political implications.

Auerbach's and others' condemnation of Browning's text may thus be based on a misreading and a failure to distinguish between important formal differences from earlier Browning poems: whereas Pompilia represents herself through her own speech, the Duchess of

5. See Cook, Appendix III, "When were the Comparini at Arezzo?," pp. 283–84.
6. Mary Poovey, *Uneven Developments*: p. 65.

Ferrara, an earlier victim of a murderous husband, is simply a silent, hanging representation.[7] Pompilia is the object of others' representations and her own, but in speaking she establishes herself, very assertively in fact, as a subject—claiming Caponsacchi as hers, for example, with "He was mine, he is mine, he will be mine"—and asserting the absolute truth of her speech (l. 1457). While it is true that Browning's poem does not employ the strategy of, for example, Augusta Webster's *A Castaway*, in which the reader encounters only the woman's representation of herself, it is not true that Pompilia is utterly silenced and marginalized, despite her ultimate silence and objectification in death. While her voice is not the public voice of *Aurora Leigh*, it is a public voice in the same sense in which that of the speaker of *A Castaway* is public: it is published and as such intervenes in the literary and social debates of Victorian Britain.

When we read the agency back into Pompilia's monologue it becomes difficult to concur with an unremittingly critical assessment of the gender politics of Browning's representation of Pompilia. Similarly, it is possible to locate agency in Pompilia's role in the narrative of *The Ring and the Book* to an extent that challenges the views of critics such as Adrienne Auslander Munich, who argues that Browning simply reproduces the Andromeda myth. She asserts "that Capponsacchi as a Perseus/St. George figure tells the reader to believe in his goodness; that she is likened to Andromeda confers upon Pompilia blameless victimhood. When regarded in this way Browning's interpretation of the myth reenacts a Victorian melodrama . . . complete with gender stereotypes."[8] Yet even a cursory examination of the poem's narrative reveals that it hardly subscribes to either the larger genre of romance or the traditional narrative pattern of the rescue of helpless female by manly deliverer. *The Ring and the Book* undercuts the genre of romance in two basic ways. The first, briefer instance is the contrast between the romantic representation that Pompilia's foster mother gives her daughter's prospective marriage to Guido and its reality. Violante tells Pompilia that she will marry a "cavalier," conjuring up an image of chivalric rescue shared with her girlfriend Tisbe. The image proves to have nothing in common with the man who presents himself:

> And when the next day the cavalier who came
> (Tisbe had told me that the slim young man
> With wings at head, and wings at feet, and sword
> Threatening a monster, in our tapestry,
> Would eat a girl else,—was a cavalier)—
> When he proved Guido Franceschini,—old

---

7. Brady suggests a reading of what Browning does to Pompilia that contests Auerbach's insistence on her silence: "Pompilia Comparini, who comes across the pages of the Old Yellow Book as an unfortunate, faceless victim, Browning has transformed into a brave, self-directed young woman" (p. 133). Cf. U. C. Knoepflmacher on Browning's earlier poetry in "Projection and the Female Other: Romanticism, Browning, and the Victorian Dramatic Monologue," *VP* 22 (1984): 139–59.
8. Adrienne Auslander Munich, *Andromeda's Chains: Gender and Interpretation in Victorian Literature and Art* (New York: Columbia Univ. Press, 1989), p. 140.

> And nothing like so tall as I myself,
> Hook-nosed and yellow in a bush of beard.
>
> (ll. 389–96)

One might conclude, however, that this undercutting of romantic expectations comes from bad casting, or tyrannical social custom, so the same scenario of rescue is tried later in the narrative with a much likelier candidate.

Giuseppe Caponsacchi lacks wings at head and feet, but as a slim, young, and good-looking nobleman he is much more apt for the part of cavalier. On close inspection, however, he is hardly a dashing man of action. On being informed that the woman whom he admires is beaten by her husband, he decides to remove himself from the situation by leaving for Rome. The initiative for the "rescue" is taken entirely by Pompilia herself, and even so he dithers for two days before going through with it.[9] His first words to her, as she reports them, suggest a passivity incongruous for a masterful rescuer: "I am yours" (l. 1447). Though this assertion might be construed as merely the rhetorlic of chivalry, the impression of Caponsacchi's fundamental passivity is borne out by the only really dramatic moment in the whole failed "rescue," which occurs after Guido overtakes them and brings the Commissary and guards to Pompilia's chamber. Pompilia, as part of her overall rhetorical strategy, minimizes the extent of her action in the incident, describing her rage at seeing Guido her "master, by hell's right" and Caponsacchi her "angel helplessly held back," euphemistically congratulating herself that she "did for once see right, do right, give tongue / The adequate protest," and ascribing her initiative to an "impulse to serve God" (ll. 1586, 1587, 1591–92, 1600) Caponsacchi, however, relates the specifics she glosses over:

> She started up, stood erect, face to face
> With the husband: back he fell, was buttressed there
> By the window all a-flame with morning-red,
> He the black figure, the opprobrious blur,
> Against all peace and joy and light and life.
> "Away from between me and hell!"—she cried:
> . . . .
> I may have made an effort to reach her side
> From where I stood i' the door-way,—anyhow
> I found the arms, I wanted, pinioned fast,
> Was powerless. . . .
> . . . .
> She sprung at the sword that hung beside him, seized,
> Drew, brandished it, the sunrise burned for joy

9. Pompilia, emphasizing as she does her passivity, does not recount this latter aspect of the narrative,—at II.145ff. she elides the days of hesitation—but Caponsacchi, whose name suggests emasculation and who bemoans throughout his monologue that he has been "ineffective help" to Pompilia, does. He also records her reproach of him and her firm conscription of him to do her will, even though he has come resolved to refuse her (7.1952, 105off.). Although I do not pursue this avenue further, Book 6, Giuseppe Caponsacchi, provides ample evidence of Pompilia's persuasive ability, and suggests that she has scripted him into her understanding of their respective roles in the central incident of *The Ring and the Book*.

O' the blade, "Die," cried she, "devil, in God's name!"
Ah, but they all closed round her.

(6. 1523–47)

The first line of this passage contains an unmistakable echo of the
twenty-second of Barrett Browning's *Sonnets from the Portuguese*,
which begins "When our two souls stand up erect and strong, / Face to
face." The parallel creates an association between the representation
of self that allowed Barrett Browning to envisage a marriage of equals,
and the strength that permits Pompilia to resist a marriage of inequal-
ity and abuse.[1] The second gesture at romance in *The Ring and the
Book* is, then, a great failure, both in terms of the cavalier's conduct
and in its practical consequences, even though Pompilia insists that it
was a rescue—"I will not have the service fail! / I say, the angel saved
me: I am safe!"—by redefining the terms: " 'T was truth singed the lies
/ And saved me, not the vain sword nor weak speech!" (ll. 1642–43,
1640–41). Yet even here, the "truth" to which she refers is her own
deed in striking at Guido. Thus, far from being a reinscription of the
romantic paradigm with a hidden agenda of inequality, *The Ring and
the Book* presents what amounts to a parody of romantic rescue con-
ventions. If any salvation occurs in the poem, it is a mutual one remi-
niscent of the mutual rescue of Marian and Aurora in *Aurora Leigh*.[2]
And the "melodrama" to which Munich alludes betrays a structural
ambivalence apparent also in Norton's writings: in both cases the
stock figures of victim and villain are clear enough, but the part of res-
cuing avenger ends up being played, at least in part, by the woman/
victim as well.

Pompilia does speak at the center of *The Ring and the Book*. Con-
sidered in terms of its engagement with the Woman Question, Robert
Browning's great work, the greatest poetical work of the Victorian age
according to many, takes on a rather different cast than that imparted
by critical tradition. Despite its archaic setting and the "philosophical"
concerns which have claimed the critical limelight, *The Ring and the
Book* is as thoroughly engaged with the controversy over women as po-
ems such as *Aurora Leigh* and addresses many of the same questions
using formal strategies similar to those of more overtly feminist texts.
On the level of narrative, *The Ring and the Book* addresses the posi-
tion of a disenfranchised wife, battered and sexually abused by a hus-
band whose rights are buttressed by Church and State alike. Despite
her cultural and political disenfranchisement, Pompilia defies those
powers, and although her bid for freedom fails, her husband is
brought to justice for his murderous insistence that she is a piece of
property rather than a person. Furthermore, the poem's exploration of

1. *The Complete Works of Elizabeth Barrett Browning*, ed. Charlotte Porter and Helen A. Clark
(New York: Thomas Y. Crowell, 1900; repr. New York: AMS, 1973), vol. 3: 237. The invoca-
tion in Sonnet 13 of the "silence of my womanhood" (p. 233) in a text crucially concerned
with revising both the genre and gender conventions of the sonnet tradition marks an invo-
luted rhetorical strategy not unlike Pompilia's.
2. See Brady, pp. 8–9, drawing on Flavia Alaya and Dorothy Mermin, for a discussion of how
Barrett Browning helped revise Browning's earlier conceptions of rescue, and on the mutu-
ality of the rescue (and larger relationship) of Pompilia and Caponsacchi.

the viability of romance as an emancipatory form creates a parody rescue plot driven by female rather than male agency. Pompilia's agency functions as a narrative subtext which is obfuscated by the discourse of female passivity which she deploys to construct her defense. This discourse, like the other discourses in the poem, is emphatically cultural rather than natural, and traceable to the position of the speaker in a particular location in the social nexus at a specific historical moment. To insist on Pompilia's agency, then, is to redefine agency not as a fixed category but as the product of particular social and linguistic parameters—in this case, paradoxically, the construction of woman through the discourse of female passivity.

Dorothy Mermin has argued that poems such as *The Ring and the Book* "rigidly adhere to conventional gender roles for women; imagine . . . a Pompilia who can write."[3] If we read Pompilia as agent both of the flight from Guido and of her own monologue, not only does it become possible that she can read and write, but the "conventional gender roles" readers of the poem have criticized must be seen as culturally produced and enforced codes rather than natural behavior. *The Ring and the Book's* renowned experimentality, its hybrid genericity contributes to this project in several ways. As narrative poetry it deconstructs the cultural myth of romance which would uphold conventional categories and definitions of gender. As dramatic poetry or closet drama it emphasizes the way agency and identity are contingent on social possibilities, and rejects the notion of a transcendent subjectivity in the form of an omniscient narrator. And Pompilia's voice within her own dramatic monologue parallels the inscription of female literary subjectivity in *Aurora Leigh* or *A Castaway*. Most of all, the multi- and trans-generic aspects of *The Ring and the Book* dialogize the poem, and make it what critics have begun increasingly to call it, a novel. It is foremost a novel in the Bakhtinian sense that it foregrounds the social imbrication, cultural contestation, and transformability of discourse.[4] This is why the poem finally, paradoxically, both asserts Pompilia as agent of her own discourse and narrative, and inscribes her as victim of social discourse and narrative; she is both literary subject as speaking subject and cultural object of her own and others' discourse. The paradox, as I have suggested elsewhere, is one that inheres in the historical moment which saw the emergence of a female political subject in Victorian Britain.[5] It suggests the need for a conception of agency predicated not much on identity as on a complex process of cultural production that may involve a subject fractured by contradictory discursive possibilities.

3. Dorothy Mermin, "Genre and Gender in *Aurora Leigh*," p. 9.
4. Bakhtin's concept of the novel is applicable to verse as well as prose texts, and its emphasis on dialogism and intertextuality is well suited to a complex and polyvocal text such as *The Ring and the Book*. See *The Dialogic Imagination*, ed. Michael Holquist, trans. Caryl Emerson and Michael Holquist (Austin: Univ. of Texas Press, 1981) and *Speech Genres and Other Late Essays*, ed. Caryl Emerson and Michael Holquist, trans. Vern W. McGee (Austin: Univ. of Texas Press, 1986).
5. Susan Brown, "Economical Representations: Dante Gabriel Rossetti's 'Jenny,' Augusta Webster's 'A Castaway,' and the Campaign against the Contagious Diseases Acts," *VRev* 17 (1991): 78–95.

This reading is not to suggest that Pompilia is necessarily adulterous, untruthful, or even literate. Convincing arguments remain for various interpretations, and I am not offering an exhaustive reading of *Pompilia*. Rather, I am arguing that gendered conventions of reading, common to the historical setting of *The Ring and the Book*, to the Victorian context of its production and reception, and to its twentieth-century critical context, have shaped and unnecessarily foreclosed readings of this and of numerous other texts. The conscription of Pompilia into a narrative of feminine victimization represents a gratous reinscription of gendered values which were actually under serious debate at the historical moment when the text materialized. A realization that the cultural and literary conventions underpinning such interpretation are actually more fluid and conflicted than hitherto recognized opens up the possibility of readings which recognize the active participation of texts in historical debate and social change.

Such readings of literary history have been largely absent from the study of Victorian poetry. As Avrom Fleishman has observed, even studies of the last decade such as Carol Christ's *Victorian and Modern Poetics* focus on "theoretical and stylistic continuities, without once considering the rest of creation as it might affect the poets and their ideas."[6]

However, although Fleishman signals his awareness of feminist criticism and makes occasional reference to Barrett Browning, he implies that "the young men who were to become Victorian poets" comprise the entire class (p. 371). Gender does not enter into Fleishman's anticipated history of Victorian poetic genres. His assertion that "the Victorians may have achieved a form of social critique—with a carefully obscured but still legible reference—in . . . the making of fresh poems in new, or newly rededicated, genres" is welcome, as is his insistence that studies of Victorian poetry are badly in need of anchoring in the social facts and ideological currents of the age" (pp. 374, 367). But it is necessary to remember how thoroughly imbricated with questions of gender both the "social facts and ideological currents" of the Victorian period were, and to insist on an understanding of genre which takes gender into account.

Since traditional understanding of *The Ring and the Book's* generic innovation has related it to the epistemological preoccupations of the poem, what implications does my attempt to make "cultural sense" (Bristow, p. 7) of the poem have? As I have already implied, Pompilia is far from peripheral to the poem's concern with truth. She is in fact on trial for infidelity, for being untrue to her position as a woman and wife, and that truth has been almost universally granted by critics of the text. Having put the woman in the text in question shifts the grounds of traditional interpretation substantially. Such a shift in reading creates an aporia in the text which unsettles attempts to fix language or meaning in the poem.[7]

---

6. Avrom Fleishman, "Notes for a History of Victorian Poetic Genres," *Genre* 18 (1985): 363.
7. There is, of course, the significant issue of the Pope's monologue, the other dramatic book of the poem which has generally been read "straight."

Why Pompilia should have been so easily identified with truth at the nexus of gender, infidelity, and hermeneutics can be deduced from John Kaye's assertion in 1855 of the essential, even biological connection between women and truth: "There is no confusion, as regards the woman's knowledge, of the true and the false. Whether her offspring be legitimate or illegitimate, she knows it to be her own. ("The 'Non-Existence' of Women," p. 543). Woman thus figures the stability of truth and knowledge within an essentializing discourse of gender, and in turn guarantees the social order, as Mary Poovey argues: "Because of the place that woman occupied in the symbolic order, she was the guarantor of truth, legitimacy, property, and make identity" (p. 80). Yet within this discursive construction, knowing the truth is not the same as divulging it, as Kaye goes on to acknowledge in contemplating the fate of "miserable delusion" suffered by a man whose wife passes off another's child as his own. Indeed, Edward Cox's hateful commentary on rape trials blandly asserts that a woman in Pompilia's situation cannot speak truly: "She has the most powerful of all motives that can influence the female mind—the protection of her own character. . . . On this subject the truth is impossible to be obtained from her" (Kaye, p. 83). The parameters of social debate which underscore the importance of the question of the truth of "woman," provide no more guidance as to Pompilia's truth or innocence than Browning's text.

Interrogating the connection between the figure of woman and the hermeneutic project of *The Ring and the Book* has far-reaching implications, which I shall here only gesture at in terms of Elisabeth Bronfen's recent claims about the text. Considering the poem in the context of a long cultural fascination with and aestheticization of women's deaths, she argues that death in the poem "produce a moment of transition in which everything is called into question. The sheer materiality of Pompilia's body liminally suspended between life and death, the threat of its irrevocable absence, lets her pose as a hermeneutic task and serve as a site of its truth" (p. 291). However, a historically situated consideration of *The Ring and the Book* suggests that much is already in transition at the discursive site of "woman," the Woman Question. Thus Pompilia's place at "the crux of a mystery story," I would insist, is neither because she is a revenant, bridging the known and unknown worlds, but because she is a woman. Her "sheer materiality" can only be rhetorical; like her position as a hermeneutic task and site of truth, it must be culturally produced and sustained.[8] And although most readings including Bronfen's do not recognize it, as a site of truth within the text Pompilia is unstable, questionable ground. In other words, the status of Pompilia, as well as the "truth" she defends, is in question in Browning's text as much as the status and "ontological" meaning of historical women was in question in the intersection of discourses on gender, property, violence, and authority

8. See the essays reprinted from *m/f* in Parveen Adams and Elizabeth Cowie, eds., *The Woman in Question* (Cambridge, Massachusetts: MIT Press, 1990) for a sense of the immense potential of historical analysis attentive to processes of signification to interrogate apparently transparent or unitary categories such as woman.

in mid-Victorian England. And the question of woman indeed has immense implications, not only for the representation and reproduction of femininity but also, as Victorianists have been arguing increasingly, for the displaced management of anxieties about such matters as masculinity, class, national identity, and empire. *The Ring and the Book* does in fact embody a representational and epistemological crisis as articulated in traditional Browning scholarship. What requires recognition is the extent to which female agency and self-representation lie at the heart of the question.

Robert Browning: A Chronology

1812	Born May 7 at Camberwell (London suburb) to Robert and Sara Anna Wiedemann Browning.
ca. 1820–26	In boarding school near his home.
ca. 1824	Wrote a volume of Byronic verse called *Incondita*, which his parents tried unsuccessfully to have published. Browning later destroyed the volume, and only two of the poems have survived.
1826	Discovered Percy Bysshe Shelley's poetry. Read *Miscellaneous Poems, Queen Mab*.
1828	Enrolled in newly founded University of London, but withdrew after only a few months.
1833	*Pauline*, anonymously published, went unsold and received scant notice.
1834	Journey to Russia in March and April.
1835	*Paracelsus* published at his father's expense.
1837	*Strafford*, a drama, was performed five nights. None of Browning's plays enjoyed commercial success, and he finally abandoned the stage.
1838	First Italian journey. Found material for *Sordello*.
1840	*Sordello* published. It was a critical failure, retarding the poet's reputation.
1841–46	Published *Pippa Passes*, first of eight pamphlets comprising *Bells and Pomegranates*. The others: (II) *King Victor and King Charles*, a drama, 1842; (III) *Dramatic Lyrics*, 1842; (IV) *The Return of the Druses*, a drama, 1843; (V) *A Blot in the 'Scutcheon*, a drama performed three nights, 1843; (VI) *Colombe's Birthday*, a drama, 1844; (VII) *Dramatic Romances and Lyrics*, 1845; (VIII) *Luria* and *A Soul's Tragedy*, both dramas, 1846.
1844	Second Italian journey.
1845	On January 10, wrote first letter to the poet Elizabeth Barrett, an invalid whose father was determined that his children should remain unmarried. On May 20, made first visit to Elizabeth at Wimpole Street.
1846	Married Elizabeth Barrett on September 12 without her father's knowledge. On September 19, they eloped to the Continent—their destination Pisa, Italy.
1847	Summer: Settled at Casa Guidi, in Florence.
1849	First collected edition of poems published. On March 9, a son, Robert Wiedemann Barrett, born. Shortly after, Browning's mother died.

1850	*Christmas-Eve and Easter-Day.*
1855	*Men and Women*, Browning's best single volume.
1855–56	Autumn-Winter: Visited London.
1860	Discovered the Old Yellow Book, source of *The Ring and the Book*, at a bookstall in Florence.
1861	June 29: Elizabeth Barrett Browning's death.
1862	Settled at 19 Warwick Crescent, London.
1863	Second collected edition of Browning's poems (called the "third").
1864	*Dramatis Personae*, a critical as well as a popular success. Browning lionized. That autumn, he began composing *The Ring and the Book.*
1866	Death of Browning's father.
1868–69	*The Ring and the Book* published; exceedingly well received. Browning's fame nearly equal to Tennyson's.
1871	*Balaustion's Adventure; Prince Hohenstiel-Schwangau.*
1872	*Fifine at the Fair.*
1873	*Red Cotton Night-Cap Country.*
1875	*Aristophanes' Apology; The Inn Album.*
1876	*Pacchiarotto and How He Worked in Distemper.*
1877	*The Agamemnon of Aeschylus.*
1878	*La Saisiaz* and *The Two Poets of Croisic.*
1879	*Dramatic Idyls.*
1880	*Dramatic Idyls: Second Series.*
1881	The Browning Society (London) founded.
1883	*Jocoseria.*
1884	*Ferishtah's Fancies.*
1887	*Parleyings with Certain People of Importance in Their Day.*
1888–89	*Poetical Works* in sixteen volumes, the last edition supervised by Browning.
1889	December 12: *Asolando* published; Browning died in Venice the same evening, at the house of his son. Burial December 31 in Westminster Abbey.

Selected Bibliography

• indicates works included or excerpted in this Norton Critical Edition.

In this listing, recent scholarship and criticism have been emphasized as most relevant to the needs of contemporary readers.

I. COLLECTED EDITIONS

Most authoritative modern collected editions have been based primarily on the "Fourth and complete edition" of *The Poetical Works of Robert Browning* (17 vols. London: Smith, Elder, 1888–94), all supervised by Browning except for the final volume. Currently, three multi-volume editions of Robert Browning's collected works remain in progress:

The Complete Works of Robert Browning (13 volumes published as of 2006), ed. Roma King, Jr. et al. and published by Ohio University Press and Baylor University (the *Ohio Browning*), prints the 1888–89 text, recording all variants.

The Clarendon Press has published 7 volumes of *The Poetical Works of Robert Browning*, ed. Ian Jack, Margaret Smith, et al. (the *Oxford Browning*). This edition also prints the text of 1888–89, recording all variants.

John Woolford and Daniel Karlin continue to edit *The Poems of Browning* in the Longman Annotated English Poets series, two volumes having been published as of 2006. This edition prints from first editions, and records substantive variants.

The Ring and the Book

The early editions of *The Ring and the Book* having textual importance are the first (4 vols., 1868–69); the second (4 vols., 1872 and 1882–83); and that included in vols. 8–10 of the 16-vol. *Poetical Works of Robert Browning*, 1888–89.

The most authoritative, readily available edition (using the 1888–89 text) is Thomas J. Collins and Richard D. Altick, eds. *The Ring and the Book*. Peterboro, ON: Broadview, 2001. Altick's annotated Penguin edition of *The Ring and the Book* (1971, rpt. 1981, 1990, now out of print) uses the text of the first edition.

II. REFERENCE WORKS AND BIBLIOGRAPHIES

Cook, A. K. *A Commentary upon Browning's* The Ring and the Book. Oxford: Oxford UP, 1920.
De Vane, William Clyde. *A Browning Handbook*. 2nd ed. New York, 1955.
Drew, Philip. *An Annotated Critical Bibliography of Robert Browning*. New York: Harvester Wheatsheaf, 1990.
Hawlin, Stefan. *The Complete Critical Guide to Robert Browning*. New York: Routledge, 2001.
Kelley, Philip, and Betty A. Coley. *The Browning Collections: A Reconstruction with Other Memorabilia*. Waco, TX: Armstrong Browning Library, 1984.
Shroyer, Richard J., and Thomas J. Collins. *A Concordance to the Poems and Plays of Robert Browning*. 7 vols. New York: AMS Press, 1996.

See also "Introduction" and "Appendices" to the *Oxford Browning*, cited above.

Other bibliographies are Leslie N. Broughton, Clark S. Northup, and Robert Pearsall, *Robert Browning: A Bibliography, 1830–1950*, Ithaca, 1953; continued by William S. Peterson in *Robert and Elizabeth Barrett Browning: An Annotated Bibliography, 1951–1970*, The Browning Institute, 1974. Annual bibliographies of studies in Victorian literature are published in the MLA International Bibliography and in the summer issues of *Victorian Studies*. See also: "Guide to the Year's Work in Victorian Poetry," published annually in *Victorian Poetry*.

III. Biographical Studies

Chapman, Alison. "Mesmerism and Agency in the Courtship of Elizabeth Barrett and Robert Browning." *Victorian Literature and Culture* 26.2 (1998): 303–19.
Finlayson, Iain. *Browning*. London: HarperCollins, 2004.
Garrett, Martin. *A Browning Chronology: Elizabeth Barrett and Robert Browning*. New York: St. Martin's, 1999; Basingstoke, Hants: Macmillan, 2000.
———. *Elizabeth Barrett Browning and Robert Browning*. British Library Writers' Lives Series. Oxford: Oxford UP, 2001.
Garrett, Martin, ed. *Elizabeth Barrett Browning and Robert Browning: Interviews and Recollections*. Basingstoke, Hants: Macmillan, 2000.
Karlin, Daniel. "The Brownings' Marriage: Contemporary Representations." *Studies in Browning and His Circle*. 21 (Nov 1997): 33–52.
———. *The Courtship of Robert Browning and Elizabeth Barrett*. Oxford: Oxford UP, 1985.
Korg, Jacob. *Browning and Italy*. Athens, OH: Ohio UP, 1983.
Markus, Julia. *Dared and Done: The Marriage of Elizabeth Barrett and Robert Browning*. Athens, OH: Ohio UP, 1998.
Maynard, John. *Browning's Youth*. Cambridge, MA: Harvard UP, 1977.
Petrioli, Piergiacomo. "The Brownings and Their Sienese Circle." *Studies in Browning and His Circle* 24 (2001 June): 78–109.
Phelan, Joseph. "Ethnology and Biography: The Case of the Brownings." *Biography* 26.2 (Spring 2003): 261–82.
Ryals, Clyde de L. *The Life of Robert Browning: A Critical Biography*. Oxford: Blackwell, 1993.
Thomas, Donald S. *Robert Browning: A Life within Life*. New York: Viking, 1982.
Wood, Sarah. *Robert Browning: A Literary Life*. New York: Palgrave/St. Martin's, 2001.

IV. LETTERS

The Brownings' Correspondence. Ed. Philip Kelley and Ronald Hudson to vol. viii; ed. Philip Kelley and Scott Lewis to vol. xv. Winfield, KS: Wedgestone, 1984–. Definitive edition, thus far extending to 1849.
Karlin, Daniel. "Letters 'Alive and Quivering': Scholarly Approaches to the Brownings' Correspondence." *Victorian Studies* 42.3 (Spring 1999–2000): 489–96.

V. ESSAY COLLECTIONS

Bloom, Harold, and Adrienne Munich, eds. *Robert Browning: A Collection of Critical Essays*, Englewood Cliffs, NJ: Prentice-Hall, 1979.
Gibson, Mary Ellis, ed. *Critical Essays on Robert Browning*. New York: G. K. Hall, 1992.
Maynard, John. *Browning Re-viewed: Review Essays, 1980–1995*. New York: Peter Lang, 1998.
Roberts, Adam, ed. *Robert Browning*. Oxford: Oxford UP, 1997.
Woolford, John, ed. *Robert Browning in Contexts*. Winfield, KS: Wedgestone, 1998.

VI. GENERAL CRITICISM

Armstrong, Isobel. *Victorian Poetry: Poetry, Poetics and Politics*. New York: Routledge, 1993.
———. *Writers and their Background: Robert Browning*. London: Bell, 1974.
Armstrong, Isobel, ed. *The Major Victorian Poets: Reconsiderations*. London: Routledge, 1969.
Booth, Wayne C. *A Rhetoric of Irony*. Chicago and London: University of Chicago P, 1974.
Bright, Michael. *Robert Browning's Rondures Brave*. Athens, OH: Ohio UP, 1996.
Bristow, J. *Robert Browning*. New York and London: Harvester Wheatsheaf, 1991.
Bullen, J. B. *The Myth of the Renaissance in Nineteenth-Century Writers*. Oxford: Clarendon, 1994.
Eagleton, Terry. *The Illusions of Postmodernism*. Oxford: Blackwell, 1996.
Erickson, L. *Robert Browning: His Poetry and His Audiences*. Ithaca: Cornell UP, 1984.
Fowler, Rowena. "Browning and Slavery." *Victorian Poetry* 37.1 (Spring 1999): 59–69.
———. "Browning's Jews." *Victorian Poetry* 35.3 (Fall 1997): 245–66.
Fraser, Hilary. "Browning and Nineteenth-Century Historiography." *AUMLA: Journal of the Australasian Universities Language and Literature Association* 71 (May 1989): 13–29.
Gibson, Mary Ellis. *History and the Prism of Art: Browning's Poetic Experiments*. Columbus: Ohio State UP, 1987.
Hair, Donald S. *Robert Browning's Language*. Toronto: U of Toronto P, 1999.
Hughes, Linda K. "Of Parts and Periodicity: Robert Browning and Victorian Serials." *Studies in Browning and His Circle* 17 (Sept 1989): 50–59.
Karlin, Daniel. *Browning's Hatreds*. Oxford: Clarendon, 1993.
• Maxwell, Catherine. "Browning's Pygmalion and the Revenge of Galatea." *English Literary History* 60 (1993): 989–1013.
———. *The Female Sublime from Milton to Swinburne: Bearing Blindness*. Manchester: Manchester UP, 2001.

————. "Not the Whole Picture: Browning's 'unconquerable Shade.'" *Word & Image: A Journal of Verbal/Visual Enquiry* 8.4 (Oct.–Dec. 1992): 322–32.

O'Neill, Patricia. *Robert Browning and Twentieth Century Criticism*. Columbia, SC: Camden House, 1995.

Ryals, Clyde de L. *Becoming Browning: The Poems and Plays of Robert Browning, 1833–46*. Columbus: Ohio State UP, 1983.

Slinn, E. Warwick. *Browning and the Fictions of Identity*. London: Macmillan, 1982.

————. *The Discourse of Self in Victorian Poetry*, Basingstoke, Hants, and London: Macmillan, 1991.

Thomas, C. F. *Art and Architecture in the Poetry of Robert Browning: An Illustrated Compendium of Sources*. New York: Whitston, 1991.

Tucker, Herbert F., Jr. "Browning as Escape Artist: Avoidance and Intimacy." *Robert Browning in Contexts*. Ed. J. Woolford. Winfield, KS: Wedgestone, 1998.

————. "Wanted Dead or Alive: Browning's Historicism." *Victorian Studies* 38.1 (Autumn 1994): 25–39.

White, Leslie. "Browning and His Audience: 'A Battle with the Age'." *Studies in Browning and His Circle* 18 (1990): 34–52.

Woolford, John. "Browning Rethinks Romanticism." *Essays in Criticism* 43.3 (July 1993): 211–27.

————. *Browning the Revisionary*. Basingstoke, Hants, and London: Macmillan, 1988.

————. "The Romantic Brownings." *Studies in Browning and His Circle* 24 (June 2001): 7–30.

Woolford, John, and Daniel Karlin. *Robert Browning* [Studies in Eighteenth- and Nineteenth-Century Literature]. London and New York: Longman, 1996.

VII. THE DRAMATIC MONOLOGUE

Dawson, Michelle. "The Victorian Monologue and the Science of the Mind." *Australasian Victorian Studies Journal* 2 (1996): 44–55.

Everett, Glenn S. " 'You'll Not Let Me Speak': Engagement and Detachment in Browning's Monologues." *Victorian Literature and Culture* 19 (1991): 123–42.

Gregory, Melissa Valiska. "Robert Browning and the Lure of the Violent Lyric Voice: Domestic Violence and the Dramatic Monologue." *Victorian Poetry* 38.4 (Winter 2000): 491–510.

Ingersoll, Earl G. "Considerations of Gender in the Dramatic Monologue." *The Modern Language Review* 86.3 (July 1991): 545–52.

• Karlin, Daniel. "Browning's Poetry of Intimacy." *Essays in Criticism* 39 (1989): 47–64.

Martin, Loy D. *Browning's Dramatic Monologues and the Post-Romantic Subject*. Baltimore: Johns Hopkins UP, 1985.

Nichols, Ashton. "Dialogism in the Dramatic Monologue: Suppressed Voices in Browning." *Victorians Institute Journal* 18 (1990): 29–51.

Roberts, Adam. "Browning, the Dramatic Monologue and the Resuscitation of the Dead." *The Victorian Supernatural*. Ed. Nicola Bown, Carolyn Burdett, and Pamela Thurschwell. Cambridge: Cambridge UP, 2004. 109–27.

Tucker, Herbert F., Jr. *Browning's Beginnings: The Art of Disclosure*. Minneapolis, MN: U of Minnesota P, 1980.

• ————. "Dramatic Monologue and the Overhearing of Lyric." *Lyric Poetry: Beyond the New Criticism*. Ed. C. Hosek and P. Parker. Ithaca: Cornell UP, 1985. Repr. in Gibson (1992).

————. "From Monomania to Monologue: 'St. Simeon Stylites' and the Rise of the Victorian Dramatic Monologue." *Victorian Poetry* 22 (1984): 121–37.

• Wagner-Lawlor, Jennifer A. "The Pragmatics of Silence and the Figuration of the Reader in Browning's Dramatic Monologues." *Victorian Poetry* 35.3 (Fall 1997): 287–302.

VIII. STUDIES OF SINGLE WORKS

1833–1852

Anderson, James E. "Robert Browning's 'Soliloquy of the Spanish Cloister': Themes, Voices, and the Words, *Hy, Zy, Hine*." *Victorian Poetry* 35.3 (Fall 1997): 319–28.

Bullen, J. B. "Browning's Pictor Ignotus and Vasari's 'Life of Fra Bartolommeo di San Marco.'" *Review of English Studies* 23 (1972): 313–19.

Case, Alison. "Browning's 'Count Gismond': A Canvas for Projection." *Victorian Poetry* 34.2 (Summer 1996): 213–22.

Fish, Thomas E. " 'Action in Character': The Epiphanies of Pippa Passes." *Studies in English Literature* 25.4 (Autumn 1985): 845–64.

Froula, Christine. "Browning's Sordello and the Parables of Modernist Poetics." *English Literary History* 52 (1985): 965–92. Repr. in Gibson (1992).

Hecimovich, Gregg. " 'Just the thing for the time': Contextualizing Religion in Browning's 'The Bishop Orders His Tomb at St. Praxed's Church.'" *Victorian Poetry* 36.3 (1998): 259–71.

Heffernan, James A. W. "Entering the Museum of Words: Browning's 'My Last Duchess' and Twentieth-Century Ekphrasis." *Icons-Texts-Iconotexts.* Ed. Peter Wagner. Berlin: de Gruyter, 1996. 262–80.

Hochberg, S. "Male Authority and Female Subversion in Browning's 'My Last Duchess.' " *LIT: Literature Interpretation Theory* 3.1 (1991): 77–84.

Ingersoll, E. G. "Lacan, Browning, and the Murderous Voyeur: 'Porphyria's Lover' and 'My Last Duchess.' " *Victorian Poetry* 28 (1990): 151–57.

Latané, David E. "Browning's *Sordello* and the Aesthetics of Difficulty." *English Literary Studies Monograph Series,* no. 40. Victoria, BC: U of Victoria P, 1987.

McCusker, J. A. "A Note on the Last Stanza of 'Soliloquy of the Spanish Cloister.' " *Victorian Poetry* 21 (1983): 421–24.

Riede, David G. "Genre and Poetic Authority in Pippa Passes." *Victorian Poetry* 27.3–4 (Autumn-Winter 1989): 49–64.

Ryals, Clyde de L. "Browning's *Paracelsus*: 'A Poem, Not a Drama'." *Genre* 12 (1979): 203–18.

Scheick, William J. "A Verbal Trace in Browning's 'Pictor Ignotus'." *Victorians Institute Journal* 20 (1992): 39–48.

Slinn, E. Warwick. "Browning's Bishop Conceives a Tomb." *Victorian Literature and Culture* 27.1 (Mar. 1999): 251–67.

Starzyk, Lawrence J. "Browning and the Ekphrastic Encounter." *Studies in English Literature 1500–1900* 38.4 (Autumn 1998): 689–706. [on *Pauline* and other poems].

Vickers, Peter. "Practical Stylistics: Cohesion in Robert Browning's *Pippa Passes*." *Studies in English Language and Linguistics* 0 (1998): 163–78.

1855–1864

Auerbach, Nina. "Robert Browning's Last Word." *Victorian Poetry* 22.2 (1984): 161–73.

Blain, Virginia. "Browning's Men: Childe Roland, Homophobia and Thomas Lovell Beddoes." *Australasian Victorian Studies Journal* 7 (2001): 1–11.

Blanton, C. D. "Impostures: Robert Browning and the Poetics of Forgery." *Studies in the Literary Imagination* 35.2 (2002): 1–25.

Bloom, Harold (ed.). *Caliban.* New York: Chelsea House, 1992.

Byatt, A. S. " 'Half-Angel and Half-Bird.' " *Browning Society Notes* 26 (2000): 7–20. Focuses on "Epistle of Karshish."

DeLaura, David J. "The Context of Browning's Painter Poems: Aesthetics, Polemics, Histories." *PMLA* 95 (1980): 367–88.

Dellamora, Richard J. "Browning's 'Essay on Shelley' and 'Childe Roland to the Dark Tower Came': Mythopoeia and the Whole Poet." *The Pre-Raphaelite Review* 2.1 (Nov 1981): 36–52.

Dooley, Allan C. "Andrea, Raphael, and the Moment of 'Andrea del Sarto'." *Modern Philology* 81.1 (Aug 1983): 38–46.

Dupras, Joseph. "The Promise of Converting Poets in Robert Browning's 'Cleon.' " *Victorian Poetry* 38.2 (Summer 2000): 249–68.

Farkas, Ann. "Digging among the Ruins." *Victorian Poetry* 29.1 (Spring 1991): 33–45.

Faurot, Margaret. " 'Bishop Blougram's Apology': The Making of the Poet Shepherd." *Victorian Poetry* 31.1 (Spring 1993): 1–18.

Fontana, Ernest. "Sexual Tourism and Browning's 'The Englishman in Italy.' " *Victorian Poetry* 36.3 (1998): 299–306.

Goldberg, Leonard S. " 'You Think You See a Monk': The Illusions of 'Fra Lippo Lippi'." *Philological Quarterly* 81.2 (Spring 2002): 247–70.

• Gray, Erik. " 'Out of me, out of me!': Andrea, Ulysses, and Victorian Revisions of Egotistical Lyric." *Victorian Poetry* 36.4 (Winter 1998): 417–30.

• Hawlin, Stefan. "Browning's 'A Toccata of Galuppi's': How Venice Once Was Dear." *RES* 41 (1990): 496–509.

Ingersoll, Earl G. "Autumn Songs: Robert Browning's 'Andrea del Sarto' in Context." *Durham University Journal* 85.54.1 (Jan 1993): 75–79.

Inglesfield, Robert. "Two Interpolated Speeches in Robert Browning's 'A Death in the Desert.' " *Victorian Poetry* 41.3 (2003): 333–47.

Maynard, John. "Browning's Duds of Consciousness (or) No Gigadibs, No Bishop." *Robert Browning in Contexts,* ed. John Woolford. Winfield, KS: Wedgestone, 1998.

Nuttall, Anthony D. "Browning's Grammarian: Accents Uncertain?" *Essays in Criticism* 51.1 (2001): 86–100.

Polette, Keith. "The Many-Walled World of 'Andrea del Sarto': The Dynamics of Self-Expatriation." *Victorian Poetry* 35.4 (Winter 1997): 493–507.

Ryu, Myung Sook. "Madness and Mask: A Reading of Browning's 'Childe Roland to the Dark Tower Came'." *Nineteenth Century Literature in English* 4 (2001): 239–59.

Sussman, Herbert. "Robert Browning's 'Fra Lippo Lippi' and the Problematic of a Male Poetic." *Victorian Studies* 35.2 (Winter 1992): 185–200.

Tebbetts, Terrell L. "The Question of Satire in 'Caliban upon Setebos'." *Victorian Poetry* 22.4 (Winter 1984): 365–81.

The Ring and the Book

Altick, Richard D., and James F. Loucks, *Browning's Roman Murder Story: A Reading of* The Ring and the Book. Chicago: U of Chicago P, 1968.

Armstrong, Isobel. "The Problem of Representation in *The Ring and the Book*. Politics, Aesthetics, Language." *Browning e Venezia*. Ed. S. Perosa. Florence: XXX, 1991.

Austin, Kay. "Pompilia: 'Saint and Martyr Both.'" *Victorian Poetry* 17 (1979): 287–301.

Bailey, Suzanne. "Somatic Wisdom: Refiguring Bodies in *The Ring and the Book*." *Victorian Studies* 41 (1998): 61–70.

Blalock, Susan. "Browning's *The Ring and the Book*: 'A Novel Country.'" *Browning Institute Studies* 11 (1983): 39–50.

Brady, Anne P. *Pompilia: A Feminist Reading of Robert Browning's* The Ring and the Book. Athens, OH: Ohio UP, 1988.

• Brown, Susan. "Pompilia: The Woman (in) Question." *Victorian Poetry* 34 (1996): 15–37.

Buckler, William E. *Poetry and Truth in Robert Browning's* The Ring and the Book. New York: New York UP, 1985.

Doane, Margaret S. "Guido Is Saved: Interior and Exterior Monologues in Book XI of *The Ring and the Book*." *Studies in Browning and His Circle* 5 (1977): 53–64.

Findlay, Linda M. "Taking the Measure of *Difference*: Deconstruction and *The Ring and the Book*." *Victorian Poetry* 29 (1991): 401–14.

Gibson, Mary Ellis. "The Criminal Body in Victorian Britain: The Case of *The Ring and the Book*." *Browning Institute Studies* 18 (1990): 73–93.

Petch, Simon. "Equity and Natural Law in *The Ring and the Book*." *Victorian Poetry* 35.1 (Spring 1997): 105–11.

———. "Law, Narrative, and Anonymity in Browning's *The Ring and the Book*." *Victorian Literature and Culture* 20 (1992): 311–33.

Pettit, Alexander. "Place, Time, and Parody in *The Ring and the Book*." *Victorian Poetry* 31.1 (Spring 1993): 95–106.

Potkay, Adam. "The Problem of Identity and the Grounds for Judgment in *The Ring and the Book*." *Victorian Poetry* 25.2 (Summer 1987): 143–57.

Rigg, Patricia D. *Robert Browning's Romantic Irony in* The Ring and the Book. Madison, NJ: Fairleigh Dickinson UP, 1999.

Roberts, Adam. "*The Ring and the Book*: the Mage, the Alchemist, and the Poet." *Victorian Poetry* 36.1 (Spring 1998): 37–46.

Rundle, Vivienne J. "'Will You Let Them Murder Me?': Guido and the Reader in *The Ring and the Book*." *Victorian Poetry* 27.3–4 (Autumn-Winter 1989): 99–114.

Shaw, W. David. "Browning's Murder Mystery: *The Ring and the Book* and Modern Theory." *Victorian Poetry* 27 (1989): 79–98.

Slinn, E. Warwick. "Language and Truth in *The Ring and the Book*." *Victorian Poetry* 27.3–4 (Autumn-Winter 1989): 115–33.

Sullivan, Mary Rose. *Browning's Voices in* The Ring and the Book: A Study of Method and Meaning. Toronto: U of Toronto P, 1969.

Tucker, Herbert F., Jr. "Representation and Repristination: Virginity in *The Ring and the Book*." *Virginal Sexuality and Textuality in Victorian Literature*. Ed. L. Davis. Albany, N.Y.: State U of New York P, 1993.

Walker, William. "*Pompilia* and Pompilia." *Victorian Poetry* 22.1 (Spring 1984): 47–63.

Ward, Candace. "Damning Herself Praiseworthily: Nullifying Women in *The Ring and the Book*." *Victorian Poetry* 34 (1996): 1–14.

Yeo, Hongsang. "Browning's Female Romance: Gender and Class in *The Ring and the Book*." *Nineteenth Century Literature in English* 4 (1998): 189–203.

Zietlow, Paul. "The Ascending Concerns of *The Ring and the Book*. Reality, Moral Vision, and Salvation." *Studies in Philology* 84 (1987): 194–218.

1871–1889

Crowder, Ashby Bland. "Browning and How He Worked in Good Temper." *Victorian Authors and Their Works: Revision, Motivations and Modes*. Ed. Judith Kennedy. Athens: Ohio UP, 1991. 72–98. [on *Pacchiarotto*]

Hair, Donald S. "A Note on Meter, Music, and Meaning in Robert Browning's 'Fifine at the Fair'." *Victorian Poetry* 39.1 (Spring 2001): 25–35.

Kennedy, Richard S. *Robert Browning's Asolando: The Indian Summer of a Poet*. Columbia: U of Missouri P, 1993.

O'Gorman, Francis. "Reviewing *Asolando*: Aspects of the Immediate Critical Reception of Browning's Last Volume." *Browning Society Notes* 27 (Dec 2000): 21–30.

Roberts, Adam. "Using Myth: Browning's 'Fifine at the Fair'." *Browning Society Notes* 20.1 (1990): 12–30.

Schwarz, Daniel. "Browning's Version of Modern Love: 'Bad Dreams'." *Victorian Poetry* 18 (1980): 400–406.

Southwell, Samuel B. *Quest for Eros: Browning and 'Fifine'*. Lexington: UP of Kentucky, 1980.

Index of Titles

821.809 B82 2ED INFCW

Browning, Robert,

Robert Browning's poetry

:authoritative texts, criticism /
CENTRAL LIBRARY

03/12   1/13